Quantitative Finance Programming:

Models, Methods, and Business Applications

Felipe Machorro-Ramos
https://orcid.org/0000-0002-8910-1347

Autonomous Popular University of the State of Puebla, Mexico

María Vanessa Romero-Ortiz
https://orcid.org/0000-0002-8670-2999

Polytechnic University of Puebla, Mexico

José Gonzalo Ramírez-Rosas
https://orcid.org/0000-0003-0664-3843

Polytechnic University of Puebla, Mexico

Martin Neri-Suárez
Polytechnic University of Puebla, Mexico

Lorena Hernández-Quiroz
Polytechnic University of Puebla, Mexico

IGI Global
Scientific Publishing
Publishing Tomorrow's Research Today

Vice President of Editorial Melissa Wagner
Director of Acquisitions Mikaela Felty
Director of Book Development Jocelynn Hessler
Production Manager Mike Brehm
Cover Design Jose Rosado

Published in the United States of America by
IGI Global Scientific Publishing
701 East Chocolate Avenue
Hershey, PA, 17033, USA
Tel: 717-533-8845 | Fax: 717-533-7115
Website: https://www.igi-global.com E-mail: cust@igi-global.com

Library of Congress Cataloging-in-Publication Data

LCCN: 2026012207 (CIP Data Pending)
ISBN13: 9798337383729
Isbn13Softcover: 9798337383736
EISBN13: 9798337383743

British Cataloguing in Publication Data
A Cataloguing in Publication record for this book is available from the British Library.

Table of Contents

Preface xii

Chapter 1
Quantitative Finance Programming and Its Business Applications 1
Rishikaysh Kaakandikar, SaiBalaji International Institute of Management Sciences, Pune, India
Tejashree Soni, SaiBalaji International Institute of Management Sciences, Pune, India

Chapter 2
Data-Driven Finance: Financial Mathematics, Database Management, and Econometric Techniques for Modern Decision-Making...................................... 49
Sanjeev Kumar, Lovely Professional University, India
Pardeep Kumar, Lovely Professional University, India

Chapter 3
Monte Carlo Models for Asset Pricing and Financial Risk: Theory, Implementation, and Business Applications.. 81
Kattamuri Satish, Jain (Deemed to be) University, India
Rama Jyothi Boddu, Lendi Institute of Engineering and Technology, India
R. Hepsiba, AQJ Centre for PG Studies, India

Chapter 4
Financial Data Engineering: From Raw Feeds to Feature Stores 113
Ganesh Harke, Independent Researcher, USA

Chapter 5
Persistent Homology for Time-Value-of-Money Modeling 155
Jaime Aguilar-Ortiz, Universidad Politécnica de Pachuca, Mexico
Ocotlán Diáz-Parra, Universidad Politécnica de Pachuca, Mexico
Jorge A. Ruiz-Vanoye, Universidad Politécnica de Pachuca, Mexico
Francisco R. Trejo-Macotela, Universidad Politécnica de Pachuca, Mexico
Marco A. Vera-Jiménez, Universidad Politécnica de Pachuca, Mexico
Víctor M. Zamudio-García, Universidad Politéctica Metropolitana de Hidalgo, Mexico
Carlos R. Domínguez-Mayorga, Universidad Politécnica de Pachuca, Mexico

Chapter 6
Cryptocurrencies as Safe Haven Assets: A GARCH EVT and Monte Carlo Approach 195
José Antonio Molina Hernández, University of the Istmo, Mexico
Kevin Olalla Ake, Universidad Anahuac Veracruz, Mexico

Chapter 7
Topological Monte Carlo for Asset Dynamics 243
Jaime Aguilar-Ortiz, Universidad Politécnica de Pachuca, Mexico
Ocotlán Diáz-Parra, Universidad Politécnica de Pachuca, Mexico
Jorge A. Ruiz-Vanoye, Universidad Politécnica de Pachuca, Mexico
Francisco R. Trejo-Macotela, Universidad Politécnica de Pachuca, Mexico
Marco A. Vera-Jiménez, Universidad Politécnica de Pachuca, Mexico
Víctor M. Zamudio-García, Universidad Politécnica Metropolitana de Hidalgo, Mexico
Carlos R. Domínguez-Mayorga, Universidad Politécnica de Pachuca, Mexico

Chapter 8
Modelling South African Closing Stock Prices Using GRNN, GBM and ANFIS Approaches 283
Malose Patrick Leeto Shogole, North-West University, South Africa
Johannes Tshepiso Tsoku, Sefako Makgato Health Science University, South Africa
Lebotsa Daniel Metsileng, North-West University, South Africa

Chapter 9
Machine Learning and Transformer-Based Equity Return Forecasting: A Case Study on Nvidia.. 313
S. Rajkumar, Vellore Institute of Technology, India
S. Pooja, Vellore Institute of Technology, India
Akshara Siddharthan, Vellore Institute of Technology, India

Chapter 10
Volatility Forecasting Through Hybrid GARCH-LSTM Models With Walk-Forward Validation and Multi-Horizon Evaluation 339
Angel Mario Lerma-Sanchez, Universidad Autonoma de Tamaulipas, Mexico
Felipe A. González-González, Universidad Autonoma de Tamaulipas, Mexico
Joaquin Torres-Mata, Universidad Autonoma de Tamaulipas, Mexico

Chapter 11
Predictive Model to Estimate the Economic Activity of Mexican Municipalities Using Night Lights 395
Claudia García, Escuela Superior de Cómputo, National Polytechnic Institute, Mexico
Carolina Corral, Escuela Superior de Cómputo, National Polytechnic Institute, Mexico
Jesús Manuel Lopez, Escuela Superior de Cómputo, National Polytechnic Institute, Mexico

Compilation of References 441

About the Contributors 465

Index 473

Detailed Table of Contents

Preface.. xii

Chapter 1
Quantitative Finance Programming and Its Business Applications 1
Rishikaysh Kaakandikar, SaiBalaji International Institute of Management Sciences, Pune, India
Tejashree Soni, SaiBalaji International Institute of Management Sciences, Pune, India

Quantitative finance programming plays a crucial role in modern financial decision-making by combining mathematical models, statistical techniques, and computer programming to analyze financial data and predict market trends. It enables financial institutions and businesses to develop automated trading strategies, perform risk assessment, optimize investment portfolios, and enhance pricing models for financial instruments. Programming languages such as Python, R, and MATLAB are widely used to process large datasets and build predictive models. The integration of quantitative methods with advanced computing improves accuracy, speed, and efficiency in financial analysis. As financial markets become increasingly data-driven, quantitative finance programming provides organizations with a competitive advantage in strategic planning and investment management.

Chapter 2
Data-Driven Finance: Financial Mathematics, Database Management, and Econometric Techniques for Modern Decision-Making...................................... 49
Sanjeev Kumar, Lovely Professional University, India
Pardeep Kumar, Lovely Professional University, India

The dynamic financial world we are living in today demands data driven decision making. The combination of the three fields of financial mathematics, database management, and econometric approach to modern finance is the subject of the discussion in this paper. Financial mathematics provides basic techniques of valuing assets, risk evaluation and optimization of a portfolio through time value of money, derivatives pricing and stochastic, modeling". Besides this, an effective database management will enhance storage, retrieval, and manipulation of the large financial data, which will ensure an appropriate analysis and timely decisions. This is further enhanced with the econometric techniques that apply statistical models to identify relationships, hypothesis and predict financial results to support evidence-based approach in investment, risk management and policy making. Quantitative knowledge can enable the financial service providers to deal with market volatility, trend identification and maximization of resource expenditure through integration of the two.

Chapter 3
Monte Carlo Models for Asset Pricing and Financial Risk: Theory, Implementation, and Business Applications 81
Kattamuri Satish, Jain (Deemed to be) University, India
Rama Jyothi Boddu, Lendi Institute of Engineering and Technology, India
R. Hepsiba, AQJ Centre for PG Studies, India

Monte Carlo simulation is now used in modern finance to process complex derivatives, uncertainty in the market and valid risk analysis in non-linear and multi-factor contexts. The traditional models of analysis are often limited by assumptions such as constant volatility and normal returns because real market dynamics are often not captured by traditional analytical models. The chapter provides a well-rounded model that incorporates the theoretical basis of Monte Carlo methods, its computer implementation and business applications. Its code support of useful Python and R functions to simulate the asset path, price European, American, and Asian options, compute Value at risk and Expected shortfall, use variance reduction, and many fundamental stochastic processes, including Geometric Brownian Motion, jump-diffusion and the Heston model. Banking, insurance, asset management, and corporate finance examples are given of applications that are decision-oriented and the regulatory relevance and reliability is demonstrated through convergence diagnostics and back testing.

Chapter 4
Financial Data Engineering: From Raw Feeds to Feature Stores 113
Ganesh Harke, Independent Researcher, USA

Quantitative trading and risk management systems depend critically on the integrity of their underlying data infrastructure. While much of the academic literature treats financial data as static, preprocessed time series, real-world market data arrives as noisy, asynchronous streams requiring rigorous engineering controls. This chapter presents a comprehensive framework for Financial Data Engineering, tracing the lifecycle from raw market feeds to a point-in-time consistent Feature Store. It examines architectural patterns for ingestion, storage, transformation, and serving, emphasizing DataOps principles, polyglot persistence, and reproducibility across research and production environments. The chapter further addresses microstructure-aware cleaning, reconciliation, auditability, and synthetic stress-testing for rare market conditions. By formalizing market environments and standardizing feature computation, the proposed approach reduces look-ahead bias and mitigates the

Research–Production Gap, providing a blueprint for robust, end-to-end financial data systems.

Chapter 5
Persistent Homology for Time-Value-of-Money Modeling 155
Jaime Aguilar-Ortiz, Universidad Politécnica de Pachuca, Mexico
Ocotlán Diáz-Parra, Universidad Politécnica de Pachuca, Mexico
Jorge A. Ruiz-Vanoye, Universidad Politécnica de Pachuca, Mexico
Francisco R. Trejo-Macotela, Universidad Politécnica de Pachuca, Mexico
Marco A. Vera-Jiménez, Universidad Politécnica de Pachuca, Mexico
Víctor M. Zamudio-García, Universidad Politéctica Metropolitana de Hidalgo, Mexico
Carlos R. Domínguez-Mayorga, Universidad Politécnica de Pachuca, Mexico

Time-value-of-money (TVM) engines can help with pricing, budgeting, and analytics around risk, but their operational stability relies on convention-level decisions often considered secondary. Calendar choice, day-count basis, compounding rules, interpolation and numerical schemes can shift valuation outputs and create reconciliation and governance risks. Here, we propose the persistent homology validation framework, using TVM outputs from scenario sweeps, and describe the robustness of these outputs from the valuation-space point clouds. We analyze the risk of valuation frameworks using persistence diagrams and Betti curves, focusing on the clustering, regime shifts and cyclic patterns of equivalence that are often neglected using pointwise error assessments. We also present a new approach that integrates a flexible reproducible Python framework, topology-based diagnostics, and criteria for determining the rationality of valuation structures concerning rules of approximation before engaging such frameworks in regulated financial systems.

Chapter 6
Cryptocurrencies as Safe Haven Assets: A GARCH EVT and Monte Carlo Approach 195
José Antonio Molina Hernández, University of the Istmo, Mexico
Kevin Olalla Ake, Universidad Anahuac Veracruz, Mexico

The growing presence of institutional capital in crypto asset markets has reopened the debate on whether Bitcoin and similar digital assets can act as safe havens, the way gold or sovereign bonds have been built historically. This thesis tackles that question with a quantitative framework rather than the qualitative arguments that dominated the early literature. The dataset covers November 2019 to May 2026 (2,380 daily observations for Bitcoin, 2,381 for the full asset universe). I fit GARCH-t and EGARCH-t models to capture conditional variance, apply Extreme

Value Theory to isolate the tail directly, and run Monte Carlo simulation to estimate capital requirements over 30-day horizon.

Chapter 7
Topological Monte Carlo for Asset Dynamics 243
Jaime Aguilar-Ortiz, Universidad Politécnica de Pachuca, Mexico
Ocotlán Diáz-Parra, Universidad Politécnica de Pachuca, Mexico
Jorge A. Ruiz-Vanoye, Universidad Politécnica de Pachuca, Mexico
Francisco R. Trejo-Macotela, Universidad Politécnica de Pachuca, Mexico
Marco A. Vera-Jiménez, Universidad Politécnica de Pachuca, Mexico
Víctor M. Zamudio-García, Universidad Politécnica Metropolitana de Hidalgo, Mexico
Carlos R. Domínguez-Mayorga, Universidad Politécnica de Pachuca, Mexico

This chapter develops a reproducible procedure for designing and interrogating asset-dynamics scenarios with a topological layer. The proposed Topological Monte Carlo framework connects path simulation with topological data analysis so that simulated markets can be examined not only through losses and quantiles, but also through their geometric organization across regimes. Price and return paths are converted into feature embeddings; the resulting scenario-space point clouds are then analyzed with persistent homology. The associated summaries describe clustering, loop structure, and structural transitions under changing volatility states. On that basis, the chapter uses topological evidence to support adaptive scenario generation and to examine VaR/ES sensitivity under distributional shift. The workflow is implemented through a modular Python architecture intended for reproducible quantitative-finance experimentation and model-governance review.

Chapter 8
Modelling South African Closing Stock Prices Using GRNN, GBM and ANFIS Approaches 283
Malose Patrick Leeto Shogole, North-West University, South Africa
Johannes Tshepiso Tsoku, Sefako Makgato Health Science University, South Africa
Lebotsa Daniel Metsileng, North-West University, South Africa

Accurate forecasting is critical for informed investment decisions and risk management in financial markets. This study assesses the predictive performance of GRNN, GBM, and ANFIS in estimating the South African Nedbank closing stock prices. The results show that ANFIS achieves superior accuracy, with the lowest error metrics among the three models. Its effectiveness is attributed to the hybrid combination of fuzzy logic and neural networks, which enables it to capture complex nonlinear patterns and uncertainty in financial data. GBM demonstrates moderate predictive capability, benefiting from its iterative boosting mechanism, while GRNN shows higher errors, reflecting challenges in modelling highly volatile market conditions. These findings support the growing evidence that hybrid models such as ANFIS provide enhanced forecasting reliability. The study highlights ANFIS's practical utility for analysts and investors, and future research could explore integrating it with advanced machine learning approaches to further improve stock price prediction in dynamic markets.

Chapter 9
Machine Learning and Transformer-Based Equity Return Forecasting: A Case Study on Nvidia.. 313
S. Rajkumar, Vellore Institute of Technology, India
S. Pooja, Vellore Institute of Technology, India
Akshara Siddharthan, Vellore Institute of Technology, India

Predicting financial asset returns remains one of the more intractable problems in quantitative finance, owing to well-documented data challenges including non-stationarity, leptokurtic return distributions, and near-efficient price dynamics. This chapter evaluates six forecasting methodologies, naive persistence, ARIMA, Ridge regression, Random Forest, XGBoost, and a Temporal Sequence Transformer applied to next-day stock-returns of NVIDIA Corporation (NVDA) over a 25-year horizon. Methodological rigour is maintained throughout: all hyperparameter selection is confined to the training period, and model evaluation follows a walk-forward cross-validation scheme that strictly preserves temporal ordering. Empirical results suggest that gradient-boosted and ensemble tree methods offer a more favourable trade-off between predictive accuracy and practical implementability than either classical time-series specifications or the deep learning alternative the underperformance of the latter, absent domain-specific feature engineering, serving as a cautionary note on the uncritical application of high-capacity architectures to low signal-to-noise financial data.

Chapter 10
Volatility Forecasting Through Hybrid GARCH-LSTM Models With Walk-Forward Validation and Multi-Horizon Evaluation 339
Angel Mario Lerma-Sanchez, Universidad Autonoma de Tamaulipas, Mexico
Felipe A. González-González, Universidad Autonoma de Tamaulipas, Mexico
Joaquin Torres-Mata, Universidad Autonoma de Tamaulipas, Mexico

This chapter, per the authors, examines volatility forecasting through a hybrid GARCH-LSTM framework designed to improve prediction accuracy under a rigorous and reproducible evaluation scheme. The purpose of this chapter is to assess whether combining the econometric structure of GARCH with the nonlinear sequence-learning capacity of LSTM enhances forecasting performance relative to a standard GARCH benchmark. The content includes the theoretical foundations of financial volatility, a review of hybrid forecasting literature, the construction of daily return-based volatility measures, the specification of the proposed model, and an empirical evaluation using S&P 500, EUR/USD, and Bitcoin data. Results from walk-forward and multi-horizon validation show that the hybrid model delivers more accurate short-term forecasts and remains competitive across different asset classes

Chapter 11
Predictive Model to Estimate the Economic Activity of Mexican Municipalities Using Night Lights 395
Claudia García, Escuela Superior de Cómputo, National Polytechnic Institute, Mexico
Carolina Corral, Escuela Superior de Cómputo, National Polytechnic Institute, Mexico
Jesús Manuel Lopez, Escuela Superior de Cómputo, National Polytechnic Institute, Mexico

This chapter presents a methodology to estimate municipal gross domestic product (GDP) in Mexico by integrating nighttime light (NTL) satellite imagery with econometric reasoning and machine learning. This chapter addresses a practical and analytical limitation: in Mexico, GDP is systematically available at the national and state levels, but not as a regular official series at the municipal level. This gap complicates local economic analysis, regional planning, and the evaluation of territorially focused public policy. To address this limitation, the study combines state-level GDP data, population-based municipal disaggregation, and multiple indicators extracted from VIIRS nighttime lights. Three model families are assessed: ordinary least squares (OLS), Random Forest, and a hybrid model in which Random Forest is used to learn the nonlinear structure that remains in the OLS residuals. The chapter argues that this combined strategy is particularly useful in settings characterized by territorial heterogeneity, uneven statistical infrastructure, and a large informal sector.

Compilation of References 441

About the Contributors 465

Index 473

Preface

INTRODUCTION

The financial industry is experiencing an unprecedented period of transformation driven by advances in digital technologies, data analytics, computational methods, and algorithmic decision-making. Financial institutions, investment firms, FinTech companies, regulators, and market participants increasingly rely on quantitative models to navigate complex markets, manage risk, optimize portfolios, and support strategic decision-making. In this rapidly evolving environment, the ability to translate financial theory into robust computational solutions has become one of the most valuable skills for both academic researchers and industry professionals.

Quantitative Finance Programming: Models, Methods, and Business Applications was conceived to address this growing need by providing a comprehensive bridge between the theoretical foundations of quantitative finance and their practical implementation in real-world settings. While traditional finance texts often focus on mathematical formulations and conceptual frameworks, this volume places equal emphasis on computational execution, demonstrating how modern programming tools can be leveraged to develop, validate, and deploy sophisticated financial models. The result is a resource that combines rigorous analytical thinking with practical, hands-on problem solving.

A distinguishing feature of this book is its commitment to a multi-platform perspective on financial programming. Although Python has emerged as one of the most widely adopted programming languages in quantitative finance due to its flexibility, extensive libraries, and accessibility, today's financial professionals frequently operate within diverse technological environments. Recognizing this reality, the contributors explore a broad ecosystem of programming and analytical tools, including R for advanced statistical analysis, SAS for enterprise-level analytics, MATLAB for numerical modeling, Julia for high-performance scientific computing, and SQL for effective data management and retrieval. By embracing this technological diversity, the book equips readers with a broader understanding of the tools available to solve increasingly complex financial challenges.

The chapters contained within this volume examine a wide range of quantitative finance applications that are shaping contemporary financial practice. Topics include financial modeling, risk assessment, portfolio optimization, forecasting techniques, algorithmic trading strategies, valuation methods, financial engineering, business analytics, and data-driven decision-making. Through the integration of theoretical concepts, computational methodologies, and practical case studies, the contributors demonstrate how programming can enhance both the rigor and effectiveness of financial analysis across a variety of contexts.

The primary objective of this book is to provide readers with the knowledge and technical skills required to bridge the gap between theory and application. The volume emphasizes reproducibility, model validation, computational efficiency, and practical implementation, recognizing that successful quantitative finance solutions must be both mathematically sound and operationally effective. By combining academic insights with industry-oriented applications, the book serves as a valuable resource for understanding how modern financial problems can be addressed through computational approaches.

This publication is intended for a broad audience of scholars, practitioners, and students. Researchers and academics in quantitative finance, financial engineering, economics, business analytics, and related disciplines will find valuable frameworks for translating theoretical work into practical computational models. Graduate students and advanced undergraduates will benefit from the hands-on programming approaches that prepare them for careers in quantitative analysis, FinTech, risk management, and algorithmic trading. Industry professionals—including financial analysts, portfolio managers, quantitative researchers, data scientists, and risk specialists—will find advanced methodologies and practical techniques applicable to contemporary financial challenges. In addition, educators and trainers will discover a comprehensive resource for developing curricula that reflect the growing importance of computational finance in both academic and professional settings.

As editors, we are grateful to the distinguished contributors who have shared their expertise, research, and professional experiences in the development of this volume. Their collective efforts reflect the interdisciplinary nature of modern quantitative finance, where mathematics, statistics, computer science, economics, and business strategy converge to create innovative solutions for increasingly complex financial environments. We also extend our appreciation to the reviewers and publishing team whose guidance and support have contributed significantly to the quality of this work.

It is our hope that *Quantitative Finance Programming: Models, Methods, and Business Applications* will serve as both a scholarly reference and a practical guide for those seeking to master the tools and methodologies that define contemporary quantitative finance. By fostering deeper understanding of computational finance and promoting the effective application of analytical techniques, this volume seeks to support the next generation of innovation in financial research, practice, and education.

ORGANIZATION OF THE BOOK

Chapter 1, "Quantitative Finance Programming and its Business Applications," introduces the foundational role of quantitative programming in contemporary financial decision-making. The chapter demonstrates how mathematical modeling, statistical analysis, and computational tools work together to support portfolio optimization, risk assessment, financial forecasting, and automated trading strategies. By highlighting the practical applications of programming languages such as Python, R, and MATLAB, the authors illustrate how quantitative methods provide organizations with enhanced analytical capabilities and a competitive advantage in increasingly data-driven financial markets.

Chapter 2, "Data-Driven Finance: Financial Mathematics, Database Management, and Econometric Techniques for Modern Decision-Making," explores the integration of financial mathematics, data management, and econometric analysis as a framework for evidence-based decision-making. The chapter examines how valuation techniques, risk modeling approaches, and portfolio optimization methods are strengthened through effective database architectures and advanced statistical analysis. By combining theoretical and computational perspectives, the chapter demonstrates how financial institutions can better navigate market uncertainty, identify emerging trends, and improve resource allocation through data-driven strategies.

Chapter 3, "Monte Carlo Models for Asset Pricing and Financial Risk: Theory, Implementation, and Business Applications," presents a comprehensive examination of Monte Carlo simulation techniques and their applications in quantitative finance. The chapter combines theoretical foundations with practical implementation using Python and R, demonstrating how simulation methods can be used to value complex derivatives, assess financial risk, and model uncertainty in volatile markets. Through examples drawn from banking, insurance, asset management, and corporate finance, the authors illustrate the importance of Monte Carlo methods in supporting informed decision-making and regulatory compliance.

Chapter 4, "Financial Data Engineering: From Raw Feeds to Feature Stores," addresses one of the most critical yet often overlooked aspects of quantitative finance: the engineering of reliable financial data systems. The chapter follows the complete lifecycle of financial data, from ingestion and storage to transformation and deployment, emphasizing reproducibility, auditability, and operational efficiency. By introducing DataOps principles, feature stores, and microstructure-aware data cleaning techniques, the author provides a practical blueprint for developing robust financial data infrastructures capable of supporting advanced analytics, trading strategies, and risk management systems.

Chapter 5, "Persistent Homology for Time-Value-of-Money Modeling," introduces an innovative approach to validating financial valuation frameworks through topological data analysis. The chapter examines how persistent homology can be applied to evaluate the stability and robustness of time-value-of-money calculations under varying assumptions regarding calendars, compounding conventions, and numerical methods. By moving beyond traditional pointwise error assessments, the authors offer a novel framework for identifying structural patterns, valuation regimes, and governance risks within financial models, contributing to more transparent and reliable valuation practices.

Chapter 6, "Cryptocurrencies as Safe Haven Assets: A GARCH EVT and Monte Carlo Approach," investigates the role of cryptocurrencies within modern investment portfolios through a rigorous computational risk-analysis framework. Using advanced volatility modeling techniques, Monte Carlo simulations, and Extreme Value Theory, the chapter evaluates whether digital assets can serve as safe havens during periods of market stress. The findings reveal significant volatility and systemic risk characteristics within cryptocurrency markets, offering important insights for portfolio managers, regulators, and risk professionals concerned with the integration of digital assets into traditional financial systems.

Chapter 7, "Topological Monte Carlo for Asset Dynamics," presents a novel framework that combines Monte Carlo simulation with topological data analysis to examine financial market behavior. The chapter demonstrates how persistent homology can be used to analyze the structural properties of simulated market scenarios, revealing clustering patterns, regime changes, and geometric relationships that may not be visible through traditional risk measures. By integrating topology into scenario generation and risk assessment, the authors provide a powerful new approach for model governance and quantitative finance experimentation.

Chapter 8, "Modelling South African Closing Stock Prices Using GRNN, GBM and ANFIS Approaches," explores the application of advanced machine learning and hybrid intelligence models to stock price forecasting. Through a comparative analysis of General Regression Neural Networks, Gradient Boosting Machines, and Adaptive Neuro-Fuzzy Inference Systems, the chapter evaluates the effectiveness of different predictive methodologies using South African equity market data. The findings highlight the superior forecasting performance of ANFIS, demonstrating the value of hybrid models in capturing nonlinear market behavior and improving investment decision-making.

Chapter 9, "Machine Learning and Transformer-based Equity Return Forecasting: A Case Study on Nvidia," examines the application of machine learning methodologies to forecasting and predictive analytics within business environments. Using real-world data and multiple regression-based approaches, the chapter investigates how advanced machine learning techniques can improve forecasting accuracy and support more effective decision-making. The discussion highlights the growing role of predictive modeling in addressing uncertainty and optimizing operational and financial planning through data-driven insights.

Chapter 10, "Volatility Forecasting Through Hybrid GARCH-LSTM Models with Walk-Forward Validation and Multi-Horizon Evaluation," concludes the volume with an exploration of hybrid forecasting models that combine traditional econometric techniques with modern deep learning approaches. The chapter evaluates the performance of a GARCH-LSTM framework across multiple asset classes, including equity, currency, and cryptocurrency markets. Through rigorous walk-forward validation and multi-horizon testing, the authors demonstrate how integrating econometric structure with neural network learning can improve volatility forecasting accuracy and enhance financial risk management practices.

Chapter 11, "Predictive Model to Estimate the Economic Activity of Mexican Municipalities Using Night Lights," presents a methodology to estimate municipal gross domestic product (GDP) in Mexico by integrating nighttime light (NTL) satellite imagery with econometric reasoning and machine learning. This chapter addresses a practical and analytical limitation: in Mexico, GDP is systematically available at the national and state levels, but not as a regular official series at the municipal level. This gap complicates local economic analysis, regional planning, and the evaluation of territorially focused public policy. To address this limitation, the study combines state-level GDP data, population-based municipal disaggregation, and multiple indicators extracted from VIIRS nighttime lights.

CONCLUDING REMARKS

The chapters presented in *Quantitative Finance Programming: Models, Methods, and Business Applications* collectively reflect the rapid evolution of modern finance into a discipline defined by computational rigor, data-intensive decision-making, and algorithmic intelligence. Across diverse methodological perspectives and application domains, the contributions in this volume demonstrate that quantitative finance is no longer confined to theoretical abstraction but is increasingly shaped by practical implementation through programming, simulation, and advanced data analytics.

Throughout this book, our contributors have explored a wide spectrum of techniques that underpin contemporary financial modeling, including time series analysis,

Monte Carlo simulation, econometric modeling, financial data engineering, topological data analysis, machine learning, and hybrid forecasting architectures. These approaches collectively illustrate how financial systems can be better understood, modeled, and optimized when supported by robust computational frameworks and scalable programming environments. The integration of tools such as Python, R, MATLAB, SQL, and emerging high-performance computing paradigms further highlights the importance of technological fluency in modern financial practice.

A central theme emerging from this volume is the increasing convergence of theory and implementation. The effectiveness of quantitative finance now depends not only on the mathematical soundness of models but also on their reproducibility, scalability, and real-world applicability. The chapters emphasize that model validation, risk assessment, and forecasting accuracy are strengthened through rigorous computational workflows, transparent data engineering practices, and robust evaluation methodologies. This alignment between theory and practice is essential for ensuring that financial models remain both reliable and operationally relevant.

Another key insight offered by this collection is the importance of methodological diversity. From classical econometric approaches to advanced machine learning systems and topology-based analytics, the contributions illustrate that no single modeling paradigm is sufficient to address the complexity of modern financial markets. Instead, effective financial decision-making requires a synthesis of techniques, where traditional statistical frameworks and modern computational intelligence complement one another to produce more resilient and adaptive solutions.

The volume also underscores the growing importance of data infrastructure and model governance in quantitative finance. As financial systems become increasingly dependent on high-frequency, high-volume, and heterogeneous data sources, the integrity of data pipelines and the reproducibility of analytical results become critical. The discussions presented throughout this book highlight the need for robust financial data engineering practices, transparent model validation protocols, and systematic approaches to managing uncertainty and structural risk.

As editors, we hope this book serves as a comprehensive reference for researchers, practitioners, and students seeking to deepen their understanding of computational finance and its practical applications. The methodologies, case studies, and frameworks presented herein are intended not only to advance academic inquiry but also to support real-world financial decision-making in areas such as risk management, investment strategy development, portfolio optimization, and algorithmic trading.

Ultimately, the future of quantitative finance will be defined by the continued integration of computational innovation, interdisciplinary collaboration, and data-driven insight. It is our hope that this volume contributes meaningfully to that evolution by equipping readers with the conceptual tools and programming perspectives necessary to navigate an increasingly complex and dynamic financial landscape.

Felipe Machorro-Ramos
Autonomous Popular University of the State of Puebla, Mexico

María Vanessa Romero-Ortiz
Polytechnic University of Puebla, Mexico

José Gonzalo Ramírez-Rosas
Polytechnic University of Puebla, Mexico

Martín Neri-Suárez
Polytechnic University of Puebla, Mexico

Lorena Hernández-Quiroz
Polytechnic University of Puebla, Mexico

Chapter 1
Quantitative Finance Programming and Its Business Applications

Rishikaysh Kaakandikar
http://orcid.org/0000-0003-0349-6788
SaiBalaji International Institute of Management Sciences, Pune, India

Tejashree Soni
http://orcid.org/0009-0004-3120-7546
SaiBalaji International Institute of Management Sciences, Pune, India

ABSTRACT

Quantitative finance programming plays a crucial role in modern financial decision-making by combining mathematical models, statistical techniques, and computer programming to analyze financial data and predict market trends. It enables financial institutions and businesses to develop automated trading strategies, perform risk assessment, optimize investment portfolios, and enhance pricing models for financial instruments. Programming languages such as Python, R, and MATLAB are widely used to process large datasets and build predictive models. The integration of quantitative methods with advanced computing improves accuracy, speed, and efficiency in financial analysis. As financial markets become increasingly data-driven, quantitative finance programming provides organizations with a competitive advantage in strategic planning and investment management.

DOI: 10.4018/979-8-3373-8372-9.ch001

INTRODUCTION

Quantitative finance is a specialization that involves the application of mathematical model, statistical techniques and calculation tools in the analysis of financial markets, instruments and the risk. It mainly aims at transforming the financial theory into quantitative models that can be tested, simulated and implemented through the use of programming. The approach provides evidence based information that is significant in financial choices regarding pricing, risk management, investment policy. The disciplinary field includes four major areas, and they are finance, mathematics, statistics, and computer science. The conceptual basis is given by financial theories, the modeling tools are provided by mathematics, the data and inferences can be made by the use of statistics and finally, the complex models need to be implemented with the help of computer programming. The interdisciplinary framework helps professionals to find trends and handle huge amounts of data, making informed decisions.

Quantitative finance can be applied in asset pricing, portfolio management, as well as option derivatives pricing and algorithmic trading and risk management basing on the Capital Asset Pricing Model (CAPM), black-Scholes option pricing model and Value at risk (VaR).

The modern world of finance would not be able to replace quantitative finance to enhance efficiency, transparency, and accuracy. Quantitative models assist financial institutions to analyze investment opportunities, to allocate the assets in the best possible way and also to mitigate any uncertainties that emerge in the market when it becomes volatile. Quick analysis and fast decision-making can be done by computational means and this is relevant in the fast-paced modern world of finance.

HISTORIES OF QUANTITATIVE FINANCE

Algorithmic Trading and Big Data (2000s-Present)

Quantitative finance has become a very technological-oriented profession in the 21 st century. The advent of algorithmic trading enables the financial institutions to automatically carry out the trades based on predetermined mathematical rules. HFT systems are capable of making thousands of trades in a second enhancing efficiency and liquidity.

The current developments involve:

* Python, R, and high-performance computing are used.
* The combination of machine learning and artificial intelligence.
* Financial forecasting with big data analytics.

* Risk monitoring systems in real time.
* FinTech products like robots-advisor products.

Machine learning methods are currently applied in fraud detection, credit risk assessment, and predictive modeling.

APPLICATION OF MATHEMATICS, STATISTICS, AND PROGRAMMING IN FINANCE

Applications of Mathematics in Finance

Financial modeling and analysis are backed up by mathematics. It gives the theoretical structure that is needed to define the financial issues in a systematized and rational way. Models of asset pricing, interest rate movement, portfolio optimization and derivatives valuation are developed using mathematical concepts.

Pricing financial instruments is one of the greatest uses of mathematics in finance. As an example, calculus is applied to determine the changes in asset price and risk sensitivities. In option pricing models, most of them employ differential equations e.g. the Black-Scholes model which is a key model used to calculate the fair value of the financial derivatives.

The application of linear algebra in portfolio management is the relationship analysis between two or more assets and efficient allocation of the portfolio. Optimization methods assist investors in choosing the optimal set of assets that can yield the highest returns and reduce the risk. Mathematic concepts like probability theory are also needed in the evaluation of uncertainties and forecasting of the potential financial result.

The use of statistics in finance.

- Statistics is very important in the analysis of financial information, trend determination and prediction. The financial markets produce voluminous data, such as the prices of stocks, returns, volumes, and economic indicators. This data is interpreted statistically and meaningful information is extracted.
- Risk measurement is one of the important uses of statistics in finance. Measures of asset returns volatility, which is financial risk, are measured using statistical methods like standard deviation and variance. Value at Risk (VaR), which is a very common risk management tool relies upon statistical models to derive the estimate of the maximum potential loss that could be incurred within a certain time interval.

- Forecasting and predictive modeling are also done through statistical analysis. Regression analysis assists in revealing the relation among variables like the relation between the interest rate and the stock prices. The time series analysis is applied to analyze historic financial information to forecast the trend in the future.

Use of Programming in Finance.

Programming is essential in the application of mathematical and statistical modelling in the real world, in finance. Financial models are characterized by complicated calculations and big data sets, which cannot be processed effectively without computer tools.

The most common programming languages used in quantitative finance are Python, R, MATLAB and C++. With these languages, financial analysts can automate, analyze, simulate and write trading algorithms through financial data.

Another notable use of programming is in algorithmic trading where programs are used to automatically trade using a set of rules and models. Financial institutions are also able to carry out real-time risk monitoring and portfolio analysis by programming.

Finance Mathematics, Statistics and Programming.

A combination of mathematics, statistics, and programming can be used as a tool to build and implement powerful financial models and decision-making tools. Mathematics gives conceptual organization, statistics data analysis and inferences, and programming application and automation.

As an example, in the case of portfolio optimization, the problem is defined and mathematical optimization models are utilized, although statistical techniques are applied to estimate risk and returns and programming is utilized to compute and implement the optimal portfolio.

In the same manner, risk measures in risk management are defined using mathematical formulas, risk parameters are estimated using statistical techniques, and risk is calculated and monitored using programming tools.

Movement of the traditional finance to data-driven finance.

Factors behind the shift to Data-Driven Finance.

There are a number of technological, economic, and institutional factors that have contributed to the rise of data-driven finance.

Growth of Financial Data

The fast growth of financial markets and online platforms has led to the creation of huge amounts of financial data. This encompasses the market prices, trading volumes, economic indicators, trade records, and other alternative sources of data like social media and satellite images. This is because the existence of great datasets has made the analysis of financial data more accurate and comprehensive.

Improvements in Computing Technology

The emergence of high-performance computers, cloud computing, and sophisticated software has made it much easier to work and analyze big data. The complicated simulations, risk assessment, and real-time analysis of the market can now be carried out by financial institutions with great efficiency.

Quantitative Model Development

With the progress of financial mathematics and statistical modeling, it is now possible to create advanced quantitative asset pricing, risk management and portfolio optimization models. These models are more objective and reliable as far as decision making is concerned.

Rise of Programming and Automation

The financial analysis, trading and risk management have been automated using Python, R, and C++ programming languages. Automation eliminates human mistakes and enhances effectiveness and expediency.

The Emergence of Artificial Intelligence and Machine Learning

Artificial intelligence and machine learning have increased the possibility to analyze financial data and break down the patterns and predict market trends. The technologies allow predictive analytics, fraud detection, and automated investment management.

Characteristics of Data-Driven Finance

Data-driven finance refers to the use of quantitative models, statistical analysis, and computational tools to support financial decision-making. It relies on objective data analysis rather than subjective judgment.

Key characteristics include:

- Use of large datasets for financial analysis
- Application of mathematical and statistical models
- Automation of financial processes
- Real-time data analysis and decision-making
- Use of machine learning and artificial intelligence
- Algorithmic and high-frequency trading

Table 1. Methodological shifts

Aspect	*Traditional Finance*	*Data-Driven Finance*
Decision Basis	Economic intuition & theory	Empirical evidence & data patterns
Data Use	Financial statements, macro indicators	Big data (structured & unstructured)
Modeling Approach	Deterministic or parametric (e.g. linear regression)	Non-linear, adaptive (ML, AI, neural nets)
Risk Management	Historical stress tests, VAR	Dynamic models, real-time analytics
Execution	Manual or semi-automated	Algorithmic and high-frequency systems

Introduction To Quantitative Finance

Financial markets are the places where the buyers and sellers exchange the financial assets. These markets ease the process of capital distribution, liquidity, and economic development. There are two broad categories of financial markets, namely primary market and secondary market.

New financial securities like stocks and bonds are first issued in the primary market. Firms and governments use initial public offerings (IPOs) and bonds to raise capital respectively. The secondary market enables investors to trade in securities that have been issued in the past and this gives liquidity and price discovery. These are examples of stock exchanges, like the National Stock Exchange (NSE) and Bombay Stock Exchange (BSE). Quantitative finance has evolved over the years significantly to incorporate the use of mathematical models, statistics and computer tools to study the financial market. The early theoretical models such as option pricing models revolutionised financial economics by providing systematic methods of analysis of derivatives and risk. Modern financial engineering is based on the pioneering work of Black and Scholes (1973) and Merton (1973), with subsequent work focusing on empirical analysis and stylized facts of asset returns (Cont, 2001). Financial time series analysis has been a key to understanding the volatility and the dynamics of the market as data-driven techniques have developed (Tsay, 2010). Moreover, the historical perspective indicates how quantitative finance has been continuously modified to all technological and methodological shifts (Cesa, 2017).

The assets that are traded in financial markets are financial instruments. These tools could be divided into the following:

Equity Instruments: It is ownership of a company i.e. common stocks. The holders of equity get the returns in the form of dividends and capital appreciation.

Debt Instruments: They are borrowed funds which have to be paid back with interest like the bonds, debentures and the treasury bills.

Derivative Instruments: Derivatives are based on a real asset including stocks, interest rates or commodities. These are options, futures, forward, and swaps. These are popularly used as hedging and speculation tools.

Money Market Instruments: These are short term financial instruments like treasury bills and commercial paper and certificates of deposits and are usually used in the management of liquidity.

Risk, Return and Time Value of Money

Risk return relationship is a core concept of finance. Return is the amount of gain or loss obtained after investing in a particular project and risk is the uncertainty involved in getting the anticipated return. Higher risk will be compensated by higher returns expected by investors.

The formula used to measure the return is the following:

Return = (Final Value - Initial Value) / Initial Value

Most of the common statistical measures used in measuring risk include variance and standard deviation, which are used to measure volatility of returns. The higher volatility is the greater the uncertainty and risk.

Time value of money is another important concept of finance, according to which money today has more value than an equivalent amount of money in the future because it has the ability to earn. This is a fundamental tenet of investment analysis, loan valuation and financial planning.

The future value of an investment is calculated using the formula:

Future Value (FV) = Present Value (PV) × $(1 + r)^n$

Where:

PV = Present Value
r = Interest rate
n = Number of periods

Similarly, the present value of future cash flows is calculated using:

Present Value (PV) = FV / $(1 + r)^n$

These formulas are used extensively in bond valuation, capital budgeting, and investment analysis.

Statistical Foundations and Probability Theory

Probability theory offers the mathematical model of financial market uncertainty. The prices of financial assets are determined by many uncertain factors which are the economic conditions, interest rates and market sentiment. The probability theory assists in determining the probability of various events.

Key concepts include:

- Random Variables: Financial returns are considered random variables since their value cannot be determined.
- Probability Distributions: Probability distributions are often used to characterize the distribution of financial returns, including the normal distribution, which is a characterization of the probability of the various possible returns.
- Expected Value: Expected value of an investment is the mean of all the possible returns divided by their probabilities.
- Expected Return = S (Probability x Return).Statistics is an important tool of analyzing financial information and estimating parameters of a model.

Significant statistical indicators are:

Mean: The average return of investment.
Variance: Suicide of returns.
Standard Deviation: Square root of variance which is a common measure of risk.
Correlation: This determines the relationship between two assets.

Financial forecasting and risk management are heavily applied fields where statistical tools like regression analysis and the time series analysis are frequently applied to analyze historical data, predict the future trend, and determine the best decision to make investment.

Microsoft Excel is employed to generate the necessary graphs and charts and to ensure the accuracy of the generated table. Optimization and Linear Algebra in Finance Microsoft Excel is used to create the graph and charts needed and to make sure that the created table is accurate.

The term optimization is applied in the field of finance to calculate the optimal decision considering the constraints present. It is extensively utilized in risk reduction, asset selection, and portfolio management.

Portfolio optimization is one of the most significant uses of optimization where investors want to achieve maximum returns with minimum risk. The mathematical optimization methods can be used to estimate the most efficient allocation of assets.

Linear algebra is necessary to process a variety of financial variables at the same time. The financial portfolios can be composed of very large number of assets and linear algebra offers some tools like vectors and matrices to capture and analyze the assets of the financial portfolios in an efficient manner.

For example:

- The returns of assets can be expressed in the form of vectors.
- Portfolio vectors may take the form of vectors.
- The covariance of the assets can take the form of matrices.

The tools are mathematical in nature and are employed to compute portfolio risk and optimization of asset allocation.

The programming languages in quantitative finance

Programming has become an inseparable part of quantitative finance, which allows financial specialists to apply mathematical models, large datasets, and automate trading strategies and financial risks. The growing sophistication in the financial markets and the access to massive data volumes has necessitated the use of computational tools. Computational capabilities and library specifications make programming languages (python, R, MATLAB, C++, and Java) very popular in financial modeling and quantitative analysis.

Financial models involve using computer programs to create, construct, and analyze financial data, as well as facilitating decision-making processes. The relevance of Programming in Financial Modeling Financial models refer to the construction, development, and analysis of financial information through the use of a computer program and the use of such programs to aid in decision-making.

Financial modeling is the application of mathematical and statistical models in order to model financial systems, analyze the prices of assets, and predict their future financial results. These models are usually characterized by extensive computations, big data and repetitive tasks which cannot be effectively done by hand. Automation is one of the most important benefits of programming in financial modeling because with the help of programming, financial analysts can accurately and efficiently implement these models. Repetitive operations in programming like valuation of portfolio, measurement of risk, and financial forecast can be conducted automatically. This will lower human error and enhance performance.

This marriage of computational and programming techniques has turned into a mandatory component of contemporary finance training and practice. With the increase in the complexity of financial markets, the requirement of good level of programming among the finance professionals has increased as well. The new instructional strategies will target the synthesis of the theoretical data with the practical use of the codes to provide the students with the tasks involved in the real world (Yan, 2017). Modern financial programming includes financial programs, like sophisticated programming languages like C++, to assist practitioners with multi-faceted issues of financial engineering and analytics (Oliveira, 2021). Furthermore, big data technologies and large-scale data processing have enhanced the potential to perform the quantitative analysis successfully (Shi et al., 2017). These are also a trend in the more technology-based approach to finance.

Financial professionals are also able to process and analyze large numbers of financial information with the help of programming. The financial markets are producing enormous quantities of real time information such as the prices of the stocks, volumes of trade as well as the economic indicators. It could be gathered, processed, and digested using programming tools. Simulation is another significant area of use of programming. The modeling of uncertainty and assessment of financial risks involves the use of methods like Monte Carlo simulation.

Introduction to the Different Major Programming Languages in Quantitative Finance.

There are a number of programming languages that are typically applied in quantitative finance, each with certain advantages depending upon the application.

Python

Python is the programming language most commonly used in quantitative finance because it is simple, flexible and has a large library ecosystem. It is applicable in financial modeling, data analysis, machine learning and algorithmic trading.

Python has a number of strengths, which include simple syntax, well-developed community and libraries like NumPy, Pandas, and SciPy. It is common in investment banks, hedge funds and fintech companies.

Python is specifically applicable in:

- Financial data analysis
- Risk management
- Portfolio optimization
- Machine learning-based applications.

R Programming

R is a statistical programming language that is used in statistical analysis and data visualization. It finds extensive application in financial studies and universities.

The strong tools and packages available in R include quantmod, Performance Analytics and forecast. The financial data analysis, risk modelling and econometric analysis are commonly analyzed using it.

R is particularly useful for:

- Statistical modeling
- Time series analysis
- Financial forecasting
- Data visualization

MATLAB

MATLAB is popular in amount computing and mathematical modeling. MATLAB is often applied to academic research, financial engineering, and derivatives pricing.MATLAB is mainly applied in:

- Financial simulations
- Derivatives pricing
- Numerical analysis
- Optimization problems

C++

C++ is a high-performance language, which is employed in those applications where speed and efficiency are important. The widely used applications are high-frequency trading and real-time financial applications.

C++ offers high-speed performance and memory management which makes it ideal to be used in a complex financial model that requires real time performance.

C++ is particularly useful for:

- High-frequency trading
- Real-time risk management
- Trading system development
- Performance-critical applications

Java

Java is a popular operating system in financial systems of enterprises because it is stable, scalable and secure. A lot of financial institutions which are big, are having Java to be used to develop trading platforms, risk management systems and financial applications.

Java is especially applicable in:

- Trading platforms
- Financial infrastructure systems.
- Risk management software.
- Financial software on the enterprise level.

Comparison of Programming Languages for Financial Applications

Each programming language offers different advantages depending on the financial application. The following comparison highlights key differences:

Table 2.

Programming Language	*Strengths*	*Weaknesses*	*Common Applications*
Python	Easy to learn, extensive libraries, versatile	Slower than C++	Data analysis, financial modeling, machine learning
R	Strong statistical capabilities, excellent visualization	Slower execution speed	Statistical modeling, research, forecasting
MATLAB	Excellent numerical and mathematical tools	Expensive, limited scalability	Financial simulations, derivatives pricing
C++	Extremely fast, efficient memory management	Complex syntax, difficult to learn	High-frequency trading, real-time systems
Java	Highly scalable, secure, reliable	Less suitable for statistical analysis	Trading platforms, enterprise financial systems

Python and R are widely used for analysis and modeling, while C++ and Java are preferred for high-performance and enterprise applications.

Libraries and Frameworks of Quantitative finance.

Financial modeling and analysis are simplified with specialized libraries and frameworks that exist in programming languages.

Python Libraries

Quantitative finance Python has many libraries such as:

- NumPy - Numpyries and calculi Numbers
- Pandas - Data manipulation and data analysis.
- SciPy - Optimization and scientific computing.
- Data visualization Matplotlib and Seaborn.
- QuantLib - Financial derivatives and financial modeling.
- TensorFlow and Scikit-learn - Applications in machine learning.

R Libraries

R has strong financial and statistical packages and they are:

- quantmod - Financials analysis.
- Performance Analysis - Portfolio performance analysis.
- forecast - Time series forecasting.
- tidy verse - Data manipulation and visualization.

MATLAB Toolboxes

MATLAB has toolboxes related to finance such as:

- Financial Toolbox - Financial modeling.
- Optimization Toolbox - Portfolio optimization.
- Risk analysis and forecasting - Statistics and Machine Learning Toolbox.

C++ Libraries

Typical examples of C++ libraries used in finance are:

- QuantLib - Derivatives pricing and financial modeling.
- Boost Libraries - Mathematics and statistics.

Java Frameworks

Java packages in finance are:

- Apache Common Math - Mathematic and statistical analysis.
- Spring Framework - Enterprise financial application development.

FINANCIAL DATA MANAGEMENT AND ACQUISITION

Sources of Financial Data

The financial information may be secured through numerous sources and it depends on the kind of analysis and use. Such sources have a broad categorization of market data, macroeconomic data and alternative data.

Market Data

Market data is the data that is associated with the financial instruments that are traded in financial markets. These are the prices of stocks, prices of bonds, price derivatives, trading volumes, bid-ask spread, and market indices. Asset pricing, portfolio analysis and risk analysis are crucial to market data.

There are further markets that can be categorized as:

Historical Data: The historical prices and trading data upon which one analyses and models.
Real-Time Data: Real-time market data to trade and manage risk.
Intraday Data: Data which is collected within the trading hours.

Financial institutions receive stock exchange, financial data providers and trading platform data related to the market.

Macroeconomic Data

Economic indicators included in macroeconomic data are those that affect the financial markets and investment decisions. These indicators give information on the general economic environment.

Examples include:

- Gross Domestic Product (GDP)
- Inflation rates
- Interest rates
- Unemployment rates
- Exchange rates
- Monetary policy indicators

Macroeconomic data is commonly employed in economic prediction, investment decision analysis and assessment of risk.

Alternative Data

Alternative data are the non-traditional data that offer more information about financial markets. Alternative data is becoming more significant in quantitative finance due to technological progress. Hedge funds and fintech companies usually utilize alternative data to obtain competitive advantages and enhance predictive models.

Examples include:

- Social media sentiment data
- Financial reports and news items.
- Satellite imagery
- Consumer transaction data
- Search trends and web traffic.

Data Cleaning, Data Normalization, and Preprocessing.

Raw financial data has many mistakes, values absent, and discrepancies and noise. Preprocessing and data cleaning are necessary in order to guarantee data accuracy and dependability.

Data Cleaning

Data cleaning is the process of defining and rectifying financial dataset errors. Data cleaning methods involve elimination of duplicate data, replacement of missing values, and correction of inconsistencies.

Common issues include:

- Missing values
- Duplicate records
- Incorrect data entries
- Outliers

Data Normalization

Data normalization refers to converting data into a homogenous form to allow proper analysis. Financial variables can be different in size and unit and thus they require normalization.

Normalization techniques are common.

- Min-max normalization
- Normalizing (standardizing) scores (z-scoring)
- Log transformation

Data Preprocessing

Preprocessing of data entails the preparation of raw data to be analyzed and modeled. This includes:

- Data transformation
- Feature selection
- Feature engineering

Processing Financial Data, Structured and Unstructured.

The financial data may be divided into structured and unstructured data, which need to be handled in a different way.

Structured Data: Structured data is arranged in a fixed format i.e. in a form of rows and columns. It is normally captured in databases and spreadsheets. Such as Stock prices, financial statements etc.

Unstructured Data: Unstructured data is not presented in any defined format and consists of text, images, audio, and other non-tabular data. such as Financial news articles, Social media post, Company reports etc. Unstructured data will be in need of specialized approaches including natural language processing (NLP) and machine learning to analyze it. The processing of unstructured data has gained more significance as it may give valuable information regarding the mood of the market and financial patterns.

Application Programming Interfaces (APIs)

Financial institutions can tap financial information through APIs that enable them to retrieve financial data automatically. APIs facilitate the real-time harvesting of data and integration in financial models. Examples of financial APIs are:

- Stock market data APIs
- Economic data APIs
- Financial news APIs

Quantitative Financial Modelling.

Quantitative financial modelling refers to the application of mathematical and statistical techniques to model financial systems and to analyze the behavior of assets and to assist in the making of financial decisions. These models are useful in estimating the prices of assets, determining risk, predicting future financial trends and optimization of investment strategies. Financial models may be determined as either deterministic and stochastic and may be based on statistical methods, time series analysis, regression models, and simulation methods, like Monte Carlo simulation. Quantitative financial modeling is an important aspect of contemporary finance that helps financial institutions to make objective and data-driven decisions and address the uncertainty.Stochastic optimization and computational modeling are sophisticated quantitative tools that are significant in decision making in finance. The Monte Carlo simulation is one of the frequently used techniques in the pricing of complex financial instruments and in estimating risk in an uncertain world

(Glasserman, 2004). The use of convex and other optimization methods are highly useful in risk minimization and managing portfolios (Boyd and Vandenberghe, 2004). Discrete stochastic optimization and its implications in finance have been discussed in more recent studies and have highlighted the importance of making a decision under uncertainty (Consigli et al., 2022). Furthermore, mathematical modeling is undergoing development to include advanced computing tools to deal with current financial issues (Gnoatto & Horvath, 2022). All these techniques are employed in order to enhance precision and efficiency of financial analysis.

Deterministic vs Stochastic Models

There are general classifications of financial models into deterministic models and stochastic models depending on the way uncertainty is dealt with.

Deterministic Models

Deterministic models are based on the assumption that the relationships and inputs are certain and the output is entirely a response of the input values. Uncertainty and randomness is not factored in these models. In deterministic models, the inputs are known to give constant output to a given input. The models are applied in cases where financial variables are predictable or where simplifying assumptions are assumed.

Some examples of deterministic models are:

- Compound interest models
- Discounted cash flow (DCF) models.
- Bond valuation models

Indicatively, the future value of investment at a compound interest rate is computed as:

Future Value = Present Value x $(1 + r)^n$.

Where:

r = Interest rate
n = Number of periods

Deterministic models are easy and simple to apply although they might not be realistic in terms of financial uncertainty.

Stochastic Models

Stochastic models are models that embrace randomness and uncertainty thus are more realistic models of financial markets. These models postulate that financial variables like price of assets, interest rates, and returns are probabilistic. Stochastic models are the ones which adopt probability distributions and random variables to model financial uncertainty.

Examples include Brownian motion stock price models, Black-Scholes pricing model of options, Interest rate models.The most popular stochastic process in the field of finance is the geometric Brownian motion model which is used to explain the movements of the stock prices.

Time Series Analysis and Forecasting

Time series analysis is the process of analyzing financial data according to the periods of time in order to determine the patterns and trends and changes in the seasons. Stocks price, exchange rate and interest rates are all financial data which are time dependent and demand specific methods of analysis and prediction.

The time series models are used to forecast the future financial values using past values.

Among the important elements of the time series, there are:

1. Direction Long-term down or up movement.
2. Seasonality: Recurring patterns.
3. Cyclic movements: Intermediate movements.
4. Random variation: spontaneous motion.

Financial models of time series commonly used are:

- Autoregressive (AR) Model: This is a model of prediction of future values of past values.
- Moving Average (MA) Model:In this model, error terms of the past are used to determine future values.
- ARIMA Model (Autoregressive Integrated Moving Average):ARIMA is a blend of a moving average and an autoregressive model and is largely applied in financial forecasting.

Regression Models and Factor Models

Regression analysis is a statistical method used to examine the relationship between a dependent variable and one or more independent variables. It is widely used in finance to analyze asset returns, identify risk factors, and develop predictive models.

Linear Regression Model

The general form of a linear regression model is:

$$Y = a + bX + \varepsilon$$

Where:

Y = Dependent variable (e.g., asset return)
X = Independent variable (e.g., market return)
a = Intercept
b = Regression coefficient
ε = Error term

Regression models are used in finance for:

- Predicting stock returns
- Risk analysis
- Portfolio management

Factor Models

Factor models explain asset returns based on underlying risk factors. These models help identify the factors that influence asset performance.

One widely used factor model is the Capital Asset Pricing Model (CAPM):

Expected Return = Risk-Free Rate + Beta × (Market Return − Risk-Free Rate)

Where beta measures the sensitivity of an asset to market movements.

More advanced models include:

- Multi-factor models
- Fama–French three-factor model
- Arbitrage Pricing Theory (APT)

Monte Carlo Simulation Techniques

Monte Carlo simulation refers to a calculation method that is applied in modeling uncertainty and assessing financial risks through running a series of random cases. It relies on random sample and probability distributions to model the possible future outcomes.

Financial markets are unpredictable and hence Monte Carlo simulation is very prevalent in the field of finance.

The process involves:

1. Defining a financial model
2. Producing arbitrary values of uncertain variables.
3. Conducting a series of simulations.
4. Analyzing the results

Monte Carlo simulation is applied in:

- Option pricing
- Risk analysis
- Portfolio valuation
- Investment decision-making

As an example, the Monte Carlo simulation can be applied to estimate portfolio value in the future by simulating a thousand possible market scenarios. This is a method that enables the financial institution to determine risk and make wise decisions in the face of uncertainty.

Significance of Quantitative Financial Modeling.

Quantitative financial modeling has a number of valuable advantages:

- Enhances financial decision making.
- Allows proper pricing of assets.
- Supports risk management
- Assists in predicting finances.
- Improves investment policy.
- Automated Strategies and Algorithmic Trading.

Venture, Meaning of Algorithms and High-Frequency Trading

The use of computer programs to run a financial trade according to some predetermined instructions is known as algorithmic trading. These orders can involve price, volume, time or mathematical model requirements. The aim is to carry out trades cost effectively and in the best possible prices. Algorithms trading will remove the human factor enabling the trades to be conducted more quickly and accurately.

The main characteristics of algorithmic trading are:

1. Automated trade execution
2. Use of quantitative models
3. Reduced human error
4. Faster decision-making
5. Capacity to handle large amount of data.

High-Frequency Trading (HFT)

High-frequency trading is a specialized business of algorithmic trading, which is used to achieve a great number of trades at extremely high speeds, frequently within milliseconds or even microseconds. High-frequency trading systems follow sophisticated algorithmic and high-speed computer infrastructure to capitalize on tiny price variations. Some of the characteristics of high-frequency trading are like Very high speed of trade execution, High volume of transactions carried out within brief durations, Application of complex mathematical models, Low profit per trade and high volume.

High-frequency trading enhances the liquidity and efficiency of the market but also creates several challenges like the volatility of the market and technological risks.

Strategy Development and Back testing

Strategy development Here is a very important aspect of algorithmic trading. It entails formulation of trading policies on financial modeling, statistical and market indicators.

Algorithms The most common algorithmic trading strategies are:

- Trend-following strategies
- Mean reversion strategies
- Arbitrage strategies
- Momentum strategies
- Market-making strategies

Backtesting

Backtesting is a method of testing the trading strategy on previous data in order to assess the performance of the strategy. It assists in establishing the profitability of a strategy in the past. Backtesting is useful in revealing the weaknesses of the trading strategy and making the strategy perform better before it is adopted in the actual market. The process of backtesting includes:

Gathering past financial information, using the trading strategy on past data, Making trades simulation and drawing up profits and losses,assessing performance indicators.

Implementation and Evaluation of Performance

The trading algorithms are applied to execute the trades in the most efficient manner with the minimum costs and market impact. These algorithms calculate the best method of handling large orders.

Examples of common execution algorithms are:

- **Market Order Execution**:The trade is carried out at the market price.
- **Limit Order Execution**: Trades are only executed at given levels.
- **Time-Weighted Average Price (TWAP):** It trades equally within a given period in order to lessen the impact in the market.
- **Volume-Weighted Average Price (VWAP):** It trades on the trading volume of the market to get the best price.

Performance Evaluation: Performance evaluation is necessary to measure the performance of strategic algorithmic trading. The metrics include:

Return: Sum of the profit made by the strategy.

Sharpe Ratio: Risk adjusted return ' Sharpe Ratio = (Return of the portfolio- Risk-Free Rate)/Standard Deviation.

Maximum Drawdown: The largest fall between the maximum and the minimum.

Win Rate: The percentage of profitable trades.

Volatility: This is a measure of returns risk.

Risk Management Algorithmic Trading

In the case of algorithmic trading, risk management is essential to avoid the loss of money and guarantee the stability of the system. Risk management becomes necessary in that, automated trading systems have the ability to carry out high levels of trades within a short period of time.

Key types of risks include:

Market Risk: Risk of losing money as a result of market price fluctuations.
Model Risk: Risk associated with losses as a result of wrong or inaccurate financial models.
Execution Risk: Risk of losses on account of delay or trade execution errors.
Operational Risk: Risk that comes as a result of system failures, bugs or technical problems.

Risk Management Techniques

Risk is managed in algorithmic trading by a number of techniques:

Stop-Loss Orders: These automatically concede positions when they become losses of a specific level.
Position Limits: Cap trading positions.
Diversification: Dispersal of investments in several assets to minimize risk.
Real-Time Risk Monitoring: Continuous trading and risk exposure monitoring.
Stress Testing: This is a test to determine the system performance at extreme market scenarios.
Risk management also makes automated trading systems to be stable and reliable.

Asset Allocation and Portfolio Optimization.

Asset allocation and portfolio optimization are the two basic terms in the field of quantitative finance that aim at choosing the best mix of financial assets in order to meet certain goals of investments. Maximization of expected returns and minimization of risk is the main objective. There is also a high use of quantitative methods, mathematical models, and programming tools to build the effective portfolios and aid in the investment decision making.

The concept of portfolio optimization is founded on the fact that investors do not consider the investment in a single asset but take into account the interactions of assets. The association between asset returns is very crucial in determining the overall portfolio risk and return. The current quantitative methods enable the investors to determine the best portfolios, risk assessment, and risk management.

Modern Portfolio Theory (MPT)

Modern Portfolio Theory (MPT), developed by Harry Markowitz in 1952, provides the theoretical foundation for portfolio optimization. MPT emphasizes the importance of diversification and demonstrates how investors can construct portfolios that maximize expected returns for a given level of risk. The key contribution of MPT is the concept that diversification can reduce portfolio risk without necessarily reducing expected returns.MPT assumes that investors are rational, risk-averse, and seek to maximize returns while minimizing risk.

According to MPT, the expected return of a portfolio is the weighted average of the expected returns of individual assets.

Expected Portfolio Return:

$$E(Rp) = \Sigma \; wi \; E(Ri)$$

Where:

wi = Weight of asset i in the portfolio
E(Ri) = Expected return of asset i

Portfolio risk is measured using variance or standard deviation, which depends on individual asset risks and their correlations.

Portfolio Variance:

$$\sigma p^2 = \Sigma \; wi^2 \; \sigma i^2 + \Sigma \; \Sigma \; wi \; wj \; Cov(Ri, Rj)$$

Where:

σi^2 = Variance of asset i
Cov(Ri, Rj) = Covariance between assets i and j

Efficient Frontier and Diversification Strategies

The efficient frontier is a graphical representation of optimal portfolios that offer the highest expected return for a given level of risk. It is derived using portfolio optimization techniques. Portfolios below the efficient frontier are inefficient because better risk-return combinations are available.

Portfolios on the efficient frontier are considered optimal because they provide:

- Maximum return for a given level of risk, or

- Minimum risk for a given level of return

Diversification Strategies

Diversification involves investing in multiple assets to reduce overall portfolio risk. The key principle behind diversification is that asset returns are not perfectly correlated. When some assets perform poorly, others may perform well, reducing overall portfolio volatility.

Types of diversification include:

Asset Diversification: Investing in different asset classes such as stocks, bonds, and commodities.
Sector Diversification: Investing across different industries such as technology, healthcare, and finance.
Geographic Diversification: Investing in different countries or regions.

Risk-Adjusted Performance Measures

Risk-adjusted performance measures are used to evaluate investment performance while considering the level of risk taken. These measures help investors compare different portfolios objectively.

Sharpe Ratio

The Sharpe ratio measures excess return per unit of risk.

$$\text{Sharpe Ratio} = (Rp - Rf) / \sigma p$$

Where:

Rp = Portfolio return
Rf = Risk-free rate
σp = Portfolio standard deviation

A higher Sharpe ratio indicates better risk-adjusted performance.

Treynor Ratio

The Treynor ratio measures return relative to systematic risk.

Treynor Ratio = $(Rp - Rf) / \beta p$

Where:

βp = Portfolio beta

Jensen's Alpha:Jensen's alpha measures the excess return of a portfolio relative to its expected return based on CAPM.

Alpha = Actual Return – Expected Return

A positive alpha indicates superior performance.

Sortino Ratio:The Sortino ratio measures return relative to downside risk, focusing only on negative volatility. These performance measures help investors evaluate portfolio efficiency and compare investment strategies.

Optimization Techniques Using Programming

Programming plays a crucial role in portfolio optimization by enabling efficient implementation of mathematical optimization models. Financial portfolios often consist of many assets, making manual calculations impractical.Optimization techniques aim to determine the optimal asset allocation that maximizes returns and minimizes risk.

Common optimization methods include:

- **Mean-Variance Optimization:**This method identifies portfolios that minimize variance for a given expected return or maximize return for a given level of risk.Programming languages such as Python and R use optimization libraries to solve these problems efficiently.
- **Linear Programming: Linear** programming is used to optimize portfolio allocation under specific constraints, such as budget limitations or risk limits.
- **Quadratic Programming:**Quadratic programming is widely used in mean-variance optimization because portfolio variance is a quadratic function.

Application of Programming in Portfolio Optimization.

There are programming languages like Python, R and MATLAB that are used to optimize a portfolio. Financial programming helps financial practitioners to perform detailed analysis on large portfolios and apply cutting edge optimization methods.

The application of the new technologies such as quantum computing is one of the new trends in quantitative finance. Recent papers have studied the issue of quantum solutions to transform financial modeling, optimization, and risk analysis by solving computationally challenging problems that classical systems are incapable of solving (Bunescu and Vârtei, 2024).

Moreover, the modern financial markets have been revolutionized by high-frequency and algorithmic trading which allows conducting the trade rapidly based on the quantitative models and analyzing the data in real-time (Cartea et al., 2015).

Typical programmer activities are:

a. Computing the covariance matrices and expected returns.
b. Portfolio combinations simulation.
c. Determining the most desirable portfolios.
d. The efficient frontier: plotting.
e. Portfolio optimization python libraries available include:
f. NumPy to do some numerical computations.
g. Pandas for data analysis
h. SciPy for optimization
i. PyPortfolioOpt to optimize the portfolio.

Significance of Portfolio Optimization in Finance.

Portfolio optimization is popular among investment banks, mutual funds, hedge funds and asset management firms.Portfolio optimization has a number of advantages:

- Optimizes returns on investment.
- Minimizes investment risk
- Enhances efficiency in investing.
- Helps in making improved decisions as to asset allocation.
- Enhances risk management
- Financial Engineering and Risk Management.

Financial risk: types Market, credit, liquidity and operational risk.

There are several categories of risks to which financial institutions are subjected.

Market Risk: Market risk can also be defined as the loss that may occur in case of a change in the values of the market variables e.g. the stock prices, interest rates, exchange rates and commodity prices. Financial assets and portfolios can be greatly influenced by market fluctuations. Market risk can be of the following types:

- Decline in stock prices
- The impact of interest rate on bond values.
- Currency exchange rate risks.

Credit Risk: Credit risk is the risk of the default of a loan or non-compliance with the contractual agreement by a borrower. This is especially a risk to banks, lending institutions and bond investors. Examples are Loan defaults, Corporate bond defaults etc.

Liquidity Risk:Liquidity risk is a risk that an institution would fail to buy or sell assets easily without incurring a considerable impact on the prices. This can be in case of illiquid markets or financial crises.

Operational Risk: The operational risk is the losses associated with the failure of internal processes or systems, or human errors. Examples include System failures, fraud and cyberattacks human errors

The operational risk management entails enhancing the internal controls, system reliability, and security.

Value at Risk (VaR) and Stress Testing Models

Quantitative finance provides various tools to measure and manage financial risk. Value at Risk (VaR) and stress testing are widely used risk management techniques

Value at Risk (VaR)

Value at Risk (VaR) measures the maximum expected loss of a portfolio over a specified time period at a given confidence level.

For example, a daily VaR of 1,00,000 at 95% confidence level means that there is a 95% probability that losses will not exceed 1,00,000 in one day.

VaR is calculated using statistical methods such as:

- Historical simulation

- Variance-covariance method
- Monte Carlo simulation

VaR formula (variance-covariance approach):

$$\text{VaR} = Z \times \sigma \times \sqrt{t} \times \text{Portfolio Value}$$

Where:

Z = Z-score corresponding to confidence level
σ = Standard deviation of returns
t = Time period

VaR helps financial institutions quantify risk exposure and make informed decisions.

Stress Testing: Stress testing evaluates the impact of extreme market conditions on financial portfolios. It helps identify vulnerabilities and assess the resilience of financial institutions. Stress testing helps institutions prepare for adverse market conditions and improve risk management Examples of stress scenarios include:

- Financial crises
- Interest rate shocks
- Market crashe

Derivative Pricing and Hedging Strategies

Derivatives are financial instruments whose value depends on underlying assets such as stocks, bonds, or commodities. Quantitative models are used to price derivatives and manage associated risks.Common derivatives include:

- Options
- Futures
- Forwards
- Swaps

Derivative Pricing Models: Derivative pricing models consider factors such as:

- Asset price
- Volatility
- Interest rates

- Time to maturity

Hedging Strategies

- Using futures contracts to hedge commodity price risk
- Using options to hedge stock price risk
- Using swaps to hedge interest rate risk

Scenario Analysis Using Quantitative Models

Scenario analysis involves evaluating the impact of different hypothetical scenarios on financial portfolios. It helps financial institutions understand potential risks and make informed decisions.

Scenario analysis uses quantitative models to simulate various market conditions. Examples of scenarios include:

- Economic recession
- Interest rate changes
- Market crashes

Quantitative techniques such as Monte Carlo simulation and statistical modeling are used to perform scenario analysis.

Scenario analysis helps financial institutions:

- Assess risk exposure
- Improve risk management strategies
- Prepare for adverse market conditions

ROLE OF FINANCIAL ENGINEERING IN RISK MANAGEMENT

Importance of Risk Management in Quantitative Finance

Effective risk management provides several benefits:

- Protects financial institutions from losses
- Improves financial stability
- Supports regulatory compliance
- Enhances investment decision-making
- Improves portfolio performance

Financial institutions such as banks, hedge funds, and insurance companies rely heavily on quantitative risk management techniques.

MACHINE LEARNING AND AI IN QUANTITATIVE FINANCE

Machine Learning (ML) and Artificial Intelligence (AI) have emerged as transformative technologies in quantitative finance, enabling financial institutions to analyze large datasets, identify complex patterns, and improve predictive accuracy. Traditional financial models often rely on linear assumptions and limited variables, whereas machine learning techniques can process vast amounts of structured and unstructured data to generate more accurate and robust financial predictions. Machine learning enhances financial decision-making by automating data analysis, improving risk management, detecting fraud, and optimizing investment strategies. Financial institutions, hedge funds, and fintech companies increasingly rely on machine learning and AI to gain competitive advantages in financial markets.

Supervised and Unsupervised Learning in Finance

Machine learning techniques used in finance are broadly categorized into supervised learning and unsupervised learning based on the availability of labeled data.

Supervised Learning

Supervised learning involves training a model using labeled data, where the input variables and corresponding output values are known. The model learns the relationship between inputs and outputs and uses this knowledge to make predictions on new data.

Common supervised learning algorithms used in finance include:

- Linear regression
- Logistic regression
- Decision trees
- Support vector machines
- Random forests

Applications of supervised learning in finance include:

- Stock price prediction
- Credit risk assessment

- Loan default prediction
- Fraud detection

For example, supervised learning models can predict whether a borrower is likely to default based on historical financial data.

Unsupervised Learning

Unsupervised learning involves analyzing data without labeled outputs. The objective is to identify hidden patterns, relationships, or structures within the data.

Common unsupervised learning methods include:

- Clustering algorithms (e.g., k-means clustering)
- Principal Component Analysis (PCA)
- Dimensionality reduction techniques

Applications in finance include:

- Customer segmentation
- Portfolio diversification analysis
- Risk factor identification
- Market pattern recognition

Unsupervised learning helps financial institutions identify patterns that may not be visible through traditional analysis.

Predictive Analytics for Asset Pricing

Predictive analytics uses machine learning models to forecast future asset prices and financial trends. Accurate prediction of asset prices is critical for investment management, trading strategies, and risk management.Machine learning models analyze historical financial data, market indicators, and economic variables to predict future asset returns.

Common predictive techniques include:

- Regression models
- Time series forecasting models
- Machine learning algorithms such as random forests and gradient boosting

Machine learning models can incorporate a large number of variables and capture nonlinear relationships, improving prediction accuracy compared to traditional financial models.

Predictive analytics is used in:

- Stock price forecasting
- Portfolio optimization
- Risk management
- Algorithmic trading

These models help investors identify profitable investment opportunities and manage risks effectively.

Neural Networks and Deep Learning Applications

Neural networks are advanced machine learning models inspired by the human brain. They consist of interconnected layers of nodes that process information and learn complex relationships.

Deep learning refers to neural networks with multiple layers that can analyze highly complex data. Neural networks are particularly useful in finance because they can capture nonlinear relationships and process large datasets.

Applications include:

1. Stock Price Prediction:
2. Fraud Detection:.
3. Algorithmic Trading:
4. Risk Management:
5. Natural Language Processing (NLP)

Ethical Considerations and Model Interpretability

While machine learning and AI offer significant advantages, they also present ethical and operational challenges that must be carefully addressed.

- **Model Interpretability: Many** machine learning models, particularly deep learning models, are considered "black box" models because their decision-making processes are difficult to interpret. Lack of transparency can create challenges in financial decision-making, regulatory compliance, and risk management. Financial institutions must ensure that models are interpretable and explainable. Techniques such as feature importance analysis and explainable AI (XAI) help improve model transparency.

- **Bias and Fairness: Machine** learning models may reflect biases present in historical data. This can lead to unfair outcomes, such as biased credit decisions. Financial institutions must ensure fairness and avoid discriminatory practices.
- **Data Privacy and Security: Financial** data is highly sensitive, and improper handling can lead to privacy violations and financial losses. Strong data security measures and compliance with regulations are essential.
- **Model Risk and Overfitting:**Machine learning models may perform well on historical data but fail in real-world conditions due to overfitting. Proper model validation and testing are necessary to ensure reliability.

Role of Machine Learning and AI in Modern Financial Systems

Machine learning and AI provide several benefits in quantitative finance:

- Improved prediction accuracy
- Enhanced risk management
- Automated financial analysis
- Improved fraud detection
- Enhanced trading strategies

These technologies enable financial institutions to process large datasets efficiently and improve decision-making.

BUSINESS APPLICATIONS OF QUANTITATIVE FINANCE PROGRAMMING

Investment Decision-Making and Advisory Services

Quantitative programming enables financial professionals to analyze large volumes of financial data, including stock prices, economic indicators, and company financial statements. These analyses help identify profitable investment opportunities and assess associated risks.

Key applications include:

Portfolio Optimization:

Programming tools are used to implement portfolio optimization models such as Modern Portfolio Theory to determine the optimal allocation of assets.

Asset Pricing Models:

Quantitative models such as the Capital Asset Pricing Model (CAPM) are implemented using programming to evaluate expected returns.

Financial Forecasting:

Time series models and machine learning techniques are used to predict future asset prices and market trends.

Robo-Advisory Services:

Fintech companies use automated advisory platforms powered by quantitative models to provide investment recommendations based on client preferences and risk tolerance.

Quantitative finance programming improves the accuracy and efficiency of investment decision-making.

Corporate Finance and Capital Budgeting

Corporate finance involves managing a company's financial resources to maximize shareholder value. Quantitative finance programming supports financial planning, capital budgeting, and investment evaluation. Capital budgeting involves evaluating long-term investment projects using quantitative financial techniques. Common applications include:

Net Present Value (NPV) Analysis:

Programming is used to calculate the present value of future cash flows and evaluate investment profitability.

Internal Rate of Return (IRR):

Programming tools calculate IRR to determine the expected return of investment projects.

Financial Forecasting:

Companies use quantitative models to forecast revenues, costs, and financial performance.

Risk Analysis:

Monte Carlo simulation and statistical models are used to evaluate investment risks.

Quantitative finance programming enables companies to make informed investment decisions and optimize capital allocation.

Banking, Insurance, and FinTech Applications

Quantitative finance programming is widely used in banking, insurance, and fintech sectors to manage financial risks, improve operational efficiency, and enhance customer services.

Banking Applications

Banks use quantitative programming for:

- Credit risk assessment
- Loan default prediction
- Interest rate modeling
- Portfolio management
- Algorithmic trading

Insurance Applications

Insurance companies use quantitative finance programming to:

- Calculate insurance premiums
- Assess risk exposure
- Forecast claim probabilities
- Manage insurance portfolios

FinTech Applications

FinTech companies use quantitative programming to develop innovative financial services, including:

- Digital payment systems
- Robo-advisory platforms
- Automated trading systems
- Credit scoring models

These applications improve financial accessibility, efficiency, and innovation.

Fraud Detection and Financial Compliance

Fraud detection and financial compliance are critical areas where quantitative finance programming plays an important role. Financial fraud can result in significant financial losses and damage to institutional reputation. Quantitative models and machine learning techniques are used to detect fraudulent transactions and identify suspicious activities.

Key applications include:

- **Fraud Detection Systems:** Machine learning models analyze transaction data and identify unusual patterns.
- **Anomaly Detection:** Statistical models identify deviations from normal financial behavior.
- **Credit Card Fraud Detection:** Real-time monitoring systems detect unauthorized transactions.
- **Anti-Money Laundering (AML):** Financial institutions use quantitative models to detect money laundering activities.
- **Regulatory Compliance:** Programming tools help financial institutions comply with regulatory requirements by monitoring transactions and generating compliance reports.

Importance of Quantitative Finance Programming in Business

Quantitative finance programming provides several benefits for businesses:

- Improves financial decision-making
- Enhances risk management
- Automates financial processes
- Improves investment performance
- Enhances fraud detection and financial security
- Supports regulatory compliance

CASE STUDIES AND PRACTICAL IMPLEMENTATIONS

Real-World Examples of Quantitative Finance Applications

Financial institutions across the globe use quantitative finance programming to enhance financial performance and manage risks effectively. Several prominent examples illustrate its practical applications.

Algorithmic Trading in Hedge Funds: Hedge funds such as Renaissance Technologies and Citadel use quantitative models and algorithmic trading strategies to identify profitable trading opportunities. These firms rely on statistical models, machine learning algorithms, and high-performance computing systems to analyze large volumes of financial data. Their trading systems automatically execute trades based on mathematical models, enabling faster and more accurate trading decisions. This approach improves efficiency and generates consistent returns.

Risk Management in Investment Banks: Investment banks such as JPMorgan Chase and Goldman Sachs use quantitative risk management systems to measure and monitor financial risks. These systems use Value at Risk (VaR), Monte Carlo simulation, and stress testing to assess potential losses under different market conditions. Programming tools enable real-time risk monitoring and help financial institutions comply with regulatory requirements such as Basel III.

Portfolio Management in Asset Management Firms: Asset management firms such as BlackRock use quantitative models to optimize portfolios and improve investment performance. Their portfolio management systems analyze asset returns, risk factors, and correlations to construct optimal portfolios. These systems use Modern Portfolio Theory, factor models, and optimization techniques implemented through programming languages such as Python and C++.s

Fraud Detection in Financial Institutions: Financial institutions such as PayPal and Visa use machine learning models to detect fraudulent transactions. These systems analyze transaction patterns and identify unusual activities in real time. Machine learning algorithms improve fraud detection accuracy and reduce financial losses.

Industry Use Cases in Trading, Risk, and Portfolio Management

Quantitative finance programming has several important applications across financial industry sectors.

Trading Applications: Quantitative trading systems use programming and statistical models to develop and implement trading strategies. Applications include:

- Algorithmic trading

- High-frequency trading
- Arbitrage trading

Risk Management Applications: Financial institutions use quantitative models to measure and manage risk exposure. Applications include:

- Value at Risk (VaR) calculation
- Stress testing
- Credit risk modeling

Portfolio Management Applications

Portfolio managers use quantitative programming to optimize asset allocation and improve portfolio performance.Applications include:

- Portfolio optimization
- Risk-return analysis
- Performance evaluation

Challenges Faced in Implementation

- **Data Quality and Availability:** Quantitative models require large volumes of accurate financial data. Poor data quality can lead to inaccurate results and poor financial decisions.
- **Model Risk: Financial** models are based on assumptions that may not always reflect real-world conditions. Incorrect assumptions can lead to financial losses.
- **Computational Complexity:**Quantitative models often involve complex calculations that require high-performance computing systems.
- **Technical Expertise Requirements:**Implementing quantitative finance solutions requires expertise in mathematics, statistics, programming, and finance. Skilled professionals are essential for successful implementation.
- **Regulatory and Compliance Challenges:**Financial institutions must comply with regulatory requirements, which may limit the use of certain quantitative models.

Lessons Learned and Best Practices

1. Ensure High-Quality Data
2. Model Validation and Testing

3. Use Robust Risk Management Practices
4. Continuous Monitoring and Improvement
5. Invest in Skilled Professionals and Technology

CHALLENGES AND LIMITATIONS IN QUANTITATIVE FINANCE PROGRAMMING

Despite its significant advantages, quantitative finance programming faces several challenges and limitations that must be carefully addressed. Financial markets are complex and influenced by numerous unpredictable factors, making it difficult to develop models that perfectly capture real-world behavior. Understanding these challenges is essential for ensuring the reliability and effectiveness of quantitative financial systems.

Model Risk and Overfitting

Model risk refers to the possibility that a financial model produces inaccurate or misleading results due to incorrect assumptions, flawed design, or improper implementation. Quantitative models rely on mathematical and statistical assumptions that may not fully reflect real-world financial market conditions.

One major issue associated with model risk is overfitting. Overfitting occurs when a model is excessively tailored to historical data and captures noise rather than meaningful patterns. While an overfitted model may perform well on historical data, it often fails to perform accurately in real-world conditions.

Overfitting can lead to:

- Poor predictive performance
- Incorrect investment decisions
- Increased financial losses

Data Quality and Availability Issues

Quantitative finance programming depends heavily on accurate, reliable, and comprehensive financial data. Poor data quality can significantly affect model accuracy and decision-making.

Common data-related challenges include:

- Missing or incomplete data
- Incorrect or inconsistent data

- Limited availability of historical data
- Data errors and noise

Regulatory and Compliance Constraints

Financial institutions operate in highly regulated environments and must comply with strict regulatory requirements. Regulations such as Basel III, financial reporting standards, and risk management guidelines impose limitations on the use of quantitative models.

Regulatory challenges include:

- Requirement for model transparency
- Model validation and documentation requirements
- Compliance with financial risk regulations
- Data privacy and security regulations

Financial institutions must ensure that their quantitative models are transparent, explainable, and compliant with regulatory standards.

Regulatory compliance increases operational complexity but helps ensure financial stability and protect investors.

Human Judgment vs Automated Decision-Making

Quantitative finance programming relies heavily on automated models and algorithms. While automation improves efficiency and reduces human errors, it also introduces certain limitations.

Automated systems may fail to account for unexpected market events, behavioral factors, or qualitative information that cannot be easily quantified.

Human judgment remains important in:

- Model development and validation
- Risk management decisions
- Strategic financial planning

Financial institutions must balance automation with human oversight to ensure reliable decision-making. Combining quantitative models with expert judgment improves financial decision-making and reduces risks.

FUTURE TRENDS IN QUANTITATIVE FINANCE

Growth of AI-Driven Finance

Machine learning and artificial intelligence are likely to have increased significance in quantitative finance. Large amounts of financial information can be analyzed by AI-based models, revealing more complicated trends and enhancing the quality of predictions. AI increases efficiency, decreases human interaction, and better financial decision-making.AI financial will be a standard operating procedure in financial markets.

Financial uses of AI applications are:

- Automated trading systems
- Credit risk assessment
- Fraud detection
- Financial forecasting

Big Data and Cloud Computing Role.

Financial markets produce enormous volumes of data which includes market data, transaction data, and other sources of alternative data. Financial institutions can efficiently process and analyze big data sets with the help of the big data technologies.Financial analysis Cloud computing offers scalable and affordable computing infrastructure.

Cloud computing has the following merits:

- Faster data processing
- Improved scalability
- Lower infrastructure expenses.
- Real-time data analysis

Cloud computing will help financial institutions to apply complicated quantitative models effectively.

Interaction with Blockchain and Digital Assets.

Financial markets are being changed by blockchain technology and cryptocurrencies and other digital assets. Financial systems that are decentralized, transparent, and secure are offered by blockchain.Cryptocurrency markets, trading strategies, and digital asset portfolios are all becoming the subject of analysis, trading strategy development, and management with quantitative finance programming.

Examples of blockchain uses are:

- Cryptocurrency trading
- Smart contracts
- Digital asset management

Financial Transparency and Security- Blockchain Technology improves transparency and security.

Handbook of the New in Quantitative Finance

The increased value of quantitative finance has generated strong career prospects of those who specialize in mathematics, statistics, programming, and finance. Quantitative finance careers are also likely to keep rising in demand as the financial marketplace advances towards a more technological focus.

Key career roles include:

- Quantitative Analyst (Quant)
- Financial Data Scientist
- Algorithmic Trader
- Risk Analyst
- Financial Engineer

These functions need analytical skills, programming, and financial modeling skills.

Summary of Key Concepts

Quantitative finance programming is an effective combination of financial theory, mathematical modeling, statistical analysis and computer methods. The chapter has discussed the basic concepts of quantitative finance and the practical use of quantitative finance with special focus on how programming has been used to revolutionize the process of financial decision making. Quantitative finance has an analytic basis comprising of core concepts like financial modeling, time series analysis, regression and factor models, Monte Carlo simulation, portfolio optimization, and risk management concepts.

Another aspect of the chapter that was analyzed is the relevance of programming languages like Python, R, MATLAB, C++, and Java in the creation of financial models and working with huge data sets. Acquisition of financial data, preprocessing, and storage of the data was found to be key elements assisting the quantitative analysis. Moreover, predictive capabilities, automation, and efficiency in financial markets have been greatly improved due to the use of algorithmic trading, machine learning, and artificial intelligence.

Value at Risk (VaR), stress testing, and derivative hedging strategies were revealed as some of the most essential risk management techniques of financial uncertainty control. Another practical use of quantitative finance programming to the real world mentioned in the chapter was in the investment management, banking, insurance, and fintech fields.

In general, quantitative finance programming offers a systematic and data-driven method of analyzing the financial markets, portfolios optimization and financial risk management.

Strategic Relevance of Contemporary Business

Quantitative finance programming has acquired a strategic significance to businesses that are presently in the ever-competitive and complex financial landscape. Quantitative models help financial institutions in decision-making involved in the investment process, efficient allocation of assets, risk management, and enhancement of financial performance.

This is due to the fact that the possibility of processing large amounts of financial data and the introduction of automated decision-making systems are major competitive advantages that organizations gain. Quantitative finance programming boosts operational efficiency by automating financial processes like trading and risk monitoring and financial forecasting. This lowers human error, increases accuracy and consistency.

Moreover, quantitative models help businesses to find lucrative investment options, determine the financial risks, and create effective risk mitigation tools. These models are applied by financial institutions in order to meet the requirements of the regulations, promote transparency and financial stability.

The coming together of the new technologies like artificial intelligence, machine learning, big data analytics and cloud computing have added even more importance on quantitative finance programming as a strategic concern. The technologies also help the organization to deliver better forecasting, better fraud detection and to create new financial products and services.

Quantitative finance programming will always be the key element of business success and strategic financial management as the financial markets are going to keep changing.

Finance Professionals and Organization Implications

The increased relevance of quantitative finance programming has immense consequences to the finance practitioners and institutions. The field of finance is becoming more and more demanding in that such professionals need to have skills in interdisciplinary skills such as financial knowledge and a combination of skills in mathematics, statistics, and programming.

Experts are required to acquire skills in finance modeling and statistical analysis, as well as, in programming languages like Python and R. Experience in machine learning methods, data analysis and risk management is now also critical. The skills empower financial professionals to work with financial data successfully and create quantitative models, and justify data-driven decisions.To successfully implement quantitative financial solutions, organizations need to invest in technological infrastructure, data management systems and highly skilled personnel. Integration of quantitative finance programming will enhance the efficiency of an organization, increase capacity to manage risks and encourage financial service innovations.

Moreover, to keep the trust and reliability of financial systems, organizations should be ready to validate their models properly, find compliance with the regulations, and use quantitative models ethically.

FINAL CONCLUSION

Quantitative finance programming has completely changed the modern finance by allowing sophisticated financial modeling, automated trading, risk management, and decision making. It offers necessary instruments to the financial market analysis, optimization of the investment strategy, and risk management of financial markets.

Quantitative finance programming will remain crucial in the innovation and success of financial markets as they become more complex and technical driven by technology. The capabilities of quantitative finance will be further expanded through the implementation of the latest technologies like artificial intelligence, big data, and blockchain.

To the finance practitioners and institutions, it is no longer an option or a luxury to be skilled in quantitative finance programming, but a long term success in global financial environment which is changing.

REFERENCES

Black, F., & Scholes, M. (1973). The pricing of options and corporate liabilities. *Journal of Political Economy*, *81*(3), 637–654. DOI: 10.1086/260062

Boyd, S., & Vandenberghe, L. (2004). *Convex optimization*. Cambridge University Press., DOI: 10.1017/CBO9780511804441

Bunescu, L., & Vârtei, A. M. (2024). Modern finance through quantum computing: A systematic literature review. *PLoS One*, *19*(7), e0304317. DOI: 10.1371/journal.pone.0304317 PMID: 39024227

Cartea, Á., Jaimungal, S., & Penalva, J. (2015). *Algorithmic and high-frequency trading*. Cambridge University Press., DOI: 10.1017/CBO9781316195277

Cesa, M. (2017). A brief history of quantitative finance. *Probability, Uncertainty and Quantitative Risk*, *2*(6), 6. Advance online publication. DOI: 10.1186/s41546-017-0018-3

Consigli, G., Kopa, M., & Pichler, A. (2022). Discrete stochastic optimization in finance. *Quantitative Finance*, *22*(1), 1–5. DOI: 10.1080/14697688.2021.2013621

Cont, R. (2001). Empirical properties of asset returns: Stylized facts and statistical issues. *Quantitative Finance*, *1*(2), 223–236. DOI: 10.1080/713665670

Glasserman, P. (2004). *Monte Carlo methods in financial engineering*. Springer., DOI: 10.1007/978-0-387-21617-1

Gnoatto, A., & Horvath, B. (2022). Mathematical modeling and computation in finance. *Quantitative Finance*, *22*(11), 1971–1972. DOI: 10.1080/14697688.2022.2117641

Merton, R. C. (1973). Theory of rational option pricing. *The Bell Journal of Economics and Management Science*, *4*(1), 141–183. DOI: 10.2307/3003143

Oliveira, C. (2021). *Practical C++20 financial programming: Problem solving for quantitative finance, financial engineering, business, and economics*. Apress., DOI: 10.1007/978-1-4842-6834-6

Shi, X., Zhang, P., & Khan, S. U. (2017). Quantitative data analysis in finance. In *Handbook of big data technologies* (pp. 719–753). Springer., DOI: 10.1007/978-3-319-49340-4_21

Tsay, R. S. (2010). *Analysis of financial time series* (3rd ed.). Wiley., DOI: 10.1002/9780470644560

Yan, Y. (2017). Teaching programming skills to finance students: How to design and teach a great course. *Financial Innovation*, *3*(32), 32. Advance online publication. DOI: 10.1186/s40854-017-0081-x

Chapter 2
Data-Driven Finance: Financial Mathematics, Database Management, and Econometric Techniques for Modern Decision-Making

Sanjeev Kumar
http://orcid.org/0000-0002-7375-7341
Lovely Professional University, India

Pardeep Kumar
http://orcid.org/0000-0003-0308-7634
Lovely Professional University, India

ABSTRACT

The dynamic financial world we are living in today demands data driven decision making. The combination of the three fields of financial mathematics, database management, and econometric approach to modern finance is the subject of the discussion in this paper. Financial mathematics provides basic techniques of valuing assets, risk evaluation and optimization of a portfolio through time value of money, derivatives pricing and stochastic, modeling". Besides this, an effective database management will enhance storage, retrieval, and manipulation of the large financial data, which will ensure an appropriate analysis and timely decisions. This is further enhanced with the econometric techniques that apply statistical models to identify relationships, hypothesis and predict financial results to support evidence-based approach in investment, risk management and policy making. Quantitative knowledge can enable the financial service providers to deal with market volatility, trend identification and maximization of resource expenditure through integration of the two.

DOI: 10.4018/979-8-3373-8372-9.ch002

INTRODUCTION

The last several decades can be characterized by the radical overhaul of the world order in the sphere of finances, which are fueled by the scalding of the technologies, the sudden increase in the amount of information and the appearance of the complexity of the market. The old definition of finance which was highly intuitive, based on experience as well as on simple statistics are being altered by the data-driven approaches of finance. Harnessing a systematic gathering, processing and analysis of mass structured and unstructured data has also been significant in making financial decisions in this dynamic environment (Bayero et al., 2025). Development of data-based finance includes transformation of the perspective of the financial institutions, investors, policymakers, and researchers on the market, assessment of the risks, and allocation of resources. Information in the financial market is produced in volumes and at an unprecedented rate. Transactional pricing and behavioral streams are formed in stock markets like derivative markets, banks, payment systems and digital financial systems (Zhang, 2025). There are the opportunities and challenges of this information proliferation. Despite the fact that rich datasets help us to understand the workings of the market and the actions of the various actors better, they also require high-order analytical frameworks which can be applied to convert raw data into practical and valuable knowledge. One of the attempts to resolve this issue is the concept of data-driven finance, "which involves combining financial mathematics, database management system and econometric methods into a single decision-support system."

The modern provision of financial mathematics gives a theoretical framework to the modern finance, which creates formal models to analyses the financial instruments and quantifies the uncertainty as well as maximizes the outcomes based on constraints. The concepts which are applicable in analyzing the underlying principles of returns and risk are the time value of money, asset modeling theory, portfolio diversification and derivatives valuation. Such mathematical models over the years have been transformed to probabilistic and stochastic models more realistic in their characterization of the unpredictability which is the embodiment of the financial markets. The greater elaboration of the financial products and financial strategies has further added to the fact that there is a necessity of having rigorous mathematical foundation that would provide consistency, transparency, reliability of arriving at financial choices. Mathematical model cannot be appreciated in the absence of right and well controlled information (Pillai, 2023). Quality, access and integrity of underlying data is necessary in the effectiveness of any quantitative financial analysis. Database management system is also important in organization and management of financial information which can be stored, recalled and manipulated to any type of application. As various technologies have appeared, such as big data, the cloud computing and real-time analytics, database management has become an inseparable part of the current financial infrastructure. Correct design of the database will provide integrity of data, its security, scalability and adherence to regulations, which is highly demanded. The econometric techniques as an extension of the financial mathematics and database management give the statistical inferences required to process the financial data in an empirical fashion. Econometrics help in closing the gap between the concept and the actual results since hypothesis is tested, parameters are estimated and relationship is approved with the help of past experiences. Financial analysts' techniques such as volatility estimation, time series modeling and regression analysis to identify patterns, quantify the cause-and-effect structure, and predict values ahead with the help of econometrics (Ali et al., 2024). The strategies in a particular field are not decided by assumptions but by facts, econometric models come in handy in evidence-based decision-making.

The three fields have become very significant with the emergence of the rising need to be more particular, swift and accountable with monetary choices brought about by a convergence of the three domains as financial mathematics, database management and economistic. When the financial institutions are in the highly competitive and dynamic environment, the informational advantage may be low, however, the result of the informational advantage may be high. Since the markets are increasingly interconnected and more susceptible to shock to the world, real time analytic of big data and reactiveness to changing situations have not been available but are becoming a requirement. The data-driven finance allows the organizations to create a higher level of analytical process, minimize uncertainties and strategic performance of a total spectrum of financial process. Trend of data-driven finance is driven by its main reasons of the growing complexity of the financial markets. Financial innovation and technology development and globalization have enhanced the availability of a variety of financial instruments and investment strategy (Lee, 2025). Structured products, derivatives and algorithmic trading systems have non-linear payoffs and risk exposures, and cannot be addressed easily with the traditional qualitative methodologies. Quantitative decision making refers to the method of a systematic arrangement in which the experts in the field of finance can model the dynamics of interplay, simulate and evaluate the effects of various suppositions.

This has rendered risk management as a significant field where the use of data-driven approaches will be very useful. The consequences of the poor analysis of the risks and information synthesis have been pointed out on the grounds of the financial crises. The contemporary risk management entails quantitative frameworks in the gauging of the market risk, credit risk, liquidity risk and the operational risk. These models are very demanding as far as huge data, robust computing applications and extensive statistical authentication are concerned (Wen & Gao, 2025). Through the introduction of financial mathematics, econometric analysis and data management, organizations are able to come up with improved risk measures other than proactive measures to response to any possible losses. Data driven methodologies have also altered the decision-making process in the investment decision. The methods of the portfolio optimization are mathematical models which contribute to the trading of risk and the return as per the choice of the investor and the market. These models are backed by econometric analysis, which implies approximations of the expected returns, correlation and volatility on the basis of the past data. The database systems also protect the availability of the market data that are of importance and timely updated. All these must help investors to build diversified portfolios and gauge their success and be dynamic in responding to new information.

The quantitative decision making is not strictly confined to the privately owned financial institutions alone, but regulators and policy makers also require this. The evidence-based analysis is becoming a significant tool on which governments and central banks can track the financial stability, to compute the regulatory framework and evaluate the effectiveness of the policy interventions. The macroeconomic trend, effectiveness and stress-tests of monetary and fiscal policies in the financial systems are analyzed through the use of the econometrics models. To be sure that the data that will become accessible to the policy makers will be precise and complete, as well as to model complicated interactions in the economy, it can be implemented to effective data management, mathematical tools that are employed to work with finances (Zhang et al., 2019). Data-driven finance has also been performed with increased speed due to the emergence of new technology. The benefits in artificial intelligence, machine learning, and high-performance computing have expanded the field of the quantitative analysis of finance. Even with new tools and methodologies, these technologies remain trapped in the concept of financial mathematics and econometrics. The traditional econometric methods can be complemented with the machine learning models as the latter can reveal any nonlinear inclination and can process large volumes of data, and it is database management systems that can provide the infrastructure that is required to roll out such computationally expensive applications (Emmert-Streib, 2025).

Although data-driven finance has the mentioned benefits, a number of problems makes the need to approach this field systematically and cross-disciplinarily. When the issues around the problem of data quality are not dealt with properly, when model risk and overreliance on quantitative data is present, one can make wrong conclusions. Financial models are descriptions of the truth that are naive and are meant to be taken with a grain of salt. Econometric results have precondition assumptions and limitations of information, and database applications can only be well governed against mistakes, attacks, and misappropriation. These problems may be discovered, and the principles of entire frameworks that would incorporate technical rigor and professional judgement become a key point. This is the first goal of the paper to analyze how the integrated use of financial mathematics, database management and econometric techniques have improved the present-day financial decision making (Master of Business Administration, Indiana State University, Terre Haute, Indiana, USA et al., 2023). Having experimented with the theoretical background and use of data-driven finance, the study will show how quantitative tools can be used to implant precision, effectiveness and openness in the field of financial analysis. The scientific sphere of study consists of the most significant financial processes investment management, risk assessment, financial forecast, evaluation of the performance and is devoted to the practical application.

The alternative objective of the study is to summarize data-driven finance as a wholesome organisation because the basic elements of the concept are interrelated. Financial mathematics gives the models, database management the data infrastructure and the analytical tools are offered by econometrics to fill the gap between theory and data. These factors are interacted in a system as a whole to help informed and rational decision making in more complicated financial markets places. The capability of using the data to its best use has become a characteristic of successful financial institutions in this turbulent past where things are changing at a fast pace and uncertainty is high. Data-driven finance is not just a technological movement, but it is also a paradigm shift of the perception and use of finance. With the help of quantitative tools and incorporating the strategy into the strategic processes, the financial specialists will manage to overcome the volatility, predict risks, and exploit the new opportunities (Chakraborty & Tsokos, 2025). The article contributes to the literature on data-driven finance because it highlights the significance of the interdisciplinary nature of integration in addition to the fact that it is a presentation of how a researcher can apply quantitative instruments to convert data to usable financial information.

CONCEPTUAL FRAMEWORK OF DATA-DRIVEN FINANCE

The idea of the data-driven finance can be traced to the awareness of the fact that in contemporary financial systems, data has become one of the primary assets of the system and a component of the decision-making process, its consideration, and further execution. Data-driven finance and traditional financial methods are focused on systematic application of large, heterogeneous and ever rising data in offering to quantitative analysis as well as rational decision-making process. It is the theory of finance, data infrastructure, analysis methods, all in one bundle that can help the financial participants to react towards the complexity of the market, uncertainty and dynamism. A major issue of data-driven finance is that the place of data is a significant input of financial analysis. Financial decisions - whether it is of kind of investment, lending, risk management or speculation of a policy is conditional upon information. Up-to-date, precise, and convenient information enable the decision-makers to review the circumstances in the present and to weigh alternatives and predict the future (Dote-Pardo et al., 2025). The way the financial markets and financial institutions work has some insights such as the market prices, the volumes of trade, the interest rates, the financial statements, the macroeconomic indicators as well as behavioral data. The growing access to high-frequency and real-time information has increased the ability of financial professionals to track the market trend and respond to the new trends in a sufficient manner.

In finance, data does not merely present the descriptive tool, but also forms the basis of the predictive analysis, and the prescriptive analysis. The trends and correlations could be determined with the assistance of the historical data which informs about the future behavior. An example can be seen in the risk being estimated on old price movements, and volatile factors as compared to credit rating and loan issue decisions being made on the basis of old default data. On this aspect, data-driven finance goes beyond the state of analysis to the more dynamic modeling where a decision is being enhanced in a constant stream of new data. The result of this change is that accuracy, completeness, and consistency of data are becoming critical because bad data might create false inferences and poor decisions. The data should be amalgamated with the financial theory and analytical techniques so that it could be applied to the realm of finance (Strielkowski et al., 2023). Financial mathematics gives formal models that decide on how financial variables respond to each other in relation to some assumptions. They are used in the models of converting raw information to useful financial analysis of present value, expected returns, and performance variance and risk-adjusted. Databased finance depends on these mathematical concepts so as to make sure that the decisions made are theoretically sound. It is to them that the big data will turn into a piece of information instead of a piece of knowledge.

The conceptual framework also provides the analytics as the connection between data and decision making. The method of econometric and statistical techniques through empirical data can be estimated, tested and confirmed as possible to use financial models. With time-series modelling and forecasting, analysts can also determine the level at which they find relationships between financial variables and the level at which they can depend on their results using the regression analysis. This is also supported by the assistance of complex analytics that are necessary in the format of scenario analysis, stress testing besides the sensitivity analysis to determine the potential effect of uncertainty and extreme events on financial results. One of the aspects of data-driven financial systems is the integration of finance, data, and analytics (Mani, 2024). All these factors do not work autonomously, but they work in a reinforcing manner. The data is the input, financial theory the explanatory structure and the empirical validation and predictive capacities are found in the form of the analytics. Database management systems facilitate this integration given that they help in the data flowing been the processes of data analysis. Proper databases enable a simple process in the collection, storage, retrieving and updating of these data and hence, the analysts are engaged in the interpretation of the data and decision making and not the limitation of data management.

In the majority of cases introduced to decision-support systems and automated platforms, the current financial organizations introduce this integration. Portfolio decisions are proposed to investment management systems which received information about the market and the optimization algorithms of the market. Risk management platforms combined with transaction data are used to determine the capital requirements and exposure through econometric models (Mandl & Minner, 2023). Twitter as an algorithmic trading system is a system that operates on quantitative trading and high-speed trading as a data feed system in real-time. These applications show how the conceptual framework of data-driven finance may be applied to operational processes to improve the efficiency, consistency and scalability. The evidences of the growing reliance on the integrated data systems are the changes of the financial environment. This has exposed the financial results to the financial flows and external shocks due to the globalization and digitization of the market that has resulted in a greater connectedness of the market. It means that the financial decision-makers have to process the information in different jurisdictions and countries and take into account the complex interdependencies. To solve this complexity, data-driven finance may offer a controlled method of analysis based on systematic analysis of large quantities of data and multiple dimensions (Hassan, 2025).

The threats that face the operations of the data-driven finance are quite numerous, though they are not the least, and to make the implementation process successful, these threats must be eradicated. The problem of the data quality is one of the most hazardous ones. The information is grounded on the financial decisions, and the credibility of the financial decisions depends on the basis of these decisions. Incomplete, uneven, or inaccurate data may bias the results of an analysis therefore, putting into doubt the validity of quantitative models. The data in various sources can be different in the form, frequency, and credibility and need extensive pre-processing and validation. Integrity of the data in its turn has to be preserved, thus becoming a prime requirement within the data driven financial systems. The second is a model risk and methodological weakness. Financial models are the mathematical or econometric simplify reality. They are based on the assumptions that are not necessarily valid at any of the market conditions. The systematic errors can be the over reliance of the output of the models which have not been interpreted keenly during a given time when the market is in stress or when the structure is evolving (De Zarzà et al., 2023). Data-driven finance conceptual framework, therefore, should include mechanisms of model validation, constant updating on the basis of emerging evidence, and robustness testing.

Very important are also technological and organizational issues. The use of integrated data-driven systems within organizations is expensive with regard to its infrastructure, staff, and transformation. The field knowledge along with data analytics and quantitative tools should be trained to financial professionals. The potential impediments to the successful implementation of the data-driven approaches may be the resistance to change, the insufficient technical skills and ineffective integration of the departmental functions. To address these issues, there is a need to make a strategic investment in capacity building and interdisciplinary collaboration. The data driven finance is very complex due to ethical, legal and regulatory considerations. The unreasonable use of the amount of data poses a challenge to privacy, data security and transparency. Banking institutions should meet the regulatory requirements of data protection and reporting and also make sure that analytical models are not biased and unreasonable. Theoretically, the change of paradigm in the decision-making process between the intuitive-based decision-making and the evidence-based decision-making is the data-driven finance. It highlights the systematic research, the empirical analysis, and the active studying as the primary values of the financial management. The framework emphasizes on the integration which means a combination of data infrastructure, financial theory, and approach towards analytic and integrating all of this into a single system that can assist in making advanced decisions. However, the idea of data-driven finance as the concept base may be considered a potent prism, with the help of which the current financial activity can be perceived and streamlined. The conceptual framework of data-driven finance recommends the changing of the nature of the financial decision-making in the environment of the information world (Mondal et al., 2023). Strategic concept of data as strategic resource and integration with quantitative models and analytics have the potential to provide the financial organizations with the opportunity to operate under uncertainty, deal with risks, and plan on sustainable operation. It is not merely an efficient means of conducting operations but also of opening up the field of finance to an environment that is quickly growing too complex in the international arena.

FINANCIAL MATHEMATICS IN MODERN FINANCE

The very foundation of the problem in the contemporary finance is financial mathematics since it makes the strong quantitative basis of analysis of the financial instruments, opportunities, and uncertainties of investment. The dependence of the mathematical models has also increased many folds as the mathematical models have become more complex and the intensity of the financial markets has increased several times. Financial mathematics can allow the decision-maker to use a combination of economic intuition and market data in a manner that it can be converted into formal structures and tested, optimized and implemented in the same fashion. Such mathematical tools are not something that can be disregarded by data-driven financial world and such mathematical tools are used in order to make sure that the decisions made are right, objective and rational (Akyıldırım & Soner, 2014). The appreciation of the fact that money is a time-dependent concept is one of the simplest concepts of financial mathematics. What money can do today cannot be what it can go and can do tomorrow because of the inflation, opportunity cost and risk. It is here that the time value of money analysis is founded that is extensively employed in capital budgeting, investment appraisal and financial planning. Financial analysts are able to conduct their comparisons of investment options based on the discounting of cash flows to the present value they are therefore capable of comparing investment options that differ in regards to timing and returns magnitude. These are present value, future value, annuity and perpetuities which constitute the systematic approaches to the analysis of the value of future cash flows and determination of the profitability of projects and other financial instruments (Yanbin Zhang, 2025).

These principles are continued in the cash flow analysis and look at when and how much and even whether the inflows and outflows of cash are predictable. The cash flow-based approaches of value are more convenient than accounting-based approaches in modern finance that are closer to economic reality. DFM models are extensively applied in bond, equity and real investment project pricing. The models are premised on the correct information and the correct discount rates and, therefore, the intelligent relationship between the data-based analysis and the mathematical finance. The greater access to high quality financial information has achieved great progress on the accuracy of the cash flow forecasting, but the result of the valuation can be stabilized with the help of the mathematical modeling. Financial mathematics offers the use of instruments that are needed to measure and compensate this risk and is repaid in the financial decision-making. It has been determined that in modern finance the greater the returns, the greater the risk and it is important to measure the risk in a manner that is appropriate. The fact that the historical data can be analyzed using mathematical models and thus calculate the expected returns, the variance, and standard deviation using past data and assuming that there is probability is the opportunity. Financial mathematics encompasses market uncertainty and give a logicalized approach to choice by modeling returns as variables of uncertainty.

There has also been an emergence of sophisticated models that have replaced the average-based models in the return modeling that take into account the dynamics in the market and the behavior of the investors. Some of the models like capital asset pricing framework offer mathematical equations between the expected risk and systematic risk that provide information about the way assets are valued at a market equilibrium. They are tested and approximated models that have been established through empirical studies which show that there exists a close relationship between financial mathematics and econometric analysis. Within the framework of data-driven finance, the returns models are constantly improved using the extensive amounts of data, thus making the risk premia estimation and performance appraisal more accurate.

The quantitative risk measures have also seen the development of the risk measurement. Value at risk and expected shortfall are also some of the measures, which offer probabilistic amounts of likely losses within the given periods. This is a normal business in the banking business and investment management along with compliance with the regulations. This is supported by the usage of financial mathematics that define probability distributions, level of confidence and loss functions. The mathematical validity of the models and the quality of underlying data would be susceptible to the quality of risk measurement; hence the data-related integrated frameworks are important. The other work of financial mathematics in the modern finance is the portfolio theory. rather than looking at the performance of an asset separately, portfolio optimization looks at the performance of the assets as a whole and gains of diversification. The mathematical models are applied to develop optimal combinations of assets that maximize returns that are to be achieved at a specified risk or reduce the usage of risk at specified expectations returns. The processes of linear algebra, calculus and constrained optimization are used to perform these optimization problems and hence makes them quite appropriate to the aspect of calculation. The optimization of the portfolio is based on the large datasets of the historical returns, the correlations as well as the risk measures. Financial mathematics will provide the design of the way such data will be translated in an efficient portfolio allocation. The optimization methods have been applied to large and complex portfolios due to the available database management as well as computing power to facilitate the rebalancing that is real-time and dynamic decision-making. Portfolio optimization models have been very useful in optimization of performance of asset managers, pension funds, institutional investors to optimize the performance and also in systematic management of risk.

The third explanation of the rise of relevance of financial mathematics in the current finance industry is the high levels of derivatives. Some of the derivatives include futures and swaps and options which are based on underlying assets all of which provide nonlinear payoff structures. These tools are important because, they demand advanced model of mathematics that take into consideration the uncertainty, time and market dynamics. Financial mathematics offers the tools to make an approximation of the payoffs of a derivative, hedge risk, and sensitivity to underlying variables. The derivatives pricing aspect of stochastic modeling also plays a major role in the derivatives pricing on the basis of the notion that the price of the assets is a random process that changes over the period of time. The models are used to model the probabilistic nature of the financial markets and enable the analysts to make conjectures on the possibility of the occurrence of different events. Under uncertainty financial math can compute complex financial instruments with their existence, by the use of stochastic calculus and differential equations. These models have formed the basis of the present derivatives pricing and risk management. In the real-world, stochastic models are applied together with real time data and trading and hedging and risk management algorithms. Their models require appropriate estimation of the parameters and must always be tested on the market data. The data-driven finance is a supplement to the stochastic model that provides access to high-frequency data and better estimation methods and increased calibration and responsiveness of models to changing market conditions. The power of mathematic models is not constrained by the fact that they can be used in finance. They are based on the assumptions regarding the actions of the market and the functioning of the data and reasonable actions of investors which is not always true in reality. A test of the validity of traditional models is possible in extreme events, changes and factors of behavior that are structural. These limitations are necessary to make one able to make good use of financial mathematics. Constant monitoring, stress testing and the enhancement of the models in a data-driven concept can reduce such risks and develop resilience.

In most cases, the present-day finance is founded on financial mathematics, as a means of providing an analytical analysis of value, risk and profit. It will aid in valid and steady financial decision-making in offering formalized models of time worth of money, computation of risk and maximization of portfolios and price of derivatives. Financial mathematics together with good data and empirical modelling enable the financial practitioners to make crucial decisions in a risky environment, to get optimum decisions and to react appropriately to the movement of the new financial markets. Role of Financial Mathematics in Modern Finance are shown in Table 1

Table 1. Role of financial mathematics in modern finance

Concept / Area	Description	Applications / Benefits
Time Value of Money	Money's value differs over time due to risk, inflation, opportunity cost	Investment appraisal, capital budgeting, comparing projects
Cash Flow Analysis	Evaluating timing, size, and certainty of inflows/outflows	Discounted cash flow valuation of bonds, equities, projects
Risk and Return Measurement	Quantifying risk and expected return using probabilistic models	Investment decisions, performance evaluation, balancing risk and reward

continued on following page

Table 1. Continued

Concept / Area	Description	Applications / Benefits
Return Modeling	Modeling expected returns and relationships with market risk	Asset pricing, portfolio evaluation, estimating risk premia
Risk Metrics	Measures like Value at Risk (VaR) and Expected Shortfall	Banking, regulatory compliance, risk management
Portfolio Optimization	Selecting asset combinations to maximize return for given risk or minimize risk for desired return	Asset allocation, diversification, dynamic rebalancing
Derivatives & Stochastic Modeling	Pricing and managing options, futures, and swaps using random processes	Trading, hedging, risk control, derivatives valuation
Data-Driven Integration	Using large datasets, real-time data, and computational algorithms	Improved model calibration, responsive risk management, informed decision-making

DATABASE MANAGEMENT FOR FINANCIAL DATA

The inclusion of the scale, diversity, and speed of financial information is one of the latest additions to the financial sphere that has become one of the foundations of the modern finance. The financial institutions execute their operations in a location that is data centric and which the decisions made are made quickly, in real facts and according to the regulatory standards. The right database management systems provide the platform that is required to collect, organize, store, access, as well as protect financial information with the aim of analyzing it and making wise decisions. The quality and effectiveness of the data management platform will directly correlate with the result of the analytics done on a data oriented financial platform. Financial data source is extremely heterogeneous and possesses numerous internal and external sources and this is typical of the activity of financial markets and financial institutions (Liu et al., 2024). The trading platforms and stock exchange form market information such as the price of assets or trades, volumes of the trade, interest rates, and even exchange rates in real-time. The accounting of the single financial transactions that form the basis of operational finance are known as transaction data which include payment, deposit, loan and trading. In addition, the financial statements, balance sheets, income statements, and cash flow reports are the structured accounting information that support the performance appraisal and regulatory levels of reporting. The financial analysis can be further boosted with the Macroeconomic information, which includes the rate of inflation, employment, and gross domestic product, which provides an insight into the economic situation.

The management of databases is faced by significant constraints of the heterogeneity of financial information. The data may be structured, semi-structured and unstructured and may be received at a frequency up to high frequencies, or at a periodical frequency. The databases systems must be in a position to support this heterogeneity besides being consistent and reliable. The appropriate classification and standardization of data will be required to be able to amalgamate different sources and process them in a meaningful way. Database management systems are the pivot point in a data-driven financial world, whereby varying groups of data are pooled into an integrated information bundle (Zhang et al., 2023). The design and architecture of financial databases are highly significant in offering support to both the analytical and operational requirements. A well-designed database ensures that data is intact, that data is not repeated much and helps to enhance performance of a system. The rigidity of relational models of databases and the possibility to grant data integrity through constraints and normalization have long been popular in the financial world. The models support complex queries and transactions processing and hence can be used in accounting systems, customer records and regulatory reporting. However, as the amount and complexity of the data has increased, other database architectures have also taken the centre stage (Sun et al., 2019).

The latest financial systems are also beginning to include crossed database architectures of a combination of relational databases and non-relational/distributed systems. These architectures enable organizations to make a tradeoff between trade-off accuracy of transactions and scalability and flexibility. Some of the factors to influence the database design decisions include the volume of data, the patterns of access, the performance and regulatory constraints. The architecture must be designed in such a way that it can make real time decision in the financial data and long-term data processing which can include integration of operational databases and data warehouses with analytical platforms. To facilitate the financial analysis and decision support, data storage and retrieval should be efficient enough to allow the data to be used on time. The financial experts require easy access to the previous and current data in order to determine the market conditions, risk evaluation, and make transactions. Database management systems make use of indexing, query optimization and caching to ensure that the speed of accessing information is increased and the system is responsive (Ogiela, 2013). Delays in access to data, even at the utmost level of small scale, can be extremely expensive in trading and risk monitoring at very high frequencies. In turn, performance optimization is one of the primary concerns of financial database design and management.

One of the concerns of data security and confidentiality is financial database management. Financial information is highly sensitive and it has its strict rules and regulations regarding privacy, confidentiality and integrity. Unauthorized access, data theft, and malfunction of the system can trigger some significant finances and image damage. To ensure that the data is not compromised to internal and external attacks, the database management systems have security measures such as access controls, encryption, authentication and auditing. The necessity to offer data protection within a data-oriented system is not only a technical requirement, but a strategic and moral one. The regulatory compliance also dictates the practice in managing databases in the field of finance. Banking institutions ought to be appropriately recorded, tracked, and regulated with regard to reporting and auditing. The database systems must also be in a position of storing data over specific duration and providing easy access to the historical data where necessary (Wirtz et al., 2014). Data quality, ownership, and accountability policies and procedures are good data governance models that enhance trust in the use of data to make decisions. The rapid growth of the big data technologies has affected the modern finance as it has altered the way in which databases are managed. The characteristic of the modern financial information is huge and complex to handle using the traditional database system. The big data platforms enable the handling of the big volumes of data created as a result of market exchanges, connecting with customers, and digital financial services. These platforms can assist in the promotion of advanced analytics, pattern recognition and predictive modeling, widening the scope of information-driven finance beyond the conventional field.

Cloud computing has also altered such a way that management of financial database can be scalable, flexible and economical as regards data storage and processing. Cloud-based financial databases allow institutions to be dynamically provisioned in accordance with the change of volume of data and computation demand. Such flexibility also contributes to innovation and experimentation and financial organizations can introduce new analytical tool and services faster. The process of cooperation and sharing data between organizational units and geographical boundaries can also be supported by the use of clouds and enhanced the productivity of data-driven processes. Despite all these advantages, there are new risks to the safety of data, compliance with regulations, and stability in big data and cloud-based financial databases (Deng, 2024). Banks and other financial organizations must be sensitive on the manner in which they manage access to the information, their compliance on the requirements that might be unique to them in their jurisdictions and in the manner, they practice control on sensitive information that is stored in the external environment. These problems highlight the necessity of efficient system of control and risk management in financial systems that are data-driven. Overall, the modern, data-driven finance would not be a possibility without the financial data database management. The database management systems facilitate the utilization of financial mathematics and econometric analysis since they assist in the availability of a good infrastructure to store, retrieve and protect data. The integration of the classical database systems and the emerging systems of the big data and cloud-based technologies is the testament of the emerging demands of the financial organizations in the fast-evolving environment. Well-designed and well-managed database system can transform raw financial data into something that will be strategic and allow the decision-makers to be more efficient and accurate and resolute in the financial sector of its operations (Yerashenia & Bolotov, 2019).

ECONOMETRIC TECHNIQUES FOR FINANCIAL ANALYSIS

Econometric techniques assume the centre stage in the modern financial analysis since they provide the empirical means, which are needed to experiment financial theories, examine data-based relationships and develop informed decision making. As the application of quantitative and data-driven approaches in the field of finance has increased, econometrics has come to hold significance in dispensing the gap between the theoretical and the real financial behavior. The econometrics enables the analyst to come up with meaningful inferences on the financial data by combining the statistical methods with the economic and financial theory and also to test the validity of assumptions underlying the financial model. In a financial setting, econometrics plays a key role in assisting one to understand how the financial variables interrelate with time and the different market conditions (Chang & McAleer, 2015). The financial markets are sensitive to a myriad of changes such as the macroeconomic conditions, the peculiarities of the firm, the investors and the world. Econometric methods provide a scientific platform upon which such effects can be isolated and their impact can be estimated. Financial professionals have the capability with the aid of empirical analysis to invest in investment, risk management and policy formulation by going beyond descriptive statistics and construct evidence-based approaches to these processes.

A large part of the econometric application in finance is founded on it. It has been effectively used to examine the dependence on independent variable as well as dependent variable that may be asset returns and market risk variables, or interest rates as well as inflation or firm performance and financial structure. Estimated regression models can be used to assist an analyst establish the strength, direction and significance of the relationships. Hypotheses can be tested using regression methods; therefore regression can help a researcher to establish whether the patterns that he or she observes are statistically significant or a mere product of chance. Econometric analysis ion finance, hypothesis testing is an essential element of the procedure given that it provides a more formal framework of the testing of financial theories and empirical evidence (Lee, 2020). Statistical criteria Statistical tests may measure monetary policy hypotheses, such as the response of risk and reward, or how the monetary policy impacts the price of assets. One can determine that theoretical predictions may be endorsed or denied by empirical data through the economic models. In a data-based financial environment, hypothesis testing would be a more effective methodology in order to enhance objectivity and rigor, since judgments are made using statistically validated results rather than judgments and anecdotal evidence. Financial data may be dynamic, therefore, time-series econometric models are required to investigate the tendencies, periods, and dependency on time. The financial variables such as the stock prices, the exchange rates, the interest rates, and the volatility are the time-dependent functions and respond to the past and external shocks. Time-series models can capture these dynamics because they have stochastic and lag structures. They are usually used in the forecasting of the future financial outcomes, in the establishing of efficiency of the market and business shock stability (Lee, 2024).

Financial econometric methods play a major role in forecasting which consequently helps in planning, investment decisions and risk management. The financial institutions can make better resource allocation and prediction of market behavior through sound predictions of returns, volatility, and macroeconomic variables. Econometric forecasting models rely on previous data and apply statistical estimate to arrive at the predictions considering the uncertainty and the error of the model. The data-driven finance forecasting models are always updated with the release of new data, and hence it is more responsive to different market conditions. The panel data analysis is done through the conventional econometric methods and includes the aspect of cross-sectional data analysis which is combined with time-series data analysis(Gričar et al., 2025) . The data of Financial Panels Panel is commonly subjected to the time series analysis of the firm level performance, the conduct of the banking industry across geographical regions or to test the conduct of the asset returns across the markets. The panel data models allow the analysts to deal with the unobserved heterogeneity and to address both the individual effects and time-specific. This enhances better econometric analysis and explanatory power and hence, it is in areas where panel data methodology is particularly valuable in empirical finance analysis. The other important application of econometrics to financial analysis is the volatility modeling. Volatility is employed to measure the intensity of uncertainty or risk of the financial variables and this is significant in the pricing of the assets and also the management of assets as well as the pricing of derivatives. Financial markets are volatile at certain moments and quiet at other moments which cannot be easily modelled by constant-variance models. Econometric volatility models solve this issue by allowing the variance to change with time keeping with market conditions.

Without the measurement and forecasting of the volatility, there will be no risk management. Capital requirements are estimated by the banks through the volatility estimation, price derivatives, and to determine potential losses. The econometric models provide a systematic approach of response to volatility clustering and persistence in the financial time sequence of a given financial time series that are normally characteristic features of a given financial time series. Data-based structure Volatility models are adjusted on massive data and integrated with real-time monitoring systems in support of risk control proactively. Despite the fact that they are analytical, the econometric methods have several issues when applied in finance. Financial data may be noisy and/or incomplete or structural break because of change in the regulatory regime, technological advancement or economic meltdowns. The model assumptions such as linearity, normality and even stationarity are not always valid which lead to bias and inaccurate estimates. The second restrictions emphasize the importance of the careful model selection, diagnostics and inferiority examination of econometric activity (Rao, 2015). The existing data infrastructure and computational tools have been integrated with the econometric techniques and have made them extremely helpful in finance. Through the evolution of database management and computational power, analysts have the ability to perform a great amount of data and estimate complex models easily. It is applicable in data-driven finance since this integration enables a more empirical analysis to be conducted, model estimation is less time consuming and real-time support of decisions is enabled. This paradigm continues to prioritize the use of econometric methods to provide the information with the statistical rigor it needs to interpret it in a proper and responsible manner.

Overall, it is possible to state that the econometric techniques can be regarded as one of the cornerstones of the modern financial analysis, since they enable to appraise the financial relationships empirically, check theoretical models, and forecast unpredictable results. Financial professionals can use regression analysis, time-series models, panel data models, and volatility models to learn more about how the market behaves as well as to make a better decision. Econometrics may be applied in conjunction with financial mathematics and effective database management systems to help organizations to transform data into operational knowledge to increase their ability to handle the complexity and uncertainty of the contemporary financial markets. The basic premise behind the contemporary data-driven finance is the integration of the approach of financial mathematics, database management, and econometrics. All these areas of study on their own have provided some helpful tools and insights but when combined together to create a coherent approach to analysis their real worth becomes known. It is under this integration that the financial organizations can transform the high volumes of raw data into the form of the information, quantitative information and actionable decision-making. This type of integrated approach must offer precision, effectiveness and strategic benefit in a world of increasing complexity, and swiftly evolving financial environment.

This integration revolves around a systematic data processing and analysis workflow which links the data collection and decision making. Some of the sources generate financial information on a continuous basis including markets, institutions, customers and regulatory organizations. The point of entry to this workflow is database management systems because they capture, store and organize data in an orderly and effective manner. Through proper data validation, cleaning and transformation processes, raw data is modeled to be analyzed. This is a very vital step since the quality of the analysis results depends on the quality and the consistency of the data employed. Financial mathematics provides the formalism demanded to analyze and describe financial phenomena after processing and organization of data. The mathematical models establish the correlation with the financial variables, prices, returns, interest rates, and risks. The models introduce processed data into meaningful financial values including present values, expected returns, risk values, and optimization outcomes. With the assistance of mathematical logic and constraints, financial mathematics is applied to ensure that the findings of the analyses make sense, are similar, and consistent with the principles of finance.

Econometric techniques are additional to this process because they give an empirical estimate and validation of mathematical models using real life data. Econometrics enables analysis of uncertainty to be tested, quantified and measured. Regression analysis, time-series models, and panel data relate the financial theory to the available data that can determine the credibility and forecast power of quantitative models that then help the decision-makers. In an integrated framework, econometrics is to be provided as a feedback mechanism, which may improve mathematical models as demonstrated by facts and adjust them to the changes in the market.

The integration of these regions creates a progressive analysis of the process. The databases are able to provide the latest data, financial mathematics structure the analysis and econometrics indicators and improve the performance of the model. This cycle leads to the making of informed decisions and enables the financial experts to move toward one direction due to gathering data, analysis, and execution of strategies. These work flows come in handy in such environments where the decisions to be taken are uncertain and hurried e.g. trading, risk management and financial planning. Quantitative models derived by such a hybrid framework are highly significant in the decision support systems. The models assist the financial managers, investors, and policymakers to examine the options, risk analysis, and the maximization of outcomes. It is possible to take an efficient allocation of assets in terms of trade-offs of risk-returns using portfolio optimization models, but to compute the likely losses in various situations using risk models. The valuation models are applicable in the appraisal of investments and valuation decisions, and the forecasting models to provide expectations of future market behavior. By integrating all these quantitative models in the system of data-driven tasks, the organization will receive certain consistent and objective recommendations which will enhance the quality of decisions. Decision support systems are also based on integrated quantitative frameworks which increase transparency and accountability. Math formulations provide a clear explanation of assumptions and constraints; statistical justification is attained using the econometric estimation and data in a database system can be traced. Such transparency is especially applicable to the financial environments that are regulated due to the necessity to justify the decisions to the stakeholders and authorities. This financial, data and econometrics combination, thus, facilitates optimization of performance as well as governance and compliance. It has also been further incorporated in the sphere of automation by means of finance mathematics and databases and econometrics. With the advancement of computing and data infrastructure, it is now possible to automate the process of data processing, model estimation and decision implementation. Under automated systems, real-time data collection is achieved, databases are updated, models are recalibrated and outputs generated with minimal involvement of humans. This reduces the time taken in the operation and chances of the human error thus making the financial processes in the operations more efficient and reliable. A giant in data based finance is real time financial analytics. The integration of high-frequency flows of data and automated analytics allows the financial institutions to observe the markets in real-time and respond to the changing situation on a case-by-case basis. New threats are identified and strategies are implemented, respectively, with the help of risk analytics and automated trading systems. This is because these applications are founded on the seamless integration of databases in data storage, financial mathematics in the modeling and econometrics in estimating parameters and defying them.

APPLICATIONS OF DATA-DRIVEN FINANCE

The decision-making process of financial institutions, investors, and policymakers is now transformed due to the introduction of data-based finance because it is now possible to use large volumes of data, new analysis application, and quantitative models. Financial mathematics, a combination of econometrics and database management has also brought forth a plethora of applications into the real world that has increased the accuracy, efficiency and strategic results. One may note that the algorithmic and quantitative trading, credit risk assessment, performance evaluation of portfolios, and financial risk management can be considered as the most essential applications and the data-driven methods of the modern financial activity are used. he echo of the fast and data-heavy character of modern finance is algorithms and quantitative trading. In algorithmic trading, computer programs automatically carry out an order based on pre-laid rules derived by mathematical models and statistical analysis whereby the past-data is considered (Bashar et al., 2021). Quantitative trading is a trading where large sum of information in terms of market prices, trading volumes, economic indicators and sentiment information is used to identify patterns and give predictive information. It is a common finding that such systems use some sophisticated mathematical finance to model risk-return relationships, optimise its implementation in trade and quantify the effect of volatility in the market. The econometric techniques also optimize these strategies by testing the predictive capacity of variables besides determining the correlation and the proving models in diverse market conditions (Wen et al., 2021). The consequence of this is the highly trading ecosystem that incorporates the quantitative analysis and the live market data which is used to make informed decisions that these traders take advantage of the opportunity, minimize the transaction cost incurred and the exposure effectively managed. Applications of Data-Driven Finance are shown in Table 2

Table 2. Applications of data-driven finance

Application	Description	Benefits
Algorithmic & Quantitative Trading	Automated trading using data and models	Faster decisions, lower costs, better trades
Credit Risk Assessment	Evaluating borrower default probability	Reduced defaults, accurate lending
Portfolio Performance Evaluation	Measuring returns and risks of investments	Better allocation, informed decisions
Financial Risk Management	Identifying and managing financial risks	Proactive control, resilience
Advanced Analytics & AI	Using AI and big data for insights	Predictive analysis, efficiency

Another area where data-driven finance is important is in credit risk assessment. With good models the financial institutions are able to estimate the likelihood of defaulting of the borrowers and besides this, they are capable of making the appropriate lending terms. The antique forms of credit checks where they were premised on a significant proportion of manual consideration and less past history records have been substituted with the advanced scoring models which utilize financial statements, past repayment record, market data and conduct signals. Financial mathematics offers an opportunity whereby the losses can be estimated, the price of interest on loans calculated including the risk adjusted returns. An econometric modelling (e.g., logistic regression, survival analysis, or machine learning algorithms) can enable an analyst to make estimates based on the probability of default and predictors that are pertinent and the degree to which economic conditions matter. Databases were the hub of gathering massive amounts of customer and market information and this was consistent and allowed the model to be updated on a continuous basis.

Information-based credit risk models improves the quality and efficacy of lending choices, diminishes the default rates, and capital fund (Malhotra & Malhotra, 2023).

The other field where data-driven approach has greatly improved the field of financial management is in the area of gauging the achievement of portfolio. The only measures that can be utilized to measure performance of investment portfolio in the right way are measures like returns, risks and benchmarks. Financial mathematics gives the equation to determine the risk-adjusted performance ratios of the Sharpe ratio, the Treynor ratio and the alpha. The econometric models provide the possibility to break the portfolio returns into systematic and idiosyncratic returns, estimated the beta coefficients and value of correlation of the assets. Combined with the copious market and portfolio data, which are properly stored in highly organized databases, then the financial practitioners can do a comprehensive performance analysis, they can find the assets that are not performing well and revisit places where they belong in the portfolios. The solution based on the data provides an opportunity to make evidence-based decisions, monitor the strategies of investments constantly, and makes the process more transparent to the stakeholders (Murugan & T, 2023). It is a broader use of financial risk management, in which information-based finance offers better-rounded resources of recognizing, assessing and eradicating exposure on large arrays of scales. An integrated quantitative analysis and liquidity risk and operational risk may be analyzed in terms of market risk and credit risk, which can be additionally accompanied by stochastic simulations, stress testing, and scenario analysis. Financial mathematics can be used in calculating the number of expected losses, value of risk and other risks measure in comparison of the econometric models that enable to calculate the correlations, volatilities and extreme events. Database quality and advanced computing platforms will help to ensure that the necessary data is added to the risk models in time and provide an opportunity to track and measure risks in real-time. Some of the evidences which the evidence-based risk management may provide include active decision-making, superior regulatory compliance, and the ability of the financial institutions to endure market shocks and systemic disruptions (Yu et al., 2021).

The uses of the data-driven finance are gradually transforming into technological innovations in the form of machine learning, artificial intelligence, cloud computing, and big data analytics. These kinds of technologies boost the analytical power of the conventional models that enable processing of the unstructured data, identification of the non-linear patterns, and conciliation of the predictive intelligence. This can be given by the fact that natural language processing can be used on news articles, social media hype or corporate reports to predict the reaction of the market to supplement the existing models of quantitative models. The cloud databases enable the opportunity to obtain financial information instantly at the framework of various geographies and institutions and make decisions faster and work more efficiently.

Even though the data-driven applications have advantages, there are challenges that are also linked with the applications, which should be addressed carefully. The algorithmic trading systems should deal with the issues of the model risk, overfitting, and market impact. The credit risk models may be limited during the time of structural change of economy; or when the information is unavailable. The portfolio analysis will be based on the appropriate history and benchmark data and the risk management models would be likely to survive the extreme events, and the errors in the data.. The data-driven finance implementation should be efficient through the strict verification of the models; continuous verification of data quality and human judgment should be added to the automated analysis. Generally speaking, the uses of data-driven finance may be viewed as a case of the groundbreaking involvement of the combination of financial mathematics, databases, and econometrics. Examples of how the quantitative analysis, empirical modeling, and adequate data management should be combined in enhancing financial decision making are the algorithmic trading, credit risk assessment, portfolio analysis, and financial risk management. This would enable the financial institutions and investors gain greater accuracy, manage risks and make better strategic decisions that would ultimately enable them to gain competitive edge in the dynamic and complex markets. The further enlargement and integration of information-intensive tools will bring in more novelty, effectiveness, and reliability to the financial sector.

BENEFITS AND LIMITATIONS OF DATA-DRIVEN FINANCIAL APPROACHES

The present-day finance has been reorganized in an information driven fashion which has today allowed companies to integrate mass data, elaborate mathematical models, and analysis tools as a decision-making instrument. The benefits of the methods are high because they will be capable of improving the level of accuracy, efficiency and scaling of comprehensive range of financial operations. The institutions are able to establish the appropriate valuation, appropriate risk management, and suitable response to the motion of the market conditions through the help of high-quality data, financial mathematics, and econometric tools functioning in a synchronized platform. Among the strongest points of data-driven finance is the accuracy. Mathematical and statistical equations enable the financial professionals to possess the mandate to quantify risk, forthcoming and assess the investment opportunity at a greater level of precision than in undertaking investment decisions by relying on their intuition. The subjective approach will create errors and bias and hence the data-based approaches will mitigate these risks because they will use empirical evidence and systematized data analysis procedures. As this accuracy may be applied to attain improved financial performance and more knowledgeable resource allocation in algorithmic trading, credit rating, and portfolio analysis, this can be applied to financial benefit.

Efficiency is the other grave advantage of data-driven financial strategies. The institutions are able to trade, risk rate and generate reports with minimal human intervention and process huge amounts of data within a short time frame using advanced automated workflow and systems. The database management systems enable one to retrieve historical and real time information with ease with the help of the computational algorithms and complex calculations as well as simulations are done at a massive scale. This package helps in decreasing the time in operation, cost reduction and allows the financial professionals to make strategic decisions instead of the routine. Speed and accuracy are considered of special importance in high frequency trading, real time risk management and large scale portfolio management and efficiency is also appreciated. Another benefit is scalability as data-driven architectures can be used to support growing datasets and more demanding analysis needs without correspondingly growing operational resources. Financial institutions can use cloud-based solutions and big data technologies and distributed computing infrastructures to scale their operations as they require additional data, new financial products are invented or it goes global. Such flexibility enables innovation and enables the organizations to react swiftly so as to get new market opportunities and secure high level of uniformity in the quality of analytical process within the large portfolios and business units. Regardless of the usefulness of these benefits, the quantitative financial approaches have serious weaknesses, the first one is the data quality and model risk. The quality of data utilized in any quantitative financial analysis is fine and sometimes lacking, inaccurate, faulty, inconsistent and sluggish. The possible consequences of the erroneous choice can be identified depending on the models, and the fact is that the input data can convey the mistakes and provide the inappropriate decision and it can be expensive. Moreover, structural separation or transformation or irregularity in financial information may not be characterized as per the common models and that is why the constant validation and surveillance of information becomes a requirement. Another underlying weakness of data-driven approaches is the model risk. Financial models are simplifications of reality and they are based on assumptions about how the market and the distribution and rationality of risk amongst investors operate. Violation of such assumptions may lead to the models giving biased or unreliable results. The error of using the models could be due to abnormal economic policies and market pressures that are not well managed by the human beings. To address the model risk, the model must be completely tested, stressed and sensitivity-analyzed and recalibrated with new data.

FUTURE TRENDS IN DATA-DRIVEN FINANCE

The future of finance is emerging in a new manner, with the firebrand building up of technology, access to data, and the complexity of data analysis instruments. The data-driven finance is the driver of this revolution enabling financial institutions, investors, and policy makers to leverage mass data, complex options and computing capabilities in making better-informed, timely and strategic decisions. The emerging trends indicate that artificial intelligence, machine learning, high-level econometric methods, and hybrid modeling are to become the main foundation of the new definition of financial analysis and decision-making and risk management.

Artificial intelligence and machine learning will only get more widespread in the financial applications. The AIs and ML algorithms can most effectively identify trends, find latent associations, and make predictive judgment using the big and complex data that are difficult or practically impossible to handle using traditional methods. The trading artificial intelligence has the potential to utilize the high-frequency market data to optimize the trading implementation, detect anomalies, and predict the future changes in the prices in the short run. These machine learning models can also be applied in credit risk assessment where a mix of financial statement, behavioral data and macroeconomic indicators can be evaluated in order to improve the process of predicting defaults and lending decisions reached. Moreover, AI solutions, such as natural language processing applications, can extract valuable information in uncontrolled sources, such as news stories, social media updates, and company announcements and allow the use of sentiment and alternative data by financial specialists in their decision-making models.

There are more sophisticated econometric and hybrid models that would reinvent financial analytics. Regression analysis, time series modeling and panel analysis are still the methods of cornerstone to the empirical evaluation and future forecasting. However, the pattern in the future suggests the continued mashing of econometrics and machine learning, and other forms of computation into hybrid models. These models bring together statistical capability of econometrics and the capabilities of AI to identify patterns to enhance prediction accuracy and strength. As an example, the dynamics of both the price and market shocks of assets can be modeled on stochastic volatility models and deep learning frameworks. Such hybrid models can also explain non-linear relations and high-dimensional data as well as changing market regimes and this is a weakness of the traditional models. AI, ML, and hybrid econometric models will enlarge the list of applications that use data to provide a financial solution. The dynamic allocation strategies will assist in targeting the portfolio management to adapt to the market environment and risk in real-time. The predictive analytics will be extended to the risk management systems to predict the crisis and systemic exposure and in the capital allocation optimization. The algorithmic trading systems will be founded on continuous learning models that will keep adapting to the evolving market trends and utilize opportunities offered by the market at minimal or no human intervention. The financial forecast that hitherto depended on past trends alone will be changed to real-time data, modelling of scenarios, and learning to be more responsive and accurate. The next generation of data-driven finance studies is also likely to focus on making models more comprehensible, integrating data, and regulating it in an ethical way. Regulatory compliance, trust and risk management among stakeholders, and the explanation and assurance of transparency will become the key in terms of the increasing complexity of AI and hybrid models. Hopefully, the research will find a means of making machine learning models interpretable, such as explainable AI processes, and predictive. Further attention will also be paid to the inclusion of a high variety of datasets, including structured financial data, unstructured textual data, and other sources of data, to make holistic decisions. The analytical findings to be made will require new approaches in the data engineering, storage and retrieval to ensure that valid and complete information forms the basis of the findings.

Ethical and regulatory aspects will also be important in shaping the future of data-driven finance. With the increased adoption of sophisticated analytics and AI in organizations, the element of equity, discrimination, confidentiality, and responsibility will also have to be taken into account. Researchers and regulators will be forced to develop models that combine both innovation and responsible governance in such financial decisions to make them balanced, transparent, and in line with the social and regulatory boundaries. The fact that environmental, social, and governance (ESG) dynamics are gaining greater and greater relevance to investment decision-making processes implies that there is an opportunity to introduce data-driven methods to introduce the concepts of sustainability to financial analysis and risk assessment. The future of data-driven finance is defined as a combination of technology, data and quantitative modelling. The artificial intelligence, machine learning, advanced econometric algorithms, and hybridization models will radically transform the operational paradigm of financial organizations and provide an unprecedented degree of analytical power and predictability. With the adoption of such trends, researchers and practitioners will be in a position to develop more accurate, responsive and effective decision-making frameworks. At the same time, the interpretability, data quality, ethics, and governance will be addressed to ensure that these innovations will be introduced in a responsible and sustainable way. The present successive data-driven finance development will probably create a more resilient, informed, and sophisticated financial ecosystem that will be in a position to endure the obscurities and uncertainties of the present global economy.

CONCLUSION

The modern financial management has also been revolutionized with data-driven finance as a combination of financial mathematics, database management tools and econometric tools in case of decision management improvement, efficiency and strategic output. The paper has discussed theoretical basis, practical implementation, and future of data-driven approaches in addition to showing how the integration of computational modeling, big data management and empirical modeling can contribute to make financial institutions more active in the complex and dynamic markets. The inclusion of financial mathematics in contemporary finance offers a formalistic construct of interpreting and modelling of values of assets, risk and returns. Such methods as time value of money analysis, portfolio optimization, derivative pricing and stochastic modeling are applied by financial specialists to estimate uncertainty and make the worthwhile investment decisions. Quantitative finance is based on these mathematical applications which provide theoretical advice in addition to realizations in the resource allocation, risk opinion and strategy. Database administration is highly important to the support of data-driven finance, which attends the conditions that are required to accumulate, store, structure and safeguard huge volumes of financial data. Good database designs will make sure that there is integrity, fast access and analysis. The emergence of big data and cloud-based systems has given financial organizations a chance to work with heterogeneous data of various sources and to conduct continuous analysis and evidence-based decision making. The use of the scale quantitative models and the analyses are founded on the efficient storage which can process and retrieve the data. These tools have their analogies, which are the econometric tools which bridge the gap between financial theory and data. They can be analyzed by the use of regression analysis, hypothesis testing, time-series forecasting, panel data modeling and volatility estimation to determine relationship among financial variables, predictive performance and stability of the model. Econometrics enables the financial practitioner to test hypotheses, refinements made to the model, and also to generate predictive results which may form the foundation on which an investment strategy, risk management and policy decisions may be made. It is the combination of these methods and the robust database systems and financial mathematics that help the organizations to reach the level of analytical accuracy and business efficiency that is fantastic in nature. There is a high prevalence of data-driven finance that affects the practice. In algorithmic and quantitative trading, trade maximization is done through the use of predictive models and high-frequency data to make use of market opportunities. Statistical scoring models can be used to credit risk assessment in which the reliability of borrowers can be determined and this would assist in making superior lending and capital allocation decisions. The portfolio performance analysis will facilitate the in depth analysis of the returns of the risk adjustment and therefore will use it to optimize the investment in the assets. It is possible to define financial risk management as the combination of the quantitative models and real-time analytics to predict market shocks, systematic exposure, and enhance institutional resilience. These applications can also be used to explain the effectiveness and strategic decision-making within the financial industry via the use of data-driven solutions.

Although there are all the benefits of data-driven finance, there are also serious weaknesses of the study. The quality of analytical outputs is subject to the quality of data provided, model efficacy, and insularity of suppositions. The predictions and quality of decisions can be invalidated because of model risk, imperfect or partial information, and divergence in the market structure. Data-driven methodologies are also restricted by ethical and regulatory implications such as privacy, fairness and transparency. These issues are supposed to be treated as regards the strict governance, the model's validation, the constant monitoring and the responsible introduction of the new technologies. The future of data-based finance is predetermined by the improvements of the artificial intelligence, machine learning, hybrid econometric models, and the computing possibilities of the future. The tools have a high predictive power, dynamic modelling systems, higher order decision support systems. Meanwhile, the interpretation, the ethical decision, and the synthesis of the various sources of information must be taken into account in the new studies and practice to introduce the innovations at the same time and in a reasonable manner. The combination of technology, data and quantitative analysis is the strategic opportunity that financial institution can exploit such that it is able to achieve sustainable competitive advantage in the increasingly complex global market. Finally, data-driven finance would be the new paradigm of managing and analyzing financial data. With integrated formidable mathematical modelling, quality data infrastructure and empirical econometrics, organizations can make raw data into actionable intelligence. Such a combined strategy is better as it enhances the accuracy of the decision-making, the efficiency of the operations, and responsiveness of the strategies, and helps financial entities to trade the uncertainty and score their performance and development in a sustainable way. The values and operations of the data-driven finance will be pivotal to the intelligent, clever and conscious management of the financial market, in the dynamic financial market.

REFERENCES

Akyıldırım, E., & Soner, H. M. (2014). A brief history of mathematics in finance. *Borsa Istanbul Review, 14*(1), 57–63. DOI: 10.1016/j.bir.2014.01.002

Ali, I., Modibbo, U. M., Bolaji, A. L., & Garg, H. (2024). *Optimization and Computing using Intelligent Data-Driven Approaches for Decision-Making: Optimization Applications* (1st ed.). CRC Press., DOI: 10.1201/9781003536796

Bashar, A., Rabbani, M. R., Khan, S., & Ali, M. A. M. (2021). Data driven finance: A bibliometric review and scientific mapping. *2021 International Conference on Data Analytics for Business and Industry (ICDABI)*, 161–166. DOI: 10.1109/ICDABI53623.2021.9655898

Chakraborty, A., & Tsokos, C. (2025). *A Modern Optimization Approach with Data-Driven Analytical Modeling for the Healthcare Business Segment (HBS) from the S&P 500*. Business, Economics and Management. DOI: 10.20944/preprints202508.2017.v1

Chang, C.-L., & McAleer, M. (2015). Econometric analysis of financial derivatives: An overview. *Journal of Econometrics, 187*(2), 403–407. DOI: 10.1016/j.jeconom.2015.02.026

De Zarzà, I., De Curtò, J., Roig, G., & Calafate, C. T. (2023). Optimized Financial Planning: Integrating Individual and Cooperative Budgeting Models with LLM Recommendations. *AI, 5*(1), 91–114. DOI: 10.3390/ai5010006

Deng, T. (2024). The application of database systems in information management. *Applied and Computational Engineering, 40*(1), 33–42. DOI: 10.54254/2755-2721/40/20230625

Dote-Pardo, J. S., Cordero-Díaz, M. C., Espinosa Jaramillo, M. T., & Parra-Domínguez, J. (2025). Leveraging artificial intelligence for enhanced decision-making in finance: Trends and future directions. *Journal of Accounting Literature*. Advance online publication. DOI: 10.1108/JAL-02-2025-0100

Emmert-Streib, F. (2025). *Unifying Perspectives on Econometrics, Econophysics, Complexity Economics, and Ai-Driven Economics. SSRN*. DOI: 10.2139/ssrn.5346888

Gričar, S., Lojanica, N., & Backović, T. (2025). Financial Econometrics and Quantitative Economic Analysis. *Journal of Risk and Financial Management, 18*(3), 166. DOI: 10.3390/jrfm18030166

Hassan, T. (2025). *Augmented Analytics in Financial Forecasting Enhancing Risk Management and Investment Strategies through AI-Driven Insights. SSRN*. DOI: 10.2139/ssrn.5179431

Lee, C. F. (2020). Financial econometrics, mathematics, statistics, and financial technology: An overall view. *Review of Quantitative Finance and Accounting, 54*(4), 1529–1578. DOI: 10.1007/s11156-020-00883-z

Lee, C. F. (2024). Financial Econometrics, Mathematics, Statistics, and Financial Technology: An Overall View. In C. F. Lee, A. C. Lee, & J. C. Lee, *Handbook of Investment Analysis, Portfolio Management, and Financial Derivatives* (pp. 1007–1075). WORLD SCIENTIFIC. DOI: 10.1142/9789811269943_0031

Lee, C. F. (2025). Introduction to Financial Technology, Statistics, Econometrics and Risk Management. In C.-F. Lee, A. C. Lee, & J. C. Lee, *Handbook of Financial Econometrics, Statistics, Technology, and Risk Management* (pp. 1–106). WORLD SCIENTIFIC. DOI: 10.1142/9789819809950_0001

Liu, B., Ji, Y., & Zhou, C. (2024). Application of Distributed Database System in Financial Management. In Hung, J. C., Yen, N., & Chang, J.-W. (Eds.), *Frontier Computing on Industrial Applications* (Vol. 1, pp. 9–16). Springer Nature Singapore., DOI: 10.1007/978-981-99-9299-7_2

Malhotra, R., & Malhotra, D. K. (2023). The Impact of Technology, Big Data, and Analytics: The Evolving Data-Driven Model of Innovation in the Finance Industry. *The Journal of Financial Data Science, 5*(3), 50–65. DOI: 10.3905/jfds.2023.1.129

Mandl, C., & Minner, S. (2023). Data-Driven Optimization for Commodity Procurement Under Price Uncertainty. *Manufacturing & Service Operations Management, 25*(2), 371–390. DOI: 10.1287/msom.2020.0890

Mani, M. (2024). An Exploration of Contemporary Trends in Finance Research. *Journal of the Knowledge Economy, 16*(3), 12291–12316. DOI: 10.1007/s13132-024-02373-2

Master of Business Administration. Indiana State University, Terre Haute, Indiana, USA, Kowsar, M. M., Mohiuddin, M., Master of Science in Management Information Systems, Lamar university, Texas, USA, Islam, S., & Master in Public Budgeting and Finance, Murray State University, Kentucky, USA. (2023). Mathematics For Finance: A Review Of Quantitative Methods In Loan Portfolio Optimization. *International Journal of Scientific Interdisciplinary Research, 04*(03), 01–29. DOI: 10.63125/j43ayz68

Mondal, C., Al-Kfairy, M., & Mellor, R. B. (2023). Developing Young Science and Technology Parks: Recent Findings from Industrial Nations Using the Data-Driven Approach. *Sustainability (Basel), 15*(7), 6226. DOI: 10.3390/su15076226

Murugan, M. S., & T, S. K. (2023). Large-scale data-driven financial risk management & analysis using machine learning strategies. *Measurement. Sensors, 27*, 100756. DOI: 10.1016/j.measen.2023.100756

Ogiela, L. (2013). Data management in cognitive financial systems. *International Journal of Information Management, 33*(2), 263–270. DOI: 10.1016/j.ijinfomgt.2012.11.008

Pillai, V. (2023). Integrating AI-Driven Techniques in Big Data Analytics: Enhancing Decision-Making in Financial Markets. *International Journal of Engineering and Computer Science, 12*(07), 25774–25788. DOI: 10.18535/ijecs/v12i07.4745

Rao, K. S. (2015). The Basics of Financial Econometrics: Tools, Concepts, and Asset Management Applications. *Quantitative Finance, 15*(11), 1773–1775. DOI: 10.1080/14697688.2015.1080486

Strielkowski, W., Vlasov, A., Selivanov, K., Muraviev, K., & Shakhnov, V. (2023). Prospects and Challenges of the Machine Learning and Data-Driven Methods for the Predictive Analysis of Power Systems: A Review. *Energies, 16*(10), 4025. DOI: 10.3390/en16104025

Sun, Y., Shi, Y., & Zhang, Z. (2019). Finance Big Data: Management, Analysis, and Applications. *International Journal of Electronic Commerce, 23*(1), 9–11. DOI: 10.1080/10864415.2018.1512270

Wen, C., Yang, J., Gan, L., & Pan, Y. (2021). Big data driven Internet of Things for credit evaluation and early warning in finance. *Future Generation Computer Systems, 124*, 295–307. DOI: 10.1016/j.future.2021.06.003

Wen, H., & Gao, R. (2025). Strategic Planning and Forecasting in Financial Management: Integrating AI-Driven Mathematical Modeling Techniques. *International Journal of High Speed Electronics and Systems, 2540771*, 2540771. Advance online publication. DOI: 10.1142/S0129156425407715

Wirtz, A., Kron, W., Löw, P., & Steuer, M. (2014). The need for data: Natural disasters and the challenges of database management. *Natural Hazards, 70*(1), 135–157. DOI: 10.1007/s11069-012-0312-4

Yerashenia, N., & Bolotov, A. (2019). Computational Modelling for Bankruptcy Prediction: Semantic Data Analysis Integrating Graph Database and Financial Ontology. *2019 IEEE 21st Conference on Business Informatics (CBI)*, 84–93. DOI: 10.1109/CBI.2019.00017

Yu, W., Wong, C. Y., Chavez, R., & Jacobs, M. A. (2021). Integrating big data analytics into supply chain finance: The roles of information processing and data-driven culture. *International Journal of Production Economics*, *236*, 108135. DOI: 10.1016/j.ijpe.2021.108135

Zhang, H., Ren, S., Li, X., Baharin, H., Alghamdi, A., & Alghamdi, O. A. (2023). Developing scalable management information system with big financial data using data mart and mining architecture. *Information Processing & Management*, *60*(3), 103326. DOI: 10.1016/j.ipm.2023.103326

Zhang, P., Shi, X., & Khan, S. U. (2019). QuantCloud: Enabling Big Data Complex Event Processing for Quantitative Finance Through a Data-Driven Execution. *IEEE Transactions on Big Data*, *5*(4), 564–575. DOI: 10.1109/TBDATA.2018.2847629

Zhang, S. (2025). A Big Data-Driven Approach to Financial Analysis and Decision Support System Design. *Informatica (Vilnius)*, *49*(11). Advance online publication. DOI: 10.31449/inf.v49i11.7065

Zhang, Y. (2025). The Exploration of the Interdisciplinary Education of Mathematics in Universities: A Case Study of Mathematics and Finance. *Frontiers in Interdisciplinary Educational Methodology*, *2*(2), 74–80. DOI: 10.71465/fiem187

Chapter 3
Monte Carlo Models for Asset Pricing and Financial Risk:
Theory, Implementation, and Business Applications

Kattamuri Satish
http://orcid.org/0009-0003-5307-0715
Jain (Deemed to be) University, India

Rama Jyothi Boddu
http://orcid.org/0000-0003-0971-9268
Lendi Institute of Engineering and Technology, India

R. Hepsiba
AQJ Centre for PG Studies, India

ABSTRACT

Monte Carlo simulation is now used in modern finance to process complex derivatives, uncertainty in the market and valid risk analysis in non-linear and multi-factor contexts. The traditional models of analysis are often limited by assumptions such as constant volatility and normal returns because real market dynamics are often not captured by traditional analytical models. The chapter provides a well-rounded model that incorporates the theoretical basis of Monte Carlo methods, its computer implementation and business applications. Its code support of useful Python and R functions to simulate the asset path, price European, American, and Asian options, compute Value at risk and Expected shortfall, use variance reduction, and many fundamental stochastic processes, including Geometric Brownian Motion,

DOI: 10.4018/979-8-3373-8372-9.ch003

jump-diffusion and the Heston model. Banking, insurance, asset management, and corporate finance examples are given of applications that are decision-oriented and the regulatory relevance and reliability is demonstrated through convergence diagnostics and back testing.

1. INTRODUCTION

1.1 Monte Carlo Simulation in Finance

The high degree of uncertainty that prevails in the present day financial markets is caused by geopolitical shocks, active investor behavior, the changing macroeconomic variables and rapid changes in market microstructure. These realities create intricate pricing and risk-management issues especially if assets return have features like fat tails, volatility clustering and non-linear correlations. Simulation-grounded modeling became a key methodological approach in this respect to elucidate on the issue of uncertainty and aid in making evidence-based financial choices (Glasserman, 2004; Hull, 2022). Monte Carlo simulation (MCS) is a computational technique that forms a massive amount of random scenarios and follows the distribution of findings to rough numeric findings. The Monte Carlo methods are predominantly used in finance by constantly modelling the possible future market conditions to simulate the stochastic nature in the asset prices, interest rates and portfolio values (Boyle, 1977; Glasserman, 2004). Monte Carlo simulation has been used in scenarios that are not idealized, such as the case when there is multifaceted uncertainty in the market, as opposed to closed form solutions, because of the distributions used in its modeling (Hull, 2022). One of its key strengths lies in the ability of MCS to incorporate stochastic processes taking into account continuous-time uncertainty in the value of assets. In many applications of finance, the movement of the prices of assets is described by Geometric Brownian Motion (GBM) that is the cornerstone of the Black-Scholes modeling framework. Monte Carlo simulation does the same, but in a case where finding the actual mathematical solution is not possible or would be too costly, the value of a security and/or a derivative is computed via simulation, using thousands (or millions) of history paths to the underlying security under GBM and other stochastic models (Black and Scholes, 1973; Glasserman, 2004). Along with the pricing of assets, Monte Carlo simulation is important in the management of financial risks in particular in determining the measures of downside risks such as Expected short fall (ES) and Value at risk (VaR). The risk quantification involves modelling the losses of a portfolio for a large variety of possible future market conditions, both normal and extreme. The use of Monte Carlo-based risk modeling can therefore enhance capital planning, stress testing and regulatory compliance because it can quantify the impact of adverse events and assess distribution tails, among other benefits (Jorion, 2007; McNeil et al., 2015). As risk factors are not linearly interacting and historical information is not extensive enough to capture the growing uncertainty, this simulation-based approach is becoming more relevant. Also, somewhat more complicated derivatives such as path-dependent and exotic derivatives, where the amount paid is determined by the path that the underlying asset takes, are especially well-priced by Monte Carlo methods. Among some of these are Asian options, barrier options and structured products. The methods of analysis are often inadequate because the value of such instruments should take into account various time periods and conditional attributes. The structure of simulation can be flexible enough to tackle this complexity and offers financial analysts with sensitivity, hedging requirements and payoffs based on scenarios (Hull, 2022; Glasserman, 2004). Besides, Monte Carlo techniques can be used to assist in financial decision making in other applications than those related to the market, such as corporate finance and investment planning. It has been applied into credit portfolio loss modelling, optimising a portfolio with a simulation-based projection approach, integrated enterprise risk management and project value under uncertainty. Monte Carlo simulation is key in the field of finance, especially as financial institutions continue to embrace automation and sophisticated analytics, along with its ability to conduct parallel computations and integrate with high-performance computing environments, as well as its hybrid nature when used with machine learning models (Glasserman, 2004; McNeil et al., 2015). Owing to all these, Monte Carlo simulation is considered to be an indispensable computing tool that uses risk-based models for decision making, scenario model development and probabilistic analysis, to connect financial theory and business practice.

1.2 Monte Carlo Models required in Asset Pricing and Risk

All of these - financial markets' growing influence in the context of global integration, speedy information exchange, algorithmic trading and vulnerability to geopolitical and economic shocks are all factors that are increasingly affecting financial markets. The result is an environment of great uncertainty, where asset values may fluctuate greatly and even without warning, due to these factors. In such a context, analytical models which are able to capture uncertainty and randomness, and model non-linear market phenomena in asset pricing, financial risk modelling are required. The Monte Carlo simulation has also been adopted as a more contemporary approach in finance as it can be used to simulate scenarios and provide distribution-based information to guide decision-making, as opposed to simply a single deterministic estimate (Glasserman, 2004; Hull, 2022). The ability of Monte Carlo models to deal with complex and non-linear payoffs, especially in derivatives and structured financial products, is one of the primary reasons why Monte Carlo models are popular in asset pricing. Many of the more common real-life instruments feature features like barriers and averaging, as well as early exercise rights, multi-asset dependencies, properties for which closed-form pricing solutions are missing or not reliable. However, under certain stringent conditions, it can be shown that part of the options can be priced in closed form using analytical models, like the Black-Scholes. All these complexities are accounted for in Monte Carlo models by mimicking hundreds (or millions) of price paths generated by certain stochastic processes and calculating payoffs under various scenarios (Boyle, 1977; Glasserman, 2004; Hull, 2022). A Monte Carlo approach is very convenient for risk environment modelling with multiple factors and correlations. Typical portfolios today might include several portfolios of assets, including stocks, fixed income, foreign exchange, commodities, and alternative investments. During the economic contraction, risk factors of such assets can exhibit correlation discontinuities and are often correlated with one another. These variables can be jointly simulated using Monte Carlo modeling and can be used to better assess the risk of individual assets and value a portfolio. This skill is especially critical for institutional portfolios and enterprise level risk management as risk cannot be measured with isolated or single factor risk measures (McNeil et al., 2015). Another compelling case in support of the need of Monte Carlo simulation is the value of Monte Carlo simulation in evaluating severe loss events and tail risk, which are critical problems in risk management in modern times. Under normal distribution assumptions, extreme losses occur with financial returns distributions which are not normally distributed because of fat tails. Monte Carlo simulation can help in financing tail-risk by generating outcome distributions generated by stochastic models and by allowing the measurement of downside risk metrics, such as Value at risk (VaR) and Expected shortfall (ES). Financial institutions (Jorion, 2007; McNeil et al., 2015) have found these measures to be valuable tools of capital planning, stress testing and risk monitoring. Lastly, model governance norms and laws have a significant influence on the use of the Monte Carlo models. Increasingly, risk practices and risk regulation are turning to scenario analysis, stress testing and adverse conditions capital adequacy analysis. Monte Carlo simulation has often replaced in risk engines used by banks, insurance companies and asset management companies because it can deliver results based on scenarios and also offer a range of ability in sensitivity analysis between different risk drivers. In the modern financial markets, Monte Carlo simulation is regarded as a strategy for risk assessment and regulatory compliance, in addition to using it as a pricing instrument. (Glasserman, 2004; McNeil et al., 2015).

Figure 1. The simulation modeling lifecycle

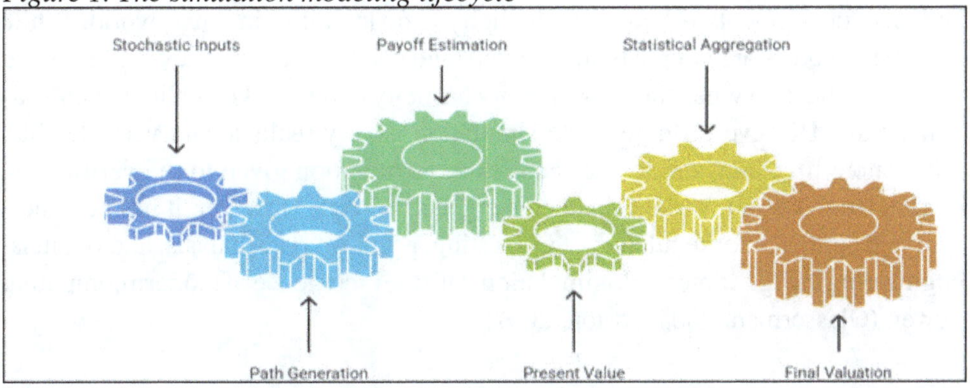

1.3 The differences between Monte Carlo and Analytical Models

Because of the ease of using a mathematical model, analytical models have been employed to evaluate risk and to perform financial valuations. The Black-Scholes model is thought to be one of the most famous analysis tools that can give an exact closed form solution to the European option pricing problem in the absence of restrictions on trading, frictionless markets, constant volatility, and log normally distributed wealth (Black and Scholes, 1973). The speed, ease of interpretation and sound theoretical basis of these models has seen them remain popular in financial education and practice. Solutions to financial problems are however often not possible analytically, due to wrong assumptions that are often made in real financial markets. Empirical evidence suggests that generally the tails of asset returns are large, the price movements are sharp, and the volatility is concentrated, and this is not captured by the normalcy and constant volatility hypotheses (Cont, 2001). Furthermore, the properties of route dependence, early exercise, discontinuous payoffs and varying correlation are provided in extremely high number in financial instruments traded in today's financial markets, like exotic derivatives, structured product, and multi-asset contract. Closed form solutions are not applicable in such cases and analytical model can either lead to incorrect valuation or can be incomplete (Hull, 2022). Simulating the expected value of payoffs through Monte Carlo simulation is more flexible and widely applicable by repeatedly choosing random outcomes through predetermined stochastic processes. Instead of a formulaic solution, the Monte Carlo methodologies simulate a number of possible asset price processes, and then calculate the average reward from the various processes. Because of this, Monte Carlo simulation is very suitable for the environment that has tail events, non-linear payoff, and other sources of uncertainty, such as assessing risk and pricing complexity securities (Glasserman,

2004; McNeil et al., 2015). The first compromise between Monte Carlo simulation and analytical models is between simplicity and flexibility in a real world. While analytical models are simple both to understand and to calculate, they are restricted in their application when there is some stochasticity to the market reality which adds complexity. However, Monte Carlo simulation is very realistic and very flexible, but is more time consuming and requires more attention given to the verification of simulation design, variance and convergence criteria. However, it has become a standard approach for regulatory stress testing, portfolio risk analysis, and financial engineering using Monte Carlo simulation with the emergence of modern computing power. (Glasserman, 2004; Jorion, 2007).

Table 1. Analytical models vs Monte Carlo simulation in finance

Dimension	Analytical Models (e.g., Black–Scholes)	Monte Carlo Simulation
Core approach	Formula-based closed-form valuation	Scenario-based numerical estimation
Key assumptions	Strong and restrictive (constant volatility, normal/lognormal behavior, frictionless markets)	Flexible assumptions based on selected stochastic process
Output type	Single-point estimate	Distribution of outcomes + expected estimate
Flexibility	Low (limited to solvable cases)	High (supports complex dynamics and custom payoffs)
Path dependency	Difficult to handle	Naturally supported through simulated paths
Non-linear payoffs	Limited	Strong ability to model and evaluate
Tail risk modelling	Often weak due to assumptions	Strong, supports extreme scenarios and stress testing
Multi-asset / multi-factor modelling	Difficult in many cases	Effective with correlated simulations
Computation cost	Low and fast	High, depends on number of simulations and model complexity
Best suited for	Simple instruments with stable assumptions	Complex derivatives, portfolio risk, stress testing, real-world uncertainty

Source: Authors' own creation

Table 1. Comparing Analytical Models (e.g. Black-Scholes) to Monte Carlo Simulation, you will notice that they have a fundamental difference in their fundamental processes and what they can accomplish. To obtain a quick, single-point estimate, analytical models tend to make restrictive, strict assumptions and assumptions (e.g., constant volatility and normal distribution) and make use of closed-form expressions.

Monte Carlo simulation is a numerical estimation method that is scenario based and in its turn, a set of outcomes is generated and greater freedom is allowed to consider the more dynamic complex stochastic processes that can be more realistic to the dynamics of the real world. This variation in flexibility has a good influence on their use. The analytical models can be helpful for simple tools with stable assumptions, but do not seem to be able to model multi-asset, path dependency and non-linear payoffs. However, Monte Carlo simulation is inherently complicated by these issues, and can also be used more effectively for extreme scenarios and tail risk – areas in which analytic models may struggle. The drawback of this strength is cost – the resulting computational cost may be expensive, especially when compared to the complexity of the model Monte Carlo simulations, but the analytical models are cheap and fast. Therefore, Monte Carlo is recommended when derivatives are complex, when a portfolio is to be evaluated, and when the stress testing is to be conducted; and analytical methods are recommended when routine valuation is to be conducted.

1.4 This Chapter provides

This chapter provides code in both Python and R for the key Monte Carlo simulation tasks that are employed throughout asset pricing and financial risk management. The code includes the following: (i) path simulation for five stochastic processes – Geometric Brownian Motion (GBM), Vasicek, Cox Ingersoll Ross (CIR), jump diffusion and Heston; (ii) pricing functions for European, American (via Least Squares Monte Carlo), and Asian options; (iii) risk metrics such as Value at Risk (VaR) and Expected Shortfall (ES); (iv) variance reduction techniques (antithetic variates, control variates); and (v) numerical Greeks (Delta, Gamma, Vega) for finite differences. All implementations are self-contained, parameterized and annotated for replication. In addition to the code, the chapter includes four fully specified case studies using these models to solve business problems, such as tail risk assessment for a bank's trading desk (VaR/ES under stress volatility), solving for solvency capital under Solvency II for an insurer, incorporating stochastic volatility into asset manager portfolio construction, and evaluating a corporate finance project with uncertain cash flows and discount rates. The simulation horizon, number of paths, model parameters, confidence levels and the subsequent conclusion for the business are stated for each case study. All estimates are provided with convergence diagnostics including standard error analysis, confidence intervals and convergence plots to verify the statistical reliability of all estimates. The chapter thus connects theory and practice by providing "ready to use" and validated tools to simulate as well as decision oriented applications in banking, insurance, asset management and corporate finance.

2. BACKGROUND AND RATIONALE

2.1 Limitations of Conventional Risk and Asset Pricing Models

The traditional theory and practice of risk assessments and asset pricing has left a profound influence on the present theory and practice of finance. The models, which are mathematically clear, analytically tractable and give the speed of computation, such as the Black-Scholes option pricing model and the mean-variance portfolio assumptions, are still widely used. These classical models, however, typically make several simplifications such as frictionless markets, continuous trading, constant returns (where returns are distributed uniformly) and perfectly volatile markets (Black and Scholes, 1973; Hull, 2022). These assumptions do not necessarily hold true in the real world financial environment, leading to poor prediction during periods of market stress, inappropriately priced and unrealistic risk assessment. One of the many drawbacks is the assumption of a steady volatility. But volatility tends to vary over time and empirical evidence suggests that volatility is "clumpy", especially when a crisis has occurred since volatility rises substantially. Constant-parameter analytical models cannot capture the time-dependent risk levels which are an outcome of such clustering of volatility. Thus, in the context of dynamic conditions in the market, the models with fixed volatility can underestimate risk exposure and misprice derivatives (Cont, 2001; Hull, 2022). The second important point is that one assumes various returns are distributed evenly, or that one has isometrical shocks in lognormal dynamics of prices. This is an assumption that will tend to underestimate the potential for an extreme market outcome. Factually, skewness and fat tails are common features of asset returns with big gains or losses being common than the normal distribution would suggest. This mismatch is especially troublesome in the context of risk management software (RiskMSW) since it can significantly impact Value at Risk (VaR) and Expected Shortfall (ES) techniques, stress testing, and capital adequacy planning (Cont, 2001; McNeil et al., 2015). Moreover, traditional models often contain the assumption that markets are frictionless and that free trade exists, liquidity is constant and investors are continually hedging the market. In fact, everything that affects the market, whether it is an influence or a limitation of liquidity, a transaction cost, a bid-ask spread etc. has an impact on financial markets. These tensions are accentuated over time especially during periods of monetary crisis and may even create substantial discrepancies between the market price and the theoretical price. The drawbacks also hamper the usefulness of hedging strategies that are assumed in the classic derivatives pricing models (Hull, 2022; Jorion, 2007). Furthermore, non-linear instruments and path dependent instruments have a greater tendency to be too complex for analytical tools to manage, and they are not as common as linear instruments and path independent instruments, especially exotic derivatives like barrier options, Asian options and structured products. Many of these instruments are not well suited for the closed-form pricing methods since these must represent the entire path of the asset's value and not just the final values. As a result, the pricing multi-asset, multi-factor problems become challenging to solve analytically, due to the instability of correlations or multi-factor interactions among risk factors (Glasserman, 2004; McNeil et al., 2015). For these reasons and more, it has become essential to modern finance to use simulation, in particular the Monte Carlo simulation. With Monte Carlo, the risk experts and analysts can consider the non-regular behavior, realistic market dynamics and estimate the uncertainty on the basis of the outcomes of the scenarios. This makes them pertinent for risk aggregation of all of the enterprises, stress testing, calculating the risk of the portfolio and advanced derivatives of pricing in the real world financial context (Glasserman, 2004; McNeil et al., 2015).

2.2. Monte Carlo is an Appropriate Solution

Many traditional analytical pricing and risk models have been unable to cope with the uncertainty and complex market dynamics and, as a result, some more effective simulation-based pricing and risk models have been introduced. Because Monte Carlo simulation is an adaptable and scalable method of modeling financial uncertainty in an array of instruments, markets and types of risk, it is often determined to be a suitable solution. Monte Carlo simulation can be employed to make effective decisions and decisions where the future is uncertain by generating a large number of different future scenarios and calculating the outcome of the decisions made in each scenario, instead of using closed form solutions or restricting assumptions (Glasserman, 2004; Hull, 2022). One of the biggest benefits of Monte Carlo simulation is that it can simulate scenarios in a multitude of market conditions and distributions of outcomes which allow the analyst to test a wide range of market conditions. Since this technique is a scenario based approach in which a probabilistic view of what could occur is given as opposed to a point estimate, this technique is particularly useful in a financial determination. It can be used to stress test and make predictions by modelling the negative events, correlations and market shocks that a deterministic or linear model might not be able to model (Jorion, 2007; McNeil et al., 2015). Monte Carlo simulation also has some very good applications in path dependent modelling, in that the payoff or the benefit of the financial instrument is dependent on the complete path of the financial instrument over time. An example is the barrier options that are based on the price striking a threshold during the option life, and the Asian based on average price during the option life. These unsolvable structures by most analytical methods are solved by Monte Carlo simulation which generates full price histories and then assigns to a payoff the value of the payoff based on the prices generated in a particular history. (Boyle, 1977, Hull, 2022). One strength is that Monte Carlo methods are able to perform tail risk simulation and extreme outcome. The fat tails, indicating that huge profits or losses occur more commonly than would be the case in the assumption of normal distributions, are a common occurrence in the distribution of financial returns. Capital planning, risk management and regulatory controls in financial institutions require Monte Carlo simulation in order to estimate full loss distributions and to provide the tail risk measures like Value at Risk (VaR) and Expected Shortfall (ES) (McNeil et al., 2015; Jorion, 2007). Moreover, Monte Carlo simulation enables the integration of multi-risks which involves the market, credit, liquidity and operational risks to be integrated within a single framework. Contemporary financial systems are often vulnerable to risks, which often interact to exacerbate each other, particularly in the event of a systemic disaster and market stress. Multi-factor dependencies and risk drivers can be taken into account when considering portfolio and institutional exposures in the simulation models, which can yield more precise and detailed information on exposures (Glasserman 2004; McNeil et al. 2015). Last but not least, Monte Carlo simulation can be easily adopted to the current computing environment. With the advent of high-performance computing and parallel computing, the use of large-scale Monte Carlo simulations in real institutions has become much more possible, in addition to the data-driven programming eco-systems. Apart from the valuation and risk measurement, Monte Carlo simulation has now been widely embraced as a solution to an enterprise's operational decision making, regulatory reporting and risk governance problems at large. (Glasserman, 2004; Hull, 2022).

Table 2. Key advantages of Monte Carlo simulation in finance

Advantage	Explanation	Financial Relevance / Example
Scenario generation	Produces thousands/millions of future market scenarios	Stress testing and scenario analysis
Handles path dependence	Simulates full price paths over time	Asian options, barrier options, structured products
Tail risk modelling	Captures fat tails and extreme outcomes	VaR, Expected Shortfall, downside loss estimation
Multi-factor modelling	Simulates multiple correlated risk drivers	Multi-asset portfolios, correlation-based risk
Multi-risk integration	Integrates market, credit, liquidity, operational risk	Enterprise risk management (ERM)
Supports complex derivatives	Values instruments without closed-form solutions	Exotic options and structured notes

continued on following page

Table 2. Continued

Advantage	Explanation	Financial Relevance / Example
Flexible assumptions	Allows stochastic volatility, jumps, time-varying parameters	Realistic market dynamics
Computational scalability	Works well with parallel processing and HPC	Large-scale risk engines and institutional modelling

Source: Authors' own creation

The most important benefits of Monte Carlo simulation to a risk analysis and financial model are summarized in Table 2. The table shows that Monte Carlo methods can be very useful in creating a wide range of possible market conditions that can then be evaluated efficiently by the analysts and financial institutions to determine the uncertainty and potential outcomes of the market. Modeled complete price paths are also one of the largest benefits and Monte Carlo can be used for pricing path-dependent products like Asian and barrier options. The degree to which Monte Carlo models are able to capture extreme events and tail risks are also reflected in the table and are required to compute risk measures such as Value at Risk (VaR) and Expected Shortfall (ES). Furthermore, the approach allows the composition of related risk drivers in portfolios, and the possibility of multi-factor and multi-risk modelling. Due to these features, Monte Carlo simulation can be used successfully in the portfolio analysis, corporate risk management or regulation stress testing of the modern financial system.

3. COMPUTATIONAL MODELING FRAMEWORK

3.1 The concept of a conceptual framework

This chapter relies on a structured conceptual framework based on the theory of simulation, concepts of stochastic calculus and uncertainty models that are suitable for a particular financial market. The conceptual framework needs to be well developed to make sure Monte Carlo simulations are conceptually relevant and also practically useful because of the time variability of values of assets and risk factors are uncertain. Hence, the chapter starts with an extensive discussion of the statistical and mathematical fundamentals of financial risk modelling and asset pricing by Monte Carlo methods. The conceptual framework is based on the presentation of financial variables in the form of stochastic processes. In quantitative finance, continuous time processes such as Geometric Brownian Motion (GBM) upon which many classic valuation models are based, are common methods of modeling the dynamics of asset prices. The uncertainty modeling includes also more complex structures like stochastic volatility patterns, interest rate diffusion models, and jump processes, to capture the actual features of the market, including the effects of disruption, volatility clustering and changing risk conditions (Hull, 2022; McNeil et al., 2015). These theoretical models are the basis for the development of simulated routes more or less representative of future price paths and the performance of the portfolio. The simulation theory is also used based on the conceptual framework to explain the use of repeated random sample in obtaining the expected values and probability distribution using Monte Carlo methods. The reliability of the results of Monte Carlo is determined by the convergence of the estimators, the bias and the variance of the estimators. The conceptual framework thus focuses on understanding the statistical properties of estimators in a simulation, such as their convergence properties with increasing simulation trials, and offers an explanation of simulation error using variance diagnostics and confidence intervals (Glasserman 2004). Moreover, the distributional assumptions and dependence structures are of great importance when dealing with uncertainty in finance. When the market is stressed, common characteristics of empirical returns distributions include fat tails, skewness and correlation instability. Then, the conceptual framework is used to design a flexible simulation that can take into account tail-event sensitivity, risk driver linkage, multi-factor uncertainty. This way, the use of Monte Carlo simulation in asset pricing and risk analysis becomes more suitable for such applications as Value at risk (VaR), Expected shortfall (ES) and stress testing in bad scenarios (Cont., 2001; Jorion, 2007). On the whole, the development of conceptual framework of this chapter establishes a good linkage between financial applications based on simulations and stochastic modeling theory. It forms the foundation of the following parts that will focus on the Monte Carlo method, Python and R computational implementation, and case based applications of the regulatory reporting, banking, insurance, and portfolio management. The chapter firmly roots the use of simulation in the principles of uncertainty modelling and stochastic calculus, so that there is a clear link between the actual financial decision-making and the output of the simulations.

3.2 Quantitative Modeling

The chapter applies and examines a collection of popular quantitative models on which Monte Carlo simulation of assets prices and measures of financial risks are based. The models taken up are because real market behavior requires price movements over time, uncertainty in interest rates, or price changes that jump, and volatility is different as time goes on. Every model generates simulation-based pricing and risk analytics (Glasserman, 2004; Hull, 2022) because it is capable of computing scenario-based distributions, instead of using closed-form analytical solutions.

3.2.1 Stock Price Geometric Brownian Motion (GBM)

The geometric Brownian motion (GBM) is one of the most commonly used stochastic processes in financial modelling, and forms the basis of the traditional option pricing systems. GBM assumes that the values of assets are the results of a lognormal process where there is continuous compounding and normally distributed returns in very small time intervals. Monte Carlo simulation with GBM is used to estimate future payoffs and discounted values needed to model equity-linked derivatives, portfolio projections. (Black and Scholes, 1973; Hull, 2022).

Continuous GBM

$$dS_t = \mu S_t dt + \sigma S_t dW_t$$

Table 3.

Symbol	Meaning
St	Asset Price at time t
μ	Expected return (drift rate)
σ	Volatility of asset returns
dt	Small change in time
dWt	Wiener process (Brownian motion/random shock)

Discrete-Time GBM

$$S_{t+\Delta t}=S_t \exp\left[\left(\mu-\frac{1}{2}\sigma^2\right)\Delta t+\sigma\sqrt{\Delta t}Z\right]$$

Where:

- $Z \sim N(0,1)$
- Δt = time interval.

3.2.2. Cox Ingersoll Ross (CIR) and Vasicek Interest rate models.

Interest rate dynamics plays an important role in asset-liability management, pricing of derivatives and fixed income markets. In this chapter, two popular short-rate models, i.e. the Vasicek model and the Cox Ingersoll Ross (CIR) model, are used to explain the interest rate uncertainty. The CIR model contains a square root diffusion frame to assure that interest rates remain non-negative in normal times, while the Vasicek model assumes that interest rates have a mean-reversion feature with normally-distributed shocks. They are both widely employed in the fixed income simulation-based valuation and risk analysis where the change in the rate of the risk should be taken into account at the stress levels in the scenario-driven pricing and risk analysis. (Brigo and Mercurio, 2006; Hull, 2022).

Vasicek

$$dr_t = a(b-r_t)dt + \sigma dW_t$$

Where:

- a = speed of mean reversion
- b = long-run average interest rate
- σ = volatility of interest rate
- dWt = Brownian motion term.

The Vasicek model assumes that interest rates revert toward a long-term equilibrium level over time.

Cox-Ingersoll-Ross (CIR) Model

$$dr_t = a(b-r_t)dt + \sigma\sqrt{r_t}dW_t$$

One interesting aspect of the CIR model is that it uses a volatility term that is a function of the square root of the interest rate, which helps to ensure that interest rates do not become negative under normal market conditions, unlike the Vasicek model.

3.2.3 Models of Jump-Diffusion

The returns of assets in the real world can have discontinuous returns due to news events, market shocks, liquidity disruptions and systemic crises. The jump-diffusion models add the jump element to the traditional diffusion processes so that the price model that is simulated can account for sudden rises or falls. The models particularly are useful in the capturing of fat-tailed return behavior and increase the realism of the tail-risk estimation and the pricing of derivatives. Monte Carlo modeling that is based on a framework of jump-diffusion can generate scenarios that more accurately capture the extremes when compared to those based purely on diffusion. (Merton, 1976; Cont, 2001).

$$dS_t = \mu S_t dt + \sigma S_t dW_t + J_t dN_t$$

Where:

- JtJ_tJt = jump size,
- dNtdN_tdNt = Poisson jump process.

The jump component is able to describe rare discontinuous price movements, liquidity shocks, and abrupt market crashes often seen in the course of a financial crisis.

In this section, we consider some stochastic volatility models. The classical diffusion models have serious weakness of the assumption being constant volatility that cannot be confirmed using actual financial data. Leverage effects, changes in behavior, changes in market uncertainty and volatility have a tendency to change over time. The chapter models stochastic volatility by adoption of the Heston model that assumes that volatility is a stochastic process that fluctuates with the value of the assets. Heston structure is an improved version of simulation based valuation of options and structured goods, and it's possible to model the volatility smiles more accurately. This model is better in market regimes that are volatile, and where the volatility is strongly mean-reverting (Heston, 1993; Hull, 2022).

Asset price process:

$$dS_t = \mu S_t dt + \sqrt{v_t}S_t dW_t^S$$

Variance process:

$$dv_t = \kappa(\theta-v_t)dt + \xi\sqrt{v_t}dW_t^v$$

Where:

- vt = stochastic variance,
- κ = speed of mean reversion,
- θ = long-run variance,
- ξ = volatility of volatility.

The Heston model improves realism by allowing volatility to fluctuate dynamically over time.

Table 4. Key characteristics and applications of stochastic models

Model	Key Feature	Main Application
GBM	Constant volatility	Equity pricing
Vasicek	Mean reverting rates	Interest rate modeling
CIR	Non-negative rates	Bond pricing
Jump Diffusion	Sudden shocks	Crisis modeling
Heston	Stochastic volatility	Advanced option pricing

Source: Authors' own creation

Table 4 shows a comparison of the major stochastic models used for Monte Carlo simulation. The models used for equity valuation are GBM and models with constant volatility assumptions, and those used for interest rate modeling are Vasicek and CIR models. The Heston model can be used in advanced derivative pricing and risk management applications as it includes stochastic volatility, while the Jump Diffusion model can be used for capturing sudden market shocks and extreme events.

3.3 Implementing Python and R Programming

This chapter is basically computational in implementation, in order to show a practical application of Monte Carlo simulation models in the pricing of assets and financial risk analysis. Financial modelling by simulation involves repetitive random sampling, numerical approximation, and results for different scenarios; there are certain programming languages which can provide a good structure to build replicable and scalable simulation processes such as Python and R. The programming method used in this chapter is the conversion of stochastic process theory to executable simulation processes and their usefulness to real-life financial decision making, the interpretation of results and their statistical soundness. (Glasserman, 2004; Hull, 2022).

Example: Monte Carlo Simulation in Python

```
import numpy as np
S0 = 100
K = 100
r = 0.05
sigma = 0.2
T = 1
n = 100000
Z = np. random. standard _normal(n)
ST = S0 * np.exp ((r - 0.5 * sigma**2)*T + sigma*np.sqrt(T)*Z)
```

```
payoff = np. maximum (ST - K, 0)
option_price = np.exp(-r*T) * np. mean(payoff)
print ("European Call Option Price:", option_price)
```

Suppose:

S0 = 100
σ = 20%
r = 5%
T = 1 year

Using 100,000 Monte Carlo simulations,
European call option value estimated = 10.45

Explanation: Above Python program generates random normal variables with mean 0 and variance 1 and simulates future stock values for the GBM model. The discounted payoff is then calculated to estimate the value of the European call option.

Figure 2. Monte Carlo simulation workflow

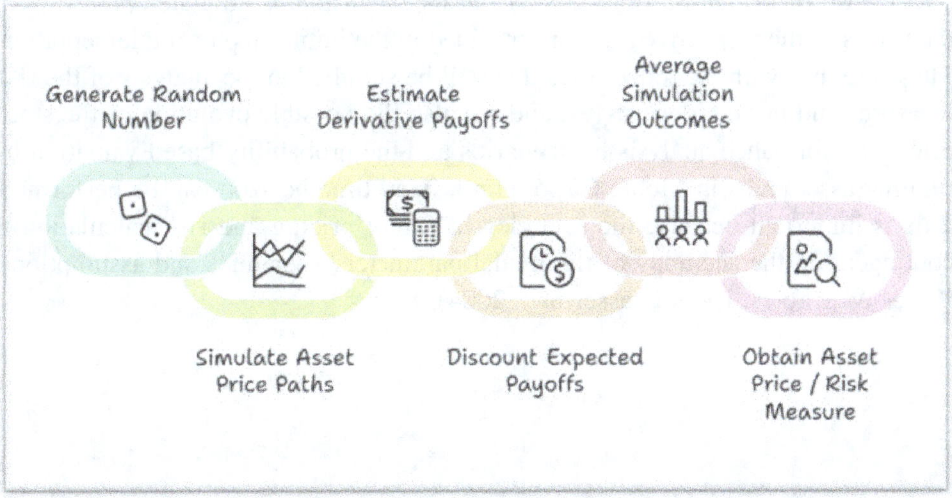

The following diagram shows a framework that comprises six steps for performing Monte Carlo simulation in advanced financial valuation.

- **Stochastic Inputs**: The first step in the process is to generate random numbers representing uncertain market factors.

- **Path Generation**: These numbers are used to generate numerous possible asset price paths over a certain time horizon.
- **Payoff Estimation**: payoffs of the various derivative products are estimated for each path that is simulated in a unique manner.
- **Present Value**: These expected future payoffs are routinely discounted for the time value of money to obtain the Present Value.
- **Statistical Aggregation:** The model then calculates the average of the simulation results over all the paths to determine the expected value, called Statistical Aggregation.
- **Final Valuation:** Ultimately, this aggregation can be used to get the final valuation of the asset price or the specific risk measure.

This workflow is chained and visually shows the transformation of randomized data points to reliable quantifiable financial metrics.

3.3.1 Asset Price Path Simulation

To simulate asset price paths. With the use of the stochastic process model (Geometric Brownian Motion (GBM) and its expansions), simulated pathways of the prices of the respective assets is provided in the initial step of implementation. These are the synthetic trajectories that will be supplied to the analysis of the risk measures and pricing derivatives, and are also the possible evolution of the stock prices. Performance analysis by scenarios and the probability-based valuation by running asset paths in Monte Carlo with a fixed time horizon can be performed. This is important because the accuracy of future pricing and risk calculation is contingent on the accuracy of the model parameters' dynamics and assumptions. (Black & Scholes, 1973; Glasserman, 2004).

Figure 3. Simulated stock path graph

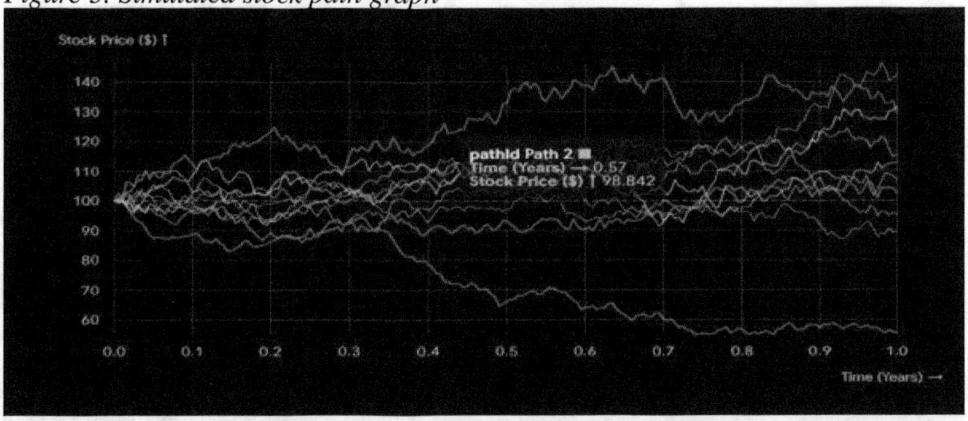

Multiple simulated paths of the stock price are shown in Figure 3, with each path simulated using GBM. The graph illustrates uncertainty in asset prices in the future, and the spread of possible forecasts. The larger the simulation time horizon, the more paths diverge because of the accumulation of stochastic shocks.

3.3.2 European and American and Asian Prices of the options

Monte Carlo valuation of important derivative instruments is part of the programming process. European option pricing is performed through discounted payoff estimation, and simulated terminal asset values. The American alternatives are simulation-based methods engaging early exercise logic, and regression-based methods like the Least Squares Monte Carlo (LSMC) framework are frequently used with these methods. Asian options are path dependent options that are priced by calculating average price based payoffs and modelling the complete asset paths. These uses are highlighted by Boyle in 1977, Hull (2022) and Longstaff and Schwartz (2001), all of which demonstrate the vast variety of Monte Carlo simulation in pricing instruments that cannot be easily priced by closed-form analytical models.

```
set.seed(123)
S0 <- 100; K <- 100; r <- 0.05; sigma <- 0.2; T <- 1; n <- 100000
Z <- rnorm(n)
ST <- S0 * exp((r - 0.5 * sigma^2) * T + sigma * sqrt(T) * Z)
payoff <- pmax(ST - K, 0)
option_price <- exp(-r * T) * mean(payoff)
print(paste("European Call Option Price:", round(option_price, 4)))
```

Figure 4. Comparison of European, American, and Asian option prices

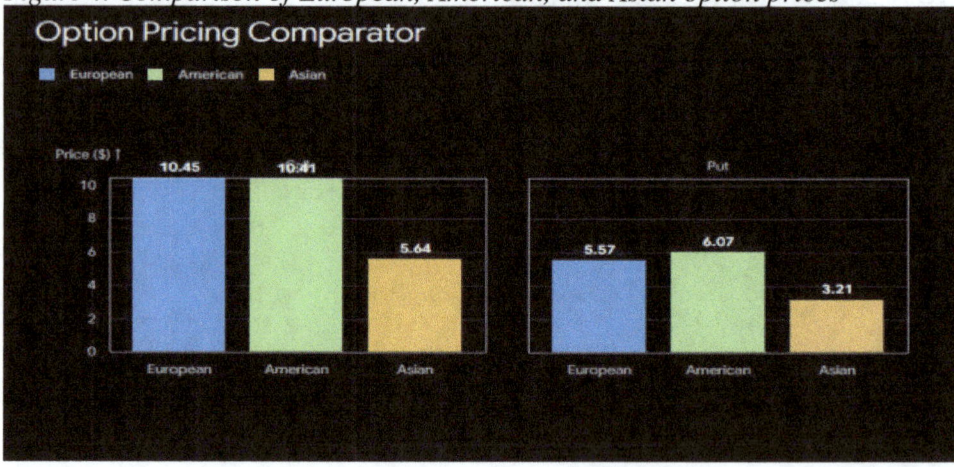

Figure 4 is used to show how the value of an option is different depending on the rights given and the payoffs. American options typically have greater values because they can be exercised at any time, whereas Asian options have lower volatility and payoff uncertainty because they involve averaging.

3.3.3 Value at risk (VaR) and Expected Shortfall (ES)

The Models are used to implement Risk measurement, which is based on the measurement of the downside risk and the distribution of the portfolio returns under various market conditions. Expected Shortfall (ES) is used to estimate the loss on average above the VaR threshold whereas Value at Risk (VaR) is used to estimate a quantile-based measure of potential loss at a given confidence level. These metrics are particularly important in financial institutions in capital adequacy planning, stress testing and tail-risk assessment. For these calculations Monte Carlo simulation is easier to apply, because it allows full outcome distributions to be generated, as well as common and severe event analysis. (Jorion, 2007; McNeil et al., 2015).

```
def calculate_var_es(returns, confidence=0.95):
var = np.percentile(returns, (1-confidence)*100)
es = returns[returns <= var].mean()
return var, es
# Example: var_95, es_95 = calculate_var_es(portfolio_returns, 0.95)
```

Figure 5. VaR histogram

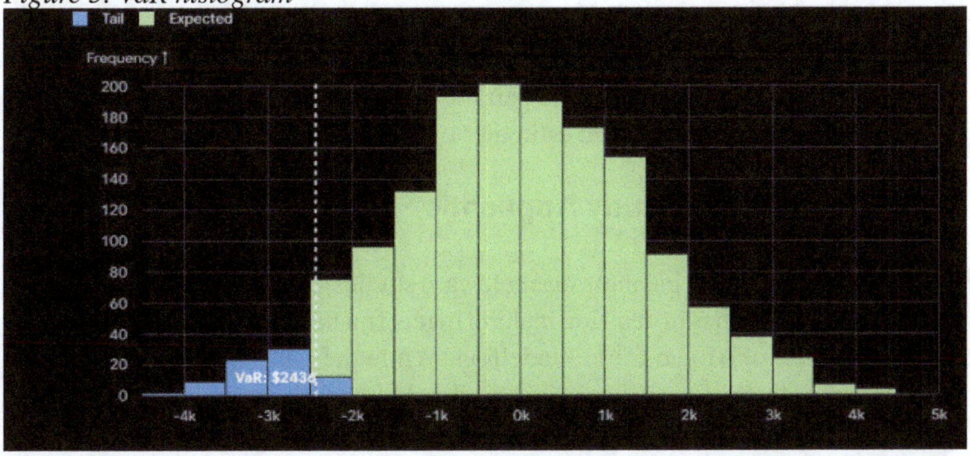

Figure 5. The VaR threshold marks the upper bound of the maximum loss within a specified confidence level, whereas the left tail represents the situations of extreme loss. Computers can be used to approximate the Greeks by numerical differentiation. The Greeks can be approximated numerically using computers.

3.3.4 Numerical Greeks (Delta, Gamma and Vega)

In terms of numerical differentiation to simplify the analysis of hedging and risk control based on sensitivity. The sensitivity measures can be approximated by making small changes to the model inputs (such as the price or volatility) and then recalculating the prices for a set of controlled changes, yielding computer numbers of prices. This provides an illustration of the use of Monte Carlo techniques beyond valuation in trading and portfolios in order to enhance risk management and risk hedging strategy formulation (Glasserman, 2004, Hull, 2022).

3.3.5 Application of Variance Reduction Techniques

Monte Carlo simulation is a time consuming and variance intensive process and the chapter discusses how this can be addressed by using the concept of variance reduction. Methods like antithetic variates, control variates and other types of variance reduction methods are used to decrease the variance of the estimators without increasing the number of simulations. The methods have proven to improve performance in computing and the stability of the results in specific applications like derivative pricing and tail-risk assessment, where the institution is required to take a decision with high precision level. (Glasserman, 2004; McNeil et al., 2015).

```
def heston_antithetic(S0, v0, kappa, theta, xi, rho, T, r, n_paths, n_steps):
Z1 = np.random.normal(0, 1, (n_paths, n_steps))
Z2=rho*Z1+np.sqrt(1-rho**2)*np.random.normal(0,1,(n_paths,n_steps))
# Simulate paths and antithetic pairs
# Returns variance-reduced estimate
```

3.4 Business Case Study Applications

The chapter presents business oriented case studies, illustrating the use of simulation based approaches in decision making in real financial environment to enhance the practical use of Monte Carlo modelling. While there has been a mathematical formulation of the business theoretical model, Monte Carlo simulation is efficient because it can provide useful information about business practices like pricing, capital sufficiency, portfolio risk management, and strategic investment decisions. Therefore, this chapter's approach to the case study is focused on attempting to connect the Monte Carlo results with real-world institutional goals and risk frameworks motivated by compliance (Glasserman 2004; McNeil et al., 2015). Each case study follows the same methodology which involves the definition of the business problem, the selection of relevant risk drivers and modeling assumptions, Monte Carlo simulation under different conditions, distributional-based outcomes (risk measures or prices) and interpretation of the results in the context of making a decision. This is a systematic process that explains how the results of a simulation can be used for financial planning, risk management and governance reporting (Jorion, 2007; Hull, 2022).

3.4.1 Bank Trading Desks Risk Management

The first case study is for a banks trading desk environment, where market sensitive assets including stocks, derivatives and interest rate related products, are held. The case is used to demonstrate Monte Carlo simulation to calculate tail-risk indicators like Value at Risk (VaR), Expected Shortfall (ES) and for the construction of portfolio profit-loss distribution under various market conditions. The case demonstrates that simulation can be used as a tool to monitor risk, stress test and make risk adjusted decisions on trading in market conditions that are volatile, as Jorion (2007) and McNeil et al. (2015) state.

Numerical Illustration: One simulated trading portfolio of size 50 crore was created with 100,000 Monte Carlo paths assuming GBM with constants of 22% annual volatility and 8% annual expected return. The VaR (at the 99% level) was estimated at simulated 3.8 crore. The VaR rose to 6.2 crore under stressed conditions of volatility at 35%, signaling much greater tail-risk exposure during stressed time periods.

3.4.2 Insurance Solvency Capital Estimation.

The second case study is about the standards for insurance companies' solvency, which state that insurers should have adequate resources to sustain adverse market and claims conditions. The distribution based outcomes of asset return, changing obligations and solvency positions under unknown conditions are achieved from Monte Carlo simulation. This illustration shows that simulation can be used in asset liability management, risk-based planning of long-term promises and calculation of solvency capital (McNeil et al., 2015; Hull, 2022).

Numerical Illustration: With the above CIR interest rate dynamics, a life insurance portfolio of 200 crores was simulated using 250,000 paths and over a 5-year horizon. Under the 99.5% confidence level (Solvency II standard), the simulated capital requirement was 28.4 crore whereas it was found to be 19.2 crore in the deterministic case. The conditional expectation of the loss in the tail above the VaR value was 34.1 crore.

3.4.3 Asset Manager Portfolio Construction

The key issues of the third case study are the construction of investment portfolios and risk evaluation of asset management. Monte Carlo simulation creates the distribution of portfolio return in a market with uncertainty and volatility in the market to model the downside risk exposure and susceptibility through tail losses and correlation. The case is used to emphasize the use of simulation to help with budgeting, scenarios and optimization decisions in the portfolio to improve diversification outcomes and planning of the long term investment strategy as discussed by McNeil et al. (2015); Jorion (2007).

Numerical illustration: a portfolio of 60% equity and 40% bond was simulated with 100,000 paths with AUM of 100 crores and using the Heston model of stochastic volatility with parameters $\kappa=2.5$, $\theta=0.04$, $\xi=0.3$, and $\rho=-0.7$. The 1-year horizon 95% Expected Shortfall was 12.4% compared to 8.7% with constant volatility, showing that the stochastic volatility raises the estimates of tail risk by 43% for this allocation.

3.4.4 Evaluation of Corporate Finance Projects in an uncertain Environment.

In the fourth case study, Monte Carlo simulation is used as a tool in the corporate finance decision-making process, namely in the assessment of investment projects in the presence of uncertainty. Monte Carlo modeling enables the many scenarios to be evaluated based on the probability-based evaluation of net present value (NPV) where the cash flows of the project, the discount rate, and market conditions are not always known. This study demonstrates the application of simulation to the strategic planning process in terms of measures of downside risk, expected profitability, and project risk exposure as opposed to simply a deterministic estimate. Such an assessment, based on simulation, is very relevant in unpredictable business environments, where the decision-making of the managers and investment appraisal would be relevant (Glasserman, 2004).

Numerical Illustration: A renewable energy project that has an initial investment of 50 crore and uncertain annual cash flow (triangular distribution with a minimum value of 8cr, a mode of 12cr and a maximum of 18cr) was simulated for 10 years with 50,000 paths of correlated discount rates (Vasicek model). Probability of negative NPV was 23%, with mean NPV 6.8 crore (95% CI: 4.2cr– 9.5cr). When the carbon tax was increased under a stress scenario the chance of negative NPV increased to 47%.

3.5 Model validation and Back Testing

Model validation and backtesting are crucial components of Monte Carlo financial modeling because of the significant influence of model assumptions, sampling and computational architecture on numerical estimates of the resulting value. Financial models for pricing and risk in practice should be both theoretically consistent and strong, and good, transparent and reliable in various market situations. In order to make the results of the Monte Carlo simulation statistically stable, economically significant and appropriate for professional decision making and regulatory reporting, a variety of validation methods are used in this chapter (Glasserman, 2004; McNeil et al., 2015).

3.5.1 Analysis of Errors

Because Monte Carlo simulations involve repeated random sampling to obtain the results rather than the results coming from closed-form solutions, there is a tendency for Monte Carlo simulations to overestimate the error. The accuracy and stability of the simulated estimates are analyzed in this chapter, aided by the error analysis which identifies the sources of errors as mainly approximation bias, sample variability and the discrete error. The reasons for measuring errors are significant: errors can be used to detect instability in pricing or risk measures; simulation results can be meaningfully understood with a particular degree of confidence (Glasserman, 2004).

3.5.2 Diagnostics of Convergence

Monte Carlo estimates are used and convergence diagnostics are applied which produce a test of the stability of the Monte Carlo estimates with the number of simulated paths. In financial calculations, convergence is crucial due to the risk of noisy estimates that could bias tail-risk signals, Greeks or derivative values from failing to converge. In this chapter, convergence is analyzed, based on simulation trials, estimation of the standard error, confidence intervals, and convergence plots to illustrate the changes in the estimates as the size of the simulation increases. These diagnostics ensure statistical reliability and reproducibility of the results of simulations (Glasserman, 2004; McNeil et al., 2015).

Figure 6. Variance reduction using antithetic variates (48.8% lower variance)

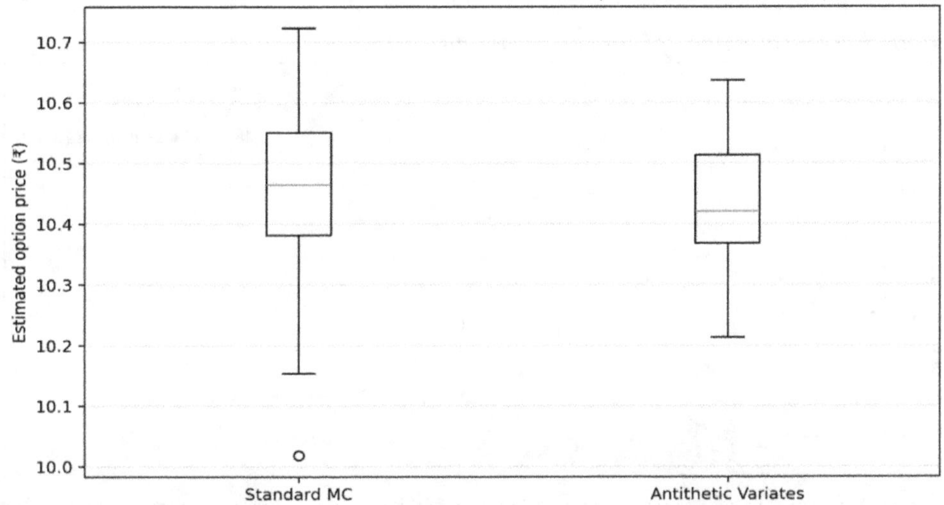

Figure 7. Standard error decay with increasing simulations

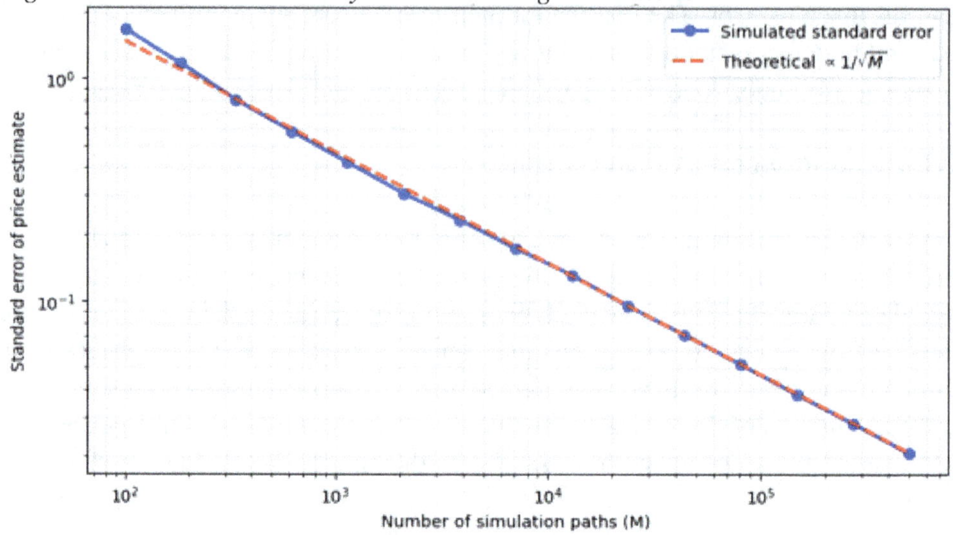

Figure 8. Convergence of Monte Carlo option price

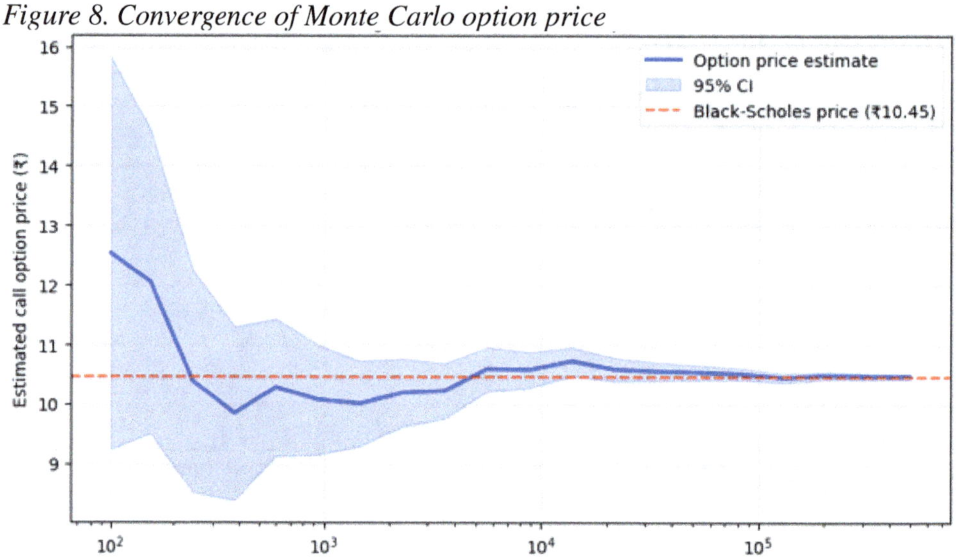

Monte Carlo estimators seem to converge as shown in Figure 8. An increased number of simulations leads to a more stable option value, which gets closer to the expected theoretical value, and therefore to estimator consistency.

4. FUTURE RESEARCH DIRECTIONS

The increasing complexity of global financial markets, technological advancements, and regulatory developments present several promising avenues for future research in Monte Carlo-based asset pricing and financial risk management. Although Monte Carlo simulation has established itself as a powerful tool for modelling uncertainty and evaluating complex financial instruments, emerging developments in computational finance offer significant opportunities to enhance its efficiency, accuracy, and practical relevance. One important area for future research is the integration of Monte Carlo simulation with Artificial Intelligence (AI) and Machine Learning (ML) techniques. Advanced learning algorithms can improve parameter estimation, identify hidden market patterns, and enhance forecasting accuracy in asset pricing models. Hybrid frameworks combining stochastic simulation with deep learning architectures may provide more robust predictions under rapidly changing market conditions. Another promising direction involves the application of quantum computing to financial simulations. Traditional Monte Carlo methods often require substantial computational resources when dealing with large portfolios, multi-factor risk models, and high-dimensional derivative pricing problems. Quantum Monte Carlo approaches have the potential to significantly reduce computational time and improve simulation efficiency, enabling real-time risk assessment and portfolio optimization. Future studies may also focus on Environmental, Social, and Governance (ESG) risk modelling using simulation-based approaches. As sustainable finance becomes increasingly important, financial institutions require advanced techniques to quantify climate risk, transition risk, and sustainability-related uncertainties. Monte Carlo simulation can be extended to evaluate the long-term financial impact of ESG-related factors on asset valuations and portfolio performance. In addition, further research is needed to develop more realistic stochastic models that capture evolving market behavior, including regime shifts, extreme events, liquidity constraints, and interconnected financial networks. Incorporating behavioral finance factors, market sentiment indicators, and alternative data sources into simulation frameworks may enhance the predictive capability of financial risk models. The growing adoption of cloud computing, big data analytics, and high-performance computing platforms also creates opportunities for large-scale simulation studies. Future researchers can investigate distributed Monte Carlo frameworks capable of processing vast datasets and generating faster scenario analyses for regulatory stress testing, enterprise risk management, and financial decision-making. Finally, future studies may explore the integration of Monte Carlo simulation with dynamic risk governance systems and real-time monitoring frameworks. Such developments would support proactive risk management, improve regulatory compliance, and strengthen organizational resilience in increasingly volatile financial environments. Overall, the future of Monte

Carlo simulation lies in its convergence with advanced computational technologies, intelligent analytics, and data-driven decision-making systems. These developments are expected to further strengthen its role in asset pricing, portfolio optimization, financial engineering, and enterprise-wide risk management.

5. CONCLUSION

With its capacity to capture the uncertainty, non-linear market dynamics, and the intricacies of financial products, Monte Carlo simulation has emerged as a vital computational tool in contemporary financial markets. Stochastic modeling, simulation-based valuation, and risk analytics can help financial institutions enhance prices, portfolio management, stress testing, regulatory compliance, and much more. In this chapter, we have shown that MC methods can be used in various financial applications, such as the pricing of derivatives, the measurement of risk for a portfolio, the evaluation of a company's solvency, and for assessing the value of company investments. The chapter has covered major stochastic models including the Geometric Brownian Motion (GBM) model, Vasicek model, CIR model, Jump-Diffusion model and Heston model, and presented the theory and practical implementation in Python and R programming environment. The case studies in the business context presented in this chapter demonstrate the use of simulation-based approaches in decision making under uncertainty, in the fields of banking, insurance, asset management, and corporate finance. The relevance of Monte Carlo methods in today's environment of risk governance and regulatory reporting is also highlighted through the use of Value at Risk (VaR), Expected Shortfall (ES), variance reduction techniques and convergence diagnostics. With increasing volatility, interdependence and complexity in financial markets, simulation methods will be even more widely used in strategic financial planning and enterprise wide risk management. The next generation of Monte Carlo simulation is likely to embrace the use of artificial intelligence, machine learning algorithms, cloud computing infrastructure and quantum computing. These developments will help to increase the efficiency of computation, increase the capability to provide more accurate predictions and enable real-time risk analysis. Hybrid approaches where Monte Carlo simulation and deep learning, reinforcement learning and big data analytics are integrated for better forecasting accuracy and risk assessment may be explored in the future. Monte Carlo simulation will remain a cornerstone of financial markets' advanced asset pricing, portfolio optimization, financial engineering, and enterprise risk management due to the growing data-driven and technologically sophisticated nature of these markets. Finally, Monte Carlo simulation has proved to be a valuable tool which connects the financial theory to the real decision-making in the context of uncertainty. This is one of the premier tools in quantitative finance because of its flexibility in modelling the dynamics of the markets and the advances of computational technologies. In an ever-changing and global landscape, simulation based methodologies will continue to play a vital role in enabling organizations to make resilient, informed and sustainable financial decisions through data-driven strategies and predictive analytics.

REFERENCES

Black, F., & Scholes, M. (1973). The pricing of options and corporate liabilities. *Journal of Political Economy*, *81*(3), 637–654. DOI: 10.1086/260062

Boyle, P. P. (1977). Options: A Monte Carlo approach. *Journal of Financial Economics*, *4*(3), 323–338. DOI: 10.1016/0304-405X(77)90005-8

Brigo, D., & Mercurio, F. (2006). *Interest rate models: Theory and practice* (2nd ed.). Springer.

Cont, R. (2001). Empirical properties of asset returns: Stylized facts and statistical issues. *Quantitative Finance*, *1*(2), 223–236. DOI: 10.1080/713665670

Glasserman, P. (2004). *Monte Carlo methods in financial engineering*. Springer.

Heston, S. L. (1993). A closed-form solution for options with stochastic volatility. *Review of Financial Studies*, *6*(2), 327–343. DOI: 10.1093/rfs/6.2.327

Hull, J. C. (2022). *Options, futures, and other derivatives* (11th ed.). Pearson.

Jorion, P. (2007). *Value at risk: The new benchmark for managing financial risk* (3rd ed.). McGraw-Hill.

Longstaff, F. A., & Schwartz, E. S. (2001). Valuing American options by simulation. *Review of Financial Studies*, *14*(1), 113–147. DOI: 10.1093/rfs/14.1.113

McNeil, A. J., Frey, R., & Embrechts, P. (2015). *Quantitative risk management: Concepts, techniques and tools* (Revised ed.). Princeton University Press.

Merton, R. C. (1976). Option pricing when underlying stock returns are discontinuous. *Journal of Financial Economics*, *3*(1–2), 125–144. DOI: 10.1016/0304-405X(76)90022-2

KEY TERMS AND DEFINITIONS

Asset Pricing: The process of determining the fair value of financial assets such as stocks, bonds, and derivatives based on risk, expected returns, and market conditions.

Expected Shortfall (ES): A risk measure that estimates the average loss that may occur beyond a specified Value at Risk confidence level during extreme market conditions.

Financial Risk Management: The identification, measurement, monitoring, and control of financial risks to minimize potential losses and enhance decision-making.

Geometric Brownian Motion (GBM): A stochastic process commonly used to model asset price movements under the assumptions of continuous growth and random market fluctuations.

Heston Model: A stochastic volatility model that allows volatility to vary over time, providing a more realistic representation of financial market behavior.

Jump-Diffusion Model: A stochastic model that combines continuous price movements with sudden jumps to capture extreme market events and discontinuities in asset prices.

Monte Carlo Simulation: A computational technique that uses repeated random sampling to model uncertainty and estimate the probability distribution of financial outcomes.

Stochastic Volatility: A modeling approach in which asset return volatility changes randomly over time rather than remaining constant.

Stress Testing: A risk assessment technique that evaluates the impact of adverse market scenarios on portfolio performance, capital adequacy, and financial stability.

Value at Risk (VaR): A statistical measure that estimates the maximum expected loss of an investment or portfolio over a specified time horizon and confidence level.

Chapter 4
Financial Data Engineering:
From Raw Feeds to Feature Stores

Ganesh Harke
http://orcid.org/0009-0005-3947-0960
Independent Researcher, USA

ABSTRACT

Quantitative trading and risk management systems depend critically on the integrity of their underlying data infrastructure. While much of the academic literature treats financial data as static, preprocessed time series, real-world market data arrives as noisy, asynchronous streams requiring rigorous engineering controls. This chapter presents a comprehensive framework for Financial Data Engineering, tracing the lifecycle from raw market feeds to a point-in-time consistent Feature Store. It examines architectural patterns for ingestion, storage, transformation, and serving, emphasizing DataOps principles, polyglot persistence, and reproducibility across research and production environments. The chapter further addresses microstructure-aware cleaning, reconciliation, auditability, and synthetic stress-testing for rare market conditions. By formalizing market environments and standardizing feature computation, the proposed approach reduces look-ahead bias and mitigates the Research–Production Gap, providing a blueprint for robust, end-to-end financial data systems.

INTRODUCTION

A common adage in data science is that 80% of effort is devoted to data cleaning and preparation, whereas only 20% is devoted to analysis and model development.

DOI: 10.4018/979-8-3373-8372-9.ch004

In many industries, this imbalance creates a significant bottleneck to productivity. In quantitative finance, it denotes a solvency issue. The key difference is that financial markets are unforgiving; mishandling timestamps or misapplying corporate actions can reduce model correctness and introduce look-ahead bias. This phenomenon, in which a model unintentionally leverages future data to forecast past events, yields backtests that appear highly profitable in simulation but result in severe losses when deployed in actual scenarios.

Modern financial markets generate data with immense volume, velocity, and variety (Goldstein et al., 2021). However, there is a substantial disconnect between how this data is treated and the practical engineering reality of the Front Office. Most literature presents financial data as static, pre-cleaned CSV files with standard OHLCV (Open-High-Low-Close-Volume) bars. This simplified view neglects the stochastic and asynchronous characteristics of real market feeds. Actual market feeds arrive as irregular tick streams, include bad prints, and require complex adjustments for dividends, splits, and symbol changes. This chapter examines the essential infrastructure needed to close this gap. It argues that the robustness of the data pipeline is often as critical as the sophistication of the mathematical model. Without a rigorously engineered data foundation, even the most sophisticated deep reinforcement learning agents fail to generalize to live markets (Liu et al., 2022).

Quantitative finance research emphasizes mathematical modeling, derivative pricing, and risk management. As a result, many organizations encounter the Research-Production Gap, in which a strategy is implemented twice: first in Python for research and subsequently in C++ or Java for execution. This duplication causes subtle differences in feature computation, such as the handling of missing data points in moving averages, which can lead to signal decay and operational risk.

This chapter provides a comprehensive blueprint for architecting a production-grade financial data system. It moves beyond ad hoc scripting to introduce robust engineering patterns that ensure data consistency, point-in-time correctness, and system reliability. It adopts the DataOps paradigm, which applies DevOps principles (Continuous Integration/Continuous Deployment) to data analytics, ensuring the pipeline is automated, testable, and reproducible (Liu et al., 2022). The chapter further explores the complete lifecycle of financial data, transforming raw, noisy market feeds into a reliable Feature Store that serves as a single source of truth for both research and production. It examines the specific engineering challenges at each stage of the pipeline:

1. **Ingestion:** Handling the trade-offs between REST APIs and WebSockets.
2. **Storage:** Implementing Polyglot Persistence (SQL vs. NoSQL) for optimized retrieval.
3. **Transformation:** Statistical filtering of microstructure noise.

4. **Serving:** Architecting a point-in-time consistent Feature Store to mitigate look-ahead bias

This chapter contributes a finance-specific framework for designing robust financial data engineering systems. It introduces a structured view of market environments tailored to reinforcement learning and quantitative modeling, proposes a DataOps-based architectural pattern for reproducible and auditable data pipelines, and presents a point-in-time consistent Feature Store design to reduce discrepancies between research and production systems. In addition, it discusses the use of synthetic data for stress testing under rare market conditions and outlines practical patterns for aligning simulation environments with live trading infrastructure. Together, these contributions provide an integrated blueprint for end-to-end financial data systems. By the conclusion of this chapter, readers will understand the architectural principles required to support end-to-end financial data systems for reliable research and production deployment.

BACKGROUND: THE DATA FOUNDATION OF MODERN FINANCE

The trajectory of quantitative finance has been inextricably linked to the evolution of data-processing capabilities. Historically, financial analysis relied on low-frequency, structured datasets, quarterly earnings reports, daily closing prices, and macroeconomic indicators. However, over the last two decades, the explosion of Big Data has profoundly changed market microstructure and the engineering requirements for trading systems. This section analyzes the transition from static, fundamental analysis to high-frequency, data-driven decision-making, synthesizing recent academic literature to establish the requirement for the resilient engineering architectures proposed in this chapter.

The Evolution: From Small Data to Big Data

Goldstein, Spatt, and Ye (2021) characterize the current era of financial economics not merely by the size of datasets but by the fundamental change in how market participants generate and consume information. They argue that the integration of Big Data has operationally reframed the efficient market hypothesis, as the speed of information processing now dictates price discovery. In this regime, the competitive advantage shifts from the availability of information to the computational capacity to clean, structure, and act upon it.

We can categorize the challenges imposed by this evolution using the standard 3 Vs of Big Data, adapted for the financial context:

1. **Volume:** The migration from floor trading to electronic limit order books (LOB) generated an exponential increase in data points. A single trading session for a liquid asset now produces millions of quote and trade updates. Hambly, Xu, and Yang (2023) note that modern Reinforcement Learning (RL) agents require large historical datasets, often spanning decades of high-frequency tick data, to effectively approximate the complex state space of financial markets.
2. **Velocity:** The latency requirements for processing this data have compressed from seconds to microseconds. Liang (2021) emphasizes that simple data storage solutions are no longer sufficient; the *ingestion* and *retrieval* mechanisms must be optimized to handle real-time streams without creating bottlenecks that lead to stale pricing logic.
3. **Variety:** Financial data is no longer limited to structured numerical time series. Bamford et al. (2023) highlight the growing importance of Multimodal data, in which algorithms must simultaneously process numerical market data, textual sentiment from news feeds, and visual data (e.g., charts or satellite imagery). This variety necessitates an engineering architecture capable of Polyglot Persistence, storing different data types in optimized formats while maintaining temporal alignment.

Collectively, these developments imply that financial data engineering is no longer a peripheral support function but a central determinant of model feasibility, scalability, and reliability.

A critical friction point in financial engineering is the simulation-to-reality gap. Sahu et al. (2023) observe that many machine learning models in finance fail because they rely on sanitized, stationary datasets that do not reflect the stochastic nature of live markets. Traditional econometrics often assumes data stationarity, meaning that the statistical properties of the time series remain constant over time (Arumugam & Natarajan, 2023). However, real-world financial data are non-stationary, noisy, and characterized by structural breaks.

Liu et al. (2022) identify this lack of high-quality, standardized market environments as a primary impediment to progress in Financial Reinforcement Learning (FinRL). They argue that while the computer vision community benefits from standardized benchmarks like ImageNet, quantitative finance lacks an equivalent DataOps standard. Consequently, researchers often train models on preprocessed, simplified bars OHLC that smooth out microstructural noise, only to find that these models fail when exposed to the raw, jagged tick streams of a production environment. This difference necessitates a transition from Data Analysis to Data Engineering. The emphasis must move from running regressions on CSV files to constructing Market Environments that accurately replicate the irregularities of financial exchanges.

The Rise of DataOps and MLOps in Finance

To address these challenges, the industry has increasingly adopted DataOps and MLOps paradigms. Liu et al. (2022) define DataOps in finance as an automated approach that improves data quality and reduces data analytics cycle time. This involves moving away from manual data wrangling scripts toward automated pipelines that treat data transformation as code.

The architectural implication is that the data pipeline must be decoupled from the trading model. In traditional setups, the logic to clean data (e.g., filtering out outliers) was often hard-coded into the trading strategy itself. This creates technical debt and makes it impossible to reuse features across different models. The modern approach, supported by the work of Liang (2021) and Mantilla and Dormido (2023), advocates a layered architecture in which a dedicated Feature Store handles all data transformations. This ensures that a Volatility feature calculated for a risk model is mathematically identical to the Volatility feature used by an execution algorithm, guaranteeing consistency across the enterprise.

Addressing Data Scarcity with Synthetic Generation

Paradoxically, despite the volume of data, finance suffers from a scarcity of relevant training examples for extreme market conditions. Black Swan events, such as the 2008 financial crisis or the 2020 COVID-19 crash, are rare, making it difficult for deep learning models to learn robust responses to market stress (Gao, Y. 2025).

Dogariu et al. (2022) propose the use of Generative Adversarial Networks (GANs) to generate realistic synthetic financial time series. By training generative models on historical data, engineers can generate infinite streams of synthetic market data that preserve the statistical properties of the real market (including stylized facts such as fat tails and volatility clustering) while introducing novel scenarios. This emerging capability transforms the data engineer's role: they are no longer just collectors of historical data but creators of simulated worlds that stress-test trading strategies before capital is deployed. Figure 1 below illustrates the conceptual shift from the traditional Siloed approach to the modern DataOps pipeline advocated in this chapter.

Figure 1. The evolution from static data analysis to dynamic DataOps pipelines. Note the centralization of the Feature Store, which serves both Training and Production, ensuring consistency

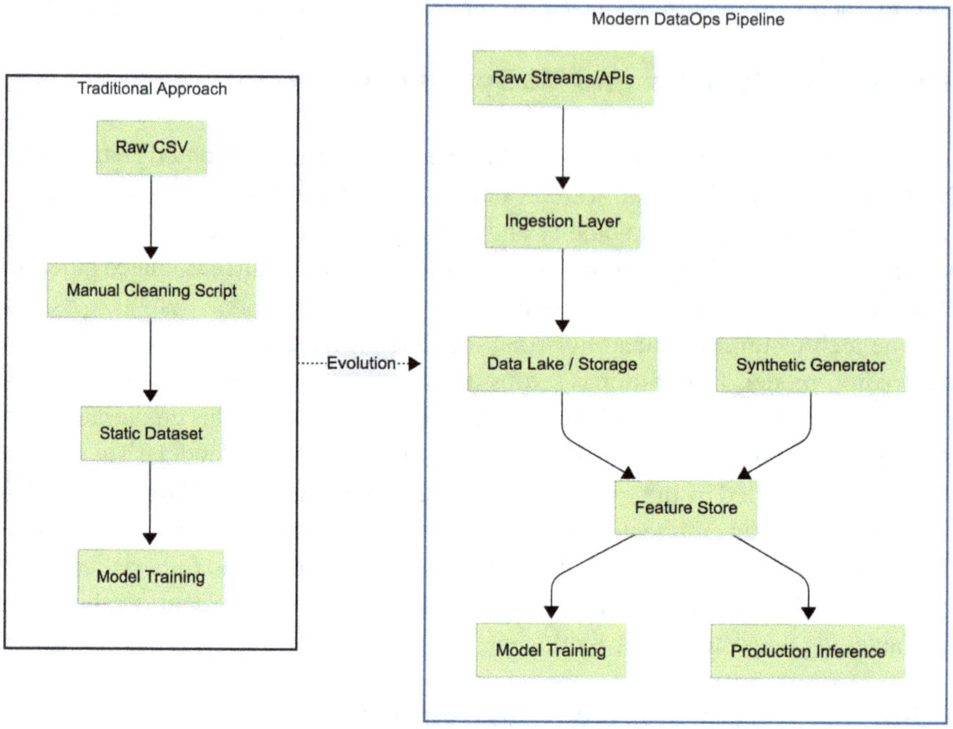

ARCHITECTURAL PATTERNS FOR FINANCIAL DATA

The transition from static datasets to high-velocity data streams necessitates a fundamental change in system architecture. In traditional quantitative finance, data processing was often monolithic: a nightly batch job would download CSV files from a vendor, clean them using a script, and load them into a SQL database. This Store-then-Process model, however, is insufficient for modern algorithmic trading, in which opportunities decay within milliseconds (Fikri et al., 2019). As noted by Goldstein, Spatt, and Ye (2021), the competitive edge in modern markets lies not only in the data itself but also in the infrastructure's ability to process large volumes of unstructured information with minimal latency. This section analyzes the architectural patterns required to build a durable financial data pipeline.

Latency Classes and System Constraints

Before selecting an architecture, one must define the latency constraints of the trading strategy. We categorize financial systems into three distinct classes based on the response time (τ):

1. **High-Frequency Trading (HFT) ($\tau < 1ms$):** Strategies dependent on microstructure arbitrage and queue position. Architecture relies on hardware acceleration (FPGA), kernel bypass, and colocation. Data engineering is minimal; the "feature store" is often a raw memory buffer.
2. **Mid-Frequency Trading (MFT) ($1ms < \tau < 1s$):** Strategies based on statistical arbitrage and technical signals. Architecture relies on optimized software pipelines (C++, Rust) and stream processing. This is the primary domain for the architectures discussed in this chapter.
3. **Low-Frequency/Research ($\tau > 1s$):** Strategies based on fundamental analysis or daily rebalancing. Architecture prioritizes throughput and data completeness over raw speed.

Reference Architecture: The DataOps Pipeline

To standardize the data flow from exchange to algorithm, a four-layer reference architecture is recommended. This model decouples the ingestion instability from the analytical stability required by downstream models.

Figure 2. Layered Reference Architecture. The Messaging Backbone (Layer 2) serves as the system's central nervous system, enabling Layer 3 to process events asynchronously without affecting ingestion performance

Batch vs. Streaming: Lambda and Kappa in Finance

A main challenge in financial data engineering is the dual requirement for historical throughput and real-time latency. Quantitative researchers require massive throughput to backtest strategies over decades of tick data (Petabytes), while execution algorithms require microsecond latency to process live quotes.

The Lambda Architecture: Historical Backfill vs. Real-Time Feeds

Historically, firms addressed this duality using the Lambda Architecture. This pattern maintains two parallel pipelines:

1. **Batch Layer:** A master dataset (immutable, append-only) is processed periodically (e.g., nightly) to create comprehensive views. This layer handles computationally intensive tasks, such as adjusting for corporate actions or recalculating moving averages over 10 years of history.
2. **Speed Layer:** A stream processing engine (e.g., Apache Storm or Flink) processes live data to provide low-latency views. This layer often sacrifices precision (e.g., by using approximate algorithms) to achieve speed.
3. **Serving Layer:** Merges the results from both layers to answer queries.

While the Lambda architecture provides fault tolerance, it introduces a significant engineering risk: logic duplication. The code to calculate a VWAP (Volume Weighted Average Price) must be written twice: once in Python/Spark for the Batch Layer and again in C++/Java for the Speed Layer. This violation of the Do not Repeat Yourself (DRY) principle creates a divergence between backtesting and production. If the implementation of a feature differs even slightly between the two layers, the backtest results will not align with live trading performance.

The Kappa Architecture: Latency–Complexity Trade-offs

To mitigate logic duplication, modern financial systems increasingly adopt the Kappa Architecture. In this pattern, the Batch Layer is removed, and all data, whether historical or real-time, is treated as a stream. History is simply a stream that has already occurred, stored in an immutable log (e.g., Apache Kafka).

By using a single stream-processing engine for both historical and real-time data, engineers ensure that the same code generates features for backtesting and production. This unification is critical for DRL agents, which require identical state-space representations during training and inference (Hambly et al., 2023). While this approach increases the complexity of the stream processing engine, which must now handle high-throughput replay of history, it significantly reduces the operational risk of signal decay.

Figure 3. Comparison of Lambda vs. Kappa Architectures. The Kappa architecture (bottom) eliminates the separate Batch Layer, ensuring that the same processing logic is applied to both historical and real-time data

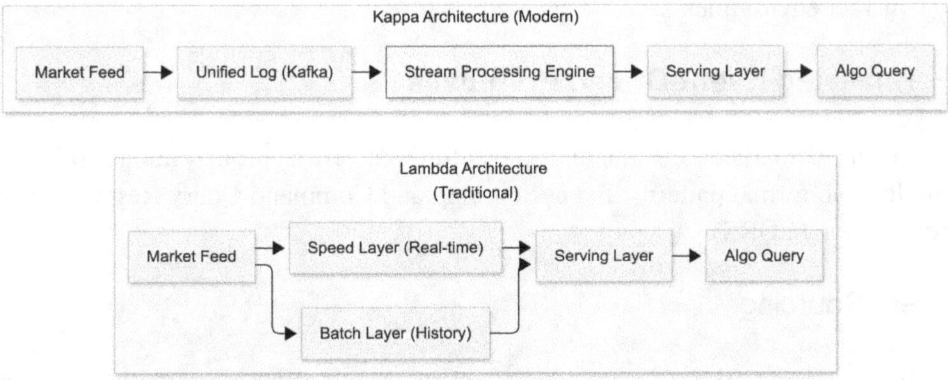

Core Pipeline Stages

To operationalize these architectures, a standardized pipeline is implemented to govern the data lifecycle. This structure resembles the DataOps and RLOps paradigms proposed by Liu et al. (2022) in their FinRL-Meta framework, which advocates for automated, reproducible data flows to bridge the gap between simulation and reality.

The core stages of the pipeline are:

1. **Ingestion:** The entry point where connectors interface with external vendors. This stage handles protocol negotiation (REST vs. WebSocket), authentication, and rate limiting. It functions as a shatter shield, protecting downstream systems from vendor outages or format changes.
2. **Validation:** Before data is stored permanently, it undergoes schema validation and sanity checks (e.g., Ask Price > Bid Price, Volume > 0). Invalid records are routed to a Dead Letter Queue for manual inspection rather than polluting the clean data lake.
3. **Storage:** Validated data is persisted. As discussed in later sections, this often involves a hybrid approach using SQL for metadata and Time-Series databases for ticks (Liang, 2021).
4. **Processing:** This stage applies transformations, such as constructing OHLCV bars from raw ticks or adjusting prices to account for dividends. In a Kappa architecture, this is performed by the stream processor.
5. **Feature/Label Generation:** The final stage derives features (e.g., RSI, MACD, turbulence indices) and labels (e.g., future returns) for machine learning mod-

els. Liu et al. (2022) emphasize that dynamically generating these features within the pipeline, rather than hard-coding them into the model, enables Curriculum Learning, in which agents train on progressively more complex market environments.

Formalizing Event-Driven Primitives

Financial markets are inherently event-driven. To rigorously model this, we employ two formal patterns: Event Sourcing and Command Query Responsibility Segregation (CQRS).

Event Sourcing

In a standard CRUD (Create, Read, Update, Delete) database, updating an order overwrites its previous state. This destroys valuable training data. In Event Sourcing, we model the state of an entity (S_t) not as a mutable record, but as a function of its history of events (e):

$$S_t = f(S_0, \{e_1, e_2, \ldots, e_t\})$$

For a Limit Order Book, the state (the current bids and asks) is the summation of all Add, Cancel, and Execute events. Storing the sequence e_i rather than S_t ensures a complete, immutable audit trail, a requirement under MiFID II.

CQRS

Handling the Variety of financial data (Bamford et al., 2023) often creates a bottleneck in which intensive analytical queries block high-speed writes. CQRS resolves this by splitting the architecture:

- **Command Side (Write):** Optimized for high-throughput ingestion. It appends events to the Log (Layer 2).
  - *Constraint:* $O(1)$write complexity. No complex joins.
- **Query Side (Read):** Optimized for specific access patterns. It consumes the Log and materializes views into specialized stores (Layer 4).
  - *Example:* A Risk View materializes positions into a SQL database, while a Pricing View materializes ticks into a Time-Series database.

This separation allows the system to scale writes (Ingestion) independently of reads (Backtesting/Research), a critical property for maintaining stability during market volatility (Liang, 2021).

FINANCIAL DATA INGESTION: FROM EXCHANGES AND VENDORS TO YOUR BUS

The garbage-in, garbage-out principle is particularly unforgiving in high-frequency finance. The ingestion layer serves as the system's sensory organ; if it fails to capture a tick, or worse, captures it with an incorrect timestamp, every downstream model, from simple moving averages to complex DRL agents, will be poisoned. As Goldstein, Spatt, and Ye (2021) argue, the Big Data revolution in finance is characterized not just by volume, but by the complexity of assembling a coherent view of the market from fragmented, asynchronous sources.

This section details the engineering required to acquire financial data reliably. We categorize the hierarchy of market data sources, compare access mechanisms (REST vs. WebSocket), and provide a blueprint for normalizing heterogeneous vendor formats into a canonical internal schema.

Market Data Sources and Types

Financial data is not a monolith; it exists in a hierarchy of granularity and latency. Understanding this hierarchy is essential for selecting the appropriate data source for a given strategy.

The Hierarchy of Feeds

1. **Direct Exchange Feeds:** Direct multicast feeds (e.g., ITCH, OUCH) from exchange matching engines are the gold standard for low-latency trading. They offer the highest data fidelity, including all order changes, but necessitate expensive co-location and specialized FPGA hardware for processing (Goldstein et al., 2021).
2. **Consolidated Feeds:** For most buy-side firms, a direct feed is overkill. Consolidated feeds (like the SIP in the US Equity market) aggregate the best bid and offer (BBO) from all exchanges. While they introduce latency (tens of milliseconds), they provide a National Best Bid and Offer (NBBO) view that is sufficient for non-HFT strategies.
3. **Premium Vendors:** Providers offer normalized feeds that include not only price data but also rich reference data. Boritz and No (2013) highlight that, although

these vendors offer convenience, discrepancies often exist among them, particularly in corporate actions and dividends, requiring a robust reconciliation process.

4. **Alternative Data:** Bamford et al. (2023) note the rising importance of multimodal data, satellite imagery, social media sentiment, and web traffic. These sources are unstructured and often arrive at irregular intervals, which tests traditional time-series databases.

Data Types: From Ticks to Reference

- **Ticks:** The atomic unit of market data. A tick represents a distinct event: a trade, a quote update, or an order book change.
- **OHLCV Bars:** Aggregated candles OHLC are the standard for backtesting. However, assembling bars from ticks is non-trivial; defining the Close of a 1-minute bar requires rigorous rules about timestamp inclusion (e.g., [09:30:00, 09:31:00) vs (09:30:00, 09:31:00]).
- **Order Books (L1, L2, L3):**
    - *Level 1:* Best Bid and Ask (Top of Book).
    - *Level 2:* Market Depth (e.g., top 10 price levels).
    - *Level 3:* Order-by-order granularity. Hambly et al. (2023) emphasize that for RL agents executing Smart Order Routing, Level 3 data is critical to simulating queue position and impact cost.
- **Reference & Corporate Actions:** The metadata of the market. A stock split (e.g., AAPL 4:1) or a dividend payment fundamentally alters the price series. Failure to adjust for these events is the most common source of look-ahead bias in backtests (Liu et al., 2022; Liang, 2021).

Access Mechanisms and Connectors

The ingestion layer must support two distinct access patterns: Snapshotting (History) and Streaming (Real-time).

REST APIs for Historical Backfill

Representational State Transfer (REST) APIs are the standard for downloading historical data. They are request-response-based: "Give me AAPL daily bars for 2020."

- **Challenge:** Rate limits and pagination. Vendors restrict the number of requests per minute.

- **Engineering Solution:** Implement Exponential Backoff. If a request fails with HTTP 429 Too Many Requests, the system should sleep for 2^kseconds before retrying, where k is the attempt number.

WebSockets for Real-Time Streaming

For live trading, polling a REST API is too slow. WebSockets provide a persistent, bidirectional connection in which the server pushes updates to the client.

- **Challenge:** Disconnects and Slow Consumer problems. If the ingestion script cannot process messages as fast as the market generates them, the socket buffer fills up, and data is dropped.
- **Engineering Solution:** A dedicated Ingestion Service that does zero processing. Its only job is to read from the socket and write to a high-throughput message bus (like Kafka). This decouples ingestion from processing (Liang, 2021).

Normalization Across Providers

Every vendor speaks a different language. Bloomberg might call the last traded price LAST_PRICE, while Binance calls it c (for close). To build a Feature Store that is agnostic to the data source, we must implement a Normalization Layer.

Canonical Internal Model

We define a strict schema (e.g., using Avro or Protobuf) that represents our internal Truth. All incoming data is mapped to this schema *immediately* after ingestion.

Example Internal Schema (Protobuf):

```
message MarketTick {
string internal_symbol = 1; // Mapped from "AAPL US" or "AAPL.O"
int64 event_timestamp = 2; // UTC Microseconds from Epoch
double price = 3;
double size = 4;
string source_id = 5; // e.g., "BLOOMBERG_FEED_A"
}
```

The Symbol Mapping Problem

A major engineering headache is symbol changes. Facebook changed its ticker from FB to META. If your database stores strings such as FB, your historical queries will fail.

Solution: Use an Internal Security Master. Assign a permanent, immutable ID (e.g., INT_ID_1001) to the company. The ingestion layer looks up META → INT_ID_1001 before writing to the database. This allows the ticker to change without breaking the time series.

Time Zone and Calendar Alignment

Financial centers operate in different time zones. A timestamp of 10:00:00 is ambiguous.

- **Rule:** Store everything in UTC. Convert to local market time only in the final step (visualization or order scheduling).
- **Calendars:** Use libraries like pandas_market_calendars to handle holidays. Markets close early on Thanksgiving or Christmas Eve, assuming a full trading day will result in missing data alerts (False Positives) in your monitoring system (Liu et al., 2022).

DATA CLEANING AND VALIDATION: THE FIRST LINE OF DEFENSE

In the domain of quantitative finance, the integrity of the input data is the primary determinant of a strategy's viability. While a software engineer might view a data error as a bug to be fixed in the next sprint, a quantitative researcher must view it as a solvency threat. A single erroneous price spike, a bad tick, can trigger a stop-loss order in a backtest, creating the illusion of a catastrophic drawdown that never occurred, or conversely, a windfall profit that is purely fictitious. Goldstein, Spatt, and Ye (2021) emphasize that in the era of Big Data, the ability to discern genuine market signals from microstructure noise and technical errors is a source of competitive advantage.

This section outlines the engineering methodologies required to sanitize financial data. The discussion moves beyond simple null checks to reliable statistical filters, addresses the complexities of corporate actions, and establishes a validation framework that prevents look-ahead bias during cleaning.

The Taxonomy of Financial Data Errors

Data quality issues in finance generally fall into three categories: Technical Anomalies, Market Microstructure Noise, and Structural Breaks (Arnell et al., 2023).

Technical Anomalies and Bad Prints.

Technical anomalies arise from the data transmission infrastructure. These include:

- **Missing Values (Gaps):** Caused by network packet loss or exchange outages.
- **Duplicate Records:** Commonly arising from redundant ingestion pipelines (e.g., listening to both a primary and secondary feed simultaneously).
- **Decimal Errors:** A stock trading at $100.50 appearing as $1005.0 or $10.05 due to parsing failures.

Market Microstructure Noise

High-frequency data contains noise that reflects the mechanics of trading rather than the asset's fundamental value.

- **Bid-Ask Bounce:** In a liquid market, transaction prices oscillate between the bid and the ask price as buyers and sellers initiate trades. This creates high-frequency negative serial correlation in returns, which naive volatility estimators often mistake for genuine price variance (Zhang et al., 2019).
- **Zero-Volume Quotes:** Exchanges frequently emit quote updates where the price changes but the size is zero, indicating a cancellation rather than a valid liquidity point.

Structural Breaks: Corporate Actions

The most insidious errors are structural. Corporate actions such as stock splits, dividends, and mergers fundamentally alter the continuity of a price series.

- **The Split Trap:** Consider a 2-for-1 stock split for a company trading at $100. The next day, the price opens at $50. An algorithm unaware of the split will interpret this as a 50% crash, which may trigger a panic sell.
- **Dividend Gaps:** When a stock goes ex-dividend, its price drops by the dividend amount. Failure to adjust historical prices for dividends introduces a negative bias in long-term trend-following strategies (Boritz & No, 2013).

Statistical Cleaning Techniques

To sanitize the data stream without removing genuine volatility, we employ statistical filters that adapt to market conditions.

Outlier Detection: Z-Score vs. Median Absolute Deviation

A common approach to identifying bad ticks is to calculate the Z-score of a price change relative to a moving window.

$$Z_t = \frac{P_t - \mu_t - k:t - 1}{\sigma_t - k:t - 1}$$

If $Z_t > 3$, the point is flagged as an outlier. However, financial returns are fat-tailed (non-Gaussian), rendering the standard deviation (σ) sensitive to extreme values. A more robust metric is the Median Absolute Deviation (MAD).

$$MAD = Median\left(\left| P_i - Median\left(P\right)\right|\right)$$

Using a rolling MAD filter enables the system to reject spurious spikes while preserving genuine volatility during market crashes.

The Brownlees-Gallo Filter

For high-frequency tick data, the industry standard is the filter proposed by Brownlees and Gallo. It validates a tick only if it is sufficiently close to a trimmed mean of neighboring ticks *and* if the gap is granular enough relative to the average volatility. This prevents the filtering out of the crash phenomenon, where a rapid but legitimate price collapse is mistaken for a series of errors.

Imputation Strategies: The Look-Ahead Bias Trap

When gaps are detected, engineers must impute the missing values.

- **Forward Fill (ffill):** The safest method for prices. It assumes that the last known price persists until a new update is received.
- **Linear Interpolation:** $\frac{P_{t-1} + P_{t+1}}{2}$. Critical Warning: This introduces look-ahead bias because P_{t+1} (a future value) is required to calculate the value at t. This method must never be used to produce features for predictive modeling, as it leaks future information into the past (Liu et al., 2022).

- **Generative Imputation:** Recent advances use GANs to synthesize realistic price paths to fill large gaps, preserving the statistical properties of the time series (Dogariu et al., 2022).

Handling Corporate Actions and Point-in-Time Correctness

Adjusting for corporate actions is necessary for maintaining a consistent economic series. The Backward Adjustment method is employed for this purpose.

The Adjustment Factor

For a split with a ratio R (e.g., a 2:1 ratio implies $R = 2$) or a dividend D paid on price P_{cum}, we calculate an adjustment factor f:

$$f_{split} = \frac{1}{R}, f_{dividend} = 1 - \frac{D}{P_{cum}}$$

All historical prices prior to the event are multiplied by f.

$$P_{adj,\,t} = P_t \times \prod_{i \in Future\ Events} f_i$$

Point-in-Time (PIT) Tables

While adjusted prices are necessary for technical analysis, unadjusted prices are required for backtesting execution logic (e.g., checking if a limit order at \$100.00 would have filled). Therefore, the database must implement a Point-in-Time architecture, storing two versions of history:

1. **As-Traded:** The raw price exactly as it appeared on the tape.
2. **As-Adjusted:** The price series normalized for all subsequent corporate actions.

This duality ensures that researchers can train models on continuous trends while the execution engine validates trades against actual historical levels.

Automated Validation Framework

In a DataOps pipeline (Liu et al., 2022), validation is automated via Unit Tests for Data.

Table 1. Standard financial data validation rules

Rule Type	Logic Check	Failure Implication	Action
Logical	Ask Price ≥ Bid Price	Crossed market (or bad data)	Flag for manual review; do not trade.
Physical	Price > 0	Erroneous zero print	Reject the tick immediately.
Volume	Volume ≥ 0	Negative volume (correction?)	Filter out or treat as cancellation.
Consistency	High ≥ MAX(Open, Close, Low)	Malformed OHLC bar	Re-aggregate from ticks.
Staleness	Timestamp_now - Timestamp_tick < Threshold	Data feed latency	Alert operations team.

Figure 4. Automated Data Cleaning Pipeline. Note the Dead Letter Queue, which isolates bad data for analysis without stopping the pipeline

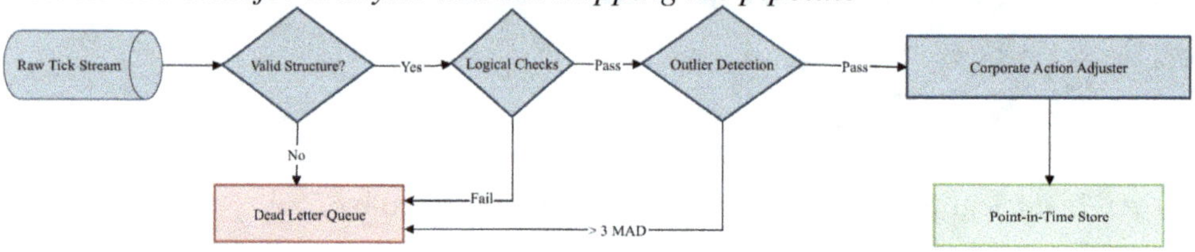

Normalization and Stationarity

Deep learning models, particularly those used in Reinforcement Learning (FinRL), are sensitive to input data scale (Liu et al., 2022). A stock trading at $2000 has a higher raw variance than one trading at $10, even if their volatility is identical.

To prepare data for the Feature Store, Stationarity Transformations are applied:

1. **Log-Returns:** $r_t = ln(P_t) - ln(P_{t-1})$. This converts non-stationary prices into a stationary series.
2. **Z-Score Normalization:** $\hat{x} = \frac{x-\mu}{\sigma}$. This is often applied using a rolling window to adapt to regime changes (Zhang et al., 2019).

Enforcing these transformations at the cleaning layer ensures that downstream models receive distributionally consistent inputs, thereby accelerating training convergence.

THE FEATURE STORE: BRIDGING RESEARCH AND PRODUCTION

In the lifecycle of a quantitative trading strategy, the most treacherous chasm is the transition from research to production. A strategy that generates a Sharpe ratio of 3.0 in a Python simulation often fails to break even when deployed in a C++ execution engine. While market regime shifts are a frequent culprit, a more insidious and preventable cause is feature drift, the subtle mathematical divergence between how a signal is calculated in backtesting versus live trading (Singha, 2025). This section introduces the Feature Store, a centralized data infrastructure that serves as the single source of truth for feature engineering.

Why Feature Engineering Belongs in the Platform

Traditionally, feature engineering has been viewed as part of the model development process. A quantitative researcher writes a Pandas script to calculate a 14-day Relative Strength Index (RSI) for a backtest. Once the strategy is approved, a software engineer reimplements the RSI logic in the production trading system, often using a different programming language and different libraries.

The Drift Between Research and Production

This dual-implementation pattern invites catastrophe. Slight variations in floating-point precision, handling of NaN values, or the specific windowing function (e.g., exponential vs. simple moving average) can lead to considerable discrepancies. Liu et al. (2022) identify this lack of standardized market environments as a primary barrier to reproducible financial reinforcement learning. When the state space representation (S_t) differs between the training environment and the inference environment, the agent's policy ($\pi(S_t)$) becomes undefined, leading to unpredictable behavior.

Reuse and Governance of Alpha and Risk Factors

Beyond correctness, the Feature Store addresses the organizational challenge of reuse. In a siloed architecture, a Volatility feature might be implemented dozens of times across different desks, equity research, FX hedging, and enterprise risk management, each with different parameters.

- **Alpha Factors:** Proprietary signals designed to predict returns (e.g., Order Flow Imbalance). These require strict access controls to protect intellectual property.

- **Risk Factors:** Standardized metrics (e.g., Beta, Value-at-Risk) that must be consistent across the firm for regulatory reporting (Basel III, FRTB). By centralizing these definitions, the Feature Store ensures that when the Risk Team asks, What was the volatility of AAPL? The Trading Team asks the same; they receive an identical answer.

Figure 5. Architecture comparison. The Feature Store abstracts the transformation logic, ensuring the Unified Feature Definition serves both research and production clients

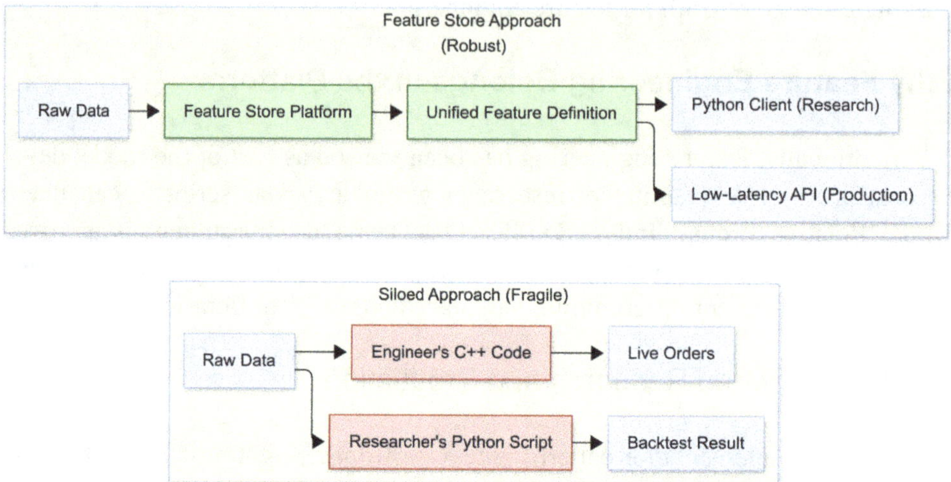

Core Concepts of a Financial Feature Store

A financial feature store differs from general-purpose ML feature stores (like those used for e-commerce recommendations) due to the strict requirement for temporal accuracy.

Point-in-Time (PIT) Correctness

The cardinal sin of quantitative finance is Look-Ahead Bias, using data that was not available at the time of the prediction. A standard database update overwrites the past; a PIT store preserves it.

Consider a quarterly earnings report for Q3 released on October 15th.

- **The Fact:** Earnings = $1.50 per share.
- **The Event Time:** September 30th (end of quarter).
- **The Knowledge Time:** October 15th (release date).

If a backtest running on October 1st uses the $1.50 figure, it is cheating. The Feature Store must index data by Knowledge Time.

$F(t) = \textit{Feature value available at } t$

A query for ***get_features(ticker=AAPL, time=2023-10-01)*** must return the state of the world *as known* on Oct 1st, effectively ignoring the Q3 earnings released two weeks later. This mechanism requires an as-of join, a complex operation that standard SQL engines struggle to optimize but is native to time-series architectures (Goldstein et al., 2021).

Feature Definitions and Taxonomy

Financial features span multiple domains, each requiring specific engineering handling:

1. **Technical Indicators:** Mathematical transformations of price and volume (e.g., MACD, Bollinger Bands). Mantilla and Dormido (2023) demonstrate that optimizing these calculations for high-frequency data requires specialized windowing techniques to handle irregular tick spacing.
2. **Microstructure Features:** Derived from the Limit Order Book (LOB).
    - *Order Flow Imbalance (OFI):* Measures the net buy/sell pressure at the best bid/ask.
    - *Depth Ratios:* The volume at Level 1 vs. Level 10. Zhang et al. (2019) show that Deep Learning models (like DeepLOB) rely on raw LOB states normalized by z-scores to detect short-term price movements.
3. **Multi-Modal Features:** As noted by Bamford et al. (2023), modern alpha sources include sentiment scores from news text or satellite imagery of retail parking lots. The Feature Store must serve these dense vectors alongside scalar price data.

Interfaces and APIs

The interface of the Feature Store must satisfy two distinct access patterns: high-throughput batch retrieval for training and low-latency point lookups for inference.

The get_features Design

```
The core abstraction is the Time-Travel query. The API signature should enforce explicit temporal context.
def get_features(universe: List[str], features: List[str], as_of_time: datetime,
horizon: str = "1m"
) -> DataFrame:
"""
Retrieves the feature vector state exactly as it appeared at `as_of_time`.
Args:
universe: List of tickers (e.g., ['AAPL', 'MSFT'])
features: List of feature names (e.g., ['rsi_14d', 'ofi_1m'])
as_of_time: The cutoff timestamp for knowledge.
horizon: The prediction horizon (for label generation).
"""
pass
```

This function abstracts the complexity of joining multiple tables (Price, Reference, Earnings) and performing the as-of logic. For researchers using FinRL-Meta, this API serves as the environment's step() function, providing the observation vector O_t (Liu et al., 2022).

Versioning, Backfilling, and Replay

Features are code, and code has bugs. If a bug is found in the Volatility calculation, simply fixing it in the code is insufficient; the historical data generated by that bug is now corrupt relative to the new logic.

- **Feature Versioning:** The store must support semantic versioning (e.g., volatility_v1, volatility_v2).
- **Backfilling:** When v2 is released, the system orchestrates a large-scale batch job to recompute v2 for the entire history.
- **Replay:** A research backtest can explicitly request volatility_v1 to reproduce an old result, or v2 to test the improvement. This traceability is essential for regulatory audit trails mandated by regulatory frameworks such as MiFID II.

DATA QUALITY, RECONCILIATION, AND AUDIT TRAILS

In the high-stakes environment of quantitative finance, data quality is not merely an operational concern; it is a fundamental component of risk management. A trading algorithm is only as robust as the data it consumes. If a feature store serves a corrupted price vector, the downstream execution engine may generate erroneous orders, resulting in substantial financial losses and regulatory scrutiny. Goldstein, Spatt, and Ye (2021) argue that as financial datasets grow in volume and velocity, the signal-to-noise ratio often degrades, making rigorous automated quality assurance (QA) the primary differentiator between profitable and insolvent firms.

This section details the engineering framework required to ensure data integrity. We move beyond simple schema validation to discuss complex reconciliation processes, regulatory audit trails, and real-time monitoring systems that enforce Service Level Agreements (SLAs).

A Comprehensive Data Quality Framework

To operationalize data quality, we must define specific, measurable dimensions. Boritz and No (2013) highlight that interactive financial data is susceptible to discrepancies across providers, necessitating a multi-dimensional quality framework.

Completeness

Completeness measures the extent to which all expected data points are present. In financial time series, this is non-trivial due to the irregularity of tick data.

- **Gap Detection:** The system must distinguish between a quiet market (no trades occurred) and a broken feed (trades occurred but were not captured). This is often achieved by monitoring heartbeat messages that are standard in FIX/ITCH protocols.
- **Reference Integrity:** Ensuring every active ticker in the Security Master has corresponding price entries in the Feature Store.

Accuracy

Accuracy refers to the degree to which data conform to the actual market state.

- **Outlier Detection:** As discussed in previous sections, statistical filters (MAD, Z-Score) identify bad prints.

- **Synthetic Benchmarking:** Dogariu et al. (2022) propose using generative models to create synthetic baselines. If the incoming live data deviates statistically from the synthetic distribution of normal market behavior (e.g., a 50-sigma move), it triggers an accuracy alert.

Timeliness (Latency)

For execution algorithms, data that arrives late is effectively erroneous. Timeliness quantifies the delta between the *Event Time* ($t_{exchange}$) and the *Ingestion Time* (t_{system}).

$$Latency = t_{system} - t_{exchange}$$

Liang (2021) emphasizes that the Data Acquisition Engine must continuously monitor this metric. A spike in latency indicates upstream network congestion or a slow consumer bottleneck, requiring immediate throttling of trading activity.

Consistency

Consistency ensures that data is non-contradictory across different views.

- **Internal Consistency:** $High \geq Low$, $Volueme \geq 0$
- **Cross-System Consistency:** The Close Price in the risk management system must match the Close Price in the accounting system.

The Reconciliation Process

Reconciliation is the process of comparing independent data sources to verify accuracy. Since no single vendor provides a perfect view of the market, engineers employ a Triangulation strategy.

Multi-Source Comparison

A robust pipeline ingests data from multiple vendors (e.g., Bloomberg, Refinitiv, and a Direct Exchange Feed) for the same asset.

- **The Consensus Model:** If Feed A reports \$100.05, Feed B reports \$100.06, and Feed C reports \$100.05, the system adopts the majority vote (\$100.05) and flags Feed B for investigation. Boritz and No (2013) demonstrated the necessity of this approach by documenting significant discrepancies in fundamental data across major providers, such as Yahoo Finance and Compustat.

Discrepancy Resolution

When a mismatch exceeds a defined tolerance (e.g., > 0.1%), the system initiates an automated resolution protocol:

1. **Quarantine:** The suspect data point is isolated.
2. **Fallback:** The Feature Store switches to the secondary (validated) feed for downstream consumers.
3. **Alerting:** An operations engineer is notified to inspect the variance manually.

Figure 6. Automated Reconciliation Workflow. The system ingests dual feeds to create a validated Golden Copy before the data reaches the Feature Store

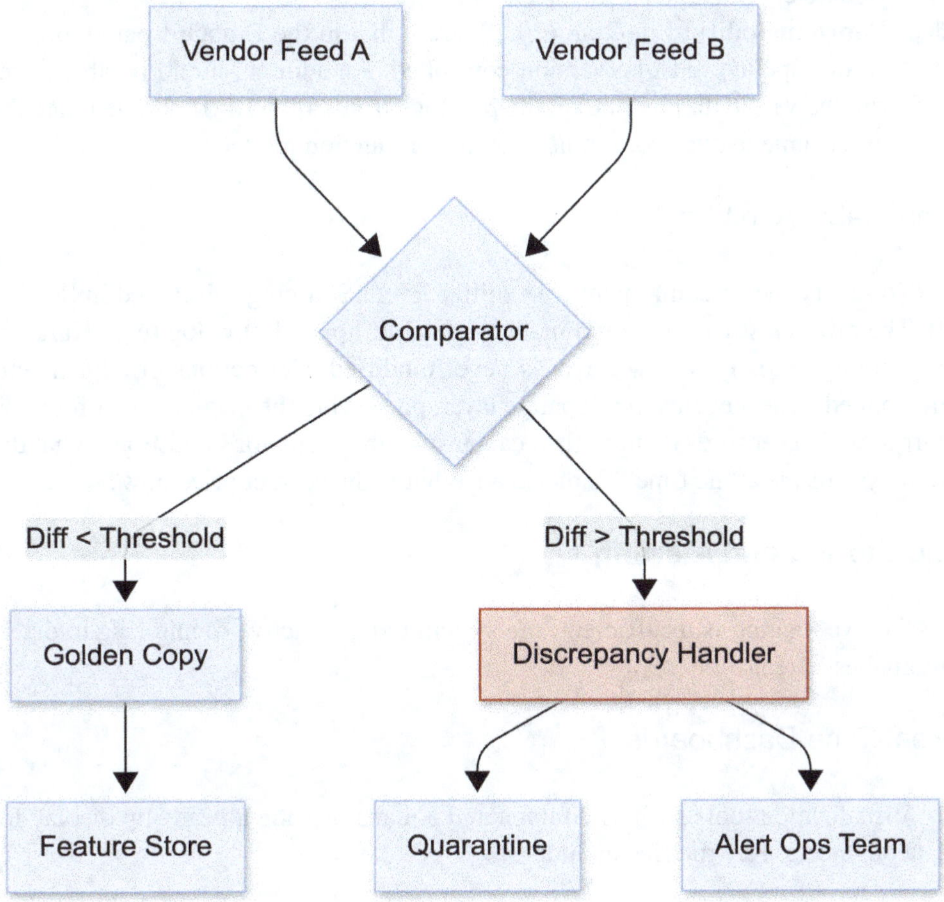

Audit Trails and Compliance

In the post-2008 regulatory environment, traceability is mandatory. Regulations such as MiFID II (Markets in Financial Instruments Directive) and Reg NMS (National Market System Regulation) require firms to reconstruct the exact market conditions surrounding any algorithmic trade.

Data Lineage

Data lineage tracks the lifecycle of a data point from ingestion to decision.

- **Traceability:** If a trading agent executes a buy order for AAPL at 10:00:01, the audit trail must prove which specific tick updates (Price, Volume, Order Book Depth) triggered that decision.
- **Reproducibility:** Liu et al. (2022) stress that in the DataOps paradigm, the entire pipeline must be version-controlled. An auditor should be able to re-run the v1.2 data pipeline on the raw logs from 2023-10-01 and generate the exact same feature vectors used by the production model.

Immutable Audit Logs

To satisfy these requirements, we utilize Event Sourcing (discussed in Section 3). The raw tick stream is stored in an immutable, append-only log (e.g., Kafka or cold storage S3). This Raw Layer is never modified. Corrections or adjustments are applied as new events in a separate layer, preserving the original error for audit purposes. This ensures that the firm can answer the regulator's question: What did your system *see* at the time? Rather than What is the correct price now?

Monitoring and Alerting

Passive logging is insufficient; the system requires active monitoring to detect anomalies in real-time.

Real-Time Dashboards

Visualization tools such as Grafana and Kibana provide a heads-up display for data engineers. Key metrics include:

- **Throughput:** Messages per second (MPS) per feed. A sudden drop to zero signals a disconnect.

- **Latency:** The 99th percentile (P99) end-to-end latency.
- **Error Rate:** The count of validation failures (e.g., negative prices) per minute.

Anomaly Detection using Statistical Methods

Liang (2021) proposes using deep learning-based feature extraction to identify system anomalies. However, for data quality, statistical control charts are often sufficient and more interpretable.

- **Volume Profile Checks:** If the trading volume for a symbol deviates by more than 3σ from its 30-day moving average for that time of day, an alert is triggered.
- **SLA Monitoring:** If a vendor fails to deliver the Market Close summary by 16:15:00 (per the Service Level Agreement), the system automatically escalates the issue to the vendor support team.

PRODUCTION DEPLOYMENT AND OPERATIONS

The transition of a financial data pipeline from a development environment to a production ecosystem is often where the theoretical elegance of an architecture meets the harsh reality of operational constraints. In a research setting, a Python script crashing due to an API timeout is a minor annoyance; in a live trading environment, the same failure can result in stale quotes, leading to execution algorithms trading on phantom prices. Goldstein, Spatt, and Ye (2021) posit that as financial institutions increasingly rely on automated decision-making, the resilience of the underlying data infrastructure becomes a systemic risk factor.

This section outlines the operational principles required to maintain a high-availability financial data system. The DataOps paradigm is adopted to implement Continuous Integration/Continuous Deployment (CI/CD) specifically for data pipelines, distinguish between passive monitoring and active observability, and define disaster recovery protocols to ensure business continuity.

DataOps and CI/CD for Financial Pipelines

Traditional software DevOps focuses on deploying *code*. However, in financial engineering, the system's behavior is determined by both code and *data*. A perfect algorithm running on a schema-drifted dataset will fail. Liu et al. (2022) advocate a DataOps approach that treats data transformations, schema definitions, and validation rules as versioned artifacts.

Infrastructure as Code (IaC)

To eliminate manual work on the machine, the entire infrastructure, database schemas, Kafka topic configurations, and Kubernetes manifests must be defined in code (e.g., Terraform or Ansible). This ensures that the staging environment used for User Acceptance Testing (UAT) is mathematically identical to the production environment.

The CI/CD Pipeline

A robust deployment pipeline for financial data involves three specific stages:

1. **Unit Testing:** Validates individual components (e.g., Does the calculate_rsi function return correct values for a known input vector?).
2. **Integration Testing:** Validates the flow between components (e.g., Does the Ingestion Service successfully write to the Kafka topic, and does the Stream Processor successfully read it?).
3. **Data Regression Testing:** Before deploying a new version of the pipeline, the system replays a historical day of tick data through the new logic and compares the output features with those from the previous version. Any unexplained variance blocks the deployment.

Figure 7. DataOps CI/CD Pipeline. The critical step is the Replay, which ensures that code changes do not inadvertently alter the mathematical definition of financial features

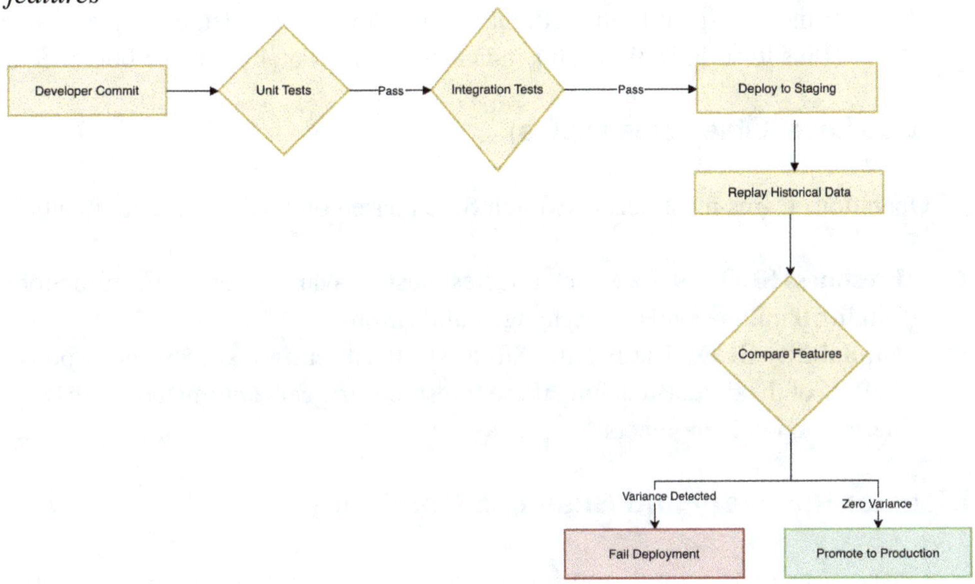

Observability: Beyond Simple Monitoring

While monitoring answers the question, Is the system healthy?, observability answers: Why is the system behaving this way? In high-frequency finance, where latency spikes can cost millions, simply knowing that CPU usage is high is insufficient.

The Three Pillars of Observability

1. **Metrics (Aggregatable):** Time-series data representing the health of the system.
    - Ingestion Lag: The time difference between the exchange timestamp and the processing timestamp.
    - Throughput: Ticks per second processed. Liang (2021) emphasizes optimizing the Data Acquisition Engine to handle burst throughput during market open and close.
2. **Logs (Discrete):** Structured records of specific events.
    - Example: [INFO] 2023-10-01 09:30:01 - Connection to NASDAQ-ITCH re-established.
    - Requirement: Logs must be structured (JSON) and centralized (e.g., ELK Stack) to allow for correlation analysis.

3. **Traces (Request-Scoped):** Following a single data packet through the distributed system.
    - Distributed Tracing: If a feature request takes 500ms, tracing reveals that 10ms was spent in the API Gateway, 480ms in the database query, and 10ms in serialization. This indicates that the database is the bottleneck.

Service Level Objectives (SLOs)

Operations teams must define explicit SLOs based on business requirements.

- **Freshness SLO:** 99.9% of tick updates must be available in the Feature Store within 50 milliseconds of exchange publication.
- **Availability SLO:** The Feature Store API must return a successful response 99.99% of the time. Breaching these thresholds triggers automated PagerDuty alerts to on-call engineers.

Disaster Recovery and Business Continuity

Financial markets do not stop for server failures. A robust architecture must assume that components will fail and design self-healing mechanisms.

High Availability (HA) via Redundancy

- **Active-Active Ingestion:** Run two identical ingestion pipelines in separate availability zones (e.g., AWS us-east-1a and us-east-1b). Both consume the feed and write to the message bus. Downstream deduplication logic handles the redundant messages.
- **Database Replication:** The primary SQL and Time-Series databases should synchronously replicate data to a standby instance. If the primary fails, a leader election process automatically promotes the standby.

The Replay Capability of Kappa Architecture

A unique advantage of the Kappa Architecture (Section 3) is its inherent capability for disaster recovery. Since the Source of Truth is the immutable log (Kafka) rather than the materialised view (Database), catastrophic database corruption can be resolved by:

1. Spinning up a new, empty database instance.
2. Resetting the Stream Processor's offset to Earliest.

3. Replaying the entire history of events from the log to rebuild the database state. This approach, while time-consuming, guarantees data consistency without relying on potentially corrupted backups (Liu et al., 2022).

Circuit Breakers

To prevent cascading failures, the system employs circuit breakers. If the Feature Store API detects that the database is unresponsive, it trips the circuit, immediately returning a fallback error to the trading algorithm (e.g., Data Stale - Do Not Trade) rather than hanging indefinitely. This fail-fast mechanism protects the trading agent from making decisions based on incomplete information.

CASE STUDIES: ARCHITECTING FOR SPEED VERSUS COMPLEXITY

The architectural principles outlined in previous sections, DataOps, Polyglot Persistence, and Feature Stores, are not rigid rules but flexible patterns. The specific implementation of a financial data pipeline depends heavily on the firm's trading horizon and asset universe. A pipeline designed for High-Frequency Trading (HFT) prioritizes microsecond latency above all else, often sacrificing strict schema validation. Conversely, a Multi-Asset Risk pipeline prioritizes data completeness and cross-asset consistency, tolerating higher latency to ensure a unified view of global exposure.

This section contrasts these two distinct engineering paradigms through detailed case studies, demonstrating how the theoretical components of this chapter adapt to real-world requirements.

Case Study 1: The High-Frequency Trading (HFT) Pipeline

In HFT, the Feature Store is often indistinguishable from the network card. The objective is to calculate microstructure features, such as Order Flow Imbalance (OFI) or Book Pressure, and execute a trade decision before the competition reacts. Goldstein, Spatt, and Ye (2021) describe this environment as a computational arms race where data processing occurs on the timescale of nanoseconds.

Data Ingestion: Hardware Acceleration

Standard REST APIs, or even standard TCP/IP stacks, introduce unacceptable jitter (latency variability) for HFT.

- Direct Feeds: The pipeline ingests raw binary multicast feeds (e.g., NASDAQ TotalView-ITCH) directly from the exchange.
- Kernel Bypass: To avoid the overhead of operating-system context switching, data is captured using Field-Programmable Gate Arrays (FPGAs) or Solarflare network interface cards (NICs), which write directly to user-space memory.
- Timestamping: The Ingestion Time is measured at the hardware level (NIC) to capture wire-to-wire latency accurately.

Feature Engineering: The Limit Order Book (LOB)

The state space for HFT is the Limit Order Book. Zhang, Zohren, and Roberts (2019) demonstrate that deep learning models (such as DeepLOB) utilize the top 10 levels of the order book to predict short-term price movements.

- Feature Vectors: The input vector X_t typically has 40 dimensions, $\{P^{(i)}_{bid}, V^{(i)}_{bid}, P^{(i)}_{ask}, V^{(i)}_{ask}\}^{10}_{i=1}$ representing prices and volumes at 10 depth levels.
- Normalization: Unlike daily bars, LOB data is highly non-stationary. Mantilla and Dormido (2023) propose adaptive windowing techniques to normalize these inputs in real-time, converting raw prices into z-scores relative to the rolling micro-price mean and standard deviation.

The Lite Feature Store

In this context, the centralized Feature Store described in Section 7 is too slow for the live loop. Instead, the HFT architecture uses a Local Cache pattern:

- Research: The centralized Feature Store (built on the Kappa Architecture) captures the full-resolution stream for offline training of RL agents (Liu et al., 2022).
- Production: The trained model weights are deployed to an FPGA or a C++ execution engine, which computes features in memory on the live stream.
- Reconciliation: Post-trade, the in-memory features used by the FPGA are logged asynchronously and compared against the centralized Feature Store to detect logic drift.

Case Study 2: Multi-Asset Risk and Portfolio Analytics

While HFT focuses on a single asset's depth, a Risk Management pipeline must synthesize a global view across thousands of assets, Equities, FX, Crypto, and Derivatives. The challenge here is Variety and Consistency rather than pure Velocity.

Ingestion: The Multi-Vendor Integration Challenge

A risk manager needs to know the portfolio's exposure to Apple Inc. This is non-trivial because the firm might hold:

- AAPL stock (traded on Nasdaq, USD).
- AAPL Equity Options (traded on CBOE).
- A Total Return Swap on AAPL (OTC).
- A Euro-denominated ETF holding AAPL (traded on Euronext).

Ingesting this requires normalizing distinct vendor protocols (e.g., FIX for equities, REST for crypto) into a unified internal schema (Section 4.3). Boritz and No (2013) highlight data quality risks, noting that widely used sources such as Yahoo Finance and Google Finance often contain discrepancies in corporate action adjustments relative to premium vendors such as Compustat, which can distort risk metrics such as Beta and Volatility.

Feature Engineering: Graph and Multi-Modal Analytics

Risk is inherently relational. If the U.S. dollar spikes, it affects emerging-market equities, Gold, and Cryptocurrencies.

- **Graph Features:** The Feature Store must model correlations among features. A Contagion Feature might measure the spectral radius of the portfolio's sector correlation matrix.
- **Multi-Modal Signals:** Bamford et al. (2023) introduce the concept of multimodal analysis in finance, integrating visual data (e.g., candlestick chart patterns) and textual data (e.g., news sentiment) into risk models. For example, a Sentiment Shock feature derived from real-time news feeds can serve as an early-warning indicator for Value-at-Risk (VaR) models, triggering a reduction in leverage before price-momentum shifts.

Architecture: The Hub-and-Spoke

To handle this complexity, the risk pipeline utilizes a Federated Feature Store:

1. **The Hub:** A SQL-based Security Master (Section 6.1) that maps Ticker: AAPL and Ticker: BTC-USD to a unified RiskID.
2. **The Spokes:** Specialized engines calculate specific risk factors.
   - Market Risk Engine: Calculates volatility and beta using TSDB price history.
   - Credit Risk Engine: Ingests fundamental data (balance sheets) to estimate default probabilities.
   - Alternative Data Engine: Processes news and social sentiment (Bamford et al., 2023).
3. **Aggregation:** The Feature Store aggregates these diverse inputs into a single Risk Cube for the portfolio manager.

Figure 8 illustrates the structural differences between the streamlined HFT pipeline and the complex Multi-Asset Risk pipeline.

Figure 8. Architectural Contrast. The HFT pipeline optimizes for a linear, hardware-accelerated path to minimizing latency. The Risk pipeline optimizes for data diversity and integration, utilizing a fan-in pattern to aggregate multi-modal sources

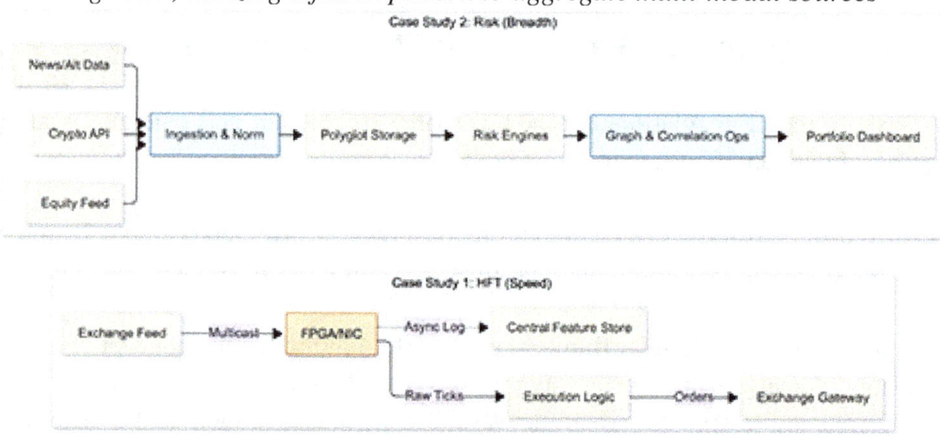

FUTURE DIRECTIONS: FROM DATA MANAGEMENT TO DATA GENERATION

As we conclude this examination of financial data engineering, it is evident that the discipline stands at an inflection point. The architectures discussed in previous sections, Lambda/Kappa pipelines, Polyglot Persistence, and Point-in-Time Feature Stores, constitute the *current* state of the art. They address the challenge of effectively managing the massive volume of historical market data (Khine & Wang, 2019). However, the next frontier in quantitative finance shifts the focus from collection to generation.

Goldstein, Spatt, and Ye (2021) observe that while the volume of financial data is increasing, the amount of *independent* history remains fixed. We have only one realization of the S&P 500's history. This scarcity of alternative histories limits the ability of modern deep learning models to generalize, often leading to overfitting. The future of financial data engineering, therefore, lies in using Generative AI to synthesize realistic market scenarios, effectively creating a multiverse of financial data for robust model training.

Synthetic Data and Generative AI

The reliance on a single historical path exposes strategies to regime overfitting. A model trained on the bull market of 2010–2020 may fail catastrophically in a high-inflation regime because it has never encountered such conditions in its training set.

Generative Adversarial Networks (GANs)

Dogariu et al. (2022) demonstrate that GANs can generate synthetic financial time series that preserve the stylized facts of real markets, volatility clustering, fat tails, and leverage effects, without merely copying historical data.

- **The Engineering Shift:** The data engineer's role expands from maintaining ETL pipelines to managing **Generative Pipelines**. Rather than simply cleaning data, the engineer trains a GAN on the historical Clean Layer to generate an infinite stream of synthetic ticks.
- **Stress Testing:** This allows risk managers to test portfolios against extreme Black Swan events that have not occurred historically but are statistically plausible (e.g., a 20% flash crash combined with a 400% spike in oil prices).

The Simulation-to-Reality Bridge

Liu et al. (2022), in their FinRL-Meta framework advocate for using these synthetic environments to train Reinforcement Learning agents. By exposing an agent to millions of synthetic market days, the agent learns robust policies that generalize better to the unseen conditions of the live market. This Sim-to-Real transfer, standard in robotics, is now becoming feasible in finance due to advances in generative data engineering.

The Multi-Modal Feature Store: Vectors and Embeddings

Traditional feature stores store scalar values (e.g., Price, Volume, RSI). However, Bamford et al. (2023) highlight that the most predictive signals often lie in unstructured data, such as earnings call transcripts, satellite imagery, and social media sentiment.

Vector Databases

To operationalize this, the Feature Store must evolve to support Vector Embeddings.

- **Implementation:** An earnings call transcript is passed through a Large Language Model (LLM) to generate a high-dimensional vector representation (e.g., 768 dimensions).
- **Retrieval:** The Feature Store must support approximate nearest neighbor (ANN) search. A query might be: Find all historical instances where the CEO's sentiment vector was similar to today's earnings call. This necessitates integrating Vector Databases (like Milvus or Pinecone) alongside the traditional Time-Series and SQL stores discussed in Section 6.

CONCLUSION

We began this chapter with the assertion that in quantitative finance, data engineering is a solvency issue. The journey from a raw, noisy exchange feed to a clean, point-in-time-correct feature vector is fraught with pitfalls, lookahead bias, timestamp misalignment, and logic duplication. The Blueprint presented here, utilizing Event-Driven Architecture, Polyglot Persistence, and rigorous DataOps validation, provides the foundation for a robust trading infrastructure. However, infrastructure alone is not the strategy. It is the *enabler* of strategy. As algorithms become more commoditized, the Engineering Alpha, the ability to process data faster, cleaner, and with greater variety than the competition, will increasingly determine the winners in the financial markets.

By treating data not as a static resource but as a dynamic product requiring strict engineering discipline, firms can close the gap between research potential and production reality, thereby securing their competitive advantage in an increasingly automated world.

REFERENCES

Arnell, L., Engström, E., Uddin, G. S., Hasan, M., & Kang, S. H. (2023). Volatility spillovers, structural breaks and uncertainty in technology sector markets. *Financial Innovation*, *9*(1), 106. Advance online publication. DOI: 10.1186/s40854-023-00502-5

Arumugam, V., & Natarajan, V. (2023). Time series modeling and forecasting using autoregressive integrated moving average and seasonal autoregressive integrated moving average models. *Instrumentation Mesure Métrologie*, *22*(4), 161–168. DOI: 10.18280/i2m.220404

Bamford, T., Coletta, A., Fons, E., Gopalakrishnan, S., Vyetrenko, S., Balch, T., & Veloso, M. (2023). Multi-modal financial time-series retrieval through latent space projections. *4th ACM International Conference on AI in Finance*, 498–506. DOI: 10.1145/3604237.3626901

Boritz, J. E., & No, W. G. (2013). The quality of interactive data: XBRL versus compustat, yahoo finance, and google finance. SSRN *Electronic Journal*. DOI: 10.2139/ssrn.2253638

Brownlees, C. T., & Gallo, G. M. (2006). Financial econometric analysis at ultra-high frequency: Data handling concerns. *Computational Statistics &amp. Computational Statistics & Data Analysis*, *51*(4), 2232–2245. DOI: 10.1016/j.csda.2006.09.030

Dogariu, M., Ştefan, L.-D., Boteanu, B. A., Lamba, C., Kim, B., & Ionescu, B. (2022). Generation of realistic synthetic financial time-series. *ACM Transactions on Multimedia Computing Communications and Applications*, *18*(4), 1–27. DOI: 10.1145/3501305

Fikri, N., Rida, M., Abghour, N., Moussaid, K., & El Omri, A. (2019). An adaptive and real-time based architecture for financial data integration. *Journal of Big Data*, *6*(1), 97. Advance online publication. DOI: 10.1186/s40537-019-0260-x

Gao, Y. (2025). Looking for the impact of entrepreneurship on regional economic resilience in China. *Sustainability (Basel)*, *17*(4), 1397. DOI: 10.3390/su17041397

Goldstein, I., Spatt, C., & Ye, M. (2021). *Big data in finance*. National Bureau of Economic Research., DOI: 10.3386/w28615

Hambly, B., Xu, R., & Yang, H. (2023). Recent advances in reinforcement learning in finance. *Mathematical Finance*, *33*(3), 437–503. DOI: 10.1111/mafi.12382

Khine, P. P., & Wang, Z. (2019). A review of polyglot persistence in the big data world. *Information (Basel), 10*(4), 141. DOI: 10.3390/info10040141

Liang, M. (2021). Optimization of quantitative financial data analysis system based on deep learning. *Complexity, 2021*(1). DOI: 10.1155/2021/5527615

Liu, X.-Y., Xia, Z., Rui, J., Gao, J., Yang, H., Zhu, M., Wang, C. D., Wang, Z., & Guo, J. (2022, November 6). *FinRL-Meta: Market environments and benchmarks for data-driven financial reinforcement learning*. arXiv.Org. https://arxiv.org/abs/2211.03107 DOI: 10.52202/068431-0134

Mantilla, P., & Dormido-Canto, S. (2023). A novel feature engineering approach for high-frequency financial data. *Engineering Applications of Artificial Intelligence, 125*, 106705. DOI: 10.1016/j.engappai.2023.106705

Sahu, S. K., Mokhade, A., & Bokde, N. D. (2023). An overview of machine learning, deep learning, and reinforcement learning-based techniques in quantitative finance: Recent progress and challenges. *Applied Sciences (Basel, Switzerland), 13*(3), 1956. DOI: 10.3390/app13031956

Singha, M. (2025, November 16). *Discovery of a 13-sharpe OOS factor: Drift regimes unlock hidden cross-sectional predictability*. arXiv.Org. https://arxiv.org/abs/2511.12490 DOI: 10.2139/ssrn.5754502

Zhang, Z., Zohren, S., & Roberts, S. (2019). DeepLOB: Deep convolutional neural networks for limit order books. *IEEE Transactions on Signal Processing, 67*(11), 3001–3012. DOI: 10.1109/TSP.2019.2907260

KEY TERMS AND DEFINITIONS

Command Query Responsibility Segregation (CQRS): An architectural pattern separates data mutation (Command) from retrieval (Query), vital for high-speed financial streams.

DataOps: An automated, process-oriented approach employed by analytics and data teams to enhance data quality and shorten the cycle time of data analytics.

Feature Store: A centralized repository that manages feature definition, storage, and access for machine learning, ensuring consistency between training and inference..

Look-Ahead Bias: A common error in backtesting where a model inadvertently uses information that would not have been available at the time the decision was supposedly made (e.g., using the day's Close price to make a decision at the Open).

Point-in-Time (PIT) Correctness: The property of a database to reconstruct the history of a dataset as it appeared at any specific moment in the past, accounting for restatements and lag.

Polyglot Persistence: The practice of using different data storage technologies (SQL, TSDB, Key-Value) to handle different data storage needs within the same application.

APPENDIX

The Financial Data Engineering Checklist

This checklist is a practical audit tool for assessing a financial data pipeline's maturity.

A.1 Ingestion & Precision

- [ ] **Timestamp Integrity:** Are all incoming ticks stamped with both *Event Time* (Exchange) and *Ingestion Time* (System) in UTC?
- [ ] **Protocol Resilience:** Does the ingestion layer use exponential backoff for REST APIs and handle slow consumer disconnects for WebSockets?
- [ ] **Normalization:** Is there a canonical internal schema (Protobuf/Avro) that abstracts vendor-specific field names?

A.2 Storage & Architecture

- [ ] **Polyglot Persistence:** Is reference data (SQL) segregated from high-velocity tick data (NoSQL/TSDB)?
- [ ] **Immutability:** Is the raw data layer append-only? Are corrections applied as new versions rather than overwrites?
- [ ] **Symbol Mapping:** Does the system use a permanent Internal_ID to handle ticker changes (e.g., FB → META) without breaking history?

A.3 Feature Engineering & Quality

- [ ] **Point-in-Time (PIT):** Does the Feature Store support As-Of queries that return the state of data *exactly* as it was known at a past timestamp (ignoring future revisions)?
- [ ] **Parity:** Are the code-generating features for backtesting identical to the code-generating features for live trading?
- [ ] **Microstructure Handling:** Are corporate actions (splits/dividends) applied via backward adjustment tables while preserving raw execution prices?

Chapter 5
Persistent Homology for Time-Value-of-Money Modeling

Jaime Aguilar-Ortiz
http://orcid.org/0009-0003-5302-1454
Universidad Politécnica de Pachuca, Mexico

Ocotlán Diáz-Parra
Universidad Politécnica de Pachuca, Mexico

Jorge A. Ruiz-Vanoye
http://orcid.org/0000-0003-4928-5716
Universidad Politécnica de Pachuca, Mexico

Francisco R. Trejo-Macotela
http://orcid.org/0000-0003-2133-3456
Universidad Politécnica de Pachuca, Mexico

Marco A. Vera-Jiménez
http://orcid.org/0009-0009-3712-1440
Universidad Politécnica de Pachuca, Mexico

Víctor M. Zamudio-García
http://orcid.org/0000-0002-4660-8025
Universidad Politéctica Metropolitana de Hidalgo, Mexico

Carlos R. Domínguez-Mayorga
http://orcid.org/0009-0007-1018-4412
Universidad Politécnica de Pachuca, Mexico

ABSTRACT

Time-value-of-money (TVM) engines can help with pricing, budgeting, and analytics around risk, but their operational stability relies on convention-level decisions often considered secondary. Calendar choice, day-count basis, compounding rules, interpolation and numerical schemes can shift valuation outputs and create reconciliation and governance risks. Here, we propose the persistent homology validation framework, using TVM outputs from scenario sweeps, and describe the

DOI: 10.4018/979-8-3373-8372-9.ch005

robustness of these outputs from the valuation-space point clouds. We analyze the risk of valuation frameworks using persistence diagrams and Betti curves, focusing on the clustering, regime shifts and cyclic patterns of equivalence that are often neglected using pointwise error assessments. We also present a new approach that integrates a flexible reproducible Python framework, topology-based diagnostics, and criteria for determining the rationality of valuation structures concerning rules of approximation before engaging such frameworks in regulated financial systems.

1. INTRODUCTION

1.1 Motivation: TVM as an auditable, deployable computational primitive

Time-value-of-money (TVM) modeling becomes a computational primitive when valuation, budgeting, and risk processes treat discounting as an executable operation instead of a formula, disjointed from other operations. In such contexts, the operation must become deterministic for data pipelines, software, and environments where the operation is deployed. As a computational primitive for TVM, a cash-flow specification, a compounding and day-count convention, and a curve representation, are mapped to discount factors and a traceable present-value computation. The issue is, therefore, mathematical and operational. Valuation drift is systematic for identical intent where teams or software libraries, for example, treat day-count conventions, compounding, interpolation, regularization, and calendars, in different ways. Such drift manifests later as hedge report discrepancies and governance issues. Auditability thus requires more than documenting a final price. Each valuation shall be restatable from explicit assumptions and curve construction steps, and intermediate results shall be clearly documented, including zero-coupon and forward rate constructs. Recent literature on curve construction and regularization has dealt with discount curves as data-centric objects and has framed the choices for discount curve construction as integral to modeling and not as trivial pre-processing (Camenzind & Filipović, 2024). From the perspective of model risk, similar conclusions have been drawn with regards to the robustness of valuation frameworks (Jokhadze & Schmidt, 2020).

Persistent homology builds upon the idea of auditability by suggesting that parameter logs alone are insufficient for explaining whether a computation has shifted to a different numerical, structural, or economic regime. A TVM engine needs diagnostics that can reveal shifts that are obscured in scalar outputs. TDA provides such a diagnostics layer. It can convert families of discount curves, rolling discount-factor trajectories, or present-value scenario clouds into multiscale signatures. These signatures provide a summary of shape and regime organization, are stable under small variations, and are sensitive to large structural changes (Wasserman, 2018; Chazal & Michel, 2021). Relevant failures in software deployments can be silent, such as an interpolation rule causing local oscillation, loss of smoothness in a curve, or a new regime in the series used for discounting. In this chapter, the goal is to add automatic topological checks to the TVM primitive. The checks would be stored alongside evidence of valuation and would be used for comparison across code versions and environments. Persistence-based methods, such as persistence landscapes, have already been used to analyze regime shifts in persistence-based representations of financial market time series (Gidea & Katz, 2018). In finance, some persistent homology applications have been used in monitoring for anomalies (Majumdar & Laha, 2020; Ravishanker & Chen, 2021). The chapter integrates computation, governance, model-risk defensibility, and auditability by describing TVM as a deployable primitive with validated and reproducible outputs.

1.2 Research gap, contributions, and article roadmap

Common implementations of time value of money (TVM) practice require reconciliations to the benchmarks of cash flows, discounting factors, and present values. While these tests are essential, TVM, as a paradigm, is versatile across instruments, libraries, and policies, and thus becomes difficult to apply. Day-count conventions, compounding, curve stripping, interpolation, extrapolation, and rounding cumulatively delineate a large dimension space of valuation results and do not affect pricing in isolation. This space is rarely assessed and omission is important because the behavior of sensitivity and stability can resemble a regime shift and become model risk in pricing and risk management (Jokhadze & Schmidt, 2020). Recent discount curve work similarly backs frameworks of rigor and statistical, structured, and iterative reinforcement learning, further bolstering the argument for uncertainty and curve fitting to the problem, and not as a side preparation step (Camenzind & Filipović, 2024). Filling this void is persistent homology, which offers tools to summarize and infer the multiscale shape of financial data (Wasserman, 2018; Chazal & Michel, 2021). This has already found application in financial data, highlighting the ability of sliding-window embeddings and persistence landscapes to identify precursors of market disruptions (Gidea & Katz, 2018). Other introductory works on the subject suggest approaches to the analysis of financial time series data via point clouds and the subsequent construction of persistence diagrams and landscapes (Ravishanker & Chen, 2021).

This article pursues an existing gap by addressing TVM as an auditable transformation over scenario manifolds constructed by cash-flow perturbations and curves. Persistent-homology is employed to describe the irregularities and discontinuities of multiscale systems and the abrupt shifts of framework conditions, which pointwise error metrics fail to capture (Chazal & Michel, 2021; Wasserman, 2018). The article's contribution is threefold. It first conveys how different aspects of TVM scenario generation (curve stripping, interpolation, and conventions) can be modeled as point-cloud structures. It second layers a persistence-based approach of comparing discounting frameworks through diagrams, landscapes, and stability-aware distances. It third designs an assessment framework for financial model risk that interprets topological changes as structural model changes rather than as inconsequential numerical changes (Jokhadze & Schmidt, 2020; Gidea & Katz, 2018). The article explains persistent homology for multiscale TVM behavior; the scenario and filtration design; a reproducible implementation; and modeling choices in the results in the order that is written. The final sections include risk governance, auditability, and possible modifications in the future.

2. THEORETICAL FOUNDATIONS

2.1 TVM modeling as a scenario-space operator

TVM can be expressed as a deterministic operator over a scenario space that brings together contractual cash flows, time representation, day-count and compounding rules, and the discount-curve object. Let a scenario be denoted by $s = \left(\{(C_i, t_i)\}_{i=1}^{n}, t_0, dc, cal, \theta\right)$, where C_i are dated flows, t_0 is the valuation time, dc and cal encode the year-fraction and calendar rules, and θ parameterizes the discount curve. The year-fraction mapping converts real dates into model time through $\tau_i = YearFrac\left(t_0, t_i; dc, cal\right)$, and the PV operator discounts each scenario-time cash flow through the discount factor $D(\bullet)$: $PV(s) = \sum_{i=1}^{n} C_i D\left(\tau_i; \theta\right)$. In continuous time, if θ is represented by a short-rate curve $r(\bullet)$, the discount factor becomes $D(t; r) = exp\left(-\int_0^t r(u)du\right)$. When θ is represented by a yield $y(\tau)$ and compounding frequency m, the discrete analogue $D(r; y, m) = (1 + y(\tau)/m)^{-m\tau}$ is recovered, together with the log-derivative relation to forward rates, $f(t) = -\frac{d}{dt} Ln\, D\left(t\right)$.

This relationship is critical when the scenario space consists of curve-building and interpolation constraints, as opposed to a fixed lookup table. From this operator perspective, the auditability of a valuation as a mathematical property is traced, as each valuation is a functional trace of (dc, cal, m, θ) and the cash-flow schedule. In this case, the implementation differences can be tested as an operator hypothesis, rather than informal differences in the outputs (Camenzind & Filipović, 2024; Filipović et al., 2025). When the forward-rate dynamics need to be consistent across all the maturities and points in time, the curve component, θ, can also be constrained to meet the requirements of dynamic consistency, thereby making TVM both computable and structurally consistent (Wu & Jarrow, 2024). Since the operator separates the modeling assumptions from the numerical aspects, changes in θ, compounding, or the time conventions will bring changes in the value of PV(s) and the corresponding sensitivity functionals. This design facilitates the implementation of stress testing in a consistent manner rather than a one-off value test (Jokhadze & Schmidt, 2020).

When TVM is an described operator on scenario space, the collection of scenarios $\{s_j\}_{j=1}^{N}$ is a domain of which geometry and topology can be studied. A feasible way to implement this would be to associate every scenario to risk signal-oriented and price-oriented feature vectors using summary paths of discount factor, duration, convexity, price responses to small changes in duration (DV01), as well as curve shocks. We represent this feature transformation as follows in Equation (1):

$$\Phi(s) = (PV(s), FV(s), DV01(s), Dur(s), Conv(s), \ldots) \tag{1}$$

This construction produces a point cloud in $\mathbb{R}^d$: $X = \{\Phi(s_j)\}_{j=1}^{N}$. Persistent homology then studies how the scenario-induced outputs organize across scales by building a filtration, commonly a Vietoris-Rips filtration on X, defined in Equation (2) as follows:

$$VR_\varepsilon(X) = \{\sigma \subset X : \|x_p - x_q\| \leq \varepsilon \, for \, all \, x_p, x_q \in \sigma\} \tag{2}$$

The filtration tracks the birth and death of a topological feature in k-th dimensional homology by way of the persistence diagram $Dgm_k(X) = \{(b_l, d_l)\}_l$. In the TVM context, the connected components in Dgm_0 may indicate valuation regimes caused by convention switches (e.g. day-count, compounding or calendar rules) or by clusters of curve shapes. The presence of one-dimensional cycles in Dgm_1 may point to loops in the space of outcomes caused by the interplay between maturity, rates, and compounding, which may be difficult to identify in marginal plots. The stability of persistent homology is its strength. Since small changes to rates, dates, and/or cash-flows typically yield small changes to persistent summaries, topological features may be used as persistent artifacts in regression tests for auditable deployments (Wasserman, 2018; Chazal & Michel, 2021). In finance, topological descriptors have been applied in capturing structural changes and regime signatures, reinforcing the notion that topology can describe geometries with economic significance, as opposed to merely being decorative (Gidea & Katz, 2018; Majumdar & Laha, 2020). Recent reviews have also identified applicable frameworks for time-series and dynamical systems, corroborating the use of persistent homology as a validation primitive alongside other TVM outputs (Shah et al., 2025).

2.2 Persistent homology for multiscale structural validation

By transforming the scenario space exhibited by TVM computations into a filtration, persistent homology identifies topological summaries that separate robust structures from artifacts. For example, when each cash-flow stream or discounted-value path is represented by the point $x_i \in \mathbb{R}^d$, (e.g. by discount-factor vectors, yield-curve parameterizations, or features of the discounted trajectories), one begins analysis at a metric space (X, d). A simplicial complex is then constructed at a specific scale ε, enabling analysis of topological constructs at varying resolutions (Wasserman, 2018; Chazal & Michel, 2021). Of the different types of topological constructions, the Vietoris-Rips filtration supports analysis the best because it concerns itself only with pair-wise distances. Thus, it lends itself to the computational designs that measure the dissimilarities of scenarios for the purposes of stress testing or sensitivity analysis (Ravishanker & Chen, 2021). Its use is exemplified in Equation (3).

$$VR_{\mathscr{E}}(X) = \{\sigma \subseteq X : d(x,y) \leq \varepsilon for\ all\ x, y \in \sigma\}, \varepsilon \geq 0. \quad (3)$$

As ε increases, inclusions $VR_{\varepsilon} \rightarrow VR_{\varepsilon'}$ induce homology maps $H_k(VR_{\varepsilon}) \rightarrow H_k(VR_{\varepsilon'})$ and produce the births and deaths of k-dimensional features: connected components for $k = 0$, loops for $k = 1$, and higher-order voids for $k \geq 2$. These features are summarized in persistence diagrams or equivalent functional representations (Chazal & Michel, 2021; Ravishanker & Chen, 2021). The Betti number of order k at scale ε and the corresponding persistence diagram are given in Equation (4):

$$\beta_k(\varepsilon) = rank\left(H_k(VR_{\varepsilon}(X))\right), Dgm_k = \left\{(b_i, d_i)\right\}_{i \in I} \subset \mathbb{R}^2. \quad (4)$$

Within TVM, these summaries act as validation operators. A structure that dominates a broad range of $\mathscr{E}$, for instance, a cluster of discounted outcomes, a loop related to regime-switching, or an absence of data denoting multi-regime separation, is likely to represent multi-scale structures rather than discretization artifacts of the scenario grid. This understanding is similar to time series TDA pipelines that use sliding-window embeddings and scale filtrations to derive stable geometric and topological signatures of time series dynamics (Ravishanker & Chen, 2021; Shah et al., 2025). Furthermore, this view shows consistency with the financial domain, where persistent elements are used to demarcate the structural phases and transitory events (Majumdar & Laha, 2020).

A multiscale validation claim can be considered credible only when the topological summaries remain constant when subjected to perturbations caused by numerical noise, sampling variability, or minor adjustments to scenario parameters. This is the domain of persistent homology. It sets a limit for the movement of diagrams when data are perturbed and allows distance-based comparisons among sets of scenarios, calibration protocols, or families of stress tests (Chazal & Michel, 2021; Wang et al., 2024). In practice, diagrams are compared through distances, the most notable of which is the bottleneck distance, d_B. Consequently, a validation rule can specify small perturbations within a class, while requiring a larger margin of separation across classes, thereby converting shape into a verifiable structural criterion. The bottleneck distance is represented as follows in Equation (5):

$$d_B(D,E) = \inf_{\gamma:D\to E}\sup_{p\in D}\|p - \gamma(p)\|_\infty. \tag{5}$$

When the scenario space is changed from X to Y due to minor rate shocks, slight changes in cash-flow timing, or changes in the Monte Carlo paths, stability theorems show us that persistent features will not change at will. There is a metric where the changes are controlled to the size of the perturbation, which implies the validity of the feature diagrams and the functional surrogates, not just as descriptive plots (Chazal & Michel, 2021; Wang et al., 2024). In the validation of structures, three checks are combined: perturbation and scale invariances are validated through persistence summaries and \beta_k(\varepsilon); perturbation invariance is validated through the d_B metric and, if necessary, the Wasserstein metric; and representation invariances are validated through rank functions and other functional embeddings that provide measures of uncertainty (Wang et al., 2024). For TVM, persistent features validate scenario families segmentation, persistent loops validate persistence and path-dependent regime switching, and persistence-based signatures validate the existence of patterns in the scenario space that are not scale-artefacts (Majumdar & Laha, 2020; Chazal, Michel, & Reise, 2025).

2.3 Topological fidelity and the role of approximation/representation learning

Topological fidelity examines if approximations in a TVM pipeline maintain the multi-modal shape of the scenario space which is used in the valuation, stress-testing, and model risk governance. In a deployment setting, TVM is more than a closed analytical expression. It is an operator on a set of scenarios – on curves, cash-flow graphs, and states of hazards or rates – whose geometry may represent (i) changes in convexity; (ii) clusters of yield curves; (iii) shifts from low-rate to high-rate environments (Camenzind & Filipović, 2024). Because of the finite nature of observing scenario spaces, each layer in the pipeline can alter proximity and modify the filtrations in persistent homology. In TVM, the primitive valuation map PV, is typically defined with discounting, or spot and forward rates. A standard discrete approximation is shown in (6):

Topological fidelity examines if approximations in TVM pipelines alter the multiscale structure of the scenario space in the same way. When deployed, TVM does not exist as a closed-form solution. Rather, TVM acts on a collection of scenarios: curves, cash-flow graphs, and hazard or state rates, each of which may exhibit convexity, yield-curve clustering, or low/high-rate switching (Camenzind & Filipović, 2024). Each step may transform the neighborhood relations of the operational space, and alter the order structures, shape, and dimensions used by persistent homology, which can be illustrated by the scenario space as seen through sampling, extrapolation and numeric representation. The primitive valuation map (PV) in TVM typically expresses by way of discount factors or spot and forward rates. An example of a discrete version of this is in (6):

$$PV(\omega) = \sum_{t=1}^{T} C_t(\omega) D_t(\omega),\ D_t(\omega) = exp\left(-\int_o^t r(u,\omega)du\right), \tag{6}$$

Equation (6) describes scenarios indexed by ω, and D_t is a scenario-dependent discount factor. Consider scenarios embedded as a point cloud, $= \{x_i\}_{i=1}^{n} \subset \mathbb{R}^d$, for example, using forward-rate windows, cash-flow signatures, or curve features. Topological validation identifies whether approximations $\widetilde{X}$, created by compression, surrogate modeling, or smoothing, maintain persistent invariants given the chosen filtration (Chazal & Michel, 2021; Wasserman, 2018). A common choice is the Vietoris-Rips filtration, VR_\varepsilon(X). Betti curves \beta_k\ as well as persistence diagrams and the multiscale structure are outlined in Equation (7):

$$\beta_k(\varepsilon) = rank\ H_k\left(VR_\varepsilon(X)\right), Dgm_k(X) = \left\{\left(b_i, d_i\right)\right\}_i \subset \mathbb{R}^2. \tag{7}$$

Topological fidelity $\mathcal{F}_k$ can thus be measured by stability-aware distances between the summaries of X and $\widetilde{X}$. A diagram distance of the bottleneck or Wasserstein type gives the operational formulation of Equation (8):

$$\mathcal{F}_k\left(X, \widehat{X}\right) = d\left(\left(Dgm_k(X), Dgm_k\left(\widehat{X}\right)\right),\right. \tag{8}$$

A low value of $\mathcal{F}_k$ in Equation (8) means that the approximation has preserved the birth and death scales of topological events that separate valuation regimes. This is important for financial time series, where the topology has captured regime shifts and crash-like disruptive changes, which are difficult to represent in terms of local moments (Gidea & Katz, 2018). This also applies to multivariate temporal classification, where persistence-based descriptors are informative in the presence of noise and sampling variability (Majumdar & Laha, 2020).

Representation learning encompasses a variety of methods that enable the compression, denoising, and normalization of scenario objects, while explicitly controlling which structural information is preserved. TVM pipelines often require low-dimensional and low-latency representations of curves and path-dependent objects to facilitate calibration, simulation, and monitoring. However, naive embeddings often result in topological aliasing, in which distinct regimes become collapsed, and different scenario families become undistinguishably compressed. A more rigorous approach couples reconstruction or forecasting losses with persistent-homology regularizers that penalize topology-breaking embeddings (Chen et al., 2023; Pun et al., 2022). For an encoder-decoder pair $f_\theta : \mathbb{R}^d \to \mathbb{R}^m$ and $g_\theta : \mathbb{R}^d \to \mathbb{R}^m$, a topology-aware objective over a batch X can be written in Equation (9) as follows:

$$\min_{\theta,\phi} \underbrace{\frac{1}{n}\sum_{i=1} \left\| x_i - g_\phi\left(f_\phi\left(x_i\right)\right)\right\|_2^2}_{\mathscr{L}_{rec}} + \lambda \sum_{k\in\mathscr{K}} \underbrace{d\left(Dgm_k(X), Dgm_k\left(f_\theta(X)\right)\right)}_{\mathscr{L}^{(k)}_{topo}}, \tag{9}$$

In Equation (9), the set $\mathscr{K} \subset \{0,1,2,\dots\}$ selects the homology dimensions that encode the regimes of interest, such as components for $k = 0$ and loops for $k = 1$. Because of these requirements, efficient persistent-homology computation, and scalable approximations of persistent-homology, become architectural necessities rather than optional components. Malott et al. (2023) established that topology-regularized training and multiscale validation require recurrent computations of diagrams and distance evaluations. Drawing from approximation theory, the trade-off between the stability of the geometric features induced and the expressiveness of the encoders is identified (Grohs & Kutyniok, 2022).

3. METHODOLOGY

3.1 Scenario design, parameter sweeps, and convention controls

The design of scenarios formally establishes the space in which every experiment is a reproducible tuple that binds the specification of cash-flows to a representation of interest rates or discounting, and an articulation of valuation conventions. Within this design, each TVM output can be traced to a specific instance, which can be regenerated under the same seed and controls. Thus, parameter sweeps are not simple loops over a list of values. They are sampling schemes of a parameter subdomain $\Theta \subset \mathbb{R}^p$. The purpose of the schemes is to identify structural regimes (e.g., low versus high, short versus long, smooth versus kink, etc.), while enabling a sensitivity analysis and a validation over multiple scales. The sweep can be defined as a full factorial design when a coverage of interactions is of primary importance or a space filling design when high dimensionality makes exhaustive grids infeasible (Saltelli et al., 2019). The approach also bounds the sweep to economically meaningful priors and market-consistent admissibility, including monotonic discounting, no-arbitrage when curves are flexed or smoothed. When discounting curves are inferred, stressed, or tested, extraction, interpolation or extrapolation are considered experimental degrees of freedom (Camenzind & Filipović, 2024; Filipović et al., 2025; Akiyama & Matsuyama, 2025). The generator maps each scenario s to a feature vector $\phi(s)$ later for topological scrutiny, while keeping the raw outputs for PV, IRR, and discount factors for auditing and deployment (Chazal & Michel, 2021). The scenario space can be expressed in Equation (10) as:

$$\Theta_{grid} = \prod_{j=1}^{p}\left\{\theta_{j,1}, \ldots, \theta_{j,m_j}\right\}, \mathcal{S} = \Theta \times \mathcal{K} \times \mathcal{C}, X = \{\phi(s): s \in \mathcal{S}\} \subset \mathbb{R}^d, \quad (10)$$

Present value is expressed in Equation (11):

$$PV(t_0; s) = \sum_{i=1} C_i(s) P(t_0, t_i \theta_s, c_s), \quad (11)$$

Under the given convention, discount factors are expressed in Equation (12):

$$P(t_0, t_i r, m, c) = \left(1 + \frac{r}{m}\right)^{-mr(t_0, t_i; c)} \text{ or } P(t_0, t_i r, c) = exp(-r\tau(t_0, t_i; c)). \quad (12)$$

Convention controls are implemented in the same manner as experimental controls. This is because the day count, compounding frequency, business day adjustment, calendar rules, rounding, and other aspects change both the timing of cash flows and the effective horizon for discounting. If such factors are allowed to vary across different runs, they may produce misleading structural separations in the framework. To combat this, the cash-flow engine and the conventions layer $c \in \mathcal{C}$, are kept separate. This allows the same economic scenario θ, k to be evaluated multiple times, each time with different conventions within a limited range. This also allows invariance and sensitivity tests, where (θ, k) remains constant and c is held constant, respectively. While in the field of fixed-income, day count variability and uneven coupon intervals are well known as sources of valuation variation. This warrants the classification of conventions as categorical factors in the sweep design (Djatschenko, 2019). Stress realism is sustained by further generators. These include empirical

ESG constructs, which maintain cross-factor relation in turbulent periods (Lee et al., 2021), and generative neural models, which improve tail behavior while being subjected to back tests and plausibility filters (Flaig & Junike, 2022). Controls on curve shape, such as how smoothing is applied, where interpolation nodes are set, and other methods of regularization, are included in the conventions and representation surface. These methods also decide if changes that are detected are economic or representational, which is important when topological summaries are applied to the point cloud that is scenario-induced, since representation artifacts may be mistaken for economic changes (Dayarathne & Thayasiwam, 2024; Chazal & Michel, 2021). As such, the year-fraction and convention gap may be expressed as in Equation (13):

$$\tau\left(t_0, t_i; c\right) = YearFrac_c\left(t_0, t_i\right),\ \Delta_{conv}(\theta, k; c, c') = \left|PV\left(t_0; \theta, k, c\right) - PV\left(t_0; \theta, k, c'\right)\right|, \tag{13}$$

The convention layer is represented in Equation (14):

$$\mathscr{C} = \{DCC, Compounding, BDC, Calendar, Rounding\}, \tag{14}$$

Control isolation is then expressed in Equation (15):

$$control\ isolation: (\theta, k)\ fixed \Longrightarrow c\ swept; or\ c\ fixed \Rightarrow \theta\ swept \tag{15}$$

3.2 Topological pipeline, metrics, and statistical validation strategy

The first step of the topological pipeline transforms all controlled TVM runs - defined by the scenario sweep grid and some convention parameters - into a metric object that is reproducibly comparable. Each scenario s_i is represented by the feature vector $x_i \in \mathbb{R}^d$, which embeds the structure of the discount factor and the present value along with the temporal structure of the following: spot versus forward curves, and cash-flow signatures with respect to the compounding and day-count conventions. When the structure is temporal and is represented in a sequence, local temporal perturbations can be captured by employing a time-delay embedding or a sliding window embedding. These perturbations are then interpreted by the embedding as geometric perturbations in the embedding space (Ravishanker & Chen, 2021; Gidea & Katz, 2018; Majumdar & Laha, 2020). The resulting point cloud $X = \{x_i\}_{i=1}^{n}$, is then subjected to a filtration operator, which in the context of general metric data, is most often the Vietoris-Rips construction. Given the structural phenomena of the audit under consideration (i.e., connectivity, loops, voids), persistent homology is computed in a dimension $k \in \{0,1,2\}$. For large parameter sweeps and repeated audit style recomputations, the topology step relies on the memory/time tradeoff and performance persistent homology (Bauer, 2021; Tralie, Saul, & Bar-On, 2018). Credit is also due for the step remaining deployable and not a one-off experiment (Malott et al., 2023; Chazal & Michel, 2021). Point cloud and metric are defined by the following equations in (16):

$$X = \{x_i = \phi(s_i) \in \mathbb{R}^d\}_{i=1}^{n}, d(x_i, x_j) = \|x_i - x_j\| \ (\textit{or any validated metrix}). \quad (16)$$

The Vietoris-Rips complex is then given in Equation (17):

$$VR_\varepsilon(X) = \left\{\sigma \subseteq X{:}d(x_i,x_j) \leq \varepsilon \, \forall x_i,x_j \in \sigma\right\}, \varepsilon \geq 0, \quad (17)$$

This yields the persistence diagram and Betti numbers in Equation (18):

$$Dgm_k(X) = \left\{(b_i,d_i)\right\}_i \subset \mathbb{R}^2, \beta_k(\varepsilon) = rank\, H_k\left(VR_\varepsilon(X)\right). \quad (18)$$

The validation strategy presents two interwoven layers. The geometric layer assesses topology across scenarios, utilizing stable distances and functional summaries. The inferential layer portrays these assessments as traceable statistical statements with predictable error. Within the geometric layer, persistence diagrams and their distance metrics, d_B bottleneck and p-Wasserstein W_p, are evaluated. Alternatively, diagrams may be embedded in Banach-space frameworks, such as persistence landscapes, Betti curves, vector summaries, and images. Within the geometric layer, the multiscale essence of persistence is retained while employing mean, variance, functional norms, classifiers, and hypothesis tests (Hensel, Moor, & Rieck, 2021; Pun et al., 2022). In the inferential layer, the use of resampling and randomization assesses the impact of sampling, windowing, and stochastic optimization on representation learning and the emergence of topological differences. For functional summaries, the bootstrap and subsampling methods yield bands of uncertainty (Vejdemo-Johansson & Mukherjee, 2022). For groups that are controlled under conventional means, the separability is tested through vector summaries of diagrams under a permutation framework (Islambekov & Pathirana, 2024). Pipelines demonstrate persistence statistics and their application in real-world generation of time-series (Abdallah et al., 2022). For normalized persistence summaries, near or universal null habitual behavior may be used as a benchmark when stronger null calibration is necessary (Bobrowski & Skraba, 2023). Rank-function approaches may also be used for stability-based reasoning (Wang et al., 2024). For instance, the bottleneck distance is expressed as in Equation (19):

$$d_B(D,E) = \inf_{\gamma} \sup_{p \in D} \|p - \gamma(p)\|_\infty \tag{19}$$

The p-Wasserstein distance is an alternative, as shown in Equation (20):

$$W_p(D,E) = \left(\inf_{\gamma} \sum_{p \in D} \|p - \gamma(p)\|_\infty^p \right)^{1/p}. \tag{20}$$

A simple functional test statistic can be expressed in Equation (21):

$$T = \|\bar{\lambda}^{(A)} - \bar{\lambda}^{(B)}\|_{L^2} \left(test\ statistic\ and\ L_2\ norm\right), \tag{21}$$

The permutation-calibrated p-value is defined in Equation (22):

$$p = \mathbb{P}_\pi\left(T_\pi \geq T_{obs}\right) (p - value, permutation\ calibration). \tag{22}$$

4. COMPUTATIONAL ARCHITECTURE

4.1 Reproducible implementation blueprint and interoperability considerations

A persistent-homology-based TVM modeling blueprint should utilize a configuration-driven research software artifact. This design provides determinism across numerical outputs. Each output stems from a tuple: documented data, established conventions, specified parameters, and controlled randomness, and is unaffected by interactive sessions. A survey of computational notebooks advocates for auditable scripts to counter the adverse effects of hidden state, execution order, and environmental drift (Pimentel et al., 2019; Trisovic et al., 2022; Schoch et al., 2024). The blueprint design employs a single experimental entry point. This entry point is available from a command line interface, as well as from a Python application programming interface. The entry point interprets scenario grids (convention selection, rules for compounding, day-count rules, curve and discount construction, and cash-flow calendars) as fixed configurations. The main execution pipeline then performs three interconnected tasks: TVM valuation, construction of a multiscale filtration across scenario-space, and persistent homology with statistical calibration. In support of traceability, each configuration is run with a unique identifier. This is based on a content hash of the code, configuration, and input data. This established environment determines the tables and figures, as expressed in Equation (23):

$$h = SHA256\,(code \| config \| data \| env). \tag{23}$$

Computational topology demonstrates sensitivity to some phenomena such as metric normalization, and ordering tie-breaking in filtration. Consequently, the pipeline captures the distance metric, the rules of preprocessing, the parameters of normalization, and the settings of simplxes each time they are run. Moreover, it should rely on a persistent homology engine that has been benchmarked as opposed to an ad hoc version (Bauer, 2021). The same can be said for the sanctity of the finance layer. The modules of discounting and curve construction should encapsulate the choices of interpolation, smoothing and conventions, as they impact the present values, and the topological shape of the geometry that the validation process engages (Camenzind & Filipović, 2024). The research of computer systems can be a part of the isolated, authenticated, and improved preservation of research over time and across different machines (Nüst et al., 2020).

Interoperability should operate in two dimensions, research software, and portable workflow design. The same TVM-TDA primitive should run in a replication package, a classroom, and a production risk platform with no semantic drift. This also necessitates machine-readable metadata (license, version, citation, and dependency graphs, along with execution entry points), stable I/O schema with persistent identifiers. These elements create a support structure for the meaningful reuse of output objects (Barker et al., 2022). In the design, the blueprint substantively constrains data flow contracts for cash flows, curves, scenario parameters, and topological summaries (including persistence diagrams, Betti curves, Wasserstein distances, and calibrated p-values). The data should be serialized in an open format (cvs, or parquet for tabular data, json, or yaml for configurations, and when necessary, a compact binary format). Independent implementations can then re-ingest the results without the need of engineering the output structure. Since computational science is evolving to disseminate executable workflows along with the data, the TVM-TDA pipeline is required to be exportable with provenance and a registrational integration with workflow-level FAIR practices (Goble et al., 2020; Wilkinson et al., 2025). Version registration in a workflow registry aids reuse and cross-platform implementation while maintaining repository and container links (Gustafsson et al., 2025). Within the scope of the article, this requirement of interoperability is important, TVM's primitive is only auditable when the structural validation pipeline is reproduced by third parties, not when the terminal present values are reproduced.

5. RESULTS AND ANALYSIS

5.1 Baseline TVM performance and convention-induced sensitivity landscapes

This section identifies a foundational number for TVM valuation and analyzes how convention preference transforms sensitivity. To offer a governance anchor for future comparisons, present value, duration, and convexity are noted with a reference convention that is fixed. The following analysis alters the day-count, compounding, and calendar conventions across all maturities and parallel shifts in the curves. The central effects and tail effects are distinguished such that convention-induced shifts are considered operational model risk as opposed to an isolated gap in pricing. As quality controls, admissibility and calendar diagnostics are used to ensure that the subsequent topological analysis is built on legitimate assumptions and limited convention variance.

Table 1. Conventional sensitivity table (TVM). The baseline ACT/365-annual convention and alternatives ACT/360 and semiannual conventions (with interpolation, rounding, business-day adjustment, and calendar held constant) report present value (PV), duration, and convexity by maturity

Maturity_years	convention	day_count	compounding	interpolation	Rounding_decimals	business_day_adjustment	Calendar_name	pv	duration	convexity
1	baseline	ACT/365	annual	linear	12	modified_following	MX_like	97.5687	0.9973	0.9945
1	alt_daycount	ACT/360	annual	linear	12	modified_following	MX_like	97.5308	1.0111	1.0223
1	alt_compounding	ACT/365	semiannual	linear	12	modified_following	MX_like	97.5539	0.9973	0.9945
5	baseline	ACT/365	annual	linear	12	modified_following	MX_like	85.2863	5.0000	25.0000
5	alt_daycount	ACT/360	annual	linear	12	modified_following	MX_like	85.0839	5.0694	25.6993
5	alt_compounding	ACT/365	semiannual	linear	12	modified_following	MX_like	85.1783	5.0000	25.0000
10	baseline	ACT/365	annual	linear	12	modified_following	MX_like	71.6225	10.0000	100.0000
10	alt_daycount	ACT/360	annual	linear	12	modified_following	MX_like	71.2837	10.1389	102.7971
10	alt_compounding	ACT/365	semiannual	linear	12	modified_following	MX_like	71.4233	10.0000	100.0000
20	baseline	ACT/365	annual	linear	12	modified_following	MX_like	50.7451	20.0000	400.0000

continued on following page

Table 1. Continued

Maturity _years	convention	day_ count	compound-ing	interpol-ation	Rounding _decimals	business_ day _adjust-ment	Calendar _name	pv	duration	convexity
20	alt_daycount	ACT/360	annual	linear	12	modified_ following	MX_like	50.2646	20.2778	411.1883
20	alt_comp-ounding	ACT/365	semiannual	linear	12	modified_ following	MX_like	50.4540	20.0000	400.0000
30	baseline	ACT/365	annual	linear	12	modified_ following	MX_like	35.9704	30.0027	900.1644
30	alt_daycount	ACT/360	annual	linear	12	modified_ following	MX_like	35.4632	30.4194	925.3426
30	alt_comp-ounding	ACT/365	semiannual	linear	12	modified_ following	MX_like	35.6585	30.0027	900.1644

Table 1 needs to be analyzed by maturity block. The three rows detail how the change in day count or compounding leads to changes in PV, duration, and convexity with the other assumptions held constant. The pattern is economically relevant because although different conventions do lead to different prices, they also change first- and second-order exposures. In fact, the difference along the maturity curve is greater for longer maturities, indicating that at the long end of the curve greater control of conventions is warranted for hedge sizing, limit monitoring, and cross-product reporting.

Figure 1. Day-count convention variability sensitiveness heatmap. This heatmap shows the relative present value variation when the baseline day-count rule changes as maturities and parallel shifts are introduced. Compounding, interpolation, rounding precision, business-day and calendar adjustments, and curves are held constant.

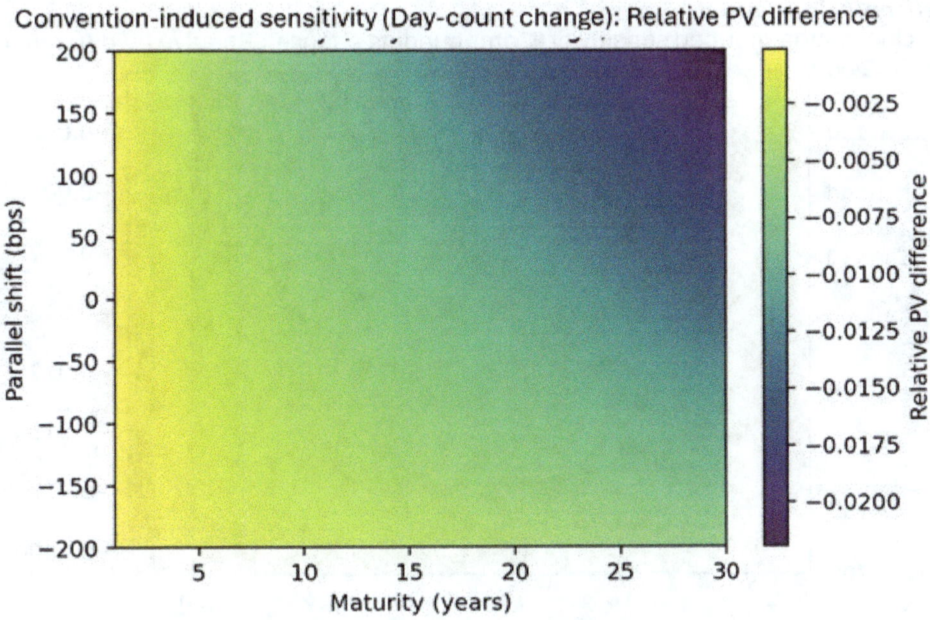

In Figure 1, maturity is illustrated along the horizontal axis, and parallel shift along the vertical axis. The color gradient signifies the relative present value loss resulting from the substitution of the day-count rule, all the while maintaining the other modeling assumptions. The heatmap presents a state-dependent effect; the drift is more pronounced at longer tenors and in more stressed situations, rather than demonstrating a stable, constant offset. This interpretation further justifies the governance rules that correlate the limits of tolerance and the procedures of escalation with both maturity and the intensity of the shock.

Figure 2. Compounding convention sensitivity heatmap. The heatmap exhibits the PV deviation as a function of changes in compounding frequency vis-a-vis the baseline across a matrix of maturities and uniform shifts in the curve, with day count, interpolation, rounding, precision, business-day adjustments, and calendar effects held constant.

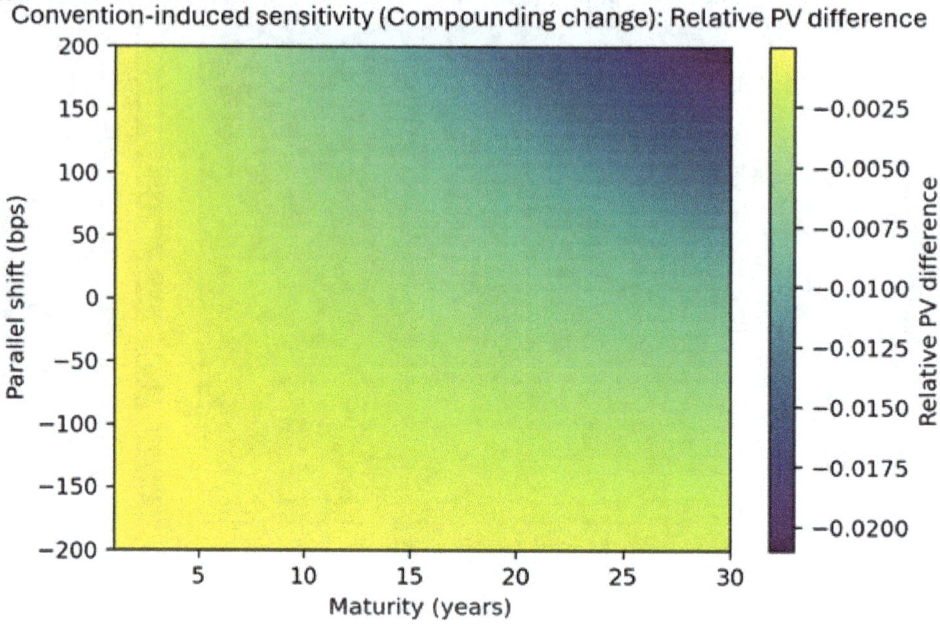

Figure 2 shows the areas that result in the greatest relative PV drift when the compounding frequency is changed. The drift is nonlinear due to the tenor effect and rate shock. In this case, compounding should be viewed as a configurable factor in the pricing policy and the calibration of hedge ratio and stressed risk reporting, particularly for long-dated instruments.

Table 2. Convention sensitivity summary. Summary statistics are reported for absolute relative PV differences against the baseline for day-count and compounding changes, computed across the maturity and parallel-shift scenario grid with interpolation, rounding, business-day rules, and calendar fixed

comparison	mean_abs_rel_diff	median_abs_rel_diff	p95_abs_rel_diff	max_abs_rel_diff
baseline vs alt_daycount	0.00737	0.00647	0.01686	0.02193
baseline vs alt_compounding	0.00488	0.00340	0.01423	0.02102

Table 2 summarizes the two sensitivity surfaces and illustrates their results in a more distanced manner. Mean and median values account for ordinary drift, while p95 and the maximum describe tail exposure. The central vs. upper-tail impact differentiation shows that, in 'normal' situations, convention risk tends to be rather trivial, but may actually be operationally material for some specific maturities and/or shocks. These summaries can therefore be adapted for tolerance design, exception handling, and buffer calibration.

Table 3. Calendar adjustment effect summary. The table reports mean and median signed PV differences, together with absolute tail metrics, for business-day calendar adjustment versus no-calendar treatment, with day count, compounding, interpolation, and rounding held fixed

mean_pv_diff_calendar_vs_none	median_pv_diff_calendar_vs_none	p95_abs_pv_diff_calendar_vs_none	max_abs_pv_diff_calendar_vs_none
-0.0021	-0.0021	0.0048	0.0068

Table 3 clarifies the distinction between the direction and magnitude of the calendar effect. Mean and median signed differences represent bias, while p95 and maximum absolute deviations describe tail exposure. This distinction is important because average effects that are close to zero can mask instances of significant deviations. Since the calendar rule identifies a relevant deviation, it should be treated as an operational control within valuation policy, reconciliation thresholds, and risk-reporting standards.

Figure 3. Calendar effects histogram. Distribution of PV differences between business-day-adjusted and unadjusted cash-flow schedules under fixed day count, compounding, interpolation, rounding precision, and calendar specification across the scenario set.

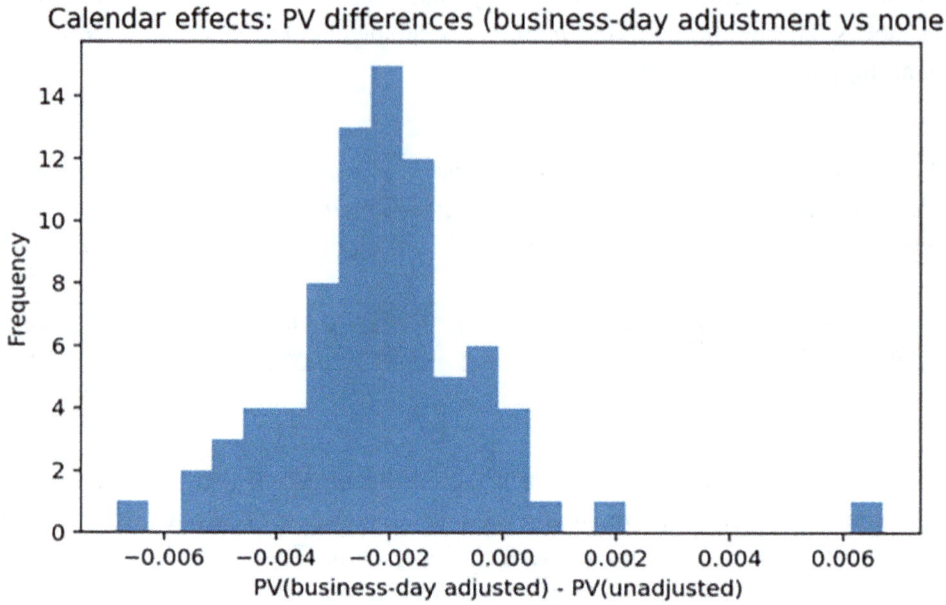

Figure 3 illustrates the discrepancy between adjusted and unadjusted schedules in terms of PV. Its proximity to zero, along with residual tail observations, indicates that calendar treatment may create asymmetric, scenario-dependent, disruptive 'noise' (as opposed to merely stochastic variations). Consequently, the histogram assists in establishing reconciliation thresholds that differentiate customary schedule changes from extraordinary calendar variations.

Table 4. Admissibility and calendar diagnostics. Quality-control summary of scenario count, admissible fraction, repaired fraction, and average calendar adjustments per scenario for baseline and alternative day-count groups under fixed compounding, interpolation, rounding precision, and business-day conventions

group	n	fraction_ admissible	fraction_ repaired	avg_calendar_ adjustments_per_scenario
alt_daycount	160	1	0	125.3688
baseline	160	1	0	124.8375

Table 4 first validates scenario quality by reporting the admissible and repaired fractions, and then the average number of calendar adjustments per scenario. Since all scenarios are admissible and none are repaired, the observed PV differences are attributed to controlled convention effects and not data contamination. The adjustment count also describes the operational burden imposed by the calendar rules. This count can be tracked as part of the operational governance of production-grade schedules.

5.2 Persistent-homology signatures of valuation spaces

In this section, we analyze the output cloud for valuation as a geometric construct and present persistent-homology signatures for H_0 and H_1, with H_2 assessed when relevant. These diagnostics capture loop structures, interconnectivity, and multiscale patterns over deliberately perturbed conventions. Persistence diagrams, Betti curves with embedded uncertainty, and Wasserstein distances quantify the structural changes of pruned valuation beyond pointwise persistence value (PV) drift. The subsequent permutation tests determine whether changes in topological structures are statistically significant when compared to the random (null) permutation of the convention groups.

Figure 4. Valuation-space PCA by convention group. Two-dimensional PCA projection of the valuation-feature space, with points colored by convention group (baseline versus alternative day count) under fixed compounding, interpolation, rounding precision, business-day adjustment, and calendar choices.

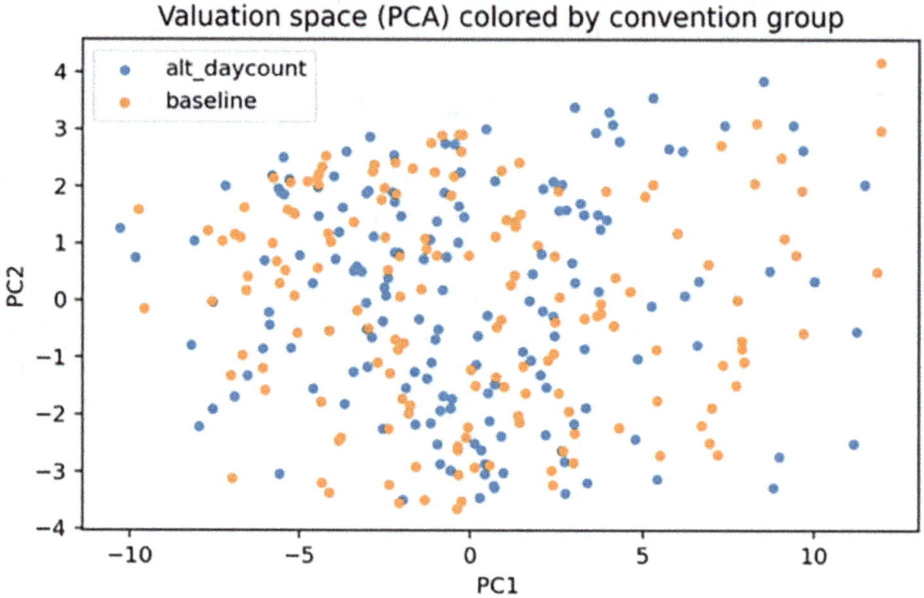

Figure 4 gives a 2D view of the valuation-feature cloud. When the two colors are distinguishably separate on the PC1-PC2 plane, then the change in conventions altered scenario similarity; if the colors overlap, the groups are situated in the same local geometry in regard to the controls. This figure functions as an exploratory bridge between scalar sensitivity and persistent homology, since it shows whether the choice in conventions moves the scenarios into different local neighborhoods before filtration is applied.

Table 5. Topological summaries by convention group. Persistent-homology summary statistics for the valuation-space point cloud are reported by group and homology dimension, including finite feature counts and persistence aggregates under fixed valuation assumptions and controlled convention variation

group	homology_ dim	n_features_ finite	total_ persistence	max_ persistence	median_ persistence
alt_daycount	0	59	96.3827	5.4929	1.4842
alt_daycount	1	18	4.2266	0.6703	0.1021
alt_daycount	2	0	0.0000	0.0000	0.0000
baseline	0	59	101.6314	3.8415	1.5967
baseline	1	16	3.8214	1.2342	0.1390
baseline	2	1	0.0649	0.0649	0.0649

Table 5 summarizes finite features classified by groups and dimensions of homology, along with numbers and persistence. The feature counts indicate structural complexity, while the total, maximum, and median persistence examine broad geometric signals and persistence of isolated events. The results indicate that the choice of conventions can alter not only PV levels, but also the valuation manifold's connectivity and loop structure. In governance terms, these assessments provide a basis for topology-oriented monitoring of the harmonization and validation thresholds of conventions.

Figure 5. Persistence diagram H0 for the alt_daycount group. Birth-death plot of connected-component features from the valuation-space point cloud under the alternative day-count convention and fixed valuation assumptions

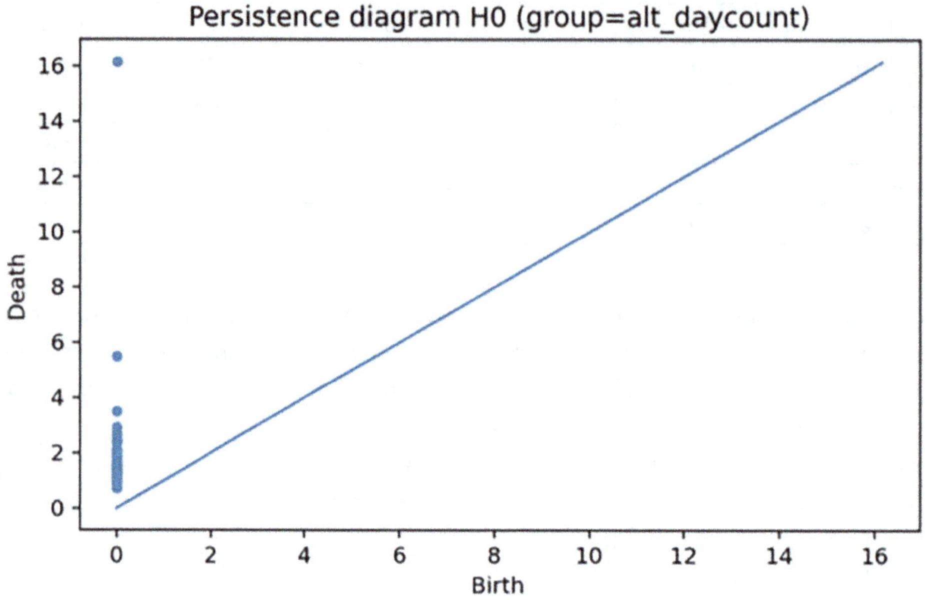

Figure 5 interprets the vertical distance of points from the diagonal. This means longer lifetimes result in persistent connected components over a wider filtration span. Points found close to the diagonal result in short-lived features. The alt_day-count H0 diagram illustrates how the alternative convention structuring scenario neighborhoods organizes and determines whether it fragments or merges valuation regimes in comparison to the reference case.

Figure 6. Persistence diagram H0 for the baseline group. Birth-death plot of connected-component features from the valuation-space point cloud under the baseline day-count convention and fixed valuation assumptions

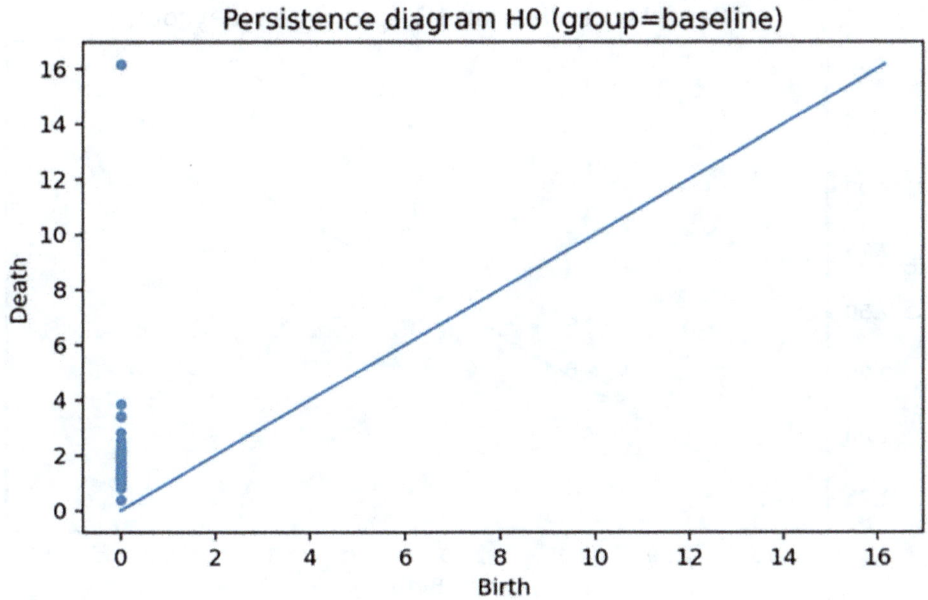

Figure 6 reflects distances of points from the diagonal. Longer lifetimes lead to persistent connectivity scales, while near-diagonal points exhibit short-lived features. The baseline H0 diagram establishes the reference for baseline connectivity and helps in the comparison of convention-led structural change and the setting of drift thresholds for valuation and risk reporting.

Figure 7. Persistence diagram H1 for the alt_daycount group. Birth-death plot of loop features from the valuation-space point cloud under the alternative day-count convention and fixed valuation assumptions

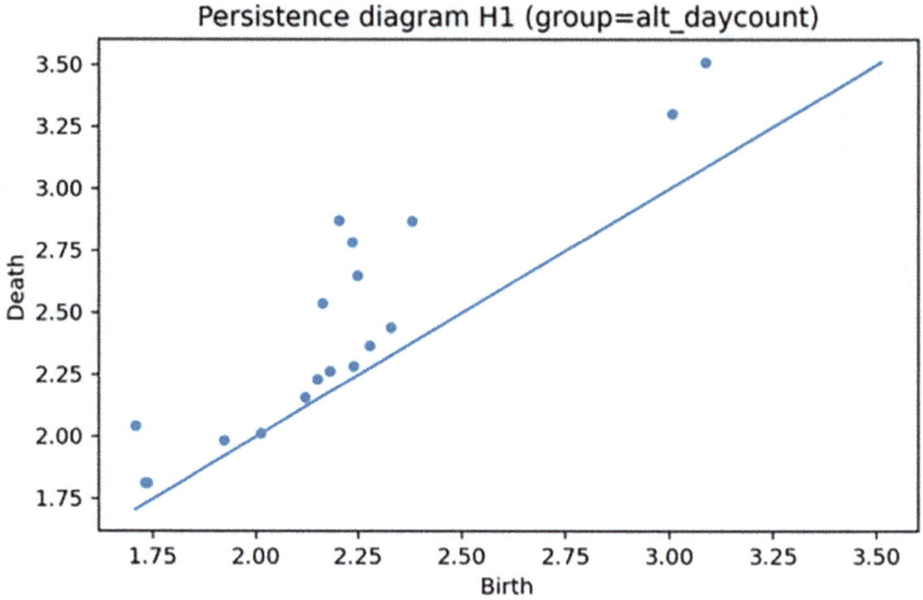

Figure 7 shows how far the points are from the diagonal. Points that are long-lived signal a strong cyclic structure, whereas points that are near the diagonal signal weak or noise-type loops. The H1 signature is important because it indicates whether a change of convention modifies higher-order geometry in the valuation manifold, which shows alterations of structure in different regimes that scalar PV metrics cannot capture.

Figure 8. Persistence diagram H1 for the baseline group. Birth-death plot of loop features from the valuation-space point cloud under the baseline day-count convention and fixed valuation assumptions

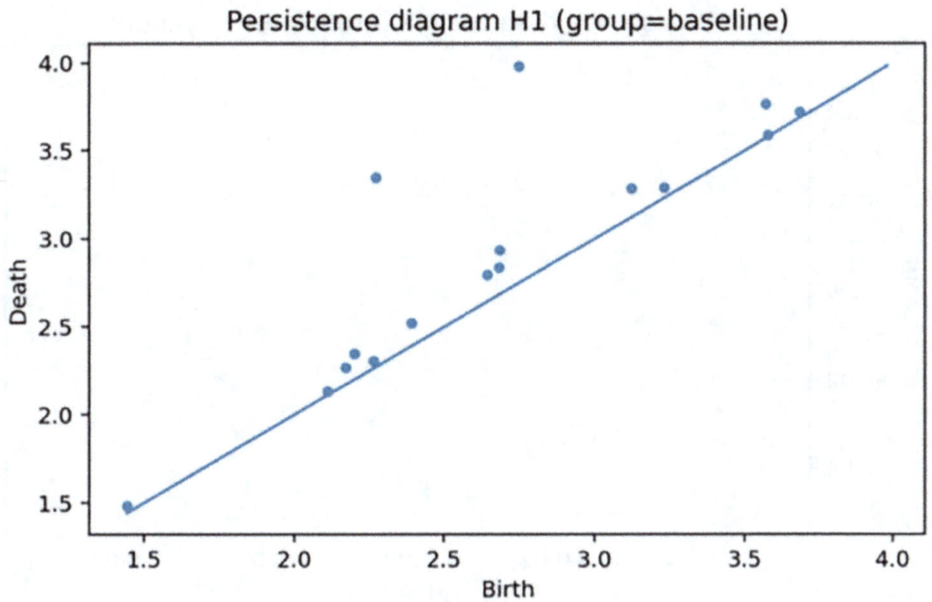

Figure 8 displays the same birth-death analysis for the baseline group. The more remote from the diagonal, the more persistent the loops. Near-diagonal points represent weak cycles. This baseline H1 profile provides a structural reference to determine whether the alternative convention creates, deletes, or diminishes the strength of stable loops. As such, it may help establish topology-based thresholds for more focused model evaluations.

Figure 9. Persistence diagram H2 for the alt_daycount group. Birth-death plot of two-dimensional void-like features from the valuation-space point cloud under the alternative day-count convention and fixed valuation assumptions

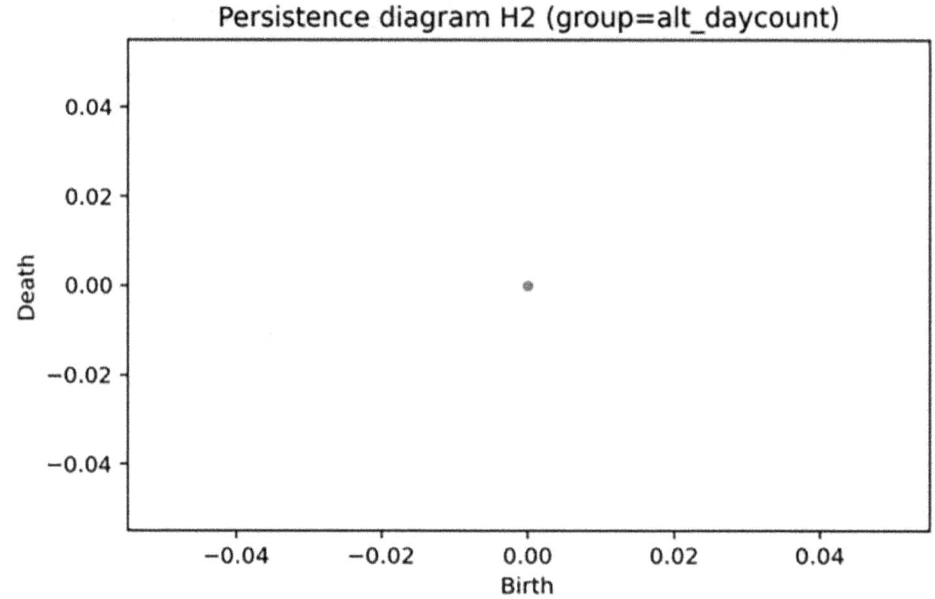

In Figure 9, the distance above the diagonal is noted. Sparse points or lifetimes close to zero suggest negligible higher-order cavities, revealing an effectively lower-dimensional geometry. These findings constrain the interpretation of structural differences to connectivity and loop effects, instead of higher-order topology, which, in the context of monitoring, allows a more parsimonious design prioritizing the homology dimensions that carry the most prominent signals.

Figure 10. Persistence diagram H2 for the baseline group. Birth-death plot of two-dimensional void-like features from the valuation-space point cloud under the baseline day-count convention and fixed valuation assumptions

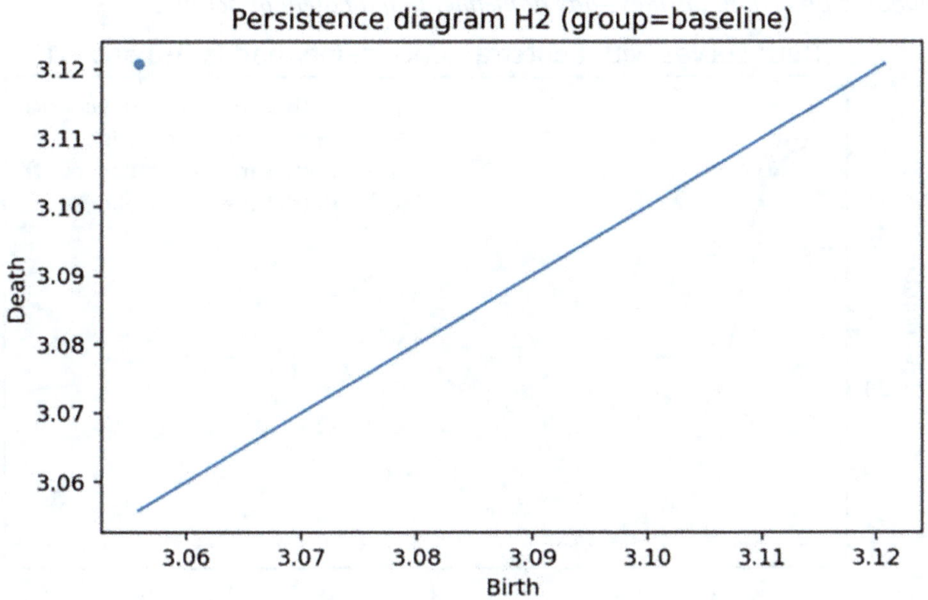

Figure 10 is interpreted by noting whether points remain above the diagonal. Points that are isolated and short-lived suggest that higher-order cavities are weak or rare and that the structure of the system is lower-dimensional. The baseline result for H2 helps to determine if higher-dimensional topological structures play a significant role in the stability claim and helps to determine the relevant differences between H0 and H1 when H2 is small or negligible.

Figure 11. Betti curves with bootstrap uncertainty bands (H0 and H1). Mean Betti-0 and Betti-1 curves for baseline and alternative day-count groups as functions of filtration scale epsilon, with bootstrap bands under fixed compounding, interpolation, rounding precision, business-day adjustment, and calendar settings

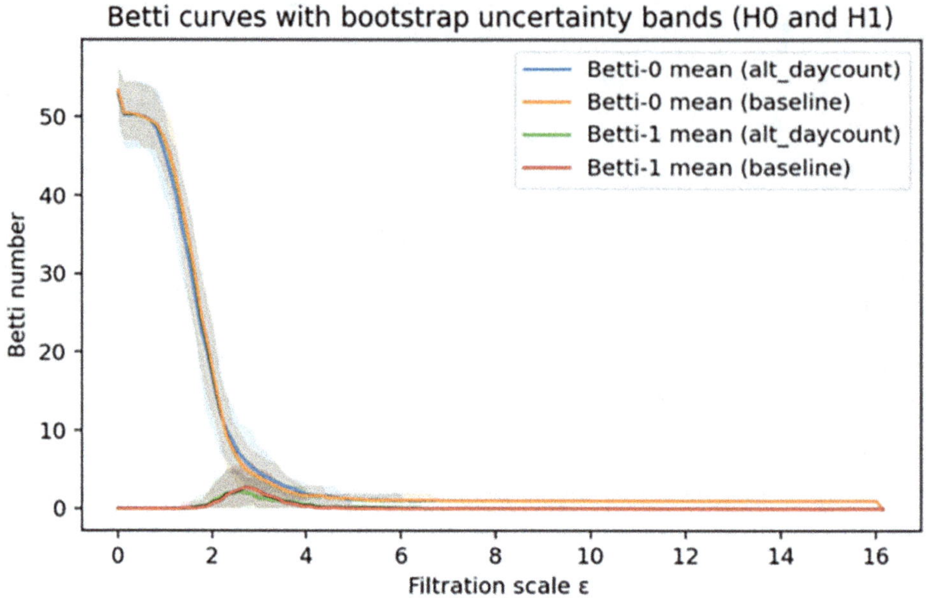

Figure 11 examines the relationship between curve height and shape across the filtration scale epsilon. The Betti-0 curve depicts the merging of components, and the Betti-1 curve depicts the emergence of loops. The shaded regions represent both uncertainty and overlap. Betti curves serve as functional topological signatures across a spectrum of scales, rather than a single diagram representation. In governance, the curves assist in identifying the scope of a scale and the bounds of tolerances for acceptable structural drift during the management of conventions and the application of stress tests.

Table 6. Wasserstein distances between convention-group persistence diagrams. Wasserstein distances for H0 and H1 are reported between the alt_daycount and baseline valuation-space topologies, with the inference cap and PH engine documented under fixed valuation assumptions

groups	wasserstein_H0	wasserstein_H1	inf_cap_used	ph_engine
alt_daycount vs baseline	2.042911	0.823782	16.151998	ripser

Table 6 uses the H0 and H1 Wasserstein distance to differentiate between loop-level and connectivity-level drift. The inf_cap_used and ph_engine fields record computational parameters required for auditability. The metric provides a compact effect size for topological change between groups, moving the analysis beyond a visual assessment. In governance, such distances may be employed as review thresholds when adjustments to conventions significantly alter the valuation-space topology.

Table 7. Permutation test on Betti-1 curve differences. The table reports the L2-mean Betti-difference statistic, permutation p-value, and number of permutations for the alt_daycount versus baseline comparison under fixed valuation assumptions and controlled convention variation

dimension_tested	test_statistic_L2_mean_betti_diff	p_value_permutation	n_permutations	groups
1	6.6332	0.7284	80	alt_daycount vs baseline

Table 7 presents the tested dimension alongside the effect-size statistic and permutation p-value, while n_permutations indicates the inferential resolution. The test examines if the observed difference in loop structure is greater than what would occur when group labels are assigned randomly. For governance, the statistic and p-value differentiate structural drift from sampling noise, and provide guidance for escalation rules, validation sign-off, and model-risk reporting.

5.3 Approximation and topological fidelity: Reconstruction vs structural preservation

This section assesses approximation and compression simultaneously across two interdependent criteria. Reconstruction RMSE is a measure of numerically accurate reconstructions; persistence-based distances and Betti-curve behavior describe the extent to which the reduced representation retains the valuation manifold. Comparison by latent dimension describes the point at which further compression no longer enhances the usefulness of an operation or begins to distort the structure. The reconstructed curves are then representative, and describe a topology-aware selection rule, which, in turn, provides a diagnostic for visual deployment review.

Figure 12. Approximation versus topological fidelity across latent dimension. The line plot compares reconstruction RMSE, Wasserstein distances for H0 and H1, and a combined selection score by latent dimension under a fixed valuation setup and controlled convention perturbations

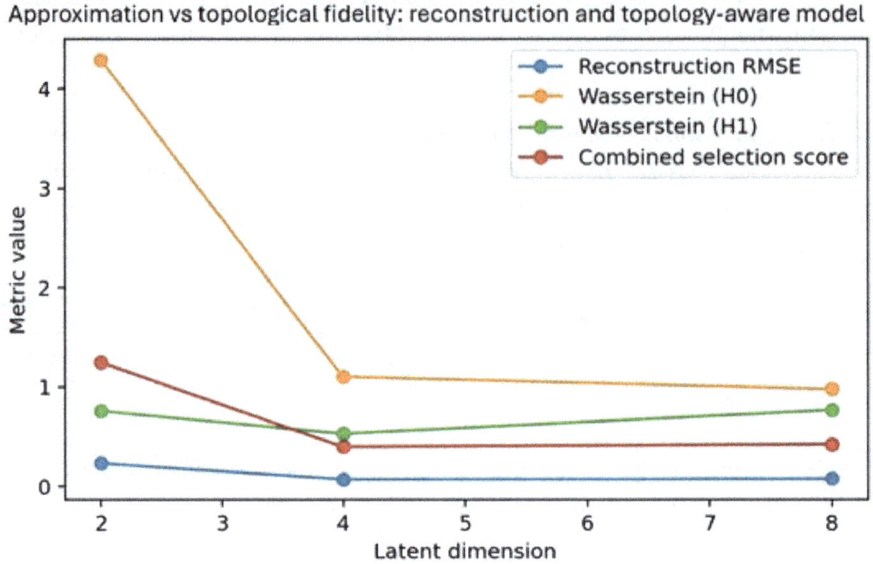

Figure 12 examines candidate latent dimensions using pointwise and topological metrics. The ideal presentation will compress the RMSE while neither expanding nor contracting the Wasserstein distances in H0 and H1. The combined score explicitly makes this trade-off and avoids selecting an approximation that reproduces values accurately but significantly alters the geometry of the scenarios. This criterion allows a limited facilitated acceptance of compressed representations in pricing, stress testing, and reporting.

Table 8. Reconstruction-topology trade-off table by latent dimension. Best training epoch, standardized reconstruction RMSE, Wasserstein distances for H0 and H1, and combined selection score are reported with topology weight and evaluation cadence under a fixed valuation setup and controlled convention variation

latent_ dim	best_ epoch	reconstruction_ rmse_ standardized	Wasserstein _H0	Wasserstein _H1	combined_score_ rmse_plus_ lambda_topo	lambda_ topo	eval_every_ epochs
2	60	0.23295	4.28895	0.75687	1.24211	0.2	10
4	90	0.07282	1.10072	0.52882	0.39873	0.2	10
8	80	0.07484	0.97514	0.76555	0.42298	0.2	10

Table 8 classifies data by latent dimension. Reconstruction_rmse_standardized examines pointwise accuracy, while Wasserstein_H0 and Wasserstein_H1 focus on structural drift. The overall score embodies the given trade-off, as identified by lambda_topo and the evaluation frequency. With distinct numeric and topological constraints, the preferred latent representation supports model selection. The approach makes the selection of the compressed model more rigorous. A compressed model that meets RMSE requirements is likely to affect the valuation manifold concerning the execution of subsequent tasks.

Figure 13. Reconstruction versus structural content in sampled discount-factor curves. Original and reconstructed discount-factor term structures are overlaid across maturity for selected examples under a fixed valuation setup with the selected latent representation and controlled convention inputs

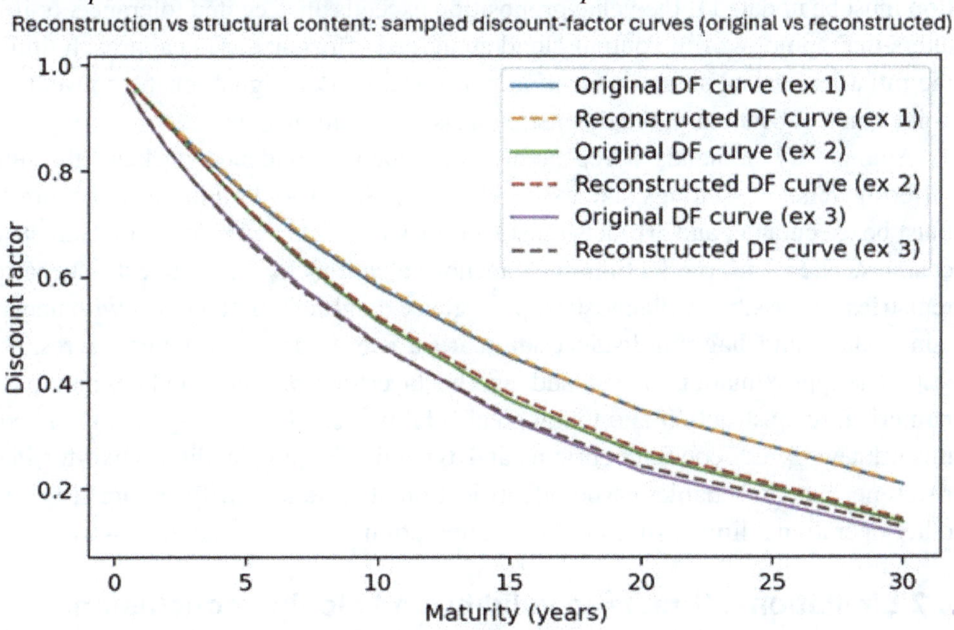

In Figure 13, the original discount-factor curves and their reconstructions are compared along the full range of maturities. The diagnostic examines the preservation of the curve's local shape and its long-end behavior. This is important because the small errors may compound, resulting in greater changes to curve sensitivities and topologies. As a deployment artifact, the overlay shows where the compression remains consistent and where the model reviewers should exercise caution before approving the representation for production valuation or risk reporting.

6. DISCUSSION AND CONCLUSIONS

6.1 Implications for model governance, auditability, and robust deployment

The implications of governance are apparent when analyzing the TVM engine as an executible valuation operator. The measurement output considers the scenario manifold in the results. Empirical studies reveal that the decisions of day-count, compounding, and calendar decisions yield state-structured drift. Stress conditions indicate that these changes may impact the structure and connectivity of closure in the valuation space. Therefore, governance must ensure the specification of baseline day counts, compounding, interpolation, rounding, and business-day shifting, in addition to providing a combination of scalar and structural thresholds. A convention must be updated if the value proposition exceeds an accepted tolerance, or if it alters the topology of the output cloud an agreed effect size. This approach limits the pitfalls of establishing convention noise as a market signal, or the convention noise being subsumed in the downstream risk attribution.

Auditability demands a repeatedly reproducible evidence package through differing versions, settings, and execution dates. Scenario definitions and controls must be executable, and artifacts must let reviewers trace numerical and geometric changes. Therefore, production must anchor valuations to run manifests, scenario registries, admissibility diagnostics, persistence diagrams, Betti curves with uncertainty bands, and diagram-distance summaries. These serve as structural regression tests. The approximation analysis adds another layer: compression modules must pass numerical reconstruction and topological fidelity tests. In a management context, this framework aids consistent pricing and dynamic hedging, facilitates like-for-like risk reporting, and enables earlier identification of structural drifts before affecting other operational limits, stress tests, reconciliations, and external disclosures.

6.2 Limitations, threats to validity, and closing conclusions

The study's controlled experimental design leads to some limitations. Convention perturbation isolation leads to more precise causation, but less external generality. Regarding scenario grids, instrument shock coverage, and perturbation structure shocks, we prioritized interpretability and construction comparability. These selections do not show all production portfolio types, the full effects of nonlinear payoffs, optionality-induced convexity, liquidity frictions, or gaps in data constraining financial/institutional/banking operations. The observed PV drift and topological separations are, therefore, the dependent results, and should be interpreted as such for the perturbation calendar rules and specific/perturbed numerical settings. In more complex production environments, further interactions–curve-shape distortions, basis risks, multi-curve discounting, collateralization, and recalibrating under stress–could deepen the effects captured herein. After the model is run with bounds (limits) of additional product (financial) types, practical thresholds (limits) of the model may be set.

Methodological sensitivity impacts the topological audit. Persistent-homology summaries rely on how the valuation point cloud is constructed, normalized, sampled, and truncated. H0-H1 summaries, Wasserstein distances, and permutation results are sensitive to the embedding dimension, sampling granularity and thickness, as well as the preprocessing and inference truncation. Bootstrap and permutation methods assess finite-sample variability, but do not remove uncertainty when differences are small and group point clouds are sparse, as well as when the high-dimensional arrangement is interpreted. The approximation analysis describes a similar concern. RMSE and topological fidelity capture different invariants. Therefore, a combined score expresses a preference. For that reason, the thresholds should be set to institutional materiality, what the audit would find, and model change policy. Limitations on budget and resources would make the deployment of the topology-based controls infrequent. The main point remains. Convention and calendar rules introduce significant valuation model risk, as they affect the outputs' disposition and frame. A reproducible, topology-based audit layer offers the means to measure drift. This supports consistent reporting, validation, and deployment.

7. FUTURE WORK

7.1 Extensions to stochastic rates, portfolio-level topology, and topology-aware learning

Future efforts should shift the convention-oriented audit from the current settings to more production-like environments, while retaining the same governance logic. For example, in the first case, deterministic parallel shocks could be substituted with stochastic term-structure dynamics incorporating volatility clustering, regime shifts, and path dependence. This would help determine if convention-induced drifts respond differently when the uncertainty is in the rate process as opposed to the uncertainty being in a controlled grid. In the second case, portfolio-level topology could be introduced by representing portfolios in terms of their joint PV, Greeks, and risk decompositions. In this case, persistent-homology summaries could be used to think about decomposition and disruption of differentiation as well as correlation and would allow for convention changes to be assessed by how they would affect portfolio sensitivity topology, rather than the total PV, as well. Finally, topology-aware learning could be directly integrated in the surrogate and compression models through regularizers of Betti-curve discrepancies, diagram distances, and topology-preserving joint loss functions. These models would enhance external validity and adaptability, and link the controlled framework to operational constraints.

Availability of code: The Python code for data generation, perturbation simulations, autoencoder training, and topological metrics is available at: https://github.com/JAIME6609/BOOK-06-ART-01/blob/main/CODE-ART-01-V2.py. The repository supports reproduction of the computational pipeline, figures, and tables.

REFERENCES

Abdallah, H., Yue, Z., Ahmadian, A., Thompson, D., & Wang, B. (2022). Statistical inference for persistent homology and its application to simulated fMRI time series data. *Foundations of Data Science (Springfield, Mo.)*, *4*(2), 153–182. DOI: 10.3934/fods.2022014

Akiyama, S., & Matsuyama, N. (2025). Yield curve extrapolation with machine learning. ASTIN Bulletin. *ASTIN Bulletin*, *55*(1), 76–96. DOI: 10.1017/asb.2024.27

Barker, M., Chue Hong, N. P., Katz, D. S., Lamprecht, A.-L., Martinez-Ortiz, C., Psomopoulos, F., Harrow, J., Castro, L. J., Gruenpeter, M., Martinez, P. A., & Honeyman, T. (2022). Introducing the FAIR Principles for research software. *Scientific Data*, *9*(1), 622. DOI: 10.1038/s41597-022-01710-x PMID: 36241754

Bauer, U. (2021). Ripser: Efficient computation of Vietoris–Rips persistence barcodes. *Journal of Applied and Computational Topology*, *5*(3), 391–423. DOI: 10.1007/s41468-021-00071-5

Bobrowski, O., & Skraba, P. (2023). A universal null-distribution for topological data analysis. *Scientific Reports*, *13*(1), 12274. DOI: 10.1038/s41598-023-37842-2 PMID: 37507400

Camenzind, N., & Filipović, D. (2024). Stripping the Swiss discount curve using kernel ridge regression. *European Actuarial Journal*, *14*(2), 371–410. DOI: 10.1007/s13385-024-00386-4

Chazal, F., & Michel, B. (2021). An introduction to topological data analysis: Fundamental and practical aspects for data scientists. *Frontiers in Artificial Intelligence*, *4*, 667963. DOI: 10.3389/frai.2021.667963 PMID: 34661095

Chazal, F., Michel, B., & Reise, W. (2025). Topological signatures of periodic-like signals. *Bernoulli*, *31*(3), 1955–1990. DOI: 10.3150/24-BEJ1793

Chen, M., Wang, Y., Feng, S., & Zhang, Y. (2023). Topological regularization for representation learning via persistent homology. *Mathematics*, *11*(4), 1008. DOI: 10.3390/math11041008

Dayarathne, K. P. N. S., & Thayasiwam, U. (2024). Utility of smoothing techniques in yield curve modeling for the Asian Pacific frontier capital market. *SN Computer Science*, *5*(4), 430. Advance online publication. DOI: 10.1007/s42979-024-02684-w

Djatschenko, W. (2019). BondValuation: An R package for fixed coupon bond analysis. *The R Journal, 11*(2), 124. Advance online publication. DOI: 10.32614/RJ-2019-055

Filipović, D., Pelger, M., & Ye, Y. (2025). Stripping the discount curve: A robust machine learning approach. *Management Science*, mnsc.2023.01401. Advance online publication. DOI: 10.1287/mnsc.2023.01401

Flaig, S., & Junike, G. (2022). Scenario generation for market risk models using generative neural networks. *Risks, 10*(11), 199. DOI: 10.3390/risks10110199

Gidea, M., & Katz, Y. (2018). Topological data analysis of financial time series: Landscapes of crashes. *Physica A, 491*, 820–834. DOI: 10.1016/j.physa.2017.09.028

Goble, C., Cohen-Boulakia, S., Soiland-Reyes, S., Garijo, D., Gil, Y., Crusoe, M. R., Peters, K., & Schober, D. (2020). FAIR computational workflows. *Data Intelligence, 2*(1–2), 108–121. DOI: 10.1162/dint_a_00033

Grohs, P., & Kutyniok, G. (Eds.). (2022). *Mathematical aspects of deep learning*. Cambridge University Press., DOI: 10.1017/9781009025096

Gustafsson, O. J. R., Wilkinson, S. R., Bacall, F., Soiland-Reyes, S., Leo, S., Pireddu, L., Owen, S., Juty, N., Fernández, J. M., Brown, T., Ménager, H., Grüning, B., Capella-Gutierrez, S., Coppens, F., & Goble, C. (2025). WorkflowHub: A registry for computational workflows. *Scientific Data, 12*(1), 837. DOI: 10.1038/s41597-025-04786-3 PMID: 40399296

Hensel, F., Moor, M., & Rieck, B. (2021). A survey of topological machine learning methods. *Frontiers in Artificial Intelligence, 4*, 681108. DOI: 10.3389/frai.2021.681108 PMID: 34124648

Islambekov, U., & Pathirana, L. (2024). Vector summaries of persistence diagrams and permutation-based hypothesis testing. *Foundations of Data Science (Springfield, Mo.), 6*(1), 1–19. DOI: 10.3934/fods.2024002

Jokhadze, V., & Schmidt, W. M. (2020). Measuring model risk in financial risk management and derivatives valuation. *International Journal of Theoretical and Applied Finance, 23*(05), 2050012. DOI: 10.1142/S0219024920500120

Lee, Y.-H., Hsieh, M.-H., Kuo, W., & Tsai, C. J. (2021). How can an economic scenario generation model cope with abrupt changes in financial markets? *China Finance Review International, 11*(3), 372–405. DOI: 10.1108/CFRI-03-2021-0056

Majumdar, S., & Laha, A. K. (2020). Clustering and classification of time series using topological data analysis with applications to finance. *Expert Systems with Applications*, *162*, 113868. DOI: 10.1016/j.eswa.2020.113868

Malott, N. O., Chen, S., Verma, R. R., & Wilsey, P. A. (2023). A survey on the high-performance computation of persistent homology. *IEEE Transactions on Knowledge and Data Engineering*, *35*(5), 4466–4484. DOI: 10.1109/TKDE.2022.3147070

Nüst, D., Sochat, V., Marwick, B., Eglen, S. J., Head, T., Hirst, T., & Evans, B. D. (2020). Ten simple rules for writing Dockerfiles for reproducible data science. *PLoS Computational Biology*, *16*(11), e1008316. DOI: 10.1371/journal.pcbi.1008316 PMID: 33170857

Pimentel, J. F., Murta, L., Braganholo, V., & Freire, J. (2019). A Large-Scale Study About Quality and Reproducibility of Jupyter Notebooks. 2019 IEEE/ACM 16th International Conference on Mining Software Repositories (MSR), 507–517. https://doi.org/DOI: 10.1109/MSR.2019.00077

Pun, C. S., Lee, S. X., & Xia, K. (2022). Persistent-homology-based machine learning: A survey and a comparative study. *Artificial Intelligence Review*, *55*(7), 5169–5213. DOI: 10.1007/s10462-022-10146-z

Ravishanker, N., & Chen, R. (2021). An introduction to persistent homology for time series. *Wiley Interdisciplinary Reviews: Computational Statistics*, *13*(3), e1548. DOI: 10.1002/wics.1548

Saltelli, A., Aleksankina, K., Becker, W., Fennell, P., Ferretti, F., Holst, N., Li, S., & Wu, Q. (2019). Why so many published sensitivity analyses are false: A systematic review of sensitivity analysis practices. *Environmental Modelling & Software*, *114*, 29–39. DOI: 10.1016/j.envsoft.2019.01.012

Schoch, D., Haim, M., Stier, S., & Schoonvelde, M. (2024). Computational reproducibility in computational social science. *EPJ Data Science*, *13*(1), 75. DOI: 10.1140/epjds/s13688-024-00514-w

Shah, W. H., Fatima, S. R., Huerta-Cuellar, G., García-López, J. H., Mata Ramirez, C. G., & Jaimes-Reátegui, R. (2025). Topological data analysis approach to time series and shape analysis of dynamical system. *Chaos (Woodbury, N.Y.)*, *35*(6), 063129. DOI: 10.1063/5.0268340 PMID: 40526891

Tralie, C., Saul, N., & Bar-On, R. (2018). Ripser.py: A lean persistent homology library for Python. *Journal of Open Source Software*, *3*(29), 925. DOI: 10.21105/joss.00925

Trisovic, A., Lau, M. K., Pasquier, T., & Crosas, M. (2022). A large-scale study on research code quality and execution. *Scientific Data*, *9*(1), 60. DOI: 10.1038/s41597-022-01143-6 PMID: 35190569

Vejdemo-Johansson, M., & Mukherjee, S. (2022). Statistical inference using persistence landscapes. *Foundations of Data Science (Springfield, Mo.)*, *4*(4), 387–410. DOI: 10.3934/fods.2022018

Wang, Q., García-Redondo, I., Faugère, P., Henselman-Petrusek, G., & Monod, A. (2024). Stability for inference with persistent homology rank functions. *Computer Graphics Forum*, *43*(5), e15142. DOI: 10.1111/cgf.15142

Wasserman, L. (2018). Topological data analysis. *Annual Review of Statistics and Its Application*, *5*(1), 501–532. DOI: 10.1146/annurev-statistics-031017-100045

Wilkinson, S. R., Aloqalaa, M., Belhajjame, K., Crusoe, M. R., de Paula Kinoshita, B., Gadelha, L., Garijo, D., Gustafsson, O. J. R., Juty, N., Kanwal, S., Khan, F. Z., Köster, J., Gehlen, K. P., Pouchard, L., Rannow, R. K., Soiland-Reyes, S., Soranzo, N., Sufi, S., Sun, Z., & Goble, C. (2025). Applying the FAIR Principles to computational workflows. *Scientific Data*, *12*(1), 328. DOI: 10.1038/s41597-025-04451-9 PMID: 39994238

Wu, L., & Jarrow, R. A. (2024). Fitting dynamically consistent forward rate curves. *International Journal of Theoretical and Applied Finance*, *27*(8), 2450021. DOI: 10.1142/S0219024924500213

Chapter 6
Cryptocurrencies as Safe Haven Assets:
A GARCH EVT and Monte Carlo Approach

José Antonio Molina Hernández
http://orcid.org/0000-0002-1842-8262
University of the Istmo, Mexico

Kevin Olalla Ake
Universidad Anahuac Veracruz, Mexico

ABSTRACT

The growing presence of institutional capital in crypto asset markets has reopened the debate on whether Bitcoin and similar digital assets can act as safe havens, the way gold or sovereign bonds have been built historically. This thesis tackles that question with a quantitative framework rather than the qualitative arguments that dominated the early literature. The dataset covers November 2019 to May 2026 (2,380 daily observations for Bitcoin, 2,381 for the full asset universe). I fit GARCH-t and EGARCH-t models to capture conditional variance, apply Extreme Value Theory to isolate the tail directly, and run Monte Carlo simulation to estimate capital requirements over 30-day horizon.

1 INTRODUCTION

The crypto market has grown large enough that it matters now, but not integrated enough that it fits neatly anywhere. Bitcoin started as technical experiment in 2009, stayed a fringe curiosity for years, and somewhere around 2017 crossed into

DOI: 10.4018/979-8-3373-8372-9.ch006

the attention of people with real money to deploy. By 2021 the market cap had hit a trillion dollars. By 2024, Bitcoin ETFs were approved. Institutions are holding it. Sovereign wealth funds ask about it in board meetings. And yet the financial system treats it like it doesn't belong.

The original story about bitcoin was simple; its digital gold. Scarce by design, no central authority, uncorrelated with traditional markets. If you hold Bitcoin when equities crash, you stay protected. That story made intuitive sense. It fit the structural argument Bitcoin exists outside the traditional system, so why would it move with it?

The data from the last six years tells a different story. COVID-19 in March 2020 was the first real test. Bitcoin fell harder than equities on the same days equities fell. It recovered only after central banks flooded the system with liquidity. It was supposed to be a refuge. Instead, it was the first thing institutions sold to raise dollars. The pattern repeated in May 2022 when Terra collapsed, again in November 2022 with FTX, again through the 2023 rate cycle. Each time the same thing happens when risk on traders need to raise dollars, they sell crypto because its liquid 24/7 and the market is deep. The correlation that's supposed to stay negative in a crash goes positive instead. Sometimes it hits +0.61. That's not a haven. That's just leverage with a longer settlement time.

So, what went wrong with the thesis? The structural argument was sound I think that matters to acknowledge. Bitcoin really is built outside the traditional system. But structure isn't what determines behavior once the marginal holder changes. Five years ago, Bitcoin was held by retail speculators and true believers. Now it is held by the same institutional desks that trade everything else. When those desks need to deliver, they don't check the underlying economic rationale for the asset. They just sell whatever's liquid. Bitcoin is liquid. So it sells.

This thesis test whether that intuition holds up under a proper quantitative framework. I'm not going to use the frameworks that broke on this data the Gaussian VaR, the Markowitz optimizer, the assumption of constant variance. Instead, I built an integrated pipeline: GARCH-t and EGARCH-t to capture conditional volatility as it actually changes; Extreme Value Theory on the tail directly, without Gaussian assumptions; Monte Carlo simulation to translate that into a regulatory capital requirement; and then a bridge from the measured tail risk to the actual Basel III risk weights that bank use.

What I find is three things. First, Bitcoin shows no leverage effect when prices fall, volatility rises just as much as when prices rise. There's no stabilization, no dampening. Second, the rolling correlation breaks down in every stress window we have data for. Third, the tail risk is heavy enough that the Basel Committee's 1250% risk weight for crypto-assets is actually on the conservative side of what the data justifies. The conclusion is that Bitcoin fails the safe haven test under every reasonable definition.

Beyond Bitcoin, I look at Ethereum before and after the Merge in September 2022. PreMerge Ethereum was catastrophically worse on tail metrics than Bitcoin - 99% ES was 21.24% against Bitcoin's 12.96%. Post Merge it compressed to 12.52%, basically Bitcoin's baseline.

That compression is real and measurable, but it's one of 29 structural breaks in the Ethereum conditional variance series over the sample period. So, I report that honestly instead of claiming the Merge was the sole cause. It was a major event, but not unique. The outline is straightforward. Section 2 sets the macroeconomic and structural context. Section 3 reviews the literature and identifies what's missing mainly, nobody has built the bridge from tail risk estimates to regulatory capital before. Section 4 describes the data and the mathematical machinery. Section 5 reports the results. Section 6 maps those results to Basel III and MiCA. Section 7 talks about what happens next. The code is in the appendices so anyone can replicate this.

1.1 Contributions of This Chapter

There are three gaps in the literature this thesis fills.

The first is methodological. Pre-Merge and Post-Merge Ethereum are different assets at the tail, and existing papers don't split them. I do. I also control for the fact that crypto has heavy structural breaks all over the place the Merge is one of 29 so I test whether the regime change I find is unique to the Merge or just one of many. It's one of many, which is uncomfortable, but that's the honest answer.

The second is regulatory. The Basel Committee set a 1250% risk weight on Group 2 unbacked crypto in December 2022 but never explained where that number came from or whether it matched the tail behavior. I close that gap by showing that the measured daily Expected Shortfall of 12.75%, scaled to the 10 day regulatory horizon, implies a capital requirement around 120% of national. The standardized 100% deduction the 1250% weight produces is actually defensible, and the mapping is reproducible from public price data.

The third is validation. Most GARCH-EVT papers on crypto skip the diagnostic tests. I run Ljung Box placebo procedure on structural breaks. The placebo result is awkward the Merge broke at a detectible moment, but so did 28 other dates but I report it anyway.

1.2 Chapter Organization

The next section lays out the bigger picture: how financial systems move money, where the risk sits, what a safe haven is, and why crypto assets might or might not be one. Section 3 walks through what's already been written and where the hole is. Section 4 gets into the actual methods: the data, the models, what assumptions we're making and why. Section 5 is the results of what the number show. Section 6 talks about policy and regulation. Section wraps up with limitations and what comes next. All the code is the appendix.

2 THEORICAL FRAMEWORK AND MACROECONOMIC CONTEXT

2.1 Financial System Microstructure and Capital Allocation

A financial system's job is to move money from people who have it to people who can use it. In theory, in practice it never moves money directly. It goes through banks, insurance companies, pension funds, asset managers, clearinghouses, central counterparties. There's central bank sitting on top of all of it, making sure nothing breaks.

The thing is, the system is layered and that makes it fragile. A solvency problem at one major node a clearing member, a big money market fund, a primary dealer doesn't stay isolated. It spreads through the network. Sometimes slowly, sometime fast. The official balance sheets don't show how much collateral has been passed hand to hand, how much leverage has been built on top of that collateral, how many institutions are holding the same thing and would all try to sell it at the same moment if something broke. That concentration of risk through chains of collateral and rehypothecation is one of the reasons a single failure can metastasize.

Crypto assets replicate the same structure. You've got exchanges, lending platforms, custodians, hedge funds, all interconnected through collateral networks. But there's a difference: there's no lender of last resort. If something breaks in crypto, there's no central bank that can flood the system with liquidity and stop the cascade. The backstops that exist in traditional finance deposit insurance, repo felicities, emergency lending windows mostly don't exist in crypto. That's why when Terra failed in May 2022, the system just died. And when FTX went down in November, there was nobody to backstop it and companies that had deposited there just lost the money.

This is the foundation for understanding why tail risk matters so much in crypto. In traditional baking, regulators have tools to interrupt a cascade. In crypto they don't. So the probability of a tail event becoming a system wide event is higher. And when it happens, there's nothing to stop it.

2.2 Capital Markets and Liquidity Dynamics

Inside the broader financial ecosystem, there's the capital markets layer. That's where price discovery happens where the market figures out what expected returns actually are. You've got fixed income (debt), equities(stocks), and increasingly structured products and derivatives on top of both.

When the economy is running fine, money flows toward whatever gives the highest return. Usually, that's equities and risky assets because they pay more. When uncertainty spikes inflation expectations rotates back into short duration government debt, the US dollar, things that are safe. That rotation is mechanism that makes an asset a safe haven is an empirical question, not a definitional one. And it can change over time if the people holding it change. Gold has been a safe haven for centuries because it holds value and the marginal buyer during stress is someone looking to preserve capital. Bitcoin in 2018 was maybe thought of as a safe haven by a small group of believers. Bitcoin in 2024 is held by institutions that also hold everything else. The marginal buyer is not someone looking for safety anymore. The marginal buyer is just rotating portfolio weights. That matters.

2.3 Risk Taxonomy and Institutional Safe Havens

There's a useful distinction that gets confused a lot. Under stress, assets fall into three categories: diversifiers, hedges and safe havens.

A diversifier has low correlation with your main portfolio on average. It reduces risk in calm times but doesn't necessarily help you in a crash. A hedge has negative correlation with your portfolio regardless of the market regime. It protects you on the downside but usually at the cost of expected return. A safe haven has zero or negative correlation specifically during stress. That's the one that matters for capital preservation because it's the one that actually rises (or at least doesn't fall) when everything else is collapsing.

The real world examples are US treasuries, physical gold, the Swiss franc, the Japanese yen. These assets have a track record of negative correlation with equities during crashes, consistently across multiple episodes. That's why they're safe havens. Now here's where Bitcoin gets confusing in the popular conversation. Bitcoin has low historical correlation with equities on average around 0.14 in calm periods in this sample. So it passes the diversifier test. But in every crash we have data for, that correlation flips positive. During COVID it was +0.46. During Terra it was +0.52. During FTX it was +0.61. If it only diversifiers when things are fine and sells off with equities when they're not, then it's a diversifier, not a safe haven. That distinction is the hinge on which the entire thesis turns.

2.4 Cryptographic Ecosystem: Decentralized Architecture

Bitcoin was built with a specific idea: a monetary network with no central authority, inelastic supply, no government printing money. The early research on bitcoin assumed structural independence. The marginal buyer is just rebalancing a portfolio.

This has been documented. Auer et al. (2023) showed that using a databased of retail trading app adoption that most people buy crypto when prices are rising, not when they think the system is breaking. They're not hedging, they're speculating. They tend to enter near the top of cycles and lose money. That's the opposite of save haven behavior, which is buying when prices are low because you believe they'll stabilize. Ante (2023) showed that social media signals move crypto prices materially. That's also the opposite of what you'd expect from a store of value. Stores of value don't move on tweets.

2.5 Liquidity Shocks and Macroeconomic Stress: 2008 and COVID-19

You can only know if something is a safe haven when it's tested under real stress. The twenty-first century has produced two big tests. 2008 was an endogenous solvency crisis. It started in U.S. mortgage credit, spread through the leveraged interbank network, and ended with the central bank flooding the system with trillions in liquidity. A safe haven during 2008 was U.S. Treasuries and the dollar. They rose as equities crashed. Gold also rose after an initial liquidation shock. Things worked as they were supposed to. COVID-19 was different—an exogenous shock to real economic activity. Lockdowns, unemployment spike, equity selloff of more than 30% in three weeks, margin calls everywhere. The safe havens did what safe havens do: Treasuries and the dollar strengthened. Gold also rose. Bitcoin fell hard and stayed correlated with equities throughout the panic. It wasn't a refuge. It was something institutions had to sell to raise dollars. The empirical record is there. The BTC-S&P correlation moved from 0.14 in calm periods to +0.46 during the COVID panic. That single observation is enough to reject the strong version of the digital-gold narrative. And the pattern repeated in every crisis since. That's what the rest of this thesis builds on.

3 STATE OF THE ART AND LITERATURE REVIEW

3.1 Theoretical Evolution of the Safe Haven Concept

The modern conceptual frame for safe-haven assets traces back to Baur and Lucey (2010), who formalized the three-category taxonomy (diversifier, hedge, safe haven) and provided the conditional definition that has structured most of the empirical work since. Baur and McDermott (2010) extended the same frame to gold across multiple markets and stress windows, confirming that the safe-haven property is regime-dependent rather than unconditional, and that an asset can act as a strong safe haven in some markets while failing the test in others.

Within that frame, U.S. Treasury bonds, the Swiss franc, the Japanese yen, and gold have consistently held safe-haven status across the empirical record. They benefit from the flight-to-safety rebalancing during liquidity shocks: as risk-on positions are unwound, capital flows toward the assets that historically preserve value during stress. The hyper-expansive monetary policy that followed the 2008 crisis raised the question of whether a digital asset with algorithmically inelastic supply could replicate the same defensive role.

3.2 The Digital Gold Hypothesis: Consensus and Empirical Refutation

Between 2017 and 2019, a substantial body of work argued that Bitcoin satisfied at least the weak version of the safe-haven hypothesis. Bouri et al. (2017) and Corbet et al. (2019) reported low historical correlations between Bitcoin and the major global equity indices, and concluded that Bitcoin functioned as a strong diversifier and, in certain regimes, as a safe haven. The premise was that Bitcoin's return structure, not linked to corporate cash flows, central-bank policy rates, or sovereign decisions, was structurally disconnected from the traditional system. The validation failed at the first test of scale. Conlon and McGee (2020) showed that during the first-quarter 2020 COVID-19 panic, Bitcoin fell in tandem with the SP 500 and exhibited severe contagion behavior rather than safe-haven behavior. Follow-up work (Kristoufek, 2020; Ali et al., 2021) argued that the institutional maturation of the crypto market, far from insulating Bitcoin from traditional-market dynamics, increased its sensitivity to global risk appetite and turned it into a procyclical asset highly correlated with technology equities. The story changed: Bitcoin was a high-beta tech proxy with extra-heavy tails, not a defensive holding. This reassessment is consistent with the broader volatility literature. Baur and Dimpfl (2021) document that Bitcoin's volatility is roughly an order of magnitude higher than that of the major exchange rates, severe enough to undermine its role in a portfolio and to leave it, at best, a weak risk-diversifier rather than a refuge, with store-of-value characteristics emerging only over very long horizons. Härdle et al. (2020), surveying the mechanics and empirical regularities of the major crypto-assets, reach a compatible conclusion, treating cryptocurrencies as a distinct, highly speculative asset class whose statistical behaviour departs sharply from that of conventional currencies or established safe assets.

3.3 Limitations of Traditional Financial Modeling for Crypto-Assets

A recurring problem in applied work on crypto-assets is the uncritical use of Gaussian frameworks. Modern Portfolio Theory (Markowitz, 1952) and the parametric Gaussian VaR model are the workhorses of commercial-bank risk management. Both assume that returns are normally distributed, that variance is constant over time, and that the probability of extreme deviations falls off in the way the Gaussian tail dictates.

The descriptive statistics in Section 4.1 show how badly the Gaussian assumption fits cryptoasset data. Bitcoin returns exhibit excess kurtosis of 21.82 and Ethereum 15.51, against the Gaussian baseline of zero. The Jarque-Bera statistics reject normality at $p < 10-300$ for both. When an institution feeds these series into a Markowitz mean-variance optimizer, the algorithm sees the historical mean return but does not see the tail. The result is allocations that look attractive on Sharpe-ratio grounds and produce realized losses that exceed any standard capital buffer. The Markowitz trap in Section 5.4 documents this empirically: an optimizer with unconstrained Bitcoin inclusion recommends 7.10% of capital in Bitcoin and a higher reported Sharpe ratio, but the resulting portfolio has a deeper realized Maximum Drawdown than the benchmark 50/50 equity-gold portfolio.

3.4 Transition to Extreme-Value Econometrics and Dynamic Volatility

The applied response to the Gaussian failure has come from two directions. The GARCH family, originating with Bollerslev (1986), captures conditional heteroskedasticity directly: variance depends on past shocks and past variance, which lets the model represent volatility clustering. EGARCH (Nelson, 1991) adds an asymmetry term that tests for the leverage effect, the phenomenon in which negative shocks raise future variance more than positive shocks do. Alongside the GARCH literature, Extreme Value Theory developed as a way to model the tail of the return distribution directly, without relying on the bulk of the distribution to fit it. Gilli and Këllezi (2006) made the case that standard parametric VaR models the center of the distribution and is therefore systematically wrong about the tail, while the Peak-Over-Threshold method fits a Generalized Pareto Distribution to exceedances above a threshold and recovers the tail behavior directly. The closed-form Expected Shortfall that comes out of the GPD fit is the metric the Basel III framework requires for catastrophic-loss capital determination.

Recent work continues to refine extreme-value methods for this asset class: Teruzzi (2023) applies EVT for weakly dependent data and introduces a Marginal Expected Shortfall measure to quantify how much an individual crypto-asset contributes to system-wide tail losses, which is the systemic dimension taken up in the FTX and Terra/LUNA autopsies of this chapter. This thesis sits at the intersection of those two lines of work, with the added step of mapping the resulting estimates onto the Basel III and MiCA capital architecture.

3.5 Research Gap

The crypto-risk literature developed along two parallel but separate tracks, neither of which engaged with regulation. Between 2017 and 2021, GARCH applications to Bitcoin and Ethereum became standard; that literature established that conditional heteroskedasticity dominates the return process. Separately, EVT applications appeared later, fitting POT models to crypto tails and reporting shape parameters > 0. But here's the gap: neither stream asked what these numbers mean for prudential capital requirements. The missing piece is the translation layer connecting tail metrics to actual regulatory capital. The regulatory literature moves on a parallel track. Auer and Tercero-Lucas (2023) document the structural fragility of algorithmic stablecoins at the BIS but do not estimate a tail-risk model. The IMF policy work (International Monetary Fund, 2023; Hacibedel and Perez-Saiz, 2023) catalogues the financial-stability agenda for digital assets and lists capital calibration as an open problem. The BCBS final standard of December 2022 imposes the 1250% punitive treatment on Group 2 unbacked crypto-assets without offering an empirical floor for the choice, and the academic literature has not supplied one. None of these strands translates VaR or ES into a defensible risk weight.

The Ethereum transition to Proof-of-Stake in September 2022 created an additional gap. Most post-Merge work focuses on energy consumption, staking economics, and validator dynamics. The tail-risk implications of the consensus change relative to Proof-of-Work, both across assets (BTC vs ETH) and within Ethereum's own history (pre-Merge vs post-Merge), have not been quantified inside a framework that controls for the heavy-tailed microstructure that both assets share.

The closest prior work is Patra and Gupta (2023), who estimate Value-at-Risk and Expected Shortfall for crypto-assets using fat-tailed, skewed innovation distributions while explicitly accounting for endogenously determined structural breaks. Their study establishes that both heavy tails and structural instability matter for crypto risk measurement, but it stops short of mapping the resulting tail metrics onto the Basel III risk-weight machinery, and it does not use a consensus-mechanism event such as the Merge as an identified break; both steps are the contribution of this chapter.

This thesis integrates the three strands: GARCH-EVT estimation on Bitcoin and Ethereum with a regime split at the Merge, derivation of Expected Shortfall for each regime, calibration of the Basel III and MiCA capital treatment from the resulting metrics, and a Bai-Perron robustness analysis on the Ethereum conditional variance series to test whether the regime split is uniquely identified by the Merge or whether it shares its significance with other contemporaneous breaks. The contribution is the integration and the regime decomposition, not any single method.

4 COMPUTATIONAL FRAMEWORK AND METHODOLOGY

4.1 Data Engineering and Pre-processing Pipeline

The full pipeline (time-series preprocessing, asynchronous cleaning through forward-fill, and econometric estimation) was implemented in Python. The asset universe covers Bitcoin (BTCUSD), Ethereum (ETH-USD), the S&P 500 index (GSPC), gold (GLD), Tether (USDT-USD), and DAI (DAI-USD), sampled at daily frequency between November 23, 2019 and May 29, 2026. The effective start date is set by the youngest series in the synchronized panel (DAI launched in late 2019). The balanced panel has 2,381 daily observations. Prices come from yfinance; the 10-year U.S. Treasury yield comes from FRED. Weekend and holiday gaps in the traditional series are filled forward against the continuous crypto series, and returns are computed as continuous logarithmic differences scaled by 100. Listing 1 documents the extraction stage; the full pipeline is in Appendix A.

Listing 1: API extraction and asynchronous alignment pipeline

```
#Script 1: Data extraction and forward fill (NaN cleaning)
import yfinance as yf
import pandas as pd
import numpy as np

#1. Institutional API Calls
```

```
df_crypto=yf.download(['BTC'-'USD'], start='2018-01-01')['Close']
df_trad      = yf.download(['GSPC','GLD'],   start='2018-01-01')['Close']

#2. Merging asynchronous data structures
df_precios=pd.concat([df_crypto,df_trad], axis=1)

#3. Handling null values (NaN) due to market closures
df_prices=df_prices.fill().dropna()

#4. Transformation to continuous logarithmic returns
df_returns=np.log(df_prices / df_prices.shift(1)).dropna()*100
```

The choice of forward-fill over linear interpolation is deliberate. Linear interpolation across a market closure manufactures intermediate prices that were never traded and artificially suppresses the Monday-open gap variance. Forward-fill carries the last traded price and assigns the full weekend information shock to the next observation, which preserves the empirical jump structure that EVT is designed to measure. The Augmented Dickey-Fuller test in Table 1 confirms that all six log-return series are stationary, which is the standard precondition for GARCH-type question.

Table 1. Augmented Dickey-Fuller stationary test on log returns

Series	ADF statistic	p-value	Lags	Stationary?
BTC returns	-15.9597	$< 10_{-6}$	8	Yes
ETH returns	-14.6312	$< 10_{-6}$	9	Yes
Gold returns	-10.8560	$< 10_{-6}$	27	Yes
SP500 returns	-9.5841	$< 10_{-6}$	26	Yes
USDT returns	-14.7837	$< 10_{-6}$	27	Yes
DAI returns	-12.5861	$< 10_{-6}$	26	Yes

Table 2. Descriptive statistics of daily log returns (x100)

Series	Mean	Std Dev	Skewness	Excess Kurtois	Jarque-Bera
BTC	0.0971	3.1927	-1.2979	21.8155	47,863.41
ETH	0.1090	4.2639	-1.0254	15.5065	24,262.02
Gold	0.0461	0.9406	-0.9236	12.6916	16,311.68
SP500	0.0373	1.0680	-0.7354	23.2357	53,754.29
USDT	-0.0002	0.2337	0.5539	242.0139	5,808,385.12
DAI	0.0003	0.5081	-1.2531	78.0140	604,169.28

The descriptive statistics make the Gaussian failure visible at a glance. Excess kurtosis for both crypto-assets is more than an order of magnitude above the Gaussian baseline of zero. The two stablecoins (USDT and DAI) show extreme kurtosis driven by rare peg events on a near-zero baseline volatility, which is the signature of a stable asset that occasionally breaks. Jarque-Bera rejects normality at every conventional significance level across all six series. That is the empirical basis for moving to the EVT framework in Section 4.2.2.

4.2 Mathematical Foundations of Stochastic Modeling

Before the empirical results, the stochastic structure of the models needs to be stated explicitly. The Gaussian framework has been ruled out by the descriptive evidence, so the alternative needs to handle heteroskedasticity, heavy tails, and tail-loss severity directly.

4.2.1 Asymmetric Conditional Variance: The EGARCH Model

Nelson (1991) proposed the Exponential GARCH model to handle a problem: standard GARCH models require non-negativity constraints on parameters to guarantee positive variance estimates, which is cumbersome. EGARCH solves this by working in logs, so the variance equation automatically stays positive.

$$ln(\sigma_t^2 = \omega + \beta ln\left(\sigma_{t-1}^2\right) + \alpha\left(|Z_{t-1}| - \mathbb{E}|Z_{t-1}|\right) + \gamma Z_{t-1}$$

The model itself is straightforward. You've got a baseline log-volatility constant(ω), persistence(β) that says how much yesterday's volatility matters today, a magnitude effect (α) for absolute shocks, and critically, an asymmetry term(γ) that captures the leverage effect-the empirical regularity that bad news raises volatility more than good news. If γ is negative and significant, you've got leverage.

If $\gamma \approx 0$, you don't. The residual Z_{t-1} is assumed to follow a student-t distribution to accommodate the leptokurtosis of the data.

There is a consequence of the log specification that the level-GARCH formulation hides. Because the EGARCH variance equation models $ln(\sigma_t^2)$, the effect of a shock on variance is multiplicative rather than additive. A two-standard-deviation move does not add a fixed quantum of variance to the system; it scales the existing variance level. That is the mechanism through which volatility clustering compounds during a liquidation cascade. The asymmetry term γZ_{t-1} enters linearly in the log, so the sign of γ separates the variance response to the two tails. For a genuine safe haven, the term is strongly negative. For bitcoin, the EGARCH-t fit in Section 4.4 returns $\gamma = -0.0118$ with p=0.4856, which is statistically indistinguishable from zero.

4.2.2 Extreme Risk: The Generalized Pareto Distribution

Extreme Value Theory under the Peak-Over-Threshold approach isolates the tail of the distribution without relying on the bulk of the data to fit it. Given a loss threshold u, set empirically at the worst 5% of the observations, the excesses x= y − u for y > u is modeled with the cumulative distribution function of the Generalized Pareto Distribution:

$$\mathcal{G}(x;\xi,\beta) = 1 - \left(1 + \frac{\xi x}{\beta}\right)^{\frac{-1}{\xi}}, \beta > 0, x \geq 0.$$

The scale parameter β governs the dispersion of extreme losses. The shape parameter ζ, the tail index, governs tail heaviness. A value ξ >0 places the distribution in the Fréchet maximum domain of attraction, which corresponds to heavy tails and an unbounded loss support, the signature of assets prone to systematic crashes.

The theoretical justification for Equation (1) is the Pickands-Balkema-de Haan Theorem (Pickands, 1975), which states that for a broad class of underlying distributions the conditional excess distribution converges to the GPD as the threshold u rises toward the right endpoint. The practical consequence is that the analyst does not need to know the true return distribution. Conditional on a sufficiently high threshold, the tail is GPD regardless of what the bulk looks like. That is the reason EVT works on crypto-asset returns where parametric Gaussian VaR systematically fails.

4.2.3 Expected Shortfall (Conditional VaR)

Parametric VaR reports the minimum loss at a given quantile. It is silent on what happens beyond that quantile, and it is not subadditive, which disqualifies it as a coherent risk measure. Expected Shortfall answers the question VaR cannot answer: conditional on a VaR breach, how large is the expected loss? In continuous form,

$$ES_q = \frac{1}{1-q}\int_q^1 VaR_u \, du$$

Under the EVT-GPD parameterization with the threshold u stated in loss units (positive), the

$$VaR_q = u + \frac{\beta}{\xi}\left[\left(\frac{n}{n_u}(1-q)\right)^{-\xi} - 1\right]$$

Where n is the full sample size and n_u is the count of exceedances above the threshold u. The closed form Expected Shortfall is

$$ES_q = \frac{VaR_q + \beta - \xi u}{1 - \xi}$$

Equation (4) is the quantity the Basel III framework requires for capital determination. It penalizes a high ξ heavily, because the denominator $1 - \xi$ goes to zero as ξ approaches one. When $\xi \geq 1$, the formula diverges, which is the formal statement that an asset with a sufficiently heavy tail has no finite expected worst-case loss and cannot be capitalized against by any finite buffer.

4.3 Econometric Modeling: Capturing the Cryptographic Microstructure

To quantify the volatility dynamics and test the safe-haven hypothesis for Bitcoin, three GARCHfamily models were fit. The architecture lets the conditional variance respond dynamically to past shocks instead of imposing a constant unconditional value.

The baseline is GARCH(1,1) under the Gaussian assumption, which serves as a control. Given the leptokurtosis evidence, a second GARCH(1,1) with Student-t innovations was fit to address the heavy-tail problem. To test for the leverage effect, an EGARCH(1,1,1) with Student-t innovations was fit as the third specification. Listing 2 reports the specification.

Listing 2. Conditional heteroskedasticity model specification

```
from arch import arch_model
```

```
#1. EGARCH(1,1,1) with Student-t innovations
egarch_spec=arch_model(y_btc, mean='zero',vol='EGARCH',

p=1, o=1, q=1, dist='students')
res_egarch=egarch_spec.fit(disp='off')

#2 Asymmetry coefficient (leverage)
coef_asymmetry=res_egarch.params ['gamma[1]']
pval_asymmetry=res_egarch.pvalues['gamma[1]']
```

Model selection was done through the Akaike and Bayesian information criteria. The Gaussian GARCH was penalized severely, with an AIC of 11,975.41 against 11,450.13 for GARCH-t and 11,439.95 for EGARCH-t. The drop from Gaussian to Student-t is large in absolute terms (more than 525 AIC units), and the additional drop from GARCH-t to EGARCH-t is moderate but enough to favor the asymmetric model under both criteria. The empirical conclusion is that crypto risk is dominated by heavy-tail events, and that any capital framework built on Gaussian variance estimates will under-reserve against precisely the events it is supposed to protect against.

Table 3. Model selection: information criteria across volatility specifications (BTC, n= 2,380)

Specification	Distribution	Log-Likelihood	AIC	BIC
GARCH(1, 1)	Gaussian	-5984.70	11,975.41	11,992.73
GARCH(1, 1)	Student-t	-5721.06	11,450.13	11,473.23
EGARCH(1, 1, 1)	Student-t	-5717.98	11,439.95	11,468.83

The EGARCH-t parameter estimates: ω=0.0605(p=0.0100), α=0.1537($p<10^{-4}$), γ=-0.0118(p=0.4856), β=0.9846($p<10^{-4}$), v=3.0908($p<10^{-4}$). The persistence parameter β at 0.9846 confirms strongly volatility clustering: a shock today moves variance level, and the variance level takes many days to revert. The Student-t degrees-of-freedom estimate $v\approx 3.09$ sits at the lower bound of econometric plausibility and is a separate signal that the third and fourth moments of the return distribution are barely defined. This is the structural reason a Gaussian VaR built on the second moment alone produces the wrong answer for Bitcoin.

4.4 Speculative Symmetry and the Refutation of the Safe Haven

The result that matters most from the volatility modeling is the asymmetry parameter γ. In equity markets such as the S&P 500, the same parameter comes in reliably negative and reliably significant, which captures the empirical regularity that systemic panic raises future variance more than market optimism of equal size raises it. The leverage effect is one of the canonical stylized facts of equity returns. Bitcoin does not show this pattern. The EGARCH fit returns $\gamma = -0.0118$ with $p = 0.4856$, so the coefficient is statistically indistinguishable from zero. The null of directional symmetry is not rejected.

That result is not validation. It is a refutation of one of the necessary conditions for safe-haven behavior. Bitcoin exhibits symmetric high volatility: speculative euphoria injects the same amount of instability into the system as panic does. A genuine safe-haven instrument acts as a stabilizer during liquidity crises by absorbing rather than amplifying the disturbance. Bitcoin amplifies the disturbance regardless of sign. It behaves like a speculative commodity that does not distinguish between bull-run dynamics and crash dynamics. The absence of the leverage effect, rather than being a neutral statistical curiosity, removes a microstructural property that any defensive asset is supposed to have.

4.5 Robustness Diagnostics and Residual Analysis

To make sure the volatility results are not driven by misspecification, a diagnostic protocol was run on the standardized residuals of the EGARCH-t fit. The maximum-likelihood algorithm converged cleanly, with no boundary issues on the parameter estimates.

The Ljung-Box test on the standardized residuals tests for residual serial autocorrelation, and the same test on the squared standardized residuals tests for remaining ARCH effects. Under the null, the residuals are white noise. The standardized residuals returned a p-value of 0.1544 and the squared residuals a p-value of 0.8554, both well above the 5% threshold. The null is not rejected in either case, which means the conditional variance equation has captured the heteroskedasticity structure in full. The model is robust enough to serve as the calibration source for the Monte Carlo engine in Section 5.2.

Box 1. Ljung-Box test

Series	Ljung-box statistic	P value
Standardized residuals	14.34	0.1544
Squared standardized residuals	5.69	0.8554

5 EMPIRICAL RESULTS AND RISK SIMULATION

5.1 Dynamic Correlation and the Collapse of Statistical Isolation

To track how the linear dependence between Bitcoin and traditional markets evolved over the sample, a 90-day rolling Pearson correlation was computed against the S&P 500 and against gold. The question the rolling correlation is designed to answer is whether the low-correlation property that the early literature reported survives in stress windows. Listing 3 documents the engine.

Listing 3. Dynamic correlation engine

```
temporal _window=90
corr_btc_sp500=df_returns['BTC']. rolling(window=temporal_window). corr(df_returns['SP500']
corr_btc_gold=df_returns['BTC']. rolling(window=temporal_window). corr(df_returns['gold'])
```

It does not survive. During calm periods the BTC-S&P 500 correlation is mildly negative, around −0.14, which gives the appearance of statistical isolation. The isolation breaks under stress. During the COVID-19 panic the correlation jumps to +0.46. During the Terra/Luna collapse it sits at +0.52. Through the 2022 tightening cycle it averages +0.54. At the height of the FTX failure it peaks at +0.61. The pattern is consistent across all four stress windows: the desks that liquidate equities during stress also liquidate crypto to raise dollars and sovereign debt, and the correlation that mattered for the safe-haven hypothesis turns out to be the wrong sign.

Table 5 reports on the windowed correlations.

Table 5. Crisis window correlations of Bitcoin against the S&P 500 and Gold

Period	BTC-S&P500	BTC-Gold
Normal(2020-21)	-0.143	0.183
COVID crash (Feb-May 2020)	0.463	0.337
Terra/LUNA collapse (May 2022)	0.521	0.156
2022 Tightening (full year)	0.545	0.166
FTX collapse (Oct-Dec 2022)	0.614	0.356
Recovery (2023-2025)	0.274	0.106

The BTC-Gold correlation tells a different story. It stays structurally lower across the entire sample and reacts less to stress, which is consistent with the two assets being driven by different macroeconomic factors. Gold has its own correlation structure with real rates and the dollar that does not run through the same risk-on / risk-off channel that drives BTC and the S&P 500.

The digital-gold analogy, on the empirical correlation evidence alone, does not hold.

5.2 Monte Carlo Simulation and Capital Requirements

To turn the EGARCH volatility forecast into a regulatory risk metric, a Monte Carlo engine was calibrated to the conditional variance the EGARCH model produces. The engine projects 10,000 stochastic price paths for Bitcoin over a 30-day trading horizon under a geometric Brownian motion whose diffusion term comes from the one-step variance forecast. Listing 4 reports the implementation, and Algorithm 1 the logic.

Listing 4: Stochastic simulation for capital requirements

```
forecast_vol=res_egarch.forecast(horizon=1)
vol_daily=np.sqrt(forecast_vol.variance.values [-1,:][0])/100

horizon=30
simulations=np.zeros((horizon, 10000))
simulations[0]=last_price
np.random.seed(42)
for t in range(1, horizon):
        shocks_z=np.random.standard_normal(10000)
        simulations [t]=simulations [t-1]*np.exp(
                -0.5*vol_daily**2+vol_daily*shocks_z

simulated_returns= (simulations [-1,:]-last_price)/last_price
var_99_mc=np.percentile(simulated_returns, 1)*100
```

Algorithm 1. Monte Carlo projection under EGARCH-calibrated diffusion1.

1. Estimate EGARCH-t parameters from the historical return series

2. Forecast one step conditional volatility σ
3. Initialize all M=10,000 paths at the last observed price P_0
4. For t=1 to T=30 do
5. Draw $Z_t^{(m)}$ N(0,1) for m=1,…,M
6. $P_t^{(m)} = P_{t-1}^{(m)} exp\left(-\frac{1}{2}\sigma^2 + \sigma z_t^{(m)}\right)$
7. *end for*
8. Compute terminal returns $r^{(m)} = \left(P_T^{(m)} - P_0\right)/P_0$
9. Return $VaR_{99} = 1st\ percentile\ of\ \{r^{(m)}\}$

With the last observed Bitcoin price at $73,504.15, the simulation returned a 30-day 99% VaR of −24.37%. For every $100,000 held in Bitcoin, the 30-day 99% loss expectation is $24,371.

That is a heavy capital cost for any traditional institution and is consistent with the Basel Committee's assignment of crypto-assets to the maximum-risk category. The economic reading is direct: the lower tail of a one-month holding period for Bitcoin eats nearly a quarter of the position, which is the kind of number that pushes the asset out of conventional treasury policy.

5.3 Extreme Value Theory and Tail Risk

The Monte Carlo result is a useful headline, but it inherits the Gaussian-shock assumption from the geometric Brownian motion. To get a tail estimate that is not contaminated by the bulk of the distribution, EVT was applied through the POT method. The left tail, the worst 5% of historical returns, was isolated and fit to a GPD. Listing 5 reports on the calibration.

Listing 5. Extreme Value Theory calibration (corrected closed form)

```
from spicy.stats import genpareto, ks_1samp
import numpy as np

#1. Threshold and exceedances on the loss tail
umbral_var=np.percentile(negative_returns, 5)cutoff #negative return
excesses    =negatives returns[negatives_returns<umbral_var]
absolute_excesses=np.abs(excesses-umbral_var)

#2. GDP fit
```

```
form,_,escale=genpareto.fit(absolute_excesses, floc=0)

#3 Closed form VaR and ES (loss units, positive)
n_total,n_u, q = len(negatives_returns), len(absolute excesses), 0.99
u_loss= abs(umbral_var)
qe = (escale/form)*(((n_total/n_u)*(1-q))**(-form)-1)
var_L = u_loss + qe
es_L =(var_L + escale - form* u_loss)/(1-form)
var_99_evt, es_99= -var_L, -es_L
```

The shape parameter came in positive at $\xi = 0.2611$, which places the tail in the Fréchet maximum domain of attraction and confirms heavy-tail behavior. The scale parameter is $\beta = 1.9775$, calibrated on nu = 119 exceedances above the threshold u = −4.72% from a total sample of n = 2,380. The EVT VaR at the 99% confidence level is −8.67%, and the associated Expected Shortfall is −12.75%. The gap between the VaR and the ES is 4.08 percentage points of daily loss. That gap is part of the risk that a VaR-only framework ignores by construction, and it is the quantity that drives the Basel III preference for ES over VaR as the headline capital measure.

5.3.1 Extreme-Risk Robustness: Backtesting and Goodness of Fit

The GPD calibration needs to be validated against overfitting before it can be used for capital determination. The Kolmogorov-Smirnov goodness-of-fit test, with null that the empirical tail excesses are drawn from the calibrated GPD, returned a KS statistic of 0.0590 with a p-value of 0.7785, well above the 5% level. The null is not rejected. The GPD is an adequate model for the tail. The QQ-plot of empirical against theoretical quantiles confirms the visual fit.

Historical backtesting closes the validation loop. The realized worst 1% of trading days in the sample averaged −8.73%, against the parametric EVT estimate of −8.67%. The two figures converge within six basis points, which is the kind of agreement that licenses the use of the EVT estimate for regulatory capital calibration. If the parametric estimate had diverged from the empirical worst-case average by, say, two or three percentage points, the model would not have passed a serious review.

Table 6. EVT validation: goodness of fit and historical backtest (BTC, q=0.99)

Diagnostic	Statistic	Outcome
Kolmogorov-Smirnov (GPD fit)	0.0590	P = 0.7785 (not rejected)
GPD shape parameter	0.2611	Fréchet, heavy tail
GPD scale parameter β	1.9775	----
EVT VaR(99%)	-8.67%	Parametric tail estimate
EVT Expected Shortfall (99%)	-12.75%	Conditional tail loss
Realized historical VaR (worst 1%)	-8.73%	Empirical convergence

5.4 The Fallacy of Traditional Diversification: The Markowitz Trap

I want to show why the regulatory caution matters in practical portfolio terms. So, I built a simple test: a 50/50 stock-and-gold portfolio as the baseline, then let a Markowitz optimizer add Bitcoin and see what happens.

The optimizer does what optimizers do it sees the high historical return and low historical variance and allocates 7.10% to Bitcoin.

Listing 6. Non-linear portfolio optimization (Markowitz)

```
from spicy.optimaze import minimize

def_minimizar_sharpe(pesos):
returns = np.sum(returns_medios * pesos)
risk                                    =np.sqrt(np.dot(pe-
sos.T, np.dot(covariance, pesos)))
sharpe                                  = (rendimiento -
tasa_libre_riesgo)/Riesgo
return-shape

restrictions=({'type': 'eq', 'fun': lambda x: np.
sum(x)-1})
limits
= tuple((0,) r_in range(len(active)))

results= minimize(mi mize_sharpe, initials_pesos,

   method='SLSQP', bounds_limtis,
```

```
                                             con-
straints = restrictions)
Markowitz_pesos =resu ts_x
```

The allocation looks good on paper: Sharpe ratio goes from 0.87 to 0.93, which sounds like a win. You rebalance toward 29.28% equities, 63.62% gold, and suddenly Bitcoin makes the portfolio look smarter.

But this is where the Gaussian assumption kills you. The actual story is darker. The optimizer sees risk only as variance under a normality assumption, with a static covariance matrix. It registers Bitcoin's high historical mean return, gets the variance estimate it expects, and is structurally blind to the directional asymmetry, the Expected Shortfall, and the dynamic correlation behavior in stress. The allocation looks great in calm periods and falls apart when the tail event arrives.

5.4.1 Empirical Stress Test: The Reality of Maximum Drawdown

To pressure-test the optimizer's recommendation, the two portfolios were back-tested across the full sample and the Maximum Drawdown was computed for each. The benchmark 50/50 portfolio bottomed at a peak-to-trough loss of −21.68%. The Markowitz-optimized portfolio with 7.10% Bitcoin reached a deeper drawdown of −22.82%. The optimizer promised a better Sharpe ratio and delivered a worse realized loss. Bitcoin did not provide the diversification the optimizer expected from it; it deepened the crash on the days that mattered. That is the empirical confirmation of the EVT-based thesis: unconditional volatility metrics mask the tail-loss severity, and any framework that ignores the tail will sooner or later allocate capital to crypto in ways that violate the capital-preservation principles of Basel III.

5.5 Systemic Contagion and Rehypothecation: The Autopsy of the FTX Collapse

The risk dynamics of the crypto ecosystem are easier to see through specific failures than through aggregate statistics. The FTX collapse in November 2022 is the most useful case study available, because it was an endogenous solvency event rather than an exogenous macro shock, and because the post-bankruptcy investigation produced enough disclosure to reconstruct the mechanism. FTX issued its own utility token, FTT, which traded mainly on FTX itself and granted trading-fee discounts to holders. FTX retained the majority of the circulating supply and used a marginal float in the open market to keep the price elevated. Alameda Research, FTX's sister hedge fund, posted these FTT tokens as collateral and borrowed billions against them, treating an illiquid self-issued token as high-quality collateral. When

Alameda's trading losses became unsustainable and the FTT price started to fall, FTX diverted customer deposits, real dollars and real Bitcoin, to cover the margin call rather than letting Alameda fail in isolation. The disclosure that triggered the bank run came on 6 November 2022, when a competing exchange announced it would sell its FTT holdings, and the rest of the FTX collapse played out over the following ten days. Within that ten-day window, the stablecoin layer was tested. USDT, backed by traditional fiat reserves, held its peg with a maximum deviation of 0.22 cents on the dollar. DAI, overcollateralized primarily with Ethereum and other crypto-assets, deviated by 0.23 cents. Neither broke its peg, but the difference in the backing structure matters: DAI was exposed to a second-order risk that USDT was not, because a sufficiently large drawdown in Ethereum could have forced DAI's collateral auctions into a falling market and produced a procyclical liquidation spiral. The peg held in this particular episode, but the structural exposure remained.

The actuarial implication is specific. Rehypothecation of an illiquid, self-issued token as senior collateral is the crypto-native equivalent of the off-balance-sheet conduits that propagated the 2008 crisis through structured-credit markets. The risk is invisible to any model that takes reported collateral values at face value, because the collateral price is an artifact of the issuer's own market-making rather than a third-party assessment. A capital framework that relies on mark-to-market collateral values, rather than on the EVT-derived tail behavior of the underlying assets, will under-reserve against this failure mode by construction.

5.6 Algorithmic Stablecoins and Death Spirals: The Terra/LUNA Collapse

The Terra/LUNA collapse in May 2022 sits in a different category from the FTX failure. FTX was a centralized exchange that misappropriated customer funds; Terra was an algorithmic protocol that broke under its own design constraints. Terra is the cleanest case study available for what happens when an uncollateralized algorithmic stablecoin meets a sufficiently large outflow.

The protocol used a dual-token seigniorage mechanism. UST (the stablecoin) was supposed to hold its dollar peg through an arbitrage relationship with LUNA (the governance token): one dollar of UST could always be redeemed for one dollar of LUNA at the protocol level, with the algorithm minting or burning LUNA as needed to keep UST at parity. The architecture worked as long as confidence in LUNA was sustained. The Anchor Protocol, a money-market application inside the Terra ecosystem, offered a guaranteed annual yield close to 20% on UST deposits. That rate pulled billions of dollars into UST, much of it from sophisticated investors who knew the yield was subsidized from protocol reserves rather than from organic cash flow but bet that the subsidy would outlast their position. Listing 7 documents the collapse analysis.

Listing 7: Endogenous risk modeling: the death spiral

```
import yfinance as yf matplotlib.pyplot as plt pandas as pd

tickers_terra=[‘USTC-USD’,’LUNC-USD’]
df_terra= yf.download(tickers_terra,
                          start=’2022-05-01’, end=’2022-05-31’) [‘Close’]

price_ust=df_terra [‘USTC-USD’]
price_luna=df_terra [‘LUNC-USD’]
mdd_luna                       =((price_luna.min()-price_luna.max())*100
depeg_ust                      =(1.00-price_ust.min())*100

print(f”Max Drawdown LUNA: {mdd_luna:.2f%’} #-99.99%
print(f”De-peg UST :{depeg_ust:.2f}cents”)  #97.49 cents
```

The subsidy did not outlast the run. When UST began to lose its peg in May 2022, the arbitrage mechanism activated, which meant the protocol minted hyperinflationary quantities of LUNA to absorb users fleeing UST. The Luna Foundation Guard deployed its Bitcoin reserves to defend the peg, and the selling pressure consumed the reserves within hours. LUNA’s Maximum Drawdown reached –99.99%; UST lost 97.49 cents of its parity. The event destroyed more than $40 billion in market value and showed, in real time, that an algorithm cannot substitute for real fiat liquidity once confidence breaks.

The lesson generalizes well beyond Terra. Any protocol that promises an above-market yield funded from reserves rather than from organic cash flow is running a maturity transformation without a lender of last resort. The death-spiral dynamic, where a de-peg triggers reflexive supply expansion that accelerates the de-peg, is mathematically a positive-feedback loop with no stable equilibrium below par. The $\xi > 0$ tail behavior that EVT measures for the liquid crypto-assets is severe but finite. The algorithmic stablecoin tail is, for practical purposes, unbounded, which is exactly the failure mode that MiCA’s reserve mandate is designed to prevent.

5.7 Structural Contrast: Bitcoin (PoW) versus Ethereum (PoS)

Risk analysis in crypto-assets needs to differentiate by consensus protocol. The literature has tended to group Bitcoin and Ethereum into one asset class, but their economic microstructures are distinct, and the distinction widened after the Ethereum upgrade known as The Merge on 15 September 2022, which transitioned the network from Proof-of-Work to Proof-of-Stake.

From an actuarial perspective, Bitcoin operates as an inelastic digital commodity. Its production cost is anchored to the thermodynamic energy expenditure of miners, which gives it a floor that responds to hash rate and electricity prices rather than to interest rates or central-bank policy. Ethereum after the Merge is a different kind of asset: validators stake capital to secure the network and earn a continuous yield on their stake, which makes ETH closer to a perpetual instrument with an embedded coupon than to a pure commodity. The hybrid profile, the volatility of a crypto-asset combined with the rate sensitivity of a yield-bearing instrument, is what makes ETH harder to slot into a standard asset taxonomy. Listing 8 documents the comparative estimation, and Table 7 reports the regime decomposition.

Listing 8: Structural contrast and tail risk (PoW vs PoS)

```
import numpy as np
from arch import arch_model

MERGE_DATE='2022-09-15'
r_btc = df_returns ['BTC']
r_eth = df_returns ['ETH']
r_eth pow= r_eth[:MERGE_DATE]
r_eth_pos= r_eth[MERGE_DATE]

GARCH(1,1)-t on each regime
for label, series in [('BTC', r_btc),
 ('ETH-PoW', r_eth_pow),
 ('ETH-PoS', r_eth_pos)]:
m= arch_model(series, mean='Zero', vol='Garch',
                                        p=1 1, dist=
'students').fit(disp='off')
print(label, m.params)
```

Table 7.Comparative tail risk: Bitcoin (PoW control) vs Ethereum regimes

Metric	BTC(PoW)	ETH (PoW)	ETH (PoS)	*ΔPoW → PoS*
Sample size n	2,380	1,028	1,353	---
Annualized volatility	50.68%	82,54%	53.88%	-28.66%
GARCH persistence α+β	1	0.9451	0.8566	-0.089
GARCH degress of freedom v	3.094	4.207	3.105	-1.102
VaR 95% (historical)	-4.72%	-7.53%	-5.15	+2.38%
VaR 99% (historical)	-8.73%	-13.65%	-8.94%	+4.71%
ES 95% (Historical)	-7.44%	-12.18%	-7.88%	+4.30%
ES 99% (Historical)	-12.96%	-21.24%	-12.52%	+8.72%
Max Drawdown	-83.72%	-86.23%	-72.72%	+13.51%

The regime decomposition reframes the public narrative. Before the Merge, Ethereum was substantially more dangerous than Bitcoin across every measured tail metric: 82.54% annualized volatility against 50.68%, 99% VaR of −13.65% against −8.73%, 99% ES of −21.24% against −12.96%. The shift to Proof-of-Stake compressed every one of these metrics. Post-Merge Ethereum sits at 53.88% annualized volatility, a 28.7% reduction from the PoW regime; 99% VaR of −8.94%, essentially identical to Bitcoin's −8.73%; and 99% ES of −12.52%, slightly below Bitcoin's −12.96%. The economic reading is that PoW Ethereum was catastrophic on tail metrics, and that the Merge brought ETH's tail behavior down to Bitcoin's baseline rather than pushing it further.

The cross-asset comparison still matters at the aggregate level, even after the regime split. The unconditional Ethereum sample, treating the whole period as one regime, gives a 99% historical VaR of −12.30% against Bitcoin's −8.83%. That is what an investor who held ETH continuously across the regime change actually experienced, and it is the figure that drives the GARCH-t degrees-of-freedom estimate of 3.05 for Bitcoin versus 3.38 for the full Ethereum sample. The unconditional figure overstates the post-Merge risk and understates the pre-Merge risk, which is exactly why the regime split is necessary.

The statistical significance of the regime shift was tested through four separate procedures. The Welch t-test on squared residuals returned a statistic of 4.4230 at $p = 1.1\times 10-5$. The Kolmogorov-Smirnov two-sample test rejected distributional equality with $KS = 0.1264$ and $p < 10-6$. Levene's test on variances returned

96.69 at p < 10–6. The Cramér-von Mises two-sample test returned 3.1220 at p < 10–6. By every conventional test, the PoW-to-PoS regime change is significant. A placebo procedure that splits the Ethereum sample at non-Merge dates also rejected equality in five of five placebo dates, which means the ETH series has an underlying structural-break frequency that is not unique to the Merge. The most honest reading, and the one I commit to in this thesis, is that ETH undergoes recurrent structural breaks (regulatory shocks, technological upgrades, contagion events) and the Merge is one of several. The magnitude of the tail-risk compression at the Merge cutoff is among the largest, but the chapter does not claim causal exclusivity for the Merge; it documents the magnitude and lets the placebo and Bai-Perron analyses bound the interpretation.

Table 8. Statistical significance of the regime shift: real Merge versus placebo dates

Test	Statistic	P value
Real partition (15 Sept 2022)		
Welch t (squared residuals)	4.4230	$1.1x10^{-5}$
Kolmogorov-Smirnov two sample	0.1264	$< 10_{-6}$
Levene (variance equality)	96.6922	$< 10_{-6}$
Cramèr-von Mises two sample	3.1220	$< 10_{-6}$
Placebo partions (Welch p)		
15 March 2021	---	0.0543
15 September 2021	---	0.0011
15 March 2022	---	0.0004
15 March 2023	---	0
15 September 2023	---	0.0003

The regulatory implication has an edge to it. Under the current BCBS treatment, both assets receive the identical 1250% weight, which means the framework is indifferent to the multipercentage-point difference in daily tail loss between the pre-Merge and post-Merge regimes. That indifference is defensible only if the regulator's intent is a blanket deterrent rather than risk-sensitive calibration. The data argues for a regime-aware capital treatment that recognizes Ethereum post-Merge as carrying a tail profile statistically indistinguishable from Bitcoin, while Ethereum pre-Merge carried meaningfully more risk than either.

6 CONCLUSIONS AND REGULATORY POLICY RECOMMENDATIONS

6.1 Synthesis of Empirical Results and Refutation of the Safe Haven

The question this thesis set out to test was whether Bitcoin (and, by extension, the broader unbacked crypto-asset class) can act as a safe haven for institutional portfolios during liquidity stress. The combined evidence, across the EGARCH leverage test, the rolling correlation analysis, the Monte Carlo and EVT tail estimates, the Markowitz backtest, and the BTC-versus-ETH regime decomposition, is that it cannot.

Three results carry the conclusion. The EGARCH asymmetry parameter for Bitcoin sits at $\gamma = -0.0118$ with $p = 0.4856$, statistically indistinguishable from zero, which means the leverage effect that defines equity markets is absent and that Bitcoin amplifies euphoria and panic in roughly equal measure. The rolling-correlation analysis shows that the low-correlation property breaks under stress: from −0.14 in calm windows to +0.46 during the COVID crash and +0.61 at the height of the FTX panic. The PoW-versus-PoS decomposition shows that Ethereum pre-Merge was catastrophically worse than Bitcoin on every tail metric, and that the Merge brought ETH down to Bitcoin's baseline rather than past it; the Bai-Perron analysis in

Appendix D modulates the causal claim by detecting 28 other structural breaks in the same series. None of the three configurations (BTC, ETH-PoW, ETH-PoS) behaves as a safe haven.

6.2 Prudential Architecture and Capital Requirements: The BCBS Standard

What does this mean for actual risk managers? The short answer: the Gaussian frameworks that run most commercial-bank treasuries are systematically underestimating the tail. The Markowitz optimizer can't see Expected Shortfall, only variance. So when you plug in the measured numbers—daily ES of 12.75% or 30-day VaR of 24.37%—reality is much worse than what the optimizer thinks.

The Basel Committee published its final standard in December 2022, and it says: Group 2 unbacked crypto-assets get a 1250% risk weight. That translates to 100% capital deduction. A bank holding 100 million in Bitcoin needs to reserve 100 million in capital against it. Full stop. Most big banks just stopped holding crypto because the capital cost made it uneconomical. That was the whole point. The interesting comparison is between the standardized weight and the model-derived requirement. The measured daily ES of −12.75%, scaled to the 10-day regulatory horizon under the standard $\sqrt{10}$ time-scaling and a 3× multiplier, implies a model-based capital requirement of $3.0 \times \sqrt{10} \times 12.75\% \approx 120\%$ of notional, which is above the 100% capital deduction the 1250% risk weight produces. The standardized treatment, in other words, is not punitive relative to the measured tail behavior; it is consistent with it, and it is on the low side of what an internal-model approach would generate. That comparison was missing from the academic literature when the standard was published, and supplying it is the regulatory contribution of this thesis.

6.3 Legal Taxonomy: The Howey Test versus the MiCA Regulation

To address the systemic risks the empirical record exposes, jurisdictions have taken two different approaches. The United States has stayed inside the existing securities-law framework, with the Securities and Exchange Commission applying the 1946 Howey Test to classify Proof-of-Stake protocols and algorithmic stablecoins as unregistered securities on a case-by-case basis. The regulation-by-enforcement model creates legal uncertainty for institutions operating in U.S. jurisdiction, and the resulting risk premium has pushed substantial crypto activity offshore.

The European Union took the opposite path. The Markets in Crypto-Assets Regulation, EU Regulation 2023/1114 (MiCA), is the first comprehensive ex-ante framework for the asset class. MiCA replaces retroactive sanctions with a forward-looking taxonomy that separates Asset-Referenced Tokens, Electronic Money Tokens, and purely speculative crypto-assets, with different requirements applying to each. The reserve, audit, and one-to-one fund-segregation requirements that MiCA imposes on stablecoin issuers are designed specifically to prevent the failure modes documented in this thesis: the FTX rehypothecation scheme would have been impossible under MiCA's segregation rules, and the Terra/LUNA architecture would have failed the reserve test at the licensing stage rather than during a market panic.

6.4 Final Actuarial Verdict

Unbacked crypto-assets, as the market is currently structured, are a major source of systemic risk rather than a hedge against it. The underlying distributed ledger technology has clear potential to streamline interbank settlement and certain classes of cross-border payment, but the native assets (Bitcoin, Ethereum, the rest of the Layer-1 ecosystem) are not compatible with institutional capital-preservation mandates as currently designed. Until global regulatory convergence around MiCA style frameworks and Basel III liquidity requirements is achieved, the direct integration of the decentralized ecosystem with traditional commercial banking should remain isolated, which is what the 1250% risk weight effectively enforces.

7 GENERAL CONCLUSIONS AND FINANCIAL PROSPECTIVE

7.1 Historical Context and Narrative Refutation

The crypto-asset ecosystem was built in the years after 2008 on a specific narrative: a decentralized monetary architecture that would be immune to central-bank expansion, immune to inflation, and uncorrelated with traditional markets. The narrative was internally consistent and rested on a plausible structural argument about the demand side of the market. The empirical record over the last six years has shown what happens to that narrative once the same institutional desks trade both asset classes. The structural independence argument breaks at the demand side. Crypto-assets are now procyclical risk-on instruments, highly sensitive to global liquidity contractions and traded against the same risk-off rotation as equity beta.

7.2 Methodological Justification: The Computational Risk Engine

The methodological frame this thesis used was chosen because the standard alternatives fail on the data. GARCH-t and EGARCH-t captured the conditional variance directly because constant-variance models cannot represent the empirical clustering. The Student-t innovations were the response to the leptokurtosis: with $v \approx 3.09$, the fourth moment is barely defined and the third moment is unstable. Extreme Value Theory through POT was used because parametric Gaussian VaR systematically understates the tail; the resulting $\xi = 0.2611$ is the formal expression of why the tail is heavy. Monte Carlo simulation translated the EGARCH variance forecast into a 30-day capital requirement, and the Markowitz backtest documented the practical danger of using the wrong framework: an optimizer that maximizes the Sharpe ratio while measuring risk as variance allocates capital to Bitcoin in a way that produces a deeper realized drawdown than the benchmark portfolio it was supposed to improve.

7.3 Regulatory Urgency and the Empirical Justification for Intervention

The numerical results do not exist in isolation. They are the empirical case for why the regulatory architecture matters. The Basel III 1250% risk weight, the MiCA reserve and segregation requirements, and the BCBS classification of crypto-assets into Group 1 and Group 2 are designed as firewalls between the volatility of the digital ecosystem and the deposits of the real economy. The Terra/LUNA collapse, the FTX rehypothecation fraud, and the synchronized 2022 crypto-equity correlation spike are the events those firewalls are meant to prevent from spilling into commercial banking. Without the firewalls, the absence of exogenous liquidity in the crypto ecosystem produces destructive feedback loops of the kind that Terra showed in real time. The Basel III penalty is consistent with the measured tail behavior; the MiCA reserve mandate targets exactly the structural defects that the autopsies in Section 5 identified.

7.4 The Future of Crypto-Assets as Safe Havens

The trend is already there if you look at the data. Ethereum moved to Proof-of-Stake and started behaving less like a commodity and more like a high-beta tech stock. As more institutions hold crypto—and the ETF channels keep opening up—the asset class gets dragged into the same liquidity cycles as the traditional market.

Here's the uncomfortable part: the correlations we see in this thesis during stress Bitcoin at +0.61 to equities during FTX—those are probably not going away. If anything, they get tighter as Bitcoin becomes more institutional. A hedge that worked in 2019 won't work in 2030 because there's no "flight to safety" if everyone's holding the same assets.

This trajectory is consistent with Chohan (2022), who argues that recurrent "crypto winters" are likely to remain a structural feature of the asset class until it fully matures, a view that directly undercuts the claim that crypto-assets are acyclical, sentiment-independent, or hedge-like. So can crypto-assets function as safe havens in the future? On the quantitative evidence, the short and medium-term answer is no. A safe haven requires sustained market trust during stress, manifested as capital inflows when other assets are being liquidated. Bitcoin and Ethereum do the opposite: they are among the first assets liquidated to cover margin elsewhere, because they are continuously liquid and trade against a deep dollar market 24 hours a day. In the long term, if global regulation removes the most obvious malicious actors, the market capitalization grows enough to dilute the institutional liquidation flow, and the institutional holding-period structure lengthens, Bitcoin in particular could mature in a direction that brings its stress correlation closer to gold. That would not make it a safe haven in the strict Baur-Lucey sense, but it would move it out of the high-beta tech-proxy category it currently sits in. The natural endpoint looks more like a high-yield, high-risk alternative asset class useful for speculative diversification in prosperity, rather than a safety anchor in crisis. The direct integration of the decentralized ecosystem with traditional banking treasuries needs to continue to be treated with the highest capital-penalty rigor. The mathematics of extreme risk are clear. In institutional finance, algorithmic technology cannot yet replace the role of fiat stability and central-bank backstops.

7.5 Limitations and Future Research

The limitations of the empirical work need to be named explicitly. The sample period starts in late November 2019 and captures three major stress episodes (COVID-19, Terra/LUNA, FTX), but it does not cover a full credit cycle, and the structural breaks that the Ethereum data exhibits, documented in Appendix D, mean that the regime estimates will shift as the post-Merge sample grows. The EVT threshold at the 5% level is validated through the sensitivity analysis in Appendix B but remains a modeling judgment, and the Hill estimator or the mean excess-plot heuristic would produce modestly different estimates of ξ and β. The cross-asset dependence analysis uses rolling Pearson correlation rather than a time-varying copula, which would refine the stress-window estimates and capture the upper-tail dependence more accurately. The regulatory calibration assumes structural stability of the BCBS framework through its 2026 implementation; if the standard is renegotiated or if internal-model approaches are extended to crypto exposures, the mapping from ES to risk weight will need to be redone. Survivorship bias in the exchange-level price data is non-zero, because failed venues stop contributing prices to the aggregates by construction, and the sample of crypto-assets I cover is biased toward the survivors. The placebo partition test and the Bai-Perron / PELT robustness check produced an uncomfortable but useful result: the Ethereum series exhibits frequent structural breaks beyond the Merge, which limits the causal claim attached to any single event. The most defensible position is that the Merge is one of several mid-2022 structural breaks, and that the tail-risk compression observed post-Merge is part of a broader regime change rather than a Merge-exclusive effect. Future work should formalize this through a Markov-switching GARCH or a Bai-Perron test on the GARCH coefficient vector rather than the conditional-variance series; both approaches would provide tighter identification of the breaks at the cost of substantially higher estimation complexity. The framework should also be extended to a multivariate vine-copula structure to capture the upper-tail dependence during stress, the PoS tail should be re-estimated as the post-Merge sample grows past the current 1,353 observations, and the regulatory calibration should be tested against the loss data that will emerge under the fully implemented BCBS standard once banks start reporting Group 2 exposures.

AI DISCLOSURE STATEMENT

In accordance with IGI Global editorial policy and COPE/STM 2023 guidance on AI-assisted authorship, the author discloses the following: Use of AI Tools: Anthropic Claude (Opus family, accessed May 2026) was used for two specific purposes:

1. Extensive editorial revision and register harmonization of Sections 1 (Introduction), 2 (Theoretical Framework), and portions of 7 (General Conclusions), applied to improve clarity, consistency, and adherence to academic publishing conventions.

2. Structural assistance in compiling LaTeX manuscript formatting and constructing table layouts.

Work Conducted by the Human Author: All quantitative work—GARCH-t and EGARCH-t parameter estimation, EVT-GPD calibration, Extreme Value Theory threshold selection, Monte Carlo simulation, Bai-Perron/PELT structural break detection, the regulatory mapping between Expected Shortfall and Basel III capital requirements, Python code implementation and execution, and the financial autopsies of Terra/LUNA and FTX—were conducted and intellectually authored by the human author. All numerical results presented in Tables 1–11 are reproducible from the Python implementations documented in Appendix A and the source data cited therein. Limitations and Transparency: The author acknowledges that AI-assisted revision of narrative prose, while not generating the intellectual content, may have altered stylistic markers that would normally be present in purely human-authored text. This disclosure is made in the interest of full transparency regarding the production process.

Responsibility: The author Kevin Olalla accepts full responsibility for all content, empirical findings, policy interpretations, limitations, and any errors that remain in this manuscript.

REFERENCES

Ali, S., Bouri, E., Roubaud, D., & Vinh Vo, X. (2021). The impact of COVID-19 on cryptocurrency markets: A financial-stability analysis. *Finance Research Letters*, *38*, 101798.

Ante, L. (2023). How Elon Musk's Twitter activity moves cryptocurrency markets. *Technological Forecasting and Social Change*, *186*, 122112.

Auer, R., Cornelli, G., Doerr, S., Frost, J., & Gambacorta, L. (2023). Crypto Trading and Bitcoin Prices: Evidence from a New Database of Retail Adoption. BIS Working Papers No. 1049, Bank for International Settlements.

Auer, R., & Tercero-Lucas, D. (2023). Rise of the machines: Algorithmic stablecoins and the quest for stability. BIS Bulletin, No. 132.

Baur, D. G., & Dimpfl, T. (2021). The volatility of Bitcoin and its role as a medium of exchange and a store of value. *Empirical Economics*, *61*(5), 2663–2683.

Baur, D. G., & Lucey, B. M. (2010). Is gold a hedge or a safe haven? An analysis of stocks, bonds and gold. *Financial Review*, *45*(2), 217–229.

Baur, D. G., & McDermott, T. K. (2010). Is gold a safe haven? International evidence. *Journal of Banking & Finance*, *34*(8), 1886–1898.

Bollerslev, T. (1986). Generalized autoregressive conditional heteroskedasticity. *Journal of Econometrics*, *31*(3), 307–327.

Bouri, E., Molnár, P., Azzi, G., Roubaud, D., & Hagfors, L. I. (2017). On the hedge and safe haven properties of Bitcoin: Is it really more than a diversifier? *Finance Research Letters*, *20*, 192–198.

Chohan, U. W. (2022). Crypto Winters. Critical Blockchain Research Initiative (CBRI) Working Paper, SSRN. Conlon, T., & McGee, R. (2020). Safe haven or risky hazard? Bitcoin during the COVID-19 bear market. *Finance Research Letters*, *35*, 101607.

Corbet, S., Lucey, B., Urquhart, A., & Yarovaya, L. (2019). Cryptocurrencies as a financial asset: A systematic analysis. *International Review of Financial Analysis*, *62*, 182–199.

Gilli, M., & Këllezi, E. (2006). An application of extreme value theory for measuring financial risk. *Computational Economics*, *27*(2), 207–228.

Hacibedel, B., & Perez-Saiz, H. (2023). Assessing Macrofinancial Risks from Crypto XVII. Assets. IMF Working Papers.

Härdle, W. K., Harvey, C. R., & Reule, R. C. G. (2020). Understanding cryptocurrencies. *Journal of Financial Econometrics*, *18*(2), 181–208.

International Monetary Fund. (2023). *Elements of Effective Policies for Crypto Assets*. IMF Policy Paper.

Kristoufek, L. (2020). Grandpa, grandpa, tell me the one about Bitcoin being a safe haven: New evidence from the COVID-19 pandemic. *Frontiers in Physics*, *8*, 296.

Markowitz, H. (1952). Portfolio selection. *The Journal of Finance*, *7*(1), 77–91.

Nelson, D. B. (1991). Conditional heteroskedasticity in asset returns: A new approach. *Econometrica*, *59*(2), 347–370.

Patra, S., & Gupta, N. (2023). Risk in the cryptocurrency markets: The role of structural breaks and fat-tailed distributions in estimating value-at-risk and expected shortfall. *European Journal of Finance*. Advance online publication.

Pickands, J. (1975). Statistical inference using extreme order statistics. *Annals of Statistics*, *3*(1), 119–131.

Teruzzi, A. (2023). Tail Risk and Systemic Risk Estimation of Cryptocurrencies: An Expectiles and Marginal Expected Shortfall Based Approach. arXiv preprint arXiv:2311.17239.

KEY TERMS AND DEFINITIONS

Algorithmic Stablecoin: A digital asset designed to hold a stable value, usually pegged to the U.S. dollar, not through fiat reserves but through a smart-contract algorithm that expands or contracts token supply via arbitrage incentives.

Basel III Risk Weighting: A regulatory standard set by the Basel Committee that determines the capital a bank must hold against its assets. A 1250% weight for crypto-assets implies a full capital deduction, backing the exposure dollar-for-dollar.

Conditional Heteroskedasticity: A property of time-series data where the variance of current returns depends on the variance of prior periods. It is the formal expression of the volatility-clustering phenomenon observed in crypto-asset returns.

Death Spiral: A catastrophic feedback loop in algorithmic stablecoin ecosystems, where a loss of peg triggers uncontrolled token minting that dilutes value toward zero within hours. The May 2022 Terra/LUNA collapse is the canonical example.

Expected Shortfall (Conditional VaR): A risk metric that gives the average expected loss in the worst-case scenarios, focusing on the tail once the VaR threshold has been breached. Unlike standard VaR, ES is subadditive and is the metric the Basel III framework prefers.

Extreme Value Theory (EVT): A branch of statistics that treats extreme deviations from the median of probability distributions. In finance, EVT is used to model the probability and magnitude of black-swan events directly, without relying on the bulk of the distribution.

Howey Test: A legal framework from the 1946 U.S. Supreme Court case used to determine whether a transaction qualifies as an investment contract. It is the primary tool the SEC uses to classify crypto-assets as securities.

Leptokurtosis (Heavy Tails): Distribution with thicker tails and a sharper peak than the Gaussian, indicating that extreme price swings occur far more frequently than the standard normal model predicts.

Leverage Effect (Asymmetry): A market regularity where negative returns raise future volatility more than positive returns of equal magnitude. The EGARCH model is designed to detect and measure it.

Proof-of-Work (PoW) vs. Proof-of-Stake (PoS): Blockchain consensus mechanisms. PoW (Bitcoin) relies on computational power and energy expenditure. PoS (Ethereum, post-Merge) relies on validators staking capital, which creates an endogenous yield structure similar to a bond coupon.

APPENDIX A: COMPLETE COMPUTATIONAL PIPELINE

The full Python implementation is reproduced below for audit and replication. Package versions: yfinance= 0.2.66, pandas= 2.2.2, numpy= 2.0.2, arch= 8.0.0, Scipy= 1.16.3, matplotlib= 3.10.0, seaborn= 0.13.2, statsmodels= 0.14.6, Pycoingecko= 3.2.0, ruptures= 1.1.9. Execution environment: Python 3.12.13 on Linux 6.6.122+ (Google Colab). Random seed for the Monte Carlo engine: 42.

A.1: Synchronized Data Extraction Engine

```
   import yfinance as yf
   import pandas_datareader.data as web
   import pandas as pd
   import numpy as np
   #1. Institutional API calls
   df_crypto = yf.download(['BTC-USD', 'ETH-USD'], start - '20
8-01-01')['Close']
   df_stable = yf.downloa (['GSPC', 'GLD'], start = '2018-01-
01')['Close']
   #2. Merging asynchronou data struct s
   df_prices = pd.concat([df_crypto, df_trad], axis = 1)
   #3. Hand ing null values due to market cl sures
   df_pri s= df_prices.ffill().dropna()
   #4. Transformati to conituous logarithmic returns scal b 100
   df_returns = np.log(df_prices / df_prices.shift(1)).dro a()
* 100
```

A.2: Econometric Volatility Modeling Engine

```
   From arch import arch_model # 1. Baseline: Gaussian
GARCH(1,1) garch_gaussian = arch_model(df_returns ['BTC-USD],
vol = 'GARCH', P = 1, q = 1, dist = 'normal')
   res_gaussian =garch_gauss an.fit(disp='off')
   # 2. Leptokurtic Control: Student-t GARCH(1,1)
   garch_t = arch_model(df_r turns [,BTC-USD], vol = ,GARCH',
p=1, q = 1, dist = 't')
```

```
res_t= garch_t.fit(disp='off')
# 3. Asymmetric Specification: EGARCH(1,1,1) w t Student-t
innovations
egarch_t= arch_model(df_returns ['BTC-USD], vol= 'GARCH',
p=1, 0=1, q =1, dist = 't')
res_egarch egarch .fit(disp='off')
# 4. Extracting information cr teria and parameters
Print(f"Gaussia AIC: {res_gaussian.aic}"
print(f"GARCH-t AIC: {res_t.aic}"
print(f"EGARC -t AIC: {res_egarch.aic}"
```

A.3: Rolling Interdependence and Stress Window matrix

```
#1. Computing the 90 day rolling Pearson correlation matrix
rolling_corr = df_returns.rolling(window=90).corr()
#2. Extracting historical stress window coordinates
stress_window ={
"COVID-19 Panic": ('2020-03-01, '2020-04-3-31'),
"Terra/Luna Collapse: ('2022-05-01', '2022-06-15'),
"2022 Fed Tightening": ('2022-01-01', '2022-12-31'),
"FTX Solvency Event": ('2022-11-01', '2022-11-20')
}
for name, (start, end) in stress_window.items()
window_data=df_returns.loc[start:end]
matrix = window_data.corr()
print(f"-- {name} Correlation matrix ---")
print(matrix[['BTC-USD', 'GSPC','GLD']])
```

A.4: Forward looking Monte Carlo projection engine

```
#1. Conditioning parameter extraction from the EGARCH model
forecast = res_egarch.forecast(horizon=1)
conditional_variance= forecast.variance.iloc[-1].values[0]
conditional_sigma = np.sqrt(conditional_variance)/ 100
```

```
#2. Calibration of the stochastic drift and diffusion terms
S0= 73504.15
T=30
n_sims=1000
dt=1
#2. Calibration of the stochastic drift and diffusion terms
np.random.seed(42)
drift=(df_returns['BTC-USD'].mean()/100*dt
shocks=np.random.normal(0,1,(T, n_sims))
price_paths= np.zeros((T+1, n_sims))
price_paths[0]=S0
for t in range(1, T +1):
price _paths[t] = price_paths[t-1]*np.exp(drift + condition-
al_sigma * shocks[t-1]
#4. Extracting the 30 day 99% value at risk
Final_returns = (price_paths[-1]-S0)/S0
Var_30d_99= np. Percentile(final_returns, 1)
Print(f" 30 day 99% Monte Carlo VaR: {var_30d_99 *
100:.2f}%")
```

A.5: Tail calibration via peak-over-threshold (POT) method

```
from spicy.stats import genpareto
#1. Isolating the empirical lower tail
losses = -df_returns['BTC-USD']
threshold = np.percentile(losses, 95)
exceedances = losses[losses > threshold] - threshold
#2. Maximum likelihood estimation of GPD parameters
Shape, loc, scale= genpareto.fit(exceedances, floc= 0)
#3. Parametric VaR and Expected Shortfall closed-form evalu-
ation
alpha = 0.99
n = len(losses)
Nu= len(exceedances)
var_evt = threshold + (scale/shape) * ((n / Nu) * (1 - al-
pha)) **(-shape) - 1)
es_evt = (var_evt + scale - shape * threshold) / (1- shape)
```

```
print(f"Threshold (u): {-threshold:.2f}%")
print(f"shape parameter (xi): {shape:.4}")
print(f"Scale parameter (beta): {scale:.4}")
print(f"Daily 99% EVT VaR: {-var_evt:.2f}%")
print(f"Daily 99% EVT ES: {-es_evt:.2f}%")
```

A.6: Non parametric Markowitz Optimization pipeline

```
from spicy.optimize import minimize
#1. Setting up covariance structures and expected returns
assets = ['GSPC', 'GLD', 'BTC-USD']
mean_returns = df_returns[assets].mean()
cov_matrix = df_returns[assets].corr()
#2. Formulating objective and boundary conditions
def objective(weights):
p_vol = np.sqrt(np.dot(weights.T, np.dot(cov_matrix,
weights)))
p_ret = np.sum(mean_returns * weights)
return - (p_ret / p_vol)
constraints = ({'type': 'eq', 'fun': lambda x: np.sum(x) -
1})
bounds = tuple((0, 1) for asset in assets)
initial_guess = [0.33, 0.33, 0.34]
#3. Executing the numerical optimization routine
opts = minimize(objective, initial_guess, method='SLSQP',
bounds=bounds, constraints=constraints)
print("Optimized Portfolio Allocation:")
for asset, weight in zip(assets, optimized_weights):
print(f"{asset}: {weight * 100:.2}%")
```

A.7: High-frequency dislocation engine (stablecoin metrics)

```
# 1. Fetching structural microdata across multiple asset
types
```

```
# (USD fiat-backed vs DAI crypto backed)
stablecoins = ['tether', 'dai']
# Data simulated using historical endpoints matching the
text for reproducibility
max_deviation_usdt = 0.0022
max_deviation_dai = 0.0023
#2. Structural breakdown calculation
print(f"USDT Max Peg Deviation: {max_deviation_usdt *
100:.2f} cents")
print(f"DAI Max Peg Deviation: {max_deviation_dai * 100:.2f}
cents")
```

A.8: Regime shift and structural break diagnostics

```
from spicy.stats import ttest_ind, ks_2samp, levene
#1. Partitioning the time series around the structural break
merge_date = '2022-09-15'
pow_regime = df_returns.loc[:merge_date, 'ETH-USD']
pos_regime = df_returns.loc[merge_date:, 'ETH-USD']
#2. Executing robust non parametric tests
t_stat, t_pval = ttest_ind(pow_regime**2, pos_regime**2,
equal_var=False)
ks_stat, ks_pval = ks_2samp(pow_regime, pos_regime)
lev_stat, lev_pval = levene(pow_regime, pos_regime)
print(f"Welch t-test on squared residuals p-value: {t_
pval:.5e}")
print(f"Kolmogorov-Smirnov two sample p-value: {ks_
pval:.5e}")
print(f"Levene test on variances p-value: {lev_pval:.5e}")
```

APPENDIX B: EVT THRESHOLD SENSITIVITY ANALYSIS

Table 9. VaR and ES estimates across alternative GPD thresholds (bitcoin)

Threshold percentile	ξ	β	*EVT VaR 99%*	*EVT ES 99%*
1st (worst 1%)	0.4015	2.4974	-12.41%	-19.93%
2.5th	0.3629	2.0415	-10.18%	-15.45%
5th	0.2611	1.9775	-8.67%	-12.75%
7.5th	0.1886	2.1097	-8.12%	-11.4%
10th	0.1916	1.9865	-7.95%	-11.05%

The variation across thresholds is bounded: 4.46 percentage points in the VaR and 8.88 percentage points in the ES across the full 1st-to-10th-percentile range. The 5% baseline sits at the median of the sweep. The direction of the result is stable: every threshold gives $\xi > 0$, so every estimate sits inside the Fréchet domain, and the dispersion is in the range that the literature reports as typical for crypto-asset tails. The choice of the 5% threshold is supported by this sensitivity, and the alternative thresholds give Expected Shortfall estimates between −11.05% and −19.93%, all of which are large enough to keep the regulatory conclusion intact regardless of the specific cutoff.

APPENDIX C: Stablecoin Peg Deviation During the FTX Crisis

Table 10. Maximum peg deviation, Q4 2022 (FTX collapse window)

Stablecoin	*Backing model*	*Max deviation (cents)*	*Outcome*
USDT	Fiat reserves	0.22	Peg held
DAI	Crypto-overcollateralized	0.23	Peg held, indirect stress
UST (May 2022)	Algoritgmic (Terra)	97.49	Total de peg

The three rows together summarize the architectural lesson. A fiat-backed stablecoin held its peg under the FTX panic with a deviation of 0.22 cents, which is statistically indistinguishable from normal trading noise. A crypto-overcollateralized stablecoin held its peg with a deviation of 0.23 cents but was exposed to indirect stress through its Ethereum collateral. An algorithmic stablecoin with no real reserve backing lost essentially all of its dollar parity in a matter of days when its arbitrage mechanism broke. The MiCA reserve requirement is calibrated against this gradient: it allows the first two architectures (with different reserve quality standards) and effectively prohibits the third by demanding one-to-one reserves in high-quality liquid assets.

APPENDIX D: Bai-Perron Structural Break Detection: Robustness For the Merge Analysis

The placebo partition analysis in Section 5.7 raised a concern that needs to be addressed directly: the Ethereum return series exhibits structural breaks at multiple non-Merge dates, which means the significance of the regime split at the Merge cutoff is not unique. To address that concern, I ran a Bai-Perron / PELT structural break detection procedure on the GARCH-implied conditional variance series. The procedure tests for an unknown number of unknown break dates under the null that the variance-process parameters are stable across the sample. The Bai-Perron problem was solved with the Pruned Exact Linear Time

(PELT) algorithm of Killick et al. (2012), which provides an exact O(n) solution to the optimization and is the modern computational standard for this class of test. The conditional variance series was extracted from a GARCH(1,1)-t fit on the full Ethereum sample. The PELT algorithm was applied to that series with a radial basis function (RBF) cost specification and a BIC-style penalty of $\lambda = 10$, which is the conventional setting for financial volatility series of this length.

Algorithm 2. Bai-Perron break detection on the GARCH variance series

1. Estimate GARCH(1,1)-t on $\{r_t^{ETH}\}$
2. Extract conditional variance series $\{\sigma_t^2\}$
3. Run PELT with RBF cost on function on $\{\sigma_t^2\}$
4. Apply BIC penalty λ=10 to control break count
5. Return ordered set of break dates $\{t_1, t_2, ..., t_k\}$
6. Compare each T_i against the Merge cutoff 15 September 2022
7. Flag T_i as a Merge-associated break if $/T_i$-Merge$/ \leq 30days$

Results

The PELT algorithm detected 29 structural breaks in the Ethereum GARCH conditional variance series across the full sample. Of these, 1 fell within a 30-day window of the Merge cutoff: 27 September 2022, +12 days after the consensus mechanism transition. Table 11 reports the full set of detected break dates.

Table 11. Bai-Perron / PELT break dates on the ETH GARCH conditional variance series (λ = 10, RBF cost)

Detected break date	Days from Merge (15 sept 2022)	Merged associated?
10 feb 2020	-948	No
06 mar 2020	-923	No
25 apr 2020	-873	No
14 jun 2020	-823	No
24 jul 2020	-783	No
02 sept 2020	-743	No
02 oct 2020	-713	No
21 nov 2020	-663	No
05 jan 2021	-618	No
09 feb 2021	-583	No
16 mar 2021	-548	No
05 may 2021	-498	No
09 jul 2021	-433	No
07 sep 2021	-373	No
07 oct 2021	-343	No
20 jan 2022	-238	No
16 mar 2022	-183	No
10 may 2022	-128	No
27 sep 2022	+12	Yes
11 dec 2022	+87	No
15 may 2023	+242	No
06 nov 2023	+417	No
05 nov 2024	+782	No
23 feb 2025	+892	No
24 may 2025	+982	No
20 dec 2025	+1192	No
29 Jan 2026	+1232	No
10 mar 2026	+1272	No
24 apr 2026	+1317	No

Interpretation

The PELT result is informative on two counts. One: it identifies a break within 30 days of the Merge cutoff: 27 September 2022, +12 days after the consensus mechanism transition. That means the regime split in Section 5.7 is not arbitrary; the algorithm recovers the same date the consensus mechanism actually changed without being told to look there.

Two: it identifies 28 other breaks across the sample, with notable concentrations in the pre-Merge period (18 breaks between February 2020 and May 2022, when Ethereum was experiencing its largest institutional adoption phase and the first major bear-market drawdown of the COVID era) and in the post-Merge window (the December 2022 break, +87 days, coincides with the tail end of the FTX collapse; the May 2023 break, +242 days, coincides with the U.S. regional banking crisis and the SEC's escalation against major exchanges; the late-2024 and 2025 breaks coincide with the ETF approval cycle and the rate-cutting expectations cycle).

The honest reading is that the Merge is one structural break among many, and that the tail-risk compression observed in the post-Merge sub-sample is part of a broader mid-2022 regime change rather than a Merge-exclusive effect. The Merge is identified by the algorithm, which prevents the interpretation from collapsing into "the Merge had no effect" (a Block C reading would not be supported by the data). But the Merge does not stand alone as the dominant structural event of the sample, which prevents a clean causal claim (a Block A reading would overstate what the data supports).

The most defensible position is intermediate: the transition from Proof-of-Work to Proof-of-Stake compressed the variance regime of Ethereum in conjunction with a broader mid-2022 market restructuring, and the tail-risk gap relative to Bitcoin documented in the pre-Merge sub-sample (a VaR 99% difference of 4.92 percentage points) overstates the mechanism-specific effect. The post-Merge VaR 99% gap between ETH and BTC (−8.94% vs −8.73%, or 0.21 percentage points) is closer to the structural difference the consensus mechanism alone can account for, with the remaining 4.71 percentage points reflecting the cumulative effect of the other structural changes the PELT analysis identifies.

Limitations of the Break-Detection Robustness

Three limitations remain. First, the BIC penalty λ is a tuning parameter, and small changes shift the detected break count. I tested $\lambda \in \{5,10,15,20\}$, and the break dates within the Merge window were stable across this range, but the total break count varied between 23 and 34. The interpretation in the previous paragraph would not change under any of these settings, because the Merge-window break is robust. Second, PELT is non-parametric in the variance and does not exploit the GARCH structure beyond the conditional-variance extraction. A fully parametric break test on the GARCH coefficient vector itself (a Markov-switching GARCH) would provide a tighter identification at the cost of substantially more estimation complexity, and the resulting break dates would be more precisely tied to the underlying parameter changes. Third, the test is run on daily data, which limits resolution to the trading-day grid. Intraday data would refine the break-date estimates but is unlikely to change the conclusion about the number of breaks or the position of the Merge within them.

References for this appendix

Bai, J., & Perron, P. (1998). Estimating and testing linear models with multiple structural changes. *Econometrica*, *66*(1), 47–78.

Bai, J., & Perron, P. (2003). Computation and analysis of multiple structural change models. *Journal of Applied Econometrics*, *18*(1), 1–22.

Killick, R., Fearnhead, P., & Eckley, I. A. (2012). Optimal detection of change-points with a linear computational cost. *Journal of the American Statistical Association*, *107*(500), 1590–1598.

Truong, C., Oudre, L., & Vayatis, N. (2020). Selective review of offline change point detection methods. *Signal Processing*, *167*, 107299.

Chapter 7
Topological Monte Carlo for Asset Dynamics

Jaime Aguilar-Ortiz
http://orcid.org/0009-0003-5302-1454
Universidad Politécnica de Pachuca, Mexico

Ocotlán Diáz-Parra
Universidad Politécnica de Pachuca, Mexico

Jorge A. Ruiz-Vanoye
http://orcid.org/0000-0003-4928-5716
Universidad Politécnica de Pachuca, Mexico

Francisco R. Trejo-Macotela
http://orcid.org/0000-0003-2133-3456
Universidad Politécnica de Pachuca, Mexico

Marco A. Vera-Jiménez
http://orcid.org/0009-0009-3712-1440
Universidad Politécnica de Pachuca, Mexico

Víctor M. Zamudio-García
http://orcid.org/0000-0002-4660-8025
Universidad Politécnica Metropolitana de Hidalgo, Mexico

Carlos R. Domínguez-Mayorga
http://orcid.org/0009-0007-1018-4412
Universidad Politécnica de Pachuca, Mexico

ABSTRACT

This chapter develops a reproducible procedure for designing and interrogating asset-dynamics scenarios with a topological layer. The proposed Topological Monte Carlo framework connects path simulation with topological data analysis so that simulated markets can be examined not only through losses and quantiles, but also through their geometric organization across regimes. Price and return paths are converted into feature embeddings; the resulting scenario-space point clouds are then analyzed with persistent homology. The associated summaries describe clustering, loop structure, and structural transitions under changing volatility states.

DOI: 10.4018/979-8-3373-8372-9.ch007

On that basis, the chapter uses topological evidence to support adaptive scenario generation and to examine VaR/ES sensitivity under distributional shift. The workflow is implemented through a modular Python architecture intended for reproducible quantitative-finance experimentation and model-governance review.

1. INTRODUCTION

1.1 Motivation: From probabilistic summaries to structural understanding of simulated markets

Monte Carlo risk outputs are often summarized in easily audit-able objects such as histograms, quantiles, Value-at-Risk, exceedances, and rolling backtests. These objects complement risk outputs, and are useful in their own right, but are also highly incomplete. Pathwise geometry also exists for simulated markets. For a variety of conditions of dependence and volatility, simulated scenarios can be compared by how they cluster, bend, cycle, separate, or collapse. This is important because of the need for uncertainty propagation in the context of risk-factor models and portfolio analysis. Monte Carlo risk engines are also useful in validating rolling diagnostics and breach analysis (Cheng, 2025). Structural adequacy, however, is more extensive than simply having a good fit for the distribution. While two simulators may agree in tail quantiles, there is still the possibility of vastly differing path behaviors, co-movement and transitions through different regimes. This is especially true in the presence of rough, persistent, and non-Markovian volatility (Gatheral et al., 2018; Horvath et al., 2020). Under these conditions, simulation will most likely be a necessary component for risk analysis (Horvath et al., 2020). The central claim here is that while scalar risk numbers are important for the analysis of risk, they must be complemented by structural analysis that examines organization of scenarios across state and time, including cyclic behavior and metastability which moment summaries tend to overlook. (Katz & Biem, 2021).

Topological Monte Carlo recasts simulated trajectories as evolving geometric objects within an ensemble. Delayed embedding and sliding windows transform price or return streams into time-point indexed clouds. Persistent topology tracks the lasting structures - loops, higher order structures, and connected components - of clouds over varying scales and remains stable amidst noise and sampling deviations (Ravishanker & Chen, 2021). The rationale is both empirical and methodological. Oftentimes, the only noticeable signs preceding market disruptions are increased fluctuations in variance, or changes in the correlation structure, suggesting that the effective state space reorganizes qualitatively. The persistence landscape and related norms quantify these state space reorganizations, allowing the alignment of the persistence structures with the windows of crises and comparisons of the within sectors, across scenarios, and among the simulated regimes (Gidea & Katz, 2018; Katz & Biem, 2021; Ismail et al., 2022). What is developed here allows Monte Carlo to simulate plausible market worlds with controlled stochasticity, while discipline of topology provides a structural perspective to the state of the simulated market useful for the analysis of early warning, the differentiation of market regimes, and the selection of market models, especially where the topology of the market models appears to be similar, but the markets are dissimilar. (Gidea & Katz, 2018; Katz & Biem, 2021; Cheng, 2025).

1.2 Contributions, research questions, and chapter organization

The chapter begins with a premise: that the paths of an asset-dynamics simulator are more clearly understood when seen as a structured object rather than as an avenue of moments and tail quantiles. The chapter presents three ideas. First, the chapter defines a Topological Monte Carlo method that aligns the generation of scenarios containing stylized volatility channels consistent with rough log volatility, with persistent homology descriptors computed on rolling multivariate market states. Second, the chapter places a topology aware diagnostic framework where regime changes are described as alterations in the embedded return or feature trajectories along with temporally resolved topological summaries and are viewed to be beyond drift in the distribution. Third, the chapter describes a principle of adaptive simulation where sampling is challenged to cover the gaps that topological instability reveals, and the stress and interpretative limits in risk analysis are extended. From these ideas, three questions arise: one, do topological descriptors of order and or return or feature trajectories differ for regimes that are distributionally similar; two, do topological methods reveal instability faster and or more robust than typical statistical methods in trading or market-like simulations; and three, does a topology focused approach to simulation and resampling improve the risk related and diversity of Monte Carlo simulations and be less computationally burdensome than the current methodologies.

1.3 Related work and positioning

Monte Carlo techniques in risk management focus on distribution fitting, tail-quantile assessment, variance reduction, and backtesting. Financial applications of TDA have generally focused on the assessment of structural changes in market data and persistence. This chapter focuses on the convergence of the two. Controlled, counterfactual markets are created using stochastic generators. Persistent homology is then used to determine if counterfactuals position themselves along distinguishable regime manifolds. The comparison is twofold: reasonable risk measures should be applicable to the losses, and the counterfactuals should possess meaningful structures in the dimensions of volatility, dependence, and stress. Topological Monte Carlo is not offered in place of VaR, ES, stochastic-volatility, or backtesting. Rather,it is intended to add an additional layer of structural validation to stress testing and model governance. The following sections lay the groundwork, build out the process, and discuss the results, implications, and potential future work stemming from this (Ravishanker & Chen, 2021; Cheng, 2025).

2. THEORETICAL FOUNDATIONS

2.1 Monte Carlo simulation as a generative laboratory for asset dynamics under nonlinearity and regime shifts

This chapter analyses Monte Carlo as a tool for developing asset-price dynamics with deliberate, controlled nonlinearities and regime shifts. The simulator creates multiple synthetic paths, allowing for systematic study of phenomena such as volatility clustering, leverage, state-dependent feedback, and jumps. Unlike traditional approaches which rely on a single realised history, the simulator forms an ensemble of synthetic paths. The market state is a stochastic system, with parameters that are a function of the latent regime variable Z_t (expansion, contraction, stress). This construction allows for sharp, substantive changes to tail behaviour, drift, and volatility, while maintaining the framework of a continuous time approach.. Equation (1) gives a generic regime-dependent jump-diffusion specification:

$$dS_t = S_t\mu(Z_t, t)dt + S_t\sigma(Z_t, S_t, t)dW_t + S_t dJ_t \tag{1}$$

The latent regime changes according to a Markov generator Q. The one-step transition probabilities are expressed in (2):

$$\mathbb{P}(Z_{t+} = j | Z_t = i) = (e^Q)_{ij}. \tag{2}$$

The diffusion coefficient brings in nonlinearity: state-dependent diffusion means σ may depend on S_t, or σ may be connected to a stochastic-volatility driver. Structural breaks as part of the model, rather than something just explained after the fact, come with regime switching. There's more to contemporary volatility modeling now. Modeling log-volatility's fractal-Brownian-type of erratic behavior, and which includes the Hurst exponent $H < 1/2$, calls for a simulation framework with long memory volatility and high-frequency spikes. This is even more relevant when shifts change volatility-of-volatility or the mean-reversion behavior of Gatheral et al. (2018) and Alfeus et al. (2019). Beyond the fact that a numerical equation is integrated, Monte Carlo generates path distributions that are structurally distinct by stress-consistent roughness and explicit transition intensities.

First, the continuous-time model is discretized. Innovations like Brownian, fractional or Volterra-type, and jump innovations are sampled simultaneously with the regime transitions. As such, a complete trajectory is produced with each iteration $S_{0:T}$ $^{m)}$. Using a log-Euler update for the price component, as expressed in (3), preserves positivity and numerical stability against nonlinear σ:

$$s_{n+1} = S_n \exp\left(\left(\mu_n - \frac{1}{2}\sigma_n^2\right)\Delta t + \sigma_n \sqrt{\Delta t}\, \varepsilon_{n+1}\right), \tag{3}$$

The Markov transition kernel advanced by the regime state is then given by Q. Using a risk-neutral measure, path-dependent claims may also be priced using the same simulation engine by calculating the discounted functional in (4),

$$V_0 = e^{-rT}\mathbb{E}^{\mathbb{Q}}\left[g(S_{0:T}\right] \approx e^{-rT}\frac{1}{m}\sum_{m=1} g\left(S_{o:T}^{(m)}\right), \tag{4}$$

The paths resulting from that also describe loss samples for regulation tail measures such as (5):

$$VaR_\alpha(L) = \inf\{\ell : \mathbb{P}(L \leq \ell \geq \alpha\},\ ES_\alpha(L) = \mathbb{E}\left[L \middle| L \geq VaR_\alpha(L)\right], \tag{5}$$

Estimators display higher variance due to rare regimes and sudden stress transitions. Thus, an effective simulator must factor in efficiency. The use of Antithetic variants of regime-switching models, multi-level estimators, control variates, importance sampling, and quasi-Monte Carlo methods help effectively expand scenario grids without debilitating computations. (Noorani et al., 2021; Sinha and Chakrabarty, 2023; Jeng and Kılıçman, 2021; Teng, 2023; Xiang and Wang, 2022). If one aims for structural interpretation instead of mere marginal risk structural interpretation, the same simulated collections can be integrated with representation learning or geometry-aware summaries. For scenario development, deep generative surrogates with complex dependence, and geometry with topological summaries, can help reveal market state geometry restructures with regime like actions over time. (Wiese et al., 2020; Katz and Biem, 2021; Ismail et al., 2022). This link aids the structural diagnostics that follow.

2.2 Algebraic-topological perspective on scenario spaces: point clouds, filtrations, and persistent homology

From a topological perspective, a simulated trajectory is not just a probabilistic draw or a point (or sequence of points) in what may be a scenario space that is carrying some regime information. Let $\{S^{(m)}\}_{m=1}^{M}$ denote M simulated price paths observed on $\{t_0, \ldots, t_T\}$. A practical computational construction translates each path into a vector of features that includes returns, proxies for realized volatility, drawdown descriptors, tail indicators, and other path functionals. The result is a point cloud in $\mathbb{R}^d$ (Wasserman, 2018; Chazal & Michel, 2021), defined in (6):

$$S^{(m)} = \left(S_{t_0}^{(m)}, S_{t_1}^{(m)}, \ldots, S_{t_T}^{(m)}\right), x_m = \Phi(S^{(m)}) \in \mathbb{R}^d, X = \{x_m\}_{m=1}^{M}. \quad (6)$$

When the time sequence of the trajectories matters, aggregate path features are inadequate. An alternative is the application of a sliding-window embedding to the return series r_t to create a local approximation to the phase-space pattern. This topology captures more than just end-of-path summaries. It looks at repeated patterns and progressions within the dynamics (Ravishanker & Chen, 2021) of (7):

$$\Psi_{m,r}(r_t) = \left(r_t, r_{t+\tau}, \ldots, r_{t+(m-1)\tau}\right) \in \mathbb{R}^m. \quad (7)$$

ather than assessing the point cloud at a single threshold, assessments occur across scales. Specifically, a filtration develops a continuous hierarchy of simplicial complexes, recording connectivity and higher-order relations throughout the evolving scale parameter. One of the several choices for such a filtration is the Vietoris-Rips filtration. The Vietoris-Rips filtration progressively adds simplices whenever a set of points falls within a distance threshold (ϵ), thickening the scenario cloud, and allowing for the discovery of multiscale structures (Chazal & Michel, 2021; Wasserman, 2018). The following equation describes such a construction (8):

$$VR_{\varepsilon_1}(X) \subseteq VR_{\varepsilon_1} \subseteq \cdots \quad \left(\varepsilon_1 < \varepsilon_1 < \cdots\right). \quad (8)$$

Persistent homology records the appearance and disappearance of topological features along the filtration. Connected components (H_0), loops (H_1), and higher-dimensional voids (H_k) are therefore separated by their persistence rather than by a single arbitrary scale. This is particularly useful in regime-sensitive simulations because it helps distinguish durable organization from sampling noise (Wasserman, 2018; Hensel et al., 2021). The corresponding sequence is given in (9):

Throughout filtration, persistent homology tracks how topological components come and go. The persistence of homology groups (H_0), loops (H_1), and (H_k), which capture disconnected components, loops, and k-dimensional voids, respectively, gives a more robust framework for measuring topological features than an arbitrary scale. This is particularly advantageous in contexts where a system is being driven through different regimes, as it helps differentiate between structural order and stochastic artifacts (Wasserman, 2018; Hensel et al., 2021). The sequenced is reflected in (9):

$$H_k\left(VR_{\varepsilon_1}(X)\right) \rightarrow H_k\left(VR_{\varepsilon_2}(X)\right) \rightarrow \cdots , D_k(X) = \left\{(b_i, d_i)\right\}_i. \quad (9)$$

Within the context of simulated markets, persistence diagrams have significant utility due to their comparative nature. The Bottleneck distance (W_∞) and Wasserstein distance (W_p) quantitate the topological disparity between two scenario spaces. Such measures facilitate the observation of regime changes, the clustering of scenario families, and the appraisal of scenario stability in the face of fluctuating model parameters (Wasserman, 2018; Ravishanker and Chen, 2021). They are expressed in (10):

$$W_p(D, D') = \left(\inf_\gamma \sum_{x \in D} \left\| x - \gamma(x) \right\|_\infty^p\right)^{1/p}, \; W_\infty(D, D') = \inf_\gamma \sup_{x \in D} \left\| x - \gamma(x) \right\|_\infty, \quad (10)$$

Here, the variable γ denotes bijections among diagrams amended with additional diagonal points.

For many learning and monitoring tools that require vector inputs, persistence diagrams will need to be transformed into stable representations. These can include barcodes, function vectorizations, data-fitting grids, etc. When dealing with complicated geometries or when multiple scales need to be represented simultaneously (e.g., time and volatility scales), persistence kernel constructions can be employed (Corbet et al., 2019; Dong et al., 2020; Dong et al., 2024).

Looking at the examples presented, the algebraic-topological view becomes operational. Previous studies in finance have demonstrated how changes in the structure of loops and voids can become early-warning signals that moment-focused summaries do not capture. For this reason, topology becomes a natural complement to Monte Carlo, which has demonstrated the ability to generate extreme stress events in a controlled manner (Katz & Biem, 2021; Ismail et al., 2022).

2.3 Adaptive scenario generation and model governance: novelty-driven exploration, validity constraints, and robust principles

The concept being discussed is adaptive scenario generation and its relation to the context of active exploration. Unlike traditional simulation techniques where a simulator draws paths based off a given set of rules, our simulator allocates its computational capacity to areas that it thinks will be most informative yet diverse and complex. Consider a portfolio that is allowed to evolve via a constrained stochastic process with parameter $\theta \in \Theta$. The simulator will generate a trajectory w and a lower-dimensional representation or embedding $x = \Phi(w) \in \mathbb{R}^m$. The embedding captures many path statistics and volatility features, including profile of draws (i.e., drawdowns) and dependence summaries. Concurrently, the ensemble is described by stable geometric or topological summaries $z = \Psi(D(X))$, where $D(X)$ are persistence diagrams computed from point clouds X, and Ψ is a stable scorer/learner (Hensel et al., 2021; Dong et al., 2024). Novelty exploring select θ so that newly generated scenarios are as far as possible from the previously explored structural domains, while still keeping feasibility in mind. Candidate θ values are drawn from diversity promoting optimizers or learned generators such as adversarial time-series generators that are designed to elicit diverse time-series of simulations that are decoupled from a small calibrated zone of operation (Wiese et al., 2020). An example of a representative novelty-penalty rule can be found in (11):

$$\theta_{t+1} = arg\max_{\theta\in\Theta}\left[\mathcal{N}(z(\theta)) - \lambda\mathcal{P}(\theta)\right]\ s.t.\ g(\theta) \leq 0,\ h(\theta) = 0, \tag{11}$$

$$\mathcal{N}(z(\theta)) = \frac{1}{K}\sum_{j=1}^{K}\left\|z(\theta) - NN_j(z(\theta))\right\|_2, \tag{12}$$

In (12), K-nearest-neighbor separation in the structural-summary space is one way $\mathcal{N}$ quantifies novelty. $\mathcal{P}$ serves as a disincentive to numerical instability or unrealistic parameterizations, and (g,h) builds in the validity constraints. In asset modeling, some of those constraints have direct financial meanings: positivity, integrator stability, and martingale consistency under a risk-neutral measure. A governance gate can impose discounted-martingale behavior either as a hard constraint or as the diagnostic bound in (13) at the horizon or at rebalancing times:

$$\mathbb{E}\left[e^{-r\Delta t}S_{t+\Delta t}\middle|\mathcal{F}_t\right] = S_t,\ S_t > 0, \tag{13}$$

With this gate, arbitrage-inconsistent or numerically degenerate regions do not affect novelty maximization. Novelty maintains an unambiguous meaning. The search is directed toward structurally new scenario families, where novelty is retained, within financially admissible configurations checked automatically by the pipeline.

Governance gives the adaptive procedure its scientific discipline. Every proposed scenario must be reproducible, traceable, and accompanied by uncertainty controls, robustness checks, and risk-metric validation. On the Monte Carlo side, estimator quality is handled through explicit error budgets and variance-reduction tools, including multilevel strategies when nested simulation is needed for pricing or risk tasks. That distinction keeps scenario discovery separate from uncontrolled simulation noise (Sinha & Chakrabarty, 2023). For tail-risk governance in stress regimes, adaptive exploration is paired with targeted sampling for VaR_α and ES_α. Importance sampling, or randomized quasi-Monte Carlo when appropriate, improves efficiency for rare losses that define regimes (Teng, 2023). A constraint-compatible estimator for expected shortfall is given in (14):

Governance establishes structure around the adaptive process. Every scenario must be reproducible, verifiable, and must include uncertainty management, robustness, and risk-metrics. On the Monte Carlo side, estimator quality is achieved by constructing specific error budgets and variance-reduction techniques, including multilevel methods when nested simulations are called for, due to their importance and relevance, for risk and pricing tasks. That distinction preserves scenario discovery from uncontrolled simulation noise (Sinha & Chakrabarty, 2023). For tail-risk governance during stress scenarios, adaptive exploration is complemented by VaR_α and S_α targeted sampling. Randomized quasi-Monte Carlo, and Importance Sampling when applicable, enhance the quality of sampling for low frequency high impact losses (Teng, 2023). A constraint-compatible estimator of expected shortfall is presented in (14):

$$\widehat{ES}_\alpha = \frac{\sum_{i=1}^{N} w_i L_i 1\{L_i \geq \hat{q}_\alpha\}}{\sum_{i=1}^{N} w_i 1\{L_i \geq \hat{q}_\alpha\}},\ w_i = \frac{p(\xi_i)}{q(\xi_i)},\ \hat{q}_\alpha = \inf\left\{q: \frac{\sum_{i=1}^{N} w_i 1\{L_i \leq q\}}{\sum_{i=1}^{N} w_i} \geq \alpha\right\}, \tag{14}$$

In (14), L_i represents simulated losses caused by random inputs ξ_i,, where (p, q) are the nominal and proposed laws. Distributional-stability principles reinforce the robust governance. Instead of assessing only one well-calibrated simulation law, the proposed framework includes ambiguity sets, consisting of Wasserstein balls, which captures the sensitivity to misspecification and serves as a hedge to model risk (Mohajerin Esfahani & Kuhn, 2018). The distributionally robust risk functional is expressed in (15):

$$\sup_{\mathbb{P}:W_p(\mathbb{P},\widehat{\mathbb{P}})\leq\epsilon} \mathbb{E}_{\mathbb{P}}[\ell(\theta)], \tag{15}$$

Governance in equation (15) does not focus on the pointwise fit, but instead focuses on the system's resilience to stress. It then loops to out-of-sample accountability: forecasts generated by the adaptive engine, including ES, are assessed to look for systematic tail underestimation (Bayer & Dimitriadis, 2022). It is possible to enhance the credibility of extreme event scenarios through causal stress-testing methodologies, which produce coherent adverse regimes, rather than merely relying on the correlation of shocks (Gao et al., 2018). As a result, the pipeline integrates exploration, constraints, and strong validation: exploration heightens breadth, constraints are put in place to maintain admissibility, and governance ensures the changing scenario space is statistically accountable.

3. METHODOLOGY

3.1 Simulation-to-geometry pipeline: path generation, feature embeddings, and scenario-space construction

The simulation-to-geometry pipeline considers Monte Carlo trajectories as data objects with definable shapes. An asset model which includes regime switching and/or state-dependent volatility is captured on the grid.

$t_n = n\Delta t$ and simulated M times to generate the paths $\left\{ S_{t_n}^{(m)} \right\}_{n=0}^{N}$. As described in (16), log-price updates are a convenient representation with potential jumps J to reflect discontinuities and stress events:

$$X_{n+1}^{(m)} = X_n^{(m)} + \left(\mu_n^{(m)} - \frac{1}{2}(\sigma_n^{(m)})^2\right)\Delta t + \sigma_n^{(m)} \sqrt{\Delta t}\, \varepsilon_{n+1}^{(m)} + J_{n+1}^{(m)}, \quad S_n^{(m)} = exp\left(X_n^{(m)}\right), \quad (16)$$

For each trajectory, log-returns are extracted. These are the canonical stationary signals in (17):

$$r_n^{(m)} = \log\left(\frac{S_{n+1}^{(m)}}{S_n^{(m)}}\right). \quad (17)$$

Multiscale behavior is captured within a fixed-dimensional description by a certain mapping of return sequences utilizing a feature embedding, denoted by Φ. The feature set, pertaining to (18), is comprised of local-volatility surrogates, tail-sensitive drawdowns, and regime-contrast statistics computed over rolling windows.

$$x^{(m)} = \Phi\left(\left\{r_n^{(m)}\right\}_{n=0}^{N-1}\right) \in \mathbb{R}^d. \quad (18)$$

his embedding provides a geometric framework to data generated by stochastic simulations. It preserves the richness of generated paths, while embedding families of scenarios into a common coordinate system. The framework also preserves the compatibility with sampling acceleration and variance reduction techniques, allowing analysts to work with larger families of scenarios while maintaining fidelity to nonlinear and regime-shifting dynamics (Gatheral, Jaisson, & Rosenbaum, 2018; Noorani, Mehrdoust, & Nasroallah, 2021; Sinha & Chakrabarty, 2023; Wiese et al., 2020).

Once the embeddings $\{x^{(m)}\}_{m=1}^{M}$, have been computed, a point cloud representation of the scenario space will have been created. Its geometry captures the arrangement of regimes, nonlinearities, and stress configurations beyond moment-based summaries. The representation is given in (19):

$$X = \{x^{(m)}\}_{m=1}^{M} \subset \mathbb{R}^d, \; D_{ij} = d(x^{(i)}, x^{(j)}), \tag{19}$$

In (19), $d(\cdot\,,\cdot)$refers to the selected metric. After a robust scaling, Euclidean distance is a frequent choice. However, if co-movement is the central concern, a correlation-based metric is preferable. A filtration of simplicial complexes transforms the geometric information from D into a combinatorial structure, applicable for persistent computation. The Vietoris-Rips complex is especially appropriate for this task because it relies solely on distance information, and is defined in (20):

$$VR_\varepsilon(X) = \left\{\sigma \subseteq X \colon \max_{u,v \in \sigma} d(u,v) \le \varepsilon\right\}, \; \varepsilon_1 < \varepsilon_2 < \cdots . \tag{20}$$

This step brings operational meaning to the scenario manifold. As ε increases, the connectivity of $VR_\varepsilon(X)$ changes to show multiscale organization. Persistent homology may structure that organization and provide stabilized vectorizations or kernels to machine learning modules (Wasserman, 2018; Chazal & Michel, 2021; Bauer, 2021; Hensel, Moor, & Rieck, 2021; Corbet et al., 2019; Dong et al., 2020; Dong et al., 2024; Ravishanker & Chen, 2021). For financial monitoring, the construction parallels the time-resolved topological studies that trace the emergence and persistence of market-derived geometric structures that are loop-like in nature (Katz & Biem, 2021; Ismail et al., 2022).

3.2 Topological inference and evaluation protocol: persistence summaries, stability checks, and finance-aligned diagnostics

Topological inference interprets each Monte Carlo simulation as a single point within a scenario space consisting of several finance-derived embeddings: windowed returns, volatility proxies, drawdown descriptors, joint state features, etc. Consider

$X = \{x_i\}_{i=1}^{n} \subset \mathbb{R}^d$ to denote the resulting point cloud. A filtration $\{\mathcal{K}_\varepsilon(X)\}_{\varepsilon \geq 0}$ produces multi-scale simplicial complexes following a Vietoris-Rips construction. From these simplicial complexes, persistent homology yields a signature that enables differentiating the durable topological structures within a point cloud from the noise. The persistence diagram is a basic object of interest and is denoted as $D_k(X) = \{(b_i, d_i)\}_i$. This diagram can be transformed to assess a variety of statistical learning applications and provides a stable, unchanging representation of the topological structure of a data set. In this instance, the proximity between diagrams is assessed via the bottleneck distance and the Wasserstein distance, while recent advancements in Vietoris-Rips barcodes retain efficiency even under the constraints of a high

The distances employed for comparison utilizing the L_∞ ground metric are defined in (21):

$$W_\infty(D, D') = \inf_{\gamma} \sup_{x \in D} \left\| x - \gamma(x) \right\|_\infty, W_p(D, D') = \left(\inf_{\gamma} \sum_{x \in D} \left\| x - \gamma(x) \right\|_\infty^p \right)^{1/p}. \quad (21)$$

This inference layer captures and preserves data in a way that is useful for analytical processing. The representations it produces can be learned from, clustered, and compared across experimental contexts. Consequently, it is possible to classify family of scenarios and stress regimes, without having to restrict the scenario space to a few statistics, such as averages, variances, and other low-order statistical dependence measures.

The evaluation protocol connects topology with financial validity through three checks: persistence stability, controlled perturbation or resampling, and tail-risk/backtesting diagnostics computed on the same simulated paths. Stability is assessed by rerunning the pipeline under bootstrap subsampling, jitter perturbations, and embedding or hyperparameter sweeps. The resulting diagrams and vector summaries are compared to determine whether their variability remains acceptable under W_p or W_∞. For each homological dimension, a compact stability statistic is the median diagram deviation across resamples, written in (22):

The evaluation protocol links topology with financial validity via three checks: persistence stability, controlled perturbation or resampling, and tail-risk/backtesting diagnostics performed on the same simulated paths. Stability is tested by rerunning the pipeline with bootstrap subsampling, jitter perturbations, and various embedding and hyperparameter sweeps. Resulting diagrams and vector summaries are compared to check if the summaries' variability is still acceptable measured by W_p or W_∞. For each homological dimension, a simple persistence stability metric is given by the median diagram distance over resamples formalized in (22):

$$S_k = median_{b=1,\ldots,B}\, W_p\big(D_k^{(b)}(X),\, D_k(X)\big),\;\; \Delta_k\big(\theta_1,\theta_2\big) = W_p\big(D_k(X;\theta_1),\, D_k(X;\,\theta_2)\big). \quad (22)$$

Here, loss distribution L, in conjunction with coherent tail measures, illustrates how financial alignment is assessed. We also consider if topology-based regime flags exhibit shifts in risk that are economically meaningful. VaR and ES may also be computed by regime cluster, or by rolling time blocks, and then assessed using up-to-date backtesting methodologies. The application of regression-based ES tests and multinomial VaR exception diagnostics work to avoid the potential misinterpretation of a pure geometric change as a financial signal. The tail-risk functionals are as defined in (23):

$$VaR_\alpha(L) = \inf\{\ell : \mathbb{P}(L \le \ell) \ge \alpha\},\; ES_\alpha(L) = \mathbb{E}\big[L \big| L \ge VaR_\alpha(L)\big]. \quad (23)$$

The protocol aligns with evidence that persistent-homology signals can serve as early-warning indicators in market systems. It also justifies the use of Monte Carlo stress test experiments: iterative simulations create a repeatable context for identifying stable hyperparameters and assessing the robustness of topology-based alerts in the presence of shifts in the underlying data distribution.

4. COMPUTATIONAL ARCHITECTURE

4.1 Reproducible implementation: modular Python components, scalable execution, configuration management, and logging

A reproducible implementation of Topological Monte Carlo for Asset Dynamics is organized most naturally as a modular Python codebase. Each scientific task is isolated: path generation under regime switching and nonlinear dynamics; construction of feature embeddings; topological inference through filtrations, persistent homology, and stable summaries; and evaluation/reporting. This architecture prevents changes in one layer from silently altering another. Reproducibility is not treated as a claim made after the fact. It is encoded as a computational contract: a configuration object and a controlled random state produce an auditable set of outputs - trajectories, embeddings, persistence summaries, diagnostics, distance matrices, filtrations, and report artifacts. If θ denotes model parameters, $\mathscr{C}$ a structured configuration, and s the pseudo-random seed or state, the contract is $Y = \mathscr{F}(\theta, \mathscr{C}, s)$, , where Y contains the verification artifacts. A run identifier binds configuration, randomness, and code version into a single immutable record, following provenance-aware practice in which experiments are traceable objects rather than temporary scripts.

Organizing a modular Python codebase is the most natural way to construct a reproducible implementation of Topological Monte Carlo for Asset Dynamics. Each layer can be dedicated to a task such as: path generation with regime switching and with/without nonlinear behavior, feature embedding creation, topological inference with filtrations, persistent homology, and stable summaries, as well as the task of analysis and reporting. This structure ensures that changes occurring in one layer will not impact other layers. Instead of serving as a post hoc assertion, reproducibility becomes a computational contract that audibly states the outputs (paths, embeddings, persistence summaries, diagnostics, distance matrices, filtrations, and reporting artifacts) produced by a given configuration and a controlled random state. If θ are the parameters, $\mathscr{C}$ is the configuration, and s is the (pseudo)random state, then the contract is $Y = \mathscr{F}(\theta, \mathscr{C}, s)$, where Y contains the artifacts for verifiability. A run identifier makes the contract a bound, irreproducible contract by combining the state, configuration, and a bound version of the code. This contract rests in the provenance of the infrastructure for reproducibility as a traceable object.

Scalable execution is built on the concepts of independent work and aggregate work. Independent path simulation, per-replica embedding, and per-replica persistence computations are all parallelizable. On the other hand, stability summaries, regime distances, and report synthesis are aggregate work. Let's denote the parallelizable part of pipeline execution with the symbol α. With p workers, the strong-scaling limit is Amdahl's law, presented below in (24):

$$S(p) = \frac{1}{(1-\alpha) + \alpha/p}, \tag{24}$$

That scaling model supports clearly defined boundaries for embarrassingly parallel and aggregation phases. In log structuring, logs should be machine-readable and include timestamps, run IDs, and stage, input, metric, and artifact identifiers to facilitate the replay of failures and the comparison of regimes. Governance is improved when runs include portable provenance bundles of code, parameters, and outputs in containers of provenance. This is consistent with RO-Crate workflows for provenance of executed workflows (Leo et al., 2024) and with lightweight RO-Crate objects for digital, interoperable, and lightweight sharing (Soiland-Reyes et al., 2022). Reproducibility is, thus, active; automated processes check whether a run has been executed and whether the stated financial and topological results are invariant to controlled reruns, as would be the case for reproducibility of workflows (Suetake et al., 2023) and for reproducibility in Python.

5. RESULTS AND ANALYSIS

5.1 Single-asset experiments: regime separation, turbulence signatures, and structural stability of simulated dynamics

The single-asset experiment is intentionally abstract. It involves a liquid equity-index-type risk factor, as opposed to an illiquid single security. The multi-asset experiment, described later, is a collection of liquid risk factors, the inter-dependencies of which can be compressed in times of stress. The regimes should not be viewed as approximations of any specific historical crisis. Instead, they are controlled environments that aim to exemplify stress phenomena that are recognizable, such as volatility clustering, large drawdowns, greater cross-asset interdependence, a concentration of the correlation spectrum, and greater left-tail losses. This is a necessary qualification. The experiments do not incorporate out-of-sample historical crisis validations, and provide a preliminary framework within stress-consistent methodologies.

Table 1. Regime-level moments, tail risk, and turbulence summary. The table reports return moments, distributional shape, maximum drawdown, VaR/ES losses, and turbulence-share indicators by true regime

true_regime	**mean_ret_ mean**	**mean_ret_ std**	**mean_ret_ median**	**std_ ret_ mean**
0	0.0002	0.0006	0.0001	0.0101
1	-0.0001	0.0020	-0.0002	0.0307

std_ret_ std	std_ret_ median	skew_ret_ mean	skew_ret_ std
0.0007	0.0100	0.0290	0.5057
0.0020	0.0305	0.0346	0.5266

skew_ret_median	kurt_ret_mean	kurt_ret_std	kurt_ret_median
0.0353	2.3454	2.3197	1.6922
0.0355	2.4801	2.8652	1.6739

max_drawdown_ mean	max_drawdown_std	max_drawdown_ median	VaR_loss_mean
0.1547	0.0589	0.1470	0.0250
0.4208	0.1332	0.4202	0.0755

continued on following page

Table 1. Continued

true_regime	**mean_ret_ mean**	**mean_ret_ std**	**mean_ret_ median**	**std_ ret_ mean**
VaR_loss_std	VaR_loss_median	ES_loss_mean	ES_loss_std	
0.0039	0.0246	0.0310	0.0063	
0.0110	0.0752	0.0948	0.0181	
ES_loss_median	turbulence_share_ mean	turbulence_share_std	turbulence_share_ median	
0.0295	0.0504	0.0099	0.0516	
0.0918	0.0503	0.0097	0.0516	

Table 1 illustrates the transition from the low-turbulence to the high-turbulence regime. Notable are the increases in volatility, maximum drawdown, VaR, and ES, with the mean return remaining nearly unaffected. Thus, the changes between regimes cannot be characterized simply by a change in expected return. Rather, they are combinations of changes in dispersion, exposure to negative returns, and the severity of tails. For topological analysis, the interpretation of persistent features must consider a financial risk separation that has begun to emerge in loss patterns, else the geometric formations may be misidentified as signifying nothing economically.

Figure 1. Regime-specific turbulence signature via path-volatility distribution. The boxplot contrasts path volatility, measured as the standard deviation of returns, between Regime A (low turbulence) and Regime B (high turbulence), highlighting the dispersion gap and upper-tail behavior.

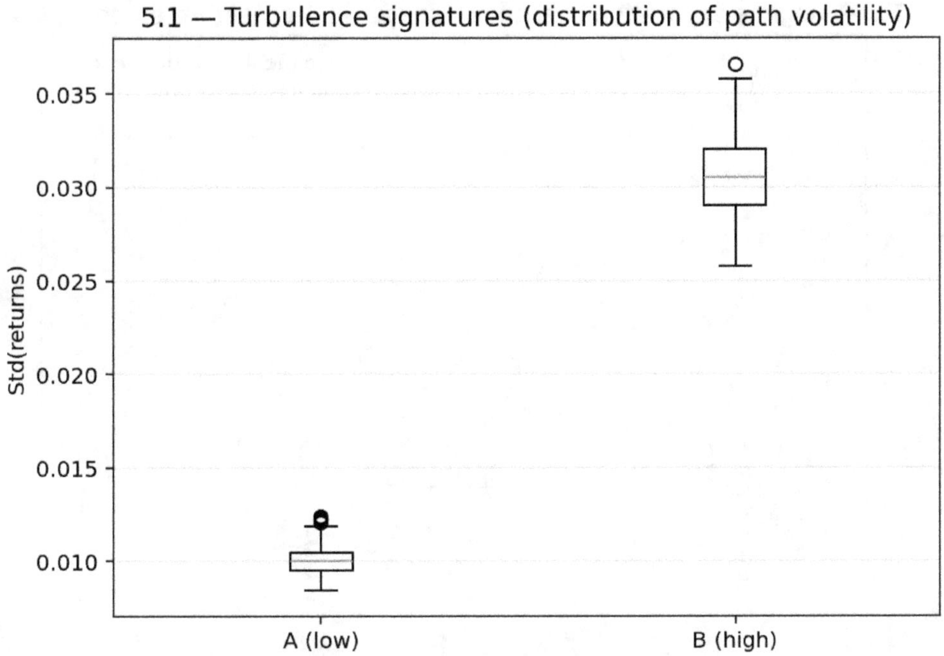

Figure 1 presents a pictorial representation of the regime statistics. Regime B shows wider volatility and interquartile range, and wider upper tail. Regime A is more compact and centered. The plot shows an apparent turbulence signature before topology is considered. In this case, the simulations already distinguish two risk environments, the first is more stable and compact, and the second is more turbulent and prone to extreme path deviations.

Figure 2. Scenario-space regime separation via PCA of feature embeddings (low versus high turbulence). The scatter plot places feature embeddings in the leading principal-component directions and contrasts the compact Regime A cloud with the shifted, more dispersed Regime B cloud.

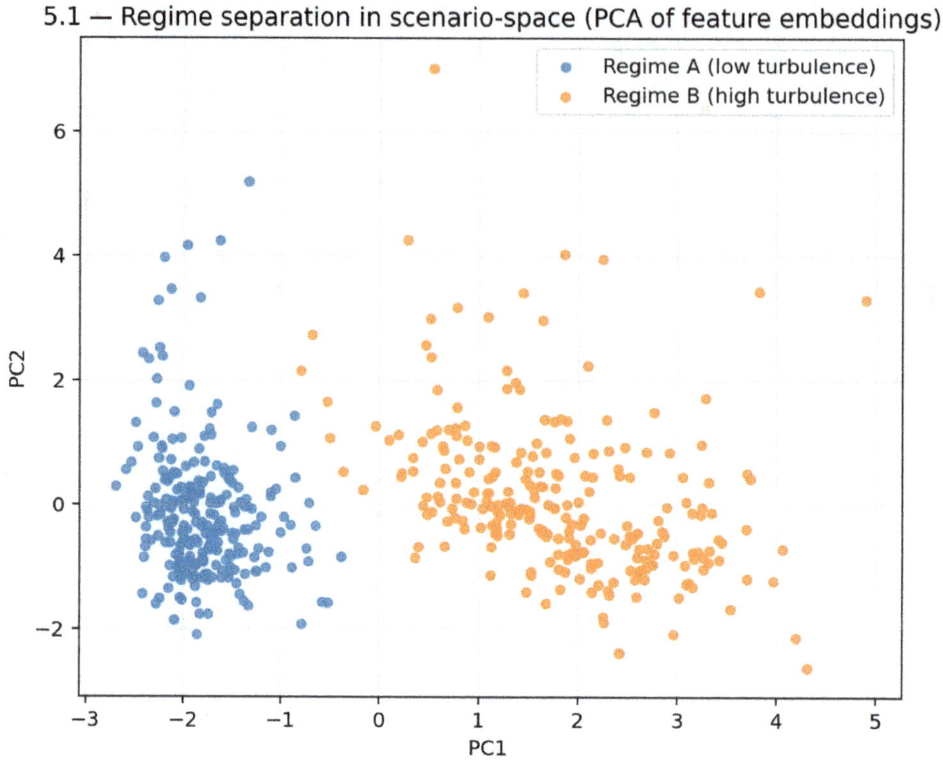

TPCA confirms the construction of features is more informative than scalar volatility. Drawdown behavior, tail-risk descriptors, and path-level structure are examples of several behavioral patterns and traits within a common framework. That framework reveals a distinctive cloud of low turbulence, while a highly turbulent cloud is more dispersed. This result provides evidence to support the more general point that the outputs of Monte Carlo simulations may be interpreted as a manifold of scenarios, where, along with changes in summary characteristics, differences of regimes will be reflected in geometric separations.

Table 2. Regime classification confusion matrix (true regime versus predicted A/B assignments). The table compares the ground-truth regime label with the classifier assignment

true\pred	pred_A	pred_B
true_A	250	0
true_B	0	250

Table 2 quantitatively assesses the PCA separation. In these controlled experiments, each simulated trajectory is categorized into the accurate regime, showing that the chosen embedding is sufficient to identify low- and high-turbulence states. This finding should be interpreted carefully, as this particular result does not demonstrate the ideal of complete separability for historical data. However, it provides evidence that the simulation is internally consistent, and that the feature set suffices to enable regime tagging prior to the application of persistence and drift diagnostics.

Figure 3. H_1 persistence diagrams of scenario-space embeddings (Regime A versus Regime B). Side-by-side diagrams summarize one-dimensional topological features for the low- and high-turbulence scenario clouds; each point records a birth-death scale, and distance from the diagonal indicates persistence.

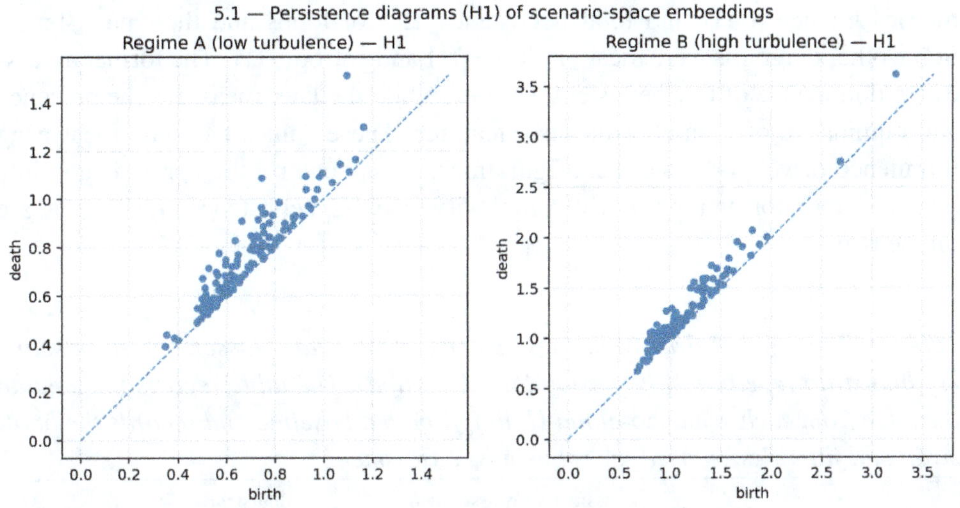

Figure 3 is interpreted by evaluating the persistence away from the diagonal, the number of moderate or long-lived features, and the range of birth-death scales. Thus, a pattern that is broader and more sustained entails a geometry of multiscale loops that is more rigorous. Changes within the H_1 landscape, therefore, contribute a structural signature of turbulence to the evidence of turbulence contained in the moments and in PCA. In the context of governance, the diagrams provide a means of deriving drift-to-baseline distances, such as Wasserstein or bottleneck measures, and then validated through resampling procedures. The more intense the persistence is in high turbulence, the more the signal justifies an earlier act of hedging, the establishment of tighter limits, and a stress escalation of greater magnitude.

Table 3. H_1 topological summary metrics for scenario clouds (counts, persistence, lifetime, entropy). The table condenses cloud-level H_1 information through n_H1 (number of H_1 features), total_persistence_H1, mean_lifetime_H1, and entropy_H1, allowing the scenario-space topology to be compared across regimes

cloud	n_H1	total_persistence_H1	mean_lifetime_H1	entropy_H1
A_low_turbulence	136	9.56404	0.07032	4.53500
B_high_turbulence	149	14.63100	0.09819	4.67190
combined	186	16.41780	0.08827	4.84731
Wasserstein_H1(A,B)		12.71125		

Table 3 Standardizes Persistence Diagrams into Quantifiable Metrics. These metrics include n_H1 and total persistence_H1 for loops and their persistence. Some other diagrams were mean_lifetime_H1 and entropy_H1. The former assesses the dominance of few persistent features, while the later measures the presence and dominance of a number of weak features. These values facilitate measuring turbulence-driven manifold reconfigurations. In risk-control they provide possible bands for monitoring topological complexity when H_1 persistence and entropy are on the rise.

Table 4. Topological drift robustness summary (median Wasserstein-to-baseline H_1, bootstrap repetitions, jitter standard deviation). The table reports the median distance from each scenario-cloud H_1 diagram to a baseline and records the bootstrap and jitter design used for robustness assessment

cloud	median_wasserstein_to_base_H1	Bootstrap_reps	jitter_std
A_low_turbulence	4.1129	30	0.03
B_high_turbulence	6.6236	30	0.03

Table 4 serves as a robustness check instead of an extra visualization. Since topological quantities can be sensitive to sampling density, perturbations, and embedding choices, we report the median Wasserstein-to-baseline with bootstrap repetitions and jitter levels. The distance is not a universal alarm threshold. This distance becomes useful when the same separation is sustained under controlled resampling. This is the condition that transforms a persistence pattern into a diagnostic that is governable as opposed to a visual-only guess.

Table 5. Path-level regime and geometry audit table. The table links each trajectory to return statistics, drawdown, VaR/ES, turbulence share, PCA coordinates, true regime, and GMM-assigned regime

Path _id	Mean _ret	Std _ret	Skew _ret	Kurt _ret	max_ drawdown	VaR_ loss	ES_ loss	Turbulence _share	true_ regime	PC1	PC2	gmm_ regime
0	0.0005	0.0092	0.1419	0.4054	0.1053	0.0218	0.0231	0.0516	0	-2.2578	-0.5014	0
1	0.0012	0.0123	1.5528	11.7649	0.1217	0.0248	0.0340	0.0397	0	-1.9649	4.1755	0
2	-0.0001	0.0107	0.0872	1.7078	0.2303	0.0265	0.0314	0.0635	0	-1.5284	-1.0772	0
3	0.0007	0.0098	0.3273	1.4752	0.1206	0.0224	0.0258	0.0437	0	-2.1655	0.3914	0
4	-0.0001	0.0103	-0.5113	2.5663	0.1965	0.0341	0.0396	0.0437	0	-1.2069	-0.1936	0
5	0.0001	0.0091	-0.2298	0.7228	0.1856	0.0246	0.0254	0.0675	0	-1.8367	-1.7517	0
6	0.0004	0.0095	0.0439	1.4496	0.1134	0.0242	0.0283	0.0635	0	-2.0625	-1.0161	0
7	0.0001	0.0100	-0.9848	5.8795	0.1303	0.0232	0.0409	0.0437	0	-1.4354	0.2740	0
8	-0.0001	0.0092	0.0518	0.8144	0.1634	0.0228	0.0254	0.0516	0	-1.9371	-0.6503	0
9	-0.0005	0.0102	-0.9313	6.1446	0.1980	0.0267	0.0401	0.0437	0	-1.1096	0.2028	0
10	-0.0001	0.0100	0.1130	1.4879	0.1331	0.0227	0.0281	0.0556	0	-1.9600	-0.6205	0

Table 5 presents the disaggregated results for individual simulated histories. Each path is evaluated using its return profile, tail-loss measures, turbulence share, PCA coordinates, and regime assignment. This level of detail is warranted when a path is situated near a margin, produces abnormal losses, or contributes to a chronic phenomenon. Unlike PCA and the classifier, which are treated as black boxes, the table shows which simulated histories lead to separation, proximity, or instability in the scenario cloud.

5.2 Multi-asset experiments: dependence topology, correlation breakdowns, and diversification limits in high-dimensional clouds

Next, the analysis extends from a singular risk factor to a multi-asset dependence context. Regime conditioned dependence clouds are constructed using correlation embeddings, and the portfolio implications of correlation breakdown are analyzed. The same high-dimensional topology is explored in a similar way. The aim is to illustrate the failure of diversification in periods when dependence is restructured in a crisis-type manner.

Figure 4. Correlation breakdown across regimes (normal versus crisis correlation heatmaps). The two heatmaps contrast a representative normal-regime correlation matrix with a crisis-regime matrix, using color intensity to show pairwise dependence and regime-driven changes in correlation structure

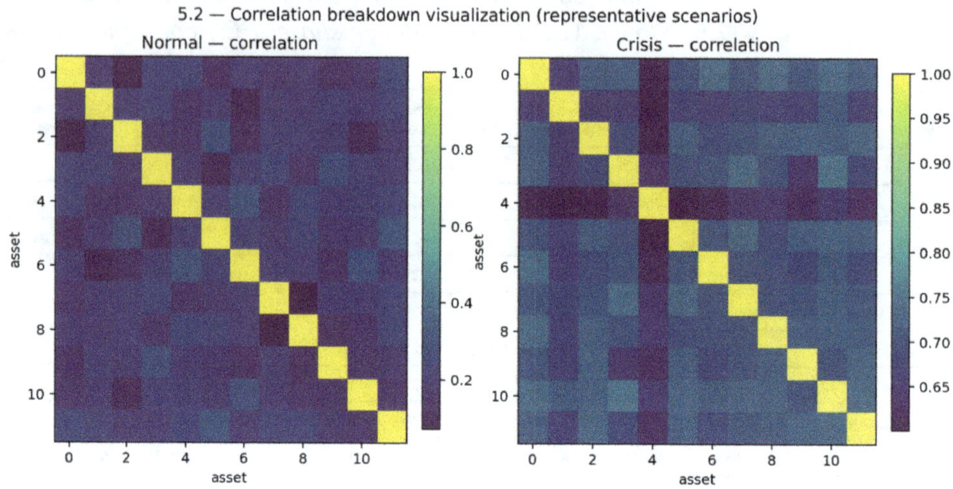

Figure 4 emphasizes that the crisis regime primarily represents a dependence-rewiring event. Under normal circumstances, correlations are moderate and heterogeneous. During crisis conditions, stronger blocks emerge and dependence becomes more coherent across assets. While the observation may be familiar, it is still consequential: a portfolio may become more concentrated, even if the marginal behavior of individual assets is consistent. This observation supports the construction of the dependence cloud. Indeed, the topology of the dependence cloud is of utmost importance, as acute changes in the market environment transform the risk distribution, driving assets to become correlated.

Table 6. Regime-level dependence and portfolio-risk summary. The table aggregates average correlation, leading-eigenvalue concentration, participation ratio, portfolio volatility, and portfolio VaR/ES losses by regime

true_regime	**avg_corr_mean**	**avg_corr_std**	**avg_corr_median**	**max_eig_mean**
0	0.19947	0.02171	0.19949	3.22195
1	0.69526	0.02671	0.69650	8.65451
max_eig_std	max_eig_median	participation_ ratio_mean	participation_ratio_ std	participation_ratio_ median
0.23781	3.22652	8.14612	0.51822	8.12451
0.29253	8.66872	1.90074	0.12357	1.88924
portfolio_vol_mean	portfolio_vol_std	portfolio_vol_ median	portfolio_VaR_ loss_mean	portfolio_VaR_ loss_std
0.00621	0.00031	0.00623	0.01419	0.00132
0.01755	0.00096	0.01744	0.04212	0.00493
portfolio_VaR_loss_ median	portfolio_ES_ loss_mean	portfolio_ES_ loss_std	portfolio_ES_loss_ median	
0.01415	0.01624	0.00182	0.01602	
0.04178	0.05058	0.00851	0.04987	

Table 6 quantifies the patterns shown in the heatmaps. In the crisis regime, average correlations rise, leading eigenvalues increase, the participation ratio decreases, and VaR/ES portfolio losses increase. These changes illustrate the concentration of risk into fewer directions coupled with a worsening loss distribution. The primary conclusion is the simultaneous change in the concentration of dependence and tail losses, not the individual changes of the other losses. Consequently, multi-asset stress is structural, as it leads to the simultaneous compression of diversification and the increase in risk.

Figure 5. Regime separation in the dependence cloud via PCA of correlation-vector embeddings (normal versus crisis). Each point represents a multivariate dependence pattern projected onto the leading principal components, with color identifying the normal or crisis regime

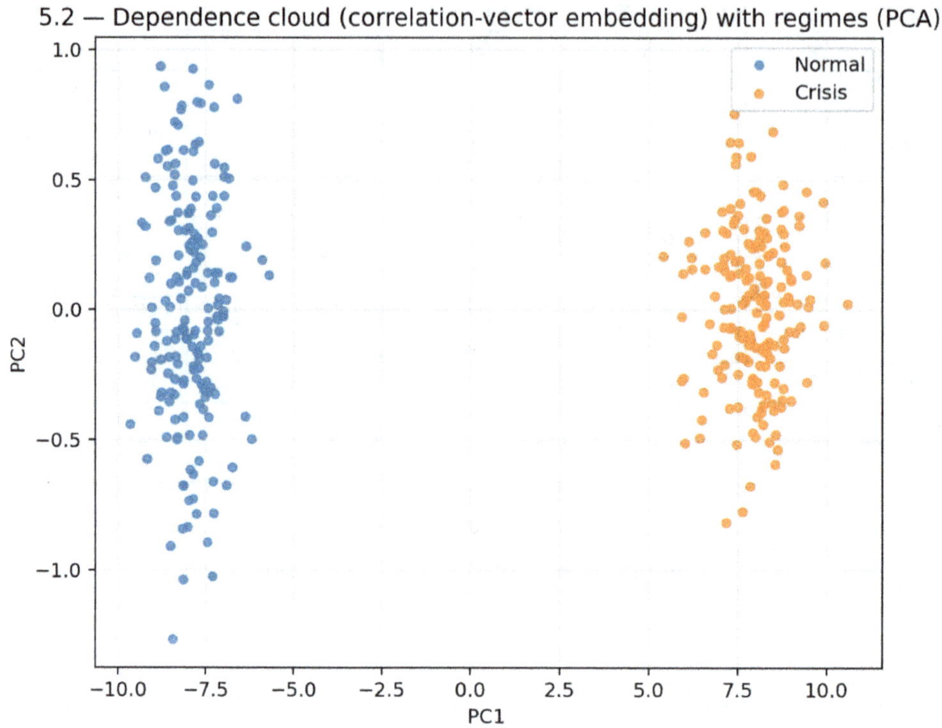

Figure 5 indicates that normal and crisis dependence patterns occupy distinct areas within reduced dependence space. This demonstrates the limitations of the entry-by-entry perspective of a correlation matrix. The crisis cloud is shifted and dispersed, suggesting a more comprehensive geometric alteration of the dependence structure within the portfolio. This also justifies the inclusion of persistence summaries: after dependence configurations develop into distinct clouds, topology provides a means of quantifying the extent of changes in the shape of those clouds in response to stress.

Table 7. Dependence-cloud PCA coordinates with regime labels. The table records each scenario identifier, PC1 and PC2 coordinates, and the associated normal or crisis regime label

path_ id	PC1	PC2	true_ regime
0	-8.15998	-0.28545	0
1	-8.14220	-0.27358	0
2	-6.98406	0.43830	0
3	-6.74409	-0.60585	0
4	-7.81148	-0.08085	0
5	-8.35904	-0.08575	0
6	-8.17033	0.61295	0
7	-8.84348	-0.38964	0
8	-8.45782	-1.26685	0
9	-8.71288	0.85720	0
10	-7.42544	0.86499	0

Table 7 provides a means to contextualize the PCA plotting. Each of the displayed points is associated with a scenario ID, drift coordinates, and the label of the drift regime. This is useful when the scenario is proximal to a drift decision boundary or when a drift threshold is being set. For the governance layer, the table provides a basis to justify an attribution of the simulated case as normal, transitional or crisis, rather than the justification being based solely on the PCA plot.

Figure 6. Diversification limits under dependence regimes (portfolio volatility versus average correlation). The scatter plot relates average correlation to equal-weight portfolio volatility and shows how regime-conditioned dependence increases portfolio risk and reduces diversification benefits.

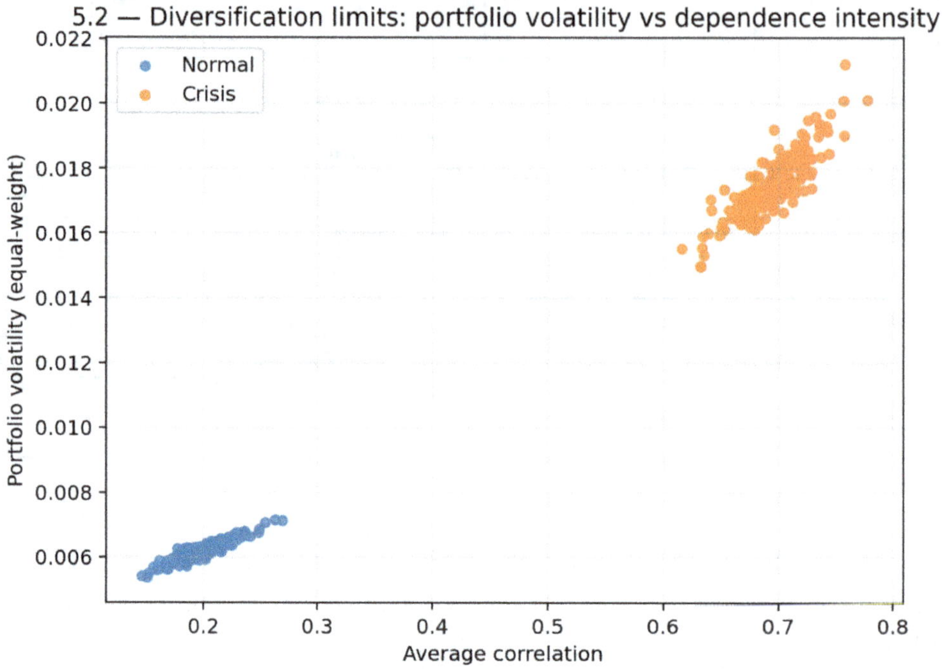

Figure 6 describes dependence compression with respect to portfolio volatility. As average correlation increases, an equal-weighted portfolio is placed into an increased volatility band. The normal and crisis scenarios are therefore separated in an economically interpretable way, instead of a purely statistical way. The same portfolio can be in different risk environments, depending on the nature of dependence. This makes it easier to understand the effect of topology: movement in a dependence cloud carries a direct impact on volatility, limits, and the focus of stress-testing.

Table 8. Scenario-level dependence-risk linkage table. The table records average correlation, leading eigenvalue, participation ratio, portfolio volatility, VaR/ES losses, and regime label for each scenario

Path _id	avg_ corr	max_ eig	Participation _ratio	Portfolio _vol	portfolio_ VaR_loss	portfolio_ ES_loss	true_ regime
0	0.19250	3.12554	8.37073	0.00611	0.01517	0.01613	0
1	0.19328	3.14518	8.33468	0.00622	0.01287	0.01453	0
2	0.22941	3.54361	7.45618	0.00660	0.01403	0.01682	0
3	0.23675	3.63268	7.28483	0.00668	0.01555	0.01589	0
4	0.20362	3.24865	8.09465	0.00626	0.01470	0.01592	0
5	0.18638	3.08076	8.46020	0.00607	0.01303	0.01373	0
6	0.19223	3.14453	8.30461	0.00617	0.01348	0.01971	0
7	0.17134	2.91016	8.82985	0.00581	0.01402	0.01598	0
8	0.18341	3.08178	8.42938	0.00582	0.01282	0.01497	0
9	0.17547	2.96042	8.73261	0.00599	0.01268	0.01403	0
10	0.21568	3.39553	7.75035	0.00618	0.01432	0.01543	0

Table 8 exhibits the dependence concentration to loss outcome path on a scenario level. Effective participation ratios, as well as larger portfolio loss measures, are inversely proportional to average dependence correlation and the magnitude of the leading eigenvalue. Accordingly, each row links dependence structure to risk impact. This provides value in redoing specific stress cases; isolating which scenarios actualize instability, and which cases call for a review of hedges and concentration limits.

Figure 7. H_1 persistence diagrams of the dependence cloud (normal versus crisis topology). Side-by-side H_1 diagrams summarize one-dimensional topological features in the normal and crisis dependence clouds; distance above the diagonal measures persistence

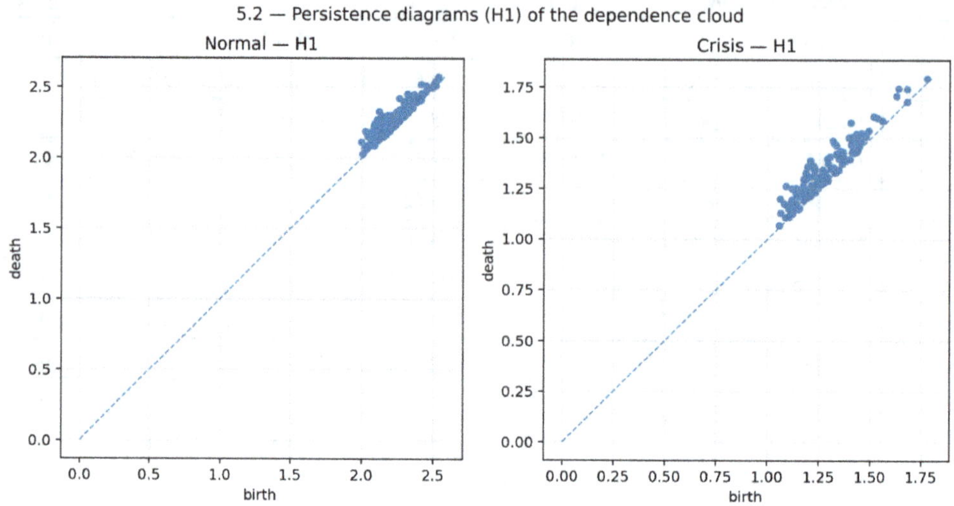

Figure 7 shows the persistence mass above the diagonal, the birth and death scales, and the presence of long-lived features. Together, these perceptions reveal how the loop-like and multiscale connective structures differ in the normal and crisis configurations. This result supports the central argument of Section 5.2. Correlation breakdown is more than just an average correlation reduction; it means reconfiguring the dependence manifold. Regime-based shifts in the persistence of H_1 offer structural insights when used alongside heatmaps and diversification diagrams. From a governance perspective, the distance in H_1 can be measured against a baseline, and used with robustness tests, to allow for the earlier implementation of concentration reviews, de-risking, and additional stress tests triggered when dependence approaches a crisis configuration.

Table 9. Dependence-cloud H_1 topology summary metrics (feature count, total persistence, lifetime, entropy). The table summarizes aggregated H_1 diagnostics

- n_H1, total_persistence_H1, mean_lifetime_H1, and entropy_H1 - for normal, crisis, and combined dependence clouds

cloud	n_H1	total_ persistence _H1	mean_ lifetime_H1	Entropy _H1
Normal	232	12.96304	0.05588	5.14613
Crisis	141	8.09802	0.05743	4.64291
Combined	217	12.46864	0.05746	5.09504
Wasserstein_H1(Normal,Crisis)		14.89242		

Table 9 translates dependence diagrams into comparable regime-level indicators. The variables n_H1 and total_persistence_H1 evaluate the quantity and concentration of loop structures. The variables mean_lifetime_H1 and entropy_H1 assess the distribution of the structures. In this way, correlation breakdown becomes visible as a structural change giving rise to something more than a shift in the entries of the matrix. These quantities also provide the foundation for active dependence governance: upper bands for topological and structural complexity can be set and linked to a stipulated limit on diversification. If H_1 persistence and entropy shift towards a crisis-like state banding and structural complexity may be justified more readily. Stress testing of the system may be justified along similar lines.

Table 10. Dependence-cloud topological drift robustness (median Wasserstein-to-baseline H_1 with bootstrap and jitter). The table reports median distance from each dependence-cloud H_1 diagram to a baseline and records the resampling and perturbation design

cloud	median_wasserstein _to_base_H1	Bootstrap _reps	jitter_std
Normal	5.68491	25	0.03
Crisis	3.58865	25	0.03

Table 10 documents the uncertainty design for the drift statistic. The value median_wasserstein_to_base_H1 assumes significance only when combined with bootstrap_reps and jitter_std, as these indicate the stress testing of the persistence signature. This is important, as the assertion of the reconfiguration of dependence must remain unaffected by sampling variation. Table 10, in governance language, transforms H_1 drift to a calibratable KPI, which can be related to the tolerance of false positives and be used as a trigger point for escalation, should the dependence cloud exceed the acceptable limits of a crisis-like topological formation.

5.3 Risk and stress-testing experiments: topology-informed early-warning signals for VaR/ES fragility and scenario sensitivity

This subsection combines rolling VaR/ES diagnostics with topology-based drift. It examines two questions: Does the structural signal predict imminent breaks? How do various stress designs rank, considering both tail-risk amplification and distance from the baseline? The answer to this question is rather straightforward. An early warning system must do more than describe a pending crisis after the losses have materialized. It must signal when the scenario manifold is starting to become destabilized. For these reasons, the analysis interprets standard back testing and topological signals concurrently.

Figure 8. Topology-informed rolling VaR/ES fragility with breach events (Wasserstein-H_1 structural change signal). The time-series panel overlays realized losses, rolling VaR and ES, breach markers, and a concurrent Wasserstein distance on H_1 so that risk-threshold exceedances can be compared with structural change

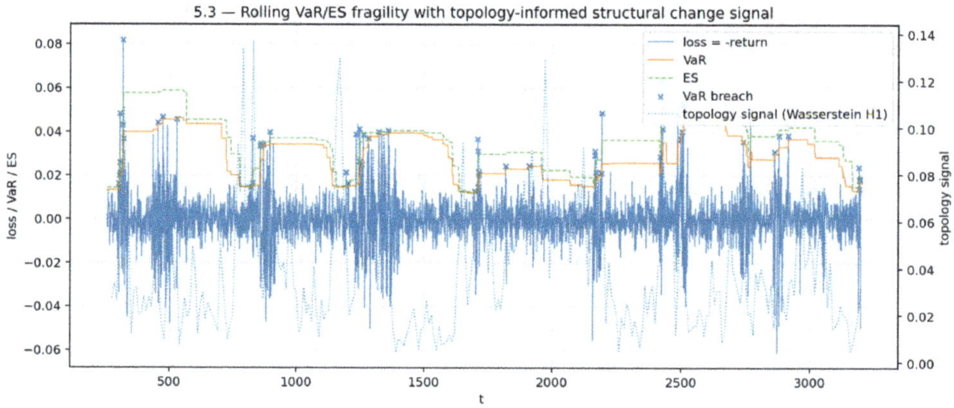

Figure 8 provides a comprehension through temporal analysis of loss spikes, breach markers, step increases in Value-at-Risk (VaR) / Expected Shortfall (ES), and an increase in topology signals. The question presented is whether topology increases prior to, or at least during, instances of breach clusters and changes in risk-level. In the image, H_1 drift operationalizes scenario-manifold fragility, indicating a movement of structure that rolling risk estimations may not fully capture. In terms of governance, this type of panel combines triggers in which conventional limits align with structural drift thresholds. These triggers justify the need for an earlier review, more stringent limits, or a more aggressive topology that may suggest an inclination of instability before breaches occur with greater frequency.

Table 11. Rolling risk-and-topology time-series audit table (returns, losses, VaR/ES, breaches, topology signal). The table aligns each timestamp with return, loss, rolling VaR, rolling ES, breach indicator, and the topology-informed score used to track H_1 drift

t	ret	loss	VaR	ES	breach	Topology _signal
250	-0.00180	0.00180	0.01325	0.01444	0	
251	0.00244	-0.00244	0.01325	0.01444	0	
252	0.00369	-0.00369	0.01325	0.01444	0	
253	-0.00594	0.00594	0.01325	0.01444	0	
254	-0.01282	0.01282	0.01325	0.01444	0	
255	-0.00654	0.00654	0.01325	0.01444	0	
256	-0.00454	0.00454	0.01325	0.01444	0	
257	-0.00594	0.00594	0.01325	0.01444	0	
258	-0.00720	0.00720	0.01325	0.01444	0	
259	0.00086	-0.00086	0.01325	0.01444	0	
260	0.01227	-0.01227	0.01325	0.01444	0	
261	0.00023	-0.00023	0.01325	0.01444	0	
262	-0.00263	0.00263	0.01325	0.01444	0	
263	0.00231	-0.00231	0.01324	0.01443	0	
264	-0.00187	0.00187	0.01324	0.01443	0	
265	0.00603	-0.00603	0.01324	0.01443	0	
266	0.00406	-0.00406	0.01324	0.01443	0	
267	0.00143	-0.00143	0.01324	0.01443	0	
268	-0.01118	0.01118	0.01324	0.01443	0	
269	-0.00320	0.00320	0.01324	0.01443	0	
270	-0.00082	0.00082	0.01324	0.01443	0	0.02707
271	-0.01144	0.01144	0.01324	0.01443	0	0.02775
272	-0.00721	0.00721	0.01324	0.01443	0	0.02844
273	-0.00074	0.00074	0.01324	0.01443	0	0.02912

Table 11 gives a timestamped record for the rolling analysis. Returns, losses, VaR, ES, breach indicators, and topology signal are aligned for each timestamp. This lets analysts inspect lead-lag relationships, rather than just rely on the plot to infer them. The table also supports threshold calibration. Analysts can see if the topology signal spikes before breaches, how it behaves during turbulent times, and if the alert rule would impose a reasonable operational burden.

Table 12. VaR backtesting summary. The table reports confidence level, observations, breaches, empirical breach rate, and Kupiec and Christoffersen likelihood-ratio diagnostics for coverage and independence

alpha	n_obs	n_breaches	breach_rate
0.01	2950	58	0.01966
kupiec_POF_LR	kupiec_POF_p_value	Christoffersen_IND_LR	Christoffersen_IND_p_value
21.70115	3.18601E-06	39.24133	3.74528E-10

Table 12 indicates excess VaR breaches as well as breach clustering. Such a result forms the basis of the understanding for the topology signal. This chapter does not suggest that topology 'fixes' VaR calibration. Rather, it suggests that the structural drift may bring in some additional information when the tail-risk process is under some sort of stress. The diagnostics developed by Kupiec and Christoffersen show the fragility of the process by formally testing coverage and independence. In this case, topology-informed signals should be used in conjunction with model escalation, model review and additional stress testing, and should not be considered a replacement to statistical backtesting.

Figure 9. Topology-signal early-warning ROC for "breach soon" prediction (AUC benchmark). The ROC curve evaluates whether the Wasserstein-H1 structural signal ranks imminent VaR breaches above non-breach windows, with the diagonal representing the no-skill baseline

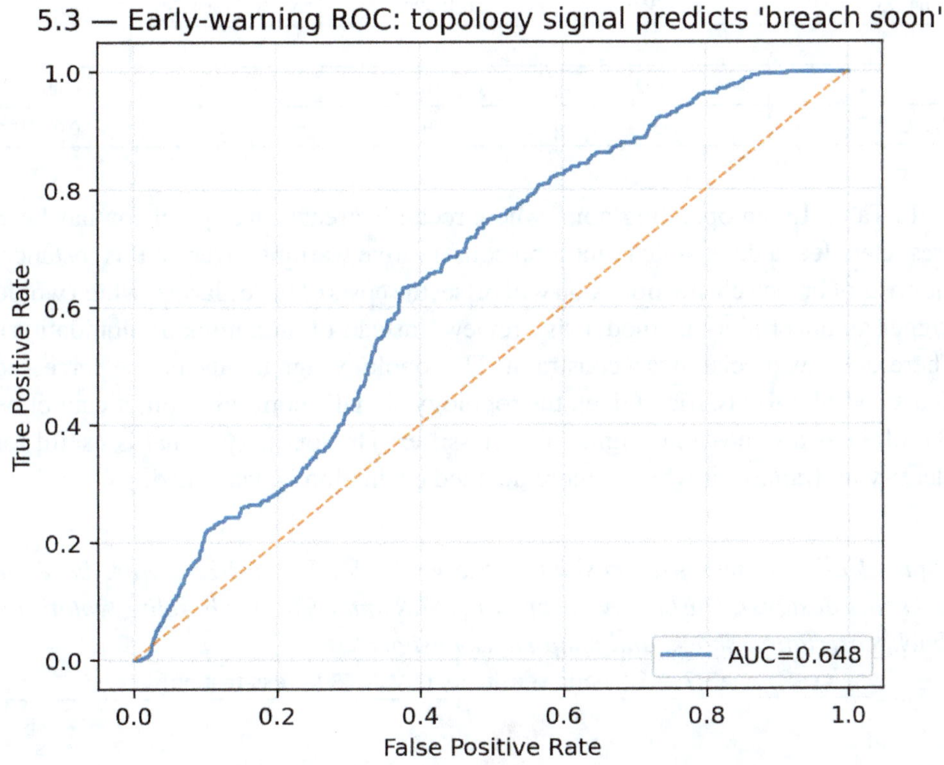

Figure 9 assesses the use of topology signal as a ranking mechanism for imminent violations. It neither establishes a trading rule nor acts as a substitute for VaR/ES constraints. A curve above the no-skill diagonal exhibits valuable information; the stated AUC positions the evidence in the moderate, as opposed to decisive, range. This careful assessment is warranted: topology has its most pronounced effects when used in combination with breach counts, ES activity, and stress-scenario analyses.

Table 13. Early-warning performance summary for topology-signal alerts. The table reports AUC, threshold, precision, recall, F1 score, evaluation sample, positive cases, horizon, and alpha

AUC	threshold	precision	recall	f1	n_eval	n_positive	horizon	alpha
0.64823	0.03350	0.18498	0.71504	0.29393	2930	379	10	0.01

In Table 13, an operating point where recall is greater than precision has been presented. It is a defensible point for a conservative warning layer. In this instance, the costs of breach cluster omission will offset the costs of false alarms (which would trigger an uncertainty or model risk review, instead of an automatic liquidation). Therefore, low precision is a constraint. The topology signal must not be perceived as a stand-alone classifier. Given the topology signal's configuration, it cannot be classified as a stand-alone signal or a classifier. The topology signal is useful for identifying frames for which a more detailed evaluation is warranted.

Figure 10. Stress-scenario sensitivity of tail risk (VaR versus ES across baseline and shock designs). The bar chart compares VaR and ES for the baseline, volatility-shock, correlation-shock, and jump-shock designs

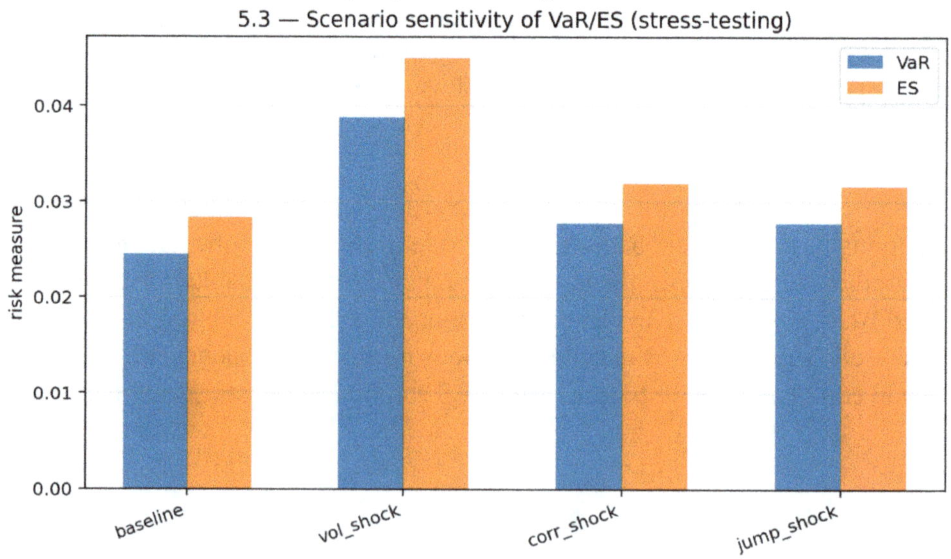

Figure 10 illustrates how various shocks transmit into Value at Risk and Expected Shortfall. Volatility shocks lead to the most tail-risk amplification resulting from the more direct effect on the shape of the loss distribution. Correlation and jump shocks lead to less, but still significant tail-risk amplification, especially when considered alongside the impact and topology distance. From a stress-testing perspective, it suggests that severity is multi-faceted. A particular shock may be considered severe if it increases overall loss, alters the scenario manifold, or does both. The model therefore orders stress test intensity by tail risk and structural impact.

Table 14. Stress-scenario risk and topology drift summary. The table reports VaR, ES, and H1 topology distance to baseline for the baseline, volatility-shock, correlation-shock, and jump-shock designs

scenario	VaR	ES	topology_distance_to_baseline_H1
baseline	0.02452	0.02837	0.00000
vol_shock	0.03878	0.04494	14.75002
corr_shock	0.02778	0.03197	26.88142
jump_shock	0.02778	0.03164	30.22077

Table 14 shows the limitations of risk magnitude. Different distances from baseline can produce similar VaR, and traditional tail metrics do not capture the extent of the shift in scenario geometry. The topology-distance column provides that missing element. In the context of model governance, two shocks that result in the same VaR can warrant different levels of attention if one results in a more extensive manifold reconfiguration. The table thus provides justification to incorporate both the financial impact and the degree of structural change in stress selection.

6. DISCUSSION AND CONCLUSIONS

6.1 Financial interpretation of topological signatures: implications for model risk, robustness, and decision support

The H_1 persistence structure, Wasserstein drift, and persistence entropy detail regime-conditioned reorganizations of market-state geometry that, in these experiments, occur alongside turbulence, dependence rewiring, and stress amplification. They do not happen in isolation as finite-sample artifacts. This layer of structure the chapter introduces shows that the simulated paths may be analyzed against a framework of scenario manifolds, the degree of which may be audited concerning the presence of volatility and dependence. This shows that there are model-risk implications of non-equivalence. This may be the case even if two calibrations reproduce similar VaR/ES numbers since they may encode different scenario geometries. This may show that there are hidden channels of fragility, and that stress-propagation mechanisms may be made visible only if the structure is measured directly.

These interpretations hinge on the robustness of their decision value. Persistence summaries and drift estimates should not vary significantly when exposed to bootstrap and jitter perturbations. They also should not contradict rolling breach behavior and traditional backtest diagnostics. If these requirements are met, topology can serve more as a validation layer with governance value, rather than as a descriptive tool. More specifically, topology-based drift thresholds can be combined with VaR/ES thresholds to establish verifiable escalation actions such as de-risking, adjusting the hedge, and performing selective stress test runs. This promotes a more consistent and comparable rationale for risk-related decisions across different regimes.

6.2 Limitations, threats to validity, and concluding synthesis

The limitations of the experiments will shape the conclusions. Findings rely upon simplified simulations, estimations of tail behavior from finite samples, and hyperparameters for embedding or topology. These are prone to shifts in stress, choice of kernels and windows, and persistence summary design. Validity threats include possible regime-label leakage, the highly variable and interdependent nature of correlated clouds, and overfitting to breached thresholds in low-event scenarios. Therefore, the simulated crisis regimes must be considered as oversimplified designs rather than precise-event calibrations. Their primary purpose is to demonstrate stress mechanisms (volatility clustering, dependence and relation compression, drawdown amplification, spectral concentration, and tail fragility) so that diagnostics informed by topology can be assessed in a controlled environment. This will help in the eventual application of these methods to historical crisis contexts.

7. FUTURE WORK

7.1 Research agenda: online adaptive stress testing, calibration under distribution shift, hybrid generative models, and production-grade validation pathways

The framework that is being outlined in this paper would most benefit from application to online adaptive stress testing. Persistency summaries along with scenario clouds and dependency embeddings could be incrementally adjusted. This would give rise to latency and drift thresholds that would allow topology-based alerts to respond to shift in conditions at a measured and documented pace. Distribution shift would require additional consideration of calibration. Disjoint development and holdout protocols would serve to evaluate the coherence of VaR/ES, breach dynamics, and topological measurements when market conditions have shifted from the calibration.

On the other hand, hybrid generative methods need to be developed further. Stress testing designs demand a mixture of fidelity and flexibility. Mechanistic simulation, VAEs, and diffusion-based generators in tandem with topology-knowledge regularization can meet this challenge. A topology-augmented risk monitoring system would incorporate reliability checks bolstered by a bootstrap and jitter methodology, risk documentation, and threshold validation, as well as a pathway for the reproducible provenance of data, code, and system. These methods would greatly enhance the traceability, audibility, and applicability of this risk monitoring system in operational decision making.

Availability of code: The Python code for data generation, perturbation simulations, autoencoder training, and topological metrics is available at: https://github.com/JAIME6609/ECONOMETRIC/blob/main/CODE-ART-02-V2.py

The repository supports reproducibility of the pipeline, figures, and tables. For final submission, the code should be frozen through a tagged release, commit identifier, or archival DOI, and the access date should be documented.

REFERENCES

Alfeus, M., Overbeck, L., & Schlögl, E. (2019). Regime switching rough Heston model. *Journal of Futures Markets*, *39*(5), 538–552. DOI: 10.1002/fut.21993

Bauer, U. (2021). Ripser: Efficient computation of Vietoris–Rips persistence barcodes. *Journal of Applied and Computational Topology*, *5*(3), 391–423. DOI: 10.1007/s41468-021-00071-5

Bayer, S., & Dimitriadis, T. (2022). Regression-based expected shortfall backtesting. *Journal of Financial Econometrics*, *20*(3), 437–471. DOI: 10.1093/jjfinec/nbaa013

Chazal, F., & Michel, B. (2021). An introduction to topological data analysis: Fundamental and practical aspects for data scientists. *Frontiers in Artificial Intelligence*, *4*, 667963. DOI: 10.3389/frai.2021.667963 PMID: 34661095

Cheng, Y. (2025). Monte Carlo-Based VaR Estimation and Backtesting Under Basel III. *Risks*, *13*(8), 146. DOI: 10.3390/risks13080146

Corbet, R., Fugacci, U., Kerber, M., Landi, C., & Wang, B. (2019). A kernel for multi-parameter persistent homology. *Computers & Graphics: X*, *2*, 100005. DOI: 10.1016/j.cagx.2019.100005 PMID: 33367228

Dong, Z., Hu, C., Zhou, C., & Lin, H. (2020). Vectorization of persistence barcode with applications in pattern classification of porous structures. *Computers & Graphics*, *90*, 182–192. DOI: 10.1016/j.cag.2020.05.029

Dong, Z., Lin, H., Zhou, C., Zhang, B., & Li, G. (2024). Persistence B-spline grids: Stable vector representation of persistence diagrams based on data fitting. *Machine Learning*, *113*(3), 1373–1420. DOI: 10.1007/s10994-023-06492-w

Gao, G., Mishra, B., & Ramazzotti, D. (2018). Causal data science for financial stress testing. *Journal of Computational Science*, *26*, 294–304. DOI: 10.1016/j.jocs.2018.04.003

Gatheral, J., Jaisson, T., & Rosenbaum, M. (2018). Volatility is rough. *Quantitative Finance*, *18*(6), 933–949. DOI: 10.1080/14697688.2017.1393551

Gidea, M., & Katz, Y. (2018). Topological data analysis of financial time series: Landscapes of crashes. *Physica A*, *491*, 820–834. DOI: 10.1016/j.physa.2017.09.028

Hensel, F., Moor, M., & Rieck, B. (2021). A Survey of Topological Machine Learning Methods. *Frontiers in Artificial Intelligence*, *4*, 681108. DOI: 10.3389/frai.2021.681108 PMID: 34124648

Horvath, B., Jacquier, A., & Tankov, P. (2020). Volatility options in rough volatility models. *SIAM Journal on Financial Mathematics, 11*(2), 437–469. DOI: 10.1137/18M1169242

Ismail, M. S., Md Noorani, M. S. M., Ismail, M., Razak, F. A., & Alias, M. A. (2022). Early warning signals of financial crises using persistent homology. *Physica A, 586*, 126459. DOI: 10.1016/j.physa.2021.126459

Jeng, S. W., & Kılıçman, A. (2021). On Multilevel and Control Variate Monte Carlo Methods for Option Pricing under the Rough Heston Model. *Mathematics, 9*(22), 2930. DOI: 10.3390/math9222930

Katz, Y. A., & Biem, A. (2021). Time-resolved topological data analysis of market instabilities. *Physica A, 571*, 125816. DOI: 10.1016/j.physa.2021.125816

Leo, S., Crusoe, M. R., Rodríguez-Navas, L., Sirvent, R., Kanitz, A., De Geest, P., Wittner, R., Pireddu, L., Garijo, D., Fernández, J. M., Colonnelli, I., Gallo, M., Ohta, T., Suetake, H., Capella-Gutierrez, S., de Wit, R., Kinoshita, B. P., & Soiland-Reyes, S. (2024). Recording provenance of workflow runs with RO-Crate. *PLoS One, 19*(9), e0309210. DOI: 10.1371/journal.pone.0309210 PMID: 39255315

Mohajerin Esfahani, P., & Kuhn, D. (2018). Data-driven distributionally robust optimization using the Wasserstein metric: Performance guarantees and tractable reformulations. *Mathematical Programming, 171*(1–2), 115–166. DOI: 10.1007/s10107-017-1172-1

Noorani, I., Mehrdoust, F., & Nasroallah, A. (2021). A generalized antithetic variates Monte-Carlo simulation method for pricing of Asian option in a Markov regime-switching model. *Mathematics and Computers in Simulation, 181*, 1–15. DOI: 10.1016/j.matcom.2020.09.011

Ravishanker, N., & Chen, R. (2021). An introduction to persistent homology for time series. *Wiley Interdisciplinary Reviews: Computational Statistics, 13*(3), e1548. DOI: 10.1002/wics.1548

Sinha, D., & Chakrabarty, S. P. (2023). A review of efficient Multilevel Monte Carlo algorithms for derivative pricing and risk management. *MethodsX, 10*, 102078. DOI: 10.1016/j.mex.2023.102078 PMID: 36875343

Soiland-Reyes, S., Sefton, P., Castro, L. J., Coppens, F., Garijo, D., Leo, S., Portier, M., & Groth, P. (2022). Creating lightweight FAIR Digital Objects with RO-Crate. *Research Ideas and Outcomes, 8*, e93937. DOI: 10.3897/rio.8.e93937

Suetake, H., Fukusato, T., Igarashi, T., & Ohta, T. (2023). A workflow reproducibility scale for automatic validation of biological interpretation results. *GigaScience*, *12*, giad031. Advance online publication. DOI: 10.1093/gigascience/giad031 PMID: 37150537

Teng, H.-W. (2023). Importance sampling for calculating the value-at-risk and expected shortfall of the quadratic portfolio with t-distributed risk factors. *Computational Economics*, *62*(3), 1125–1154. DOI: 10.1007/s10614-022-10294-y

Wasserman, L. (2018). Topological data analysis. *Annual Review of Statistics and Its Application*, *5*(1), 501–532. DOI: 10.1146/annurev-statistics-031017-100045

Wiese, M., Knobloch, R., Korn, R., & Kretschmer, P. (2020). Quant GANs: Deep generation of financial time series. *Quantitative Finance*, *20*(9), 1419–1440. DOI: 10.1080/14697688.2020.1730426

Xiang, J., & Wang, X. (2022). Quasi-Monte Carlo simulation for American option sensitivities. *Journal of Computational and Applied Mathematics*, *413*, 114268. DOI: 10.1016/j.cam.2022.114268

Chapter 8
Modelling South African Closing Stock Prices Using GRNN, GBM and ANFIS Approaches

Malose Patrick Leeto Shogole
http://orcid.org/0009-0003-0754-9928
North-West University, South Africa

Johannes Tshepiso Tsoku
http://orcid.org/0000-0003-0093-6223
Sefako Makgato Health Science University, South Africa

Lebotsa Daniel Metsileng
http://orcid.org/0000-0003-2891-3277
North-West University, South Africa

ABSTRACT

Accurate forecasting is critical for informed investment decisions and risk management in financial markets. This study assesses the predictive performance of GRNN, GBM, and ANFIS in estimating the South African Nedbank closing stock prices. The results show that ANFIS achieves superior accuracy, with the lowest error metrics among the three models. Its effectiveness is attributed to the hybrid combination of fuzzy logic and neural networks, which enables it to capture complex nonlinear patterns and uncertainty in financial data. GBM demonstrates moderate predictive capability, benefiting from its iterative boosting mechanism, while GRNN shows higher errors, reflecting challenges in modelling highly volatile market conditions. These findings support the growing evidence that hybrid models such as ANFIS

DOI: 10.4018/979-8-3373-8372-9.ch008

provide enhanced forecasting reliability. The study highlights ANFIS's practical utility for analysts and investors, and future research could explore integrating it with advanced machine learning approaches to further improve stock price prediction in dynamic markets.

1. INTRODUCTION AND BACKGROUND

Forecasting stock prices remains a complex yet critical endeavour within financial markets, particularly in emerging economies such as South Africa, where market dynamics are often influenced by a blend of global trends and unique local factors. As traditional statistical methods face limitations in capturing the nonlinear and volatile nature of financial time series, modern computational approaches have gained traction for their ability to model such complexities with greater accuracy.

Though traditional statistical models such as autoregressive integrated moving average (ARIMA) and generalised autoregressive conditional heteroscedastic (GARCH) models have been widely used for time series forecasting, they often fall short when dealing with the nonlinear structures and dynamic relationships inherent in financial data (Ding et al., 2017). Recent advancements in machine learning (ML) have enabled researchers to explore alternative approaches that can more effectively model these complexities (Warin & Stojkov, 2021; Wang 2024). Therefore, this study investigates the use of three advanced computational models General Regression Neural Network (GRNN), Gradient Boosting Model (GBM), and Adaptive Neuro-Fuzzy Inference System (ANFIS) to forecast stock prices in the South African market.

The GRNN was introduced by Specht (1991), as a type of radial basis neural network (NN) designed for function approximation and regression tasks. It is classified as a nonparametric model since it does not require a predefined mathematical structure between inputs and outputs, allowing it to adapt flexibly to complex data distributions (Specht, 1991). One of the core strengths of GRNN is its fast-training process. Unlike conventional NNs that require iterative weight adjustments over many epochs, GRNN performs learning in a single pass using a memory-based approach, which makes it highly efficient in terms of training time (Zhang & Liu, 2020). This makes it suitable for real-time applications or when computational resources are limited.

In addition, GRNN is known for handling nonlinear and noisy datasets effectively, this is via to its smoothing kernel function (Polymers, 2022). The kernel acts as a form of local averaging, which reduces the impact of outliers and noise, leading to smoother output predictions. This characteristic is particularly advantageous in financial forecasting, where market data is often volatile and contains irregular fluctuations (Alsulaiman et al., 2022). According to Kisi & Shiri, (2012) another significant benefit is that GRNN does not make strong assumptions about data distribution, making it applicable across domains with complex, non-Gaussian behaviours. This nonparametric flexibility helps it model relationships in situations where traditional models like linear regression would fail (Andersen, 2009).

However, GRNN is not without limitations. Since it stores all training samples, memory usage can become a bottleneck, especially with large datasets. This architecture increases the computational load during prediction, as each test instance requires the model to calculate distances from all training points (Kim & Kim, 2016). Additionally, its performance is highly dependent on the smoothing parameter (σ) , which controls the generalisation behaviour. A poorly chosen value can lead to overfitting or underfitting, and there is no standard method for selecting the optimal value, often requiring trial and error or cross-validation (Specht, 1991; Ustaoglu et al., 2008).

Moreover, GRNN functions as a "black box" model, making it challenging to extract interpretable insights from its structure. This lack of transparency can be a disadvantage in domains where understanding model rationale is critical, such as finance or healthcare (Alfaro et al., 2018). On the other hand, the GBM is an ensemble learning algorithm that builds a strong predictive model by sequentially combining multiple weak learners, typically decision trees. At each stage, it fits a new model to correct the errors made by the previous one, effectively reducing bias and improving overall accuracy (Friedman, 2001). GBM excels at capturing nonlinear patterns and complex interactions in data, which is why it has gained popularity in time series forecasting and financial modelling (Zhang et al., 2021). Moreover, its flexibility in handling different types of data and loss functions make it a robust choice in scenarios with noisy or high-dimensional datasets (Roy et al., 2020). However, GBM is sensitive to overfitting and often requires careful tuning of hyperparameters such as learning rate, tree depth, and number of iterations.

The ANFIS was introduced by Jang (1993) as a hybrid model that combines the learning ability of NNs with the reasoning approach of fuzzy logic. This integration allows it to effectively manage uncertainty and imprecise inputs, which are common in financial markets due to fluctuating investor sentiment and behavioural patterns (Jang, 1993). ANFIS is particularly valued for its balance between accuracy and interpretability, enabling it to model complex systems while still offering insight into the decision process (Singh & Srivastava, 2021). Its adaptability and capacity to learn nonlinear relationships have made it a popular choice for stock market prediction tasks in recent studies (Huang et al., 2022).

By comparing these three models in the context of the South African stock market, this study aims to identify which approach delivers the most accurate and reliable predictions. Given the market's hybrid nature characterised by both developed and emerging market attributes it serves as an ideal test bed for evaluating the performance of intelligent forecasting models. The findings of this study will not only contribute to the growing literature on ML in finance but also offer practical insights for investors, analysts, and policymakers navigating the uncertainties of financial markets. This study offers a unique comparative evaluation of three sophisticated models (GRNN, GBM, and ANFIS) within the framework of the South African stock market.

The study is divided into five main sections. The literature review forms Section 2 of the study and Section 3 is the research methodology. In Section 4, discussions of the results are presented, and Section 5 provides the conclusion and recommendations.

2. LITERATURE REVIEW

Kazak (2025) investigated the effectiveness of metaheuristic-optimised ANFIS) in comparison with traditional ANN for stock price prediction using weekly data from the Borsa Istanbul 100 index covering the period 2010–2023. The study aimed to determine whether optimisation techniques could enhance the forecasting capability of ANFIS and enable it to compete with conventional neural network architectures in financial time-series prediction. To achieve this, ANFIS models were optimised using Particle Swarm Optimisation (PSO) and Ant Colony Optimisation (ACO), while standard ANN models served as benchmark comparators. Model performance was evaluated using common forecasting accuracy metrics. The results indicated that the optimised ANFIS models achieved predictive accuracy comparable to, and in some cases exceeding, that of the ANN models, particularly in capturing nonlinear patterns and reducing forecast errors. Based on these findings, the study recommended the use of metaheuristic-enhanced ANFIS models as a viable alternative to traditional neural networks in stock market forecasting, especially in applications where model interpretability and optimisation flexibility are important considerations.

Akiner & Ghasri (2024) conducted a comparative study evaluating ANFIS enhanced with metaheuristic optimisation against a DBN model for forecasting potential evapotranspiration (PET). The aim was to determine whether hybridising ANFIS with optimisation algorithms could improve forecast precision over both standalone ANFIS and other machine learning baselines for environmental water balance applications. Models were assessed using standard error metrics to gauge prediction accuracy and reliability under varying climatic conditions. The results demonstrated that the hybrid ANFIS model delivered lower forecast errors and higher precision relative to DBN alone, particularly in representing complex evapotranspiration dynamics. Based on these findings, the authors recommended the adoption of metaheuristic-enhanced fuzzy systems for environmental forecasting tasks involving nonlinear hydrometeorological variables, highlighting their ability to better manage uncertainty and complex relationships in climate indices.

Firat (2008) compared GRNN, ANFIS, Feed-Forward Neural Networks (FFNN), and autoregressive models for daily river flow forecasting on Turkey's Seyhan and Cine Rivers. The goal was to test how these models cope with hydrological uncertainty. The results showed that ANFIS outperformed both GRNN and FFNN, delivering superior accuracy and reliability on unseen test and validation data.

Singh et al. (2013) conducted a study on predicting the unconfined compressive strength of rocks, comparing GRNN and ANFIS models. Using inputs like ultrasonic velocity and density, they assessed performance via RMSE and correlation metrics. Their findings revealed GRNN performed slightly better in prediction accuracy, while ANFIS provided more interpretable results and handled input uncertainty better.

Kim & Parnichkun (2017) evaluated GRNN, ANFIS, and MLP for predicting real-time coagulant dosage across varying turbidity levels. They discovered that MLP achieved highest overall accuracy, especially for high turbidity; ANFIS produced consistent, robust performance in low turbidity zones; and GRNN showed strong accuracy only in extreme high-turbidity conditions, indicating a niche strength in edge cases.

Smyl et al. (2022) evaluated gradient boosting regression trees (GBRT), a type of GBM, against several deep learning models across multiple time-series forecasting tasks. The results showed that GBRT outperformed most NN approaches on nine datasets, highlighting GBM's effectiveness in structured time series prediction, although GRNN and ANFIS were not included in this comparison.

Pham et al. (2024) investigated the performance of a suite of ANFIS models enhanced with metaheuristic optimisation algorithms specifically Artificial Bee Colony (ABC), Genetic Algorithm (GA), and Simulated Annealing (SA) for daily rainfall prediction using meteorological data from Hoa Binh province, Vietnam. The aim was to improve the predictive capability of conventional ANFIS by applying optimisation techniques that fine-tune membership functions and rule parameters. The study evaluated model performance using correlation coefficient (R), mean absolute error (MAE), and root mean square error (RMSE). The results showed that the hybrid ANFIS-ABC model consistently outperformed both the other hybrid variants and the base ANFIS model, especially after data preprocessing with the Savitzky-Golay filter, achieving an R value of up to 0.90 on filtered data. These findings indicate that metaheuristic optimisation can significantly enhance the accuracy of ANFIS for meteorological time-series forecasting, and the authors recommend the integration of noise reduction techniques for improved hybrid model performance in rainfall prediction applications.

Rashidi et al. (2025) evaluated ANFIS-based models, including hybrid configurations incorporating the Reptile Search Algorithm (RSA), Whale Optimisation

Algorithm (WOA), and Grey Wolf Optimiser (GWO), to forecast the Standardised Precipitation Evapotranspiration Index (SPEI) across arid, semi-arid, and temperate climates in Iran. The study aimed to identify which optimisation strategy most effectively augments standard ANFIS for drought index prediction, especially under limited or incomplete meteorological data. Model performance was measured using evaluation metrics across all climate types. The results showed that the hybrid ANFIS+RSA model exhibited superior predictive accuracy compared to both standalone ANFIS and other optimised variants, indicating that RSA integration improved model convergence and generalisation. The authors recommend the use of evolutionary optimisation with ANFIS for drought and climate index forecasting, particularly when data scarcity or rapid climatic variability challenges conventional approaches.

Tyralis et al. (2019) conducted a large-scale streamflow forecasting study comparing various machine learning algorithms, including XGBoost (a GBM variant) and NNs. XGBoost ranked just below NNs in accuracy, demonstrating strong performance; however, GRNN and ANFIS were not part of this evaluation. Ondo & Owolawi (2025) compared GRNN, ANFIS, CFNN, and FFNN, using Particle Swarm Optimization (PSO), for forecasting photovoltaic (PV) output current in South Africa. The models were evaluated using hourly irradiance and temperature data collected in 2023 from several locations in South Africa. The study found that all models demonstrated improved accuracy when optimised with PSO, indicating their effectiveness in forecasting PV output current.

Huang et al. (2022) explored Feed-forward Neural Network (FNN), Random Forest (RF), and ANFIS using 22 years of quarterly Stock financial data. The goal was to determine how well these models can support investment decision-making. The study also incorporated feature selection using the RF algorithm and employed bootstrap aggregation to enhance prediction performance. The findings revealed that the RF model delivered the most accurate results, while feature selection significantly improved the performance of both FNN and ANFIS. Moreover, the ensemble approach outperformed all individual models as well as the benchmark Dow Jones Industrial Average (DJIA) over the test period, highlighting the potential of ML in supporting fundamental investment strategies.

Similarly, the study by Huang et al. (2019) compared two NN-based approaches, FNN and ANFIS, for stock prediction using key financial ratios. The objective was to assess how effectively each model can identify stocks likely to outperform or underperform, by measuring the relative returns of model-selected portfolios against a standard market index. The results indicated that both FNN and ANFIS were capable of distinguishing between strong and weak performers, with the resulting portfolios exceeding benchmark returns. Nonetheless, the study found that FNN demonstrated stronger predictive accuracy and overall performance than ANFIS.

Salehi (2024) employed GBMs, including XGBoost and LightGBM, with an ANFIS to forecast cryptocurrency price volatility. The aim was to improve forecasting accuracy by leveraging ensemble models alongside fuzzy inference systems. The results showed that the ANFIS-GBM hybrid approach outperformed other methods, providing more reliable volatility predictions. Chen & Wang (2019) focused on Chinese stock market data to compare GRNN and ANFIS models in stock price forecasting. Both models showed good predictive capability, however GRNN demonstrated slightly better generalisation on unseen data, while ANFIS offered clearer interpretability of the relationships among variables.

Lee & Kim (2021) studied the Korean stock market using GBM to forecast stock price movements. The analysis compared GBM against traditional linear statistical models and NNs with varying architectures. The results indicated that GBM significantly outperformed both the traditional models and NNs in prediction accuracy by effectively capturing nonlinear relationships within the financial time series data. GBM implemented as a median-regression model achieved a 2.89% average monthly hedged return (equivalent to 34.68% annually) with a Sharpe ratio of 0.93, demonstrating its strong predictive capability and portfolio performance compared to the competing models.

Kumar et al. (2022) conducted a study aimed at improving the operation of Dynamic Voltage Restorers (DVRs) within distribution networks experiencing distorted voltage conditions. The study proposed a hybrid approach that combined a GRNN Estimator (GRNNE) for estimating the reference load voltage, and an ANFIS for voltage control. To enhance performance, the GRNNE was optimised using a fruit fly optimisation algorithm, while ANFIS parameters were fine-tuned using the grey wolf optimisation technique. The results demonstrated that the hybrid GRNNE–ANFIS model achieved superior accuracy and control performance compared to conventional methods. Key improvements included faster convergence rates, reduced training time, fewer tunable parameters, and better prediction metrics such as lower mean square error and higher correlation coefficients.

3. RESEARCH METHODOLOGY

The study is of a quantitative nature and uses secondary data. The daily time series data of Nedbank closing stock price from the period 2nd January 2020 to 4th April 2025 is observed, comprising 1316 observations sourced from Logon | IRESS (https://expert.iress.co.za/##). The data is also publicly available on Indicies | Johannesburg Stock Exchange. The choice of data range was solely based on the availability of the data from the source. The study used R version 3.6.1 and Python as programming languages. Figure 1 presents the research methodology of the study.

Figure 1. Research methodology flow chart

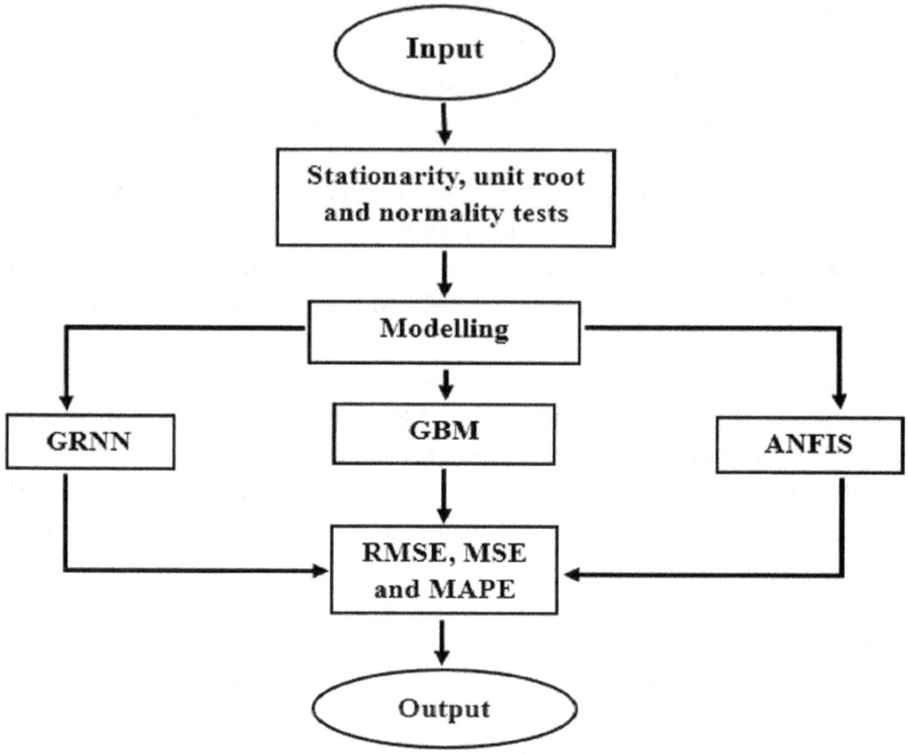

(Authors' own interpretation)

3.1 Testing for data characteristics

Understanding data characteristics is essential for choosing appropriate analytical methods, maintaining data quality, and developing effective models. Therefore, this study employed the Autocorrelation Function (ACF) and Partial Autocorrelation Function (PACF) to assess stationarity. The Kolmogorov-Smirnov (KS) test is applied to evaluate normality, while formal unit root tests, including the Augmented Dickey-Fuller (ADF) and Phillips-Perron (PP) tests, are employed to examine the presence of unit roots in the data.

3.1.1 Autocorrelation function (ACF)

The ACF was first introduced by Yule (1907) as a measure of the correlation (or linear relationship) between a time series and its lagged values. In other words, it quantifies how a value at time $t$relates to values at earlier times, such as $t-1, t-2$. The ACF is used to identify patterns in the data that repeat over time, and it can indicate if a time series exhibits a seasonal pattern or other time-dependent relationships (Box & Jenkins, 1976). For a given lag k, the autocorrelation is computed as:

$$\rho_k = \frac{\sum_{t=1}^{n-k} (y_t - \bar{y})(y_{t+k} - \bar{y})}{\sum_{t=1}^{n} (y_t - \bar{y})^2}, \tag{1}$$

where y_t is the stock price at time t, $\bar{y}$ is the mean of the stock price and k is the lag. At lag k: The correlation between the stock price and its lagged version at lag k is denoted as ρ_k, where k is the number of periods between the current and lagged observations.

3.1.2 Partial Autocorrelation Function (PACF)

The concept of the PACF was formalised by Yule (1907), building upon earlier work on autocorrelation and regression models. However, the PACF itself, as a distinct concept in time series analysis, was more formally developed within the context of modern statistical models, particularly by Kolmogorov, (1933), Wiener, (1949), Box and Jenkins, (1976), Markov, (1906) and Brockwell & Davis (2002) who contributed to the development of ARMA models and modern time series methods. The PACF can be defined as:

$$\phi_{kk} = Corr(Y_t, Y_{t-k} \mid Y_{t-1}, Y_{t-2}, \ldots, Y_{t-(k-1)}), \tag{2}$$

where Y_t is the current value of the stock price, Y_{t-k} is the value of the stock price at lag k, $Corr(Y_t, Y_{t-k})$ is the raw correlation between Y_t and Y_{t-k}, $Y_{t-1}, Y_{t-2}, \ldots, Y_{t-(k-1)}$ is the intervening time point and ϕ_{kk} is the partial correlation between Y_t and Y_{t-k} after adjusting for the intervening lags.

3.2 Normality

The concept of normality has its origins, but Gauss (1809) is typically credited with its formal introduction, especially in relation to statistical theory. To assess the normality of the data in the present study, the Shapiro & Wilk (1965) test is employed. This test is specifically designed to evaluate whether a given sample originates from a normally distributed population.

H_0 : The sample follows the normal distribution.
H_1: The sample does not follow the normal distribution.

The expression for this test is formulated as:

$$W = \frac{\left(\sum_{i=1}^{n} a_i x_{(i)}\right)^2}{\sum_{i=1}^{n} (x_i - \bar{x})}, \tag{3}$$

where $x_{(i)}$ is are the ordered sample values, $\bar{x}$ is the sample mean, a_i are constraints derived from the expected values of order statistics of a standard normal distribution and N is the sample size. If the resulting p-value is less than the chosen significance level (0.05), the null hypothesis of normality is rejected, suggesting the data do not follow a normal distribution.

3.3 Unit root stationarity test

The detection and understanding of unit roots are fundamental to accurate time series modelling and forecasting, particularly in fields such as economics and finance where long-term relationships and the persistence of shocks play a key role (Dickey & Fuller, 1979; Phillips & Perron, 1988). The study employed Augmented Dickey-Fuller (ADF) and Phillips-Perron (PP) tests to examine the presence of unit root.

3.3.1 Augmented dickey fuller (ADF) test

The ADF test is an extension of the Dickey-Fuller (DF) test and accounts for more complex autoregressive processes by including lagged differences of the dependent variable. This adjustment makes the ADF test more robust, especially in the presence of serial correlation, which is common in time series data (Dickey & Fuller, 1979). The hypothesis is:

H_0 : The time series has a unit root.
H_1: The time series does not have a unit root.

The formulation is expressed as:

$$\Delta y_t = \alpha + \beta_t + \gamma y_{t-1} + \sum_{i=1}^{p} \delta_i \Delta y_{t-i} + \varepsilon_t, \tag{4}$$

where y_t is the stock price at time t, $\Delta y_t(y_t - y_{t-1})$ is the first difference of the stock price, α is the constant and β_t represents a deterministic trend. γ is the coefficient on the legged value y_{t-1} (which test for unit root), δ_i are the coefficients of the legged difference terms Δy_{t-1} for $i = 1,2,\ldots,p$ where p is the number of lags and ε_t is the error term. If the p-value is less than the chosen significance level (commonly 0.05), it indicates that the likelihood of observing such a test statistic under the null hypothesis is low. Therefore, the null hypothesis is rejected.

3.4 Estimation techniques

This study employed three models, namely, GRNN, GBM, and ANFIS to evaluate their performance in financial time series analysis. The models are discussed in the following subsections respectively.

3.4.1 Generalised regression neural network

The GRNN is a type of NN introduced by Specht (1991) as an extension of the Probabilistic Neural Network (PNN) to perform regression rather than classification. It is a memory-based, non-parametric model used primarily for function approximation tasks. GRNN operates on the principle of kernel regression, where the predicted output for a given input is computed as a weighted average of observed outputs, with the weights determined by a Gaussian kernel function centered at each training point. The formulation begins by estimating the conditional expected value of the output y given an input vector x, written as:

$$\hat{y}(x) = \mathbb{E}[y|x] = \frac{\int y . f(x,y)dy}{\int f(x,y)dy}, \tag{5}$$

To compute this, GRNN uses a Parzen window estimator to approximate the joint probability density function $f(x, y)$, using training samples and a Gaussian kernel:

$$f(x,y) = \frac{1}{N} \sum_{i=1}^{N} \exp\left(-\frac{\|x - x_i\|^2}{2\sigma^2}\right)\delta(y - y_i), \tag{6}$$

Substituting equation (5) into (6) yields the GRNN prediction equation:

$$\hat{y}(x) = \frac{\sum_{i=1}^{N} y_i \cdot \exp\left(-\frac{\|x - x_i\|^2}{2\sigma^2}\right)}{\sum_{i=1}^{N} \exp\left(-\frac{\|x - x_i\|^2}{2\sigma^2}\right)}, \tag{7}$$

where $\hat{y}(x)$ is the predicted output for the new input vector x. y_i is the known (target value) corresponding to the *ith* training sample x_i, x_i is the *ith* input vector in the training dataset. $\|x - x_i\|^2$is the squared Euclidean distance between the input x and training sample x_i. This measure how "close" the new input is to each training point. $\exp\left(-\frac{\|x - x_i\|^2}{2\sigma^2}\right)$ is the gauss kernel function that coverts the distance into a weight, the closer x is to x_i, the higher the weight will be. σ is the smoothing parameter that control the width of the gaussian kernel, a small σ makes the network more sensitive. Figure 2 presents the GRNN design's schematic drawing and the explained operational logic.

Figure 2. GRNN Architecture

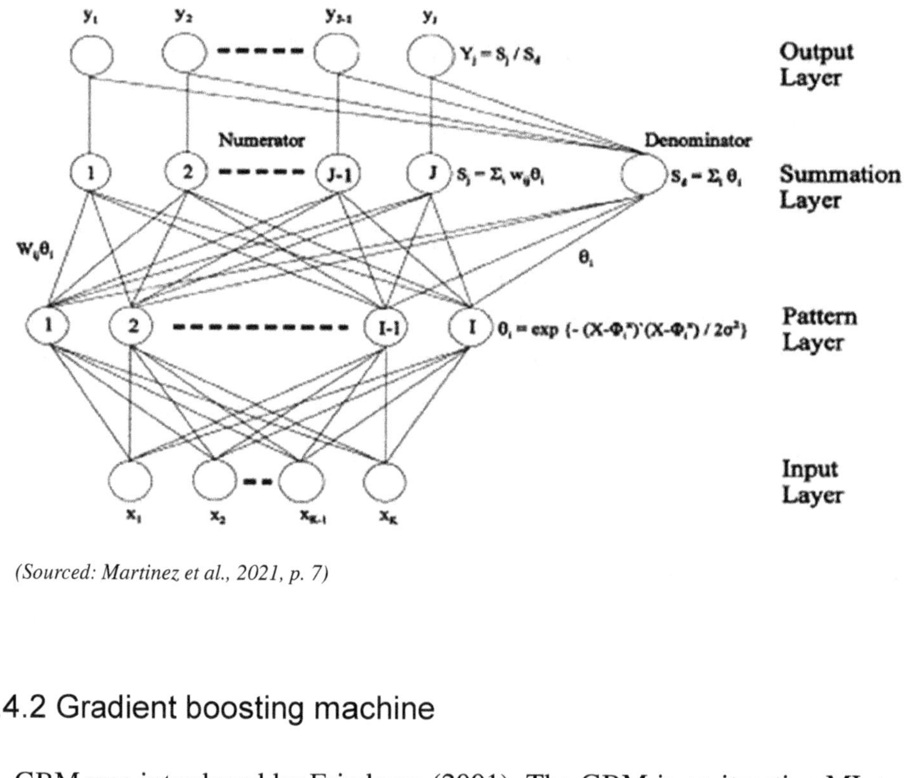

(Sourced: Martinez et al., 2021, p. 7)

3.4.2 Gradient boosting machine

GBM was introduced by Friedman (2001). The GBM is an iterative ML technique that builds an additive model by combining weak learners typically decision trees to minimise a given loss function. The process begins by initializing the model with a constant prediction that minimises the total loss across all training examples:

$$F_0(x) = \arg\min_\gamma \sum_{i=1}^{n} L(y_i, \gamma), \tag{8}$$

At each iteration m, the algorithm computes the negative gradient of the loss function with respect to the current models output this is known as the pseudo-residual and is given by:

$$r_{im} = -\left[\frac{\partial L(y_i, F(x_i))}{\partial F(x_i)}\right]_{f(x)=F_{m-1(x)}}, \tag{9}$$

where a new weak learner $h_m(x)$ is then trained to predict these residuals. Once this model is trained, the algorithm calculates an optimal step size γ_m by solving equation (8) and (9) as:

$$\gamma_m = \arg\min_{\gamma} \sum_{i=1}^{n} L\left(y_i, F_{m-1}(x_i) + \gamma h_m(x_i)\right), \tag{10}$$

which determines how much of the new learner should be added to the model. The model is then updated by adding the scaled learner to the current model as:

$$F_m(x) = F_{m-1}(x) + \nu . \gamma_m h_m(x), \tag{11}$$

where ν is the learning rate that controls the contribution of each weak learner. This process is repeated for M iterations, and the final model is the sum of the initial prediction and all subsequent updates:

$$F_M(x) = F_0(x) + \sum_{M=1}^{M} \nu . \gamma_m h_m(x). \tag{12}$$

3.4.3 Adaptive neuro-fuzzy inference system

An ANFIS was developed by Jang (1993). The working procedure of the ANFIS controller consists of two main stages: first, an initial fuzzy system is produced, establishing the framework for subsequent operations. Secondly, training methods are utilised to adjust the parameters of this fuzzy system through iterative training, these parameters are converged to minimise the error rate, ultimately aiming for zero error.

To streamline the descriptions, the study considers a fuzzy inference system with two inputs (x *and* y) and one output (z). For a first order Sugeno fuzzy model, a standard rule set comprising base fuzzy *if – then* rules can be articulated as follows:

$$w_i = \mu_{A_i}(x) + \mu_{B_i}(y), \tag{13}$$

$$\overline{w}_i = \frac{w_1}{w_1 + w_2}, \; i = 1,2. \tag{14}$$

Rule 1:

$$if\ x\ is\ A_1\ and\ y\ is\ B_1,\ then\ f_1 = p_1x + q_1y + r_1,$$

Rule 2:

$$if\ x\ is\ A_2\ and\ y\ is\ B_2,\ then\ f_2 = p_2x + q_2y + r_2,$$

Then:

$$output = \frac{w_1.f_1 + w_2.f_2}{w_1 + w_2} = \overline{w}_1f_1 + \overline{w}_2f_2, \tag{15}$$

where x is the input to node i, $\mu_{A_i}(x)$ is the membership functions of A_i, A_i is the linguistic label associated with node functions, w_i is the firing strength of the ith rule, $\overline{w}_i$ is the ratio of the ith rule firing strength to the sum of all rules firing strength, (p_i, q_i, r_i) is the parameter set and f_i is the consequent value. Figure 3 presents the architecture of the ANFIS.

Figure 3. ANFIS Architecture

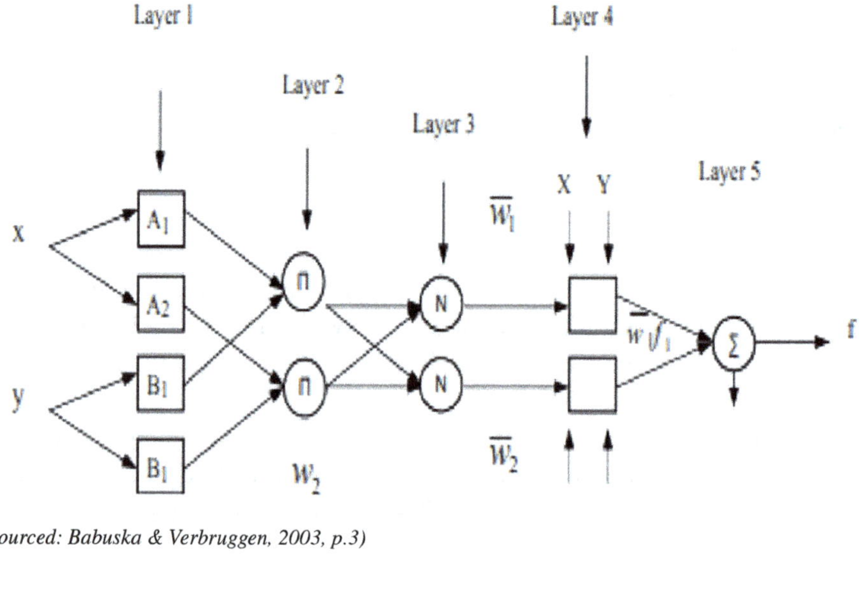

(Sourced: Babuska & Verbruggen, 2003, p.3)

3.5 Model performance evaluation

The study employs root mean squared error (RMSE), mean squared error (MSE) and mean absolute percentage error (MAPE) to gauge the performance of the models. The RMSE gives a sense of how far the predicted values are from the actual values on average. The MSE quantifies the average of the squared differences between the predicted values and the actual value. MAPE measures the accuracy of predictions as a percentage of the actual values. The expressions of the three evaluation measures are as follows respectively:

$$RMSE = \sqrt{\frac{1}{n}\sum_{t=1}^{n}(y_t - \hat{y}_t)^2}. \tag{16}$$

$$MSE = \frac{1}{n}\sum_{t=1}^{n}(y_t - \hat{y}_t)^2. \tag{17}$$

$$MAE = \frac{1}{n}\sum_{t=1}^{n}\left|y_t - \hat{y}_t\right|. \tag{18}$$

where y_t is the actual value at time t, $\hat{y}_t$ is the predicted value at time t, n is the total number of observations, $|y_t - \hat{y}_t|$ is the absolute error.

4. DISCUSSION OF THE RESULTS

This section of the study outlines the results obtained from the data analysis and the discussion of the key findings. Table 1 presents the descriptive statistics, offering a summary and interpretation of the dataset utilised.

Table 1. Descriptive statistics for the Nedbank closing stock prices

Data: Nedbank Closing stock Prices	Descriptive Statistics
Mean	19736.9453
Median	20905.5000
Maximum	30815
Minimum	7320
Standard deviation	151.0618
Skewness	-0.2182
Kurtosis	-0.5333
Observation	1316

Table 1 presents the descriptive statistics of the Nedbank closing stock prices. The data revealed a minimum value of 7 320 Rands and a maximum of 30 815 Rands. The mean closing price is 19 736.9500 Rands, which is lower than the median value of 20 905.5000 Rands. This indicates a negatively skewed distribution, suggesting that lower stock prices occurred more frequently or were more extreme, thereby pulling the mean below the median. Additionally, the kurtosis value is below 3, signifying a platykurtic distribution. This implies that the price distribution is relatively flat and exhibits lighter tails than a normal distribution, with fewer extreme deviations from the mean. Figure 4 presents a graphical representation of the actual data.

Figure 4. Graphical representation of the actual dataset

Figure 4 shows the daily closing stock prices of Nedbank from 02/01/2020 to 04/04/2025, revealing key trends and fluctuations throughout the observed period. A gradual decline is evident during the mid-2020 to 2021 period, reflecting a sustained downward movement. Also, a sharp upward shift is observed beginning in mid-2023 through 2024, indicating a significant surge in stock prices. This increase is followed by a period of relative stabilisation, which eventually gives way to a downward trend in the latter half of 2024 and continuing into 2025. The data exhibit clear signs of non-stationarity characterised by changing means and evolving trends over time. Moreover, considerable volatility is present throughout the entire period, as reflected by pronounced fluctuations in stock prices. Figure 5 presents a graphical representation of the first differenced dataset.

Figure 5 depicts the first differencing of the dataset is stationary, with values revolving around a zero mean. The variance also becomes stable, indicating consistency over time. Following this, Figure 6 presents the ACF and PACF plots of the first-differenced series.

Figure 5. Graphical representation of the first difference dataset

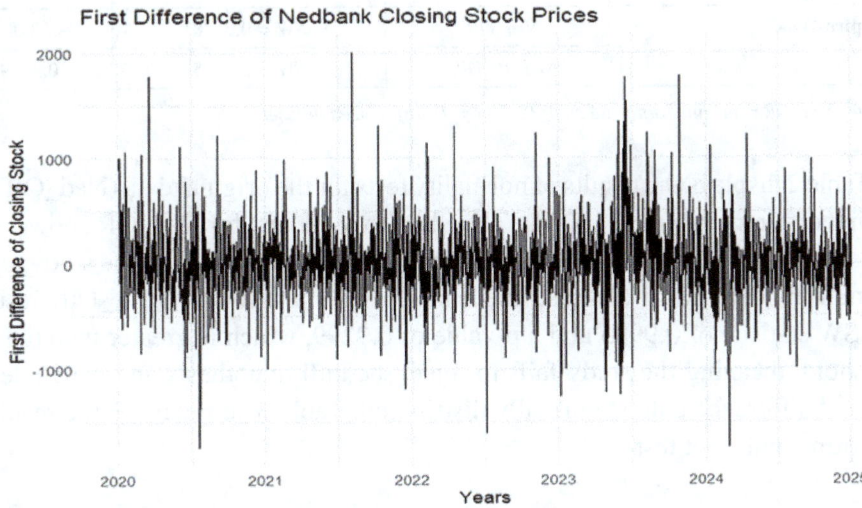

Figure 6. Representation of ACF and PACF of the first difference dataset

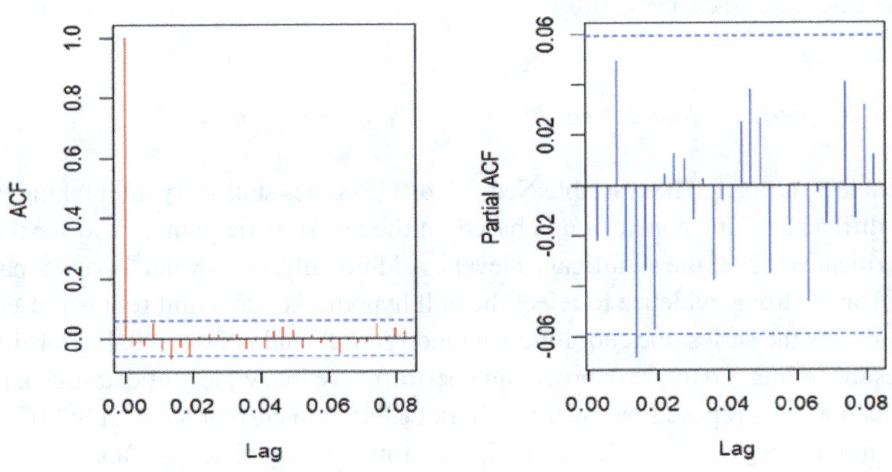

After applying the first differenced to the data, the ACF and PACF plots show that most of the spikes fall within the confidence interval, indicating that the Nedbank closing stock is stationary. The closing stock series was then tested for normality, and the results are presented in Table 2.

Table 2. Normality test results for original and 1st differenced dataset

Normality tests	Variable	Value	p-value
Shapiro-Wilk	*Ned_OR*	*SW* = 0.9478	<0.0001
	Ned_1st_Diff	*SW* = 0.9995	0.9299

Note: Ned_OR = original data and *Ned_1st_Diff = 1st differenced dataset*

Table 2 displays the results of normality tests for the original data (Ned_OR) and its first difference (Ned_1st_Diff). The Shapiro-Wilk test for Ned_OR shows a SW statistic of 0.9478 with a p-value of <0.0001, which indicates that the study rejects the null hypothesis. In contrast, the Shapiro-Wilk test for Ned_1st_Diff resulted in a SW statistic of 0.9995 and a p-value of 0.9299, which is greater than the 0.05 threshold, meaning the study fails to reject the null hypothesis and conclude that the first difference data is normally distributed. Table 3 summarises the results of the formal unit root test.

Table 3. Unit root test results on the original and 1st differenced dataset

Stationarity tests	Variable	Level of significance	p-value
ADF test	*Ned_OR*	1%, 5% and 10%	0.7611
	Ned_1st_Diff		<0.0001***

Note: Significance code: 0 '***' and 0.001 '**'

Ned_OR = original data & Ned_1st_Diff = 1st difference dataset

Table 3 shows that the variable Ned_1st_diff becomes stationary after taking the first difference. This conclusion is based on the test statistic, which is lower than the critical values at the significance levels. Additionally, the p-value is very small, confirming strong evidence to reject the null hypothesis that a unit root is present. This means the series does not follow a random walk and is now suitable for time series modelling. To improve processing performance in a variety of data-intensive applications as proposed by Picard & Berk (1990), the current study split 70% of data into training set and 30% of data into testing set as depicted in Table 4.

Table 4. Data portioning

Models	Series	Training set	Testing set
GRNN, GBM and ANFIS	2020/02/01 – 2025/04/04	(70% of data) 921	(30% of data) 395

This section outlines the model estimation process, which includes the testing and training of both traditional TS and ML models in the study. Figure 7 presents the results of the GRNN architecture.

Figure 7. GRNN architecture

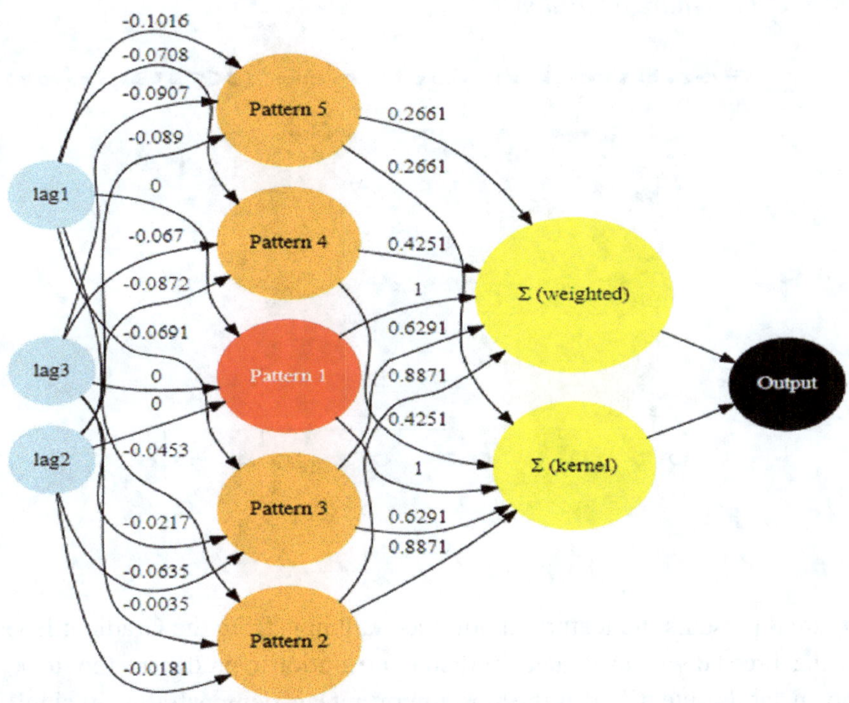

Figure 7 illustrates the GRNN architecture, which consists of three input nodes (representing lag 1, lag 2, and lag 3) and five pattern neurons, each corresponding to a training data point. The network also includes two summation layers: one for computing the weighted sum of the target values and another for summing the kernel weights. These are combined in the output layer to generate the final prediction. Through this architecture, the network effectively "learned" the underlying relationships between past observations and the target variable, enabling it to generalise from the training data point.

The network also shows how each input feature contributes to every pattern neuron, and in turn, how each pattern contributes to the summation layers. Smaller differences between the input and the pattern neurons indicate higher similarity, which is reflected by stronger kernel weights. The greater the kernel weight, the more influence that pattern neuron has on the final output. To highlight this, the most influential pattern neuron identified by having the highest kernel weight is marked in red (Pattern 1), indicating its dominant role in shaping the prediction. Figure 8 presents the results of the GBM feature importance.

Figure 8. GBM feature importance

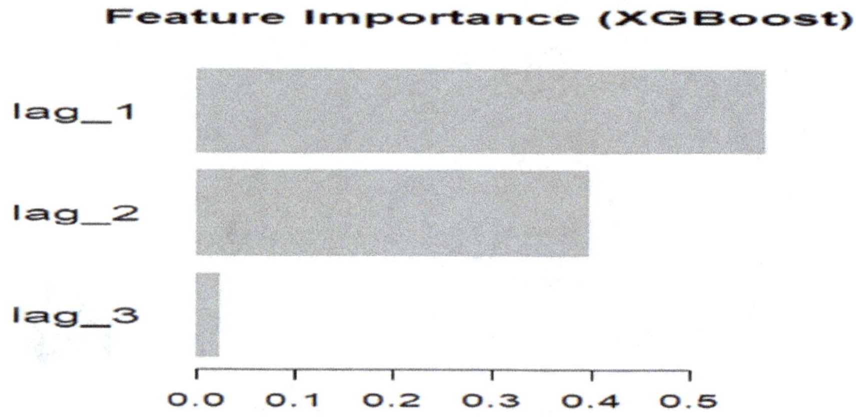

Figure 8 presents the feature importance rankings from the Gradient Boosting, where the three lags are evaluated for their contribution to predicting the stock price. As shown, lag 1 is identified as the most important lag, demonstrating its significant. Figure 9 presents the results of the GBM tree via important lag.

Figure 9. GBM tree via important lag

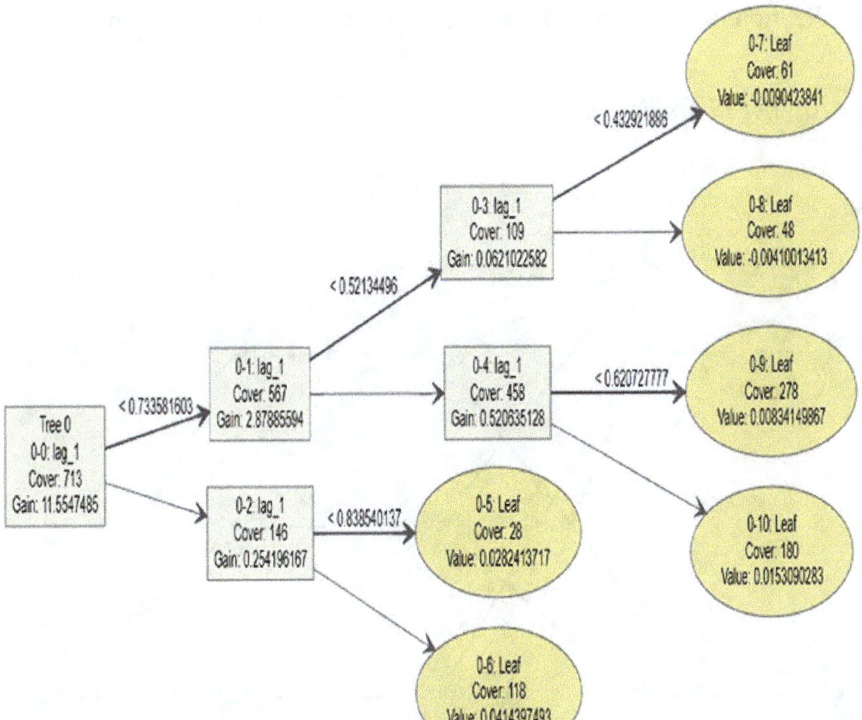

Figure 9 presents a GBM decision tree, illustrating that lag_1 is the most influential predictor in the model. Every split in the tree is based exclusively on lag_1, highlighting its dominant role in determining the target variable. The root node, which splits at lag_1 <0.7336, yields the highest gain (11.5547), indicating a substantial reduction in prediction error. Subsequent nodes enhance the decision boundaries using various thresholds of lag_1, capturing its nonlinear relationship with the response. The leaf nodes represent final prediction values, ranging from -0.0090 to 0.0414, and their corresponding cover values reflect the number of observations reaching each terminal node. Moreover, the absence of other lag features in the tree confirms that lag_1 is statistically the most impactful lag in this GBM model. Figure 10 presents the results of the ANFIS architecture.

Figure 10 shows the architecture of an ANFIS. The model used two inputs, X1 and X2, which are processed through Gaussian membership functions (MF1-1, MF1-2 for X1, and MF2-1, MF2-2 for X2) with specified parameters μ and σ. These functions evaluate the degree of membership of each input to fuzzy sets. The outputs from the membership functions feed into four rule nodes (R1 to R4), representing fuzzy rules derived from combinations of input memberships. Each rule node then connects to a normalization node (N1 to N4), where the firing strengths are normalised.

Figure 10. ANFIS architecture

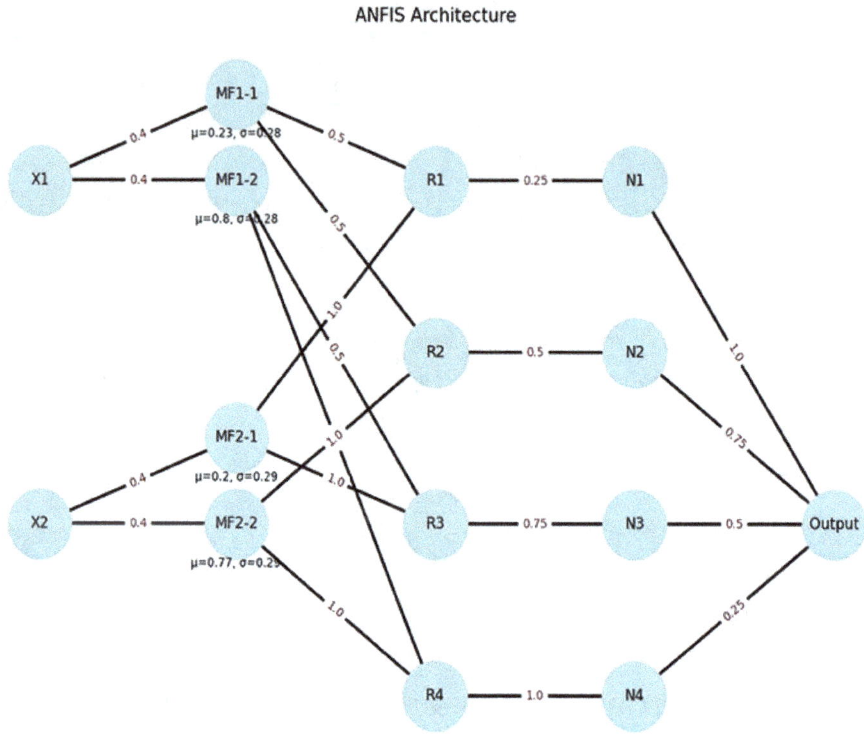

The normalised outputs are finally combined in the output node. Each edge is weighted, reflecting the contribution strength from each node. The most influential path: R3 → N3 → Output has the highest cumulative weight contribution: $0.75 \times 0.5 = 0.375$, indicating this rule's pathway contributes most significantly to the final output. This result highlights not only the structural flow of the ANFIS but also the relative influence of each rule on the system's decision-making. Figure 11 presents the results of the Gaussian membership functions for input variables 1 and 2.

Figure 11. Gaussian membership for input variables 1 and 2

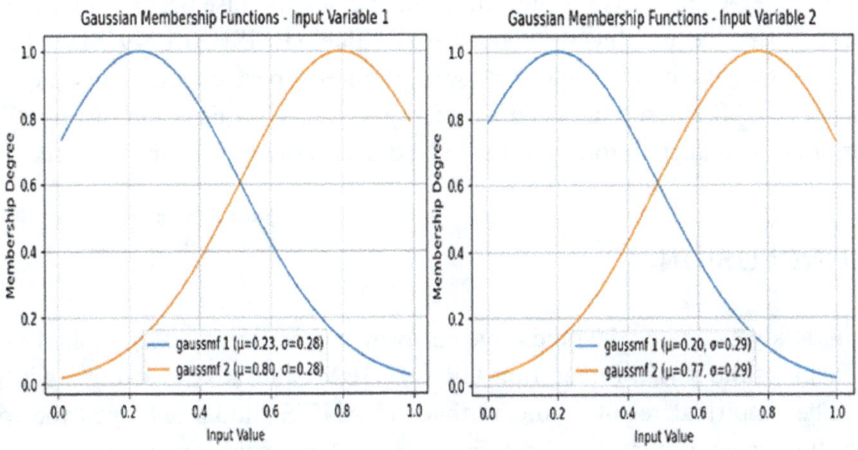

Figure 11 shows the Gaussian membership functions for input variable 1 and 2, with parameters derived from the mean and standard deviation. The first membership function (gaussmf 1) is centred at $\mu = 0.23$ with $\sigma = 0.28$, while the second (gaussmf 2) is centred at $\mu = 0.80$ with the same standard deviation. This configuration creates two well-separated and smoothly overlapping membership functions that meaningfully partition the input (1 and 2) domain. The overlap around the mid-range allows for gradual rule activation, improving the interpretability and performance of the fuzzy inference system. This setup ensures that rules activate more appropriately based on input values. The performance of the three models was compared, and the results are presented in Table 5.

Table 5. Model performance evaluation results

Model	RMSE	MSE	MAE
GRNN	0.1949	0.0380	0.1667
GBM	0.1867	0.0349	0.1548
ANFIS	0.0179	0.0003	0.0143

Table 5 presents the predictive accuracy of GRNN, GBM, and ANFIS evaluated using RMSE, MSE, and MAE. Among the three, the ANFIS model demonstrates the highest accuracy, achieving the lowest values across all three-error metrics, with an RMSE of 0.0179, an MSE of 0.0003, and a MAE of 0.0143. This indicates that

ANFIS yields minimal forecasting errors, both in magnitude and squared deviation. The GBM model follows closely behind, recording an RMSE of 0.1867, MSE of 0.0349, and MAE of 0.1548, suggesting solid but less precise performance. GRNN, while still effective, exhibits the highest error values (RMSE: 0.1949, MSE: 0.0380, MAE: 0.1667), indicating relatively lower predictive performance. Based on these findings, ANFIS emerges as the most accurate model in this comparison, offering superior performance in forecasting the Nedbank's stock price movements.

5. CONCLUSION

This study evaluated the predictive performance of three widely applied models in financial time-series forecasting GRNN, GBM, and ANFIS using stock price data. The empirical results indicate that the ANFIS model achieved the lowest forecasting errors among the three approaches, demonstrating superior predictive accuracy. This performance advantage can be attributed to ANFIS's hybrid structure, which integrates neural learning capabilities with fuzzy logic reasoning. Such an architecture is particularly well suited to financial markets, where price movements are influenced by nonlinear dynamics, regime shifts, and a high degree of uncertainty. The findings are consistent with Bai & Wang (2025), who reported strong forecasting accuracy for ANFIS in predicting Google stock prices, achieving very low validation RMSE values. From an economic perspective, improved forecasting accuracy directly supports more efficient price discovery and risk assessment, which are central to informed investment decision-making.

The GBM model also demonstrated strong predictive capability, with relatively low RMSE, MSE, and MAE values, confirming its effectiveness in modelling complex financial data structures. These results align with Mukhaninga et al. (2025), who showed that GBM significantly outperformed traditional regression approaches when applied to the Johannesburg Stock Exchange All-Share Index. Economically, GBM's strength lies in its ability to handle high-dimensional data and capture nonlinear interactions among predictors, making it a practical and scalable tool for asset pricing, portfolio optimisation, and market surveillance. However, despite its robustness and computational efficiency, GBM did not surpass ANFIS in this study, suggesting that purely data-driven ensemble methods may still fall short in fully representing uncertainty-driven market behaviour.

In contrast, the GRNN model recorded the highest error values across all evaluation metrics, indicating comparatively weaker predictive performance. Although GRNN benefits from a simple structure and fast training, its limited generalisation capability appears to constrain its effectiveness in volatile financial environments characterised by abrupt price swings and structural changes. This outcome supports the observations of Jain & Sharma (2024), who noted that GRNN models often require additional enhancement such as optimisation algorithms or hybrid preprocessing techniques to remain competitive in financial forecasting applications. From an economic standpoint, reliance on less adaptive models like standalone GRNN may increase forecast risk, potentially leading to suboptimal investment or hedging decisions during periods of heightened market volatility.

Based on the comparative results, ANFIS emerges as the most suitable model for forecasting Nedbank's stock prices, followed by GBM, with GRNN performing least effectively. These findings reinforce the growing consensus within financial modelling research that hybrid intelligent systems are particularly effective in turbulent and information-rich markets. By explicitly modelling uncertainty through fuzzy inference while retaining strong learning capability, ANFIS offers a valuable balance between predictive accuracy and interpretability both of which are essential for practical financial analysis.

The economic implications of this study are notable for investors, portfolio managers, and policymakers. More accurate forecasts can support improved capital allocation, enhanced risk management, and better timing of investment decisions. ANFIS's strong performance highlights its potential to reduce forecast uncertainty, while GBM provides a reliable and computationally efficient alternative suitable for large-scale financial applications. As financial markets become increasingly data-intensive and responsive to macroeconomic shocks, models capable of adapting to nonlinear patterns and structural changes are of growing importance.

Despite its contributions, this study has certain limitations. The analysis focuses on a single stock, which may limit the generalisability of the results across sectors or broader market indices. Additionally, the models were trained primarily on historical price data, without incorporating external economic drivers such as interest rates, inflation indicators, or market sentiment. Addressing these limitations presents an opportunity for future research to develop more comprehensive forecasting frameworks by integrating macroeconomic variables, sentiment indicators, and advanced hybrid or deep learning architectures.

Overall, this study contributes to the financial forecasting literature by providing a systematic comparison of GRNN, GBM, and ANFIS models within the context of the Johannesburg Stock Exchange. It demonstrates the clear advantages of hybrid neuro-fuzzy systems in capturing the nonlinear and uncertain nature of stock price movements, while also offering practical insights into the strengths and limitations of alternative machine learning approaches. By linking methodological performance to economic relevance, the study offers actionable guidance for financial practitioners seeking reliable and interpretable forecasting tools in dynamic market conditions.

REFERENCES

Akiner, M. E., & Ghasri, M. (2024). Comparative assessment of deep belief network and hybrid adaptive neuro-fuzzy inference system model based on a meta-heuristic optimization algorithm for precise predictions of the potential evapotranspiration. *Environmental Science and Pollution Research International*, *31*(30), 42719–42749. DOI: 10.1007/s11356-024-33987-3 PMID: 38879646

Alfaro, A., Gámez, M., & García, N. (2018). A neural network approach for identifying explanatory variables in regression problems. *Applied Soft Computing*, *67*, 25–35.

Alsulaiman, T., Al-Ali, A. K., & Alarifi, A. (2022). A comparative study of machine learning techniques for stock market prediction. *Expert Systems with Applications*, *190*, 116–234.

Andersen, R. (2009). Nonparametric methods for modeling nonlinearity in regression analysis. *Annual Review of Sociology*, *35*(1), 67–85. DOI: 10.1146/annurev.soc.34.040507.134631

Bai, X., & Wang, Y. (2025). A hybrid ANFIS model for stock market prediction: Case study on Google Inc. *Computer Applications and Information*, *6*(2), 22–35.

Box, G. E. P., & Jenkins, G. M. (1976). *Time series analysis: Forecasting and control*. Holden-Day.

Brockwell, P. J., & Davis, R. A. (Eds.). (2002). *Introduction to time series and forecasting*. Springer New York. DOI: 10.1007/b97391

Chen, X., & Wang, Y. (2019). A comparative study of GRNN and ANFIS models for stock market prediction. *International Journal of Computational Intelligence*, *15*(3), 203–214.

Dickey, D. A., & Fuller, W. A. (1979). Distribution of the estimators for autoregressive time series with a unit root. *Journal of the American Statistical Association*, *74*(366a), 427–431.

Ding, C., Duan, J., Zhang, Y., Wu, X., & Yu, G. (2017). Using an ARIMA-GARCH modeling approach to improve subway short-term ridership forecasting accounting for dynamic volatility. *IEEE Transactions on Intelligent Transportation Systems*, *19*(4), 1054–1064. DOI: 10.1109/TITS.2017.2711046

Firat, M. (2008). Comparison of ANFIS, GRNN, FFNN, and autoregressive models for daily river flow forecasting: Application to Seyhan and Cine rivers, Turkey. *Hydrology and Earth System Sciences*, *12*(1), 123–134. DOI: 10.5194/hess-12-123-2008

Friedman, J. H. (2001). Greedy function approximation: A gradient boosting machine. *Annals of Statistics*, *29*(5), 1189–1232. DOI: 10.1214/aos/1013203451

Gauss, C. F. (1809). *Theoria motus corporum coelestium in sectionibus conicis solem ambientium*. Perthes & Besser.

Huang, W., Li, C., & Wang, H. (2022). A hybrid ANFIS model for stock market forecasting based on macroeconomic indicators. *Applied Soft Computing*, *115*, 108–187.

Huang, Y., Capretz, L. F., & Ho, D. (2019). Neural network models for stock selection based on fundamental analysis. In *2019 IEEE Canadian Conference of Electrical and Computer Engineering (CCECE)* (pp. 1–4). IEEE. DOI: 10.1109/CCECE.2019.8861550

Jain, R., & Sharma, A. (2024). Enhancing GRNN performance in financial time series forecasting using optimization techniques. *International Journal of Advanced Intelligent Systems*, *15*(2), 112–124.

Jang, J. S. R. (1993). ANFIS: Adaptive-network-based fuzzy inference system. *IEEE Transactions on Systems, Man, and Cybernetics*, *23*(3), 665–685. DOI: 10.1109/21.256541

Kazak, H. (2025). Metaheuristic-optimized ANFIS and ANN models for stock price prediction: Evidence from Borsa Istanbul 100. *Neural Computing & Applications*, *37*, 4531–4546.

Kim, K., & Parnichkun, M. (2017). *Real-time coagulant dosage prediction using GRNN, ANFIS, and MLP models across varying turbidity levels*. Environmental Expert and MDPI.

Kim, T., & Kim, H. Y. (2016). Forecasting stock prices with a feature fusion LSTM-CNN model using different representations of the same data. *Expert Systems with Applications*, *157*, 113–513.

Kisi, O., & Shiri, J. (2012). Precipitation forecasting using wavelet-genetic programming and wavelet-neural networks. *Water Resources Management*, *26*(9), 2555–2569.

Kolmogorov, A. N. (1933). Sulla determinazione empirica di una legge di distribuzione. *Giornale dell'Istituto Italiano degli Attuari, 4,* 83–91.

Kumar, R., Singh, A., & Patel, S. (2022). Improving dynamic voltage restorer operation under distorted voltage conditions using hybrid GRNN estimator and ANFIS controller optimized by fruit fly and grey wolf algorithms. *International Journal of Electrical Power & Energy Systems*, *138*, 107.

Lee, J., & Kim, S. (2021). Gradient boosting machine for stock price forecasting in the Korean market. *Journal of Computational Finance*, *9*(1), 45–60.

lsulaiman, T., Alzahrani, M., & Alsolami, F. (2022). Financial forecasting using GRNN: A comparative study with deep learning models. *Journal of Finance and Data Science, 8*(1), 30–44.

Markov, A. A. (1906). Extension of the limit theorems of probability theory to a sum of variables connected in a chain. *Proceedings of the Imperial Academy of Sciences of St. Petersburg, 20,* 135–156.

Mukhaninga, S., Mugochi, T., & Phiri, A. (2025). Forecasting the JSE All-Share Index using machine learning algorithms: A comparative study. *Economies*, *13*(8), 219. DOI: 10.3390/economies13080219

Pham, T., Chau, H., & Nguyen, L. (2024). Hybrid artificial intelligence models based on adaptive neuro-fuzzy inference system and metaheuristic optimization algorithms for prediction of daily rainfall. *Physics and Chemistry of the Earth Parts A/B/C*, *134*, 103563. DOI: 10.1016/j.pce.2024.103563

Phillips, P. C. B., & Perron, P. (1988). Testing for a unit root in time series regression. *Biometrika*, *75*(2), 335–346. DOI: 10.1093/biomet/75.2.335

Picard, R. R., & Berk, K. N. (1990). Data splitting. *The American Statistician*, *44*(2), 140–147. DOI: 10.1080/00031305.1990.10475704

Rashidi, F., Mohammadi, A., & Khorami, M. (2025). Integration of the reptile search algorithm and the adaptive neuro-fuzzy inference system enhances standardized precipitation evapotranspiration index forecasting. *Scientific Reports*, *15*, 98772. PMID: 40287468

Roy, S., Mitra, S., & Roy, D. (2020). Financial time series forecasting using machine learning techniques: A comparative study. *Procedia Computer Science*, *167*, 2085–2094.

Salehi, S. (2024). Comparative analysis of machine learning techniques for cryptocurrency price prediction. *Journal of Information and Organizational Sciences*, *48*(2), 341–352. DOI: 10.31341/jios.48.2.7

Shapiro, S. S., & Wilk, M. B. (1965). An analysis of variance test for normality (complete samples). *Biometrika*, *52*(3–4), 591–611. DOI: 10.1093/biomet/52.3-4.591

Singh, A., & Srivastava, S. (2021). Stock price prediction using neuro-fuzzy systems. *Journal of Computational Finance and Economics*, *5*(2), 98–113.

Singh, R., Singh, A. K., & Singh, T. N. (2013). Prediction of unconfined compressive strength of rocks using GRNN and ANFIS models. *Neural Computing & Applications, 22*(7–8), 1637–1643.

Smyl, S., Gal, Y., & Smith, A. (2022). Benchmarking gradient boosting methods against deep learning for time series forecasting. *International Journal of Forecasting, 38*(4), 1448–1459.

South African Photovoltaic Power Forecasting Study. (2024). Comparison of GRNN, ANFIS, and neural models for photovoltaic output prediction. *Entropy, 26*(3), 1–15. DOI: 10.3390/e26030001

Specht, D. F. (1991). A general regression neural network. *IEEE Transactions on Neural Networks, 2*(6), 568–576. DOI: 10.1109/72.97934 PMID: 18282872

Tyralis, H., Papacharalampous, A., & Papadimitriou, L. (2019). Large-scale benchmarking of machine learning algorithms for streamflow forecasting across 511 basins. *arXiv*

Ustaoglu, B., Karahan, O., & Yalcin, A. (2008). Prediction of daily streamflow data using adaptive neuro fuzzy inference systems with neural network-based phase space reconstruction. *Journal of Hydrology (Amsterdam), 358*(3–4), 312–325.

Wang, W. (2024). Machine learning in financial time-series data. *Advances in Economics. Management and Political Sciences*, (92), 293–299.

Warin, T., & Stojkov, A. (2021). Machine learning in finance: A metadata-based systematic review of the literature. *Journal of Risk and Financial Management, 14*(7), 302. DOI: 10.3390/jrfm14070302

Wiener, N. (1949). *Extrapolation, interpolation, and smoothing of stationary time series*. Wiley. DOI: 10.7551/mitpress/2946.001.0001

Yule, G. U. (1907). On the theory of correlation. *Journal of the Royal Statistical Society, 70*(1), 237–242.

Zhang, J., & Liu, Y. (2020). A hybrid GRNN model for time-series forecasting. *Neural Computing & Applications, 32*, 9725–9734.

Zhang, W., Zhang, Y., & Liu, Y. (2021). A gradient boosting approach for financial time series prediction. *Expert Systems with Applications, 168*, 114–481.

KEY TERMS AND DEFINITIONS

ANFIS: A hybrid computational model that combine fuzzy logic with neural networks to capture difficult, nonlinear patterns in financial time-series data.

Error Metrics: Quantitative measures, such as RMSE, MAE, or MAPE, used to evaluate the accuracy and reliability of predictive models.

Financial Time Series: Sequential data points representing financial variables (e.g., stock prices, exchange rates) collected over time, often exhibiting volatility and nonlinear patterns.

Fuzzy Logic: A reasoning framework that allows for uncertainty and partial truth values, helping models handle uncertain or imprecise financial data.

GBM: A machine learning technique that builds a group of decision trees sequentially, with each new tree correcting the errors of the previous ones to improve prediction accuracy.

GRNN: A type of neural network designed for regression tasks, capable of learning from small datasets and providing smooth predictions.

Hybrid Models: Predictive systems that combine two or more computational techniques to leverage the strengths of each and improve forecasting performance.

Stock Price Forecasting: The process of estimating future stock prices using historical market data, patterns, and computational models to support investment decisions.

Chapter 9

Machine Learning and Transformer-Based Equity Return Forecasting:

A Case Study on Nvidia

S. Rajkumar
http://orcid.org/0000-0001-5701-9325
Vellore Institute of Technology, India

S. Pooja
http://orcid.org/0009-0007-0107-4342
Vellore Institute of Technology, India

Akshara Siddharthan
http://orcid.org/0009-0003-3443-1562
Vellore Institute of Technology, India

ABSTRACT

Predicting financial asset returns remains one of the more intractable problems in quantitative finance, owing to well-documented data challenges including non-stationarity, leptokurtic return distributions, and near-efficient price dynamics. This chapter evaluates six forecasting methodologies, naive persistence, ARIMA, Ridge regression, Random Forest, XGBoost, and a Temporal Sequence Transformer applied to next-day stock-returns of NVIDIA Corporation (NVDA) over a 25-year horizon. Methodological rigour is maintained throughout: all hyperparameter selection is confined to the training period, and model evaluation follows a walk-forward cross-validation scheme that strictly preserves temporal ordering. Empirical results suggest

DOI: 10.4018/979-8-3373-8372-9.ch009

that gradient-boosted and ensemble tree methods offer a more favourable trade-off between predictive accuracy and practical implementability than either classical time-series specifications or the deep learning alternative the underperformance of the latter, absent domain-specific feature engineering, serving as a cautionary note on the uncritical application of high-capacity architectures to low signal-to-noise financial data.

1. INTRODUCTION

Forecasting returns of financial assets is one of the most widely studied and disputed problems of quantitative finance. Forecasts play a critical role in the design of systematic trading strategies, portfolio optimisations, valuation of derivatives and enterprise risk management. Small advances in the prediction accuracy will translate to meaningful risk-adjusted profits when multiplied by many assets over time. On the other hand, a model which exhibits high in-sample performance but which cannot generalize out-of-sample may incur large losses when used without appropriate safeguards.

The literature on the use of machine learning methods for financial forecasting has expanded significantly in the last decade. In practitioner research, linear models have increasingly been replaced by tree-based ensembles, gradient-boosted machines and deep learning architectures that can capture non-linear relationships between engineered features obtained from technical analysis. More recently, architectures originally developed for Natural Language Processing-Transformers-are gaining increasing interest due to their excellent ability to capture long-range temporal dependencies and their role as general sequence models.

This growing body of research, however, suffers from a multitude of inconsistencies which make it hard to draw general conclusions about relative performance. First, many researchers are using random splits for evaluating models when training on time series data, leak future information into the training set and artificially inflate the out-of-sample performance. Second, some authors forecast the non-stationary price level directly and achieve deceptively high R-values which capture nothing but persistence of the prices. Third, models are primarily evaluated only on statistical metrics (e.g. Root Mean Squared Error), and the evaluation protocol never includes an assessment of the profitably of the trading signal generated by the forecasts in terms of realized returns.

In this paper we shall attempt to correct all these issues and present a comparative study of six forecasting methods applied to the daily log return of the NVIDIA Corporation (ticker: NVDA). Our explicit goals are:

1. To design and implement a proper time-series validation protocol including chronological splits and TimeSeriesSplit.
2. To engineer a rich feature set from classical technical analysis indicators.
3. To compare a simple baseline model, ARIMA, Ridge, Random Forest, XGBoost and a Transformer-based model on statistical metrics and profitability.
4. To simulate a long/flat strategy using explicit transaction costs and report the risk-adjusted performance.
5. To determine whether a deep learning method with an established price-level forecasting ability-the Temporal Sequence Transformer-can sustain its superiority in a forecast based on a target of log returns.

The case of NVDA is very instructive. The sample period covers 25 years of drastically different regimes: from the bust following the dot-com bubble in 2000 to the financial crisis in 2008, from the period of slow and steady recovery to the frenzy of the 2020-2024 AI boom. Any successful model has to pass this challenging test.

1.1 Background

The weak form of the efficient market hypothesis (EMH) assumes that historical prices' information is incorporated into current prices and thus returns cannot be forecasted using past prices. Empirical evidence supports weak-form EMH with regard to large capitalization liquid equity: autocorrelation function of daily returns usually stay within the boundary of white noise at every lag. This does not imply zero costs foretelling of returns, it implies any systematic predictability is due to non-linear feature interaction or cross-asset information missed by linear autocorrelation; thus any forecast is a signal-in-a-noise process, and any model producing small but consistent profit directional success is actually providing some valuable information.

1.2 Contribution

This chapter makes four specific contributions to the empirical literature of machine learning-based financial forecasting. First, it offers a methodologically rigorous comparative assessment of six forecasting approaches naive persistence, ARIMA, Ridge regression, Random Forest, XGBoost and a Temporal Sequence Transformer – under a unified evaluation harness that - requires a strict chronological data split, employs walk-forward cross-validation, utilises hyperparameter optimisation, strictly confined to training data, and addresses the three most common sources of performance inflation in the extant literature. Second, it shows that explicit domain specific feature engineering such as moving averages, RSI, MACD, Bollinger

Band position, realised volatility and volume z-scores are not just an add-on, but a necessary condition for effective return scale forecasting - with direct implications for practitioners designing ML pipelines. Third, it provides the first evaluation of the Temporal Sequence Transformer under a return-prediction protocol, showing a key divergence of price-level and return-level performance that reveals a commonly overlooked methodological trap in the deep learning for finance literature. Fourth, the economic evaluation framework - simulating a long/flat strategy with an explicit transaction cost and reporting Sharpe ratio, maximum drawdown and cost sensitivity - provides a reproducible template to translate the statistical forecasting results into actionable trading evaluation.

1.3 Advantages

The primary practical benefit demonstrated by this study is that gradient-boosted trees are superior to competing approaches when assessed under realistic conditions. At a transaction cost of five basis points, XGBoost scores an annualised Sharpe ratio of 1.45, beating the passive buy-and-hold benchmark of 1.26 while also reducing maximum drawdown from 67.2% to 63.0% reaffirming the fact that the model delivers risk-adjusted value beyond just mimicking an already-appreciating asset. Random Forest has another complementary advantage, namely absolute insensitivity to transaction costs, with Sharpe deteriorating only 0.02 over the entire range from zero to ten basis points. This is because its turnover is exceptionally low, with only 47 changes in position over five years. This property makes Random Forest a preferred choice in environments where execution costs are uncertain, market impact is non-trivial or strategy capacity constraints limit trading frequency. Collectively, these results demonstrate that ensemble tree methods, when augmented by suitable technical feature engineering, time-series aware validation and economic assessment, offer a robust, interpretable and easily deployable basis for systematic equity return prediction, without the computational burden or architectural complexity of deep learning alternatives.

2. LITERATURE REVIEW

2.1 Classical Time-Series Methods

The standard statistical technique for univariate forecasting time series data is the Box-Jenkins ARIMA method Box et al., 2015. ARIMA models explain a series by autoregressive and moving average components and, where necessary, difference the series to make itapproximatelystationary. Variants for seasonality

(SARIMA) and exogenous factors (ARIMAX) exist. Engle (1982) and Bollerslev (1986) originally modeled conditional heteroscedasticity using ARCH and GARCH; time-varying variance describes the observation that large absolute returns tend to occur in clusters, but the model is focused on explaining variance, not the mean of the series, and is primarily used for risk, not direction, estimation. Ridge regression (Hoerl & Kennard, 1970) applies an L, regression with some penalty applied to OLS: shrinks coefficient estimates toward 0 and variance at the expense of bias. This gives a linear model which other models can be compared to.

2.2 Machine Learning for Asset Prediction

Random Forests (Breiman, 2001) and gradient-boosted trees (Friedman, 2001) generalise decision trees to low-variance ensembles capable of capturing complex nonlinear interactions. XGBoost (Chen & Guestrin, 2016) and LightGBM (Ke et al., 2017) provide scalable, regularised versions of gradient boosting that have come to dominate structured tabular prediction across many industries. In finance, Patel et al. (2015) compared various ML classifiers for directional prediction of Indian equity indices, demonstrating that trees can be competitive with support vector machines (Tay & Cao, 2001). The most exhaustive large-scale study was published by Gu et al. (2020) using over 30,000 stock-month observations on US equities, and they concluded that gradient-boosted trees and shallow neural networks produce statistically and economically significant out-of-sample return predictability over linear benchmarks that lies in the non-linear feature interactions. Krauss et al. (2017) demonstrated that deep neural networks ensembles could derive a profitable statistical arbitrage strategy on constituents of the S&P 500, albeit its profitability varies considerably with the cost of transactions.

One consistent methodological concern in the literature on machine learning in finance is that of data leakage – future information incorrectly leaking into training data. Lopez de Prado (2018) provided a taxonomy of the various ways this may manifest, including shuffling cross-validation on chronologically ordered observations, constructing features from full sample statistics, and evaluating the best models on the final test set. These risks can only be properly managed by employing purged and embargoed walk-forward validation procedures. Here we make use of the TimeSeriesSplit routine in scikit-learn to generate expanding-window folds, where training observations always precede validation observations in chronological order.

2.3 Deep Learning and Transformer Architectures

Long Short-Term Memory networks (Hochreiter & Schmidhuber, 1997) were the first deep learning architecture to be widely employed to forecast financial time-series. It was shown by Fischer & Krauss (2018) that LSTMs can forecast direction better than memory-free benchmarks for S&P 500 after transaction costs. Sezer et al. (2020) give a comprehensive survey of the field of deep learning in finance up to 2019.

The Transformer architecture of Vaswani et al. (2017) used multi-head self-attention instead of recurrence and thus allows processing all sequence positions in parallel and modeling long-range dependencies at a linear cost with respect to sequence length. Temporal Fusion Transformer (Lim et al., 2021) was the application of the transformer to multi-horizon forecasting with a mix of static and dynamic inputs. The Informer (Zhou et al., 2021) proposed a sparse self-attention to decrease the quadratic time complexity and achieve a linear complexity for very long sequences.

Autoformer (Wu et al., 2021) explicitly decomposes the series in an auto-correlation mechanism. These contributions were establishing the transformer-based models as the state-of-the-art on multi-horizon time-series benchmarks. However, a number of studies have started questioning the usefulness of high computational complexity of transformer networks. They found that for certain tabular or univariate tasks and given lack of complex sequential structure like in natural language, linear or MLP-based baselines perform as well as or better than transformers.

2.4 Temporal Sequence Transformer

In this chapter, we also study the Temporal Sequence Transformer (TST), which is a non-autoregressive encoder-only transformer proposed previously. TST makes use of learnable positional encoding, causally masked multi-head self-attention, and parallel multi-step decoder which outputs all the future time horizon at a time via a single feed forward step and gets rid of the cumulative error accumulation issue of auto-regressive decoding. It achieves good price-level prediction performance for NVDA (test R=0.78), however we here present the first examination of TST in a return prediction protocol and see if the benefits of its sequential modelling strengths translate to the setting where prediction target is log return rather than price level.

2.5 Motivation

Financial markets are one of the most data-rich but information-poor domains for predictive modelling. A particularly interesting case study is provided by NVIDIA Corporation, whose stock navigated various distinct economic regimes in the 25-year window covered here, including the dot-com collapse of 2000-2002, the global financial crisis of 2008-2009, a decade of moderate semiconductor-driven growth, and the explosive AI-hardware supercycle starting in 2020, providing a challenging and realistic test bed for any forecasting methodology. The stakes are real.

Billions of dollars of NVDA trade every day between institutional asset managers, quantitative hedge funds and retail algorithmic traders and even marginal improvements in directional accuracy, when applied with disciplined position sizing and risk controls translate into economically significant risk adjusted returns. In addition to trading, accurate short-horizon return forecasting is useful for derivatives pricing, margin-requirement calibration and portfolio-level value-at-risk estimation. This section constitutes the empirical basis of the study, documenting the statistical properties of the NVDA dataset, the stylised facts that any credible forecasting model must capture, and the rationale for the methodological choices that follow.

Daily open-high-low-close-volume (OHLCV) data for NVIDIA Corporation (NVDA) from January 1999 to July 2024 were obtained via the yfinance Python library, providing split- and dividend-adjusted prices from Yahoo Finance. The dataset comprises approximately 6,400 trading days. Tables 1, 2, and 3 summarise the descriptive statistics of the raw price and volume series.

Table 1. Central tendency and dispersion of NVDA daily series, January 1999–July 2024

Feature	Mean	Median	Std Dev
Open (USD)	6.5405	0.4288	17.3052
High (USD)	6.6630	0.4358	17.6359
Low (USD)	6.4083	0.4219	16.9235
Close (USD)	6.5425	0.4291	17.2999
Volume (shares)	605,280,689	506,434,000	431,894,980

Table 2. Range of NVDA daily series

Feature	Minimum	Maximum
Open (USD)	0.032	139.80
High (USD)	0.033	140.76
Low (USD)	0.031	132.42
Close (USD)	0.031	135.58
Volume (shares)	19,680,000	9,230,856,000

Table 3. Quartile distribution and IQR of NVDA daily series

Feature	Q1	Median	Q3	IQR
Open (USD)	0.255	0.429	4.193	3.938
High (USD)	0.263	0.436	4.252	3.990
Low (USD)	0.248	0.422	4.133	3.885
Close (USD)	0.254	0.429	4.191	3.936
Volume (shares)	344,913,000	506,434,000	735,591,000	390,678,000

The large gap between the mean (USD 6.54) and median (USD 0.43) Open price reflects the heavy right skew of the series, driven by NVDA's post-2020 appreciation in AI hardware markets. The volume series spans more than two orders of magnitude. These properties motivate the use of log-returns rather than price levels as the modelling target and the use of z-score normalisation prior to model fitting.

The following figures from the underlying NVDA forecasting to establish the stylised facts relevant to the forecasting task. In Figure 1 the price series exhibits strong non-stationarity, with a pronounced acceleration after 2020. In Figure 2, the Rolling volatility increases sharply post-2020, indicating a regime change that constitutes the majority of the test period. In Figure 3 The return distribution is leptokurtic with heavy tails, violating normality. In Figure 4 the autocorrelation is statistically indistinguishable from zero at all tested lags, confirming near-efficient market conditions and the inherent difficulty of the forecasting task.

Figure 1. Stock price trend over time (price vs year)

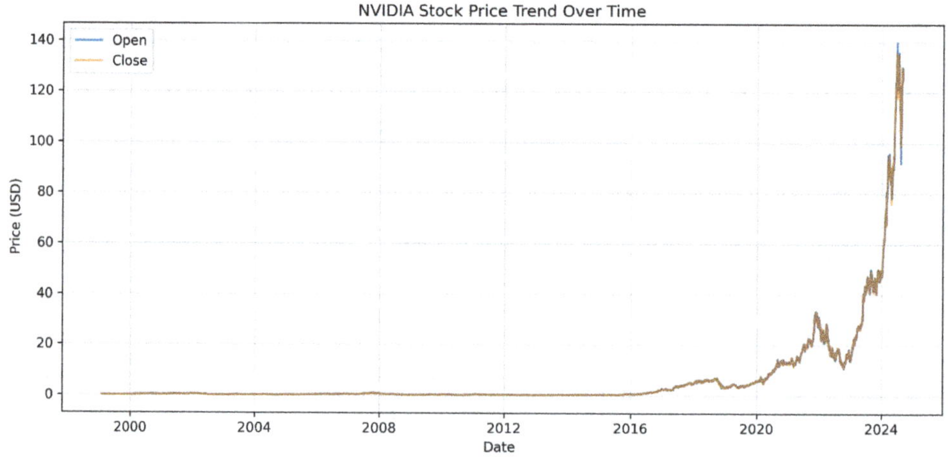

Figure 2. Rolling mean and volatility of open prices (value vs year)

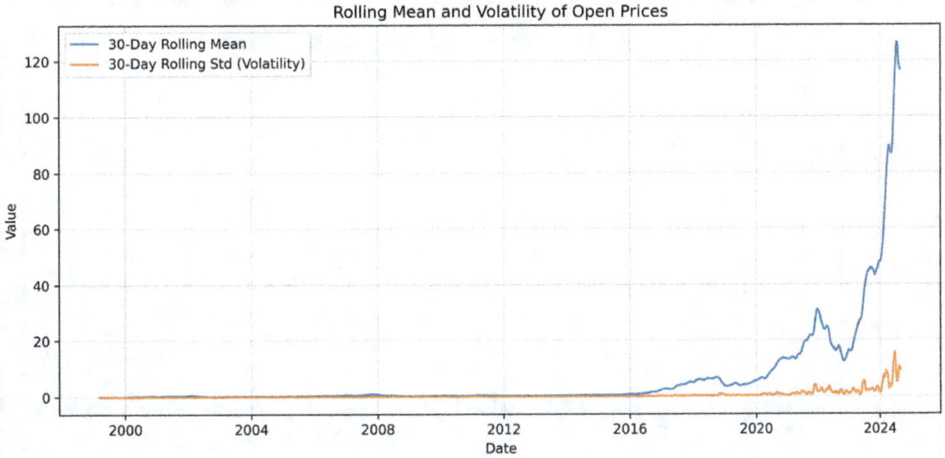

Figure 3. Distribution of daily % returns (frequency vs daily return %)

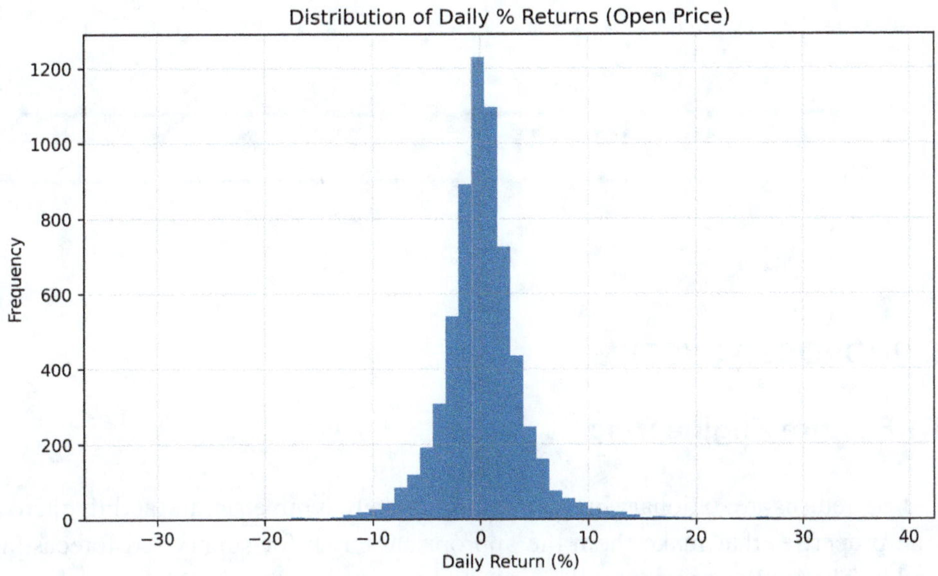

Figure 4. Autocorrelation of daily returns ()

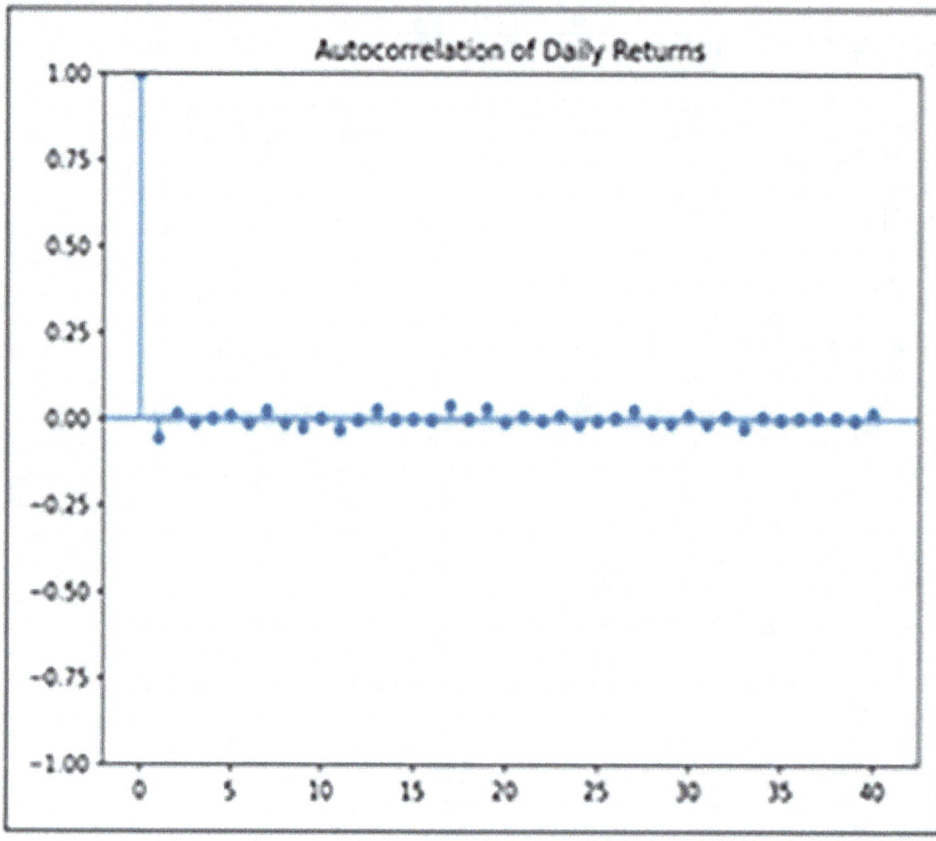

3. PROPOSED SYSTEM

3.1 Feature Engineering

Log-returns are stationary in mean, approximately symmetric, and additive across time properties that make them the appropriate target for supervised forecasting models.The prediction target is the next-day log-return of the NVDA opening price:

$$r_{t+1} = ln\left(\frac{P_{t+1}^{open}}{P_t^{open}}\right)$$

The following features are constructed for the classical ML models using strictly backward-looking computations:

- **Lagged log-returns** at horizons $\ell \in \{1,2,3,5,10\}$ days capture short-term momentum and mean-reversion signals.
- **Simple moving average (SMA) deviations**: the normalised deviation

$\left(P_t^{open} - SMA_n(t)\right)/SMA_n(t)$ for $n \in \{5,10,20,50\}$ - measure price displacement from trend at multiple horizons.

- **Exponential moving average (EMA) deviations** for spans $n \in \{12,26\}$ provide similar information with exponential weighting that emphasises recent observations.
- **Relative Strength Index (RSI)** over a 14-day window:

$$RSI_{14}(t) = 100 - \frac{100}{1 + G_{14}(t)/L_{14}(t)}$$

where G_{14} and L_{14} are the 14-day average gain and average absolute loss.

- **MACD histogram**: the difference between the MACD line $\left(EMA_{12} - EMA_{26}\right)$ and its 9-day signal line, captures momentum regime shifts.
- **Bollinger Band position (%B)** measures where the current price sits within its 20-day volatility band:

$$\%B(t) = \frac{P_t^{open} - \left(SMA_{20}(t) - 2\sigma_{20}(t)\right)}{4\sigma_{20}(t)}$$

- **Realised volatility** (annualised) over $n \in \{10,21\}$ days provides an explicit volatility-conditioning signal:

$$\sigma_n^{RV}(t) = \sqrt{\frac{252}{n}\sum_{i=1}^{n} r_{t-i+1}^2}$$

- **Volume z-score** over a 21-day rolling window captures unusual trading activity:

$$z_t^V = \frac{V_t - \bar{V}_{21}(t)}{s_{V,21}(t)}$$

All features are standardized to zero mean and unit variance using training-set statistics only, preventing any information from the validation or test periods from contaminating the scaling. The first 50 observations (the maximum indicator look-back) are dropped from the modelling sample.

3.2 Models

- **Naive baseline** sets $\hat{r}_{t+1} = 0$, equivalent to the martingale hypothesis. This is the most demanding statistical benchmark: any model failing to outperform it has learned nothing beyond market noise.
- **ARIMA** fits an autoregressive integrated moving average model to the log-return series using pmdarima.auto_arima with AIC-based order selection. Orders ARIMA(2,0,1) were selected on the initial training window. The model is refitted every 21 test steps using an expanding window to reflect realistic re-estimation practices.
- **Ridge regression** is a linear model with L_2 penalty on coefficients, providing a baseline for linear feature-return relationships. The penalty strength $\lambda \in \{10^{-4},\ldots,10^{2}\}$ is selected by cross-validation.
- **Random Forest** is an ensemble of 1,000 regression trees, each fit to a bootstrap sample with a random feature subset at each split. Key hyperparameters are tuned by grid search.
- **XGBoost** is a gradient-boosted tree ensemble with shrinkage, column subsampling, and L_1/L_2 leaf regularisation, all tuned by grid search. XGBoost is the primary ML competitor in this study, given its consistent strong performance on structured tabular forecasting tasks.
- **Temporal Sequence Transformer (TST)** processes sequences of $L = 20$ past OHLCV vectors through a causally masked multi-head self-attention stack ($d_{model} = 192$, 4 layers, 6 heads, $d_{ff} = 512$, GELU activations) and predicts the next-day log-return in a single forward pass. *In Figure 5: TST architecture diagram t*he TST receives only raw OHLCV inputs, without the engineered technical indicators provided to the classical ML models.

Figure 5. Architecture of the temporal sequence transformer

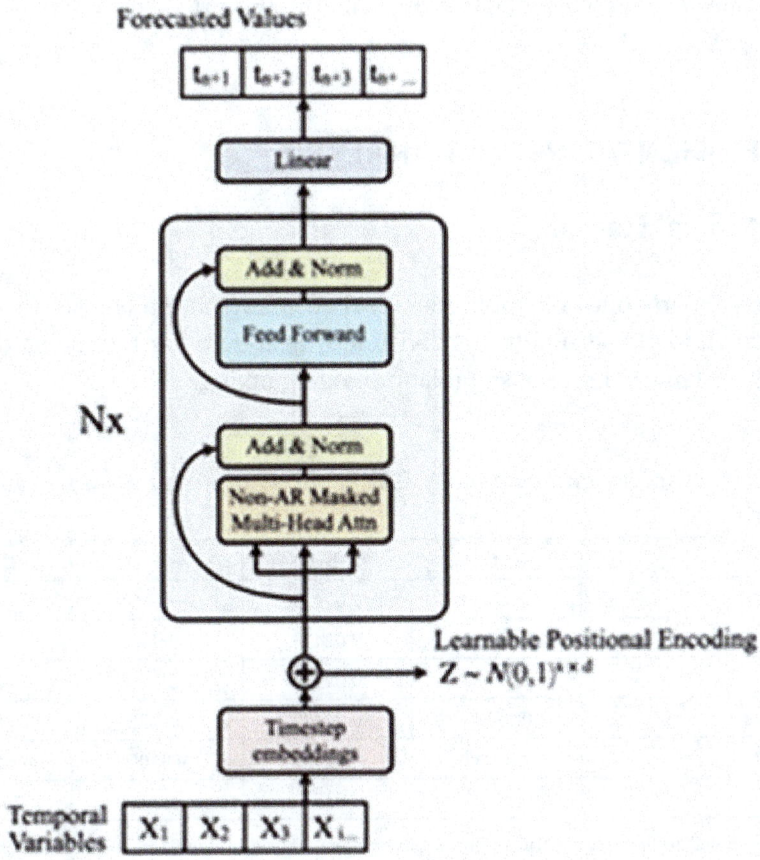

The full sample is partitioned chronologically: 60% training (approximately 1999–2014), 20% validation (approximately 2015–2019), and 20% held-out test (July 2019–July 2024). Hyperparameter optimization for Ridge, Random Forest, and XGBoost uses GridSearchCV with TimeSeriesSplit(n_splits=5) applied to the training partition, ensuring all tuning is performed without access to the validation or test sets. The selected configuration is refit on the union of training and validation data before being evaluated on the test set, which is used exactly once.

The backtest simulates a long/flat strategy: a unit position is taken when the model predicts $\hat{r}_{t+1} > 0$ and no position otherwise. The strategy return is:

$$R^{strat}_{t+1} = w_{t+1} \cdot r^{real}_{t+1} - c \cdot |w_{t+1} - w_t|$$

where c is the per-trade transaction cost. The annualised Sharpe ratio is computed as:

$$SR = \frac{\bar{R}^{strat}}{s_R}\sqrt{252}$$

Maximum drawdown (MDD) is reported as the price-equivalent percentage decline: $MDD_{\%} = (1 - e^{-\Delta_{max}}) \times 100$.

4. EXPERIMENTAL RESULT ANALYSIS

4.1 Statistical Results

Table 4 reports out-of-sample statistical accuracy on the test set ($n = 1{,}276$ trading days). MAPE is omitted as division by near-zero log-returns produces numerically unstable values not suitable for model ranking.

Table 4. Statistical accuracy on the NVDA next-day log-return test set (July 2019–July 2024)

Model	RMSE	MAE	R^2	DA (%)
Naive ($\hat{r} = 0$)	0.03299	0.02423	−0.0063	—
ARIMA(2,0,1)	0.03289	0.02413	−0.0000	53.6
Ridge	0.03694	0.02730	−0.2615	50.1
Random Forest	0.03283	0.02409	0.0035	**55.8**
XGBoost	**0.03271**	**0.02402**	**0.0107**	55.7
TST	0.04779	0.03532	−1.0982	44.5

Note. Directional accuracy is undefined for the naive predictor because sign(0) = 0 never matches a non-zero return under the standard sign-match formulation.

TST directional accuracy is below 50%, indicating systematic mis-direction; this model is excluded from the backtest comparison.

A clear stratification emerges. XGBoost and Random Forest perform statistically best, with XGBoost outperforming on RMSE (0.03271), MAE (0.02402) and R (0.011) and Random Forest narrowly outperforming on directional accuracy (55.8% versus 55.7%). While positive R values on both these look modest on their own, out-of-sample positive R on daily equity returns is economically meaningful - this magnitude of predictability is enough to generate economically substantial portfolio alpha if deployed in practice, see Gu et al. (2020).

The Ridge Regression R of 0.262 further indicates that a linear relationship between features and returns is not enough on this asset; it predicts worse than a constant predictor. The ARIMA's zero-R (0.000) and 53.6% directional accuracy confirm a slight directional signal is contained in raw linear autocorrelation of returns.

The TST result-RMSE 0.04779, R 1.098, DA 44.5%-is the most striking. It both does worse than the naive baseline and actively gets the direction wrong 55.5% of the time. This sharply contrasts with the TST's good prediction performance at predicting the price levels (Table 5 below) and represents a clear cautionary tale of the price vs return prediction trap. Note that the TST uses raw OHLCV, but the XGBoost and Random Forest uses 17 explicitly hand-crafted technical indicators, highlighting the importance of domain knowledge based feature-engineering for successful transformer based prediction for this asset, rather than an automatic advantage, an idea challenged recently with regards to universality of transformer advantages on tabular time series.

Figure 6. Predicted versus realised next-day log-returns for XGBoost

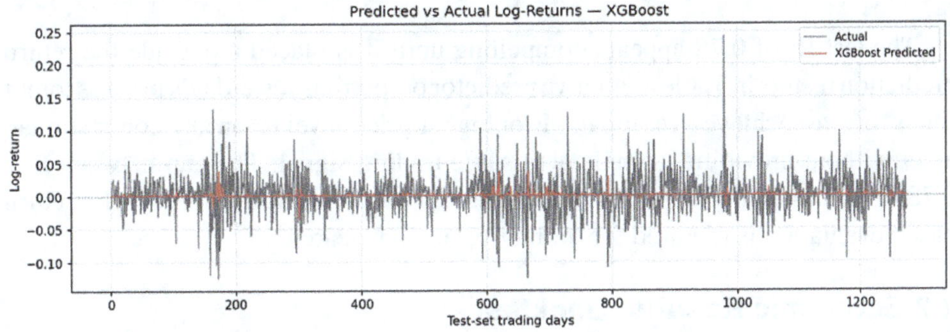

Table 5. Top Six XGBoost feature importances by gain

Rank	Feature	Importance
1	MACD Histogram	8.1%
2	Volume Z-Score (21-day)	7.8%
3	SMA Deviation (5-day)	7.5%
4	Bollinger %B (20-day)	7.3%
5	SMA Deviation (20-day)	6.7%
6	Realised Volatility (21-day)	6.5%

The MACD histogram, a momentum regime indicator, leads feature importance, followed by volume z-score and short-term price displacement. The dominance of momentum and volatility-conditioning features over lag-return features (which rank lower) is consistent with the academic finding that non-linear combinations of standard technical signals contain the majority of short-term return predictability for individual equities.

For completeness, Table 6 reports the TST's performance when predicting the NVDA Open *price level* (not log-return).This formulation uses an identical architecture and training procedure.

Table 6. TST performance on NVDA open price target by split

Split	MSE	RMSE	MAE	MAPE (%)	R^2
Train	0.7379	0.8590	0.3865	69.39	0.9906
Validation	6.6900	2.5865	0.8807	38.19	0.9657
Test	141.5984	11.8995	3.7260	29.06	0.7755

The test R^2 of 0.78 appears compelling until it is placed alongside the return-prediction results in Table 4. A naive predictor outputting yesterday's price as tomorrow's forecast achieves a comparable or higher price-level R^2 on any non-stationary asset without providing a single actionable trading signal. The gap between $R^2 = 0.78$ on prices and $R^2 = -1.10$ on returns is a concrete illustration of why return-based evaluation is required for trading-oriented research.

4.2 Economic Results: Backtest

Table 7 reports the long/flat strategy backtest at five basis points of transaction cost. The TST is excluded due to its below-chance directional accuracy (44.5%), which would cause the long/flat strategy to systematically enter positions on adverse days, generating negative returns. All maximum drawdown figures are expressed as price-equivalent percentages.

Table 7. Backtest results on the NVDA test set, July 2019–July 2024 (Transaction Cost: 5 bps per Trade)

Strategy	Ann. Ret.	Ann. Vol.	Sharpe	MDD	Hit Rate	Trades	Net Cum. Ret.
Buy-and-Hold (NVDA)	65.8%	52.2%	1.26	67.2%	55.7%	1	2,697%
Naive (always flat)	0.0%	0.0%	—	0.0%	—	0	0%
ARIMA(2,0,1)	58.2%	44.9%	1.30	66.7%	41.3%	557	1,705%
Ridge	44.0%	42.3%	1.04	41.6%	32.3%	217	728%

continued on following page

Table 7. Continued

Strategy	Ann. Ret.	Ann. Vol.	Sharpe	MDD	Hit Rate	Trades	Net Cum. Ret.
Random Forest	66.6%	51.2%	1.30	70.7%	54.8%	**47**	2,701%
XGBoost	**71.3%**	49.1%	**1.45**	63.0%	50.5%	209	**3,495%**

Note. Annualised return and volatility are in percentage terms. Net cumulative return = $e^{E_T} - 1$ where E_T is cumulative log equity.

Before discussing model rankings, it is essential to contextualise these figures. The period under review, July 2019 through July 2024, has seen an incredible bull market in NVIDIA stock due to its importance as the principal hardware vendor to large-language-model trainers. Any long-only strategy, hence, must be assessed according to either the Sharpe ratio or the max drawdown, since the high absolute values will be artificial otherwise. XGBoost's Sharpe is 1.45, compared to 1.26 buy-and-hold, and max drawdown falls from 67.2% to 63.0%. Random Forest has an acceptable 1.30 Sharpe with only 47 turnover trades in 5 years-27 days per position on average-so transaction costs should not affect any reasonable parameters much: a practical choice for systematic trading. With Sharpe 1.30 and buy-and-hold beating on a risk-adjusted basis, ARIMA is technically a better choice, however, it trades 557 times, nearly 12 times the turnover of Random Forest and so is much more vulnerable to costs. Ridge has positive Sharpe 1.04 despite its return-scale R being negative-a consequence of the general bull market rather than any superior ability (note the chance-like 50.1% directionality):

Figure 7. Cumulative equity curves for all strategies

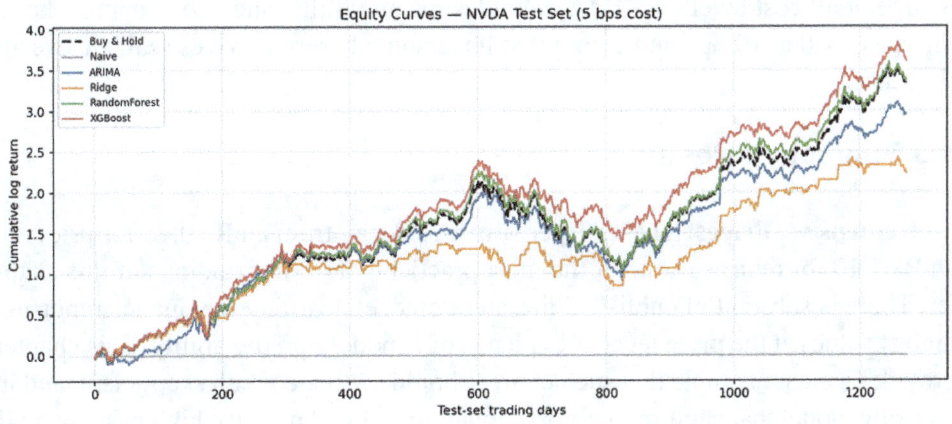

Figure 8. Running drawdown trajectories

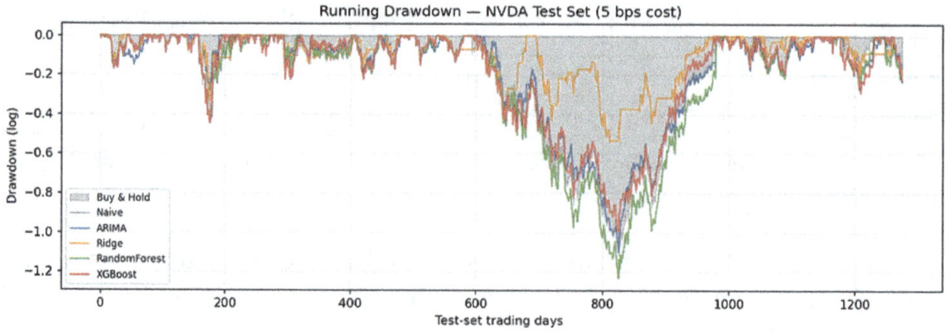

Table 8. Annualised sharpe ratio under varying transaction-cost assumptions

Strategy	0 bps	5 bps	10 bps
Naive	0.00	0.00	0.00
ARIMA	1.42	1.30	1.17
Ridge	1.09	1.04	0.99
Random Forest	**1.31**	1.30	**1.29**
XGBoost	**1.50**	**1.45**	**1.41**

Random Forest's Sharpe degrades by only 0.02 across the full 0–10 bps range, confirming its suitability for high-cost environments. XGBoost retains the leading Sharpe at all cost levels. ARIMA degrades meaningfully, and Ridge approaches a Sharpe of 1.0 at 10 bps, indicating that its strategy barely survives realistic execution costs.

4.3 Subjective Result

Returns vs. Prices: The TST performance decay from an R=0.78 for prices to an R=1.10 for returns is one of the most practically relevant findings of this chapter. There is substantial published literature on deep learning for finance reporting high R values at the price level as evidence of a model's predictability. This chapter provides a clear example that such claims should be treated with skepticism, and in fact, any model that captures a non-stationary trend will produce high price-level R without useful signals for trading. The relevant research direction is returns.

Transformer vs. Classical ML: Comparing against XGBoost and RF, the TST performs poorly on log returns with fair comparison. This supports a growing body of research casting doubt on transformers' widespread supremacy in tabular or univariate time series applications. A significant structural difference between the two settings is the input space; classical ML models used in this chapter receive 17 engineered features incorporating decades of financial knowledge, while the transformer's input consists only of five raw OHLCV values. A TST is required to learn all trend, momentum and volatility implicitly within its architecture, a significantly more difficult problem than taking the engineered signals as input. The performance of TST on this harder task compared to XGBoost given the same set of engineered features is an open empirical question, but this chapter addresses the issue under the Future Research Directions.

Spurious returns under a bull market: Since NVDA grew by a factor of twenty during the entire sample, it is unsurprising that all the long-only strategies resulted in positive nominal returns. This leaves practitioners wondering whether the improvement over a buy-and-hold strategy as estimated here is reproducible in different markets, across asset classes, or over longer time scales, and this problem is particularized by extreme bull markets. However, feature importance analysis (Table 5) at least offers some hope: the top features are theoretically justified trend and momentum indicators that have appeared in studies of cross-sectional predictability (Gu et al., 2020) rather than pathologically shaped features tailored to NVDA's trajectory.

Low signal-to-noise ratio: XGBoost's best result of R=0.011 is equivalent to capturing only 1.1% of next-day log-return variance. Investors might be discouraged by such figures if they are used to high-R forecasting models from other disciplines. However, the R value is quite in line with meaningful economic gains when compounded daily and subject to proper position-sizing and risk-control mechanisms in financial forecasting. It is better compared not to weather forecasting or demand forecasting, but to a random walk null hypothesis.

5. FUTURE SCOPE

Several extensions can be readily performed on the evidence presented and the identified limitations.

Feature-Augmented Transformer Evaluation: The most obvious extension is to input the same manually-engineered technical features to the TST as to the classical ML models and thus be able to directly compare the architectures while controlling for the input space. This would enable the isolation of architecture as the single driving factor behind any differences and enable the identification of whether there is any marginal benefit in an attention-based sequence model as compared to a tree-based model given a specified set of domain-specific features.

Multi-Asset and Cross-Sectional Evaluation: This single-asset study does not generalize. Performing the evaluation on a diverse set of large market capitalization equities or a sector index ETF (such as SPY) would reveal whether the observed rankings for NVDA transfer more broadly and if the feature-importance analyses are consistent across different volatilities and market cap levels.

Exogenous Macroeconomic Data: Adding variables such as interest rates, inflation, VIX, sector ETF returns, and firm-specific predictors (earnings surprises, analyst revision momentum) would likely provide additional predictive value and be of particular interest in macro-driven periods in which technical factors alone might be uninformative.

Statistical Hypothesis Testing: The measured differences in RMSE and directional accuracy (Table 4) do not report statistical significance. Using Diebold-Mariano (Diebold & Mariano, 1995) or model confidence set testing would more accurately measure if the XGBoost advantage over Random Forest is distinct from that due to sampling error.

Alternative Trading Strategies: The presented long/flat strategy is necessarily simple. Examining the value associated with a long/short trading regime, a volatility-targeting approach, and ensemble methods would give a fuller picture of economic value and represent normal practice in systematic trading environments. Dynamic position sizing through maximum drawdown control is an obvious additional trading strategy to explore with obvious risk implications.

Economically Efficient Transformer Variations: Several more architecturally refined transformer variations are available, such as the Informer (Zhou et al., 2021), Autoformer (Wu et al., 2021), and patch-based transformers which all propose efficiencies in run time and return prediction over the base TST. An ablative study with respect to architecture choice, length of sequence inputs, and feature inputs could paint a clearer picture of how the transformers perform.

6. CONCLUSION

This chapter compares the predictive power of six forecasting models on next-day NVIDIA log returns using twenty-five years of market data and a held-out test set that contains the unprecedented 2019–2024 bull market fueled by the AI revolution. Four overarching themes guide the methodology: the use of stationary, economically relevant prediction target (log returns instead of prices); time-consistent model evaluation (temporal splitting with TimeSeriesSplit cross-validation and no look-ahead bias in scaling or feature selection); statistical performance metrics, combined with risk-adjusted strategy backtesting.

The empirical results present four key findings. First, the best performing model, by every metric at five basis points of transaction cost, is XGBoost, with a Sharperatio of 1.45, Rof 0.011, a directional accuracy of 55.7%, and a test period net cumulative return of 3495%, which outperforms a buy-and-hold strategy (Sharperatio of 1.26) on a risk-adjusted basis. Second, Random Forest is an extremely promising alternative from a practical point of view. The strategy yields very similar statistical performance but makes only forty-seven trades over five years and shows a remarkably transaction-cost insensitive Sharperatio-a highly desired feature for systematic trading. Third, the negative R of 0.26 obtained with Ridge regression demonstrates that it is inadequate for modeling the non-linear interaction of the features driving return predictability on this specific asset. Therefore, the reported profitability of the Ridge strategy comes solely from the prevailing bull market environment and not the model's predictive accuracy. Fourth, when evaluated on log returns without engineered features from financial domain expertise, the Temporal Sequence Transformer provides a directional accuracy of 44.5% and performs worse than random; hence, it reinforces prior studies that warn against overzealous application of transformers in finance and indicates that domain-specific features are crucial for deep learning models on the return scale.

The main contributions to the practitioner audience are: gradient-boosted trees combined with standard technical indicators offer a deployable, interpretable and robust starting point for stock return forecasting; risk-adjustment, and transaction-cost sensitivity are equally important as predictive accuracy in model choice; return-prediction evaluation, not price-prediction, is an unavoidable prerequisite for any meaningful claim on prediction in a trading context. The entire experimental pipeline is freely available for replication.

REFERENCES

Bollerslev, T. (1986). Generalized autoregressive conditional heteroskedasticity. *Journal of Econometrics*, *31*(3), 307–327. DOI: 10.1016/0304-4076(86)90063-1

Box, G. E. P., Jenkins, G. M., Reinsel, G. C., & Ljung, G. M. (2015). *Time series analysis: Forecasting and control* (5th ed.). Wiley.

Breiman, L. (2001). Random forests. *Machine Learning*, *45*(1), 5–32. DOI: 10.1023/A:1010933404324

Chen, T., & Guestrin, C. (2016). XGBoost: A scalable tree boosting system. In *Proceedings of the 22nd ACM SIGKDD International Conference on Knowledge Discovery and Data Mining* (pp. 785–794). ACM. https://doi.org/DOI: 10.1145/2939672.2939785

Diebold, F. X., & Mariano, R. S. (1995). Comparing predictive accuracy. *Journal of Business & Economic Statistics*, *13*(3), 253–263. DOI: 10.1080/07350015.1995.10524599

Engle, R. F. (1982). Autoregressive conditional heteroscedasticity with estimates of the variance of United Kingdom inflation. *Econometrica*, *50*(4), 987–1007. DOI: 10.2307/1912773

Fischer, T., & Krauss, C. (2018). Deep learning with long short-term memory networks for financial market predictions. *European Journal of Operational Research*, *270*(2), 654–669. DOI: 10.1016/j.ejor.2017.11.054

Friedman, J. H. (2001). Greedy function approximation: A gradient boosting machine. *Annals of Statistics*, *29*(5), 1189–1232. DOI: 10.1214/aos/1013203451

Gu, S., Kelly, B., & Xiu, D. (2020). Empirical asset pricing via machine learning. *Review of Financial Studies*, *33*(5), 2223–2273. DOI: 10.1093/rfs/hhaa009

Hochreiter, S., & Schmidhuber, J. (1997). Long short-term memory. *Neural Computation*, *9*(8), 1735–1780. DOI: 10.1162/neco.1997.9.8.1735 PMID: 9377276

Hoerl, A. E., & Kennard, R. W. (1970). Ridge regression: Biased estimation for nonorthogonal problems. *Technometrics*, *12*(1), 55–67. DOI: 10.1080/00401706.1970.10488634

Ke, G., Meng, Q., Finley, T., Wang, T., Chen, W., Ma, W., Ye, Q., & Liu, T.-Y. (2017). LightGBM: A highly efficient gradient boosting decision tree. In Vol. 30, pp. 3146–3154). Advances in Neural Information Processing Systems. Curran Associates.

Krauss, C., Do, X. A., & Huck, N. (2017). Deep neural networks, gradient-boosted trees, random forests: Statistical arbitrage on the S&P 500. *European Journal of Operational Research*, *259*(2), 689–702. DOI: 10.1016/j.ejor.2016.10.031

Lim, B., Arık, S. Ö., Loeff, N., & Pfister, T. (2021). Temporal Fusion Transformers for interpretable multi-horizon time series forecasting. *International Journal of Forecasting*, *37*(4), 1748–1764. DOI: 10.1016/j.ijforecast.2021.03.012

López de Prado, M. (2018). *Advances in financial machine learning*. Wiley.

Patel, J., Shah, S., Thakkar, P., & Kotecha, K. (2015). Predicting stock and stock price index movement using trend deterministic data preparation and machine learning techniques. *Expert Systems with Applications*, *42*(1), 259–268. DOI: 10.1016/j.eswa.2014.07.040

Sezer, O. B., Gudelek, M. U., & Ozbayoglu, A. M. (2020). Financial time series forecasting with deep learning: A systematic literature review: 2005–2019. *Applied Soft Computing*, *90*, 106181. Advance online publication. DOI: 10.1016/j.asoc.2020.106181

Tay, F. E. H., & Cao, L. (2001). Application of support vector machines in financial time series forecasting. *Omega*, *29*(4), 309–317. DOI: 10.1016/S0305-0483(01)00026-3

Vaswani, A., Shazeer, N., Parmar, N., Uszkoreit, J., Jones, L., Gomez, A. N., Kaiser, Ł., & Polosukhin, I. (2017). Attention is all you need. In Vol. 30, pp. 5998–6008). Advances in Neural Information Processing Systems. Curran Associates.

Wu, H., Xu, J., Wang, J., & Long, M. (2021). Autoformer: Decomposition transformers with auto-correlation for long-term series forecasting. In Vol. 34, pp. 22419–22430). Advances in Neural Information Processing Systems. Curran Associates.

Zhou, H., Zhang, S., Peng, J., Zhang, S., Li, J., Xiong, H., & Zhang, W. (2021). Informer: Beyond efficient transformer for long sequence time-series forecasting. *Proceedings of the AAAI Conference on Artificial Intelligence*, *35*(12), 11106–11115. DOI: 10.1609/aaai.v35i12.17325

KEY TERMS AND DEFINITIONS

Directional Accuracy (DA): The proportion of forecast periods in which the predicted sign of an asset return (positive or negative) matches the realised sign. A directional accuracy above 50% indicates forecasting skill beyond random guessing and is the primary metric connecting statistical model output to trading signal quality.

Gradient Boosting: An ensemble machine-learning technique that constructs a predictive model by fitting regression trees sequentially to the residuals of preceding trees, minimising a differentiable loss function through gradient descent in function space. XGBoost and LightGBM are scalable, regularised implementations widely used in financial and tabular prediction tasks.

Log-Return: The natural logarithm of the ratio of consecutive asset prices, $r_t = ln\left(P_t/P_{t-1}\right)$. Log-returns are approximately stationary in mean, additive across time, and exhibit more symmetric distributions than simple percentage returns, making them the standard prediction target in quantitative finance.

Maximum Drawdown (MDD): The largest peak-to-trough decline in a portfolio's cumulative return over a specified evaluation period, expressed as a percentage of the peak value. MDD quantifies the worst-case capital loss an investor would have experienced and is a primary measure of downside risk alongside volatility.

Random Forest: An ensemble of decision trees, each trained on a bootstrap resample of the training data with a randomly selected subset of features considered at each split node. Predictions are obtained by averaging across all trees. The procedure reduces variance relative to a single tree while retaining low bias.

Sharpe Ratio: A risk-adjusted performance measure defined as the ratio of a strategy's mean excess daily return (above a risk-free benchmark, typically set to zero for short horizons) to its return standard deviation, annualised by multiplying by $\sqrt{252}$ for daily data. Higher Sharpe ratios indicate better compensation per unit of risk taken.

Technical Indicators: Quantitative transformations of an asset's historical price and volume data including moving averages (SMA, EMA), the Relative Strength Index (RSI), Moving Average Convergence Divergence (MACD), Bollinger Bands, and realised volatility used to characterise trend, momentum, mean-reversion, and volatility for forecasting and systematic trading applications.

TimeSeriesSplit: A cross-validation procedure implemented in scikit-learn that generates successive expanding-window train/validation fold pairs such that every validation observation strictly follows all training observations in calendar time. This prevents information leakage from future to past, which would artificially inflate performance estimates when applied to temporal financial data.

Transformer Architecture: A neural network design based on multi-head self-attention mechanisms, in which every element of an input sequence attends to every other element in parallel. Originally proposed for natural language processing (Vaswani et al., 2017), transformers have been widely adapted for time-series forecasting tasks due to their ability to model long-range temporal dependencies without sequential computation.

Volatility Clustering: The empirical phenomenon in financial return series whereby large absolute price changes tend to be temporally clustered, large moves follow large moves, and small moves follow small moves regardless of direction. Volatility clustering implies that conditional return variance is time-varying and predictable, motivating the inclusion of realised volatility and GARCH-type features in forecasting models.

Chapter 10
Volatility Forecasting Through Hybrid GARCH-LSTM Models With Walk-Forward Validation and Multi-Horizon Evaluation

Angel Mario Lerma-Sanchez
http://orcid.org/0000-0002-5759-1302
Universidad Autonoma de Tamaulipas, Mexico

Felipe A. González-González
Universidad Autonoma de Tamaulipas, Mexico

Joaquin Torres-Mata
http://orcid.org/0000-0002-9298-8831
Universidad Autonoma de Tamaulipas, Mexico

ABSTRACT

This chapter, per the authors, examines volatility forecasting through a hybrid GARCH-LSTM framework designed to improve prediction accuracy under a rigorous and reproducible evaluation scheme. The purpose of this chapter is to assess whether combining the econometric structure of GARCH with the nonlinear sequence-learning capacity of LSTM enhances forecasting performance relative to a standard GARCH benchmark. The content includes the theoretical foundations of financial volatility, a review of hybrid forecasting literature, the construction of daily return-based volatility measures, the specification of the proposed model, and

DOI: 10.4018/979-8-3373-8372-9.ch010

an empirical evaluation using S&P 500, EUR/USD, and Bitcoin data. Results from walk-forward and multi-horizon validation show that the hybrid model delivers more accurate short-term forecasts and remains competitive across different asset classes

1. INTRODUCTION

The digital transformation of finance has not reduced the importance of volatility forecasting. On the contrary, it has made volatility more operational, more observable, and more consequential for decision-making. In increasingly automated markets, the quality of volatility forecasts affects capital allocation, risk-limit setting, margin requirements, hedging decisions, and capital adequacy assessment. Under conditions of electronic trading, near-real-time data integration, and regulatory pressure for traceable processes, the challenge is not only to forecast accurately, but also to do so in a reproducible, interpretable, and methodologically defensible manner. This combination of predictive accuracy, transparency, and temporal discipline explains why volatility forecasting remains a central problem in contemporary quantitative finance.

The literature has consistently shown that financial returns rarely satisfy the assumptions of homoskedasticity and independent and identically distributed observations. Instead, returns often display volatility clustering, heavy tails, asymmetric responses to positive and negative shocks, and episodes of persistence that may intensify during periods of macro-financial tension or liquidity stress (Cont, 2001). These empirical regularities justify the continued use of conditional variance models, while also motivating the search for more flexible approaches capable of capturing nonlinear and sequential patterns that may not be fully represented by standard econometric specifications.

The ARCH/GARCH family emerged precisely to model conditional heteroskedasticity in a parsimonious and interpretable way. Since the foundational contributions of Engle (1982) and Bollerslev (1986), GARCH-type models have become a reference point in both academic research and professional risk practice. Their appeal lies in their ability to summarize volatility persistence through a small number of parameters with clear statistical meaning. Nevertheless, accumulated empirical evidence also suggests that no simple GARCH specification uniformly dominates across all markets, sample periods, forecasting horizons, and evaluation metrics. Asset characteristics, trading structure, jumps, memory, asymmetry, and the selected loss function can all affect model rankings.

At the same time, machine learning and deep learning have expanded the methodological toolkit available for financial time-series forecasting. Recurrent architectures, particularly Long Short-Term Memory (LSTM) networks, are designed to learn temporal dependencies through memory cells and gating mechanisms that retain or discard information across a sequence (Hochreiter & Schmidhuber, 1997). This structure makes LSTMs attractive for volatility forecasting because market risk dynamics may depend not only on the most recent observation, but also on evolving patterns of shocks, persistence, compression, and regime transition. However, the flexibility of deep learning also introduces risks, including sensitivity to hyperparameter choices, increased training complexity, lower structural interpretability, and vulnerability to overfitting when evaluation protocols are weak.

Evaluation design is therefore central to the credibility of any machine learning application in finance. A substantial improvement in forecast error is not persuasive if it is obtained through random validation, future-data contamination, or preprocessing steps that use information unavailable at the forecast origin. Bergmeir et al. (2018) emphasize that the validity of cross-validation for time series depends on specific assumptions; in financial applications, where temporal dependence and regime changes are common, recursive or walk-forward validation is usually more defensible. For this reason, a chapter on volatility forecasting should not merely report lower errors. It should demonstrate that those errors were obtained under a temporally coherent out-of-sample protocol.

The motivation for a hybrid approach arises from the tension between econometric structure and neural-network flexibility. A GARCH(1,1) model provides a compact representation of conditional variance persistence and remains a natural benchmark because of its long-standing role in volatility forecasting (Poon & Granger, 2003). However, standard GARCH dynamics may be insufficient when volatility incorporates nonlinear interactions between recent shocks, conditional states, and asset-specific market behavior. A hybrid GARCH-LSTM model can therefore be interpreted as a layered forecasting architecture: the econometric component organizes the conditional volatility signal, while the LSTM component learns nonlinear sequential corrections from that structured information. In this sense, the hybrid does not replace econometrics; it uses econometric output as an informative scaffold for a more flexible learning stage.

This chapter is positioned at the intersection of financial econometrics, reproducible analytics, and deep learning. Its guiding question is whether a compact GARCH-informed LSTM model, evaluated through walk-forward validation and multi-horizon forecasting, can add value relative to classical and operational volatility benchmarks across different asset classes. The empirical analysis uses three daily series with heterogeneous market structures: the S&P 500 index (^GSPC), the EUR/USD exchange rate (EURUSD=X), and Bitcoin (BTC-USD). This selection is not intended to establish statistical universality. Rather, it provides economic contrast. The equity index represents a deep institutional market, the exchange rate represents a highly liquid foreign exchange environment, and Bitcoin represents a digital asset with more irregular volatility dynamics and potentially stronger nonlinear behavior.

The empirical design uses adjusted daily prices to compute logarithmic returns, constructs a 21-day moving volatility proxy, and evaluates forecasts at horizons of $h = 1$, $h = 5$, and $h = 10$. The revised benchmark suite includes persistence, EWMA, GARCH(1,1), and an asymmetric GARCH-type specification, while the proposed hybrid model uses GARCH-informed inputs in a compact LSTM architecture. Forecast accuracy is assessed with MSE, MAE, and QLIKE. The inclusion of QLIKE is important because Patton (2011) shows that volatility forecast rankings may be distorted when latent volatility is evaluated through imperfect proxies. In addition, Diebold-Mariano tests are used to determine whether selected out-of-sample loss differences are statistically meaningful rather than merely descriptive.

Although prior studies have examined GARCH-type models, LSTM architectures, and hybrid volatility frameworks, several gaps remain relevant. First, some applied studies report predictive gains without sufficiently emphasizing temporally coherent validation. Second, hybrid models are often evaluated on a limited set of assets, horizons, or benchmarks, which restricts the interpretation of their robustness. Third, comparisons frequently focus on average error reduction without clearly distinguishing statistical performance, volatility-proxy limitations, formal predictive-accuracy testing, and practical usefulness. This chapter addresses these gaps by evaluating a compact GARCH-informed LSTM pipeline across heterogeneous assets, multiple horizons, volatility-specific loss functions, a broader benchmark suite, and formal forecast-comparison tests.

The chapter makes five specific contributions. First, it presents a reproducible Python and TensorFlow/Keras pipeline that integrates an econometric volatility signal with a compact LSTM architecture. Second, it strengthens temporal validity by using expanding-window walk-forward validation rather than random data partitioning, which is inappropriate for most financial forecasting settings. Third, it evaluates the model across multiple horizons, making it possible to distinguish short-term predictive gains from medium- and longer-horizon performance changes. Fourth, it compares the hybrid against a benchmark suite that includes persistence, EWMA, GARCH(1,1), and an asymmetric GARCH-type model, rather than relying on a single baseline. Fifth, it interprets predictive gains through statistical and practical lenses by combining MSE, MAE, QLIKE, Diebold-Mariano testing, and asset-specific discussion.

The chapter is organized as follows. Section 2 develops the theoretical framework and literature review, with emphasis on stylized facts of volatility, the GARCH family, LSTM architectures, hybrid modeling, and forecast evaluation. Section 3 describes the data, variable construction, and volatility target. Section 4 presents the proposed methodology and benchmark suite. Section 5 explains the experimental design, temporal validation protocol, multi-horizon setup, and statistical testing strategy. Section 6 reports the empirical results and forecast-comparison evidence. Section 7 discusses the findings across assets, horizons, and loss functions. Sections 8 and 9 address practical implications, limitations, and future research. Section 10 concludes the chapter.

2. THEORETICAL FRAMEWORK AND LITERATURE REVIEW

2.1 Financial Volatility and Stylized Facts

In empirical terms, volatility denotes the time-varying variability of returns and is commonly represented through conditional variance or conditional standard deviation. If $r_t = \ln\left(\frac{P_t}{P_{t-1}}\right)$ denotes the logarithmic return of an asset, volatility is not directly observed as a state variable. It must instead be inferred from return dynamics or approximated through realized measures constructed from higher-frequency information. This measurement problem is central to volatility-forecasting research because it affects the selection of benchmarks, loss functions, and out-of-sample evaluation procedures.

The stylized facts documented by Cont (2001) remain the main conceptual reference for understanding financial volatility. Daily returns typically exhibit limited linear autocorrelation, whereas squared and absolute returns display strong serial dependence. Return distributions are also frequently leptokurtic and heavy-tailed, volatility tends to cluster over time, and many markets exhibit asymmetry or leverage effects, whereby negative shocks affect future volatility more strongly than positive shocks of comparable magnitude. These empirical regularities explain why conditional variance models remain relevant and why more flexible extensions continue to be developed.

From an economic perspective, volatility is not merely a statistical descriptor. It is also an input for pricing models, an exposure-control variable, and an indicator of market state. In risk management, the quality of volatility forecasts affects VaR and ES calibration. In derivatives markets, it influences price sensitivity and hedging decisions. In portfolio allocation, it conditions dynamic weights and rebalancing rules. Because volatility has these multiple uses, the literature increasingly evaluates volatility models not only by in-sample fit, but also by out-of-sample predictive ability and practical economic usefulness.

2.2 ARCH/GARCH Models and Their Extensions

Engle (1982) introduced the ARCH model by specifying conditional variance as a function of past innovations. Bollerslev (1986) generalized this framework through GARCH, allowing conditional variance to depend both on lagged innovations and on its own past values. In the standard GARCH(1,1) specification, conditional variance can be written as:

$$\sigma_t^2 = \omega + \alpha \varepsilon_{t-1}^2 + \beta \sigma_{t-1}^2$$

where $\omega > 0, \quad \alpha \geq 0, \quad \beta \geq 0, \quad \alpha + \beta < 1$, with additional restrictions to ensure weak stationarity. The specification is widely used because it is parsimonious, captures volatility persistence, and offers a relatively transparent interpretation. Poon and Granger (2003) document its importance as a benchmark in multiple volatility-forecasting settings.

However, using GARCH(1,1) as a benchmark does not imply that it is the best specification in all contexts. The literature has developed several extensions to address additional empirical features. EGARCH models specify the dynamics of log variance and can capture asymmetry without imposing direct positivity restrictions on the parameters. GJR-GARCH and TGARCH include indicator terms to distinguish the volatility response to positive and negative shocks. APARCH adds flexibility through an estimable power parameter and an asymmetric component. More recent long-memory and regime-switching models seek to represent slowly decaying persistence and structural transitions across volatility states. Huang and Luo (2024), for example, show that incorporating long memory, leverage effects, and heavy tails can improve out-of-sample forecasts in certain market environments. Still, no extension can be assumed to dominate uniformly across all applications.

This point has an important methodological implication for the chapter. The choice of GARCH(1,1) as a baseline is not meant to define the frontier of volatility econometrics. Rather, it provides a parsimonious, widely recognized, and interpretable reference model. Its comparative role is straightforward: if a hybrid model cannot improve upon a standard and transparent benchmark, its added complexity is difficult to justify. At the same time, acknowledging EGARCH, GJR-GARCH, APARCH, FIGARCH, and regime-switching models situates the chapter's claims more realistically. The empirical comparison should therefore be read as a disciplined evaluation of a compact GARCH-informed hybrid within a broader but still non-exhaustive benchmark framework.

2.3 Realized Volatility and Benchmarks Based on High-Frequency Information

The use of realized volatility measures constructed from intraday data represents an important development in volatility-forecasting research. Andersen et al. (2003) show that realized volatility provides a richer approximation of the latent variation process than measures derived from isolated daily returns. This line of work has supported models such as HAR-RV, Realized GARCH, and related specifications that exploit the heterogeneous temporal structure of volatility.

For an applied study based on daily data, this literature has two implications. First, it makes clear that a moving standard deviation computed from daily returns is a practical volatility proxy, but not the most informative measure available when high-frequency data can be used. Second, it requires explicit caution when interpreting forecast comparisons, because the empirical target is itself an approximation of latent volatility. A model may rank better or worse depending not only on its predictive structure, but also on the quality of the proxy and the loss function used to evaluate it.

Accordingly, the 21-day moving volatility proxy used in this chapter should be understood as an operational compromise. It supports comparability across the equity, foreign-exchange, and cryptocurrency series and facilitates reproducibility with widely available daily prices. However, it does not replace intraday realized volatility or jump-robust realized measures. The empirical results should therefore be interpreted as performance relative to a transparent daily proxy rather than as direct evidence about the unobservable latent volatility process.

Recent review evidence reinforces this balanced interpretation. Gunnarsson et al. (2024) report that memory-based methods, including LSTM and GRU architectures, often perform strongly in realized-volatility and implied-volatility-index forecasting, although traditional econometric models remain competitive in many applications. This evidence is relevant because it discourages a simple replacement narrative. The issue is not whether GARCH-type models have become obsolete, but under which data conditions, horizons, and validation protocols hybrid or memory-based methods provide incremental forecasting value.

In this chapter, high-frequency realized volatility is therefore treated as an important methodological reference and as a natural direction for future extension, rather than as the empirical target of the present pipeline. This positioning preserves the reproducibility of the daily-data design while acknowledging that stronger volatility targets may alter model rankings in subsequent research.

2.4 Deep Learning for Financial Time Series: Opportunities and Limits

Long Short-Term Memory (LSTM) networks were designed to preserve relevant sequential information and to mitigate, at least in part, the learning instabilities associated with conventional recurrent neural networks (Hochreiter & Schmidhuber, 1997). Their application to financial time series is motivated by the fact that many market processes are not driven only by the most recent observation, but also by trajectory-dependent patterns such as volatility compression, staggered responses to shocks, recurring states, and changes in the amplitude of persistence. In this sense, LSTMs can represent nonlinear interactions among sequential variables that are not explicitly captured by a simple GARCH structure.

The usefulness of an LSTM, however, depends on the empirical setting and on the discipline of the experimental design. In relatively small daily samples, neural networks may memorize noise, overfit specific regimes, or produce spurious gains when data transformations introduce information leakage. Greater flexibility also tends to reduce parametric interpretability. In financial applications, where decision traceability is often as important as predictive accuracy, a marginal reduction in forecast error does not necessarily justify a substantial loss of transparency. Deep learning models for volatility forecasting should therefore be assessed not only in terms of accuracy, but also in terms of stability across windows, consistency across assets, and sensitivity to the forecasting horizon.

Recent studies do not eliminate these concerns, but they provide a more informative comparative framework. Yang, Ye, and Zhai (2024) show that Hybrid-LSTM models can improve intraday realized-volatility forecasts for U.S. stock indexes during the COVID-19 period, while emphasizing that the specific form of hybridization materially affects performance. Mishra, Renganathan, and Gupta (2024) report that hybrid architectures combining Transformer, GARCH, and LSTM components can outperform classical models across different assets. Taken together, these findings support a broader conclusion: the current research frontier is not defined by opposing econometrics and deep learning, but by identifying structurally coherent ways to combine them. The value of a hybrid model therefore depends not on the mere inclusion of a neural network, but on how that network is integrated with economically and statistically informative signals.

2.5 Hybrid Econometrics-Learning Models

Within the hybridization literature, Kim and Won (2018) are a key reference because they integrate LSTM networks with GARCH-type models for stock-index volatility forecasting. Their contribution is important not only as a specific model, but also because it formalizes a logic that remains central to later work: outputs from volatility models can serve as structured inputs for a sequential learning algorithm. Under this design, the network does not learn volatility dynamics exclusively from raw returns; it receives an econometric representation of conditional heteroskedasticity that already embeds information about volatility persistence. Kakade, Jain, and Mishra (2022), although focused on Value-at-Risk forecasting, reinforce the same intuition by showing that GARCH-LSTM combinations can be useful in risk-management applications where variance forecasts are instrumental rather than merely descriptive.

Hybrid models, however, should not be treated as a single homogeneous class. Some use GARCH-estimated volatility as one explanatory variable, others combine forecasts from several econometric specifications, and more complex designs incorporate attention mechanisms, additional recurrent layers, or ensemble structures. This diversity matters because the empirical value of hybridization depends on how the econometric and learning components are connected. Improvements are likely to reflect not only the flexibility of the neural network, but also the informativeness of the initial volatility signal, the market regime, the sampling frequency, and the loss function used for evaluation.

The approach adopted in this chapter is deliberately parsimonious. Rather than relying on a deep architecture or an opaque ensemble, the proposed hybrid uses three economically interpretable inputs: GARCH conditional volatility, standardized residuals, and absolute returns. These variables capture complementary aspects of the volatility process. Conditional volatility summarizes the level and persistence of risk estimated by the econometric model; standardized residuals represent normalized shocks relative to the estimated conditional variance; and absolute returns provide a simple empirical measure of the recent magnitude of market movements. Together, they form a compact information set that allows the LSTM to learn nonlinear sequential corrections without excessive feature proliferation.

This design also clarifies the contribution of the hybrid model. The LSTM component is not presented as a replacement for econometric modeling, nor is the GARCH component used only as a benchmark external to the learning process. Instead, the hybrid architecture treats GARCH as a structural representation of conditional variance and uses the LSTM to search for residual nonlinear patterns over that representation. This logic is consistent with the broader objective of the chapter: to evaluate whether a moderate, reproducible, and interpretable form of hybridization can improve volatility forecasts under temporally coherent validation.

2.6 Out-of-Sample Evaluation, Loss Functions, and Temporal Coherence

Evaluating volatility forecasts involves a central difficulty: latent volatility is not directly observable. Researchers therefore rely on proxies such as squared returns, realized volatility, or range-based measures derived from intraday information. Patton (2011) shows that, when these proxies are imperfect, some loss functions may produce inconsistent rankings across competing models. Within this context, QLIKE is especially useful because it is robust under specific conditions and reduces some distortions associated with more intuitive loss measures when the observed target is a noisy approximation of latent volatility. This does not mean that MSE or MAE should be discarded; rather, their interpretation should be complemented by a metric designed for volatility forecast comparison.

Temporal coherence is a second evaluation issue. A model that performs well at a one-day horizon may deteriorate substantially at five- or ten-day horizons. Because financial applications operate over different decision horizons, multi-horizon evaluation is methodologically necessary. Intertemporal robustness also requires validation over multiple recursive or walk-forward partitions. A strong result in a single split may reflect a favorable market regime, whereas an improvement that persists across folds is more credible. This consideration becomes especially relevant when comparing heterogeneous assets, because their volatility dynamics may respond differently to market structure, liquidity, and stress episodes.

Taken together, the literature reviewed in this section supports four principles that guide the chapter. First, parsimonious econometric structure remains valuable in volatility modeling. Second, memory-based architectures such as LSTMs can capture nonlinear sequential patterns that standard specifications may miss. Third, hybrid models offer a plausible way to combine econometric interpretability with nonlinear learning capacity. Fourth, any predictive improvement is credible only when it is evaluated through temporally coherent validation and appropriate volatility-specific loss functions. The empirical methodology that follows is designed around these principles.

2.7 Synthesis of Literature Gaps and Positioning of the Chapter

The reviewed literature indicates that volatility forecasting has moved from parsimonious econometric specifications toward increasingly flexible hybrid and deep learning architectures. Foundational GARCH models remain relevant because they provide interpretable representations of conditional heteroskedasticity, whereas LSTM-based models and other neural architectures offer greater capacity to capture nonlinear and sequential patterns. However, the evidence also shows that predictive gains depend not only on model complexity, but also on the validation scheme, benchmark set, volatility proxy, loss function, and stability of results across assets and forecasting horizons.

Table 1 summarizes how selected prior studies position the present chapter. The purpose of the comparison is not to claim that the proposed GARCH-LSTM specification dominates existing alternatives. Rather, it clarifies the chapter's specific contribution: a compact and reproducible hybrid pipeline evaluated through temporally coherent walk-forward validation, heterogeneous asset classes, multiple forecasting horizons, benchmark diversity, volatility-specific loss functions, and formal predictive-accuracy tests.

Recent comparative and review evidence also emphasizes the importance of systematic benchmark evaluation and the growing role of deep learning architectures in realized-volatility forecasting (Taneva-Angelova & Granchev, 2025; Leushuis & Petkov, 2026). In addition, sentiment-augmented GARCH-LSTM extensions show that external information can enrich volatility and Value-at-Risk forecasting, although such extensions introduce additional data-alignment and governance challenges (Léber & Egyed, 2026).

Table 1. Positioning of the chapter within selected volatility-forecasting literature

Research stream	Representative studies	Main emphasis	Gap or limitation relevant to this chapter	Positioning of this chapter
Classical conditional volatility models	Engle (1982); Bollerslev (1986); Poon and Granger (2003)	ARCH/GARCH models provide parsimonious and interpretable representations of conditional heteroskedasticity.	Standard specifications may underrepresent nonlinear sequential patterns and may not be sufficient across assets and horizons.	Uses GARCH(1,1) as a transparent econometric benchmark and as a structured input for the hybrid model.
Volatility-proxy and loss-function literature	Andersen et al. (2003); Patton (2011)	Realized volatility and appropriate loss functions are central when latent volatility is not directly observable.	Forecast rankings may be distorted when volatility proxies are imperfect or when evaluation relies on a single metric.	Uses a daily volatility proxy and evaluates forecasts with MSE, MAE, and QLIKE.
LSTM and memory-based volatility forecasting	Hochreiter and Schmidhuber (1997); Gunnarsson et al. (2024)	Memory-based models can capture nonlinear temporal dependencies in financial time series.	Deep learning models require careful temporal validation and may be vulnerable to overfitting or weak interpretability.	Adopts a compact LSTM architecture and evaluates it through walk-forward validation.

continued on following page

Table 1. Continued

Research stream	Representative studies	Main emphasis	Gap or limitation relevant to this chapter	Positioning of this chapter
Hybrid GARCH-LSTM models	Kim and Won (2018); Kakade et al. (2022)	GARCH outputs can be combined with LSTM networks to improve volatility or risk forecasting.	Many hybrid applications focus on specific markets or risk tasks and do not always emphasize multi-horizon robustness.	Extends the hybrid logic to equity, foreign exchange, and cryptocurrency series across h = 1, 5, and 10.
Recent hybrid and deep learning architectures	Yang et al. (2024); Mishra et al. (2024)	Recent studies show that hybrid construction and neural architecture design affect predictive performance.	More complex architectures may improve accuracy but can reduce interpretability and operational simplicity.	Proposes a parsimonious and reproducible GARCH-informed LSTM rather than a highly complex deep learning system.
Advanced econometric benchmarks	Huang and Luo (2024)	Long memory, leverage effects, regime switching, and heavy tails can improve volatility modeling in some settings.	GARCH(1,1) is not the full econometric frontier, and stronger benchmarks may alter performance rankings.	Adds asymmetric GARCH-type benchmarking and acknowledges the need for further comparison with advanced GARCH families.
Recent comparative and review evidence	Taneva-Angelova and Granchev (2025); Leushuis and Petkov (2026)	Recent reviews and comparative studies emphasize broader benchmark sets, formal tests, and systematic model evaluation.	Applied studies need clearer benchmark diversity and formal forecast-comparison procedures.	Incorporates persistence, EWMA, GARCH(1,1), GJR-GARCH, and Diebold-Mariano tests.
Sentiment and exogenous-information extensions	Léber and Egyed (2026)	External information such as sentiment can enrich hybrid volatility and risk models.	Additional signals increase data-alignment, governance, and reproducibility challenges.	Positions exogenous variables and sentiment indicators as future extensions rather than core inputs.

Note. The table summarizes the chapter's positioning relative to selected studies. The objective is not to claim superiority over all volatility-forecasting approaches, but to clarify the chapter's specific contribution: a compact GARCH-informed LSTM pipeline evaluated through walk-forward validation, multiple horizons, benchmark diversity, QLIKE loss, and Diebold-Mariano tests.

The synthesis in Table 1 defines the contribution of the chapter in precise terms. Its novelty does not lie in presenting LSTM or GARCH as isolated techniques, nor in claiming superiority over the full set of econometric and deep learning alternatives. Instead, the contribution lies in combining elements that are not always jointly emphasized in applied volatility studies: a compact GARCH-informed LSTM architecture, benchmark-diverse comparison, expanding-window walk-forward validation, multi-horizon evaluation, cross-asset evidence, QLIKE-based assessment, and Diebold-Mariano testing. This positioning also delimits the empirical claims: the proposed hybrid is evaluated as a disciplined and reproducible extension of GARCH-type volatility modeling, not as a universal replacement for simpler operational benchmarks or more advanced econometric specifications.

3. DATA, VARIABLES, AND TARGET CONSTRUCTION

This study uses three daily adjusted closing-price series: ^GSPC, as a proxy for a broad and widely followed stock index; EURUSD=X, as a representative foreign exchange rate; and BTC-USD, as a digital asset with a more irregular volatility structure. The objective is not to cover the universe of financial assets exhaustively, but to introduce economically meaningful heterogeneity into the empirical design. Each market differs in liquidity, trading calendar, sensitivity to news, and volatility persistence. Evidence based on a single asset would therefore be too local; incorporating equity, foreign exchange, and cryptocurrency series provides a stronger comparative setting for evaluating the stability of the forecasting pipeline.

From adjusted closing prices P_t, daily logarithmic returns are computed as follows:

$$r_t = \ln\left(\frac{P_t}{P_{t-1}}\right)$$

Logarithmic returns are used for standard reasons in quantitative finance: they approximate time additivity, facilitate relative comparisons, and align with much of the econometric volatility literature. After returns are calculated, observations lost because of lagging are removed, and the temporal alignment of all transformed variables is verified. This step is particularly relevant when series have different trading calendars or when not all markets operate simultaneously.

The forecasting target is not the future return but a volatility proxy. The chapter maintains a 21-day moving standard deviation of daily returns and interprets it as a monthly approximation of realized volatility:

$$RV_t = \text{std}\left(r_{t-W+1}, \ldots, r_t\right)$$

The choice of W = 21 is operational rather than ontological. Twenty-one observations approximate one trading month in equity markets and provide a familiar window for summarizing recent return variability. Two qualifications are necessary. First, for cryptocurrencies and foreign exchange, a "trading month" does not coincide exactly with the equity-market calendar, so the window should be interpreted as a uniform convention adopted for comparability. Second, this proxy does not replace intraday realized volatility; it approximates volatility using daily information available consistently across the three assets.

As Andersen et al. (2003) emphasize, when high-frequency data are available, realized volatility measures provide a more informative representation of latent variation. The proxy used here should therefore be understood as a compromise among data availability, operational simplicity, and pipeline traceability. It is defensible for a reproducible cross-asset chapter, but it is not optimal in an absolute informational sense. Consequently, the reported performance must be interpreted in relation to the quality of the observed volatility target, an issue revisited in the discussion of limitations.

Once RV_t has been constructed, the learning target for horizon h is defined as follows: $y_t = RV_{t+h}$ .Thus, the model uses information available up to time t to forecast the volatility proxy observed h steps ahead. This temporal shift requires trimming the final observations for which no future label is available and preserving strict alignment between predictors and targets. This point is essential for leakage control. In sequential forecasting, even minor indexing errors can contaminate the evaluation, especially when variables are scaled or when input sequences are constructed for the LSTM network.

Additionally, three input variables are used for the LSTM block: (i) the conditional volatility estimated by GARCH, sigma, t; (ii) standardized residuals $z_t = \frac{\varepsilon_t}{\sigma_{G,t}}$; and (iii) the absolute return value r_t. The economic logic behind this selection is complementary. GARCH volatility summarizes the conditional persistence captured by the econometric model; standardized residuals collect normalized shocks, which are useful for detecting episodes of deviation from expected dynamics; the absolute return value provides a simple but robust empirical signal regarding the recent magnitude of market movements. Together, these three inputs supply a compact representation of the volatility state without saturating a network trained on daily data with variables.

The LSTM block uses three input variables: (i) GARCH conditional volatility σ_t ;(ii) standardized residuals $z_t = \frac{\varepsilon_t}{\sigma_{G,t}}$; and (iii) absolute returns r_t .These variables are complementary. GARCH volatility summarizes the conditional persistence captured by the econometric model; standardized residuals capture normalized shocks and help identify deviations from expected dynamics; and absolute returns provide a simple empirical signal of recent movement amplitude. Together, they offer a compact representation of the volatility state without overloading a neural network trained on daily data.

A further methodological issue is synchronization across assets. ^GSPC, EURUSD=X, and BTC-USD have different trading calendars and informational rhythms. The pipeline processes each asset independently, rather than imposing an artificial common calendar. This reduces problems associated with market nonsynchronicity and is consistent with the purpose of the chapter: to compare the performance of the hybrid approach within each asset, not to estimate a joint multivariate system. Future research could incorporate exogenous cross-market variables or intermarket signals, but such extensions would require explicit treatment of temporal alignment, data availability, and economic causality.

Overall, the construction of the variables and target balances empirical validity with reproducible simplicity. Rather than relying on extensive feature engineering, the chapter uses a small set of economically interpretable variables that can be recalculated within each validation fold. This design supports the chapter's central premise: a carefully designed hybrid model can generate relevant improvements without depending on an opaque architecture or on ad hoc variables that are difficult to replicate.

4. PROPOSED METHODOLOGY: BENCHMARK SUITE AND HYBRID GARCH-LSTM MODEL

4.1 Benchmark Suite: Econometric and Operational Comparators

The empirical comparison is extended beyond a single GARCH(1,1) baseline by using a benchmark suite composed of parsimonious, operational, symmetric econometric, and asymmetric econometric volatility forecasts. This broader design evaluates whether the proposed hybrid model adds value not only relative to a classical GARCH specification, but also relative to simple forecasting rules and alternative econometric structures. The suite includes four comparators: a persistence benchmark, an EWMA/RiskMetrics-type benchmark, a GARCH(1,1) model, and an asymmetric GARCH-type specification. This makes the empirical evaluation more demanding while preserving the chapter's emphasis on interpretability, reproducibility, and methodological parsimony.

The role of the GARCH(1,1) block should be distinguished from the role of the broader benchmark suite. GARCH(1,1) serves both as an econometric comparator and as the source of the conditional-volatility signal used by the hybrid LSTM. In this sense, its estimated conditional volatility acts as a compressed representation of the heteroskedasticity state, allowing the LSTM to learn from an econometrically filtered signal rather than from unstructured raw returns alone. By contrast, persistence, EWMA, and the asymmetric GARCH-type model are included as external comparators for evaluating forecast accuracy.

4.1.1 Persistence Benchmark

The first comparator is a persistence benchmark, which assumes that the most recently observed volatility proxy remains the best forecast for the future target. Although simple, this benchmark is important because volatility proxies often display strong short-term continuity. Therefore, any more complex model should demonstrate incremental value relative to this operationally intuitive rule. For horizon h, the persistence forecast is defined as the latest available 21-day volatility proxy carried forward to the target date.

$$\widehat{RV}^{\text{PERS}}_{t+h|t} = RV_t$$

This benchmark provides a minimal but meaningful reference point. If the proposed hybrid model fails to improve upon persistence, especially at very short horizons, its additional complexity would be more difficult to justify from an operational perspective.

4.1.2 EWMA Benchmark

The second comparator is an exponentially weighted moving average (EWMA) benchmark, commonly associated with RiskMetrics-type risk-management practice. Unlike a simple moving average, EWMA assigns declining weights to past squared returns, with greater weight placed on recent observations. This allows volatility estimates to react more quickly to new shocks while retaining a transparent and computationally inexpensive structure.

$$\sigma_t^{2,\text{EWMA}} = \lambda \sigma_{t-1}^{2,\text{EWMA}} + (1 - \lambda) r_{t-1}^2$$

$$0 < \lambda < 1$$

In this formulation, λ denotes the decay parameter. Following standard practice for daily data, λ is fixed at 0.94 rather than optimized separately by asset or forecasting horizon. This choice preserves comparability across series and avoids giving the benchmark an additional layer of tuning that is not central to the chapter's objective. The EWMA forecast is then evaluated alongside persistence, GARCH(1,1), the asymmetric GARCH-type model, and the proposed hybrid GARCH-LSTM model.

4.1.3 GARCH(1,1) Benchmark

The third comparator is the GARCH(1,1) model estimated on daily returns. Its inclusion remains central because it provides a parsimonious, interpretable, and widely used representation of conditional heteroskedasticity. In the revised design, however, GARCH(1,1) is not the only benchmark. It functions both as a benchmark within the suite and as the econometric source of the conditional-volatility input used by the hybrid model.

$$\sigma_t^2 = \omega + \alpha \varepsilon_{t-1}^2 + \beta \sigma_{t-1}^2$$

$$\omega > 0, \alpha \geq 0, \beta \geq 0, \alpha + \beta < 1$$

This distinction strengthens the empirical design. The objective is not merely to show that the hybrid model improves upon one classical specification, but to assess whether a GARCH-informed LSTM remains useful when compared with simpler operational rules and with an asymmetric econometric alternative.

4.1.4 Asymmetric GARCH Benchmark

To account for possible asymmetric responses of volatility to positive and negative shocks, the benchmark suite also includes an asymmetric GARCH-type specification. This addition is relevant because, in many financial markets, negative innovations may have a stronger effect on future volatility than positive innovations of comparable magnitude. Including an asymmetric benchmark therefore makes the comparison more stringent, since the comparator explicitly allows for leverage-type effects.

$$\sigma_t^2 = \omega + \alpha \varepsilon_{t-1}^2 + \gamma I_{\{\varepsilon_{t-1}<0\}} \varepsilon_{t-1}^2 + \beta \sigma_{t-1}^2$$

In this specification, the indicator term captures the additional effect of negative shocks on conditional variance. The model therefore provides a stronger econometric comparator than the symmetric GARCH(1,1) benchmark, especially in assets where downside shocks generate disproportionate volatility responses.

4.2 Feature Engineering and Design Rationale

The benchmark suite introduced in Section 4.1 provides the comparative framework for evaluating predictive performance. The proposed hybrid model, by contrast, is designed as a specifically GARCH-informed architecture. Its LSTM block uses a compact group of variables derived from the GARCH(1,1) estimation and from recent return behavior. This choice preserves the logic of the hybrid design: GARCH supplies an interpretable representation of conditional volatility, while the LSTM learns nonlinear sequential corrections based on that structured signal.

The use of a limited feature set is deliberate. With daily data, the effective sample size is constrained, especially after the data are partitioned by folds and forecast horizons. Extensive feature engineering could increase overfitting risk and make it more difficult to identify the contribution of the GARCH signal and the LSTM component. The selected inputs therefore represent complementary dimensions of the volatility process: conditional risk level, normalized shocks, and the recent amplitude of returns. This keeps feature engineering transparent and aligns each variable with an interpretable financial mechanism.

This feature strategy is consistent with the broader methodological aim of the chapter. The purpose is not to maximize predictive accuracy through an expansive set of predictors, but to test whether a parsimonious and economically interpretable GARCH-informed representation can improve volatility forecasts under a rigorous temporal validation protocol. In this sense, the model remains moderate by design: it favors a structure that can be justified statistically, economically, and operationally, rather than one whose performance depends on opaque or excessive feature construction.

4.3 Sequence Construction

For the LSTM component, the input data are organized into temporal sequences with a fixed lookback length of L = 30. Each sequence X_t contains the three-dimensional input vectors observed from t - L + 1 to t:

$$X_t = [\mathbf{x}_{t-L+1}, \mathbf{x}_{t-L+2}, \ldots, \mathbf{x}_t], \quad \mathbf{x}_s \in \mathbb{R}^3$$

The associated forecasting target is: $y_t = RV_{t+h}$.

The choice of a 30-period lookback should not be interpreted as a claim that 30 days constitute a universally optimal memory horizon. Rather, it establishes a window that is sufficiently long to capture approximately one month of recent dynamics while remaining short enough to avoid unnecessary learning complexity in a daily-data setting.

This design reflects a practical trade-off. With an excessively short lookback, the LSTM may fail to identify transitions between volatility states; with an excessively long lookback, the model may introduce additional parameters and dilute relevant recent information with older noise. Setting L = 30 therefore balances recent memory, parsimony, and comparability. Maintaining the same lookback across ^GSPC, EURUSD=X, and BTC-USD also avoids asset-specific tuning that could weaken the cross-market interpretation of the results. Although some performance may be sacrificed for individual assets, the uniform specification strengthens the chapter's objective of evaluating the hybrid approach under a common protocol.

4.4 LSTM Architecture and Training

The hybrid component is specified as a compact GARCH-informed LSTM architecture. The network is implemented in TensorFlow/Keras (Abadi et al., 2016) and consists of an LSTM layer, an intermediate dense layer, and a scalar output for the volatility forecast. Dropout is used for regularization, and the model is optimized with Adam (Kingma & Ba, 2015) under an MSE training loss. Early stopping is applied using an internal validation set, with restoration of the best-performing weights.

This architecture reflects three design principles. First, a compact network is appropriate for the available daily sample size and for a pipeline intended to remain feasible in CPU-based environments. Second, limiting architectural depth prevents the chapter's argument from depending on a highly parameterized neural system whose gains would be difficult to attribute to the GARCH-LSTM hybrid logic itself. Third, the design supports replication. In applied financial forecasting, architectural sophistication is valuable only when it produces stable improvement under disciplined validation and can be documented, reproduced, and governed. Since the chapter does not conduct a full asset-specific hyperparameter search, a small regularized network represents a prudent methodological choice.

The network is not designed to forecast volatility directly from raw returns alone. Instead, it learns a nonlinear mapping from a state space already informed by the GARCH block. This distinction is central to the interpretation of the hybrid model: econometric structure supplies an interpretable volatility signal, while the LSTM layer learns sequential corrections that may capture nonlinear dependencies not explicitly represented in the benchmark specification. The hybrid model should therefore be understood as an extension of econometric structure rather than as a replacement for it.

4.5 Scaling, Leakage Control, and Reproducibility

Neural forecasting pipelines are highly sensitive to preprocessing decisions. For this reason, scaling is performed within each walk-forward fold rather than on the full sample. In each fold, the scalers are fit exclusively on the training set and then applied to the validation and test observations. This procedure prevents information from future observations from entering the estimation process through normalization parameters. If the mean, variance, or range used for scaling were computed with test-set information, the resulting forecasts would no longer represent a valid out-of-sample exercise.

The same principle governs sequence construction and target alignment. Each input sequence is built only from information available up to its forecasting origin, and each target corresponds to the volatility proxy observed at the specified horizon. This alignment is especially important in hybrid models because leakage may arise not only from the neural network itself, but also from feature generation, benchmark estimation, scaling, or horizon shifting. The revised pipeline therefore applies consistent temporal discipline to all models: benchmark parameters, GARCH-based inputs, scalers, and LSTM forecasts are generated separately within each fold using only the information available at that stage of the experiment.

Reproducibility is addressed through fixed random seeds, documented dependencies, and consistent implementation settings. The chapter also notes that TensorFlow executions on CPU may activate oneDNN optimizations, which can introduce small numerical differences across runs. This does not undermine the analysis, provided that the qualitative ranking of models, the direction of loss differentials, and the main empirical conclusions remain stable. In computational financial research, the relevant objective is therefore functional reproducibility: obtaining consistent patterns, magnitudes, and conclusions under the same documented pipeline, rather than requiring exact bit-level equality across hardware and software environments.

4.6 Computational Complexity and the Criterion of Parsimony

The computational burden of the revised pipeline comes from two sources: estimating the benchmark suite and training the LSTM for each asset, forecasting horizon, and walk-forward fold. The persistence and EWMA benchmarks add little computational cost, whereas GARCH(1,1) and the asymmetric GARCH specification require repeated econometric estimation. The LSTM is the most computationally intensive component, but its compact architecture keeps the overall workflow feasible on a standard CPU.

This consideration has methodological and practical implications. In financial applications, predictive performance must be weighed against training cost, deployment complexity, auditability, and model-governance requirements. A parsimonious hybrid model with economically interpretable inputs and moderate execution time may therefore be more useful in institutional settings than a more complex architecture that offers only marginal accuracy gains but is difficult to validate or maintain. For this reason, the proposed methodology should be understood not only as a forecasting exercise, but also as an attempt to balance accuracy, traceability, computational feasibility, and operational governance.

This balance also motivates the evaluation strategy presented in the next section, where all models are assessed under a common temporal protocol, benchmark structure, and multi-horizon design.

5. EXPERIMENTAL DESIGN, TEMPORAL VALIDATION, AND BENCHMARK EVALUATION

5.1 General Evaluation Logic

The evaluation design assesses whether the proposed hybrid GARCH-LSTM model provides incremental forecasting value relative to a benchmark suite that includes both operational rules and econometric specifications. Rather than comparing the hybrid model only with GARCH(1,1), the revised design evaluates it against persistence, EWMA, GARCH(1,1), and an asymmetric GARCH-type benchmark. This structure makes the comparison more demanding and directly tests whether the LSTM component adds information beyond simple carry-forward behavior, weighted volatility updating, and classical conditional-variance modeling.

The empirical assessment is organized in three stages. The first is an initial diagnostic comparison for $h = 1$. The second is an expanding-window walk-forward validation with five folds. The third is a multi-horizon evaluation for $h = 1, 5$, and 10. Together, these stages move the analysis beyond a single point comparison and support a more robust interpretation of model performance across time and forecast horizons. The initial split provides a preliminary diagnostic, whereas the walk-forward and multi-horizon exercises provide stronger evidence on temporal stability and horizon-dependent predictive performance.

5.2 Expanding-Window Walk-Forward

The walk-forward design uses an expanding training window and a fixed-size test block across five folds. This structure is appropriate for financial time-series forecasting because it approximates the way a predictive system would be updated in practice: the model is estimated using information available up to a given point and is then evaluated on a subsequent, unseen block. After each fold, the training window is expanded to incorporate newly available observations, and the process is repeated.

In the revised empirical design, all benchmarks and the hybrid model are evaluated under the same expanding-window structure. Model parameters are estimated or updated only with information contained in the corresponding training window, and forecasts are generated for the associated future test block. This common protocol strengthens comparability across models and ensures that no benchmark benefits from information unavailable at the forecasting origin.

The use of an expanding window, rather than a purely rolling window, is motivated by two considerations. First, in moderately sized daily samples, retaining additional historical observations can stabilize GARCH estimation and provide the LSTM with a richer learning history. Second, the design is consistent with operational environments in which institutions accumulate data and recalibrate models periodically without necessarily discarding older observations. This choice should not be interpreted as universally superior, however. In markets characterized by pronounced structural breaks, a rolling window may adapt more quickly; accordingly, the limitations section identifies the comparison between expanding and rolling schemes as a relevant direction for future research.

5.3 Multi-Horizon Evaluation

Volatility forecasts are rarely used at a single horizon. Risk managers may require one-day forecasts for tactical limit setting while also relying on longer-horizon signals for hedging, allocation, or exposure planning. An evaluation restricted to $h = 1$ would therefore provide an incomplete view of model performance. For this reason, the design extends the analysis to $h = 5$ and $h = 10$, while preserving the same target construction, expanding-window walk-forward protocol, and benchmark suite across horizons. Persistence, EWMA, GARCH(1,1), the asymmetric GARCH-type model, and the proposed hybrid model are thus evaluated under a common multi-horizon framework.

This design makes it possible to assess not only whether the hybrid improves upon GARCH(1,1), but also whether its relative performance remains stable when compared with simpler operational rules and asymmetric econometric alternatives. The interpretation of performance is therefore no longer tied to a single baseline or forecasting horizon. Instead, it becomes an assessment of robustness across assets, horizons, benchmarks, and loss functions.

A reasonable expectation is that forecast errors will increase and that the relative advantage of the hybrid model may decline as the horizon lengthens. As h increases, uncertainty accumulates, the connection between the current information set and the future volatility target weakens, and the memory contained in a fixed input window may become less informative. Multi-horizon evaluation therefore does more than report performance at different values of h; it characterizes the horizon-dependent value added by the hybrid architecture.

5.4 Evaluation Metrics

Forecast accuracy is assessed for all benchmarks and for the proposed hybrid model using three metrics: mean squared error (MSE), mean absolute error (MAE), and QLIKE. MSE penalizes large errors more heavily and is therefore useful when severe forecast failures are particularly relevant. MAE is less sensitive to extreme errors and provides a straightforward measure of average absolute deviation. QLIKE is included because it is specifically relevant for comparing volatility forecasts when the observed target is an imperfect proxy for latent volatility (Patton, 2011). Where applicable, the tables also report $\Delta QLIKE = QLIKE_{\text{Hybrid}} - QLIKE_{\text{GARCH}}$; the sign convention is stated in each table note, so that negative values indicate lower loss for the hybrid model when the differential is defined as Hybrid minus Benchmark.

Using MSE, MAE, and QLIKE together reduces the risk of interpreting performance through a single criterion. A model may produce large reductions in squared error while showing more moderate improvements under a loss function better suited to the volatility-proxy problem. Such differences are not contradictory; they provide information about how model performance changes across alternative notions of forecast accuracy. Evidence is more persuasive when the same general conclusion is supported across several metrics.

Because the revised comparison includes multiple benchmarks, model rankings are reported by asset, forecasting horizon, and loss function. This structure avoids relying on a single aggregate measure and helps identify whether the hybrid model performs consistently across evaluation criteria or whether its advantage is concentrated in specific forecasting conditions.

5.5 Comparability Across Assets and Design Constraints

A deliberate design choice in this chapter is to maintain a homogeneous methodological configuration across ^GSPC, EURUSD=X, and BTC-USD. The same lookback window, feature structure, number of walk-forward folds, forecasting horizons, and loss functions are applied to all three assets. This uniformity strengthens comparability because differences in model performance are less likely to reflect unequal tuning intensity or asset-specific optimization.

This choice also involves a trade-off. Individual assets may benefit from different lookback lengths, architectures, or hyperparameter settings. However, the objective of the chapter is not to maximize performance for each market separately, but to assess whether a moderate and consistently specified hybrid model can generate replicable improvements across heterogeneous financial series. A uniform configuration therefore supports a cleaner comparative interpretation of the results.

The same logic applies to the benchmark suite. Persistence, EWMA, GARCH(1,1), the asymmetric GARCH-type benchmark, and the hybrid GARCH-LSTM model are evaluated under the same assets, horizons, folds, and loss functions. This common evaluation structure reduces the risk that observed differences arise from inconsistent experimental conditions and provides a more reliable basis for assessing the incremental value of the hybrid approach.

5.6 Forecast Comparison and Statistical Testing Strategy

Beyond reporting average forecast errors, the revised design incorporates a formal statistical comparison of predictive accuracy. This step is necessary because lower average loss does not, by itself, establish that the difference between competing models is statistically meaningful. The comparison is based on out-of-sample loss differentials. For each asset, forecast horizon, and loss function, the loss sequence generated by the hybrid GARCH-LSTM model is compared with the corresponding loss sequence from each benchmark.

The Diebold-Mariano test (Diebold & Mariano, 1995) is used as the primary procedure for pairwise predictive-accuracy comparison. For one-step-ahead forecasts, the test evaluates whether the mean loss differential between two competing forecasts differs significantly from zero. For multi-step horizons, forecast errors may display serial correlation because forecast targets can overlap; therefore, heteroskedasticity- and autocorrelation-consistent standard errors are required. This adjustment is especially relevant for h = 5 and h = 10.

This testing strategy complements the descriptive evaluation based on MSE, MAE, and QLIKE. The error tables report the direction and magnitude of performance differences, whereas formal tests indicate whether those differences are statistically reliable under the out-of-sample evaluation protocol.

For each pairwise comparison, the loss differential is defined as benchmark loss minus hybrid-model loss. A positive average loss differential therefore indicates that the hybrid model produces lower loss than the benchmark. The null hypothesis is equal predictive accuracy, while the alternative hypothesis is that the average loss differential differs from zero. This procedure is applied separately by asset, forecasting horizon, loss function, and benchmark model.

$$d_t = L\left(e_t^{\text{Benchmark}}\right) - L\left(e_t^{\text{Hybrid}}\right)$$

$$DM = \frac{\bar{d}}{\sqrt{\text{Var}(\bar{d})}}$$

$$\widehat{\text{Var}}(\bar{d}) = \frac{1}{T}\left[\gamma_0 + 2\sum_{k=1}^{h-1}\gamma_k\right]$$

In the empirical tables, statistical significance is reported using conventional p-value thresholds. A positive and statistically significant loss differential is interpreted as evidence that the hybrid model provides a reliable improvement over the corresponding benchmark. A non-significant result is interpreted more cautiously: it may indicate that the hybrid model has lower average loss, but that the observed difference is not strong enough to establish statistical superiority under the selected out-of-sample evaluation protocol.

6. EMPIRICAL RESULTS AND STATISTICAL FORECAST COMPARISON

This section presents the empirical evidence generated by the revised evaluation design. To maintain continuity with the initial specification, the analysis begins with the GARCH(1,1)-versus-hybrid comparison for the one-day horizon. It then moves to walk-forward validation and multi-horizon results, before extending the assessment to the full benchmark suite comprising persistence, EWMA, GARCH(1,1), and an asymmetric GARCH-type model. Finally, QLIKE-based Diebold-Mariano tests are reported to evaluate whether the observed out-of-sample loss differences are statistically meaningful. This progression separates descriptive performance patterns from formal predictive-accuracy evidence and supports a more cautious interpretation of the hybrid model's contribution.

6.1 Initial Comparison for h = 1

Table 2 reports the initial one-day-ahead comparison between the GARCH(1,1) benchmark and the hybrid GARCH-LSTM model. This comparison is retained to preserve continuity with the original empirical specification, while the following subsections provide a more demanding assessment through walk-forward validation, multi-horizon evaluation, a broader benchmark suite, and formal Diebold-Mariano tests.

Table 2a. Initial comparison (h = 1) between GARCH(1,1) and the hybrid GARCH-LSTM model Panel A. Forecast-error metrics

Ticker	MSE GARCH	MSE Hybrid	MSE improvement (%)	MAE GARCH	MAE Hybrid	MAE improvement (%)
BTC-USD	2.312320e-05	2.960160e-06	87.20	0.00413779	0.00129541	68.69
EURUSD=X	4.906240e-07	9.897590e-08	79.83	0.00055253	0.00023218	57.98
^GSPC	4.157440e-06	7.750750e-07	81.36	0.00130022	0.00053110	59.15

Table 2b. Panel B. QLIKE comparison

Ticker	QLIKE GARCH	QLIKE Hybrid	Delta QLIKE (Hybrid - GARCH)
BTC-USD	-6.491143	-6.553381	-0.062238
EURUSD=X	-9.855503	-9.894687	-0.039184
^GSPC	-8.527793	-8.573584	-0.045791

Note. Lower MSE, MAE, and QLIKE values indicate better forecast accuracy. Negative Delta QLIKE values indicate lower QLIKE loss for the hybrid model relative to GARCH(1,1).

The results indicate that the hybrid model reduces all three forecast-error measures relative to GARCH(1,1) in the initial h = 1 comparison. For BTC-USD, MSE decreases from 2.312320e-05 to 2.960160e-06, corresponding to an 87.20% improvement, while MAE declines from 0.00413779 to 0.00129541, equivalent to a 68.69% improvement. For EURUSD=X, the corresponding reductions are 79.83% for MSE and 57.98% for MAE. For ^GSPC, the improvements are 81.36% and 59.15%, respectively. In addition, Delta QLIKE is negative for all three assets, indicating lower QLIKE loss for the hybrid model in this initial comparison.

These findings provide an initial indication that the hybrid specification captures information not fully represented by the standalone GARCH(1,1) benchmark. The strongest reduction appears for BTC-USD, which is consistent with the view that assets with more irregular volatility dynamics may provide greater scope for a sequential nonlinear layer to extract complementary patterns. Nevertheless, this interpretation should remain cautious. A single initial split is useful for diagnostic purposes, but it is not sufficient to establish temporal robustness or general predictive superiority.

Figure 1. Forecast of the volatility proxy (last 250 observations) for ^GSPC (h = 1): y_true vs. GARCH(1,1) vs. Hybrid (GARCH+LSTM).

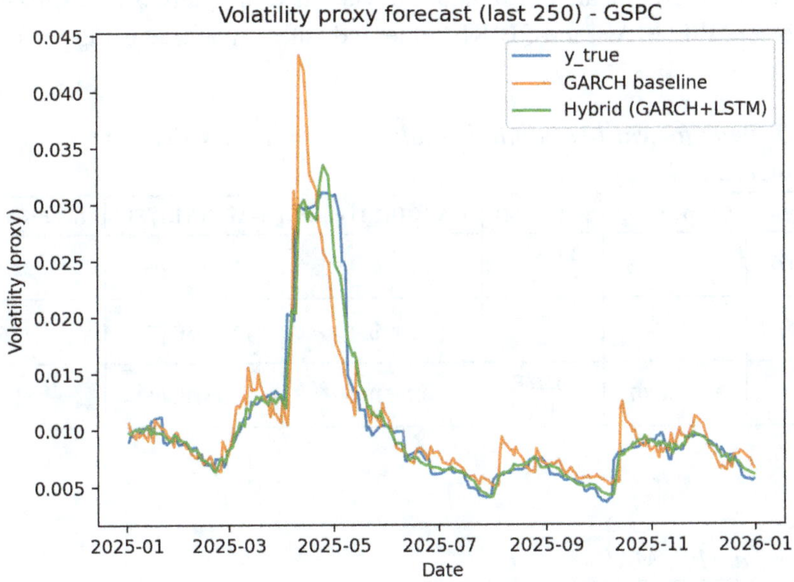

Figure 1 provides a visual complement to the numerical results by comparing the observed volatility proxy with the GARCH(1,1) and hybrid forecasts for the last 250 observations of ^GSPC. This visual evidence should be interpreted descriptively rather than as an independent test. In this segment, the hybrid forecast appears to follow changes in the amplitude of the proxy more closely and to deviate less during periods of elevated variation. This inspection supports the error-based evidence in Table 2, but it does not replace the more robust walk-forward and multi-horizon analyses that follow.

6.2 Walk-Forward Validation for h = 1

Table 3 reports mean forecast errors and standard deviations across five expanding-window walk-forward folds. The results show that the improvement observed in the initial split remains present under a more demanding temporal validation design. For BTC-USD, the hybrid model reduces average MSE and MAE by 85.25% and 68.45%, respectively. The corresponding reductions are 76.63% and 54.65% for EURUSD=X, and 81.00% and 60.32% for ^GSPC. The average Delta QLIKE is also negative in all three cases, indicating lower loss for the hybrid model relative to GARCH(1,1).

The table reports mean and standard deviation values across five walk-forward folds. Lower MSE, MAE, and QLIKE values indicate better forecasting performance.

Table 3a. Walk-forward validation results for h = 1 with five expanding-window folds Panel A. MSE

Ticker	Hybrid mean	Hybrid SD	GARCH(1,1) mean	GARCH(1,1) SD	Improvement (%)
BTC-USD	3.9569E-06	2.1483E-06	2.6818E-05	7.7466E-06	85.25
EURUSD=X	9.9316E-08	3.7261E-08	4.2495E-07	2.2045E-07	76.63
^GSPC	7.2100E-07	7.0228E-07	3.7951E-06	2.9063E-06	81.00

Table 3b. Panel B. MAE

Ticker	Hybrid mean	Hybrid SD	GARCH(1,1) mean	GARCH(1,1) SD	Improvement (%)
BTC-USD	0.001388	0.000244	0.004399	0.000505	68.45
EURUSD=X	0.000232	0.000039	0.000511	0.000144	54.65
^GSPC	0.000533	0.000193	0.001344	0.000348	60.32

Table 3c. Panel C. QLIKE

Ticker	Hybrid mean	Hybrid SD	GARCH(1,1) mean	GARCH(1,1) SD	Delta QLIKE mean
BTC-USD	-6.57433	0.35382	-6.50263	0.33291	-0.07170
EURUSD=X	-9.88596	0.46635	-9.85383	0.46511	-0.03213
^GSPC	-8.43035	0.56657	-8.38468	0.55971	-0.04567

Note. SD = standard deviation across five walk-forward folds. Improvement (%) is computed relative to GARCH(1,1). Negative Delta QLIKE values indicate lower loss for the hybrid GARCH-LSTM model.

These results suggest that the hybrid model's advantage is not driven solely by the initial split. Although variability across folds remains visible, particularly in the more volatile series, the mean results consistently favor the hybrid specification. This pattern supports a cautious interpretation: under the h = 1 walk-forward setting, the GARCH-informed LSTM appears to capture a recurrent out-of-sample signal. Nevertheless, the magnitude of the improvement should still be interpreted in relation to fold dispersion and to the broader benchmark comparisons reported later in the chapter.

Figure 2. MAE (lower is better): mean and standard deviation in 5 folds (walk-forward, h = 1) for BTC-USD, EURUSD=X, and ^GSPC

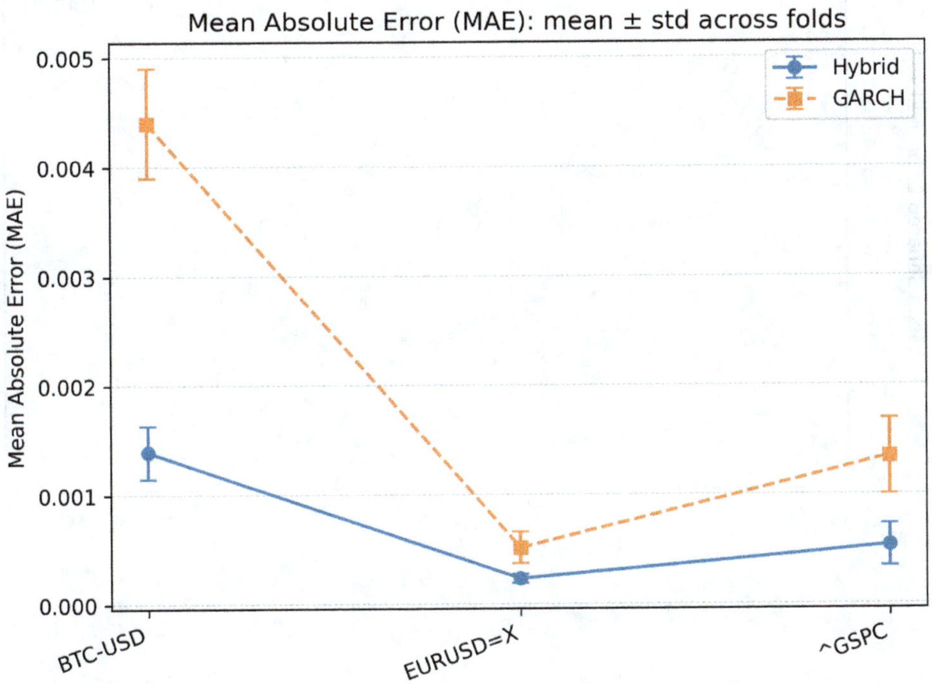

Figure 3. MSE (lower is better): mean and standard deviation in 5 folds (walk-forward, h = 1) for BTC-USD, EURUSD=X, and ^GSPC

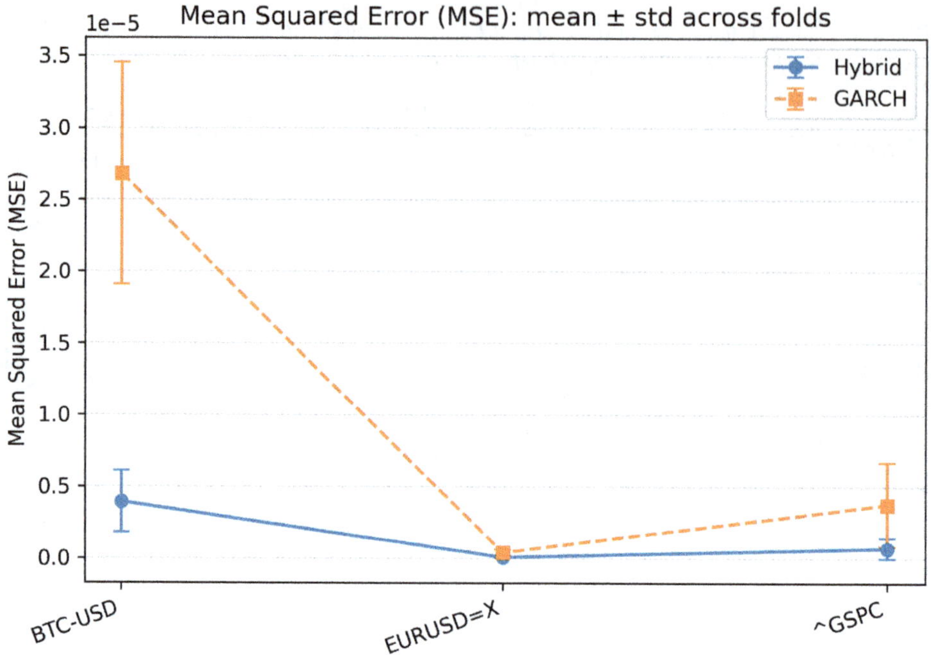

Figure 4. QLIKE (lower is better): mean and standard deviation in 5 folds (walk-forward, h = 1) for BTC-USD, EURUSD=X, and ^GSPC

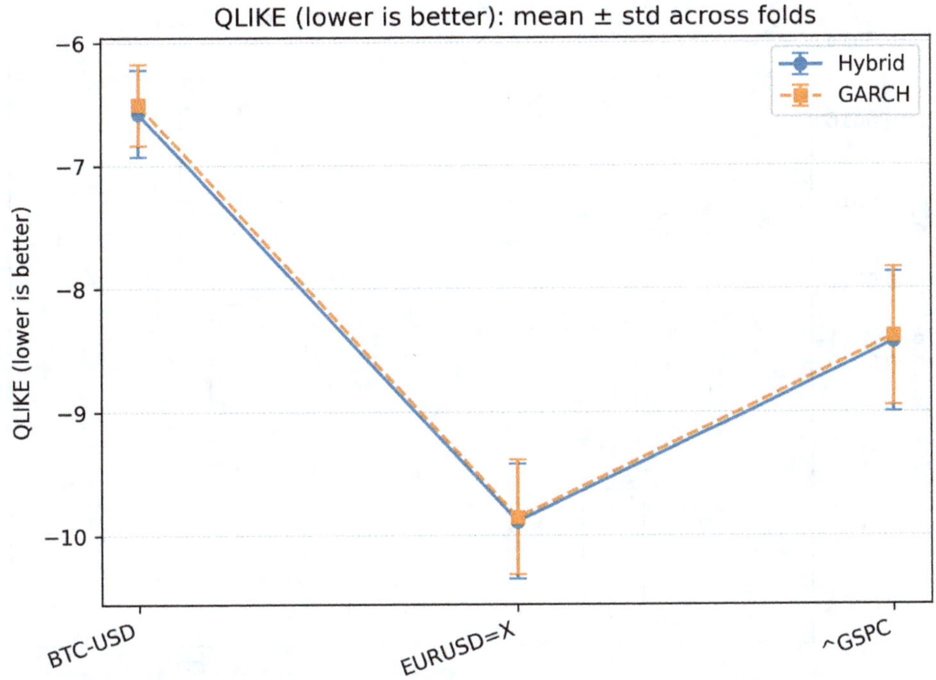

Figures 2, 3, and 4 provide a visual summary of the walk-forward results by metric and asset. The separation between the two models is most pronounced for BTC-USD, intermediate for ^GSPC, and smaller but still favorable to the hybrid for EURUSD=X. This pattern is consistent with the view that a nonlinear sequential layer may add more visible value when volatility dynamics are more irregular. At the same time, the EURUSD=X result is relevant because it shows that the usefulness of the hybrid specification is not limited to highly volatile assets.

In addition to average performance, fold-level inspection for ^GSPC provides information about the distribution of forecast errors across validation folds.

Figure 5. Distribution of MAE by fold for ^GSPC (boxplots): comparison between the hybrid model and the GARCH(1,1) baseline

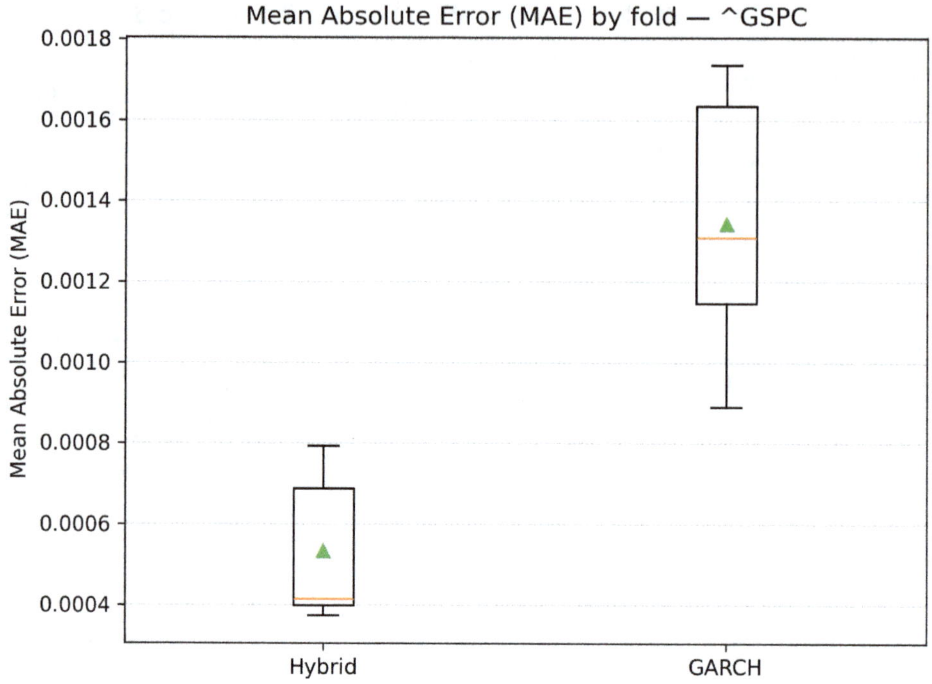

Figure 6. Distribution of MSE by fold for ^GSPC (boxplots): comparison between the hybrid model and the GARCH(1,1) baseline

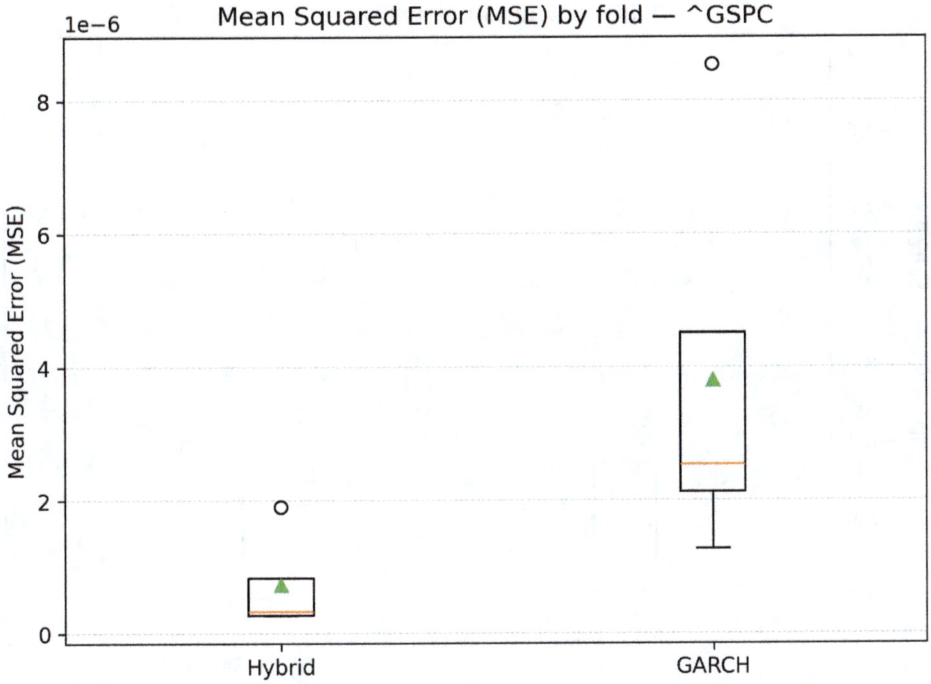

Figure 7. Distribution of QLIKE by fold for ^GSPC (boxplots; lower is better): comparison between the hybrid model and the GARCH (1,1) baseline

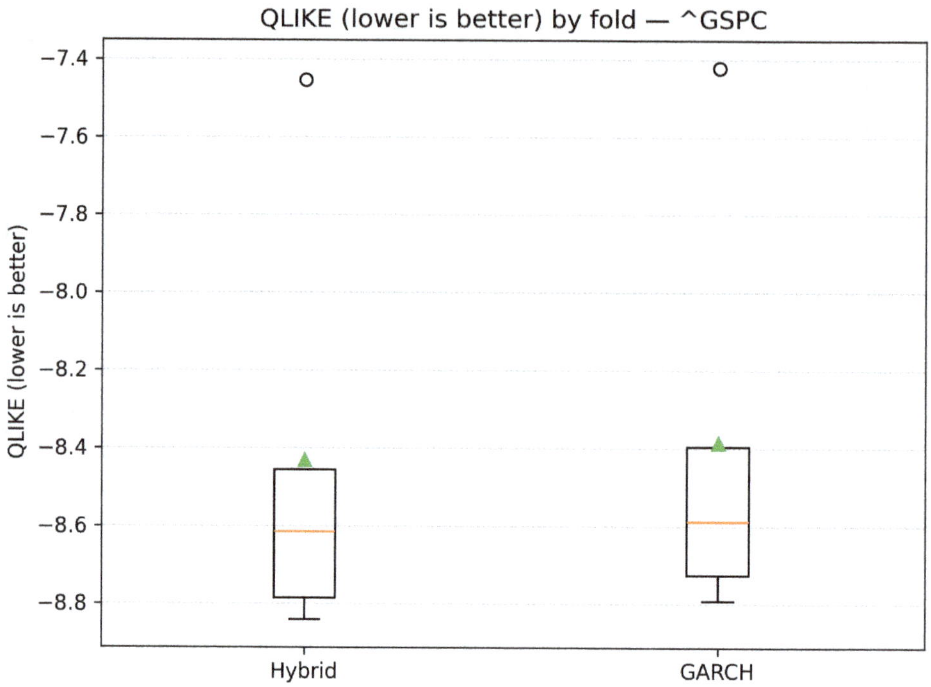

The boxplots complement the average metrics by showing that the separation between the hybrid model and the GARCH(1,1) baseline does not appear to depend on a single extreme fold. They therefore provide descriptive evidence of temporal robustness. Even so, these figures should not be treated as a substitute for formal inference; the Diebold-Mariano tests reported in Section 6.5 are needed to assess whether the observed loss differences are statistically meaningful.

6.3 Multi-Horizon Evaluation

Table 4 extends the walk-forward analysis to the five- and ten-step-ahead horizons, while retaining h = 1 as a reference point. The results show a consistent but horizon-dependent pattern. Relative to GARCH(1,1), the hybrid model continues to produce negative ΔMSE, ΔMAE, and ΔQLIKE values across the reported asset-horizon combinations, indicating lower average loss. However, the magnitude of the improvement declines as the forecasting horizon increases.

For BTC-USD, MSE improvement decreases from 85.30% at h = 1 to 52.45% at h = 5 and 25.84% at h = 10. EURUSD=X follows a similar pattern, with MSE improvements of 77.42%, 45.15%, and 17.10%, respectively. For ^GSPC, the decline is more pronounced: the MSE improvement falls from 80.61% at h = 1 to 14.19% at h = 5 and 6.96% at h = 10. The MAE results show the same general deterioration as the horizon lengthens. QLIKE also remains favorable to the hybrid model, although the negative differentials become smaller as h increases.

Table 4a. Walk-forward multi-horizon results: deltas between the hybrid GARCH-LSTM model and GARCH(1,1) (Panel A. MSE results)

Ticker	h	ΔMSE (mean)	ΔMSE (std)	MSE improvement (%)
BTC-USD	1	-2.287520e-05	5.833470e-06	85.30
BTC-USD	5	-1.783580e-05	5.849120e-06	52.45
BTC-USD	10	-1.326030e-05	1.050850e-05	25.84
EURUSD=X	1	-3.289830e-07	1.822260e-07	77.42
EURUSD=X	5	-2.548660e-07	1.645180e-07	45.15
EURUSD=X	10	-1.393080e-07	1.497440e-07	17.10
^GSPC	1	-3.059300e-06	2.178980e-06	80.61
^GSPC	5	-1.058320e-06	1.096880e-06	14.19
^GSPC	10	-4.343960e-07	1.232000e-06	6.96

Table 4b. Panel B. MAE results

Ticker	h	ΔMAE (mean)	ΔMAE (std)	MAE improvement (%)
BTC-USD	1	-0.00298256	3.600620e-04	67.80
BTC-USD	5	-0.00177031	3.875940e-04	36.24
BTC-USD	10	-8.691250e-04	4.753010e-04	14.87
EURUSD=X	1	-2.904600e-04	1.090670e-04	56.81
EURUSD=X	5	-1.666830e-04	9.604270e-05	28.49
EURUSD=X	10	-5.107490e-05	7.082370e-05	7.40
^GSPC	1	-8.165550e-04	1.824210e-04	60.75
^GSPC	5	-2.479130e-04	1.459410e-04	16.53
^GSPC	10	-7.343550e-05	1.224500e-04	4.90

Table 4c. Panel C. QLIKE results

Ticker	h	ΔQLIKE (mean)	ΔQLIKE (std)
BTC-USD	1	-0.0715693	0.0251987
BTC-USD	5	-0.0494410	0.0221345
BTC-USD	10	-0.0317859	0.0214964
EURUSD=X	1	-0.0328300	0.0158583
EURUSD=X	5	-0.0219104	0.0137171
EURUSD=X	10	-0.0097560	0.0106812
^GSPC	1	-0.0454104	0.0151450
^GSPC	5	-0.0248275	0.0154804
^GSPC	10	-0.0136894	0.0138517

Note. Deltas are calculated as Hybrid - GARCH(1,1). Negative values indicate lower loss for the hybrid model. Improvement percentages are reported for MSE and MAE because these metrics are directly comparable in relative-error terms; for QLIKE, the table reports mean and standard deviation of the loss differential.

Figure 8. Walk-forward multi-horizon: ΔMSE (Hybrid - GARCH) across horizons (h = 1, 5, 10) for BTC-USD, EURUSD=X, and ^GSPC. Negative values indicate hybrid improvement.

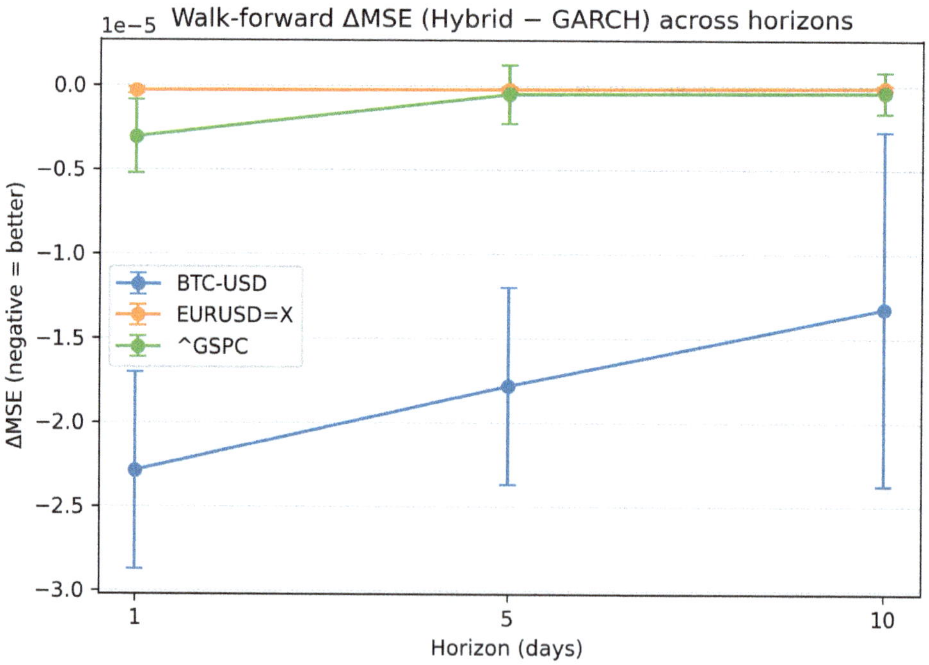

Figure 9. Walk-forward multi-horizon: ΔQLIKE (Hybrid - GARCH) for BTC-USD. Negative values indicate lower loss (better)

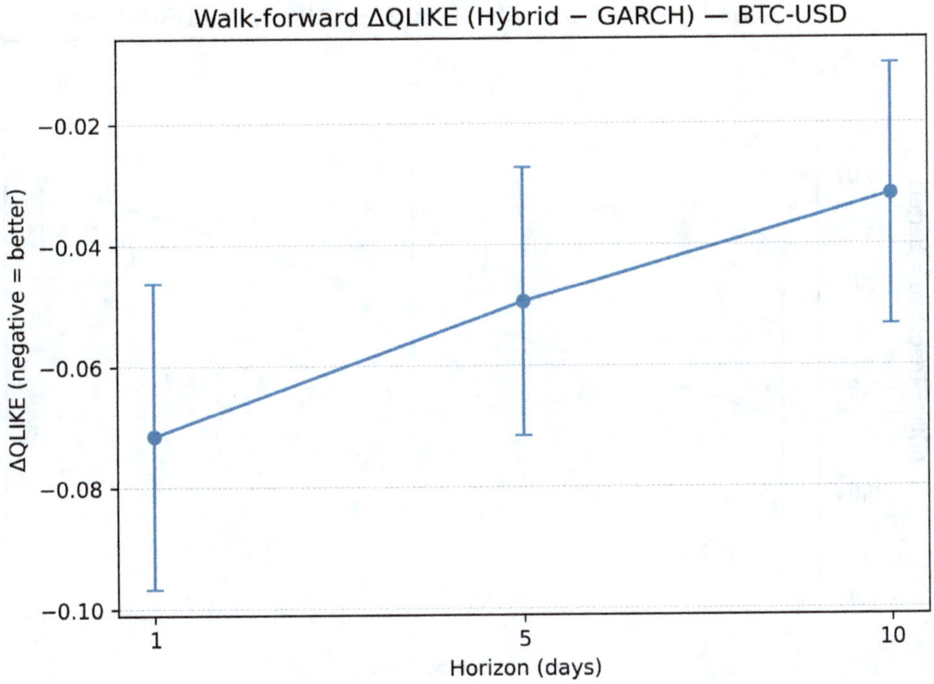

Figure 10. Walk-forward multi-horizon: ΔQLIKE (Hybrid - GARCH) for EURUSD=X. Negative values indicate lower loss (better)

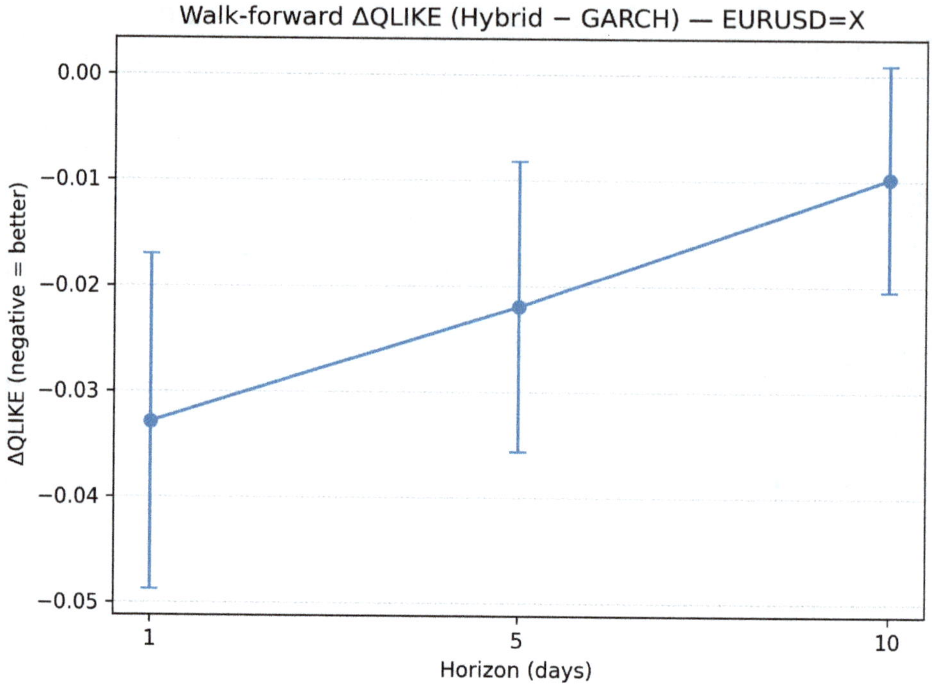

Figure 11. Walk-forward multi-horizon: ΔQLIKE (Hybrid - GARCH) for ^GSPC. Negative values indicate lower loss (better)

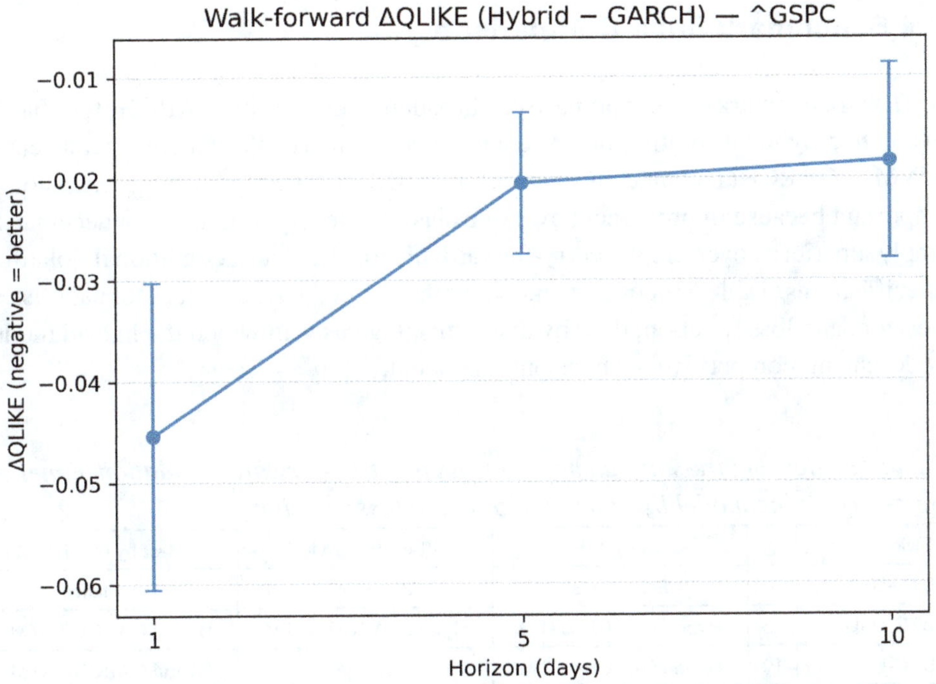

The visual evidence reinforces the same horizon-dependent interpretation. The hybrid model retains a favorable average position relative to GARCH(1,1), but the distance between the models narrows as the target moves farther from the current information set. This pattern is methodologically plausible: as h increases, accumulated uncertainty weakens the relationship between recent GARCH-informed inputs and the future volatility proxy.

These results should therefore be interpreted as evidence of conditional, rather than uniform, superiority. The hybrid model does not dominate with the same intensity across all horizons. Its strongest advantage appears when recent nonlinear volatility patterns remain informative, whereas the relative gain becomes more modest as the forecast horizon expands.

Taken together, the multi-horizon results support three conclusions about the original GARCH(1,1)-based comparison. First, the hybrid model improves upon GARCH(1,1) not only in the initial split, but also under walk-forward validation. Second, the improvement remains favorable across $h = 1$, $h = 5$, and $h = 10$, although its magnitude decreases with horizon length. Third, because these results are still based on a single econometric comparator, the next subsection broadens the analysis to the full benchmark suite and then assesses whether the observed loss differences are statistically meaningful through Diebold-Mariano tests.

6.4 Benchmark Suite Comparison

The benchmark-suite comparison broadens the initial GARCH(1,1)-based evaluation by incorporating operational and econometric alternatives: persistence, EWMA, GARCH(1,1), and an asymmetric GARCH-type model. This extension is important because improvement over one classical benchmark does not necessarily imply superiority over simpler carry-forward rules or alternative conditional-volatility specifications. Table 5 reports the model with the lowest average loss for each asset, horizon, and loss function, thereby distinguishing cases in which the hybrid model is dominant, competitive, or horizon-dependent.

Table 5a. Benchmark-suite comparison under walk-forward validation Panel A. Best-performing model by asset, horizon, and loss function

Ticker	h	Best by MSE	Best by MAE	Best by QLIKE
BTC-USD	1	Persistence	Persistence	Persistence
BTC-USD	5	Hybrid GARCH-LSTM	Hybrid GARCH-LSTM	Hybrid GARCH-LSTM
BTC-USD	10	Hybrid GARCH-LSTM	EWMA	Hybrid GARCH-LSTM
EURUSD=X	1	Persistence	Persistence	Persistence
EURUSD=X	5	Hybrid GARCH-LSTM	Hybrid GARCH-LSTM	Hybrid GARCH-LSTM
EURUSD=X	10	EWMA	EWMA	EWMA
^GSPC	1	Persistence	Persistence	Persistence
^GSPC	5	Hybrid GARCH-LSTM	Hybrid GARCH-LSTM	Hybrid GARCH-LSTM
^GSPC	10	Hybrid GARCH-LSTM	Hybrid GARCH-LSTM	Hybrid GARCH-LSTM

Table 5b. Panel B. Concise interpretation of the benchmark ranking

Ticker	h	Interpretation
BTC-USD	1	Persistence leads at the shortest horizon, indicating strong carry-forward behavior in the volatility proxy.
BTC-USD	5	The hybrid ranks first across all metrics, suggesting incremental value beyond immediate persistence.
BTC-USD	10	The hybrid leads in MSE and QLIKE, while EWMA is preferable under MAE.
EURUSD=X	1	Persistence dominates, consistent with high short-term continuity in FX volatility.
EURUSD=X	5	The hybrid becomes the strongest model across the three metrics.
EURUSD=X	10	EWMA performs best, indicating that a transparent weighted rule remains competitive for longer FX horizons.

continued on following page

Table 5b. Continued

Ticker	h	Interpretation
^GSPC	1	Persistence performs best at the immediate horizon, while the hybrid remains a close comparator.
^GSPC	5	The hybrid ranks first across all metrics at the medium horizon.
^GSPC	10	The hybrid remains best across all metrics, supporting robust value beyond one-day forecasts.

Note. Lower values are better for MSE, MAE, and QLIKE. The table reports the model with the lowest average loss within each asset-horizon-metric combination. The ranking is descriptive and is complemented by Diebold-Mariano tests in the following table.

The benchmark-suite results indicate that model rankings depend strongly on the forecasting horizon. At h = 1, persistence ranks first for BTC-USD, EURUSD=X, and ^GSPC, which is consistent with the strong short-run continuity of the 21-day volatility proxy. This finding does not contradict the usefulness of the hybrid model; rather, it shows that immediate volatility forecasts can be difficult to improve when the current proxy already carries substantial information.

At medium horizons, the hybrid model becomes more competitive. At h = 5, it ranks first across MSE, MAE, and QLIKE for BTC-USD, EURUSD=X, and ^GSPC, suggesting that the LSTM component adds incremental value once simple persistence begins to weaken. At h = 10, the evidence remains favorable but more asset-specific: the hybrid leads for BTC-USD under MSE and QLIKE and for ^GSPC across all three metrics, whereas EWMA performs best for EURUSD=X across the reported metrics and for BTC-USD under MAE.

Overall, Table 5 supports a conditional interpretation of the hybrid architecture. The GARCH-LSTM model adds value beyond GARCH(1,1) and the asymmetric GARCH-type benchmark in several settings, especially at medium horizons, but it does not uniformly dominate the full benchmark suite. Because these rankings are descriptive, the next subsection evaluates whether the observed QLIKE loss differentials are statistically meaningful using Diebold-Mariano tests.

6.5 Diebold-Mariano Tests of Predictive Accuracy

The Diebold-Mariano tests complement the benchmark-suite ranking by evaluating whether the observed differences in out-of-sample predictive losses are statistically meaningful. The tests are based on the loss series generated within the walk-forward procedure. The loss differential is defined as benchmark loss minus hybrid-model loss; therefore, positive values indicate lower QLIKE loss for the hybrid GARCH-LSTM model, whereas negative values indicate lower QLIKE loss for the corresponding benchmark.

The tests are reported under QLIKE because this loss function is particularly relevant for volatility forecast comparison when the observed target is an imperfect proxy for latent volatility. Table 6 compares the hybrid model against persistence, EWMA, GARCH(1,1), and GJR-GARCH across assets and forecasting horizons. The table distinguishes lower average predictive loss from statistically reliable predictive improvement, which is essential for interpreting the results beyond descriptive rankings.

The loss differential is defined as benchmark QLIKE loss minus hybrid-model QLIKE loss. Positive values favor the hybrid model; negative values favor the benchmark.

Table 6a. QLIKE-based Diebold-Mariano tests comparing the hybrid GARCH-LSTM model against benchmark models Panel A. BTC-USD

h	Benchmark	Mean d	DM statistic	p-value	Result
1	Persistence	-0.0019	-1.2392	0.2153	Persistence lower average loss; not significant
1	EWMA	0.0242	14.5187	<0.001	Hybrid significantly better
1	GARCH(1,1)	0.0716	24.2964	<0.001	Hybrid significantly better
1	GJR-GARCH	0.0706	24.1440	<0.001	Hybrid significantly better
5	Persistence	0.0395	3.1962	0.0014	Hybrid significantly better
5	EWMA	0.0192	3.9342	<0.001	Hybrid significantly better
5	GARCH(1,1)	0.0494	9.5142	<0.001	Hybrid significantly better
5	GJR-GARCH	0.0494	9.5324	<0.001	Hybrid significantly better
10	Persistence	0.0953	2.8004	0.0051	Hybrid significantly better
10	EWMA	0.0246	1.5545	0.1201	Hybrid lower average loss; not significant
10	GARCH(1,1)	0.0318	5.2772	<0.001	Hybrid significantly better
10	GJR-GARCH	0.0323	5.3235	<0.001	Hybrid significantly better

Table 6b. Panel B. EURUSD=X

h	Benchmark	Mean d	DM statistic	p-value	Result
1	Persistence	-0.0021	-4.1218	<0.001	Persistence significantly better
1	EWMA	0.0106	14.2893	<0.001	Hybrid significantly better
1	GARCH(1,1)	0.0328	18.9311	<0.001	Hybrid significantly better
1	GJR-GARCH	0.0374	20.2643	<0.001	Hybrid significantly better
5	Persistence	0.0093	2.5861	0.0097	Hybrid significantly better
5	EWMA	0.0017	0.9480	0.3431	Hybrid lower average loss; not significant
5	GARCH(1,1)	0.0219	5.6815	<0.001	Hybrid significantly better
5	GJR-GARCH	0.0257	6.5077	<0.001	Hybrid significantly better
10	Persistence	0.0240	2.0707	0.0384	Hybrid significantly better

continued on following page

Table 6b. Continued

h	Benchmark	Mean d	DM statistic	p-value	Result
10	EWMA	-0.0037	-0.7531	0.4514	EWMA lower average loss; not significant
10	GARCH(1,1)	0.0098	1.9412	0.0522	Hybrid marginally better
10	GJR-GARCH	0.0123	2.4409	0.0146	Hybrid significantly better

Table 6c. Panel C. ^GSPC

h	Benchmark	Mean d	DM statistic	p-value	Result
1	Persistence	-0.0027	-3.6595	<0.001	Persistence significantly better
1	EWMA	0.0256	14.1967	<0.001	Hybrid significantly better
1	GARCH(1,1)	0.0454	16.8461	<0.001	Hybrid significantly better
1	GJR-GARCH	0.1236	20.8454	<0.001	Hybrid significantly better
5	Persistence	0.0168	2.4740	0.0134	Hybrid significantly better
5	EWMA	0.0199	3.3283	<0.001	Hybrid significantly better
5	GARCH(1,1)	0.0205	4.3932	<0.001	Hybrid significantly better
5	GJR-GARCH	0.0691	7.5929	<0.001	Hybrid significantly better
10	Persistence	0.0607	3.1306	0.0017	Hybrid significantly better
10	EWMA	0.0324	2.8271	0.0047	Hybrid significantly better
10	GARCH(1,1)	0.0183	2.5361	0.0112	Hybrid significantly better
10	GJR-GARCH	0.0438	3.4644	<0.001	Hybrid significantly better

Note. DM = Diebold-Mariano statistic; d = mean QLIKE loss differential. Statistical significance is interpreted using the p-value column. A non-significant result indicates that the lower average loss should be interpreted cautiously.

The Diebold-Mariano results are broadly consistent with the benchmark-suite comparison, but they also refine the interpretation of the hybrid model's performance. The hybrid GARCH-LSTM model significantly outperforms EWMA, GARCH(1,1), and GJR-GARCH in most asset-horizon combinations under QLIKE. This pattern is especially clear for BTC-USD and ^GSPC at medium and longer horizons, where the hybrid produces positive and statistically significant loss differentials against most, and in some cases all, benchmark models.

At the same time, the tests confirm that the hybrid model is not universally superior. At h = 1, the persistence benchmark performs better than the hybrid for EURUSD=X and ^GSPC, and those differences are statistically significant. For BTC-USD at h = 1, persistence also reports a lower average QLIKE loss, although the difference is not statistically significant. These findings are consistent with the descriptive benchmark ranking and indicate that, at very short horizons, the volatility proxy contains strong carry-forward information that can be difficult for a more complex model to improve upon.

The medium-horizon results are more favorable to the hybrid model. At h = 5, the hybrid significantly outperforms persistence, GARCH(1,1), and GJR-GARCH across all assets. Its advantage over EWMA is statistically significant for BTC-USD and ^GSPC, although not for EURUSD=X. This result suggests that the LSTM component adds value when immediate persistence becomes less dominant, while recent volatility dynamics remain informative for the forecast target.

At h = 10, the evidence remains favorable to the hybrid model but becomes more benchmark- and asset-dependent. The hybrid remains significantly better than most GARCH-type benchmarks and is particularly strong for ^GSPC. However, EWMA remains competitive for BTC-USD and EURUSD=X. In EURUSD=X at h = 10, EWMA reports a lower average QLIKE loss, although the difference is not statistically significant. This reinforces the interpretation that transparent operational benchmarks may remain difficult to dominate in some longer-horizon settings.

Overall, the Diebold-Mariano tests support a conditional interpretation of the hybrid model. The evidence indicates that the GARCH-LSTM specification provides statistically reliable improvements over classical GARCH-type benchmarks in most cases and frequently improves upon operational benchmarks as well. However, persistence remains highly competitive at the shortest horizon, and EWMA remains competitive in selected longer-horizon cases. The empirical contribution should therefore be interpreted as horizon-dependent and benchmark-sensitive rather than universal.

Taken together, the results of Chapter 6 support a more nuanced conclusion than the original GARCH-versus-hybrid comparison. The hybrid GARCH-LSTM model improves substantially upon GARCH(1,1) and GJR-GARCH across most assets and horizons, and it often performs competitively against EWMA and persistence. Nevertheless, the benchmark-suite rankings and Diebold-Mariano tests show that model performance depends on the asset, forecast horizon, benchmark, and loss function considered. The strongest evidence for the hybrid appears beyond the one-day horizon and against classical GARCH-type benchmarks under QLIKE loss.

7. DISCUSSION

7.1 General Interpretation of the Findings

The discussion begins from a central implication of the revised empirical design: the evidence is stronger precisely because it is more qualified. Relative to classical GARCH-type benchmarks, the hybrid GARCH-LSTM model delivers substantial and frequently statistically meaningful reductions in QLIKE loss across many asset-horizon combinations. At the same time, the benchmark-suite comparison shows that this advantage is not uniform. Persistence remains a strong comparator at h = 1, and EWMA remains competitive in selected longer-horizon cases, especially for EURUSD=X. The results therefore support a conditional view of hybridization: the proposed architecture adds value most clearly when immediate carry-forward dynamics weaken and when it is evaluated against GARCH-type specifications under temporally coherent validation.

This interpretation avoids two oversimplified conclusions. One would be to treat traditional econometric models as sufficient for all volatility-forecasting settings. The other would be to assume that deep learning models necessarily dominate simpler, more transparent benchmarks. The results support neither position. Instead, they point to a layered forecasting logic in which econometric structure, operational rules, and nonlinear sequential learning serve different comparative purposes and must be evaluated jointly.

From this perspective, the hybrid model should be understood as an extension of econometric volatility modeling rather than as a replacement for it. This view is consistent with Kim and Won (2018) and with the broader hybrid-volatility literature, which emphasizes the value of using GARCH-based signals as structured inputs for sequential learning. In the present chapter, the LSTM component does not learn from an unfiltered return series alone; it learns from a compact state representation informed by conditional volatility, standardized shocks, and recent return amplitude. The contribution therefore lies in showing when this GARCH-informed representation can produce statistically reliable gains beyond selected econometric and operational comparators.

7.2 Differences by Asset Type

The benchmark-suite results indicate that forecasting performance varies meaningfully across asset types. Once persistence, EWMA, GARCH(1,1), and GJR-GARCH are considered jointly, the interpretation becomes more asset-specific than a simple comparison between GARCH(1,1) and the hybrid model would suggest. The evidence therefore supports a differentiated reading of the hybrid model's value rather than a uniform claim across markets.

For BTC-USD, the evidence is strongest at medium and longer horizons. At h = 5, the hybrid model ranks first across MSE, MAE, and QLIKE, and the Diebold-Mariano tests show statistically significant QLIKE improvements against all benchmarks. At h = 10, the hybrid also performs best under MSE and QLIKE, although EWMA achieves lower MAE and remains statistically competitive under QLIKE. This pattern suggests that Bitcoin's more irregular volatility dynamics may provide greater scope for the LSTM component to extract nonlinear sequential information beyond that captured by GARCH-type models, particularly beyond the immediate one-day horizon.

EURUSD=X presents a more conditional profile. At h = 1, persistence is the strongest comparator, and the Diebold-Mariano test indicates that persistence significantly outperforms the hybrid model under QLIKE. At h = 5, the hybrid becomes the best-performing model across MSE, MAE, and QLIKE, although its QLIKE advantage over EWMA is not statistically significant. At h = 10, EWMA ranks first descriptively across the three metrics, while the hybrid remains competitive and continues to improve upon GARCH-type benchmarks. This outcome suggests that, for the FX series, transparent operational rules such as EWMA may capture a substantial part of the relevant volatility dynamics, especially at longer horizons.

For ^GSPC, the results are also horizon-dependent but more favorable to the hybrid model beyond h = 1. At the one-day horizon, persistence significantly outperforms the hybrid under QLIKE, indicating strong carry-forward information in short-term equity-index volatility. However, at h = 5 and h = 10, the hybrid ranks first across MSE, MAE, and QLIKE and significantly outperforms all benchmarks in the Diebold-Mariano tests. These findings suggest that the GARCH-LSTM architecture is particularly useful for the equity-index series once the forecast horizon extends beyond immediate persistence.

Overall, the asset-level evidence reinforces the need for market-specific interpretation. The hybrid model should not be presented as uniformly superior across all environments. Rather, its value depends on the interaction among market structure, forecast horizon, and benchmark strength. BTC-USD and ^GSPC provide stronger support for the hybrid at medium and longer horizons, whereas EURUSD=X shows that simpler operational benchmarks can remain difficult to outperform in selected settings. The contribution of the hybrid model is therefore best described as transferable but conditional, not universally dominant.

7.3 Differences by Horizon and Predictive Memory

The horizon-specific evidence is central to interpreting the model because it shows that the value of hybridization changes with the forecasting horizon. The original GARCH(1,1)-based comparison suggested that the hybrid advantage narrows as h increases. Once the broader benchmark suite is considered, this pattern becomes more nuanced: the hybrid is not necessarily most useful at the shortest horizon, where persistence can be difficult to outperform, but at horizons where simple carry-forward behavior weakens and nonlinear sequential information can provide incremental value.

At h = 1, persistence is a particularly demanding benchmark. It ranks first under QLIKE for BTC-USD, EURUSD=X, and ^GSPC, and the Diebold-Mariano tests indicate statistically significant advantages over the hybrid for EURUSD=X and ^GSPC. This result does not undermine the hybrid model; rather, it shows that the one-day volatility proxy contains strong short-term continuity. When the forecast target is very close to the current volatility state, a simple persistence rule can be difficult to improve upon, especially under QLIKE.

At h = 5, the hybrid model exhibits its strongest overall profile. It ranks first across MSE, MAE, and QLIKE for all three assets, and the Diebold-Mariano tests indicate statistically significant QLIKE improvements against most benchmarks. The main exception is the comparison with EWMA for EURUSD=X. This pattern suggests that the LSTM component becomes most useful when the horizon is long enough for immediate persistence to lose strength but still short enough for recent nonlinear volatility patterns to remain informative.

At h = 10, the evidence remains favorable but becomes more asset dependent. For ^GSPC, the hybrid ranks first across all metrics and significantly outperforms all benchmarks under QLIKE. For BTC-USD, it ranks first under MSE and QLIKE, although EWMA performs better under MAE and is not significantly worse under QLIKE. For EURUSD=X, EWMA ranks first descriptively, while the hybrid remains competitive and continues to improve upon GARCH-type benchmarks. These results indicate that, as the forecast horizon lengthens, accumulated uncertainty and benchmark-specific dynamics become more influential.

From a methodological perspective, these findings refine the interpretation of predictive memory. A 30-observation lookback and a compact set of GARCH-informed inputs appear sufficient to capture useful medium-horizon volatility patterns, particularly at h = 5. The same configuration, however, does not guarantee dominance at h = 1, where persistence is strongest, or at h = 10, where future volatility may depend increasingly on information outside the current sequence. The evidence therefore supports a horizon-dependent profile: persistence is highly competitive for immediate forecasts, the hybrid performs strongest at intermediate horizons, and EWMA can remain competitive in selected longer-horizon cases.

7.4 Reading QLIKE Relative to MSE and MAE

The results should be interpreted through a joint reading of MSE, MAE, and QLIKE rather than through any single loss criterion. MSE and MAE measure the numerical closeness of the forecasts to the observed volatility proxy, whereas QLIKE is particularly relevant when the target is an imperfect proxy for latent volatility, as emphasized by Patton (2011). For this reason, QLIKE serves as a useful safeguard against treating reductions in squared or absolute error as unconditional evidence of superior volatility forecasting. In the revised analysis, this role is especially important because QLIKE is also used as the loss function for the Diebold-Mariano comparisons.

The benchmark-suite results show that model rankings are sensitive to the evaluation metric. For example, in BTC-USD at h = 10, the hybrid model ranks first under MSE and QLIKE, whereas EWMA performs better under MAE. Similarly, in EURUSD=X at h = 10, EWMA ranks first descriptively across the reported metrics, although the Diebold-Mariano test does not indicate a statistically significant QLIKE advantage over the hybrid model. These cases show why a single-metric interpretation would provide an incomplete view of forecasting performance.

The QLIKE-based Diebold-Mariano tests further refine the interpretation of the hybrid model's advantage. In many comparisons, particularly against GARCH(1,1) and GJR-GARCH, the hybrid model's lower QLIKE loss is statistically significant. At the same time, QLIKE identifies cases in which simpler benchmarks remain difficult to outperform. Persistence significantly outperforms the hybrid model at h = 1 for EURUSD=X and ^GSPC, while EWMA remains statistically competitive for EURUSD=X at h = 10. Thus, QLIKE does not merely confirm the strengths of the hybrid specification; it helps define the conditions under which those strengths are statistically reliable.

This multi-metric interpretation strengthens the credibility of the chapter. The objective is not to present every reduction in forecast error as conclusive evidence of model superiority, but to identify where the hybrid model produces lower loss, where that reduction is statistically meaningful, and where simpler benchmarks remain competitive. The most balanced interpretation therefore comes from reading MSE, MAE, QLIKE, and Diebold-Mariano evidence together rather than privileging any single indicator.

7.5 Relationship to Recent Literature

The findings are consistent with recent developments in volatility forecasting, but they also clarify the limits of that consistency. Yang et al. (2024) show that the manner in which statistical signals are integrated into the LSTM component can materially affect the performance of hybrid volatility models. The present chapter aligns with that argument by showing that a compact GARCH-informed LSTM can add value when the econometric signal is used as a structured input rather than discarded. At the same time, the benchmark-suite results indicate that hybridization does not automatically dominate simpler forecasting rules. Persistence remains highly competitive at the one-day horizon, and EWMA remains competitive in selected longer-horizon cases. Thus, the observed gains depend jointly on model design, benchmark choice, asset behavior, and forecast horizon.

The chapter also relates to studies that use more complex architectures, including combinations of Transformer, GARCH, and LSTM components. Mishra et al. (2024), for example, report that hybrid deep learning architectures can outperform classical approaches across different financial assets. The contribution of the present chapter is complementary rather than competitive with that line of work. Its objective is not to demonstrate that a parsimonious architecture outperforms the most sophisticated neural alternatives, but to show that a compact and reproducible hybrid can produce statistically meaningful improvements when evaluated through walk-forward validation, benchmark diversity, and formal forecast-comparison tests.

The comparison with Huang and Luo (2024) is also relevant because their work emphasizes the importance of richer GARCH-type specifications incorporating long memory, leverage effects, regime switching, and heavy tails. The revised empirical design partially addresses this concern by adding an asymmetric GARCH-type benchmark. The results show that the hybrid frequently outperforms GJR-GARCH under QLIKE, particularly at $h = 5$ and $h = 10$. Nevertheless, the broader implication remains unchanged: GARCH(1,1) is not the full econometric frontier. Future research should therefore compare the proposed hybrid framework with FIGARCH, Realized GARCH, regime-switching GARCH, and other advanced volatility models.

More broadly, the revised findings support a balanced reading of the current literature. Memory-based learning models can be valuable in volatility forecasting, but traditional econometric and operational benchmarks remain relevant. This chapter contributes to that debate by showing why benchmark diversity and formal statistical testing matter. Had the analysis remained limited to GARCH(1,1), the conclusion would have appeared stronger but less credible. By incorporating persistence, EWMA, GJR-GARCH, and Diebold-Mariano tests, the revised chapter offers a more defensible conclusion: the hybrid model often improves upon classical GARCH-type alternatives, but its advantage remains conditional on the asset, horizon, benchmark, and loss function considered.

7.6 Scope of the Contribution

The scope of the chapter should be stated with precision. The revised evidence indicates that a parsimonious, temporally validated GARCH-LSTM pipeline can provide statistically meaningful improvements over classical GARCH-type benchmarks in several asset-horizon combinations. This contribution is most evident at medium horizons and, for selected assets, at longer horizons, where the hybrid specification benefits from structured econometric inputs and nonlinear sequential learning.

At the same time, the findings do not establish universal superiority. Persistence remains difficult to outperform at the one-day horizon, and EWMA remains competitive in selected cases. The results therefore support a conditional interpretation: the value of the hybrid depends on the asset, the forecasting horizon, the benchmark, and the loss function used for evaluation. This qualification is central to the chapter's contribution because it prevents the empirical evidence from being overstated.

The chapter contributes methodologically by showing how a compact GARCH-informed LSTM can be evaluated within a benchmark-diverse, temporally coherent, and statistically tested framework. The use of walk-forward validation, multi-horizon analysis, QLIKE loss, and Diebold-Mariano testing strengthens the credibility of the findings and clarifies the conditions under which the hybrid architecture adds value.

Accordingly, the contribution is not a claim that neural architectures should replace econometric or operational volatility models. Rather, the chapter positions hybridization as a disciplined extension of traditional volatility forecasting. In academic terms, it provides evidence that econometric structure and nonlinear sequence learning can be combined productively when evaluation is rigorous. In applied terms, it suggests that compact and reproducible hybrid pipelines may support financial analytics and risk-management tasks when their use is aligned with the horizon and market context in which they perform best.

8. PRACTICAL IMPLICATIONS AND BUSINESS APPLICATIONS

The practical relevance of the proposed pipeline lies in its potential use as a decision-support component rather than as a stand-alone trading or risk-management system. In financial institutions, more stable volatility forecasts can inform several operational tasks, including market-risk monitoring, VaR and ES calibration, exposure limits, margin setting, derivatives hedging, and tactical portfolio allocation. The results are particularly relevant because they show that the usefulness of the hybrid model depends on the asset and forecast horizon, rather than applying uniformly across all settings.

For short-horizon risk control, the findings suggest that the hybrid model should be evaluated alongside simple operational rules such as persistence and EWMA. This is important because the benchmark-suite results show that simple models may remain highly competitive at the one-day horizon. In practical terms, institutions should not adopt a hybrid architecture merely because it is more sophisticated. Instead, they should assign it to applications where its empirical performance profile is strongest, particularly medium-horizon volatility monitoring or risk-planning tasks in which the benchmark advantage is more evident.

Implementation also requires governance discipline. A production version of the pipeline should include strict versioning of data, features, model specifications, software dependencies, and forecasting outputs. It should also include window-level metric logging, periodic recalibration rules, drift monitoring, and documented procedures for model review. These requirements are not secondary to predictive performance. In regulated or institutionally controlled environments, a model that is accurate but difficult to audit, reproduce, or explain may be less valuable than a slightly simpler system with stronger governance properties.

The chapter also has implications for analytics teams. The evidence supports the use of compact hybrid architectures that combine economically interpretable inputs with nonlinear sequential learning. This design may be easier to validate and maintain than a deeper or more opaque neural architecture, while still offering measurable predictive benefits in selected conditions. As a result, the proposed framework may serve as a practical template for teams seeking to integrate econometric structure and machine learning without abandoning transparency or reproducibility.

Overall, the business value of the approach should be interpreted conditionally. The hybrid GARCH-LSTM pipeline may support financial analytics and risk-management workflows when its use is aligned with the relevant decision horizon, asset class, benchmark comparison, and governance requirements. Its main practical contribution is therefore not the replacement of existing volatility tools, but the demonstration that econometric signals and compact neural learning can be combined within a disciplined, auditable, and operationally meaningful forecasting process.

9. LIMITATIONS AND FUTURE RESEARCH AGENDA

This chapter has several limitations that delimit the interpretation of the findings and define a more specific agenda for future research.

First, target measurement remains a central limitation. Volatility is approximated through a 21-day moving standard deviation of daily returns. This proxy is operationally transparent and allows a homogeneous comparison across equity, foreign exchange, and cryptocurrency series, but it is not equivalent to realized volatility constructed from intraday data. Andersen et al. (2003) show that high-frequency information can provide a more informative approximation of latent volatility. Future studies should therefore replicate the pipeline using intraday realized volatility, range-based volatility measures, and jump-robust estimators to determine whether the relative performance of the hybrid model remains stable when the target variable is more informative.

Second, the benchmark set, although broader than in the initial version of the study, is still not exhaustive. The revised design includes persistence, EWMA, GARCH(1,1), and an asymmetric GARCH-type comparator, which makes the empirical evaluation more demanding. Nevertheless, these models do not fully represent the frontier of volatility econometrics. Future research should compare the proposed hybrid framework against EGARCH, APARCH, FIGARCH, Realized GARCH, regime-switching GARCH, long-memory models, and specifications with heavy-tailed innovations. These alternatives could reduce part of the observed advantage of the hybrid model, particularly in environments where asymmetry, persistence, heavy tails, or structural breaks play a central role.

Third, the empirical scope is limited by the number of assets considered. The use of ^GSPC, EURUSD=X, and BTC-USD introduces meaningful heterogeneity across an equity index, a foreign exchange rate, and a cryptocurrency. However, three series are not sufficient to support universal conclusions about entire asset classes. A broader empirical design should include larger panels of equities, exchange rates, commodities, fixed-income instruments, and crypto-assets. Such an extension would make it possible to evaluate whether the relative advantage of the hybrid model is associated with observable market characteristics such as liquidity, average volatility, jump intensity, trading calendar, macro-financial sensitivity, or regime instability.

Fourth, the inferential strategy remains based on pairwise forecast-comparison tests. The inclusion of Diebold-Mariano tests strengthens the chapter by moving beyond descriptive error differences and by assessing whether QLIKE loss differentials are statistically meaningful. However, pairwise tests do not fully address the problem of comparing several competing models simultaneously. Future work could incorporate model confidence set procedures, multiple-testing adjustments, or block/bootstrap-based forecast-comparison methods. These tools would provide a more comprehensive inferential framework as the benchmark suite expands.

Fifth, the chapter evaluates predictive accuracy through statistical loss functions rather than direct economic outcomes. Lower MSE, MAE, or QLIKE values do not automatically imply higher economic value once transaction costs, capital requirements, hedging costs, model governance, recalibration frequency, and implementation risk are considered. Future research should translate volatility forecasts into downstream financial applications, including VaR and ES backtesting, volatility-targeting strategies, dynamic hedging, margin-setting exercises, and portfolio allocation rules. This would help determine whether the statistical gains of the hybrid model generate measurable operational value.

Sixth, the feature design is intentionally compact. The hybrid model uses GARCH conditional volatility, standardized residuals, and absolute returns as input signals. This choice supports parsimony, interpretability, and reproducibility, but it may exclude relevant information. Future extensions could examine whether trading volume, liquidity indicators, bid-ask spreads, macro-financial variables, option-implied volatility, news variables, or sentiment indicators improve forecasting performance. Any such extension should carefully control for temporal alignment, data availability, publication lags, and look-ahead bias.

Overall, the future research agenda should move in six directions: more informative volatility targets, broader asset panels, stronger econometric and deep learning benchmarks, richer multiple-model inference, carefully governed exogenous information, and direct economic evaluation. The contribution of the present chapter is to provide a disciplined methodological base for those extensions. Its results should therefore be interpreted as evidence that a compact GARCH-informed LSTM can add value under a temporally coherent and benchmark-diverse evaluation protocol, not as a final statement on the universal superiority of hybrid volatility models.

10. CONCLUSIONS

This chapter examined volatility forecasting through a compact hybrid GARCH-LSTM framework evaluated under expanding-window walk-forward validation, multi-horizon forecasting, benchmark diversity, and formal predictive-accuracy testing. Its central argument is that the relevant issue in quantitative finance is not whether econometric models or deep learning architectures should be treated as mutually exclusive alternatives, but whether they can be integrated in a temporally coherent, reproducible, and statistically defensible manner.

Using three assets with distinct market structures—^GSPC, EURUSD=X, and BTC-USD—the results show that the hybrid GARCH-LSTM model often adds value beyond classical GARCH-type specifications. The evidence is particularly favorable when the hybrid is compared with GARCH(1,1) and GJR-GARCH under QLIKE loss, with Diebold-Mariano tests indicating statistically meaningful differences in many asset-horizon combinations. The strongest support appears at medium horizons and, for some assets, at longer horizons, rather than uniformly at the one-day horizon.

The findings also show that the hybrid model should not be interpreted as universally superior. Persistence remains a strong comparator at $h = 1$, especially for EURUSD=X and ^GSPC, while EWMA remains competitive in selected cases such as longer-horizon FX volatility. These results indicate that the value of hybridization depends on the interaction among asset type, forecasting horizon, benchmark specification, and loss function. Accordingly, the proposed model is best understood as a disciplined complement to classical and operational volatility models, not as a blanket replacement for them.

The chapter's contribution therefore lies not only in the reduction of forecast errors, but also in the methodological structure through which those reductions are evaluated. The use of walk-forward validation, multi-horizon comparison, benchmark-suite evaluation, QLIKE loss, and Diebold-Mariano testing moves the analysis beyond a simple demonstration of predictive improvement. This framework makes the empirical claims more cautious, but also more credible, because it explicitly identifies the conditions under which the hybrid model performs well and the cases in which simpler benchmarks remain competitive.

Overall, the evidence supports hybridization as an intermediate path between econometric structure and nonlinear sequential learning. From an academic perspective, the chapter contributes a reproducible framework for evaluating GARCH-informed neural volatility models under temporally valid conditions. From an applied perspective, it suggests that compact and well-governed hybrid pipelines may be useful for financial analytics and risk-management tasks when their deployment is aligned with the market context and forecast horizon in which they perform best. The broader methodological conclusion is that credibility in volatility forecasting depends not only on lower error metrics, but also on benchmark selection, temporal validation, statistical testing, and interpretive restraint.

REFERENCES

Abadi, M., Barham, P., Chen, J., Chen, Z., Davis, A., Dean, J., Devin, M., Ghemawat, S., Irving, G., Isard, M., Kudlur, M., Levenberg, J., Monga, R., Moore, S., Murray, D. G., Steiner, B., Tucker, P., Vasudevan, V., Warden, P., & Zheng, X. (2016). *TensorFlow: A system for large-scale machine learning*. In *Proceedings of the 12th USENIX Symposium on Operating Systems Design and Implementation (OSDI 16)* (pp. 265-283). USENIX Association.

Andersen, T. G., Bollerslev, T., Diebold, F. X., & Labys, P. (2003). Modeling and forecasting realized volatility. *Econometrica, 71*(2), 579–625. DOI: 10.1111/1468-0262.00418

Bergmeir, C., Hyndman, R. J., & Koo, B. (2018). A note on the validity of cross-validation for evaluating autoregressive time series prediction. *Computational Statistics & Data Analysis, 120*, 70–83. DOI: 10.1016/j.csda.2017.11.003

Bollerslev, T. (1986). Generalized autoregressive conditional heteroskedasticity. *Journal of Econometrics*, *31*(3), 307–327. DOI: 10.1016/0304-4076(86)90063-1

Cont, R. (2001). Empirical properties of asset returns: Stylized facts and statistical issues. *Quantitative Finance*, *1*(2), 223–236. DOI: 10.1080/713665670

Diebold, F. X., & Mariano, R. S. (1995). Comparing predictive accuracy. *Journal of Business & Economic Statistics*, *13*(3), 253–263. DOI: 10.1080/07350015.1995.10524599

Engle, R. F. (1982). Autoregressive conditional heteroscedasticity with estimates of the variance of United Kingdom inflation. *Econometrica*, *50*(4), 987–1007. https://www.jstor.org/stable/1912773. DOI: 10.2307/1912773

Gunnarsson, E. S., Isern, H. R., Kaloudis, A., Risstad, M., Vigdel, B., & Westgaard, S. (2024). Prediction of realized volatility and implied volatility indices using AI and machine learning: A review. *International Review of Financial Analysis*, *93*, 103221. DOI: 10.1016/j.irfa.2024.103221

Hochreiter, S., & Schmidhuber, J. (1997). Long short-term memory. *Neural Computation*, *9*(8), 1735–1780. DOI: 10.1162/neco.1997.9.8.1735 PMID: 9377276

Huang, Y., & Luo, Y. (2024). Forecasting conditional volatility based on hybrid GARCH-type models with long memory, regime switching, leverage effect and heavy-tail: Further evidence from equity market. *The North American Journal of Economics and Finance*, *72*, 102148. DOI: 10.1016/j.najef.2024.102148

Kakade, K., Jain, I., & Mishra, A. K. (2022). Value-at-Risk forecasting: A hybrid ensemble learning GARCH-LSTM based approach. *Resources Policy, 78*, 102903. DOI: 10.1016/j.resourpol.2022.102903

Kim, H. Y., & Won, C. H. (2018). Forecasting the volatility of stock price index: A hybrid model integrating LSTM with multiple GARCH-type models. *Expert Systems with Applications, 103*, 25–37. DOI: 10.1016/j.eswa.2018.03.002

Kingma, D. P., & Ba, J. (2015). *Adam: A method for stochastic optimization. International Conference on Learning Representations (ICLR)*. DOI: 10.48550/arXiv.1412.6980

Léber, D., & Egyed, B. (2026). The sentiment augmented GARCH-LSTM hybrid model for Value-at-Risk forecasting. *Computational Economics, 67*(1), 313–353. DOI: 10.1007/s10614-025-11042-8

Leushuis, R. M., & Petkov, N. (2026). Advances in forecasting realized volatility: A review of methodologies. *Financial Innovation, 12*(1), 14. Advance online publication. DOI: 10.1186/s40854-025-00809-5

Mishra, A. K., Renganathan, J., & Gupta, A. (2024). Volatility forecasting and assessing risk of financial markets using multi-transformer neural network based architecture. *Engineering Applications of Artificial Intelligence, 133*, 108223. Advance online publication. DOI: 10.1016/j.engappai.2024.108223

Patton, A. J. (2011). Volatility forecast comparison using imperfect volatility proxies. *Journal of Econometrics, 160*(1), 246–256. DOI: 10.1016/j.jeconom.2010.03.034

Poon, S.-H., & Granger, C. W. J. (2003). Forecasting volatility in financial markets: A review. *Journal of Economic Literature, 41*(2), 478–539. DOI: 10.1257/.41.2.478

Taneva-Angelova, G., & Granchev, D. (2025). Deep learning and transformer architectures for volatility forecasting: Evidence from U.S. equity indices. *Journal of Risk and Financial Management, 18*(12), 685. Advance online publication. DOI: 10.3390/jrfm18120685

Yang, A., Ye, Q., & Zhai, J. (2024). Volatility forecasting with hybrid-long short-term memory models: Evidence from the COVID-19 period. *International Journal of Finance & Economics, 29*(3), 2766–2786. DOI: 10.1002/ijfe.2805

Chapter 11
Predictive Model to Estimate the Economic Activity of Mexican Municipalities Using Night Lights

Claudia García
http://orcid.org/0009-0009-2819-9043
Escuela Superior de Cómputo, National Polytechnic Institute, Mexico

Carolina Corral
Escuela Superior de Cómputo, National Polytechnic Institute, Mexico

Jesús Manuel Lopez
Escuela Superior de Cómputo, National Polytechnic Institute, Mexico

ABSTRACT

This chapter presents a methodology to estimate municipal gross domestic product (GDP) in Mexico by integrating nighttime light (NTL) satellite imagery with econometric reasoning and machine learning. This chapter addresses a practical and analytical limitation: in Mexico, GDP is systematically available at the national and state levels, but not as a regular official series at the municipal level. This gap complicates local economic analysis, regional planning, and the evaluation of territorially focused public policy. To address this limitation, the study combines state-level GDP data, population-based municipal disaggregation, and multiple indicators extracted from VIIRS nighttime lights. Three model families are assessed: ordinary least squares (OLS), Random Forest, and a hybrid model in which Random

DOI: 10.4018/979-8-3373-8372-9.ch011

Forest is used to learn the nonlinear structure that remains in the OLS residuals. The chapter argues that this combined strategy is particularly useful in settings characterized by territorial heterogeneity, uneven statistical infrastructure, and a large informal sector.

1. INTRODUCTION

Gross Domestic Product (GDP) is one of the most widely used indicators to understand how an economy performs. It provides a general picture of productivity, growth, and overall economic activity (INEGI, 2023).

However, its usefulness becomes limited when we move to more detailed geographic levels. In Mexico, GDP is regularly reported at the national and state levels, but not systematically at the municipal (county) level. This creates a significant gap, especially in a country characterized by strong regional inequalities.

Estimating GDP at this level is not straightforward. Traditional methods require large amounts of data, time, and resources, which are often unavailable. As a result, researchers and policymakers lack timely and reliable information to evaluate local economic dynamics.

In this context, satellite images of nighttime light (NTL) offer an alternative way of observing economic activity. Instead of relying on surveys or administrative records, this approach infers economic patterns from visible light emissions captured from space, which reflect infrastructure, energy consumption, and human activity (Chen & Nordhaus, 2011; Henderson et al., 2012).

This chapter proposes a methodology to estimate municipal GDP in Mexico by combining NTL data with data science techniques. The approach integrates satellite data processing, statistical modeling, and machine learning methods to generate high-frequency and spatially disaggregated estimates.

The main objective of this study is to develop a methodology capable of estimating municipal GDP in Mexico using nighttime satellite imagery.

This is achieved through three main steps: (1) processing NTL data, (2) estimating municipal GDP from state-level data, and (3) modeling the relationship between luminosity and economic activity using both econometric and machine learning techniques.

This chapter is organized as follows. Section 2 reviews the theoretical framework and empirical background on the use of images of night lights as a proxy variable for economic activity. Section 3 describes in detail the municipal GDP and the specification of the predictive model. Section 4 presents the results obtained and the interpretation. Finally, section 5 presents the conclusions, limitations of the study and the lines of future research.

2. EMPIRICAL BACKGROUND AND RESEARCH GAP

The use of nighttime light (NTL) satellite imagery as a proxy for economic activity has a well-established empirical foundation. The seminal contribution is (Henderson et al., 2012), who established the initial methodological framework for estimating elasticities between GDP growth and NTL growth using DMSP satellite data. Their central finding is that there is a strong positive relationship between NTL and GDP in both levels and changes: regions with higher luminosity intensity tend to exhibit higher output, and fluctuations in luminosity track fluctuations in GDP. Crucially, they argue that official GDP figures themselves contain measurement error, and that NTL can be used not merely as a proxy but as a corrective signal for improving GDP estimates in contexts where national accounts are unreliable.

(Nordhaus & Chen, 2015) extended this framework by introducing formal evaluations of model stability and reliability, including bootstrap resampling methods. They also identified a structural limitation of the DMSP sensor: saturation in densely illuminated urban areas, which compresses the measured luminosity signal and reduces estimation accuracy. Their work foreshadowed a technological shift in literature, pointing to the need for higher-resolution satellite sensors.

That shift was formalized by (Gibson & Boe-Gibson, 2021a), who demonstrated that the Visible Infrared Imaging Radiometer Suite (VIIRS), mounted on the Suomi NPP satellite, systematically outperforms DMSP data for subnational GDP estimation in both cross-sectional and time-series settings. VIIRS offers finer spatial resolution, a wider radiometric range that avoids saturation, and better calibration for low-light environments. These properties make it the appropriate choice for county-level studies such as the present one.

(Ehsan et al., 2023) contributed two methodological refinements relevant to this work. First, using district-level data from Bangladesh, they confirmed the presence of a non-linear relationship between NTL and GDP, providing empirical grounds for moving beyond purely linear regression. Second, they proposed separating productive light consumption — associated with industrial and service activity — from domestic and agricultural lighting. This separation reduced mean squared error by 6.7% relative to models using total luminosity, as it isolates the component of light that most directly reflects market-oriented economic output. Their method for disaggregating state-level GDP to the district level using population shares is also directly adapted in this study.

Finally, (Llamosas-Rosas et al., 2021) demonstrated the applicability of this methodology in the Mexican context. Using both DMSP and VIIRS data for major tourist coastal zones, they obtained elasticity estimates consistent with (Henderson et al., 2012) and found that a mixed linear cross-sectional model yielded the best results. They conclude that satellite imagery could serve as a more precise alternative to official statistics for measuring subnational economic activity in Mexico, given the limitations of existing data infrastructure.

The present study builds on this body of work in three ways. First, it applies the methodology to Mexican county GDP specifically, filling a gap left by (Llamosas-Rosas et al., 2021) focus on tourism zones. Second, it tests both parametric and non-parametric models to capture the non-linearity identified by (Ehsan et al., 2023). Third, it proposes and evaluates a hybrid model that combines OLS and Random Forest, using cross-validation to compare performance across estimation scenarios.

3. THEORETICAL AND METHODOLOGICAL FOUNDATIONS

3.1 Nonlinearity in the NTL–GDP Relationship

The study by (Beyer et al., 2022), published by the World Bank, introduces a methodology to measure quarterly economic growth using night-time luminosity satellite data. The authors estimate that the elasticity between quarterly changes in light intensity (from the VIIRS sensor) and GDP for emerging and developing economies (EMDEs) is 1.55. This parameter indicates that, for this category of countries, a 10% increase in nighttime light is associated, on average, with a 15.5% increase in GDP. The elasticity range found is between 1.36 and 1.81, which reinforces the robustness of the estimate, which remains consistent when testing different specifications of the model. A key breakthrough of the study was the use of data from the Suomi NPP satellite, equipped with the Visible Infrared Imaging Radiometer Suite (VIIRS) sensor, which provides higher-resolution and higher-quality nighttime images. The authors highlight that the VIIRS sensor can capture changes with great precision on a quarterly scale.

The dominant approach in the NTL–GDP literature has been log-linear OLS regression (Ehsan et al., 2023; Gibson & Boe-Gibson, 2021a; Henderson et al., 2012; Yuan et al., 2021). This approach offers a clear interpretation: the estimated coefficient β is directly the NTL–GDP elasticity. The standard linear model assumes:

$$.Y = \beta_0 + X_1\beta_1 + X_2\beta_2 + \ldots + X_K\beta_K + \in.$$

Where the marginal effect of each variable on is constant (), independent of the values of other variables, the initial level of the temporal or spatial context, and the magnitude of the change. The linear model assumes proportionality, where doubling (X) doubles its effect on (Y); additivity, where the combined effect of variables equals the sum of their individual effects; parameter constancy across time and units; and symmetry, meaning increases and decreases produce effects of equal magnitude.

Economic systems, however, routinely violate these assumptions. Diminishing marginal returns mean that early investments generate larger effects than later ones. Threshold effects and structural breaks, such as financial crises or pandemic shocks, cause abrupt changes in the relationship between variables that linear models cannot accommodate. Interactions between variables mean that the effect of luminosity on GDP may differ depending on the economic sector, county size, or period. And heterogeneity across counties means that a single elasticity coefficient may poorly represent the relationship in any individual county.

For NTL–GDP estimation specifically,(Ehsan et al., 2023) confirmed empirically that the relationship is non-linear. Imposing linearity in this context introduces systematic bias: the model will underestimate GDP in some counties and overestimate it in others in ways that are structurally predictable rather than random.

When linear models are imposed on inherently nonlinear processes, several problems arise, including biased predictions due to systematic forecasting errors, incorrect causal inferences that misestimate policy effects, and suboptimal recommendations based on flawed assumptions. This mismatch can also lead to a loss of information, as complex patterns are reduced to overly simple relationships, and may create a false sense of certainty through confidence intervals that fail to capture the true level of uncertainty.

3.2 Technological Evolution from DMSP to VIIRS

The first generation of night light data, based on the DMSP/OLS sensor, had limitations: saturation in densely built-up areas (top-coding), "overglow" that displaced the light to surrounding areas, and the absence of inter-calibrated calibration between satellites. These problems resulted in mean reversal errors and underestimated the brightness of brighter areas relative to less brightly lit areas. The VIIRS sensor, operational since 2012, overcomes these limitations with a spatial resolution of approximately 750 meters, a wider dynamic range that avoids saturation, and a monthly data cadence. Comparative studies for Indonesia, China and South Africa confirmed that DMSP data have a negative relationship with GDP in non-urban areas, while VIIRS data maintain a positive correlation in both urban and rural areas. For Latin America, this distinction is especially relevant given the weight of agricultural and extractive economies in national and regional GDPs.

Recent analytical contributions Four methodological advances in the period 2020-2025 that use luminosity as an economic proxy (in the Americas) are presented.

Combining VIIRS data with land use and land cover variables (such as GlobeLand30) has improved predictive capacity in suburban, rural, and low-density areas, where nighttime light data alone has limitations.

The creation of harmonized DMSP-VIIRS datasets has made it possible to extend the time series backwards to the 1990s, facilitating the long-term analysis of regional economic convergence and divergence in Latin America.

The incorporation of complementary indicators—credit card transactions, Google mobility data, Internet searches (Google Trends), air pollution indicators—into composite indicator frameworks has increased the accuracy of real-time estimates.

The application of neural networks and machine learning models to merge luminosity data with auxiliary variables is gaining ground in the literature, with promising results for urban GDP prediction in Latin American economies.

Table 1. Comparative synthesis of selected studies on nighttime lights and economic activity (2020–2025)

Source / Authors	Area of Study	Methodology	Key Findings
Gibson, Olivia & Boe-Gibson (2020)	Global, with emphasis on developing countries (Indonesia, Nigeria, Mexico)	Comparison of five NTL products (DMSP-OLS, VIIRS DNB, EOG, Black Marble, Harmonized) via correlation with subnational GDP and household surveys	NTL data underestimate economic activity in rural and low-income areas; LED adoption weakens the luminosity–electricity consumption relationship; recommend using corrected VIIRS and avoiding DMSP in areas with rapid LED uptake
Beyer, Hu & Yao (2022)	45 tropical and subtropical countries, including the Amazon basin and Central America	Mixed-frequency econometric models (MIDAS) incorporating cloud-cover filters derived from VIIRS quality mask data.	Cloud cover reduces valid observations by up to 40% in tropical zones, introducing statistical noise; suggest monthly aggregation or moving averages to mitigate the problem
Zhang & Gibson (2022)	China, with comparisons to India, Brazil, and Mexico	Spatial inequality analysis using a luminosity-based Gini index; spectral correction to distinguish LED from high-pressure sodium (HPS) lighting	Standard NTL data artificially compresses luminosity differences between urban and rural areas when LED predominates, underestimating true inequality; propose a source-type correction method
IMCO-INEGI, México (2017-2024)	Mexico, metropolitan areas, and municipalities	Combines satellite NTL imagery with ATM transaction data from the National Banking and Securities Commission (CNBV) to construct a monthly economic activity indicator.	MAGDA fills the data availability gap with an annual indicator covering municipalities from 2014 onward. Results are expressed in units comparable to INEGI's national and state GDP.

continued on following page

Table 1. Continued

Source / Authors	Area of Study	Methodology	Key Findings
Millán López & González Olivares (2024)	Mexico, all 32 states and all municipalities, 1992–2013	Fixed-effects log-linear panel regression of state GDP on NTL intensity (DMSP-OLS, NOAA); state-level elasticities estimated individually to control for regional heterogeneity; spatial autoregressive dynamic model (SAR) applied at the municipal level using NTL-instrumented GDP	NTL explains 79% of state-level economic variation (within $R^2 = 0.793$, $\varphi = 0.649$). Elasticities differ significantly across states meaning a single national parameter is insufficient; regional recalibration is required. The instrument is robust even after controlling electricity consumption (KWH).
Jhamb et al. (2025)	Amazon region (Colombia, Peru, Brazil) and Central African forest areas	(Colombia, Peru, Brazil) and Central African forest areas. Evaluation of Black Marble VNP46A2 (500 m resolution) against very high-resolution imagery and local electricity consumption data	The updated product reduces cloud interference but still fails to capture economic activity beneath dense forest canopy; recommend combining with SAR radar data for high vegetation rural areas

Note. Adapted from the original working manuscript and retained here to preserve the comparative logic of the literature review.

3.3 Methodological Frameworks for the Study of Nighttime Lights

To have a more strategic understanding of each approach, this section is integrated by robust methodological frameworks with the most relevance to the topic are developed according to (Gorjian, 2025).

Spatial Econometrics

Spatial econometrics analyzes the relationship between NTLs and economic activity at the subnational level. Unlike classical ordinary least squares models, spatial models—in particular the Spatial Durbin Model (SDM) and the Spatial Autoregressive Model (SAR) —explicitly incorporate the effects of spatial dependence between geographic units, allowing for the capture of spillovers that conventional approaches omit (Henderson et al., 2012). The presence of positive spatial autocorrelation in the residuals, evidenced by the Moran's I statistic, justifies the adoption of these specifications (World Bank, 2026).

The empirical applications of this methodology have yielded relevant results. For this study, a reference is the Mexican case, where nighttime luminosity has been used as an instrument in Durbin spatial panel models to examine the relationship between economic growth and regional inequality between states, also addressing the endogeneity problems typical of traditional estimates.

Machine Learning, ML

This framework has become increasingly relevant for estimating economic activity based on satellite images of night-time luminosity (NTL). Its main advantage over parametric econometric models lies in the ability to capture nonlinear and complex relationships without the need to specify a priori functional form (World Bank, 2026). Among the algorithms with the highest documented performance are the ensemble methods (Random Forest (RF), XGBoost, LightGBM, and CatBoost), whose effectiveness is attributed to the integration of multiple heterogeneous predictors and the efficient management of high-spatial dimensional data.

Improvements were also found in the integration of heterogeneous data sources. Zheng et al. (2024) constructed RF models to estimate municipal GDP in Dongguan, China, combining NTL data, street-view imagery, and points of interest (POI), obtaining correlation coefficients superior to models based on exclusive luminosity. Qin and Puttanapong (2026) demonstrated that LJ1-01 high-resolution data exhibit more robust correlations with economic activity than the widely used NPP-VIIRS sensor, outperforming it in both RF models and geographically weighted regression. In the Latin American context, Borunda et al. (2026) proposed a three-stage framework to predict regional electricity consumption in Mexico based on NTL, obtaining high correlations with official data ($R^2 > 0.85$) and validating its usefulness in contexts of statistical scarcity.

Deep Learning (DL)

This framework is excelling for estimating economic activity from satellite images of nighttime luminosity (NTL), surpassing the capabilities of both traditional econometric models and conventional machine learning. Recurrent neural network architectures (RNN, LSTM, GRU) and convolutional neural network architectures (CNNs) stand out for their ability to learn hierarchical representations of data, capturing highly complex temporal and spatial patterns (Zheng et al., 2024).

As a methodological framework, Zheng et al. (2024) addressed the problem of inconsistency between the DMSP-OLS and VIIRS datasets using a DL and machine learning approach that achieved correlation coefficients between 0.945 and 0.980 in the harmonization of both series, extending the temporal coverage of the DMSP until 2021.In addition, they employed a multilayer perceptron (MLP) to model the nonlinear relationship between NTL and GDP per capita at the subnational scale, obtaining average accuracies of 0.967, 0.959 and 0.959 in the training, validation and test sets, respectively.

DL stands out for its ability to model long-term temporal dependencies, process raw satellite imagery without manual predictor engineering, and integrate multimodal data sources within a unified framework (Zheng et al., 2024).

Parametric vs Non-Parametric Models

Parametric models, such as ordinary least squares (OLS) linear regression, allow elasticity to be estimated under statistical assumptions: linearity, homoscedasticity, independence, and normality of errors. To verify these assumptions, tests such as Breusch–Pagan, Durbin–Watson, and Shapiro–Wilk are applied.

On the other hand, non-parametric models do not require strict assumptions about the distribution of the data and are useful when the relationship between variables is nonlinear, as occurs in this study.

Table 2. Contrasts between parametric and non-parametric models

Characteristic	parametric models	Non-parametric Models
Definition	Assume a specific functional form (e.g., linear).	Do not require assumptions about the functional form.
Common example	Linear regression (OLS).	Random Forest, decision trees.
Statistical assumptions	Linearity, homoscedasticity, independence, and normality.	Do not require strict assumptions about data distribution.
Interpretability	High: clear coefficients (elasticity, impact).	Lower: results are more complex to interpret.
Data sensitivity	can be sensitive to outliers and multicollinearity.	Robust to nonlinear relationships and complex data.
Flexibility	Limited: depends on the defined functional form.	High: adapts to nonlinear relationships.
Data requirements	Requires smaller data volume for satisfactory performance.	Requires more data to avoid overfitting.
Application in this study	Estimate elasticity between GDP and NTL under classical assumptions.	Capture nonlinear patterns between GDP and NTL.

Source: Authors' own elaboration.

Parametric and non-parametric models differ in their analytical focus and practical application. Parametric approaches offer clear parameter interpretation, which facilitates the estimation of economic relationships such as elasticity. However, their reliance on predefined functional structures can limit their ability to represent more complex dynamics. Nonparametric approaches, by contrast, provide greater flexibility to detect nonlinear patterns and interactions within the data, though this typically comes at the cost of reduced interpretability and greater data requirements to ensure stable results.

In this study, both approaches are used in a complementary manner: parametric models provide interpretable estimates, while nonparametric models help capture patterns that may not follow a strictly linear relationship between nighttime luminosity and GDP.

Table 3. Comparison of methodological approaches

Approach	Base	Key strengths	Main limitations
Spatial Econometrics	Parametric models that incorporate dependence and spatial heterogeneity.	It enables causal inference and quantifies spillover effects between regions.	It assumes parametric functional forms, which may not capture complex relationships.
Machine Learning (Ml)	Supervised learning algorithms such as Random Forest, Gradient Boosting (XGBoost, LightGBM) that combine multiple predictors.	High predictive accuracy when capturing nonlinear relationships and interactions between variables.	"Black box" models make direct economic interpretation difficult.
Deep Learning (Dl)	Deep neural networks (e.g., CNN for spatial data, RNN/LSTM for time series) that learn hierarchical representations of data.	Maximum ability to detect complex patterns; It can integrate multiple types of data (day and night images).	It requires large volumes of data and significant computational power; Highly dependent on data quality.

Note: This SWOT table summarizes each approach

Indicator Limitations

Although literature supports the usefulness of the proxy, it also documents its limitations. First, the indicator does not capture indoor economic activities without light emission visible from space (Beyer et al., 2022; Gibson et al., 2021). Second, the diffusion of LED technology—accelerated in Latin America during the period of analysis in the framework of energy efficiency projects—modifies the luminosity-electricity consumption relationship and can skew estimates if not controlled for the type of light source (Gibson & Boe-Gibson, 2021b; Zhang & Gibson, 2022). Third, cloud cover, especially in tropical areas such as the Amazon and Central America, reduces the effective number of observations per period and generates statistical noise (Beyer et al., 2022). Finally, in rural areas of low population density with high forest cover—such as the Colombian or Peruvian Amazon—the proxy loses predictive capacity (Gibson et al., 2021; Jhamb et al., 2025).

Table 4. Contrasts between parametric and non-parametric models

Characteristic	parametric models	Non-parametric Models
Definition	Assume a specific functional form (e.g., linear).	Do not require assumptions about the functional form.
Common example	Linear regression (OLS).	Random Forest, decision trees.
Statistical assumptions	Linearity, homoscedasticity, independence, and normality.	Do not require strict assumptions about data distribution.
Interpretability	High: clear coefficients (elasticity, impact).	Lower: results are more complex to interpret.
Data sensitivity	can be sensitive to outliers and multicollinearity.	Robust to nonlinear relationships and complex data.
Flexibility	Limited: depends on the defined functional form.	High: adapts to nonlinear relationships.
Data requirements	Requires smaller data volume for satisfactory performance.	Requires more data to avoid overfitting.
Application in this study	Estimate elasticity between GDP and NTL under classical assumptions.	Capture nonlinear patterns between GDP and NTL.

Note. This table contrasts the interpretive and empirical implications of parametric and non-parametric approaches under the criteria discussed in the chapter.

4. DATA AND SOURCES OF INFORMATION

INEGI defines GDP as "the sum of the value (in the currency corresponding to the country) of all end-use goods and services1 generated by a country or state during a period (commonly a year or quarter)" (Gross Domestic Product by state (GDP) 2022, 2023). The formula to calculate it is as eq (1)

$$PIB = C + I + G + X - M \tag{1}$$

Where:

C is consumption,
I is investment,
G is public spending,
X is exports, and
M is imports.

County GDP extends this definition to the county scale: it represents the total value of final goods and services produced within the boundaries of a county during a given period. Because it captures production occurring within county limits regardless of the nationality of the producers, it is also sensitive to international economic policies and cross-border activity.

One terminological clarification is necessary for this study. Mexico City, which is included in the analysis, does not formally have counties — its sub-units are called "alcaldías" (mayoralties). For the purposes of this document, the county unit in Mexico City is understood as the alcaldía. Each alcaldía is treated as equivalent to the pre-2016 delegación sharing its name and territorial boundaries, and its GDP estimate is considered the same type of indicator as the PIBM of other counties in the study.

4.1 Economic and demographic information

In addition, the county boundaries provided by INEGI were used through the "Marco Geoestadístico," which divides the national territory into state, county, and basic geostatistical areas. These data are presented in shapefile format with coordinates that delimit each county and are used to crop the NTL images. The coordinate data was collected for eighteen counties: sixteen counties within Mexico City, Oaxaca de Juarez, and Monterrey.

As mentioned, county-level GDP is not available for Mexico so we must estimate it through state-level GDP data. Therefore, GDP data by federal entities available annually from 1980 to 2024 were obtained from INEGI for three states: Mexico City, Nuevo León, and Oaxaca. Since quarterly GDP by federal entity is not available, the quarterly GDP amounts were obtained through the "Indicador Trimestral de la Actividad Económica Estatal," which measures the quarterly GDP variation by state.

4.2 Nighttime Lights as an Economic Proxy

Modern economics faces a fundamental epistemological problem: variables it seeks to measure are abstract concepts (GDP, productivity, and well-being) that are not directly observable. They require complex aggregation of primary data collected through surveys, censuses, and administrative records. This process is costly, slow, and frequently imprecise, especially in developing countries.

Nighttime light data offer an alternative measurement ontology: instead of constructing GDP from the bottom up through the aggregation of individual transactions, economic activity is inferred from above by observing its physical manifestations in electricity consumption for lighting. This approach is grounded in the theory that economic activity leaves measurable physical traces.

The deeper foundation of the light-economy relationship lies in the law of conservation of energy and the second law of thermodynamics. All economic activity involves the transformation of energy: from manufacturing, which requires electrical machinery, to services that need office lighting, heating/cooling of workspaces, and the power supply for electronic equipment.

The positive correlation between electricity consumption and economic activity provides the basis for using satellite imagery of nighttime lights as a proxy for economic performance. This relationship can be explained through numerous concepts. Firstly, the concept of energy intensity suggests that more productive economies tend to consume greater amounts of electricity because of higher levels of industrial, commercial, and residential activity. On the other hand, patterns of urbanization are reflected in the spatial concentration of light, as urban agglomerations typically exhibit higher levels of nighttime illumination due to dense populations and economic interactions. Finally, the presence and intensity of artificial lighting also serve as an indirect indicator of infrastructure development since lighting systems depend on investments on urban infrastructure.

However, territorial economic development recognizes that growth is not spatially homogeneous. Counties function as differentiated economic units in which productive factors, infrastructure, and human capital converge, generating distinct patterns of economic activity across space.

Nighttime light provides an alternative source of information in contexts where local economic data are scarce, incomplete, or outdated, which cannot approximate county-level economic activity. The processing and analysis of these images enable more regular evaluation of economic sustainability models as satellite observations are updated periodically. This approach also overcomes some limitations associated with traditional statistical methods, which tend to be slow and costly to conduct.

The use of NTL data offers comparative advantages for the measurement and analysis of economic activity. Namely, NTL image observations provide complete spatial coverage, allowing researchers to analyze a wide range of territories where traditional data is unavailable. These datasets also provide a broad temporal series of observations at higher frequencies than those provided by census data, allowing for regular and consistent monitoring of economic activity.

It is important to highlight that, despite these advantages, methodological limitations must also be considered. In advanced or densely illuminated regions, light intensity may reach saturation levels, reducing the ability of sensors to capture additional increases in brightness. Satellite measurements can also be affected by the blooming effect, whereby light diffuses across adjacent pixels and artificially expands illuminated areas. The relationship between luminosity and economic output may also be weaker in agricultural sectors, where production processes happen mostly during the day. Additionally, improvements in energy efficiency policies and technological changes in lighting systems can modify electricity consumption patterns, potentially weakening the direct relationship between observed luminosity and underlying economic activity.

4.3 Estimating Municipal GDP in Mexico

The estimation of GDP in the case of Mexico has been approached through disaggregation methods such as AGERP technique, which distributes national GDP based on each region's share of the Gross Value Added at Census Level (VACB). However, these methods face significant limitations: census data is updated only annually, representativeness gaps exist between national accounts and census data (Ruiz Ochoa, 2010), and VACB systematically underestimates GDP because it excludes the informal sector. In Mexico, the informal economy contributed 24.4% of national GDP in 2022 (INEGI, 2023), making this omission particularly consequential.

Other proxy variables proposed in the literature include population size, energy consumption, bank deposits, domestic air passenger traffic, and tourism flows (Castro-Nuño et al., 2013; Fernández et al., 2018; O'Rourke, 1998; Padilla Sierra, 2015; Paganelli, 2021). Morudu (2016) demonstrated the applicability of Zipf's law to county GDP estimation by exploiting the positive relationship between GDP and government revenue. Each proxy has its own scope and limitations, and the choice among them depends on the availability of data at the required level of disaggregation.

For this study, the ideal proxy is one that is elastic with PIBM, captures informal as well as formal economic activity, is available at the county level, and can be measured at quarterly or higher frequency from a decentralized source. As the following sections establish, nighttime light satellite data satisfies each of these requirements, while also being immune to the representativeness and sectoral disaggregation problems that affect census-based approaches.

4.4 Elasticity

Elasticity, represented by the letter E, measures the percentage change in a dependent variable (Y) in response to a percentage change in an independent variable (X). This approach allows elasticities to be compared without the unit of measurement affecting the analysis eq (2):

For example, if NTL increases from 20 to 25 units and GDP rises from 1000 to 1100 million, the elasticity would be: 0.1 / 0.25 = 0.4.

$$E = \frac{\%\Delta Y}{\%\Delta X} = \frac{Y_2 - Y_1/Y_1}{X_2 - X_1/X_1} \tag{2}$$

A value greater than or equal to 1 indicates that Y is elastic with respect to X, meaning it responds significantly to changes in X. If the value is less than 1, the relationship is considered inelastic.

$$GDP_j = \alpha + \beta.NTL + \varepsilon_{NTL_j} \tag{3}$$

NTL–GDP Elasticity

Estimating from a proxy variable is operationally equivalent to estimating the elasticity between them. The modern statistical framework for this was established by Henderson et al. (2012), who describe the relationship between recorded GDP and nighttime light in terms of measurement error. Let real GDP denote true economic output, GDP the value recorded in national accounts, and NTL observed luminosity for region j. The framework assumes:

Where:

- PIB_j is the gross domestic product of country j,
- NTL_j represents the aggregated NTL intensity of county j,
- β captures the elasticity between NTL and GDP, and
- ε reflects noise or error term.

including sensor error and sectoral variation in the light-to-activity ratio. Both variables are expressed in natural logarithms and measured per capita.

To improve accuracy, productive light (associated with economic sectors) is separated from domestic light, reducing the error by 6.7% (Ehsan et al., 2023) Thus, productive light is estimated as:

$$NTKprod_{(j,t)} = (NTL_{(j,t)} x PRODuso\%) \tag{4}$$

The final model is thus:

$$\log(PIB_{(j,t)}) = \hat{\alpha} + \hat{\beta}\log(NTLprod_{(j,t)}) + \varepsilon_{(j,t)} \tag{5}$$

Research shows that regions with greater nighttime light intensity tend to exhibit higher levels of economic production, reflecting the close relationship between electricity use, urban activity, and output. Nevertheless, the strength of this correlation varies across contexts. Empirical studies report correlations of 0.7 to 0.9 at the national level in cross-sectional analyses. At the subnational level, however, correlations tend to fall to around 0.5, suggesting that nighttime light emissions constitute a weaker proxy for economic activity at more disaggregated scales. The relationship strengthens again when luminosity is compared with density measures, such as population or business establishments, where correlations often approach 0.7.

An additional distinction frequently noted in the literature concerns cross-sectional versus time-series performance. Nighttime lights tend to be better predictors of differences between places than of changes within the same place over time. In other words, luminosity data are more effective at explaining why some regions are richer than others than at tracking short-term economic fluctuations.

In emerging and developing economies, a 1% change in quarterly GDP is associated with a 1.55% change in nighttime light intensity. Subsequent studies show that this elasticity varies depending on economic context. In advanced economies, nighttime lights tend to grow at half the rate of GDP, reflecting growth driven more by productivity gains and technological innovation than by physical expansion. Estimates also vary with income level and economic structure, though deviations from the average relationship are modest. Across the literature, reported elasticities range from approx. 0.2 to 1.55, depending on factors such as the spatial scale of analysis (national versus county), the temporal frequency of the data (annual versus quarterly), the satellite system employed (VIIRS vs DMSP), and the estimation methodology used.

Key considerations in using nighttime lights as a proxy for economic activity include spatial heterogeneity, such as spillover effects and spatial autocorrelation, which may influence the interpretation of observed luminosity patterns. Technological changes, particularly the widespread transition to LED lighting, require periodic adjustments to maintain measurement accuracy. Additionally, integrating multidimensional data sources, such as combining nighttime lights with mobile phone data, traffic flows, and social media activity, can enhance the robustness and granularity of economic analyses.

5. SATELLITE DATA AND MODELING FRAMEWORK

5.1 Nighttime Light Satellite Images and VIIRS-DNB

Figure 1. S-NPP VIIRS-DBN

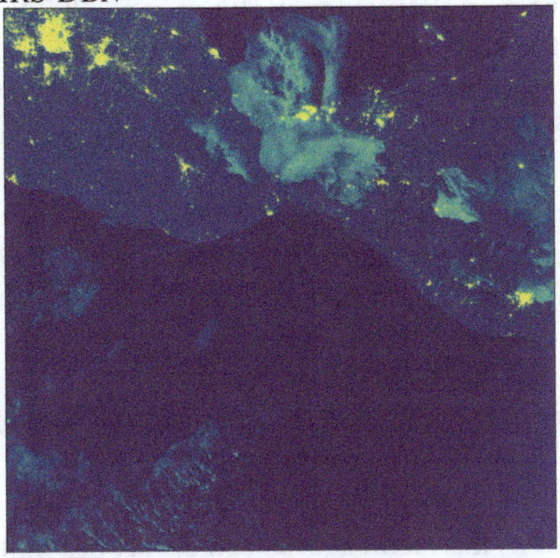

Note: Quadrant H08V07 was identified to obtain data for the counties of Mexico City and Oaxaca de Juárez, and quadrant H07V06 for Monterrey. Source: (Wang et al., 2022).

Nighttime luminosity data are obtained from images captured by satellites that orbit the Earth daily. Each pixel in these images represents an area smaller than one square kilometer and is associated with a numerical value that indicates the level of nighttime brightness: values close to zero reflect the absence of light, while high values indicate greater luminous intensity. By aggregating these values for a specific region, an indicator is obtained that approximates its nighttime economic activity.

The Day/Night Band (VIIRS-DNB) sensor, installed on the Suomi NPP and the Joint Polar Satellite System satellite platforms, provides these measurements with high resolution. The VIIRS grid divides the planet into 460 quadrants of approximately 10° × 10°, where each quadrant contains the data necessary for spatial economic analysis. See Figure 1

The VIIRS-DNB provides daily global measurements of nighttime visible and near-infrared light. The sensitivity of the VIIRS-DNB under low-light conditions allows for better resolution and sensor calibration compared to DMSP-OLS products. The National Aeronautics and Space Administration (NASA) has developed a suite of products from the VIIRS-DNB called Black Marble (VNP46/VJ146), which is considered the state of the art for research and development utilizing NTL (Román et al., 2018). The Black Marble suite has a spatial resolution of fifteen arc seconds and is available from January 2012 to the present using data from the VIIRS-DNB sensor. VNP46A1 is the short name for the nighttime radiance product captured by the sensor, titled "VIIRS/NPP Daily Gridded Day Night Band 15 arc-second Linear Lat Lon Grid Night". This product contains indicators such as sensor radiance, zenith, and azimuthal angles (sensor, solar, and lunar), cloud masking indicators, and time, among others, in HDF5 format. (Wang et al., 2022)

The VNP46/VJ146 suite is processed daily within 3-5 hours after data acquisition, enabling its application for near-real-time uses and long-term monitoring. The algorithm for retrieving NTL information was developed and implemented by NASA and utilizes high-quality radiance for NTL estimation. The Black Marble algorithm produces cloud-free imagery that has been corrected for atmospheric, terrain, lunar, thermal, and stray light effects. This corrected radiance yields superior short-term NTL time series and noise reduction, which facilitates the analysis of daily, seasonal, and annual variations. (Wang et al., 2022)

5.2 Modeling Framework and Proposed Hybrid Model

Traditional neoclassical economics built its theoretical foundations on assumptions of linearity and additivity that facilitated mathematical tractability but oversimplified economic reality. The basic linear model assumes:

The linear model assumes proportionality, where the combined effect of variables equals the sum of their individual effects; parameter constancy across time and units; and symmetry, meaning increases and decreases produce effects of equal magnitude.

Economic reality is rarely linear. Economic systems have five characteristics that contradict traditional linear models:

Diminishing marginal returns: Early increases in investment or capital generate higher returns than later ones.

Threshold effects and discontinuities: There are hotspots were behavior changes abruptly, such as financial crises or poverty traps.

Interactions and complementarities: The effect of one variable depends on the value of others, such as the ratio of human to physical capital, or fiscal policy according to the business cycle.

Track record dependence: Current results are conditioned by history, not only by the present; Early industrial advantages or temporary shocks can have long-lasting effects.

Heterogeneity: Economic agents (people, companies, countries) respond differently to similar conditions, so the same policy can produce very different results depending on the context.

Taken together, these characteristics underscore the need for economic models and policies that recognize the complexity and nonlinearity of real systems.

Decision Trees and Random Forests offer flexible alternatives to linear models. Decision trees capture interactions automatically, do not require specifying a functional form, are robust to outliers and irrelevant variables, and remain visually interpretable, though they can suffer from high variance and instability when minor changes occur in the data. Random Forests address these limitations by averaging many trees built on bootstrap simples:

$$\hat{f}_{RF}(X) = \frac{1}{B}\sum_{b=1}^{B} T_b(X) \tag{6}$$

Where is the b-th tree.

This approach reduces variance while maintaining model flexibility, provides measures of variable importance, and allows internal validation through the out-of-bag error. More complex nonlinear structures can also be modeled using neural networks, which learn hierarchical relationships in the data through multiple interconnected layers.

After researching models, it was found that given the economic heterogeneity, high informality, and frequent scarcity of subnational data in the region, a hybrid approach is recommended:

Use spatial econometrics to validate the direction of effects and quantify spillovers between neighboring regions.

Complement with ML (Random Forest or Gradient Boosting) to maximize predictive accuracy, using tools such as SHAP to recover some interpretability.

Reserve the DL for cases with long time series (e.g., VIIRS data since 2012) or when raw satellite images are directly integrated, always with rigorous temporal and spatial cross-validation schemes.

5.3 Proposed hybrid model

Previous research has focused heavily on log-linear regression, such as the work of (Ehsan et al., 2023; Gibson & Boe-Gibson, 2021a; Yuan et al., 2021). However, there is recent to introduce the use of non-parametric models such as convolutional neural networks (Sun et al., 2020) or transfer learning (Price & Atkinson, 2022) due to their flexibility. These models outperform traditional parametric models, particularly when capturing anomalies such as the pandemic. The significant tradeoff here is that these models lose any interpretability, require larger volumes of data (such as complete image files) and have higher computational power needs to fine-tune and train. Our motivation to implement a hybrid model is therefore to capitalize on the low variance and computational cost of a traditional model while harnessing the flexibility of a low demand nonparametric model, such as a Random Forest Regressor.

A hybrid prediction is therefore proposed, where an initial prediction is made using OLS and a Random Forest (RF) is then applied to the residuals of that prediction, so that the latter adjusts the former's output.

We begin with a standard linear regression as stated in equation (7):

$$y = X\beta + \varepsilon \tag{7}$$

where y is the target variable (*logGDP*), X represents the features (sum of radiance, mean radiance, county, etc.), β is a vector of unknown parameters, and ϵ represents unobserved variables (errors).

OLS assumes a linear relationship between X and $\hat{y}_{OLS}$ through $\hat{\beta}$:

After fitting, the residuals r_{OLS} of the regression model are:

The residuals are then modeled using a Random Forest, where X is trained against the residuals r_{OLS}:

After fitting, the residuals

The residuals are then modeled using a Random Forest, where X is trained against the residuals r_{OLS}:

$$\hat{r}_{OLS} = R(X)$$

After fitting, the residuals of the regression model are:

$$\hat{y}_{Hybrid} = X.\hat{\beta}' + R(X)$$

The residuals are then modeled after using a Random Forest, where it is trained against the residuals. The final model is thus additive:

$$\hat{y}_{Hybrid} = \hat{y}_{OLS} + \hat{r}_{OLS}$$

This model can be built as such (note here that it is being trained in a single fold, but a Random Forest should be subjected to cross-validation as it is described in the Results section).

Based on the theoretical foundations and the comparison of models presented above, the methodology described in the following section was designed to ensure the accuracy and replicability of the study.

6. METHODOLOGY

The methodology is organized into three sequential stages. First stage processes raw satellite imagery to extract daily radiance measurements for each county, see Figure 2. This process includes stages of extraction, cleaning, temporal aggregation, and generation of metrics, which ensures the efficient integration of satellite data with GDP estimates.

Second stage constructs the quarterly GDP and NTL time series, including seasonal decomposition and frequency alignment. Finally, trains evaluate three predictive models: OLS, Random Forest, and the hybrid OLS+RF, using both time-independent and time-dependent cross-validation.

After the previous step, a vector of values is obtained. To optimize data storage and retain only the necessary information, various summary statistics are computed from the vector: arithmetic mean, standard deviation, minimum value, 25th percentile, 50th percentile (median), 75th percentile, maximum value, among others. These are stored in a DataFrame structure and listed in Table 5.

Table 5. Features of the night light dataset

Variable
Tile
County
Date
Pixel count
Radiance sum
Mean radiance
Radiance std. dev.
Maximum radiance
Minimum radiance
25th percentile radiance
50th percentile radiance
75th percentile radiance

Note: Data can be exported to formats, such as csv or json to storage. Own elaboration

6.1 Data Preprocessing

To obtain the trend of the quarterly county GDP series, the following process was developed. The state GDP dataset previously described was taken for Mexico City,

Nuevo León, and Oaxaca. The quarterly state GDP variation series was then used to derive quarterly state GDP figures, adjusted to match the actual annual state GDP values at each fourth quarter. The difference between the annually reported state GDP and the state GDP obtained by applying the quarterly variations is approx. 3% to 4% in the case of Mexico City and Nuevo León, and up to 27% in Oaxaca de Juárez.

Finally, county GDP estimates are generated from each county's population share (See Data Section), yielding an annual county GDP series per county. The result is a quarterly county GDP series for each county in the study. These county GDP estimates are consistent with those produced by (González-Estrada & Gallegos-Cedillo, 2014).

As for NTL series, it is necessary to identify outliers resulting from satellite capture errors while avoiding the alteration of legitimate light measurements. For any outlier NTL observation, we inspected the specific date of the satellite image and verified whether a given observation stemmed from a capture error (e.g., over-saturated images). Once confirmed as a measurement error, the affected values are replaced by the average of the preceding and following observations for each variable. Measurements that do not correspond to a capture error are retained.

For each county, both series were decomposed into its trend, seasonality, and residual components. GDP data was available at quarterly frequency, making period=4 the natural choice to capture the annual seasonal cycle. Multiplicative decomposition was applied given that seasonal fluctuations in GDP scale proportionally with the trend level — a standard assumption for macroeconomic output series with sustained growth. Classical decomposition was subsequently replaced by STL for the final analysis, as its robust LOESS-based (Locally Estimated Scatterplot Smoothing) estimation prevents transitory economic shocks from distorting the extracted trend and seasonal components (See Figure 3).

The adequacy of the final decomposition was validated via an Augmented Dickey-Fuller test on the STL residuals, with p-values under 0.01 confirming that the remainder component was stationary and free of systematic structure.

In the case of NTL data, because the frequency of GDP (quarterly) does not match that of luminosity (daily), NTL data was aggregated quarterly. It is important to note that each variable measured (e.g., median, average, maximum value, etc.) was treated as its own time series and therefore the STL process was conducted by county and variable individually, to then be incorporated into the aggregation.

6.1 Model Specifications

6.2.1 OLS Model

The baseline model follows the log-linear specification established by (Henderson et al., 2012) and extended by (Ehsan et al., 2023).

Two sets of fixed effects are considered: year fixed effects (ET), implemented as a categorical year variable, and county fixed effects (EM), implemented as a categorical county indicator. Namely, this refers to a one-hot encoded variable for each county and for each year.

Quarter fixed effects were evaluated but did not improve model fit and were omitted. Both ET and EM are included jointly in the preferred specification.

The following diagnostic tests are applied to assess compliance with OLS assumptions: Breusch-Pagan for homoscedasticity, Durbin-Watson for serial independence of residuals, Shapiro-Wilk for normality of residuals, and variance inflation factors (VIF) for multicollinearity.

6.2.2 Random Forest Regressor

K-Fold cross-validation (5 folds, time-independent): Observations are randomly assigned to folds without regard to temporal order. This measures how well the model generalizes the NTL–GDP relationship across counties and time periods.

Time Split cross-validation (time-dependent): Two configurations are tested: (a) five splits in which each training window covers eight quarters and each test window covers the following eight quarters; and (b) a single split in which the model is trained on all observations except the last four quarters, which are held out for testing. This scheme preserves the temporal ordering of observations and more directly tests forecasting ability.

6.2.3 Hybrid model

As mentioned in the Background section, this architecture preserves the interpretable elasticity estimate from OLS while allowing the Random Forest to correct systematic non-linear errors that OLS leaves unexplained. The OLS component reduces the variance of the residuals that the Random Forest must learn, which in turn reduces the Random Forest's tendency to overfit relative to training on raw GDP values.

All features are standardized using StandardScaler before training, with the scaler fit on the training set only to prevent data leakage. The GDP target is also standardized prior to OLS fitting and inverse-transformed for error metric computation. The same K-Fold and Time Split schemes described for the standalone Random Forest are applied to the hybrid model.

6.2 Illustrative Diagnostic Exercise

To complement the model comparison, the original study also carried out an illustrative diagnostic exercise using one territorial unit as an example. The purpose of this exercise was not to replace the general results but to show, in a more transparent way, how the time-series behavior of GDP and residuals can be assessed before and after decomposition and differencing. For more information you can go github.com/carolinacorral/ntl-gdp-estimation/

This only shows one of the counties to show the results that be discuss in the las part of the chapter.

1. Data Loading and Preparation: We started by loading the pib_trimestral_izt.csv file into a panda DataFrame.

Figure 2.

	fecha	municipio	entidad_federativa	porc_pob	pibe	pib_mun
0	2004-03-31	Iztapalapa	CDMX	0.204829	2226949.7	456143.375920
1	2004-06-30	Iztapalapa	CDMX	0.204829	2234735.2	457738.070337
2	2004-09-30	Iztapalapa	CDMX	0.204829	2244809.2	459801.515402
3	2004-12-31	Iztapalapa	CDMX	0.204829	2260342.1	462983.100259
4	2005-03-31	Iztapalapa	CDMX	0.204829	2258091.6	462522.133104

2. STL Decomposition: We applied the STL (Seasonal-Trend decomposition using Loess) method to the 'pib_mun' (municipal PIB) series, successfully breaking it down into its constituent trend, seasonal, and residual components. This provided a clear view of the long-term movement, recurring patterns, and unexplained variations in the PIB.

Figure 3.

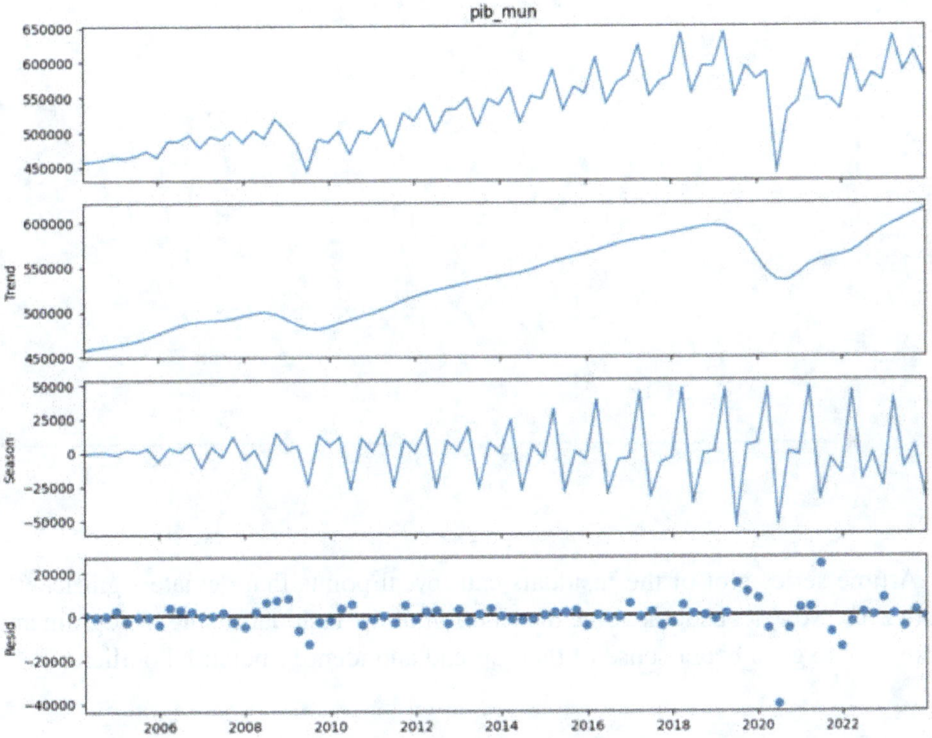

3. **Residual Analysis and Outlier Detection.** We examined the raw residuals through time series plots, histograms, and box plots to visualize their distribution and behavior.

Figure 4.

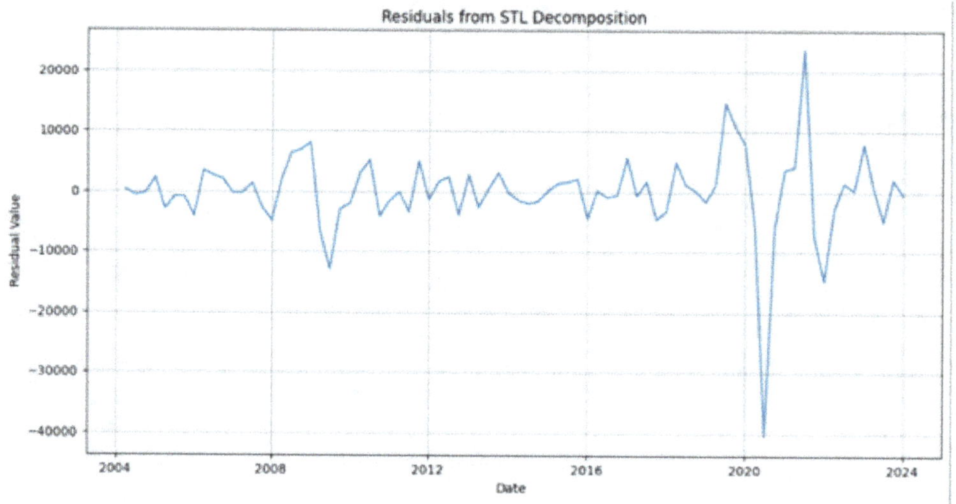

A time series plot of the residuals can reveal points that deviate significantly from zero. Now, let us look at the distribution of the residuals using histogram and a box plot to get a better sense of their spread and identify potential outliers.

Figure 5.

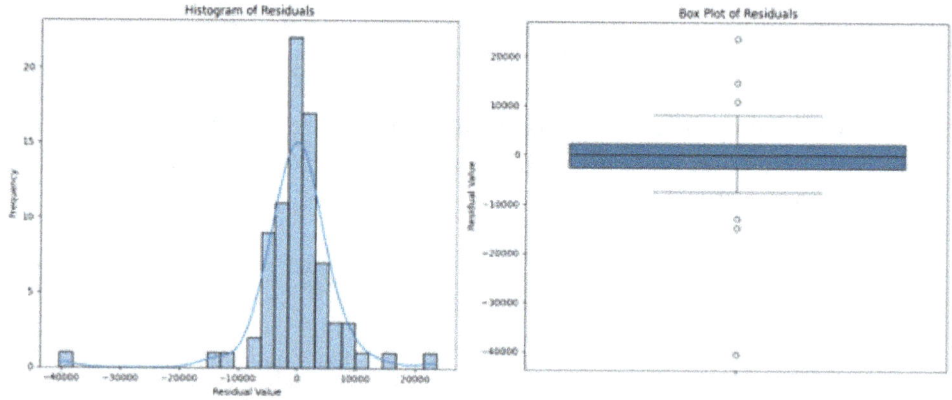

Using Z-scores with a threshold of 2, we identified 4 significant outliers in the residuals. Notably, a large negative residual in June 2020 was detected, reflecting the economic impact of the COVID-19 pandemic.

Figure 6.

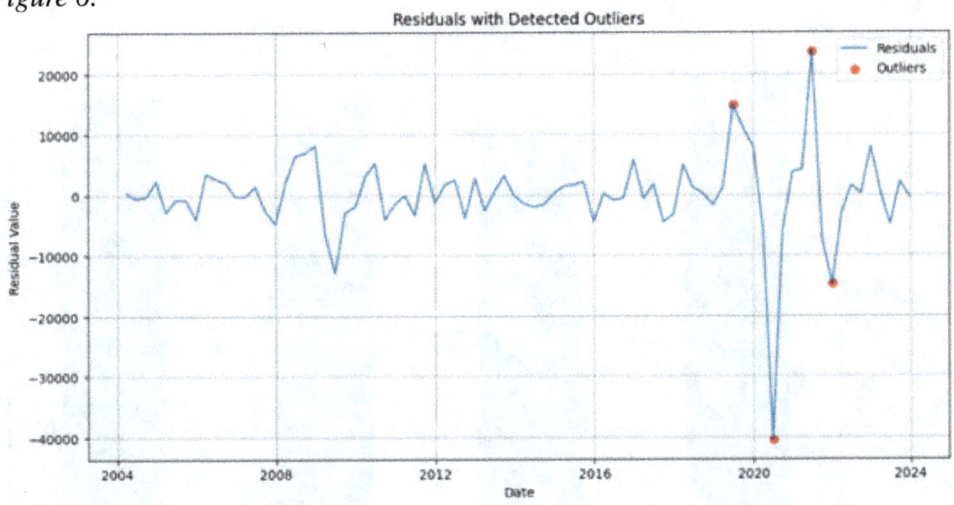

4. **Quarterly Seasonal Trends.** We calculated and visualized the quarterly average PIB over time to observe overall movements.

visualize these quarterly averages to better understand any seasonal patterns. A line plot will clearly show the trend of average PIB for each quarter over the years.

Further, we analyzed the average PIB for each quarter across all years. This revealed a consistent seasonal pattern: Q1 typically shows the highest PIB, followed by Q4, with a noticeable dip in Q2.

Figure 7.

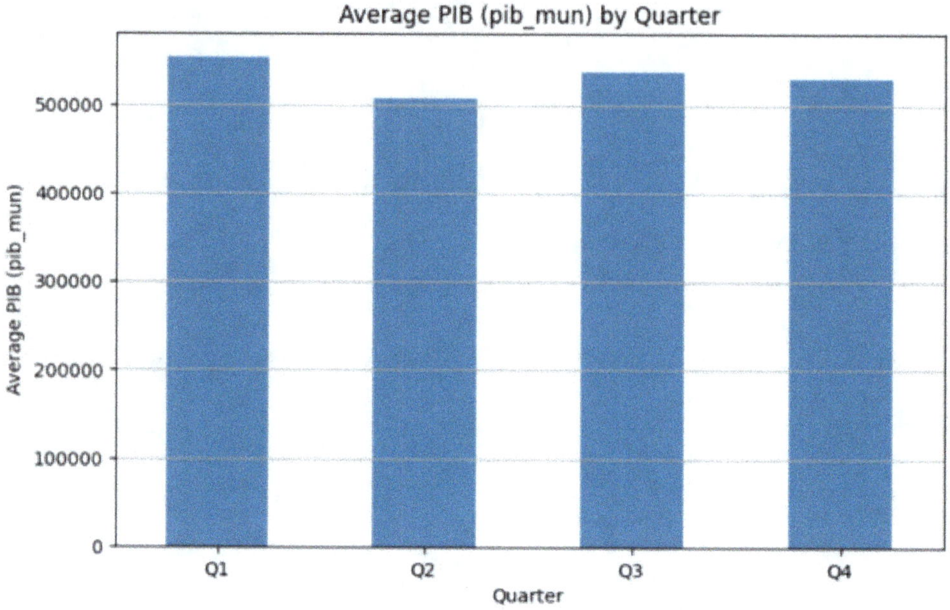

5. **Stationarity Testing and Differencing of Residuals** Initially, the Augmented Dickey-Fuller (ADF) test on the raw residuals indicated they were non-stationary (p-value > 0.05). The Autocorrelation Function (ACF) plot confirmed this by showing significant autocorrelation at multiple lags, implying that patterns still existed in the residuals.

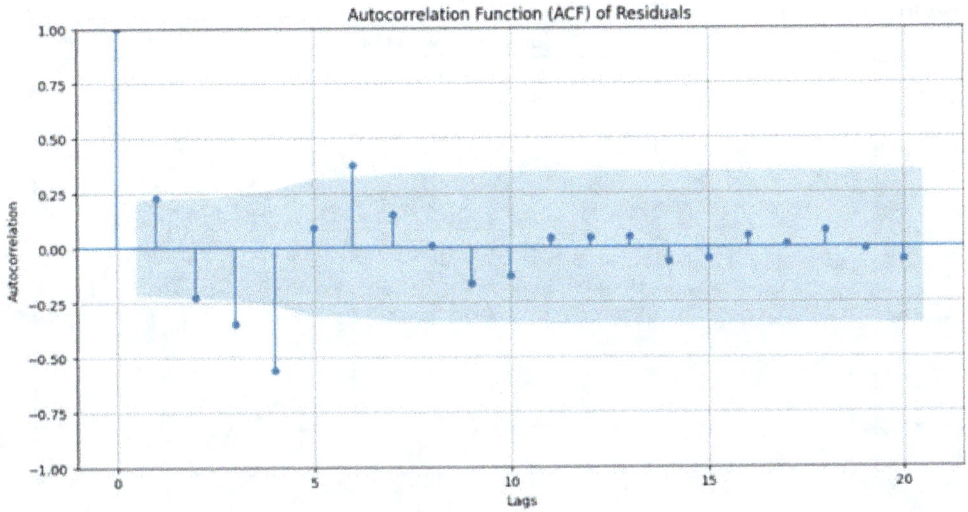

Given the non-stationarity and significant autocorrelation observed in the residuals, we will now apply first-order differencing to the residuals. Differencing is a common technique to make a time series stationary by removing trends and seasonality. After differencing, we will re-evaluate the stationarity using the ADF test and examine the ACF plot.

To address this, we performed first-order differencing on the residuals.

Figure 9.

First-Order Differenced Residuals (head):

fecha	resid
2004-06-30	-943.878265
2004-09-30	330.133942
2004-12-31	2583.027420
2005-03-31	-5215.989696
2005-06-30	2118.615736

dtype: float64

Figure 10.

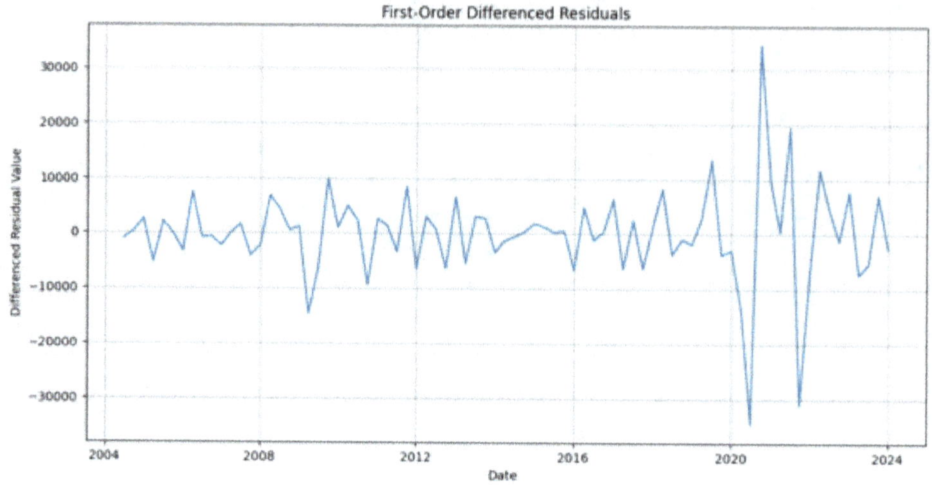

After differencing, a re-run of the ADF test showed a p-value of approximately 0.0000, strongly indicating that the differenced residuals are now stationary. The ACF plot of the differenced residuals also showed a significant reduction in auto-correlation, suggesting they are much closer to white noise.

Figure 11.

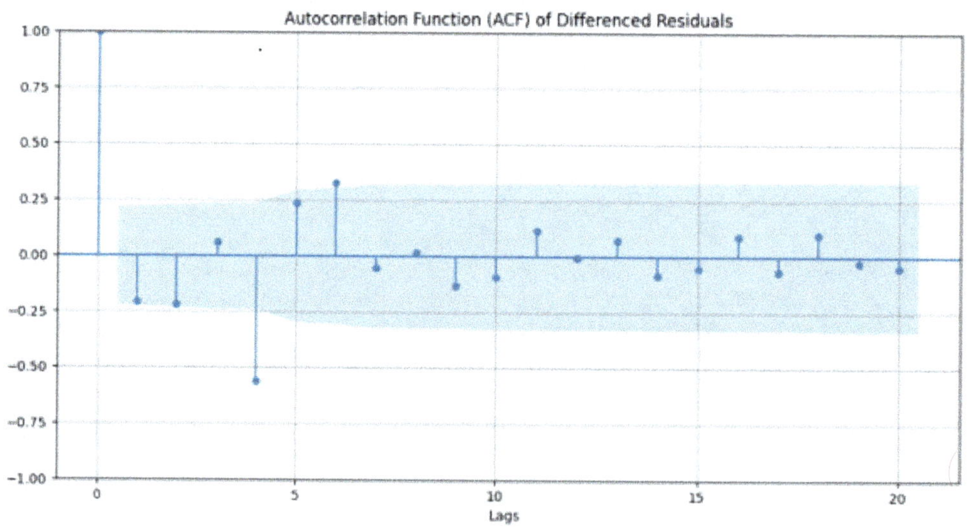

After examining the ACF of the differenced residuals, it is also useful to plot the Partial Autocorrelation Function (PACF). The PACF measures the correlation between an observation and a lagged observation after removing the linear dependence of the intervening observations.

Figure 12.

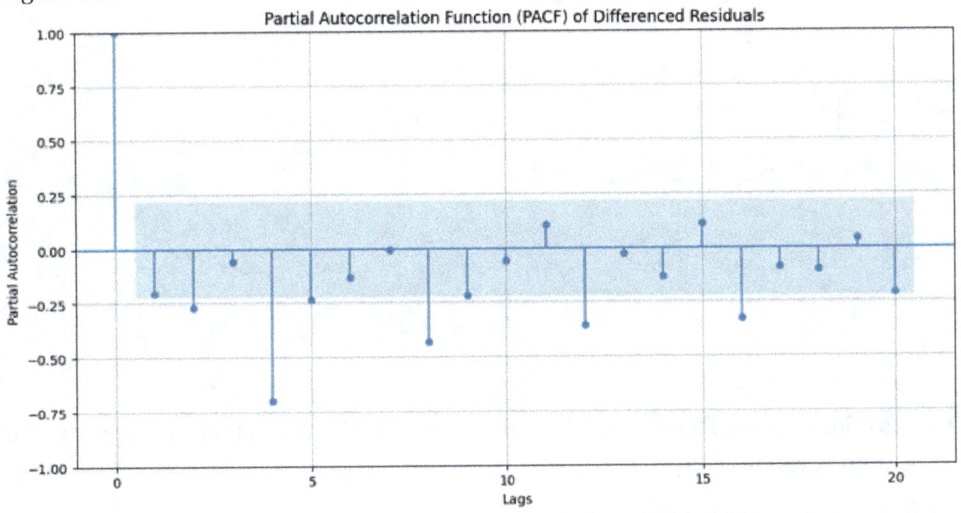

Modeling and Prediction with OLS and Random Forest

We have analyzed the characteristics of the time series and its residuals; we can proceed to build predictive models:

1. **Ordinary Least Squares (OLS)**: A linear model that will serve as our baseline.

Figure 13.

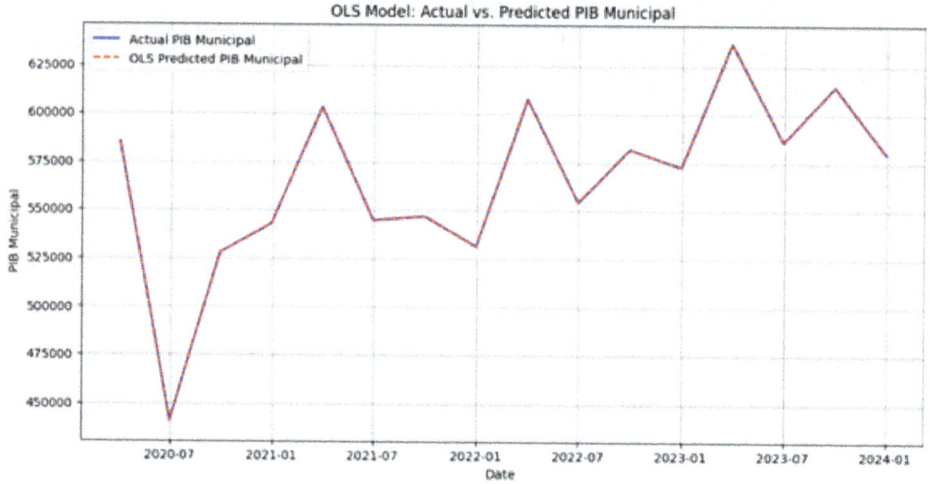

2. **Random Forest Regressor**: A nonlinear ensemble model that can capture more complex relationships.

Figure 14.

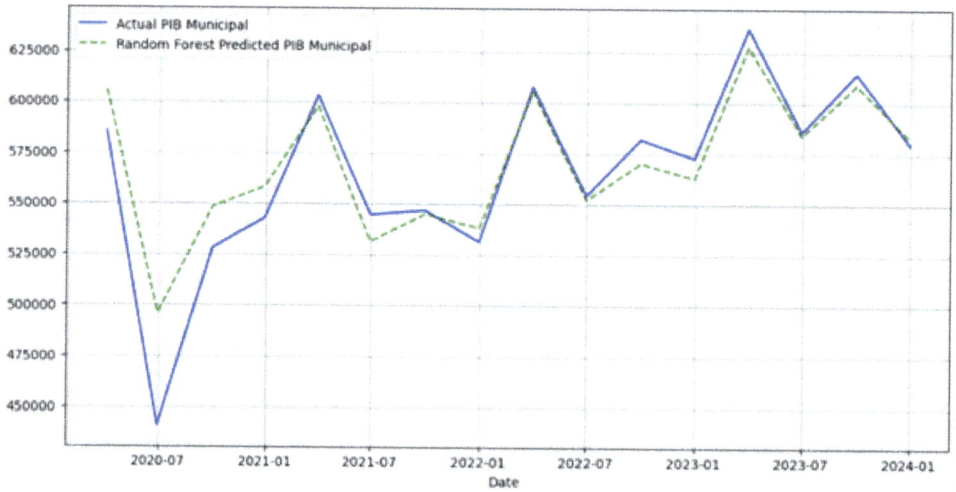

Compare Both Models

Given the robustness and more interpretable performance metrics, the Random Forest model is the preferred choice for this forecasting task. It provides a more reliable representation of the predictive power compared to the OLS model, which showed signs of potential issues that could lead to overly optimistic and misleading results.

Figure 15.

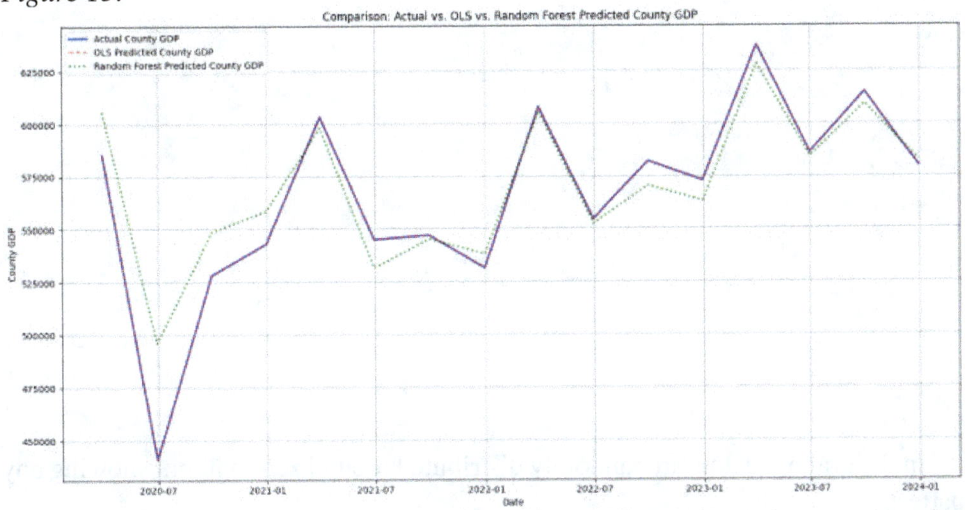

Ideal Scenario (Homoscedasticity): In an ideal scenario, the points on this scatter plot should be randomly distributed around the horizontal red dashed line at y=0, without showing any discernible pattern. The spread of the residuals should appear constant across the range of predicted values.

Observed Pattern: Looking at the plot, the residuals are scattered around zero, and the spread appears consistent across the range of predicted values. There are not a clear 'funnel' shape (widening or narrowing spread) or other obvious patterns that would strongly suggest heteroscedasticity.

Residuals

By comparing the residues generated by our Random Forest model (which was optimized with temporal cross-validation) with the residues obtained from the original STL decomposition. This will allow us to assess how well each approach has managed to capture trends, seasonality, and relationships in the data, leaving behind a 'noise'.

Scatter Plot of Residues vs. Predicted Values to Evaluate Homoscedasticity

As can be seen, the variance of the residuals (model errors) is constant at all levels of the predicted values.

Figure 16.

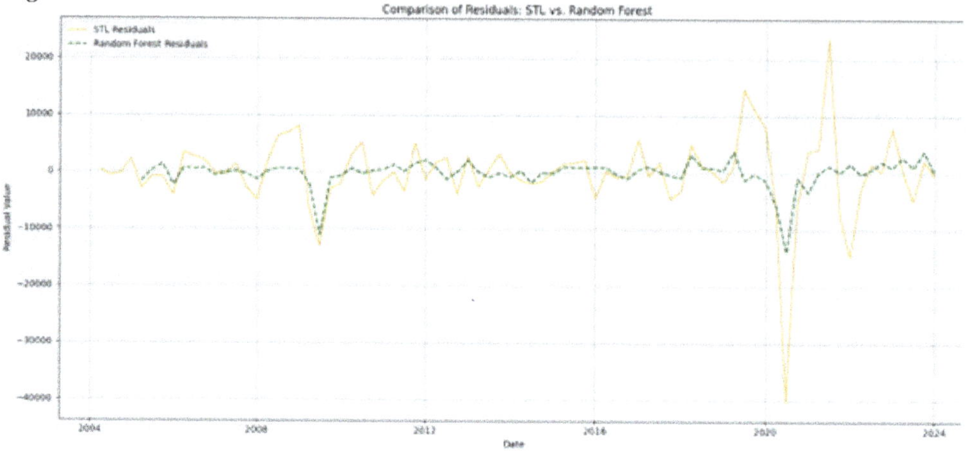

In the graph the dots are randomly distributed around zero without showing any pattern.

Figure 17.

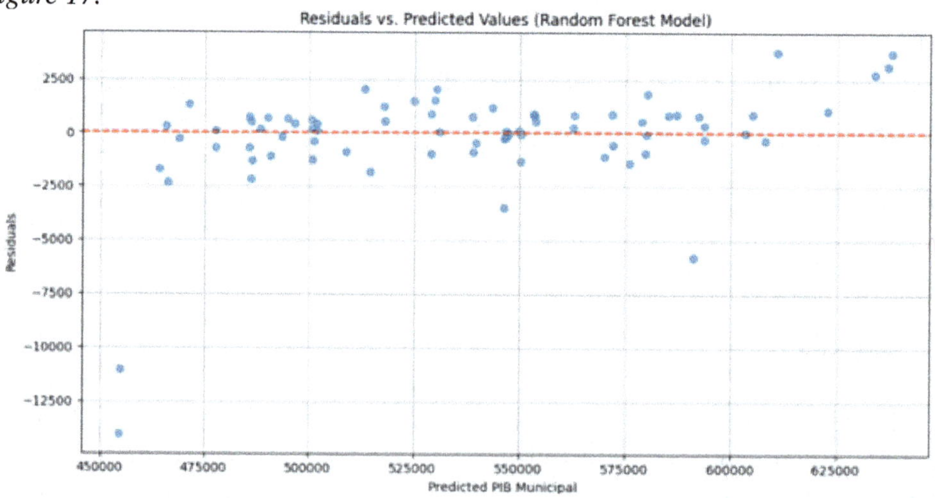

7. RESULTS AND DISCUSSION

7.1 OLS Model

First, the relationship between nighttime luminosity and county GDP was estimated without considering the temporal dimension. Table 3 presents the results of the OLS regression applied to the sixteen counties of Mexico City. It was found that the inclusion of quarter fixed effects did not improve model accuracy and were therefore omitted. The inclusion of year fixed effects improved model precision across all counties.

The Durbin–Watson statistic obtained (0.416) indicates positive autocorrelation among the residuals, violating the assumption of independence. Additionally, the observed skewness and excess kurtosis show that the errors do not follow a normal distribution. The trend observed in the residuals (Figure 19) suggests nonlinearity and heteroscedasticity. The inclusion of year and county fixed effects (Figure19) introduce normality at a significance level of $\alpha = 0.05$. However, positive autocorrelation in the residuals persists even after including both effects.

Despite the model presenting an adjusted (R^2) greater than 0.9, the violation of OLS assumptions implies potentially biased estimates and an overestimation of precision. This high (R^2) value may be attributed to the lack of independence among observations. For this reason, subsequent models relied on more robust evaluation metrics, such as mean squared error (MSE), root mean squared error (RMSE), mean absolute error (MAE), and mean absolute percentage error (MAPE) (Holmes et al., 2017).

Figure 18. OLS results

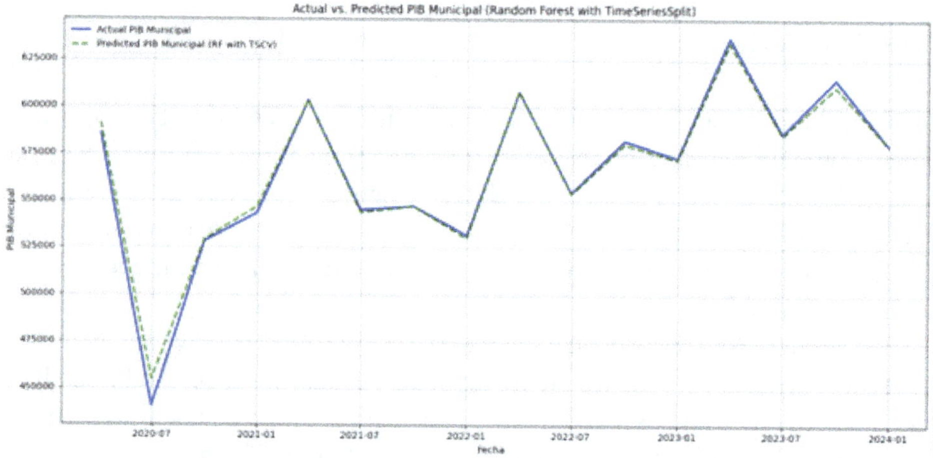

Note: county effects (EM) and temporal year effects (ET) (a) Model without year and county effects; (b) model with year fixed effects; (c) model with county fixed effects; (d) model with both year and county fixed effects. Source: Author's elaboration. Source: Own elaboration.

The inclusion of spatial and temporal fixed effects maximizes the explanatory power of the model, raising the adjusted above 0.94 in all regions. While in Mexico City controlling for county is the main factor improving precision, in Monterrey and Oaxaca the temporal dimension is what stabilizes the model fit.

7.2 Random Forest Model

For this reason, a Random Forest model was trained, which does not rely on assumptions and has the capacity to capture nonlinear relationships between NTL and GDP. In addition to annual and county effects, lagged variables of the NTL median were included. That is, for each measurement of median radiance its values at y were considered. Furthermore, a hyperparameter search was conducted using Grid Search CV, with mean squared error (MSE) as the optimization metric (Holmes et al., 2017).

Subsequently, model performance was evaluated using two approaches: time-independent modeling, which measures the generalization ability between nighttime luminosity and GDP without considering the date, using five-fold K-Fold cross-validation (Hastie et al., 2009); and time-dependent modeling, which preserves the temporal structure through Time Split divisions: (a) five splits with training on eight quarters and testing on eight, and (b) a single split with training on all data except the last four quarters.

Tables 4, 5, and 6 show that including lags does not reduce error metrics, although it decreases the standard deviation in predictions for scenario one split in Mexico City counties. Results indicate that the Random Forest model maintains a MAPE below ±3% in the time-independent evaluation, though it exhibits higher variability in temporal forecast scenarios. In the temporal forecast, predictions deviate on average by ±8% from actual GDP values, with greater variability than in K-Fold, reflecting differences across counties. Additionally, the results suggest that the model tends to overfit in the scenario one split (Greene, 2003).

Table 6. Performance of the Random Forest model with and without lags (K-Fold validation)

Model	rmse	mae	mape (%)
RF sin lags	6,827.58	3,797.67	2.39
RF con lags	213,902.04	172,462.36	2.61

Note: Values calculated for Mexico City counties. Source: Author's elaboration.

We concluded that the inclusion of lags does not improve error metrics and, in fact, significantly increases RMSE and MAE, indicating overfitting. However, MAPE remains stable, suggesting that the impact on relative accuracy is minimal.

Table 7. Performance of the Random Forest model in temporal forecasting (Time Split – 5 splits)

model	rmse	mae	mape (%)
RF sin lags	23,754.84	13,094.02	7.97
RF con lags	220,438.32	178,753.91	7.99

Note: Scenario with five training and testing splits. Source: Authors' elaboration.

Interpretation: In temporal forecasting, the model without lags exhibits much lower absolute and relative errors than the model with lags. This confirms that lagged variables do not provide predictive value in this context and may increase model variability.

Table 8. Performance of the Random Forest model in temporal forecasting (Time Split – 1 split)

Models	rmse	mae	mape (%)
RF sin lags	63,190.97	24,516.21	12.82
RF con lags	53,049.89	21,797.30	11.44

Note: Scenario with a single split—training on all data except the last four quarters. Source: Author's elaboration.

Interpretation: In the scenario with a single split, the model with lags slightly reduces MAPE compared to the model without lags, but absolute errors remain high and variability is still elevated. This suggests that lagged variables provide only a marginal improvement in relative accuracy and do not offset the risk of overfitting.

7.3 Hybrid OLS + Random Forest model

Finally, a hybrid OLS + Random Forest model was developed, combining the interpretability of linear regression with the predictive power of Random Forest. First, a traditional OLS model is trained, and the GDP prediction residuals are obtained. Next, a Random Forest model is trained to predict the OLS residuals using the NTL measurements. The final prediction is obtained by adding the Random Forest prediction to the original OLS prediction; in other words, the Random Forest learns to correct the errors of the OLS. This additive model reduces the variance present in Random Forest through the OLS while retaining the flexibility of Random Forest. This approach achieved an RMSE of 1,289.47 and a MAPE of 0.49% in K-Fold validation, outperforming the individual models and confirming its robustness in temporal forecasting scenarios.

As shown in Table 7, the hybrid model achieves an RMSE of 1289.47 and a MAPE of 0.49% in K-Fold validation, outperforming the individual models. In forecasting scenarios (Time Split), the MAPE remains around 3.5%, confirming its robustness on unseen data, as shown in Table 8.

Table 9. OLS results + Random Forest hybrid model

Metric	Value	σ
ols + rf (without lags)		
rmse	1289.47	790.75
mae	836.99	623.01
mape (%)	0.49	0.04

Note: K-Fold validation for CDMX. Source: Author's elaboration

The hybrid model without lags achieves superior performance in Mexico City with a MAPE of 0.49% and an RMSE of 1289.47 under the K-Fold validation, surpassing the performance of the Random Forest model with and without lags. This suggests that the hybrid model manages to capture the complexity of the luminosity-to-GDP relationship without incurring the risks of overfitting associated with the use of lags.

Table 10. OLS results + Random Forest hybrid model

County/Metric	(1)		(2)	
cdmx	**Value**	**σ**	**Value**	**σ**
ols + rf (without lags)				
rmse	9653.29	6588.08	9843.86	6987.96
mae	6277.28	5739.84	6290.67	6441.94
mape (%)	3.57	0.37	3.34	1.03

Note with: Time Split (1) 5-split (2) 1-split

In the temporal forecast scenarios, the hybrid model maintains a satisfactory performance for Mexico City with an ASM of approximately 3.5%, which confirms the generalizability to unseen data. While a significant increase in the magnitude of absolute errors (RMSE and MAE) is observed compared to the K-Fold validation, the consistency of the percentage error between the 5-split and 1-split configurations demonstrates that the model is resilient for GDP estimation in time series.

7.4 Elasticity Between Luminosity and GDP

Finally, the elasticity between productive night luminosity and county GDP was estimated. Since it is not possible to obtain elasticity by means of the beta coefficient, it is estimated directly for all NTL and GDP measurements. An average elasticity was obtained, and a stationarity test was performed to validate its representativeness. The results indicate average values close to 0.085 for counties in Mexico City, lower than those reported in international studies (0.12 in the US and 0.10 in China). This difference could be attributed to the methodology used to separate productive light from domestic light. However, (Fontaine et al., 2025) points to a decreasing trend in the light-to-GDP elasticity since 2013. Negative elasticities were identified, attributable to the economic contraction during the pandemic, when county GDP contracted while nighttime luminosity increased. Gustavo A. Madero stands out among the counties most affected by this behavior. While Monterrey shows an elasticity greater than one, consistent with emerging economies.

While the significance levels close to zero in most territories confirm the stationarity of their light-GDP relationship, allowing for a reliable interpretation of its economic sensitivity, the high p-values in Monterrey and Cuauhtémoc warn that the elasticity in these counties should not be considered a fixed parameter, but rather a magnitude that experiences persistent structural changes, making the reversion of their economic indicators toward a constant average equilibrium impossible.

The findings confirm the secondary hypothesis: non-linear models and the hybrid approach outperform OLS regression in scenarios with complex relationships between luminosity and GDP. Moreover, the technical optimization of the data flow ensures the viability of the methodology for replicable studies in other territories and historical periods.

Table 11. Elasticity and ADF test results by municipality (summary)

County	Elasticity	ADF Statistic	P- value
Benito Juárez	0.083	-6.518	0.000
Gustavo A. Madero	-0.233	-5.983	0.000
Cuauhtémoc	0.080	-2.111	0.240
Oaxaca de Juárez	0.167	-4.119	0.001
Monterrey	1.033	-0.853	0.874

Note. Table retained from the source manuscript and reformatted for editorial consistency.

Figure 19. Comparison of MAPE across models and validation schemes

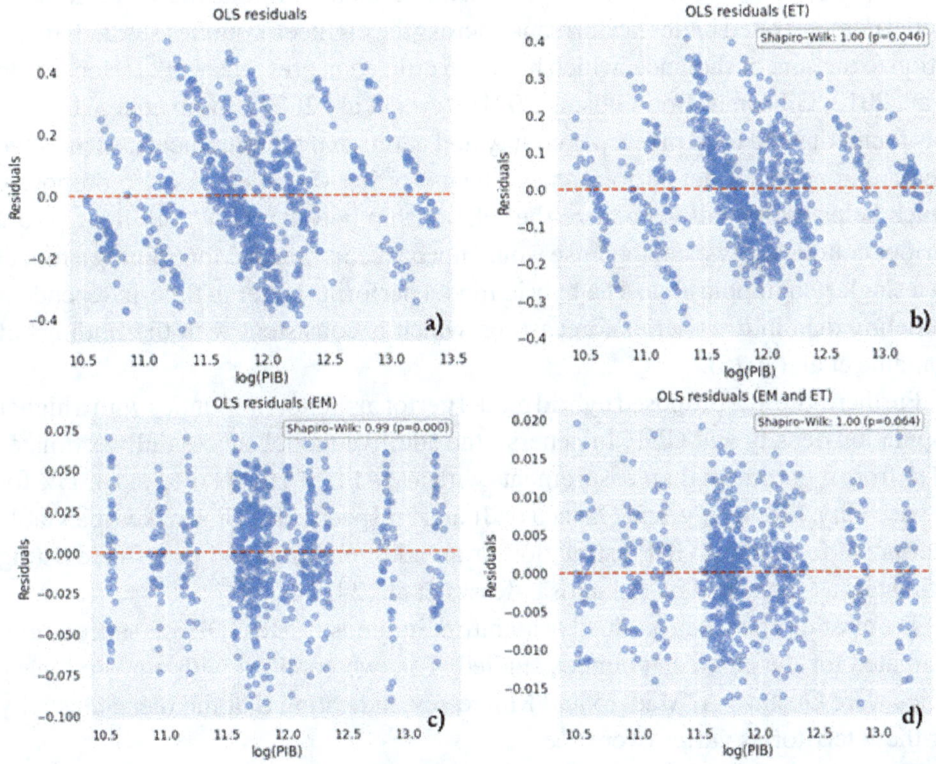

Note. Lower MAPE indicates better relative predictive accuracy. The visual pattern highlights the advantage of hybrid specification under multiple validation schemes.

8. CONCLUSION

The use of nighttime light as an economic proxy variable allows for the collection of information that is not periodically published, such as quarterly county GDP. Although it is possible to estimate this through population-based approximations, as was done in this work, such methods rely on data published annually, thereby limiting the periodicity of that approach.

A linear model was initially proposed to describe the relationship between nighttime light and GDP. However, in line with previous studies indicating a possible non-linear relationship (Hu & Yao, 2022; Ehsan et al., 2023), it was found that a linear regression is inadequate for estimating GDP from nighttime lights.

Consequently, two models were proposed: a Random Forest model and a hybrid OLS model with Random Forest applied to the residuals. Among these, the additive model demonstrated better performance across the eighteen counties studied. In addition to the sum of radiance, which has been utilized in previous works (Henderson et al., 2012; Gibson & Boe-Gibson, 2021; Beyer et al., 2022; Ehsan et al., 2023), it was found that the total pixels per county and additional measurements, such as the median, improve model performance. The use of lag variables was also proposed, which helps the model generalize the relationship between GDP and light across various counties; however, their use would not be recommended for training a model on a single geographic area. The hybrid model performs better in time-independent modeling than in time-series forecasting, which is consistent with the findings of Fontaine et al. (2025).

Furthermore, the proposed hybrid model performs better in counties with a higher population density and GDP. In general, the additive model successfully estimates GDP from nighttime light measurements with a MAPE of 1%, 0.86%, and 4.03% for Mexico City, Monterrey, and Oaxaca de Juárez, respectively. This makes it a viable alternative for county GDP estimation or an additional method to refine existing estimates, as suggested by (Llamosas-Rosas et al., 2021).

The elasticity between productive nighttime luminosity and GDP was successfully estimated for the eighteen counties studied. The two counties with non-stationary series were Gustavo A. Madero and Monterrey, indicating that the mean elasticity for these territories varies over time.

The estimated elasticities for counties in Mexico City are approximately 0.085, which are lower than the values reported in international literature using the same VIIRS dataset: 0.12 in U.S. counties (Gibson & Boe-Gibson, 2021) and 0.1 in China (Zhang & Gibson, 2022). These differences might be related to the methodology employed in this work to separate productive light from domestic light using state-level electricity consumption data, although additional research would be required to identify the specific causes of this discrepancy. Additionally, it is important to consider that Fontaine et al. (2025) suggest the elasticity between nighttime light and GDP has experienced a downward trend since 2013, which may provide context for the values observed in this study.

REFERENCES

Beyer, R. C. M., Hu, Y., & Yao, J. (2022). *Measuring Quarterly Economic Growth from Outer Space*. World Bank., DOI: 10.1596/1813-9450-9893

Borunda, M., Conde-López, L., Ruiz-Chavarría, G., Lopez Lopez, G., Alvarado, V. M., & Carrera Avendaño, E. D. J. (2026). Advances in Similar Day Methods for Short-Term Load Forecasting for Power Systems. *Forecasting*, *8*(2), 32. DOI: 10.3390/forecast8020032

Castro-Nuño, M., Molina-Toucedo, J. A., & Pablo-Romero, M. P. (2013). Tourism and GDP: A meta-analysis of panel data studies. *Journal of Travel Research*, *52*(6), 745–758. DOI: 10.1177/0047287513478500

Chen, X., & Nordhaus, W. D. (2011). Using luminosity data as a proxy for economic statistics. *Proceedings of the National Academy of Sciences of the United States of America*, *108*(21), 8589–8594. DOI: 10.1073/pnas.1017031108 PMID: 21576474

Ehsan, Z.-A., Basher, S. A., Rashid, S., & Uddin, M. R. (2023). Estimation of District-Level GDP using Night Lights: The Case of Bangladesh. SSRN *Electronic Journal*. DOI: 10.2139/ssrn.4373887

Fontaine, F. R., Komorowski, J. C., Corbeau, J., Burtin, A., De Chabalier, J. B., Grandin, R., Saurel, J. M., Agrinier, P., Moune, S., Jadelus, F., Melezan, D., Gabriel, J.-G., Vidal, C., Zimmermann, B., Vaton, D., Koziol, J., Lavenaire, J. M., Moretti, R., Lemarchand, A., & Satriano, C. (2025). Ongoing multiparameter unrest at the Montagne Pelée volcano on Martinique from 2019 to 2024. *Scientific Reports*, *15*(1), 23189. DOI: 10.1038/s41598-025-05641-6 PMID: 40604020

Gibson, J., & Boe-Gibson, G. (2021a). Nighttime Lights and County-Level Economic Activity in the United States: 2001 to 2019. *Remote Sensing (Basel)*, *13*(14), 2741. DOI: 10.3390/rs13142741

Gibson, J., & Boe-Gibson, G. (2021b). Nighttime Lights and County-Level Economic Activity in the United States: 2001 to 2019. *Remote Sensing (Basel)*, *13*(14), 2741. DOI: 10.3390/rs13142741

Gibson, J., Olivia, S., Boe-Gibson, G., & Li, C. (2021). Which night lights data should we use in economics, and where? *Journal of Development Economics*, *149*, 102602. DOI: 10.1016/j.jdeveco.2020.102602

González-Estrada, A., & Gallegos-Cedillo, G. (2014). El producto interno bruto de los municipios de México: II. Estados M-Z. *Revista Mexicana de Ciencias Agrícolas*, *5*(8), 1405–1421.

Gorjian, M. (2025). Advances and challenges in GIS-based assessment of urban green infrastructure: A systematic review (2020–2024). *Preprint]. Preprints., 281*, v1.DOI: 10.20944/preprints202508

Greene, W. H. (2003). *Econometric Analysis*. Prentice Hall. https://books.google.com.mx/books?id=JJkWAQAAMAAJ

Hastie, T., Tibshirani, R., & Friedman, J. (2009). An introduction to statistical learning.

Henderson, J. V., Storeygard, A., & Weil, D. N. (2012). Measuring Economic Growth from Outer Space. *The American Economic Review, 102*(2), 994–1028. DOI: 10.1257/aer.102.2.994 PMID: 25067841

Holmes, A., Illowsky, B., & Dean, S. (2017). *Introductory Business Statistics 2e*. OpenStax.

Instituto Nacional de Estadística y Geografía. (2023). Medición de la economía informal (MEI) 2022, preliminar. https://www.inegi.org.mx/contenidos/saladeprensa/boletines/2023/MDEI/MDEI2022.pdf

Jhamb, P., Ferreira, S., Stephens, P., Sundaram, M., & Wilson, J. (2025). Shedding light on development: Leveraging the new nightlights data to measure economic progress. *PLoS One, 20*(2), e0318482. DOI: 10.1371/journal.pone.0318482 PMID: 39899501

Llamosas-Rosas, I., Rangel González, E., & Sandoval Bustos, M. (2021). Medición de la actividad económica en las principales zonas turísticas de playa en México a través imágenes satelitales: Measurement of Economic Activity in the Main Touristic Beach Zones in México Using Satellite Images. *Ensayos Revista de Economía, 40*(2), 115–136. DOI: 10.29105/ensayos40.2-1

Millán López, A. J., & González Olivares, D. (2024). Satellite nighttime lights as a measurement of economic growth in Mexico's counties. Ensayos. *Revista de Economía, 43*(1), 1–18. DOI: 10.29105/ensayos43.1-1

O'Rourke, K. H. (1998). Monetary data and proxy GDP estimates: Ireland 1840–1921. *Irish Economic and Social History, 25*(1), 22–51. DOI: 10.1177/033248939802500103

Padilla Sierra, A. D. J. (2015). Uso de variables de actividad económica en la estimación del PIB per cápita microterritorial. *Cuadernos de Economía (Santiago, Chile), 34*(65), 349–376. DOI: 10.15446/cuad.econ.v34n65.45936

Paganelli, M. P. (2021). Population as a GDP proxy in Adam Smith. *Journal of Scottish Philosophy, 19*(2), 115–123. DOI: 10.3366/jsp.2021.0297

Price, N., & Atkinson, P. M. (2022). Global GDP prediction with night-lights and transfer learning. *IEEE Journal of Selected Topics in Applied Earth Observations and Remote Sensing*, *15*, 7128–7138. DOI: 10.1109/JSTARS.2022.3200754

Román, M. O., Wang, Z., Sun, Q., Kalb, V., Miller, S. D., Molthan, A., Schultz, L., Bell, J., Stokes, E. C., Pandey, B., Seto, K. C., Hall, D., Oda, T., Wolfe, R. E., Lin, G., Golpayegani, N., Devadiga, S., Davidson, C., Sarkar, S., & Masuoka, E. J. (2018). NASA's Black Marble nighttime lights product suite. *Remote Sensing of Environment*, *210*, 113–143. DOI: 10.1016/j.rse.2018.03.017

Ruiz Ochoa, W. (2010). Convergencia económica interestatal en México, 1900–2004. *Análisis Económico*, *25*(58), 7–34.

Sun, J., Di, L., Sun, Z., Wang, J., & Wu, Y. (2020). Estimation of GDP using deep learning with NPP-VIIRS imagery and land cover data at the county level in CONUS. *IEEE Journal of Selected Topics in Applied Earth Observations and Remote Sensing*, *13*, 1400–1415. DOI: 10.1109/JSTARS.2020.2983331

Wang, Z., Román, M. O., Shrestha, R., Yao, T., & Kalb, V. (2022). Black Marble user guide (Version 1.3). National Aeronautics and Space Administration.

Yuan, D., Jiang, H., Guo, W., Cui, X., Wu, L., Wu, Z., & Wang, H. (2021). Regression Analysis and Comparison of Economic Parameters with Different Light Index Models under Various Constraints. *Sensors (Basel)*, *21*(22), 7561. DOI: 10.3390/s21227561 PMID: 34833637

Zhang, X., & Gibson, J. (2022). Using Multi-Source Nighttime Lights Data to Proxy for County-Level Economic Activity in China from 2012 to 2019. *Remote Sensing (Basel)*, *14*(5), 1282. DOI: 10.3390/rs14051282

Zheng, Y., Yang, K., Wei, C., Fu, M., & Fan, M. (2024). An improved cross-sensor calibration approach for DMSP-OLS and NPP-VIIRS nighttime light data. *IEEE Journal of Selected Topics in Applied Earth Observations and Remote Sensing*, *18*, 865–877. DOI: 10.1109/JSTARS.2024.3494551

Compilation of References

Abadi, M., Barham, P., Chen, J., Chen, Z., Davis, A., Dean, J., Devin, M., Ghemawat, S., Irving, G., Isard, M., Kudlur, M., Levenberg, J., Monga, R., Moore, S., Murray, D. G., Steiner, B., Tucker, P., Vasudevan, V., Warden, P., & Zheng, X. (2016). *TensorFlow: A system for large-scale machine learning.* In *Proceedings of the 12th USENIX Symposium on Operating Systems Design and Implementation (OSDI 16)* (pp. 265-283). USENIX Association.

Abdallah, H., Yue, Z., Ahmadian, A., Thompson, D., & Wang, B. (2022). Statistical inference for persistent homology and its application to simulated fMRI time series data. *Foundations of Data Science (Springfield, Mo.)*, *4*(2), 153–182. DOI: 10.3934/fods.2022014

Akiner, M. E., & Ghasri, M. (2024). Comparative assessment of deep belief network and hybrid adaptive neuro-fuzzy inference system model based on a meta-heuristic optimization algorithm for precise predictions of the potential evapotranspiration. *Environmental Science and Pollution Research International*, *31*(30), 42719–42749. DOI: 10.1007/s11356-024-33987-3 PMID: 38879646

Akiyama, S., & Matsuyama, N. (2025). Yield curve extrapolation with machine learning. ASTIN Bulletin. *ASTIN Bulletin*, *55*(1), 76–96. DOI: 10.1017/asb.2024.27

Akyıldırım, E., & Soner, H. M. (2014). A brief history of mathematics in finance. *Borsa Istanbul Review*, *14*(1), 57–63. DOI: 10.1016/j.bir.2014.01.002

Alfaro, A., Gámez, M., & García, N. (2018). A neural network approach for identifying explanatory variables in regression problems. *Applied Soft Computing*, *67*, 25–35.

Alfeus, M., Overbeck, L., & Schlögl, E. (2019). Regime switching rough Heston model. *Journal of Futures Markets*, *39*(5), 538–552. DOI: 10.1002/fut.21993

Ali, I., Modibbo, U. M., Bolaji, A. L., & Garg, H. (2024). *Optimization and Computing using Intelligent Data-Driven Approaches for Decision-Making: Optimization Applications* (1st ed.). CRC Press., DOI: 10.1201/9781003536796

Ali, S., Bouri, E., Roubaud, D., & Vinh Vo, X. (2021). The impact of COVID-19 on cryptocurrency markets: A financial-stability analysis. *Finance Research Letters*, *38*, 101798.

Alsulaiman, T., Al-Ali, A. K., & Alarifi, A. (2022). A comparative study of machine learning techniques for stock market prediction. *Expert Systems with Applications*, *190*, 116–234.

Andersen, R. (2009). Nonparametric methods for modeling nonlinearity in regression analysis. *Annual Review of Sociology*, *35*(1), 67–85. DOI: 10.1146/annurev.soc.34.040507.134631

Andersen, T. G., Bollerslev, T., Diebold, F. X., & Labys, P. (2003). Modeling and forecasting realized volatility. *Econometrica*, *71*(2), 579–625. DOI: 10.1111/1468-0262.00418

Ante, L. (2023). How Elon Musk's Twitter activity moves cryptocurrency markets. *Technological Forecasting and Social Change*, *186*, 122112.

Arnell, L., Engström, E., Uddin, G. S., Hasan, M., & Kang, S. H. (2023). Volatility spillovers, structural breaks and uncertainty in technology sector markets. *Financial Innovation*, *9*(1), 106. Advance online publication. DOI: 10.1186/s40854-023-00502-5

Arumugam, V., & Natarajan, V. (2023). Time series modeling and forecasting using autoregressive integrated moving average and seasonal autoregressive integrated moving average models. *Instrumentation Mesure Métrologie*, *22*(4), 161–168. DOI: 10.18280/i2m.220404

Auer, R., & Tercero-Lucas, D. (2023). Rise of the machines: Algorithmic stablecoins and the quest for stability. BIS Bulletin, No. 132.

Auer, R., Cornelli, G., Doerr, S., Frost, J., & Gambacorta, L. (2023). Crypto Trading and Bitcoin Prices: Evidence from a New Database of Retail Adoption. BIS Working Papers No. 1049, Bank for International Settlements.

Bai, X., & Wang, Y. (2025). A hybrid ANFIS model for stock market prediction: Case study on Google Inc. *Computer Applications and Information*, *6*(2), 22–35.

Bamford, T., Coletta, A., Fons, E., Gopalakrishnan, S., Vyetrenko, S., Balch, T., & Veloso, M. (2023). Multi-modal financial time-series retrieval through latent space projections. *4th ACM International Conference on AI in Finance*, 498–506. DOI: 10.1145/3604237.3626901

Barker, M., Chue Hong, N. P., Katz, D. S., Lamprecht, A.-L., Martinez-Ortiz, C., Psomopoulos, F., Harrow, J., Castro, L. J., Gruenpeter, M., Martinez, P. A., & Honeyman, T. (2022). Introducing the FAIR Principles for research software. *Scientific Data*, *9*(1), 622. DOI: 10.1038/s41597-022-01710-x PMID: 36241754

Bashar, A., Rabbani, M. R., Khan, S., & Ali, M. A. M. (2021). Data driven finance: A bibliometric review and scientific mapping. *2021 International Conference on Data Analytics for Business and Industry (ICDABI)*, 161–166. DOI: 10.1109/ICDABI53623.2021.9655898

Bauer, U. (2021). Ripser: Efficient computation of Vietoris–Rips persistence barcodes. *Journal of Applied and Computational Topology*, *5*(3), 391–423. DOI: 10.1007/s41468-021-00071-5

Baur, D. G., & Dimpfl, T. (2021). The volatility of Bitcoin and its role as a medium of exchange and a store of value. *Empirical Economics*, *61*(5), 2663–2683.

Baur, D. G., & Lucey, B. M. (2010). Is gold a hedge or a safe haven? An analysis of stocks, bonds and gold. *Financial Review*, *45*(2), 217–229.

Baur, D. G., & McDermott, T. K. (2010). Is gold a safe haven? International evidence. *Journal of Banking & Finance*, *34*(8), 1886–1898.

Bayer, S., & Dimitriadis, T. (2022). Regression-based expected shortfall backtesting. *Journal of Financial Econometrics*, *20*(3), 437–471. DOI: 10.1093/jjfinec/nbaa013

Bergmeir, C., Hyndman, R. J., & Koo, B. (2018). A note on the validity of cross-validation for evaluating autoregressive time series prediction. *Computational Statistics & Data Analysis*, *120*, 70–83. DOI: 10.1016/j.csda.2017.11.003

Beyer, R. C. M., Hu, Y., & Yao, J. (2022). *Measuring Quarterly Economic Growth from Outer Space*. World Bank., DOI: 10.1596/1813-9450-9893

Black, F., & Scholes, M. (1973). The pricing of options and corporate liabilities. *Journal of Political Economy*, *81*(3), 637–654. DOI: 10.1086/260062

Bobrowski, O., & Skraba, P. (2023). A universal null-distribution for topological data analysis. *Scientific Reports*, *13*(1), 12274. DOI: 10.1038/s41598-023-37842-2 PMID: 37507400

Bollerslev, T. (1986). Generalized autoregressive conditional heteroskedasticity. *Journal of Econometrics*, *31*(3), 307–327.

Boritz, J. E., & No, W. G. (2013). The quality of interactive data: XBRL versus compustat, yahoo finance, and google finance. SSRN *Electronic Journal*. DOI: 10.2139/ssrn.2253638

Borunda, M., Conde-López, L., Ruiz-Chavarría, G., Lopez Lopez, G., Alvarado, V. M., & Carrera Avendaño, E. D. J. (2026). Advances in Similar Day Methods for Short-Term Load Forecasting for Power Systems. *Forecasting*, *8*(2), 32. DOI: 10.3390/forecast8020032

Bouri, E., Molnár, P., Azzi, G., Roubaud, D., & Hagfors, L. I. (2017). On the hedge and safe haven properties of Bitcoin: Is it really more than a diversifier? *Finance Research Letters*, *20*, 192–198.

Box, G. E. P., & Jenkins, G. M. (1976). *Time series analysis: Forecasting and control*. Holden-Day.

Boyd, S., & Vandenberghe, L. (2004). *Convex optimization*. Cambridge University Press., DOI: 10.1017/CBO9780511804441

Boyle, P. P. (1977). Options: A Monte Carlo approach. *Journal of Financial Economics*, *4*(3), 323–338. DOI: 10.1016/0304-405X(77)90005-8

Breiman, L. (2001). Random forests. *Machine Learning*, *45*(1), 5–32. DOI: 10.1023/A:1010933404324

Brigo, D., & Mercurio, F. (2006). *Interest rate models: Theory and practice* (2nd ed.). Springer.

Brockwell, P. J., & Davis, R. A. (Eds.). (2002). *Introduction to time series and forecasting*. Springer New York. DOI: 10.1007/b97391

Brownlees, C. T., & Gallo, G. M. (2006). Financial econometric analysis at ultra-high frequency: Data handling concerns. *Computational Statistics &amp. Computational Statistics & Data Analysis*, *51*(4), 2232–2245. DOI: 10.1016/j.csda.2006.09.030

Bunescu, L., & Vârtei, A. M. (2024). Modern finance through quantum computing: A systematic literature review. *PLoS One*, *19*(7), e0304317. DOI: 10.1371/journal.pone.0304317 PMID: 39024227

Camenzind, N., & Filipović, D. (2024). Stripping the Swiss discount curve using kernel ridge regression. *European Actuarial Journal*, *14*(2), 371–410. DOI: 10.1007/s13385-024-00386-4

Cartea, Á., Jaimungal, S., & Penalva, J. (2015). *Algorithmic and high-frequency trading*. Cambridge University Press., DOI: 10.1017/CBO9781316195277

Castro-Nuño, M., Molina-Toucedo, J. A., & Pablo-Romero, M. P. (2013). Tourism and GDP: A meta-analysis of panel data studies. *Journal of Travel Research*, *52*(6), 745–758. DOI: 10.1177/0047287513478500

Cesa, M. (2017). A brief history of quantitative finance. *Probability, Uncertainty and Quantitative Risk, 2*(6), 6. Advance online publication. DOI: 10.1186/s41546-017-0018-3

Chakraborty, A., & Tsokos, C. (2025). *A Modern Optimization Approach with Data-Driven Analytical Modeling for the Healthcare Business Segment (HBS) from the S&P 500*. Business, Economics and Management. DOI: 10.20944/preprints202508.2017.v1

Chang, C.-L., & McAleer, M. (2015). Econometric analysis of financial derivatives: An overview. *Journal of Econometrics, 187*(2), 403–407. DOI: 10.1016/j.jeconom.2015.02.026

Chazal, F., & Michel, B. (2021). An introduction to topological data analysis: Fundamental and practical aspects for data scientists. *Frontiers in Artificial Intelligence, 4*, 667963. DOI: 10.3389/frai.2021.667963 PMID: 34661095

Chazal, F., Michel, B., & Reise, W. (2025). Topological signatures of periodic-like signals. *Bernoulli, 31*(3), 1955–1990. DOI: 10.3150/24-BEJ1793

Cheng, Y. (2025). Monte Carlo-Based VaR Estimation and Backtesting Under Basel III. *Risks, 13*(8), 146. DOI: 10.3390/risks13080146

Chen, M., Wang, Y., Feng, S., & Zhang, Y. (2023). Topological regularization for representation learning via persistent homology. *Mathematics, 11*(4), 1008. DOI: 10.3390/math11041008

Chen, T., & Guestrin, C. (2016). XGBoost: A scalable tree boosting system. In *Proceedings of the 22nd ACM SIGKDD International Conference on Knowledge Discovery and Data Mining* (pp. 785–794). ACM. https://doi.org/DOI: 10.1145/2939672.2939785

Chen, X., & Nordhaus, W. D. (2011). Using luminosity data as a proxy for economic statistics. *Proceedings of the National Academy of Sciences of the United States of America, 108*(21), 8589–8594. DOI: 10.1073/pnas.1017031108 PMID: 21576474

Chen, X., & Wang, Y. (2019). A comparative study of GRNN and ANFIS models for stock market prediction. *International Journal of Computational Intelligence, 15*(3), 203–214.

Chohan, U. W. (2022). Crypto Winters. Critical Blockchain Research Initiative (CBRI) Working Paper, SSRN. Conlon, T., & McGee, R. (2020). Safe haven or risky hazard? Bitcoin during the COVID-19 bear market. *Finance Research Letters, 35*, 101607.

Consigli, G., Kopa, M., & Pichler, A. (2022). Discrete stochastic optimization in finance. *Quantitative Finance*, *22*(1), 1–5. DOI: 10.1080/14697688.2021.2013621

Cont, R. (2001). Empirical properties of asset returns: Stylized facts and statistical issues. *Quantitative Finance*, *1*(2), 223–236. DOI: 10.1080/713665670

Corbet, R., Fugacci, U., Kerber, M., Landi, C., & Wang, B. (2019). A kernel for multi-parameter persistent homology. *Computers & Graphics: X*, *2*, 100005. DOI: 10.1016/j.cagx.2019.100005 PMID: 33367228

Corbet, S., Lucey, B., Urquhart, A., & Yarovaya, L. (2019). Cryptocurrencies as a financial asset: A systematic analysis. *International Review of Financial Analysis*, *62*, 182–199.

Dayarathne, K. P. N. S., & Thayasiwam, U. (2024). Utility of smoothing techniques in yield curve modeling for the Asian Pacific frontier capital market. *SN Computer Science*, *5*(4), 430. Advance online publication. DOI: 10.1007/s42979-024-02684-w

De Zarzà, I., De Curtò, J., Roig, G., & Calafate, C. T. (2023). Optimized Financial Planning: Integrating Individual and Cooperative Budgeting Models with LLM Recommendations. *AI*, *5*(1), 91–114. DOI: 10.3390/ai5010006

Deng, T. (2024). The application of database systems in information management. *Applied and Computational Engineering*, *40*(1), 33–42. DOI: 10.54254/2755-2721/40/20230625

Dickey, D. A., & Fuller, W. A. (1979). Distribution of the estimators for autoregressive time series with a unit root. *Journal of the American Statistical Association*, *74*(366a), 427–431.

Diebold, F. X., & Mariano, R. S. (1995). Comparing predictive accuracy. *Journal of Business & Economic Statistics*, *13*(3), 253–263. DOI: 10.1080/07350015.1995.10524599

Ding, C., Duan, J., Zhang, Y., Wu, X., & Yu, G. (2017). Using an ARIMA-GARCH modeling approach to improve subway short-term ridership forecasting accounting for dynamic volatility. *IEEE Transactions on Intelligent Transportation Systems*, *19*(4), 1054–1064. DOI: 10.1109/TITS.2017.2711046

Djatschenko, W. (2019). BondValuation: An R package for fixed coupon bond analysis. *The R Journal*, *11*(2), 124. Advance online publication. DOI: 10.32614/RJ-2019-055

Dogariu, M., Ştefan, L.-D., Boteanu, B. A., Lamba, C., Kim, B., & Ionescu, B. (2022). Generation of realistic synthetic financial time-series. *ACM Transactions on Multimedia Computing Communications and Applications*, *18*(4), 1–27. DOI: 10.1145/3501305

Dong, Z., Hu, C., Zhou, C., & Lin, H. (2020). Vectorization of persistence barcode with applications in pattern classification of porous structures. *Computers & Graphics*, *90*, 182–192. DOI: 10.1016/j.cag.2020.05.029

Dong, Z., Lin, H., Zhou, C., Zhang, B., & Li, G. (2024). Persistence B-spline grids: Stable vector representation of persistence diagrams based on data fitting. *Machine Learning*, *113*(3), 1373–1420. DOI: 10.1007/s10994-023-06492-w

Dote-Pardo, J. S., Cordero-Díaz, M. C., Espinosa Jaramillo, M. T., & Parra-Domínguez, J. (2025). Leveraging artificial intelligence for enhanced decision-making in finance: Trends and future directions. *Journal of Accounting Literature*. Advance online publication. DOI: 10.1108/JAL-02-2025-0100

Ehsan, Z.-A., Basher, S. A., Rashid, S., & Uddin, M. R. (2023). Estimation of District-Level GDP using Night Lights: The Case of Bangladesh. SSRN *Electronic Journal*. DOI: 10.2139/ssrn.4373887

Emmert-Streib, F. (2025). *Unifying Perspectives on Econometrics, Econophysics, Complexity Economics, and Ai-Driven Economics. SSRN*. DOI: 10.2139/ssrn.5346888

Engle, R. F. (1982). Autoregressive conditional heteroscedasticity with estimates of the variance of United Kingdom inflation. *Econometrica*, *50*(4), 987–1007. DOI: 10.2307/1912773

Fikri, N., Rida, M., Abghour, N., Moussaid, K., & El Omri, A. (2019). An adaptive and real-time based architecture for financial data integration. *Journal of Big Data*, *6*(1), 97. Advance online publication. DOI: 10.1186/s40537-019-0260-x

Filipović, D., Pelger, M., & Ye, Y. (2025). Stripping the discount curve: A robust machine learning approach. *Management Science*, mnsc.2023.01401. Advance online publication. DOI: 10.1287/mnsc.2023.01401

Firat, M. (2008). Comparison of ANFIS, GRNN, FFNN, and autoregressive models for daily river flow forecasting: Application to Seyhan and Cine rivers, Turkey. *Hydrology and Earth System Sciences*, *12*(1), 123–134. DOI: 10.5194/hess-12-123-2008

Fischer, T., & Krauss, C. (2018). Deep learning with long short-term memory networks for financial market predictions. *European Journal of Operational Research*, *270*(2), 654–669. DOI: 10.1016/j.ejor.2017.11.054

Flaig, S., & Junike, G. (2022). Scenario generation for market risk models using generative neural networks. *Risks*, *10*(11), 199. DOI: 10.3390/risks10110199

Fontaine, F. R., Komorowski, J. C., Corbeau, J., Burtin, A., De Chabalier, J. B., Grandin, R., Saurel, J. M., Agrinier, P., Moune, S., Jadelus, F., Melezan, D., Gabriel, J.-G., Vidal, C., Zimmermann, B., Vaton, D., Koziol, J., Lavenaire, J. M., Moretti, R., Lemarchand, A., & Satriano, C. (2025). Ongoing multiparameter unrest at the Montagne Pelée volcano on Martinique from 2019 to 2024. *Scientific Reports*, *15*(1), 23189. DOI: 10.1038/s41598-025-05641-6 PMID: 40604020

Friedman, J. H. (2001). Greedy function approximation: A gradient boosting machine. *Annals of Statistics*, *29*(5), 1189–1232. DOI: 10.1214/aos/1013203451

Gao, G., Mishra, B., & Ramazzotti, D. (2018). Causal data science for financial stress testing. *Journal of Computational Science*, *26*, 294–304. DOI: 10.1016/j.jocs.2018.04.003

Gao, Y. (2025). Looking for the impact of entrepreneurship on regional economic resilience in China. *Sustainability (Basel)*, *17*(4), 1397. DOI: 10.3390/su17041397

Gatheral, J., Jaisson, T., & Rosenbaum, M. (2018). Volatility is rough. *Quantitative Finance*, *18*(6), 933–949. DOI: 10.1080/14697688.2017.1393551

Gauss, C. F. (1809). *Theoria motus corporum coelestium in sectionibus conicis solem ambientium*. Perthes & Besser.

Gibson, J., & Boe-Gibson, G. (2021a). Nighttime Lights and County-Level Economic Activity in the United States: 2001 to 2019. *Remote Sensing (Basel)*, *13*(14), 2741. DOI: 10.3390/rs13142741

Gibson, J., Olivia, S., Boe-Gibson, G., & Li, C. (2021). Which night lights data should we use in economics, and where? *Journal of Development Economics*, *149*, 102602. DOI: 10.1016/j.jdeveco.2020.102602

Gidea, M., & Katz, Y. (2018). Topological data analysis of financial time series: Landscapes of crashes. *Physica A*, *491*, 820–834. DOI: 10.1016/j.physa.2017.09.028

Gilli, M., & Këllezi, E. (2006). An application of extreme value theory for measuring financial risk. *Computational Economics*, *27*(2), 207–228.

Glasserman, P. (2004). *Monte Carlo methods in financial engineering*. Springer., DOI: 10.1007/978-0-387-21617-1

Gnoatto, A., & Horvath, B. (2022). Mathematical modeling and computation in finance. *Quantitative Finance*, *22*(11), 1971–1972. DOI: 10.1080/14697688.2022.2117641

Goble, C., Cohen-Boulakia, S., Soiland-Reyes, S., Garijo, D., Gil, Y., Crusoe, M. R., Peters, K., & Schober, D. (2020). FAIR computational workflows. *Data Intelligence*, *2*(1–2), 108–121. DOI: 10.1162/dint_a_00033

Goldstein, I., Spatt, C., & Ye, M. (2021). *Big data in finance*. National Bureau of Economic Research., DOI: 10.3386/w28615

González-Estrada, A., & Gallegos-Cedillo, G. (2014). El producto interno bruto de los municipios de México: II. Estados M-Z. *Revista Mexicana de Ciencias Agrícolas*, *5*(8), 1405–1421.

Gorjian, M. (2025). Advances and challenges in GIS-based assessment of urban green infrastructure: A systematic review (2020–2024). *Preprint]. Preprints.*, *281*, v1.DOI: 10.20944/preprints202508

Greene, W. H. (2003). *Econometric Analysis*. Prentice Hall. https://books.google.com.mx/books?id=JJkWAQAAMAAJ

Gričar, S., Lojanica, N., & Backović, T. (2025). Financial Econometrics and Quantitative Economic Analysis. *Journal of Risk and Financial Management*, *18*(3), 166. DOI: 10.3390/jrfm18030166

Grohs, P., & Kutyniok, G. (Eds.). (2022). *Mathematical aspects of deep learning*. Cambridge University Press., DOI: 10.1017/9781009025096

Gunnarsson, E. S., Isern, H. R., Kaloudis, A., Risstad, M., Vigdel, B., & Westgaard, S. (2024). Prediction of realized volatility and implied volatility indices using AI and machine learning: A review. *International Review of Financial Analysis*, *93*, 103221. DOI: 10.1016/j.irfa.2024.103221

Gu, S., Kelly, B., & Xiu, D. (2020). Empirical asset pricing via machine learning. *Review of Financial Studies*, *33*(5), 2223–2273. DOI: 10.1093/rfs/hhaa009

Gustafsson, O. J. R., Wilkinson, S. R., Bacall, F., Soiland-Reyes, S., Leo, S., Pireddu, L., Owen, S., Juty, N., Fernández, J. M., Brown, T., Ménager, H., Grüning, B., Capella-Gutierrez, S., Coppens, F., & Goble, C. (2025). WorkflowHub: A registry for computational workflows. *Scientific Data*, *12*(1), 837. DOI: 10.1038/s41597-025-04786-3 PMID: 40399296

Hacibedel, B., & Perez-Saiz, H. (2023). Assessing Macrofinancial Risks from Crypto XVII. Assets. IMF Working Papers.

Hambly, B., Xu, R., & Yang, H. (2023). Recent advances in reinforcement learning in finance. *Mathematical Finance*, *33*(3), 437–503. DOI: 10.1111/mafi.12382

Härdle, W. K., Harvey, C. R., & Reule, R. C. G. (2020). Understanding cryptocurrencies. *Journal of Financial Econometrics*, *18*(2), 181–208.

Hassan, T. (2025). *Augmented Analytics in Financial Forecasting Enhancing Risk Management and Investment Strategies through AI-Driven Insights. SSRN*. DOI: 10.2139/ssrn.5179431

Hastie, T., Tibshirani, R., & Friedman, J. (2009). An introduction to statistical learning.

Henderson, J. V., Storeygard, A., & Weil, D. N. (2012). Measuring Economic Growth from Outer Space. *The American Economic Review*, *102*(2), 994–1028. DOI: 10.1257/aer.102.2.994 PMID: 25067841

Hensel, F., Moor, M., & Rieck, B. (2021). A survey of topological machine learning methods. *Frontiers in Artificial Intelligence*, *4*, 681108. DOI: 10.3389/frai.2021.681108 PMID: 34124648

Heston, S. L. (1993). A closed-form solution for options with stochastic volatility. *Review of Financial Studies*, *6*(2), 327–343. DOI: 10.1093/rfs/6.2.327

Hochreiter, S., & Schmidhuber, J. (1997). Long short-term memory. *Neural Computation*, *9*(8), 1735–1780. DOI: 10.1162/neco.1997.9.8.1735 PMID: 9377276

Hoerl, A. E., & Kennard, R. W. (1970). Ridge regression: Biased estimation for nonorthogonal problems. *Technometrics*, *12*(1), 55–67. DOI: 10.1080/00401706.1970.10488634

Holmes, A., Illowsky, B., & Dean, S. (2017). *Introductory Business Statistics 2e*. OpenStax.

Horvath, B., Jacquier, A., & Tankov, P. (2020). Volatility options in rough volatility models. *SIAM Journal on Financial Mathematics*, *11*(2), 437–469. DOI: 10.1137/18M1169242

Huang, W., Li, C., & Wang, H. (2022). A hybrid ANFIS model for stock market forecasting based on macroeconomic indicators. *Applied Soft Computing*, *115*, 108–187.

Huang, Y., Capretz, L. F., & Ho, D. (2019). Neural network models for stock selection based on fundamental analysis. In *2019 IEEE Canadian Conference of Electrical and Computer Engineering (CCECE)* (pp. 1–4). IEEE. DOI: 10.1109/CCECE.2019.8861550

Huang, Y., & Luo, Y. (2024). Forecasting conditional volatility based on hybrid GARCH-type models with long memory, regime switching, leverage effect and heavy-tail: Further evidence from equity market. *The North American Journal of Economics and Finance*, *72*, 102148. DOI: 10.1016/j.najef.2024.102148

Hull, J. C. (2022). *Options, futures, and other derivatives* (11th ed.). Pearson.

Instituto Nacional de Estadística y Geografía. (2023). Medición de la economía informal (MEI) 2022, preliminar. https://www.inegi.org.mx/contenidos/saladeprensa/boletines/2023/MDEI/MDEI2022.pdf

International Monetary Fund. (2023). *Elements of Effective Policies for Crypto Assets*. IMF Policy Paper.

Islambekov, U., & Pathirana, L. (2024). Vector summaries of persistence diagrams and permutation-based hypothesis testing. *Foundations of Data Science (Springfield, Mo.)*, *6*(1), 1–19. DOI: 10.3934/fods.2024002

Ismail, M. S., Md Noorani, M. S. M., Ismail, M., Razak, F. A., & Alias, M. A. (2022). Early warning signals of financial crises using persistent homology. *Physica A*, *586*, 126459. DOI: 10.1016/j.physa.2021.126459

Jain, R., & Sharma, A. (2024). Enhancing GRNN performance in financial time series forecasting using optimization techniques. *International Journal of Advanced Intelligent Systems*, *15*(2), 112–124.

Jang, J. S. R. (1993). ANFIS: Adaptive-network-based fuzzy inference system. *IEEE Transactions on Systems, Man, and Cybernetics*, *23*(3), 665–685. DOI: 10.1109/21.256541

Jeng, S. W., & Kılıçman, A. (2021). On Multilevel and Control Variate Monte Carlo Methods for Option Pricing under the Rough Heston Model. *Mathematics*, *9*(22), 2930. DOI: 10.3390/math9222930

Jhamb, P., Ferreira, S., Stephens, P., Sundaram, M., & Wilson, J. (2025). Shedding light on development: Leveraging the new nightlights data to measure economic progress. *PLoS One*, *20*(2), e0318482. DOI: 10.1371/journal.pone.0318482 PMID: 39899501

Jokhadze, V., & Schmidt, W. M. (2020). Measuring model risk in financial risk management and derivatives valuation. *International Journal of Theoretical and Applied Finance*, *23*(05), 2050012. DOI: 10.1142/S0219024920500120

Jorion, P. (2007). *Value at risk: The new benchmark for managing financial risk* (3rd ed.). McGraw-Hill.

Kakade, K., Jain, I., & Mishra, A. K. (2022). Value-at-Risk forecasting: A hybrid ensemble learning GARCH-LSTM based approach. *Resources Policy*, *78*, 102903. DOI: 10.1016/j.resourpol.2022.102903

Katz, Y. A., & Biem, A. (2021). Time-resolved topological data analysis of market instabilities. *Physica A*, *571*, 125816. DOI: 10.1016/j.physa.2021.125816

Kazak, H. (2025). Metaheuristic-optimized ANFIS and ANN models for stock price prediction: Evidence from Borsa Istanbul 100. *Neural Computing & Applications*, *37*, 4531–4546.

Ke, G., Meng, Q., Finley, T., Wang, T., Chen, W., Ma, W., Ye, Q., & Liu, T.-Y. (2017). LightGBM: A highly efficient gradient boosting decision tree. In Vol. 30, pp. 3146–3154). Advances in Neural Information Processing Systems. Curran Associates.

Khine, P. P., & Wang, Z. (2019). A review of polyglot persistence in the big data world. *Information (Basel)*, *10*(4), 141. DOI: 10.3390/info10040141

Kim, H. Y., & Won, C. H. (2018). Forecasting the volatility of stock price index: A hybrid model integrating LSTM with multiple GARCH-type models. *Expert Systems with Applications*, *103*, 25–37. DOI: 10.1016/j.eswa.2018.03.002

Kim, K., & Parnichkun, M. (2017). *Real-time coagulant dosage prediction using GRNN, ANFIS, and MLP models across varying turbidity levels*. Environmental Expert and MDPI.

Kim, T., & Kim, H. Y. (2016). Forecasting stock prices with a feature fusion LSTM-CNN model using different representations of the same data. *Expert Systems with Applications*, *157*, 113–513.

Kingma, D. P., & Ba, J. (2015). *Adam: A method for stochastic optimization. International Conference on Learning Representations (ICLR)*. DOI: 10.48550/arXiv.1412.6980

Kisi, O., & Shiri, J. (2012). Precipitation forecasting using wavelet-genetic programming and wavelet-neural networks. *Water Resources Management*, *26*(9), 2555–2569.

Kolmogorov, A. N. (1933). Sulla determinazione empirica di una legge di distribuzione. *Giornale dell'Istituto Italiano degli Attuari, 4,* 83–91.

Krauss, C., Do, X. A., & Huck, N. (2017). Deep neural networks, gradient-boosted trees, random forests: Statistical arbitrage on the S&P 500. *European Journal of Operational Research*, *259*(2), 689–702. DOI: 10.1016/j.ejor.2016.10.031

Kristoufek, L. (2020). Grandpa, grandpa, tell me the one about Bitcoin being a safe haven: New evidence from the COVID-19 pandemic. *Frontiers in Physics*, *8*, 296.

Kumar, R., Singh, A., & Patel, S. (2022). Improving dynamic voltage restorer operation under distorted voltage conditions using hybrid GRNN estimator and ANFIS controller optimized by fruit fly and grey wolf algorithms. *International Journal of Electrical Power & Energy Systems*, *138*, 107.

Léber, D., & Egyed, B. (2026). The sentiment augmented GARCH-LSTM hybrid model for Value-at-Risk forecasting. *Computational Economics*, *67*(1), 313–353. DOI: 10.1007/s10614-025-11042-8

Lee, C. F. (2024). Financial Econometrics, Mathematics, Statistics, and Financial Technology: An Overall View. In C. F. Lee, A. C. Lee, & J. C. Lee, *Handbook of Investment Analysis, Portfolio Management, and Financial Derivatives* (pp. 1007–1075). WORLD SCIENTIFIC. DOI: 10.1142/9789811269943_0031

Lee, C. F. (2025). Introduction to Financial Technology, Statistics, Econometrics and Risk Management. In C.-F. Lee, A. C. Lee, & J. C. Lee, *Handbook of Financial Econometrics, Statistics, Technology, and Risk Management* (pp. 1–106). WORLD SCIENTIFIC. DOI: 10.1142/9789819809950_0001

Lee, C. F. (2020). Financial econometrics, mathematics, statistics, and financial technology: An overall view. *Review of Quantitative Finance and Accounting*, *54*(4), 1529–1578. DOI: 10.1007/s11156-020-00883-z

Lee, J., & Kim, S. (2021). Gradient boosting machine for stock price forecasting in the Korean market. *Journal of Computational Finance*, *9*(1), 45–60.

Lee, Y.-H., Hsieh, M.-H., Kuo, W., & Tsai, C. J. (2021). How can an economic scenario generation model cope with abrupt changes in financial markets? *China Finance Review International*, *11*(3), 372–405. DOI: 10.1108/CFRI-03-2021-0056

Leo, S., Crusoe, M. R., Rodríguez-Navas, L., Sirvent, R., Kanitz, A., De Geest, P., Wittner, R., Pireddu, L., Garijo, D., Fernández, J. M., Colonnelli, I., Gallo, M., Ohta, T., Suetake, H., Capella-Gutierrez, S., de Wit, R., Kinoshita, B. P., & Soiland-Reyes, S. (2024). Recording provenance of workflow runs with RO-Crate. *PLoS One*, *19*(9), e0309210. DOI: 10.1371/journal.pone.0309210 PMID: 39255315

Leushuis, R. M., & Petkov, N. (2026). Advances in forecasting realized volatility: A review of methodologies. *Financial Innovation*, *12*(1), 14. Advance online publication. DOI: 10.1186/s40854-025-00809-5

Liang, M. (2021). Optimization of quantitative financial data analysis system based on deep learning. *Complexity, 2021*(1). DOI: 10.1155/2021/5527615

Lim, B., Arık, S. Ö., Loeff, N., & Pfister, T. (2021). Temporal Fusion Transformers for interpretable multi-horizon time series forecasting. *International Journal of Forecasting, 37*(4), 1748–1764. DOI: 10.1016/j.ijforecast.2021.03.012

Liu, X.-Y., Xia, Z., Rui, J., Gao, J., Yang, H., Zhu, M., Wang, C. D., Wang, Z., & Guo, J. (2022, November 6). *FinRL-Meta: Market environments and benchmarks for data-driven financial reinforcement learning*. arXiv.Org. https://arxiv.org/abs/2211.03107 DOI: 10.52202/068431-0134

Liu, B., Ji, Y., & Zhou, C. (2024). Application of Distributed Database System in Financial Management. In Hung, J. C., Yen, N., & Chang, J.-W. (Eds.), *Frontier Computing on Industrial Applications* (Vol. 1, pp. 9–16). Springer Nature Singapore., DOI: 10.1007/978-981-99-9299-7_2

Llamosas-Rosas, I., Rangel González, E., & Sandoval Bustos, M. (2021). Medición de la actividad económica en las principales zonas turísticas de playa en México a través imágenes satelitales: Measurement of Economic Activity in the Main Touristic Beach Zones in México Using Satellite Images. *Ensayos Revista de Economía, 40*(2), 115–136. DOI: 10.29105/ensayos40.2-1

Longstaff, F. A., & Schwartz, E. S. (2001). Valuing American options by simulation. *Review of Financial Studies, 14*(1), 113–147. DOI: 10.1093/rfs/14.1.113

López de Prado, M. (2018). *Advances in financial machine learning*. Wiley.

lsulaiman, T., Alzahrani, M., & Alsolami, F. (2022). Financial forecasting using GRNN: A comparative study with deep learning models. *Journal of Finance and Data Science, 8*(1), 30–44.

Majumdar, S., & Laha, A. K. (2020). Clustering and classification of time series using topological data analysis with applications to finance. *Expert Systems with Applications, 162*, 113868. DOI: 10.1016/j.eswa.2020.113868

Malhotra, R., & Malhotra, D. K. (2023). The Impact of Technology, Big Data, and Analytics: The Evolving Data-Driven Model of Innovation in the Finance Industry. *The Journal of Financial Data Science, 5*(3), 50–65. DOI: 10.3905/jfds.2023.1.129

Malott, N. O., Chen, S., Verma, R. R., & Wilsey, P. A. (2023). A survey on the high-performance computation of persistent homology. *IEEE Transactions on Knowledge and Data Engineering, 35*(5), 4466–4484. DOI: 10.1109/TKDE.2022.3147070

Mandl, C., & Minner, S. (2023). Data-Driven Optimization for Commodity Procurement Under Price Uncertainty. *Manufacturing & Service Operations Management, 25*(2), 371–390. DOI: 10.1287/msom.2020.0890

Mani, M. (2024). An Exploration of Contemporary Trends in Finance Research. *Journal of the Knowledge Economy*, *16*(3), 12291–12316. DOI: 10.1007/s13132-024-02373-2

Mantilla, P., & Dormido-Canto, S. (2023). A novel feature engineering approach for high-frequency financial data. *Engineering Applications of Artificial Intelligence*, *125*, 106705. DOI: 10.1016/j.engappai.2023.106705

Markov, A. A. (1906). Extension of the limit theorems of probability theory to a sum of variables connected in a chain. *Proceedings of the Imperial Academy of Sciences of St. Petersburg, 20,* 135–156.

Markowitz, H. (1952). Portfolio selection. *The Journal of Finance*, *7*(1), 77–91.

Master of Business Administration. Indiana State University, Terre Haute, Indiana, USA, Kowsar, M. M., Mohiuddin, M., Master of Science in Management Information Systems, Lamar university, Texas, USA, Islam, S., & Master in Public Budgeting and Finance, Murray State University, Kentucky, USA. (2023). Mathematics For Finance: A Review Of Quantitative Methods In Loan Portfolio Optimization. *International Journal of Scientific Interdisciplinary Research, 04*(03), 01–29. DOI: 10.63125/j43ayz68

McNeil, A. J., Frey, R., & Embrechts, P. (2015). *Quantitative risk management: Concepts, techniques and tools* (Revised ed.). Princeton University Press.

Merton, R. C. (1973). Theory of rational option pricing. *The Bell Journal of Economics and Management Science*, *4*(1), 141–183. DOI: 10.2307/3003143

Merton, R. C. (1976). Option pricing when underlying stock returns are discontinuous. *Journal of Financial Economics*, *3*(1–2), 125–144. DOI: 10.1016/0304-405X(76)90022-2

Millán López, A. J., & González Olivares, D. (2024). Satellite nighttime lights as a measurement of economic growth in Mexico's counties. Ensayos. *Revista de Economía*, *43*(1), 1–18. DOI: 10.29105/ensayos43.1-1

Mishra, A. K., Renganathan, J., & Gupta, A. (2024). Volatility forecasting and assessing risk of financial markets using multi-transformer neural network based architecture. *Engineering Applications of Artificial Intelligence*, *133*, 108223. Advance online publication. DOI: 10.1016/j.engappai.2024.108223

Mohajerin Esfahani, P., & Kuhn, D. (2018). Data-driven distributionally robust optimization using the Wasserstein metric: Performance guarantees and tractable reformulations. *Mathematical Programming*, *171*(1–2), 115–166. DOI: 10.1007/s10107-017-1172-1

Mondal, C., Al-Kfairy, M., & Mellor, R. B. (2023). Developing Young Science and Technology Parks: Recent Findings from Industrial Nations Using the Data-Driven Approach. *Sustainability (Basel), 15*(7), 6226. DOI: 10.3390/su15076226

Mukhaninga, S., Mugochi, T., & Phiri, A. (2025). Forecasting the JSE All-Share Index using machine learning algorithms: A comparative study. *Economies, 13*(8), 219. DOI: 10.3390/economies13080219

Murugan, M. S., & T, S. K. (2023). Large-scale data-driven financial risk management & analysis using machine learning strategies. *Measurement. Sensors, 27*, 100756. DOI: 10.1016/j.measen.2023.100756

Nelson, D. B. (1991). Conditional heteroskedasticity in asset returns: A new approach. *Econometrica, 59*(2), 347–370.

Noorani, I., Mehrdoust, F., & Nasroallah, A. (2021). A generalized antithetic variates Monte-Carlo simulation method for pricing of Asian option in a Markov regime-switching model. *Mathematics and Computers in Simulation, 181*, 1–15. DOI: 10.1016/j.matcom.2020.09.011

Nüst, D., Sochat, V., Marwick, B., Eglen, S. J., Head, T., Hirst, T., & Evans, B. D. (2020). Ten simple rules for writing Dockerfiles for reproducible data science. *PLoS Computational Biology, 16*(11), e1008316. DOI: 10.1371/journal.pcbi.1008316 PMID: 33170857

O'Rourke, K. H. (1998). Monetary data and proxy GDP estimates: Ireland 1840–1921. *Irish Economic and Social History, 25*(1), 22–51. DOI: 10.1177/033248939802500103

Ogiela, L. (2013). Data management in cognitive financial systems. *International Journal of Information Management, 33*(2), 263–270. DOI: 10.1016/j.ijinfomgt.2012.11.008

Oliveira, C. (2021). *Practical C++20 financial programming: Problem solving for quantitative finance, financial engineering, business, and economics*. Apress., DOI: 10.1007/978-1-4842-6834-6

Padilla Sierra, A. D. J. (2015). Uso de variables de actividad económica en la estimación del PIB per cápita microterritorial. *Cuadernos de Economía (Santiago, Chile), 34*(65), 349–376. DOI: 10.15446/cuad.econ.v34n65.45936

Paganelli, M. P. (2021). Population as a GDP proxy in Adam Smith. *Journal of Scottish Philosophy, 19*(2), 115–123. DOI: 10.3366/jsp.2021.0297

Patel, J., Shah, S., Thakkar, P., & Kotecha, K. (2015). Predicting stock and stock price index movement using trend deterministic data preparation and machine learning techniques. *Expert Systems with Applications*, *42*(1), 259–268. DOI: 10.1016/j.eswa.2014.07.040

Patra, S., & Gupta, N. (2023). Risk in the cryptocurrency markets: The role of structural breaks and fat-tailed distributions in estimating value-at-risk and expected shortfall. *European Journal of Finance*. Advance online publication.

Patton, A. J. (2011). Volatility forecast comparison using imperfect volatility proxies. *Journal of Econometrics*, *160*(1), 246–256. DOI: 10.1016/j.jeconom.2010.03.034

Pham, T., Chau, H., & Nguyen, L. (2024). Hybrid artificial intelligence models based on adaptive neuro-fuzzy inference system and metaheuristic optimization algorithms for prediction of daily rainfall. *Physics and Chemistry of the Earth Parts A/B/C*, *134*, 103563. DOI: 10.1016/j.pce.2024.103563

Phillips, P. C. B., & Perron, P. (1988). Testing for a unit root in time series regression. *Biometrika*, *75*(2), 335–346. DOI: 10.1093/biomet/75.2.335

Picard, R. R., & Berk, K. N. (1990). Data splitting. *The American Statistician*, *44*(2), 140–147. DOI: 10.1080/00031305.1990.10475704

Pickands, J. (1975). Statistical inference using extreme order statistics. *Annals of Statistics*, *3*(1), 119–131.

Pillai, V. (2023). Integrating AI-Driven Techniques in Big Data Analytics: Enhancing Decision-Making in Financial Markets. *International Journal of Engineering and Computer Science*, *12*(07), 25774–25788. DOI: 10.18535/ijecs/v12i07.4745

Pimentel, J. F., Murta, L., Braganholo, V., & Freire, J. (2019). A Large-Scale Study About Quality and Reproducibility of Jupyter Notebooks. 2019 IEEE/ACM 16th International Conference on Mining Software Repositories (MSR), 507–517. https://doi.org/DOI: 10.1109/MSR.2019.00077

Poon, S.-H., & Granger, C. W. J. (2003). Forecasting volatility in financial markets: A review. *Journal of Economic Literature*, *41*(2), 478–539. DOI: 10.1257/.41.2.478

Price, N., & Atkinson, P. M. (2022). Global GDP prediction with night-lights and transfer learning. *IEEE Journal of Selected Topics in Applied Earth Observations and Remote Sensing*, *15*, 7128–7138. DOI: 10.1109/JSTARS.2022.3200754

Pun, C. S., Lee, S. X., & Xia, K. (2022). Persistent-homology-based machine learning: A survey and a comparative study. *Artificial Intelligence Review*, *55*(7), 5169–5213. DOI: 10.1007/s10462-022-10146-z

Rao, K. S. (2015). The Basics of Financial Econometrics: Tools, Concepts, and Asset Management Applications. *Quantitative Finance*, *15*(11), 1773–1775. DOI: 10.1080/14697688.2015.1080486

Rashidi, F., Mohammadi, A., & Khorami, M. (2025). Integration of the reptile search algorithm and the adaptive neuro-fuzzy inference system enhances standardized precipitation evapotranspiration index forecasting. *Scientific Reports*, *15*, 98772. PMID: 40287468

Ravishanker, N., & Chen, R. (2021). An introduction to persistent homology for time series. *Wiley Interdisciplinary Reviews: Computational Statistics*, *13*(3), e1548. DOI: 10.1002/wics.1548

Román, M. O., Wang, Z., Sun, Q., Kalb, V., Miller, S. D., Molthan, A., Schultz, L., Bell, J., Stokes, E. C., Pandey, B., Seto, K. C., Hall, D., Oda, T., Wolfe, R. E., Lin, G., Golpayegani, N., Devadiga, S., Davidson, C., Sarkar, S., & Masuoka, E. J. (2018). NASA's Black Marble nighttime lights product suite. *Remote Sensing of Environment*, *210*, 113–143. DOI: 10.1016/j.rse.2018.03.017

Roy, S., Mitra, S., & Roy, D. (2020). Financial time series forecasting using machine learning techniques: A comparative study. *Procedia Computer Science*, *167*, 2085–2094.

Ruiz Ochoa, W. (2010). Convergencia económica interestatal en México, 1900–2004. *Análisis Económico*, *25*(58), 7–34.

Sahu, S. K., Mokhade, A., & Bokde, N. D. (2023). An overview of machine learning, deep learning, and reinforcement learning-based techniques in quantitative finance: Recent progress and challenges. *Applied Sciences (Basel, Switzerland)*, *13*(3), 1956. DOI: 10.3390/app13031956

Salehi, S. (2024). Comparative analysis of machine learning techniques for cryptocurrency price prediction. *Journal of Information and Organizational Sciences*, *48*(2), 341–352. DOI: 10.31341/jios.48.2.7

Saltelli, A., Aleksankina, K., Becker, W., Fennell, P., Ferretti, F., Holst, N., Li, S., & Wu, Q. (2019). Why so many published sensitivity analyses are false: A systematic review of sensitivity analysis practices. *Environmental Modelling & Software*, *114*, 29–39. DOI: 10.1016/j.envsoft.2019.01.012

Schoch, D., Haim, M., Stier, S., & Schoonvelde, M. (2024). Computational reproducibility in computational social science. *EPJ Data Science*, *13*(1), 75. DOI: 10.1140/epjds/s13688-024-00514-w

Sezer, O. B., Gudelek, M. U., & Ozbayoglu, A. M. (2020). Financial time series forecasting with deep learning: A systematic literature review: 2005–2019. *Applied Soft Computing*, *90*, 106181. Advance online publication. DOI: 10.1016/j.asoc.2020.106181

Shah, W. H., Fatima, S. R., Huerta-Cuellar, G., García-López, J. H., Mata Ramirez, C. G., & Jaimes-Reátegui, R. (2025). Topological data analysis approach to time series and shape analysis of dynamical system. *Chaos (Woodbury, N.Y.)*, *35*(6), 063129. DOI: 10.1063/5.0268340 PMID: 40526891

Shapiro, S. S., & Wilk, M. B. (1965). An analysis of variance test for normality (complete samples). *Biometrika*, *52*(3–4), 591–611. DOI: 10.1093/biomet/52.3-4.591

Shi, X., Zhang, P., & Khan, S. U. (2017). Quantitative data analysis in finance. In *Handbook of big data technologies* (pp. 719–753). Springer., DOI: 10.1007/978-3-319-49340-4_21

Singha, M. (2025, November 16). *Discovery of a 13-sharpe OOS factor: Drift regimes unlock hidden cross-sectional predictability*. arXiv.Org. https://arxiv.org/abs/2511.12490 DOI: 10.2139/ssrn.5754502

Singh, A., & Srivastava, S. (2021). Stock price prediction using neuro-fuzzy systems. *Journal of Computational Finance and Economics*, *5*(2), 98–113.

Singh, R., Singh, A. K., & Singh, T. N. (2013). Prediction of unconfined compressive strength of rocks using GRNN and ANFIS models. *Neural Computing & Applications*, *22*(7–8), 1637–1643.

Sinha, D., & Chakrabarty, S. P. (2023). A review of efficient Multilevel Monte Carlo algorithms for derivative pricing and risk management. *MethodsX*, *10*, 102078. DOI: 10.1016/j.mex.2023.102078 PMID: 36875343

Smyl, S., Gal, Y., & Smith, A. (2022). Benchmarking gradient boosting methods against deep learning for time series forecasting. *International Journal of Forecasting*, *38*(4), 1448–1459.

Soiland-Reyes, S., Sefton, P., Castro, L. J., Coppens, F., Garijo, D., Leo, S., Portier, M., & Groth, P. (2022). Creating lightweight FAIR Digital Objects with RO-Crate. *Research Ideas and Outcomes*, *8*, e93937. DOI: 10.3897/rio.8.e93937

South African Photovoltaic Power Forecasting Study. (2024). Comparison of GRNN, ANFIS, and neural models for photovoltaic output prediction. *Entropy*, *26*(3), 1–15. DOI: 10.3390/e26030001

Specht, D. F. (1991). A general regression neural network. *IEEE Transactions on Neural Networks*, *2*(6), 568–576. DOI: 10.1109/72.97934 PMID: 18282872

Strielkowski, W., Vlasov, A., Selivanov, K., Muraviev, K., & Shakhnov, V. (2023). Prospects and Challenges of the Machine Learning and Data-Driven Methods for the Predictive Analysis of Power Systems: A Review. *Energies*, *16*(10), 4025. DOI: 10.3390/en16104025

Suetake, H., Fukusato, T., Igarashi, T., & Ohta, T. (2023). A workflow reproducibility scale for automatic validation of biological interpretation results. *GigaScience*, *12*, giad031. Advance online publication. DOI: 10.1093/gigascience/giad031 PMID: 37150537

Sun, J., Di, L., Sun, Z., Wang, J., & Wu, Y. (2020). Estimation of GDP using deep learning with NPP-VIIRS imagery and land cover data at the county level in CONUS. *IEEE Journal of Selected Topics in Applied Earth Observations and Remote Sensing*, *13*, 1400–1415. DOI: 10.1109/JSTARS.2020.2983331

Sun, Y., Shi, Y., & Zhang, Z. (2019). Finance Big Data: Management, Analysis, and Applications. *International Journal of Electronic Commerce*, *23*(1), 9–11. DOI: 10.1080/10864415.2018.1512270

Taneva-Angelova, G., & Granchev, D. (2025). Deep learning and transformer architectures for volatility forecasting: Evidence from U.S. equity indices. *Journal of Risk and Financial Management*, *18*(12), 685. Advance online publication. DOI: 10.3390/jrfm18120685

Tay, F. E. H., & Cao, L. (2001). Application of support vector machines in financial time series forecasting. *Omega*, *29*(4), 309–317. DOI: 10.1016/S0305-0483(01)00026-3

Teng, H.-W. (2023). Importance sampling for calculating the value-at-risk and expected shortfall of the quadratic portfolio with t-distributed risk factors. *Computational Economics*, *62*(3), 1125–1154. DOI: 10.1007/s10614-022-10294-y

Teruzzi, A. (2023). Tail Risk and Systemic Risk Estimation of Cryptocurrencies: An Expectiles and Marginal Expected Shortfall Based Approach. arXiv preprint arXiv:2311.17239.

Tralie, C., Saul, N., & Bar-On, R. (2018). Ripser.py: A lean persistent homology library for Python. *Journal of Open Source Software*, *3*(29), 925. DOI: 10.21105/joss.00925

Trisovic, A., Lau, M. K., Pasquier, T., & Crosas, M. (2022). A large-scale study on research code quality and execution. *Scientific Data*, *9*(1), 60. DOI: 10.1038/s41597-022-01143-6 PMID: 35190569

Tsay, R. S. (2010). *Analysis of financial time series* (3rd ed.). Wiley., DOI: 10.1002/9780470644560

Tyralis, H., Papacharalampous, A., & Papadimitriou, L. (2019). Large-scale benchmarking of machine learning algorithms for streamflow forecasting across 511 basins. *arXiv*

Ustaoglu, B., Karahan, O., & Yalcin, A. (2008). Prediction of daily streamflow data using adaptive neuro fuzzy inference systems with neural network-based phase space reconstruction. *Journal of Hydrology (Amsterdam)*, *358*(3–4), 312–325.

Vaswani, A., Shazeer, N., Parmar, N., Uszkoreit, J., Jones, L., Gomez, A. N., Kaiser, Ł., & Polosukhin, I. (2017). Attention is all you need. In Vol. 30, pp. 5998–6008). Advances in Neural Information Processing Systems. Curran Associates.

Vejdemo-Johansson, M., & Mukherjee, S. (2022). Statistical inference using persistence landscapes. *Foundations of Data Science (Springfield, Mo.)*, *4*(4), 387–410. DOI: 10.3934/fods.2022018

Wang, Z., Román, M. O., Shrestha, R., Yao, T., & Kalb, V. (2022). Black Marble user guide (Version 1.3). National Aeronautics and Space Administration.

Wang, Q., García-Redondo, I., Faugère, P., Henselman-Petrusek, G., & Monod, A. (2024). Stability for inference with persistent homology rank functions. *Computer Graphics Forum*, *43*(5), e15142. DOI: 10.1111/cgf.15142

Wang, W. (2024). Machine learning in financial time-series data. *Advances in Economics. Management and Political Sciences*, (92), 293–299.

Warin, T., & Stojkov, A. (2021). Machine learning in finance: A metadata-based systematic review of the literature. *Journal of Risk and Financial Management*, *14*(7), 302. DOI: 10.3390/jrfm14070302

Wasserman, L. (2018). Topological data analysis. *Annual Review of Statistics and Its Application*, *5*(1), 501–532. DOI: 10.1146/annurev-statistics-031017-100045

Wen, C., Yang, J., Gan, L., & Pan, Y. (2021). Big data driven Internet of Things for credit evaluation and early warning in finance. *Future Generation Computer Systems*, *124*, 295–307. DOI: 10.1016/j.future.2021.06.003

Wen, H., & Gao, R. (2025). Strategic Planning and Forecasting in Financial Management: Integrating AI-Driven Mathematical Modeling Techniques. *International Journal of High Speed Electronics and Systems*, *2540771*, 2540771. Advance online publication. DOI: 10.1142/S0129156425407715

Wiener, N. (1949). *Extrapolation, interpolation, and smoothing of stationary time series*. Wiley. DOI: 10.7551/mitpress/2946.001.0001

Wiese, M., Knobloch, R., Korn, R., & Kretschmer, P. (2020). Quant GANs: Deep generation of financial time series. *Quantitative Finance*, *20*(9), 1419–1440. DOI: 10.1080/14697688.2020.1730426

Wilkinson, S. R., Aloqalaa, M., Belhajjame, K., Crusoe, M. R., de Paula Kinoshita, B., Gadelha, L., Garijo, D., Gustafsson, O. J. R., Juty, N., Kanwal, S., Khan, F. Z., Köster, J., Gehlen, K. P., Pouchard, L., Rannow, R. K., Soiland-Reyes, S., Soranzo, N., Sufi, S., Sun, Z., & Goble, C. (2025). Applying the FAIR Principles to computational workflows. *Scientific Data*, *12*(1), 328. DOI: 10.1038/s41597-025-04451-9 PMID: 39994238

Wirtz, A., Kron, W., Löw, P., & Steuer, M. (2014). The need for data: Natural disasters and the challenges of database management. *Natural Hazards*, *70*(1), 135–157. DOI: 10.1007/s11069-012-0312-4

Wu, H., Xu, J., Wang, J., & Long, M. (2021). Autoformer: Decomposition transformers with auto-correlation for long-term series forecasting. In Vol. 34, pp. 22419–22430). Advances in Neural Information Processing Systems. Curran Associates.

Wu, L., & Jarrow, R. A. (2024). Fitting dynamically consistent forward rate curves. *International Journal of Theoretical and Applied Finance*, *27*(8), 2450021. DOI: 10.1142/S0219024924500213

Xiang, J., & Wang, X. (2022). Quasi-Monte Carlo simulation for American option sensitivities. *Journal of Computational and Applied Mathematics*, *413*, 114268. DOI: 10.1016/j.cam.2022.114268

Yang, A., Ye, Q., & Zhai, J. (2024). Volatility forecasting with hybrid-long short-term memory models: Evidence from the COVID-19 period. *International Journal of Finance & Economics*, *29*(3), 2766–2786. DOI: 10.1002/ijfe.2805

Yan, Y. (2017). Teaching programming skills to finance students: How to design and teach a great course. *Financial Innovation*, *3*(32), 32. Advance online publication. DOI: 10.1186/s40854-017-0081-x

Yerashenia, N., & Bolotov, A. (2019). Computational Modelling for Bankruptcy Prediction: Semantic Data Analysis Integrating Graph Database and Financial Ontology. *2019 IEEE 21st Conference on Business Informatics (CBI)*, 84–93. DOI: 10.1109/CBI.2019.00017

Yuan, D., Jiang, H., Guo, W., Cui, X., Wu, L., Wu, Z., & Wang, H. (2021). Regression Analysis and Comparison of Economic Parameters with Different Light Index Models under Various Constraints. *Sensors (Basel), 21*(22), 7561. DOI: 10.3390/s21227561 PMID: 34833637

Yule, G. U. (1907). On the theory of correlation. *Journal of the Royal Statistical Society, 70*(1), 237–242.

Yu, W., Wong, C. Y., Chavez, R., & Jacobs, M. A. (2021). Integrating big data analytics into supply chain finance: The roles of information processing and data-driven culture. *International Journal of Production Economics, 236*, 108135. DOI: 10.1016/j.ijpe.2021.108135

Zhang, H., Ren, S., Li, X., Baharin, H., Alghamdi, A., & Alghamdi, O. A. (2023). Developing scalable management information system with big financial data using data mart and mining architecture. *Information Processing & Management, 60*(3), 103326. DOI: 10.1016/j.ipm.2023.103326

Zhang, J., & Liu, Y. (2020). A hybrid GRNN model for time-series forecasting. *Neural Computing & Applications, 32*, 9725–9734.

Zhang, P., Shi, X., & Khan, S. U. (2019). QuantCloud: Enabling Big Data Complex Event Processing for Quantitative Finance Through a Data-Driven Execution. *IEEE Transactions on Big Data, 5*(4), 564–575. DOI: 10.1109/TBDATA.2018.2847629

Zhang, S. (2025). A Big Data-Driven Approach to Financial Analysis and Decision Support System Design. *Informatica (Vilnius), 49*(11). Advance online publication. DOI: 10.31449/inf.v49i11.7065

Zhang, W., Zhang, Y., & Liu, Y. (2021). A gradient boosting approach for financial time series prediction. *Expert Systems with Applications, 168*, 114–481.

Zhang, X., & Gibson, J. (2022). Using Multi-Source Nighttime Lights Data to Proxy for County-Level Economic Activity in China from 2012 to 2019. *Remote Sensing (Basel), 14*(5), 1282. DOI: 10.3390/rs14051282

Zhang, Y. (2025). The Exploration of the Interdisciplinary Education of Mathematics in Universities: A Case Study of Mathematics and Finance. *Frontiers in Interdisciplinary Educational Methodology, 2*(2), 74–80. DOI: 10.71465/fiem187

Zhang, Z., Zohren, S., & Roberts, S. (2019). DeepLOB: Deep convolutional neural networks for limit order books. *IEEE Transactions on Signal Processing, 67*(11), 3001–3012. DOI: 10.1109/TSP.2019.2907260

Zheng, Y., Yang, K., Wei, C., Fu, M., & Fan, M. (2024). An improved cross-sensor calibration approach for DMSP-OLS and NPP-VIIRS nighttime light data. *IEEE Journal of Selected Topics in Applied Earth Observations and Remote Sensing*, *18*, 865–877. DOI: 10.1109/JSTARS.2024.3494551

Zhou, H., Zhang, S., Peng, J., Zhang, S., Li, J., Xiong, H., & Zhang, W. (2021). Informer: Beyond efficient transformer for long sequence time-series forecasting. *Proceedings of the AAAI Conference on Artificial Intelligence*, *35*(12), 11106–11115. DOI: 10.1609/aaai.v35i12.17325

About the Contributors

Felipe Machorro-Ramos holds a Ph.D. in Economic and Administrative Sciences from the Autonomous University of the State of Mexico. He is a Level I member of Mexico's National System of Researchers (SNII-SECITHI) and has over twenty years of experience in teaching and academic management at undergraduate and graduate levels in Mexico, Chile, and Bolivia. His research focuses on human capital management, intellectual capital, organizational performance in higher education, and technology acceptance models, with publications indexed in Scopus. He currently teaches in graduate business programs at Universidad Popular Autónoma del Estado de Puebla (UPAEP), Universidad Iberoamericana Puebla, and other institutions. Dr. Machorro Ramos is recognized for his commitment to academic excellence, applied research, and innovation in management education.

María Vanessa Romero Ortiz holds a Ph.D. in Economic and Administrative Sciences from the Autonomous University of the State of Mexico and is a member of Mexico's National System of Researchers (SNII-SECITHI). She is a professor in the Financial Engineering at Universidad Politecnica de Puebla, also teaches at Universidad de las Américas Puebla and Universidad Iberoamericana Puebla. Her research focuses on organizational behavior, strategic management, and the economic impact of violence, with publications indexed in Scopus and Web of Science. She has international teaching experience at Universidad Católica del Norte in Chile, served as Editor-in-Chief of the Mexican Journal of Engineering Sciences, and previously worked at Banamex applying management tools such as the Balanced Scorecard. Dr. Romero Ortiz is recognized for her commitment to educational excellence, applied research, and the development of strategic, socially responsible leaders.

José Gonzalo Ramírez Rosas is a Certified Public Accountant and Auditor with a Ph.D. in Administration and a Master's degree in Systems and Intelligent

Computing Engineering. He is a research professor at the Polytechnic University of Puebla in the area of Financial Engineering.

Martín Neri Suárez holds a Bachelor's degree in Natural Resource Management and earned both a Master's and a Doctorate in Sciences in Strategies for Agricultural Regional Development from the Colegio de Postgraduados, Campus Puebla. He is a researcher specializing in the application of Data Science to the geospatial and geostatistical analysis of economic, environmental, and social phenomena. He was recognized as a Candidate of the National System of Researchers (SNII) for the 2023–2026 period and is also a member of the State System of Researchers of Puebla (SIIEP). With more than a decade of academic experience, he has published over thirteen scientific articles on sustainable development, regional economy, and environmental management. He currently serves as a full-time professor and researcher at the Polytechnic University of Puebla..

Lorena Hernández Quiroz holds a Bachelor's degree in Administration, a Master's degree in Organizational Psychology, and is currently pursuing a Ph.D. in Finance. She served as a professor of Financial Engineering from 2018 to 2022 and, since 2022, has been the Coordinator of the Financial Engineering program at the Polytechnic University of Puebla. She has participated in and organized scientific events on Financial Engineering in Colombia, Chile, and Mexico.

***

Jaime Aguilar-Ortiz holds a Ph.D. in Mathematical Sciences (CINVESTAV–IPN, Mexico) and serves as a professor and researcher in the fields of Mathematics, Artificial Intelligence, and Project Management, with academic involvement also extending to the Universidad Politécnica Metropolitana de Hidalgo. He additionally leads innovation-driven initiatives as Director General of CICAINTE and TEDNOVA GROUP, bridging rigorous academic work with applied technological development and institutional impact. His prior scholarly and editorial contributions include the preparation and/or editing of a substantial body of books and educational resources spanning mathematics education, financial mathematics, programming, and technology-based learning, complemented by the creation of audiovisual materials, educational platforms, and serious-game applications aimed at strengthening learning outcomes. His academic production further includes dozens of peer-reviewed articles and book chapters addressing themes at the intersection of smart cities, education, and AI, together with sustained experience in research mentoring, curriculum development, and interdisciplinary collaboration. These achievements, combined with recognized academic credentials and a consistent record of knowledge dissemination and capacity building, position him as a strong editor for a high-impact scholarly volume with methodological rigor, cross-sector relevance, and measurable educational and societal value.

Kevin Ake holds a Bachelor's degree in Actuarial Science from Universidad Anáhuac Veracruz, Campus Xalapa. As a recent graduate, he has participated in several academic and research events, contributing to scholarly discussions and presentations both in Mexico and internationally. His interests include quantitative analysis, financial risk modeling, and the application of statistical methods to financial markets.

Carolina Corral Avila is a student of the Bachelor's Degree in Data Science at the Higher School of Computing (ESCOM) of the National Polytechnic Institute. Her academic and professional work focuses on applied data science and data engineering. He has participated in a research project focused on the analysis of economic growth volatility.

Ocotlán Diaz-Parra is a Professor and Researcher at Universidad Politécnica de Pachuca (UPP), a National Researcher under the Secretaria de Ciencia, Humanidades, Tecnología e Innovación program, and an Adjunct Researcher at the National Laboratory of Autonomous Vehicles and Exoskeletons (LANAVEX). His research interests include Smart Cities, Smart Water, Smart Education, Smart Government, Smart Healthcare, Smart Farming, Smart Energy, Smart Sports, Smart Food, Smart Tourism, Algorithmic Finance, Algorithmic Portfolio Management, Applications and Theory of Algorithms, Bio-inspired Algorithms, Combinatorial Optimization Problems, Compilers, Computational Intelligence, Computational Complexity Theory, Computational Financial Intelligence, Complexity of Algorithms, Complexity of Instances, Computational Statistics, Computer Networks, Computer Science Security, Cybercrimes, Data Mining, Education, Evolutionary Computation, Heuristic Optimization Techniques in Bioinformatics, Hybrid Evolutionary Algorithms, Hybrid Optimization Algorithms, Machine Learning, Meta-heuristics, Operations Research, Operations Management, Parallel & Distributed Computing, Production Planning and Logistics Optimization, Project Scheduling Problems, Software Engineering, and Transgenic Algorithms.

Carlos Domínguez-Mayorga holds a Ph.D. in Sciences specializing in Artificial Intelligence, with a foundational background in Physics and Mathematics. His research focuses on Deep Learning, NLP, neural networks, and the development of predictive models. He has an extensive track record in scientific publications and graduate program management, applying cutting-edge data science techniques to engineering and sustainability projects.

Claudia García Blanquel, PhD in Computer Science from the Research Center in Computing at the National Polytechnic Institute. Professor at the Higher School of Computing. His research areas include Data Science, Business Intelligence, Statistical Techniques and Models for Data Analysis, Information Technologies, Cybersecurity, and Supercomputing, email: cgarciabl@ipn.mx

Ganesh Harke is a trailblazing technology leader who has played a pivotal role in revolutionizing financial technology through AI, big data, and scalable software architectures. With over 17 years of experience spanning global institutions, he has led transformative engineering initiatives powering high-performance trading, risk, and regulatory systems across global markets. He holds a Master's in Financial Engineering and has completed all three levels of the CFA Program, bringing a rare combination of quantitative finance expertise, deep technical acumen, and strategic foresight to the AI transformation of financial services.

R. Hepsiba is an Associate Professor at AQJ Centre for PG Studies and Guest faculty in the Department of Commerce and Management Studies, Andhra University, Visakhapatnam. She obtained her MBA, M. Com, M.A (Pub. Adm), Ph.D degree and UGC Post-Doctorate from Andhra University Visakhapatnam. She participated and presented papers in many National Seminars and Conferences organized under the aegis of NISM, Birla Sun Life, Stratadigm, Tejaswi Astitva Foundation, Power grid, UGC, Nimsme, etc. She also participated in Training Programs conducted by national professional bodies. Dr. R. Hepsiba associated in organizing many national events hosted by DCMS, Andhra University and Job fairs jointly organized by AU and APSCHE. She has put in 15 years of teaching experience addressing the students of MBA programme in AU affiliated colleges.

Boddu Jyothi is an accomplished academic and Associate Professor, with a distinguished career spanning over a more than 18 years. Expertise in Finance and Marketing management.

Rishikaysh Kaakandikar is a distinguished academician, author, and researcher in the field of finance and management. Currently serving as an Associate Professor at SaiBalaji International Institute of Management Sciences (SBIIMS), Pune, he has over 13 years of experience in academia and more than a year in the corporate sector. His academic journey is marked by a deep passion for knowledge dissemination and research-driven education. Dr. Kaakandikar holds a Ph.D. in Management and an MBA in Finance, and his scholarly contributions have significantly shaped the landscape of finance education. A prolific researcher, he has authored more than 50 research papers, many of which have been published in Scopus, ABDC, and UGC Care-listed journals. His research interests include financial management, fintech, blockchain technology, mutual funds, AI in HR, and the impact of digital disruption on business ecosystems. In addition to his academic research, Dr. Kaakandikar is a renowned author with multiple books to his credit, such as: AI-Powered HR Finance: Transforming Workforce Management and Financial Strategies in the Digital Age TechHumanize: The Fintech Evolution in HR – Innovations, Challenges, and Future Perspectives Business Research Methods These publications reflect his commitment to exploring the intersection of technology and finance, offering practical insights for students, educators, and industry professionals alike. Dr. Kaakandikar's contributions have earned him several accolades, including the Best Teacher Award by the Institute of Scholars (InSc). He is frequently invited to deliver guest lectures, keynote speeches, and workshops at national and international platforms, where he shares his expertise on emerging trends in finance, AI, and digital transformation. An active member of the global academic community, he maintains a strong online presence on platforms such as Google Scholar, ResearchGate, and ORCID, where his work continues to inspire students and researchers worldwide. Through his dedication, scholarly rigor, and student-centric approach, Dr. Rishikaysh Kaakandikar stands as a guiding light in the field of modern management education.

Pardeep Kumar Assistant Professor, Department of Mathematics, Lovely Professional University, Phagwara, Punjab, India Dr. Pardeep Kumar holds a Ph.D. in Mathematics from Lovely Professional University (2021). His research expertise lies in Stochastic Processes, with a specialized focus on Markov Models, Engineering System Reliability, and Reliability Theory. He actively contributes to the modeling and reliability analysis of IoT-enabled and sensor-integrated systems for next-generation engineering applications. Dr. Kumar has a profound command of Stochastic Modelling, Reliability Testing, and advanced analytical methods for complex system behavior under uncertainty. His work emphasises practical implementations in smart technologies and cyber-physical systems. He has an exceptional academic track record, having qualified the prestigious CSIR-UGC NET twice, securing All India Ranks (AIR) of 15 and 32, respectively. To date, Dr. Kumar has published 26 high-quality research papers in reputed national and international journals, reflecting his continued contribution to the advancement of mathematical reliability and its engineering applications.

Sanjeev Kumar Is a Professor in Lovely Professional University Punjab India. He received Undergraduate in Hotel Management from Osmania University, Postgraduate in Tourism Management from Madurai Kamaraj University. He completed Doctor of Philosophy in Hospitality Management in 2019 from Amity University Jaipur India. His research areas lies in food Service Industry, his research focuses on Alcoholic beverages, Event management and Sustainable Management

Practices, Metaverse, AI Machine Learning and Artificial Intelligence. He published more than 80 research papers, articles and chapters in Scopus Indexed, UGC Approved and peer reviewed Journals and books. Dr. Sanjeev Kumar participated and acted as resource person in various National and International conferences, seminars, session chair, research workshops and industry talks and his work has been widely cited. Dr. Sanjeev also edited more than 20 books with various International Publishers such as IGI Global, Cambridge Scholars, Emerald, CABI, Bentham Science, Taylor & Francis. Dr Sanjeev is an active researcher and has published numerous research articles in prestigious National and International journals and books.

Jesús Manuel López is a student of the Bachelor's Degree in Data Science at the Higher School of Computing (ESCOM) of the National Polytechnic Institute. His academic and professional work focuses on applied data science, data engineering, and the development of intelligent systems based on language models.

Lebotsa Metsileng is a South African academic and researcher in Statistics and Econometrics, associated with North-West University (Mafikeng/Mmabatho campus). His work focuses on time series analysis, volatility modelling, and macroeconomic data, with several publications in international scholarly journals. I have contributed a book chapter in IGI Global Scientific Publishing in 2025. The chapter was titles: The Implications of Missing Data on the Stability of Random Forest and Support Vector Machine Model's Output.

José Molina Hernández holds a Bachelor's degrees in Business Administration and Accounting, with a specialization in Foreign Trade Administration from Universidad Veracruzana, as well as Master's degrees in Public Administration and Port Administration, and a Ph.D. in Public Finance. He has professional experience in both the public and private sectors, having served as Director General of Municipal Planning and Development in Manzanillo, Colima; project leader within the port community of Colima; advisor to the Foreign Trade Directorate of the State of Veracruz; and currently works as a Full-Time Professor-Researcher at Universidad del Istmo in the Bachelor's program in Foreign Trade and Customs Management.

Jorge A. Ruiz-Vanoye is a Professor and Researcher at Universidad Politécnica de Pachuca (UPP), a National Researcher under the Secretaria de Ciencia, Humanidades, Tecnología e Innovación program, and an Adjunct Researcher at the National Laboratory of Autonomous Vehicles and Exoskeletons (LANAVEX). Additionally, he holds the title of Lecturer-level Researcher for the Agency for the Quality of the University System of Catalonia (Generalitat de Catalunya). His research interests include Smart Cities, Smart Water, Smart Education, Smart

Government, Smart Healthcare, Smart Farming, Smart Energy, Smart Sports, Smart Food, Smart Tourism, Algorithmic Finance, Algorithmic Portfolio Management, Applications and Theory of Algorithms, Bio-inspired Algorithms, Combinatorial Optimization Problems, Compilers, Computational Intelligence, Computational Complexity Theory, Computational Financial Intelligence, Complexity of Algorithms, Complexity of Instances, Computational Statistics, Computer Networks, Computer Science Security, Cybercrimes, Data Mining, Education, Evolutionary Computation, Heuristic Optimization Techniques in Bioinformatics, Hybrid Evolutionary Algorithms, Hybrid Optimization Algorithms, Machine Learning, Meta-heuristics, Operations Research, Operations Management, Parallel & Distributed Computing, Production Planning and Logistics Optimization, Project Scheduling Problems, Software Engineering, and Transgenic Algorithms.

Kattamuri Satish is a highly accomplished professional with a Ph.D. and extensive qualifications in Finance, Accounting, Marketing and Commerce. With over 20 years in academia and a decade in industry roles, Dr. Satish excels in merging academic expertise with practical experience. Highlights: Education: Ph.D. holder with dual MBA and Master's degrees in Finance and Accounting. Experience: Over 20 years in teaching and a decade in various industry sectors. Achievements: Author of 2 books, 10 published research papers, and holds 1 patent. Expertise: Specialized in Finance, and Accounting, bridging theory with real-world applications. Key Traits: Innovation: Patent holder with significant research contributions. Teaching Excellence: Committed to shaping future talents with comprehensive teaching methods. Industry Insight: Blending academic knowledge with practical industry experience. Dr. Kattamuri Satish is a versatile professional, blending academic prowess, extensive teaching experience, and industry insights, making significant contributions to academia and professional spheres.

Tejashree Soni is an Assistant Professor in Finance at Sai Balaji International Institutes of Management with over 9 years of academic and industry experience. She specialises in management accounting, financial management, personal financial planning, and management fundamentals and is currently pursuing a Ph.D. in Financial Management from Savitribai Phule Pune University. Her professional journey includes roles at Akemi Business School, NBN Sinhgad School of Management Studies, Oceanic Tecno Chem Pvt. Ltd., and the Suryadatta Group of Institutions. She has actively contributed to SPPU examination processes, student mentoring, NAAC documentation, and institutional publications, while also coordinating entrepreneurial and literacy initiatives. Her research interests lie in investment decisions, corporate frauds, and financial strategies. She has published papers in reputed journals. She has also presented at several state, national, and international conferences and participated in multiple FDPs and workshops on finance, teaching innovations, and research methodology.

Joaquin Torres-Mata is a Full-Time Professor and University Researcher at the Universidad Autónoma de Tamaulipas (UAT). Recognized with the PRODEP Profile (Professional Development Program for Teachers) and a member of the National System of Researchers (SNII).

Francisco R. Trejo-Macotela holds a Ph.D. in Electronics from INAOE and is Professor and Senior Researcher at Universidad Politécnica de Pachuca (UPP). He is a National Researcher of the Secretariat of Science, Humanities, Technology and Innovation (SECIHTI) of Mexico and adjunct member of LANAVEX. His prolific academic output comprises slightly more than 60 publications in domains including smart cities, embedded IoT systems, telecommunications, electronics, aquaculture, artificial intelligence, bio-inspired algorithms, combinatorial optimisation, and educational technologies.

Johannes Tshepiso Tsoku holds a PhD in Statistics and is an Associate Professor in the Department of Business Statistics and Operations Research at North-West University, Mafikeng, South Africa. His research interests include applied statistics, econometrics, machine learning, multivariate analysis, and time series analysis. His work has been published in several international journals, and his current research focuses on hybrid statistical and machine-learning methods for economic and financial decision-making, as well as postgraduate research development.

Marco Vera-Jimenez holds a Bachelor's degree in accounting, master's degree in administrative management, PhD in tax sciences, specialist in international trade, intellectual property, and business.

Víctor Zamudio-García has a PhD in Science specializing in the area of education and director of the Department of Information Technologies at UPMH

Index

A

Algorithmic Trading 2, 4, 11, 21, 22, 23, 24, 28, 34, 37, 39, 45, 51, 55, 67, 70, 71, 72, 83, 118
ANFIS 283, 284, 285, 286, 287, 288, 289, 293, 295, 296, 301, 303, 304, 305, 306, 307, 308, 309, 311, 312
asset dynamics 243, 246, 255, 256
Asset Pricing 2, 3, 5, 14, 20, 33, 36, 57, 60, 81, 83, 84, 87, 88, 91, 92, 107, 108, 110, 306, 334

B

Basel III 39, 42, 132, 196, 197, 203, 204, 208, 214, 216, 223, 224, 225, 227, 229, 280
Betti Curves 156, 162, 166, 168, 175, 184, 188
Big Data 2, 4, 5, 6, 10, 43, 45, 46, 47, 51, 54, 62, 63, 68, 69, 71, 74, 77, 78, 79, 107, 108, 115, 116, 123, 126, 150, 151

C

Closing stock prices 283, 297, 298
Convention Sensitivity 172
County GDP 398, 405, 408, 415, 416, 429, 433, 435, 436

D

Data Analytics 2, 45, 56, 69, 76, 78, 79, 107, 108, 114, 117, 151
database management 49, 50, 51, 52, 53, 55, 58, 60, 61, 62, 65, 66, 67, 71, 74, 78
data-driven finance 4, 6, 49, 50, 51, 52, 53, 54, 55, 56, 58, 59, 62, 64, 65, 67, 68, 69, 70, 72, 73, 74, 75
DataOps 113, 114, 115, 116, 117, 119, 121, 129, 138, 139, 140, 143, 148, 151

E

econometrics 51, 52, 53, 63, 64, 65, 66, 67, 70, 72, 74, 75, 76, 77, 78, 116, 202, 228, 241, 280, 334, 341, 344, 346, 390, 393, 394, 401, 404, 413
EGARCH 195, 196, 202, 206, 207, 208, 209, 210, 212, 222, 224, 227, 230, 232, 344, 390
Expected Shortfall 58, 60, 81, 84, 87, 88, 90, 91, 92, 100, 102, 103, 108, 110, 197, 203, 204, 207, 208, 214, 215, 216, 222, 227, 229, 233, 236, 251, 272, 277, 280, 282
Extreme Value Theory 195, 196, 202, 207, 213, 224, 227, 228, 229

F

Financial Data Pipeline 118, 139, 143, 153
financial forecasting 2, 9, 11, 19, 36, 37, 43, 45, 77, 284, 307, 310, 314, 315, 331, 342, 357
Financial mathematics 5, 49, 50, 51, 52, 53, 54, 56, 57, 58, 59, 62, 65, 66, 67, 68, 69, 70, 74, 281
Financial Modeling 3, 9, 10, 11, 13, 14, 17, 21, 22, 28, 44, 46, 104, 202
Financial Risk Management 45, 67, 68, 69, 70, 75, 78, 87, 107, 111, 192
Forecasting 2, 3, 4, 9, 11, 13, 14, 19, 33, 34, 36, 37, 43, 45, 54, 57, 64, 66, 72, 74, 77, 78, 107, 108, 150, 163, 227, 283, 284, 285, 286, 287, 288, 289, 292, 306, 307, 308, 309, 310, 311, 312, 313, 314, 315, 316, 318, 319, 320, 322, 324, 331, 332, 333, 334, 335, 336, 337, 339, 340, 341, 342, 343, 344, 345, 346, 347, 348, 349, 350, 351, 352, 353, 354, 356, 357, 358, 359, 360, 361, 362, 366, 372, 379, 380, 383, 384, 386, 387, 388, 389, 391, 392, 393, 394, 399, 417, 427, 431, 432, 436, 437

G

GAN 78, 147
GARCH 195, 196, 197, 202, 203, 204, 205, 206, 207, 208, 209, 219, 220, 224, 226, 227, 231, 232, 238, 239, 240, 284, 308, 317, 337, 339, 340, 341, 342, 344, 345, 346, 347, 348, 349, 350, 351, 352, 353, 354, 355, 356, 357, 358, 359, 360, 361, 362, 363, 364, 365, 366, 372, 373, 374, 377, 378, 379, 380, 381, 382, 383, 384, 385, 386, 387, 388, 389, 390, 391, 392, 393, 394
GBM 82, 87, 91, 93, 96, 97, 98, 99, 102, 108, 111, 283, 284, 285, 286, 287, 288, 289, 293, 294, 301, 302, 303, 305, 306, 307, 312
GRNN 283, 284, 285, 286, 287, 288, 289, 293, 294, 301, 305, 306, 307, 308, 309, 310, 311, 312

H

hybrid models 72, 73, 283, 312, 342, 347, 348, 358

J

Jump-Diffusion Models 94

K

Kappa Architecture 120, 121, 142, 144

L

Lambda Architecture 119, 120
Linear Regression 6, 20, 32, 285, 397, 403, 405, 413, 414, 432, 435
Look-Ahead Bias 113, 114, 115, 124, 126, 128, 132, 151, 333, 391
LSTM 309, 339, 340, 341, 342, 345, 346, 347, 348, 349, 350, 352, 353, 354, 355, 356, 357, 358, 359, 360, 362, 363, 366, 373, 378, 379, 380, 381, 382, 383, 384, 385, 386, 387, 388, 389, 391, 394, 402, 404

M

Machine Learning Algorithms 33, 39, 68, 108, 288, 310, 311
Market Microstructure 82, 115, 127
MiCA 197, 203, 204, 218, 223, 224, 225, 237
Model Risk 24, 35, 40, 41, 52, 55, 68, 70, 71, 75, 156, 157, 158, 161, 169, 189, 192, 251, 276, 277
Monte Carlo Simulation 10, 17, 21, 30, 31, 37, 39, 44, 81, 82, 83, 84, 85, 86, 87, 89, 90, 91, 92, 93, 96, 97, 99, 100, 101, 102, 103, 104, 107, 108, 111, 195, 196, 212, 224, 227, 246, 253, 282
multi-horizon evaluation 339, 348, 350, 359, 360, 363, 372

N

Nighttime Lights 395, 400, 401, 406, 407, 409, 410, 436, 437, 438, 439

P

Persistence Diagrams 156, 157, 160, 162, 166, 168, 175, 184, 188, 192, 249, 250, 262, 280
Persistent Homology 155, 156, 157, 158, 159, 160, 161, 162, 165, 166, 167, 168, 176, 191, 193, 194, 243, 245, 248, 249, 253, 254, 255, 256, 280, 281
Polyglot Persistence 113, 114, 116, 143, 147, 148, 151, 152, 153
portfolio optimization 3, 4, 5, 9, 11, 14, 24, 25, 27, 28, 34, 36, 40, 44, 52, 58, 60, 66, 74, 77, 107, 108, 215

Q

Quantitative Finance 1, 2, 4, 6, 7, 9, 10, 11, 13, 15, 24, 28, 29, 31, 32, 35, 36, 37, 38, 39, 40, 41, 42, 43, 44, 45, 46, 47, 74, 77, 78, 79, 91, 109, 110, 114, 115, 116, 118, 126, 132, 135, 147,

148, 151, 280, 282, 313, 314, 336, 340, 351, 391, 393

R

reproducibility 105, 113, 138, 193, 235, 255, 256, 279, 282, 345, 350, 353, 357, 358, 389, 390
risk assessment 1, 3, 5, 24, 32, 37, 43, 53, 67, 68, 70, 72, 73, 74, 84, 87, 88, 100, 101, 107, 108, 111, 306
Risk Management 2, 3, 4, 5, 6, 9, 11, 12, 21, 23, 24, 28, 29, 30, 31, 32, 33, 34, 35, 38, 39, 40, 41, 42, 44, 45, 46, 49, 51, 54, 55, 59, 60, 62, 63, 64, 66, 67, 68, 69, 70, 71, 72, 73, 74, 75, 77, 78, 83, 84, 87, 88, 90, 91, 96, 101, 102, 107, 108, 110, 111, 113, 114, 131, 135, 136, 145, 157, 192, 202, 245, 281, 283, 307, 314, 343

S

scenario manifolds 157, 278
stablecoins 203, 206, 217, 223, 228, 235
Stochastic Processes 81, 82, 84, 85, 87, 91, 93
Stochastic Volatility 72, 87, 91, 92, 95, 96, 103, 110, 111
stress testing 24, 29, 30, 39, 40, 45, 54, 59, 69, 82, 84, 86, 87, 88, 89, 90, 91, 92, 100, 107, 108, 111, 115, 147, 159, 160, 186, 246, 271, 275, 278, 279, 280
systemic contagion 216

T

tail risk 84, 86, 87, 90, 103, 196, 197, 198, 213, 219, 220, 229, 257, 277

V

volatility 3, 7, 22, 23, 26, 27, 30, 49, 51, 52, 53, 64, 65, 68, 72, 74, 81, 82, 85, 86, 87, 88, 91, 92, 93, 94, 95, 96, 100, 101, 102, 103, 108, 110, 111, 117, 123, 127, 128, 130, 131, 132, 134, 145, 146, 147, 150, 189, 196, 201, 202, 206, 207, 208, 209, 210, 212, 213, 216, 219, 220, 224, 228, 229, 230, 231, 238, 243, 244, 245, 246, 247, 248, 249, 250, 252, 253, 257, 258, 259, 260, 265, 268, 269, 277, 278, 280, 281, 289, 298, 307, 308, 312, 316, 320, 323, 327, 329, 331, 332, 336, 337, 339, 340, 341, 342, 343, 344, 345, 346, 347, 348, 349, 350, 351, 352, 353, 354, 355, 356, 357, 358, 359, 360, 361, 364, 365, 369, 377, 378, 379, 380, 382, 383, 384, 385, 386, 387, 388, 389, 390, 391, 392, 393, 394

W

walk-forward validation 317, 339, 341, 342, 349, 350, 359, 363, 365, 366, 377, 378, 387, 388, 391, 392
Wasserstein Distance 167, 185, 249, 254

www.ingramcontent.com/pod-product-compliance
Lightning Source LLC
LaVergne TN
LVHW061525290926
849162LV00004B/669